Critical Acclaim for RUNNING MS-DOS®:

Named "Best How-To Book" of 1990.   Computer Press Association

"RUNNING MS-DOS combines a lucid presentation of DOS commands and functions with sound advice on approaching the basic housekeeping chores that all PC users need to perform. It's presented in a highly readable format that includes plenty of useful examples."

PC World

"RUNNING MS-DOS proves how-to books don't have to be pedantic, ugly and full of mistakes. A book even the PC mavens turn to, it is written by a human being for human beings, in a strange and wonderful tongue: English."

Jim Seymour, PC Week

"This book is simply the definitive handbook of PC-DOS and MS-DOS...written for both novices and experienced users."

BYTE *magazine*

"If you're new to MS-DOS, Van Wolverton's RUNNING MS-DOS is essential. This well-written volume has become a classic and is a must-have for serious PC users. If you can only buy one DOS book, buy this one."

Compute! *magazine*

"Excellent guide for computer novices. The tone is informal yet direct. Features are clearly defined and illustrated. Good one-book reference."

Computer Book Review

"One of the most popular DOS books is Van Wolverton's RUNNING MS-DOS."

PC Magazine

"...essential for those who want to get the most out of their PCs."

Washington Post

"RUNNING MS-DOS is well organized and clearly written. Van Wolverton goes to great lengths to explain the commands rather than just show you how to use them."

PC Resource

"This is truly the cornerstone book for any serious MS-DOS user's library."

Computer Shopper

"RUNNING MS-DOS has become a sort of operating system bible for PC owners....Wolverton's easygoing style and Microsoft's lavish use of illustrations make this one of the best DOS books on the market."

Dallas Morning News

"...clearly guides you through the mazes of computer disk operating systems for any IBM PC or IBM compatible."

New York Daily News

"By far the best feature of RUNNING MS-DOS is Van Wolverton's clear and to-the-point writing. In his examples, he not only tells you how to enter MS-DOS commands, but he shows you how MS-DOS responds, so you know when you have entered commands properly. Beginners and experienced users alike will find this book helpful."

Online Today

RUNNING MS DOS®

RUNNING

MS DOS®

VAN WOLVERTON

Three books in one:

- ■ **Introduction to DOS and PCs**
- ■ **Guide to using DOS through version 5**
- ■ **Complete command reference**

Your key to MS-DOS mastery!

Microsoft
P R E S S

PUBLISHED BY
Microsoft Press
A Division of Microsoft Corporation
One Microsoft Way
Redmond, Washington 98052-6399

Library of Congress Cataloging-in-Publication Data

Wolverton, Van, 1939–
    Running MS-DOS / Van Wolverton. -- 5th ed.
      p.   cm.
    Includes index.
    ISBN 1-55615-337-6
    1. MS-DOS (Computer operating system)   2. PC DOS (Computer
operating system)   I. Title.
    QA76.76.O63W65   1991
    005.4'46--dc20   90-49856
                                                   CIP

Printed and bound in the United States of America.

1 2 3 4 5 6 7 8 9 AGAG 4 3 2 1 0

Distributed to the book trade in Canada by Macmillan of Canada,
a division of Canada Publishing Corporation.

Distributed to the book trade outside the United States and Canada by Penguin Books Ltd.

Penguin Books Ltd., Harmondsworth, Middlesex, England
Penguin Books Australia Ltd., Ringwood, Victoria, Australia
Penguin Books N.Z. Ltd., 182-190 Wairau Road, Auckland 10, New Zealand

British Cataloging-in-Publication Data available.

Acquisitions Editor: Dean Holmes
Project Editor: JoAnne Woodcock
Technical Editor: Dail Magee, Jr.

For Jeanne,

who makes it all worthwhile

CONTENTS

Acknowledgments   xiii

Introduction   xv

PART I
GETTING TO KNOW DOS

CHAPTER 1
What Is DOS?   3

CHAPTER 2
Starting DOS   9

CHAPTER 3
Getting Your Bearings   23

CHAPTER 4
A Look at Files and Diskettes   39

PART II
LEARNING TO USE DOS

CHAPTER 5
Managing Your Files   57

CHAPTER 6
Managing Your Diskettes   97

CHAPTER 7
Managing Your Devices   119

CHAPTER 8
A Tree of Files   141

CHAPTER 9
Managing Your Fixed Disk   171

CHAPTER 10
The DOS Shell   209

CHAPTER 11
Creating and Editing Files of Text   245

CHAPTER 12
The Edlin Text Editor   263

CHAPTER 13
Taking Control of Your System   279

CHAPTER 14
Creating Your Own Commands   297

CHAPTER 15
Creating Smart Commands   317

CHAPTER 16
Creating More Smart Commands   333

CHAPTER 17
Tailoring Your System   355

CHAPTER 18
DOS Is an International System   387

PART III
APPENDIXES

APPENDIX A
Installing DOS   411

APPENDIX B
Glossary   421

APPENDIX C
DOS Command Reference   433

Index   561

ACKNOWLEDGMENTS

It's been more than six years since the first edition of this book hit the shelves, and the world of computers has changed mightily. The person who bought the first edition of this book most likely had a 64 K IBM PC with two diskette drives. Those of you who buy this edition probably have an IBM PC/AT with a megabyte or more of memory and a 30- or 40-megabyte fixed disk—or, more likely, a computer made by some other company, but whose behavior is nonetheless indistinguishable from the IBM version.

But all those machines use MS-DOS, so I'd like to thank all those folks who have labored to put a DOS machine on everyone's desk. Thanks, too, to IBM and Microsoft for starting things off back in 1981.

Both DOS and this book are in their fifth version. That's uncommon longevity in the quicksilver world of personal computers. Version 5 makes more changes to DOS—and Running MS-DOS—than any other release. How do you dodge that many bullets? Easy. Get someone with the skill and patience of Dail Magee, Jr., to make sure you get it right.

The staying power of DOS is due to the remarkable proliferation of IBM and IBM-compatible computers. The staying power of this book is due, in large part, to the inspiration and efforts of three remarkable women.

My mother, Bee Forsyth Wolverton, preached the gospel of clear writing as far back as I can remember, and emphasized her message by setting—as she continues to set—a dauntingly high example. My editor, JoAnne Woodcock, cossets and cajoles me through each revision, using her skill, judgment, and patience to improve the book each time; she is without peer. And most of all, Jeanne Elizabeth Wolverton whipped the first edition into shape before anyone else ever saw it, and continues to keep me on the right track; she has been my first editor for nearly 30 years, and I've still got a lot to learn from her.

So, a special thanks to those three women who have contributed so much to this book. And a personal thanks to the people of Montana who have made Jeanne and me feel so welcome. It's good to be back.

Van Wolverton
Rubicon
Sawmill Gulch Road
Alberton, MT 59820
March 1991

INTRODUCTION

It may be tempting to skip these opening words and "get to the meat of it," but please read this introduction anyway. The information included here is both useful and brief.

You may want to know whether this book applies to you. It does, if your computer uses MS-DOS. The book itself was written with an IBM Personal Computer, but it applies equally well to any machine that uses MS-DOS.

You bought this book—or at least took the time to pick it up and glance through it—despite the hefty manual you got with your copy of DOS. Why? What else can a book like this offer? It can offer simplicity. The DOS manual is thorough and complete. It is your official, comprehensive reference guide to DOS, but its goal is really to tell you *about* DOS rather than how to *use* DOS in your everyday work.

This book does not show you how to set up your computer, nor does it describe in detail the pieces of the system, such as the keyboard or the display. These matters should be covered thoroughly in the manuals that came with your computer.

The book assumes neither that you are, nor that you aspire to become, a programmer. It doesn't try to explain how DOS works, and it leaves to the DOS manual the task of explaining some of the more technical features. The book does assume that you have access to an IBM Personal Computer or one of the many other machines that run MS-DOS, and that you want to put the machine to work. It includes scores of examples, and it is organized by what you want the computer to do, not (as a programmer would expect) by how DOS itself is structured. The examples reflect real-life situations.

You don't have to be a mechanical engineer to drive a car well, but you do need experience. You don't have to be a computer scientist to use DOS well, either, and this book starts you on your way.

WHAT'S IN THE BOOK, AND WHERE

This book covers DOS through version 5, as it is used on machines that have a fixed disk and either one or two diskette drives. Although a fixed disk is assumed, the examples are also structured to work on computers that have two diskette drives.

Part I, Chapters 1 through 4, describes the pieces of the computer system, defines some terms and concepts, and provides hands-on examples that show you the major capabilities of DOS.

Part II, the bulk of the book, includes Chapters 5 through 18. These chapters show you how to operate your computer system and manage all its parts with the DOS commands.

Chapters 5, 6, and 7 show you how to manage your files, diskettes, and computer devices such as the printer and the display. Chapter 8 describes the DOS multilevel filing system that allows you to set up a personalized computer file system that matches the way you work. Chapter 9 shows you how to manage the files and directories on a fixed disk, and it shows you some ways to protect both the disk and your work from loss or damage.

Chapter 10 takes you through a menu-based version 5 program called the Shell that makes your display visually more interesting and your work with the computer easier in many ways.

Chapters 11 and 12 are complementary chapters that describe two text-editing programs released with different versions of DOS. Chapter 11 deals with another menu-based program, the version 5 MS-DOS Editor. If you don't have the MS-DOS Editor, however, Chapter 12 describes its predecessor, the Edlin text editor that has been shipped with DOS since its first release.

Chapters 13 through 18 describe ways to tailor DOS to your own needs. Chapter 13 shows you how to take control of your system with a special set of commands called filter commands; it also shows you how to use a program named Doskey that can save time and work by recording keystrokes and commands. Chapters 14 through 16 show you how to create your own sets of commands and save them in special files called batch files. Chapter 17 shows you several techniques you can use to make DOS immediately useful in its own right, and it describes ways to help DOS use your computer more efficiently. Chapter 18 shows you how to control the way DOS displays the date and shows you how to type, display, and print characters from international alphabets.

Finally, in Part III, Appendix A tells you how to install DOS, Appendix B provides a glossary of commonly used terms, and Appendix C describes the DOS commands, with cross-references to the detailed discussions in the preceding chapters.

If you plan to use your computer for word processing, spreadsheets, database management, games, or any of the many other types of applications available for IBM and compatible computers, this book is probably all you'll need. Not only does it show you how to use DOS so you can run your programs, it shows you how to make good use of DOS without additional software.

ABOUT THE EXAMPLES

The best way to learn how to put DOS to work is to use it. This book, therefore, is devoted primarily to examples. Terms and concepts are defined as you need them and are illustrated with hands-on examples that help you see both what you do and why. Because the book covers different versions of DOS and different types of machines, there are variations in some examples; these alternatives are identified. Unless an example states it is for a particular version or computer setup, the DOS displays shown in this book are the MS-DOS version 5 responses on a computer with one fixed disk and one diskette drive. If you are using a different version of DOS or a different computer setup, the responses you see may vary somewhat. Do not be concerned.

What to Type and When

There's an awkward mismatch between a computer and a book that shows you how to use it. The computer is dynamic: It displays messages, moves data back and forth between disks and memory, prints words and pictures, and chirps now and then to announce completion of another task. When you use the computer, you enter into a dialogue: You type something, the computer responds, you type something else, and so on, back and forth, until your work is done.

A book, however, is static. It can show only snapshots of your dialogue with the system, yet it must describe that dialogue well enough so that you can take part in it. In this book, we have to show what you type and how the computer responds. We have to distinguish parts of this dialogue, such as the names of files and messages displayed on the screen, from the surrounding prose. Here are the conventions we've adopted:

▶ Hands-on examples are shown in different type, on separate lines, just as you would see them on your display. The characters you type are printed in lower-case colored type; DOS usually doesn't care whether you type in uppercase or lowercase, but lowercase seems to be easier. Here is a sample of the conventions for hands-on examples:

```
C:\> format b:
Insert new diskette for drive B:
and press ENTER when ready...
```

▶ Occasionally, similar information occurs in text. In these instances, the interaction between you and DOS is printed in italics to distinguish it from the surrounding text. For example, you may see: "Type *n* when DOS displays *Format another (Y/N)?*"

▶ Many DOS commands include options, or parameters, that allow you to specify a particular disk drive, file, or piece of equipment, or to use a particular form of the command. Options are shown in angle brackets (<>) when they represent a variable entry, such as the name of a file. When they must be entered exactly, they are shown in the form you must use. For example, here are some options of the Format command used in the preceding examples (don't worry about understanding the command at this point):

format <drive> /4 /F:<size> /Q

Now it's time to meet DOS. This book was written to be used alongside the system, so put it beside your keyboard, turn to Chapter 1, and get ready to put DOS to work.

PART I

GETTING TO
KNOW DOS

Part I describes the terms and the basic operating principles of DOS. The chapters show you how to start DOS and how to control the system with DOS commands. The information is primarily tutorial, and many examples are included. Later parts of the book contain all detailed reference information that describes the DOS commands and their capabilities.

Part I introduces you to the concept of an operating system: what it is, what it does, and why you need it. Together, these chapters give you the foundation for using DOS effectively in your daily work with the computer.

CHAPTER 1

WHAT IS DOS?

Y ou've got your computer, and you've probably got one or two programs, such as a word processor or a spreadsheet, to use with it. But what is this thing called DOS? Why do you hear so much about it, and why have hundreds of pages of instructions been written for it?

DOS IS A PROGRAM

DOS is a program, but it's not just any program. Chances are none of your other programs would work without it, because DOS controls every part of the computer system. DOS not only makes it possible for your other programs to work, it also gives you complete control over what your computer does, and how. DOS is the link between you and your computer.

To appreciate the role DOS plays, take a quick look at the pieces of your computer system and what they do.

HARDWARE MAKES IT POSSIBLE

Your computer equipment, called *hardware,* probably includes a keyboard, display, printer, and one or more disk drives. The purposes of the first three are straightforward: You type instructions at the keyboard, and the system responds by displaying or printing messages and results.

The purpose of a disk drive isn't quite so obvious, but it quickly becomes apparent as you use the system: A disk drive records and plays back information, much as a tape deck records and plays back music. The computer's information is recorded in files on disks; you'll find that disk files are as central to your computer work as paper files are to more traditional office work.

SOFTWARE MAKES IT HAPPEN

No matter how powerful the hardware, a computer can't do anything without programs, called *software.* There are two major types of software: *system programs,* which control the operation of the computer system, and *application programs,* which perform more obviously useful tasks, such as word processing.

Each program uses the hardware. It must be able to receive instructions from the keyboard, display and print results, read and write files from and to a disk, send and receive data through the computer's communications connections, change the colors on a color display, and so on through all the capabilities of the hardware.

So that each program doesn't have to perform all these functions for itself, a system program called the *operating system* manages the hardware. The operating system allows an application program to concentrate on what it does best, whether it's moving paragraphs about, tracking accounts receivable, or calculating stress in a bridge beam. DOS is an operating system.

DOS IS A DISK OPERATING SYSTEM

The operating system for IBM and IBM-compatible computers is the Microsoft Disk Operating System—MS-DOS or, for short, just DOS. DOS is called a disk operating system because much of its work involves managing disks and disk files.

What Does an Operating System Do?

An operating system plays a role something like a symphony conductor. When the score calls for the violins to play, the conductor cues the violins; when the score says the cellos should play more softly, the tympani should stop, or the entire orchestra should pick up the tempo, the conductor so instructs the musicians.

The players in the orchestra and their instruments represent the hardware. The experience and skill of the conductor represent the operating system. The score represents an application program.

When one score is replaced by another—Beethoven's Fifth Symphony is put aside and replaced by Haydn's *Surprise* Symphony, for example—the same musicians use the same instruments, and the same conductor uses the same experience and skills. A different sound, a different mood, perhaps, but the elements are the same.

When one application program is replaced by another—for example, an accounting program is put aside and replaced with a word processor—the same hardware carries out the instructions of the same operating system. A different program, a different purpose, perhaps, but the elements are the same.

DOS coordinates the computer system, just as the conductor coordinates the orchestra. Your application programs run in concert with DOS, trusting it to keep the system humming.

Much of what DOS does, such as how it stores a file on a disk or prints on the printer, is invisible to you. But DOS lets you control the things you care about, such as which program to run, what report to print, or what files to erase. These functions share an important characteristic: They need disks and disk drives.

Disk Drives

Personal computers use two main types of disk: a flexible disk in a protective plastic jacket, called a *diskette,* which you can remove from the drive, and a permanently mounted unit called a *fixed disk.* There are two types of diskette: 5.25 inches square in a flexible plastic jacket, and 3.5 inches square in a rigid plastic shell.

A fixed disk holds much more information than a diskette—from 15 to 100 times as much, or even more—and is much faster. Most personal computers have one fixed disk and one diskette drive. Machines without a fixed disk usually have two diskette drives.

To distinguish among the types of disk, this book uses *diskette* to mean either type of flexible disk, *fixed disk* to mean only a fixed disk, and *disk* to refer to both.

5

Disk Files

Just as you organize and store your written records in paper files, you organize and store computer information in disk files.

A disk file—usually called a file—is a collection of related information stored on a disk. It could be a letter, an income tax return, or a list of customers. It could also be a program, because the programs you use are stored in files.

Virtually all your computer work revolves around files. Because one of the major functions of DOS is to take care of files, much of this book is devoted to showing you how to create, print, copy, organize, and otherwise manage files.

Where Is DOS?

When your computer is turned off, DOS is stored on disk. Although it's a special type of program, DOS is still a program, and that means it's stored on disk in a set of files like any other collection of computer information.

If your computer has a fixed disk, DOS is probably already on it—placed there, perhaps, by your computer dealer, or by someone else who set up your system. If your computer does not have a fixed disk, it must use DOS from diskettes, so it should have come with a copy of DOS on two or more diskettes.

Different Versions of DOS

DOS has been revised a number of times since its release in 1981; the first version was numbered 1.00. DOS is revised to add more capability, to take advantage of more sophisticated hardware, and to correct errors. When you start up your system, DOS may display the version number you are using.

When a new version of DOS appears, a change in the number following the decimal point—3.20 to 3.30, for example—marks a minor change that leaves the new version of DOS substantially the same as the previous version. A change in the number preceding the decimal point marks a major change. Version 5.0, for example, occupies less of your computer's memory than version 4.0, yet it has more features than any of its predecessors.

Even though newer versions of DOS have much more capability, they remain compatible with earlier versions. Thus, if you start with version 2.1, you can still use all your knowledge and experience, plus your files and diskettes, when you move to a newer version of DOS.

For simplicity, this book usually refers to DOS by major version number only— for example, version 5 or version 4, rather than version 5.0 or version 4.01. It also omits references to versions of DOS earlier than version 3, but much of the information applies to these versions too. Remember, version 2 is just as much a part of DOS as version 5. It's simply older and, though it includes many of the features described here, it doesn't provide them all.

What Is Compatibility?

You've no doubt seen the term *IBM-compatible* in an article or an advertisement. What does compatibility actually mean? Compatibility essentially refers to the ability of one computer to use programs and data created for or stored on another computer. In everyday use, the most meaningful measure of compatibility is the extent to which you can use the same programs, data, and diskettes in computers of different makes or different models:

▶ If two systems are totally compatible, they can freely use the same programs and diskettes. This is the type of compatibility exhibited among different models of IBM Personal Computers and the IBM-compatible machines made by manufacturers other than IBM. On these machines, such full compatibility is made possible in part by MS-DOS: Any computer that can run MS-DOS can run programs designed for MS-DOS, and that computer can (given the proper application programs) freely use diskettes from any other MS-DOS computer.

▶ Incompatible systems might use different versions of the same program, but they can't use either programs or diskettes intended for the other computer. This is typically the situation between IBM and Macintosh computers. An IBM machine can, for example, use the IBM version of Microsoft Word, and the Macintosh can use the Macintosh version of Microsoft Word, but neither computer can use the version intended for the other. Nor can these computers easily exchange diskettes, because neither system can read files stored by the other without special hardware.

When specifics are needed, this book describes how DOS works on the IBM PS/2 (all models), IBM PC/AT, IBM PC/XT, and IBM PC. If your computer is a compatible machine, however, the descriptions apply equally to your system.

WHAT CAN YOU DO WITH DOS?

DOS coordinates the operation of the computer for your application programs. That's valuable—essential, really—but DOS has much more to offer. You can use DOS itself, controlling it with instructions called *commands,* to manage your files, control the work flow, and perform useful tasks that might otherwise require additional software.

For example, DOS includes a program that lets you create and revise files of text. Although it's not a word processor, the DOS editor is fine for short memos and lists. Using it, you can write short documents in less time than it might take using your word processing program.

You can tailor DOS to your specific needs by creating powerful commands made up of other DOS commands, and you can even create your own small applications. For example, this book shows you how to create a simple file manager—a program that lets you search a file for specific information—using nothing but DOS commands.

Versions 4 and 5 of DOS also include a separate program, called the *Shell,* that lets you choose commands and files from on-screen lists called *menus.* If you want, you can use the Shell for routine work, dispense with it and work directly with DOS, or move freely between DOS and the Shell as your work requires.

Your knowledge of DOS can range from just enough to use a single application program to mastery of the full range of capabilities in the later versions. But no matter how far you go, you needn't learn to program. It's all DOS, and it's all in this book.

CHAPTER SUMMARY

This quick tour of DOS may have introduced several new terms and concepts. Here are the key points to remember:

▶ A working computer system needs both hardware (equipment) and software (programs).

▶ DOS (the Microsoft Disk Operating System) coordinates the operation of all parts of the computer system.

▶ A file is a collection of related information stored on a disk. Most of your computer work will involve files.

▶ Besides running your application programs, DOS is valuable in its own right.

The next chapter starts you off at the keyboard.

CHAPTER 2

STARTING DOS

Now that you have been introduced to some of the things DOS does for you, it's time to start your system and do something. Whenever you start your computer, whether it is to use a word processor, an accounting program, or DOS itself, you begin by *loading* DOS into the computer's memory, its workplace. Loading the DOS program and starting it running is sometimes called "booting the system" or "booting the disk." This term is borrowed from the phrase "pulling yourself up by your bootstraps," because DOS essentially pulls itself up by its own bootstraps, loading itself from disk into memory, where it then waits for a command from you.

The examples from here on assume that you have a computer with a fixed disk, that your system is set up to use DOS, and that you are familiar with its control switches. If you need to install a more recent version of DOS on your fixed disk, refer to Appendix A. (If your computer does not have a fixed disk and you're using DOS from diskettes, have your usual startup diskette ready.)

STARTING THE SYSTEM

When you use DOS from a fixed disk, the DOS program must be copied into the computer's memory from the fixed disk (usually known to DOS as drive C). All you need to do before starting the system is make sure the latch on drive A (the diskette drive) isn't closed; otherwise, the system will try to load the DOS program into the computer's memory from the diskette in drive A.

If you're not using a fixed disk, the DOS program must be copied into the computer's memory from the diskette in drive A. Open the latch of drive A (either the left-hand or the upper diskette drive) and put in the diskette you use to start DOS—called the *system disk* in this book—with the label up and away from the machine, as in Figure 2-1. If you're using 5.25-inch diskettes, close the latch.

Turn on the system. The computer seems to do nothing for several seconds, but this is normal. Each time you turn on the power switch, the computer checks its memory and all attached devices to be sure everything is working properly. The system beeps after it has made sure that all is well, the drive lights flash, and the computer begins loading DOS into memory.

As soon as the program is loaded, DOS is running and ready to go to work.

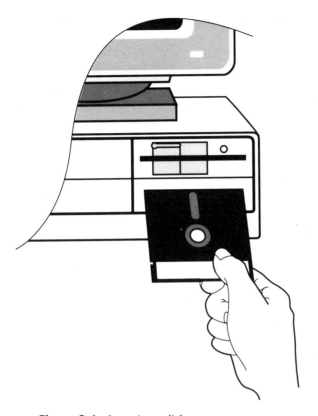

Figure 2-1. *Inserting a diskette.*

A First Look at DOS

Both DOS and the computers it runs on have evolved in the years since DOS and the IBM PC were introduced. The examples in this book are designed to work correctly with your computer and any release of DOS that supports the commands described, but there are variations in the way computers are set up and in the ways DOS can be organized, installed, and presented to the person who uses it.

One highly visible difference is how DOS looks once it is loaded into memory and ready for you to command. The following sections describe the major variations, one of which should explain what you see on your screen when you start the system.

Opening with the DOS Shell

If you're using version 4 or 5 of DOS, your system might be set up to start with the DOS Shell. If so, you'll see a display like the one on the following page.

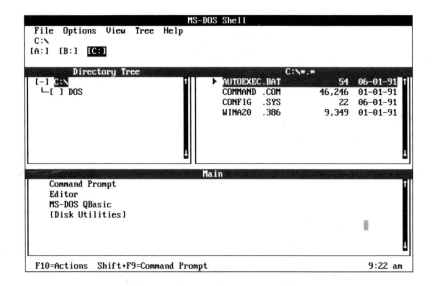

This illustration shows the opening screen of the version 5 Shell as it appears in the form called *text mode*, in which the display is made up of letters, numbers, lines, brackets, and other text characters rather than graphic images such as file folders and arrow-shaped mouse pointers. Your Shell screen might differ in some details.

Chapter 10, ''The DOS Shell,'' shows you how to use the Shell. Because the Shell is optional, however, and because you sometimes leave it to use parts of DOS, the remainder of this chapter—indeed, much of this book—takes you outside the Shell. This is done both to help you become comfortable with DOS itself and to enable users of all versions of DOS to benefit from the examples.

If you see the opening Shell screen, leave the Shell for now by pressing the F3 key. DOS responds by clearing the screen and displaying this:

    c:\>_

or this:

    c:\DOS>_

(If your computer doesn't have a fixed disk, you see A:\> instead of C:\>.)

Now you have a direct line to DOS. Go on to the heading ''The System Prompt.''

Opening Without the DOS Shell

On many systems, regardless of the version of DOS you use, DOS starts out by rapidly displaying some brief messages. If this is how your system starts, one of the messages you're likely to see tells you the version of DOS you're using. In version 5, for example, the message looks something like this:

    MS-DOS Version 5.0

If you see such a message—or any others that don't require responses from you—you can assume that DOS is settling in properly.

In a startup routine like this, DOS ends by displaying:

```
C:\>_
```

or this:

```
C:\DOS>_
```

or this (if you don't have a fixed disk):

```
A:\>_
```

and waits for your command. If your startup ends like this, DOS is ready to go to work. Go on to the heading ''The System Prompt.''

Opening with Date and Time Requests

Regardless of the version you use, DOS checks for the correct date and time as part of its standard startup routine. If your computer contains a battery-powered internal clock, DOS checks the clock for the information it needs. If your computer does not have a clock, however, the first thing that DOS does is ask you for the date and time. First, it asks for the date:

```
Current date is Tue 01-01-1980
Enter new date (mm-dd-yy): _
```

If you see this message, press the Enter key for now, even though the date isn't Tuesday, January 1, 1980. DOS next requests the time:

```
Current time is  0:01:30.00a
Enter new time: _
```

Again, just press Enter; you'll see how to set or change both the date and time later in this chapter. DOS should now display a message showing the version you're using, then end with a display like this:

```
C:\>_
```

or this:

```
C:\DOS>_
```

or this (if you don't have a fixed disk):

```
A:\>_
```

Go on to the heading ''The System Prompt.''

None of the Above

In the years since DOS appeared, many companies have developed shell programs and more sophisticated software that provide alternative ways to use a computer and manage files and applications. The DOS Shells in versions 4 and 5 are examples of such programs. Microsoft Windows is another.

If none of the preceding descriptions match what you see when you start your computer, check the documentation that came with your computer, or ask the person who set up your system whether a shell or other special program has been installed and, if so, how you can leave it temporarily to use this book.

THE SYSTEM PROMPT

The C:\> (or A:\> if you're not using a fixed disk) is called the *system prompt* or *command prompt*, because the system program (DOS) is prompting you to type a command. At this point, DOS is at what is often called *command level,* because it's ready and waiting for a command.

The system prompt identifies the *current drive,* the drive where DOS looks for a file. DOS identifies your drives by letter. On a system with one diskette drive and one fixed disk, the diskette drive is identified as both A and B, the fixed disk drive as drive C. On a system with two diskette drives, the left-hand or upper drive is drive A, the right-hand or lower drive is drive B.

When DOS is loaded from the fixed disk (drive C), DOS assumes drive C is the current drive, and the initial system prompt is C:\> or C:\DOS>. If you're not using a fixed disk, DOS is loaded from drive A; DOS assumes that drive A is the current drive, and the initial system prompt on your system is A:\>.

This book contains many examples for you to try. With a few exceptions, the examples show the system prompt as C:\> because that is the normal system prompt on a computer with a fixed disk and version 5 of DOS. If you're not using a fixed disk, proceed with the example, but bear in mind that where you see C:\> in the book, you will see A:\> on your screen.

ENTERING DOS COMMANDS

For the first few commands you enter in this session, you need only the standard typewriter keys on the keyboard. Three of those keys, Enter, Backspace, and Up arrow, are shown on the keyboards in Figures 2-2 and 2-3 and are worth separate mention.

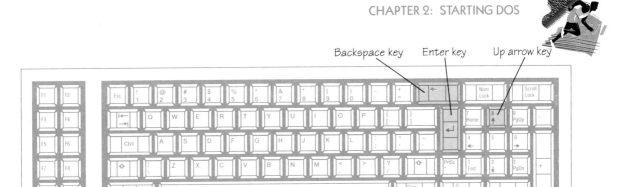

Figure 2-2. *The Backspace, Enter, and Up arrow keys on the IBM PC and PC/XT keyboards.*

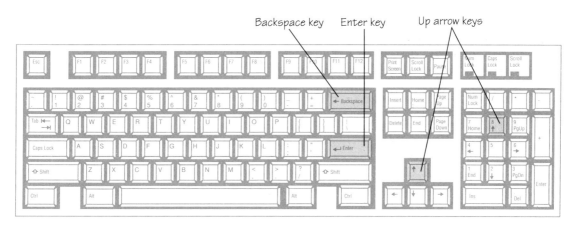

Figure 2-3. *The Backspace, Enter, and Up arrow keys on the enhanced IBM PC/AT keyboard.*

The Enter Key

The Enter key is labeled with a bent left arrow (↵), the word *Enter*, or both. Like the return key on a typewriter, it marks the end of a line. In general, DOS doesn't know what you have typed until you press Enter, so remember: End a command by pressing the Enter key.

The Backspace Key

The Backspace key is labeled with a long left arrow (←), the word *Backspace*, or both. It erases the last character you typed; use it to correct typing errors.

15

The Up Arrow Key

The Up arrow key is labeled with an upward-pointing arrow (↑). It is located on the 8 key in the calculatorlike numeric keypad on all IBM-compatible keyboards and also appears in the set of four ''direction'' keys to the left of the keypad on enhanced keyboards. The Up arrow key is often used to move a highlight on the screen, but in version 5 of DOS it also lets you repeat a command, as you'll see in a moment.

GETTING STARTED

At this point, DOS should be displaying the system prompt, followed by a blinking underline. This underline is the *cursor*. It shows where DOS will display whatever you type next. It also tells you that DOS is waiting for you to type something. It's time to put DOS to work.

The DOS commands you'll try in this chapter are easy to use and remember, so no special preparation is needed. If you have version 5 of DOS, however, you have an ''extra''—a small program named Doskey that you can load into your computer's memory and use with DOS to make some tasks more efficient. You can try Doskey in this chapter, so if you have version 5, type:

```
C:\>doskey
```

and press the Enter key. DOS responds:

```
DOSKey installed.
```

Note: If you're using DOS from diskettes and see the message Bad command or file name, *don't worry. The diskette in drive A doesn't include the part of DOS needed to carry out your command. Just ignore Doskey for now; you'll soon be able to use it without a second thought.*

Checking on Your Version of DOS

Some of the examples in this book assume you know which version of DOS you're using. If DOS identifies itself during startup, that's fine. But what if it doesn't? The easiest way to find out about DOS is to ask DOS itself. Whether you know your DOS version or not, try out the Ver (short for *version*) command. Type:

```
C:\>ver
```

and press the Enter key.

DOS responds by displaying a message that identifies the version. The exact wording depends on the computer and version of DOS you have. In Microsoft releases of version 5, for example, the message reads:

```
MS-DOS Version 5.0
```

KEEPING TRACK OF THE DATE AND TIME

It's important to know which version of DOS you use, but it's more important to know your computer keeps the correct date and time. The computer has an electronic clock that keeps time to the hundredth of a second. DOS uses this clock to keep track of both the time of day and the date.

In some computers, the clock doesn't run when the system is shut off, so each time you start the system DOS sets the date to January 1, 1980 (01-01-1980) and sets the time to midnight (0:00:00.00 or 12:00:00.00a). That's why, on systems without a battery-powered clock of some type, DOS prompts for the correct date and time at startup.

If your system doesn't keep the date and time current, and you just press Enter in response to the date and time prompts when you start the system, DOS assumes that it's midnight on January 1, 1980. Even though you might have been advised (for simplicity) to skip setting the correct date and time earlier in the chapter, it really isn't a good habit to form because DOS marks each disk file you create or change with the current time and date. Such information is useful, so it's a good idea to set the correct date and time—if necessary—each time you start the system.

Checking or Changing the Date

To check or change the date, you use the DOS Date command. Type:

```
C:\>date
```

and press Enter. DOS responds like this (you probably see a different date):

```
Current date is Fri 08-30-1991
Enter new date (mm-dd-yy): _
```

The cursor now follows the *Enter new date* request. Such a request is called a *prompt*; DOS frequently prompts you to enter information so that you don't have to memorize operating procedures.

To enter the date, you type the numbers that represent the month, day, and year, separated by hyphens, and then you press the Enter key. You don't have to type the day of the week; DOS figures out the day for you.

For this example, set the date to October 16, 1991, by typing the following (be sure to press Enter after the last number):

```
Current date is Fri 08-30-1991
Enter new date (mm-dd-yy): 10-16-91
```

Note: You can also use a slash (/) or a period to separate the numbers. Whichever you use, if you don't do it exactly right (in other words, in a way that DOS recognizes), DOS displays Invalid date *and prompts you to try again. If you make a mistake or enter the wrong date, don't be alarmed. As you'll soon see, it's easy to fix such errors.*

17

Check the date again to be sure DOS changed it for you. If you don't have version 5, you repeat your last command by typing it again. Do so now; DOS should respond with its normal date display.

If you have version 5, there's an easier way to repeat a command: Press the Up arrow key once. DOS displays:

```
C:\>date_
```

There's the Date command you just typed. Remember when you entered a Doskey command a few pages ago? Doskey starts a program that keeps track of each command you type in a special area of memory. After you have started Doskey, you can recycle previous commands by pressing the Up or Down arrow keys, as you just did.

Press the Enter key, and DOS responds just as if you had typed the Date command:

```
Current date is Wed 10-16-1991
Enter new date (mm-dd-yy): _
```

By pressing just two keys, you have repeated your last DOS command.

You'll correct the date in a moment, but first try the following exercise to see how easily you can fix typing errors.

Backspacing to Correct Typing Errors

Try out the Backspace key. Type some characters, such as the following, at random, but don't press Enter:

```
Current date is Wed 10-16-1991
Enter new date (mm-dd-yy): w710273_
```

This isn't a valid date. If you were to press enter now, DOS would display the message *Invalid date* and ask you to try again. Correct your typing ''error'' by pressing the Backspace key until all the characters are erased and the cursor is back to its original position, just to the right of the colon. The screen looks like it did before:

```
Current date is Wed 10-16-1991
Enter new date (mm-dd-yy): _
```

This time, type the correct date and press Enter—for example:

```
Current date is Wed 10-16-1991
Enter new date (mm-dd-yy): 10-1-91
```

for October 1, 1991.

Checking or Changing the Time

Just as you can control the date with the Date command, you can check or change the time with the DOS Time command. If your computer has an internal clock/calendar that keeps the date and time current even when the system is turned off, you probably won't have a lot of use for either Date or Time, but they can still come in handy—when the time changes with Daylight Saving Time, for example, or when you want to know what day of the week a certain date falls on.

Once you've seen the Date command, the Time command looks quite familiar. To try it, type:

```
C:\DOS>time
```

DOS displays its version of the time and prompts for a new time:

```
Current time is  8:22:33:55a
Enter new time: _
```

If DOS displays the correct time and you don't want to tamper with it, press Enter without typing a response. If the time is incorrect, or you feel like experimenting, type the time in the appropriate format for your version of DOS, as described below:

DOS Version	Time Format	Examples
1 through 3	24-hour clock	8:30 (before noon) or 20:30 (after noon)
4 and 5	12-hour or 24-hour clock	8:30a and 8:30p or 8:30 and 20:30

With versions 1 through 3, for example, you would type:

```
Current time is  8:22:33:55a
Enter new time: 13:15
```

to set the time to 1:15 in the afternoon. With versions 4 and 5, you could also type:

```
Current time is  8:22:33:55a
Enter new time: 1:15p
```

Versions 4 and 5 accept either form.

If you've changed to an incorrect time, reset it before continuing: If you have version 5, press the Up arrow key to recall the last command. If you don't have version 5, type *time*. Now type the correct time and press Enter to carry out the command.

CHANGING THE CURRENT DRIVE

You can change the current drive simply by typing the letter of the new drive, followed by a colon. For example, try changing the current drive to B.

You'll need a diskette, so either find one that you have used before or use one of your DOS diskettes (be careful with it).

If you have one diskette drive, insert the diskette in the drive with the label up and away from the machine. If you have two diskette drives, insert the diskette in the drive that does not currently contain your DOS startup disk.

Now type:

    C:\>b:

If you have one diskette drive, DOS displays the message:

    Insert diskette for drive B: and press any key when ready

The diskette is in the drive, so press a key. DOS responds:

    B:\>_

Now the system prompt is B:\>, confirming that DOS will look in drive B unless told otherwise.

If you're using a fixed disk, change the current drive back to drive C by typing the following:

    B:\>c:

    C:\>_

The system prompt returns to C:\>.

If you're not using a fixed disk, change the current drive back to drive A by typing the following:

    B:\>a:

    A:\>_

The system prompt returns to A:\>.

PRINTING WHAT IS ON THE SCREEN

The screen shows you a record of your commands and the responses from DOS; it normally shows a maximum of 25 lines. When all the lines are filled, each additional line causes the entire screen to shift up, or *scroll,* to make room for the new line at the bottom; the top line disappears from view.

Because a copy of what is on the display is often useful, DOS makes it easy to print what's on the screen. Locate the key labeled PrtSc (for *Print Screen,* spelled out on some keyboards). Make sure your printer is turned on, hold down the Shift key, and press PrtSc (this combination is referred to in text as Shift-PrtSc).

Each line of the screen is printed.

Note: If Shift-PrtSc does not produce a printed copy of what's on the screen, you might need to help your printer understand the instruction. With the Hewlett-Packard LaserJet Plus, for example, you press the button labeled ON LINE, press the FORM FEED button to print the page, then press ON LINE again to return the printer to its earlier status. If necessary, check the documentation that came with your printer.

CLEARING THE SCREEN

Sometimes, when the screen is filled with commands and responses, you might want to clear it before continuing with your work. You can erase everything on the screen with the Clear Screen (cls) command. Try it by typing:

```
C:\>cls
```

The screen is cleared, except for the system prompt in the upper left-hand corner.

TURNING THE SYSTEM OFF

If DOS is displaying the system prompt, all you have to do to shut the system down is turn off the power switch. You can do it anytime, except when the light on a disk drive is on; turning the power off while a drive is in use can cause you to lose the data on the disk. (If you're using an application program and decide to shut the system down, first follow the program's instructions for saving your work and quitting. When the program returns you to the DOS prompt, you can shut down without risking loss of data.)

Some devices attached to your system may have special requirements for shutting down, such as a specific sequence in which they should be turned off. Be sure you know any special instructions for the devices attached to your system.

After you shut the system down, be sure to remove any diskettes you are using and store them where they will be safe. You can remove your diskettes before you turn off the power, provided the disk drive is not in use.

CHAPTER SUMMARY

You have completed your first session with DOS. It wasn't very long, but you started the system, entered a few DOS commands, and printed what was on the screen. These are the key points:

▶ You control DOS by typing commands.

▶ DOS doesn't know what you have typed until you press the Enter key.

▶ The Backspace key erases the last character you typed.

▶ The system prompt tells you that DOS is at the command level, ready to accept a command from you.

▶ The letter in the system prompt identifies the current drive; you can change the current drive by typing the new drive letter, followed by a colon.

▶ You can check on your version of DOS with the Ver (for *version*) command.

▶ The computer keeps track of the date and time. You can also set them with the Date and Time commands.

▶ In version 5, Doskey helps you repeat commands quickly and easily.

▶ Pressing Shift-PrtSc prints the contents of the screen.

▶ Typing *cls* clears the screen.

CHAPTER 3

GETTING YOUR BEARINGS

When you venture into new territory—a different part of town, a park, a department store, a building you've never visited—you know where you're starting from, why you're there, and pretty much where you want to go. You took your first steps with DOS in the previous chapter. Now it's time to get your bearings—time to begin learning your way around, moving in the direction of one task or another, and calling a halt if you either want or need to.

That's what this chapter is all about. It introduces you to the directory of files that DOS keeps on each disk and shows you how to use the special keys on your keyboard. You use these keys to tell DOS to cancel lines or commands, to freeze the display, and to restart DOS itself. If you have version 5, you're given a closer look at Doskey, which extends your control over the keyboard and enables you to review and repeat commands you've already used.

To try the examples, start DOS as you normally do, even if your system is already running. Especially with version 5, this will ensure that the examples work as described. If necessary, press F3 to leave the DOS Shell. Don't worry about leaving your computer on while you read the text between examples; DOS is patient.

THE DIRECTORY

Recall from Chapter 1 that information stored on a disk is stored as a file. For every disk you use, DOS automatically keeps and updates a list of all the files you've saved on the disk. This list is called the *directory*.

If you create and save a new file, DOS adds it to the list for that disk. If you revise an old file, DOS keeps track of that too. The directory eliminates the need for you to keep a separate record of everything you save. You can tell DOS you want to see the directory of a particular disk whenever DOS is displaying the system prompt or, as explained in Chapter 10, when you are using the DOS Shell.

The examples in this chapter give you a look at a directory and show you different ways to display information about your files. But before you begin exploring directories, you should know a little about how DOS saves your files.

Whenever you create a file, you give it a descriptive name, called the *file name,* of up to eight characters. If you want, you can add a suffix, called the *extension,* of up to three more letters. The file name and extension help DOS distinguish one file from another and keep information where it belongs.

Whenever you ask DOS to show you the directory of a disk, DOS lists the files it finds, showing each file name (and extension, if there is one). It also shows you the size of each file, in units called *bytes,* and gives the date and the time the file was either created or last changed.

Many people have heard of a byte but aren't quite certain what it is. The easiest way to think of a byte is as the amount of storage required to hold one character in computer memory or on disk. Here are a few familiar items and their sizes, in bytes:

the letters *abcd*, 4 bytes, 1 byte per letter; the words *United States*, 13 bytes—blanks count; a double-spaced, typewritten page, 1500 bytes; this book, approximately 1,000,000 bytes.

Depending on the size and type of drives you use (fixed disk, diskette, or both), a typical diskette can hold from 362,496 to 1,457,664 bytes, and a typical fixed disk can hold anywhere from about 10,000,000 to 80,000,000 bytes—even more. For convenience, such large quantities are usually given in kilobytes (K) or megabytes (MB). One kilobyte equals 1024 bytes, and one megabyte equals 1024 kilobytes, so disk capacity can range from 360 K to 80 MB or more.

A Special Kind of Directory

Left to itself, DOS doesn't group files logically as you would do, categorizing them by type, content, or any other characteristic. DOS doesn't, for example, keep all program files in one place and all documents in another. To DOS, a file is just a file, and as it keeps track of the files you create, it keeps adding their file names to the disk directory.

The main disk directory cannot simply grow without limit, however, even though a large fixed disk can hold thousands of files. To help control growth and give you a way to keep track of similar groups of files, DOS includes commands that let you divide disk storage space into smaller, more manageable areas called *subdirectories*. Subdirectories are the disk equivalent of dividers in a file drawer.

Although you won't be working with subdirectories until later in this book, you do need to know that versions 4 and 5 of DOS normally install themselves automatically, on a fixed disk, in a subdirectory named DOS. Earlier versions of DOS, though they did not install themselves, were often placed in a subdirectory by the people who installed them. The tradition of keeping DOS in its own subdirectory is, in fact, so commonplace that this book assumes you have a DOS subdirectory if you use DOS from a fixed disk.

If you have a fixed disk, you can easily check for a DOS subdirectory. If your system prompt looks like this:

```
C:\DOS>_
```

DOS itself is telling you that you have a DOS subdirectory and it is looking at the subdirectory right now.

If your system prompt looks like this:

```
C:\>_
```

you need to check a little further. Use the Change Directory command, which tells DOS to find and focus its attention on the subdirectory you name. Type:

```
C:\>cd dos
```

If all goes well, DOS turns to your DOS subdirectory, and your system prompt probably changes to C:\DOS>. If DOS cannot find a DOS subdirectory, it responds with the message *Invalid directory* and once again displays the system prompt.

Note: The preceding two examples cover the majority of fixed disks equipped with versions 3 through 5 of DOS. If you received the Invalid directory *message, you can still try the following examples. They'll work just fine, but you should bear in mind that the file names you see might not be the same as those shown in the book.*

Chapter 8, ''A Tree of Files,'' shows you how to create, use, manage, and remove subdirectories. The next part of this chapter shows you how to browse through directories and subdirectories, finding specific files they contain.

DISPLAYING A DIRECTORY

To display the current directory (the directory DOS uses unless you specify otherwise), you simply type *dir*, the name of the Directory command. Type the command and press Enter (remember, if you don't have a fixed disk, your system prompt is A>):

    C:\DOS>dir

If you have a fixed disk and have displayed the DOS directory, the directory probably scrolled off the screen faster than you could read it. There are several ways to handle that, but one of the simplest uses what's called a command *parameter*. As you'll see in the next chapter, a command parameter lets you refine the action of a command. Here, with the Directory command, you can use a parameter typed as /p to tell DOS to *pause* after displaying a screenful of directory entries. Try it. If your directory listing was too long to fit on one screen, type:

    C:\DOS>dir /p

This time, scrolling stops when the screen is full. Press any key to see the remainder of the directory listing, one screenful at a time. Figure 3-1 shows a sampling of the DOS file names you see on a computer with a fixed disk and version 5 of DOS.

If you're using diskettes or a different version of DOS, your directory listing differs—perhaps a little, perhaps a lot. The list might be shorter, for example, or it might show some different names, dates, or times. Regardless, certain names, such as FORMAT, COMMAND, COUNTRY, KEYBOARD, and MODE appear consistently across different versions of DOS. You can check your display for one or two of those names if you want, but the real point of this example is simple: The result of a Directory command should always be a list of files stored on the disk.

Note: The Directory command is used in examples throughout the book. Unless stated otherwise, the version 5 display is shown.

```
Volume in drive C is FIXED DISK
Volume Serial Number is 1608-5A30
Directory of C:\DOS

    .              <DIR>       09-01-91    9:04a
    ..             <DIR>       09-01-91    9:04a
EGA        SYS       4885  03-01-91   12:00a
FORMAT     COM      32833  L3-01-91   12:00a
DISPLAY    SYS      15723  03-01-91   12:00a
COUNTRY    SYS      16944  03-01-91   12:00a
HIMEM      SYS      11424  03-01-91   12:00a
KEYB       COM      14442  03-01-91   12:00a
KEYBOARD   SYS      33776  03-01-91   12:00a
MODE       COM      23313  03-01-91   12:00a
SETVER     EXE      11821  03-01-91   12:00a
EGA        CPI      58848  03-01-91   12:00a
ANSI       SYS       8934  03-01-91   12:00a
DEBUG      EXE      20522  03-01-91   12:00a
DOSKEY     COM       5751  03-01-91   12:00a
EDLIN      EXE      12578  03-01-91   12:00a
EMM386     EXE      91210  03-01-91   12:00a
FASTOPEN   EXE      11890  03-01-91   12:00a
FDISK      EXE      57192  03-01-91   12:00a
MEM        EXE      39514  03-01-91   12:00a
MIRROR     COM      18089  03-01-91   12:00a
```

Figure 3-1. *A sample directory display of version 5 DOS files.*

The lines at the top of a directory listing give information about the disk itself and are explained in Chapter 6, ''Managing Your Diskettes.'' In version 5, the last two lines of a directory display show the number of files in the directory, the number of bytes of storage they occupy, and—in the last line—the number of bytes of storage remaining on the disk. (In versions before 5, the directory listing ends with a single line that gives the number of files and the number of bytes available for storage.)

Figure 3-2 shows a sample entry from a directory. The file name is DISKCOPY; note that it is eight letters long, the maximum length of a DOS file name. The next item, COM, is the file's extension. The next item tells you the file's size, and the final two entries give the date and time the file was created or last changed.

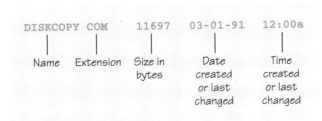

Figure 3-2. *A sample directory entry.*

SOME IMPORTANT KEYS

In the examples in the previous chapter, you used the standard typewriter portion of the keyboard to enter commands. Several other keys have important meanings to DOS. Figures 3-3 and 3-4 show where these keys are located on two common versions of the IBM keyboard. If your keyboard does not have the key used in an example, check your system's documentation for equivalent keys.

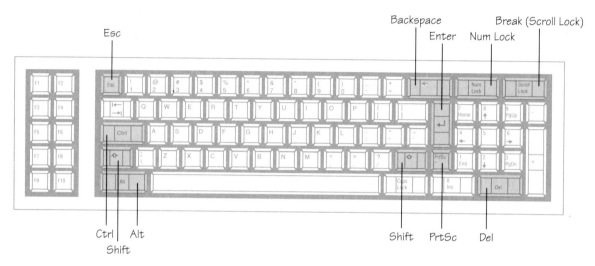

Figure 3-3. *Special keys on the IBM PC and PC/XT keyboards.*

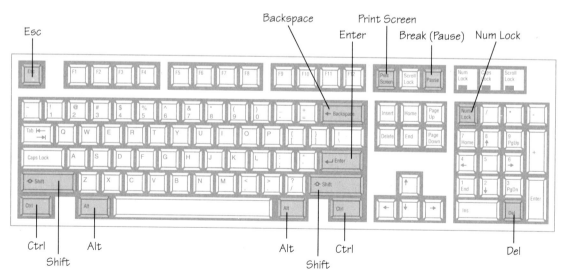

Figure 3-4. *Special keys on the enhanced IBM PC/AT keyboard.*

Shift

The Shift keys are labeled with an open arrow, the word *Shift*, or both. Like the Shift keys on a typewriter, they have no effect by themselves; they shift the keyboard to uppercase letters and special characters, such as the dollar sign.

Escape

This key, usually labeled *Esc*, cancels a line you have typed. To see how it works, type several characters (but don't press Enter):

    C:\DOS>Now is the time

To erase this line, you could repeatedly press the Backspace key, but press the Escape key instead:

    C:\DOS>Now is the time\

DOS displays a reverse slash (\) to indicate that the line was canceled and moves the cursor to the next line. DOS doesn't repeat the system prompt, but the cursor indicates it is still ready for you to type a command. Press the Enter key, and DOS displays the system prompt and the cursor on the next line:

    C:\DOS>_

Pressing the Escape key is the quickest way to cancel a line you have typed.

Control

This key, usually labeled *Ctrl*, has no effect by itself, but it is used like the Shift keys to change the effect of pressing another key. The combination of the Control key and some other key is represented in this book by Ctrl- followed by the other key. Ctrl-Break, for example, means ''hold down the Control key, then press and release the Break key.'' The Control key combinations are described in a moment.

Numeric Lock

This key, familiarly known as *Num Lock*, does two things. It switches the effect of the keys in the calculator-style number pad at the right side of the keyboard back and forth between cursor movement and numbers. On the PC and PC/XT keyboards, it is also used in combination with the Control key to freeze the display. To test the first function, press Num Lock, and then press the 4 key in the numeric pad several times:

    C:\DOS>444_

The keys produce numbers on the screen. Now press Num Lock again and press the same 4 key you pressed before:

    C:\DOS>44_

Pressing Num Lock a second time switched the keys to their cursor-movement functions. The 4 key is labeled with a left arrow in addition to the number 4; pressing it moves the cursor left, in the direction of the arrow, and erases a character just as the Backspace key does. Press Num Lock and the same 4 key again:

```
C:\DOS>444_
```

You switched back to numbers. Press Num Lock one more time to switch back to cursor movement, press Esc to cancel the line, and press the Enter key to return to the system prompt:

```
C:\DOS>444\
```

```
C:\DOS>_
```

You won't often use the arrow keys for cursor movement with DOS, but many application programs, such as word processors, require frequent cursor movements. If you have version 5, you'll also use the arrow keys for giving commands to Doskey.

Break

This key is labeled either *Scroll Lock* and *Break* or *Pause* and *Break*. When labeled *Scroll Lock* and *Break* (as on the PC and PC/XT keyboards), this key has no effect on DOS by itself, but it is used with the Control key to cancel a command you have entered. If labeled *Pause* and *Break* (as on the PC/AT keyboard), this key temporarily halts the display; when used with the Control key, it cancels a command.

Alternate and Delete

These keys, labeled *Alt* and *Del*, have no effect on DOS by themselves but are used with the Control key to restart DOS.

Print Screen

This key, labeled *Print Screen, Prnt Scrn, PrtSc*, or some close variation, is used with the Shift and Control keys to print the contents of the screen. You used Shift-PrtSc in the previous chapter; you'll use Ctrl-PrtSc, and see the difference, in a short while. (If you have an IBM PS/2 keyboard, you don't have to press Shift with PrtSc.)

Control Key Functions

Figure 3-5 shows the effects produced by holding down the Control key and pressing another key. You'll probably use these combinations fairly often with DOS, so the next few topics show you examples of each combination. When you are being shown exactly what to type, the names of the keys are separated by hyphens and enclosed in angle brackets to represent pressing a Control key combination. Thus, when you see <Ctrl-Break> in a command, it means ''press Ctrl-Break.''

Before trying the examples, you should also note that DOS displays the Control key as the symbol ^. DOS does not acknowledge all Control key commands on the screen, but when it does, it uses the symbol ^ in combination with a letter. Control-Break, for example, shows on the screen as ^C and can also be typed by holding down the Control key and typing the letter C.

Ctrl-Num Lock or Pause	Halts whatever the system is doing until you press another key. Typically used to freeze the display when information is scrolling by too fast or scrolling off the top of the screen. Can also be typed as Ctrl-S (Ctrl plus the letter S).
Ctrl-Break	Cancels whatever the system is doing. Use this when you really don't want the computer to continue what it's doing. Can also be typed as Ctrl-C (Ctrl plus the letter C).
Ctrl-PrtSc	Pressing this key combination once causes DOS to start printing every line as it is displayed; pressing Ctrl-PrtSc a second time stops simultaneous displaying and printing. Can also be typed as Ctrl-P (Ctrl plus the letter P).
Ctrl-Alt-Del	Restarts DOS. This combination is unique; no other keys can be used to do the same thing.

Figure 3-5. *Control key combinations.*

Freezing the Display

As mentioned earlier, DOS lets you temporarily halt the display by pressing Ctrl-Num Lock or the Pause key. When you do this, the display remains frozen, giving you time to read it. To start the display moving again, you simply press any key.

To test this function, type the following to display the directory. When the entries start appearing on the screen, press Pause or Ctrl-Num Lock to freeze the display:

```
C:\DOS>dir
```

Press any key, and the display resumes. You can press Pause or Ctrl-Num Lock to stop and start the display as many times as you like, so you can view displays that are many screens long.

Canceling a Command

If you enter a command and then change your mind or realize that you meant to enter some other command, you can cancel the command you entered by pressing Ctrl-Break. To test this function, type the Directory command again. This time, however, press Ctrl-Break when DOS begins to display the directory entries.

31

Here's an example:

```
C:\DOS>dir

 Volume in drive C is FIXED DISK
 Volume Serial Number is 1608-5A30
 Directory of C:\DOS

 .            <DIR>      09-01-91    9:04a
 ..           <DIR>      09-01-91    9:04a
 EGA      SYS      4885 03-01-91   12:00a
 FORMAT   COM     32833 03-01-91   12:00a
 DISPLAY  SYS     15723 03-01-91   12:00a
 COUNTRY  SYS     16944 03-01-91   12:00a
 HIMEM    SYS     11424 03-01-91   12:00a
 KEYB     COM     14442 03-01-91   12:00a
 KEYBOARD SYS     33776 03^C

C:\DOS>_
```

Your display probably stopped somewhere else in the directory, but when you press Ctrl-Break, DOS stops what it is doing, displays ^C, and returns to the command level.

Printing and Displaying Simultaneously

In the previous chapter you printed the contents of the screen by pressing Shift-PrtSc. There's another way to print from the screen: Pressing Ctrl-PrtSc tells DOS to start printing everything it displays. DOS continues to print and display simultaneously until you press Ctrl-PrtSc again.

To test this function, make sure your printer is turned on, press Ctrl-PrtSc, then enter the Directory command:

```
C:\DOS><Ctrl-PrtSc>dir
```

DOS again displays the directory of the system disk, but this time each line is printed as it is displayed. (If you're using a LaserJet or similar printer, you might have to press Ctrl-P instead.)

The directory is displayed more slowly than when you use the Directory command alone, because DOS waits until a line is printed before displaying and printing the next line. You can cancel the Directory command before the complete directory is printed by pressing Ctrl-Break. Remember to press Ctrl-PrtSc as well, to end the simultaneous displaying and printing.

If you want to print something without printing the command that creates the display, type the command, press Ctrl-PrtSc, and then press Enter. For example, when you printed the directory in the preceding example, the Directory command was the first line printed. To avoid printing the command, type:

```
C:\DOS>dir<Ctrl-PrtSc>
```

Now printing begins with the first line of the directory; the Directory command isn't printed. Cancel the command by pressing Ctrl-Break.

Be sure to press Ctrl-PrtSc again to stop printing; otherwise, DOS continues to print everything it displays, even if you go on to an entirely different task.

Shift-PrtSc versus Ctrl-PrtSc

These two methods of printing from the screen work differently and have different uses. Shift-PrtSc prints everything on the screen and stops. Ctrl-PrtSc, as you just saw, alternates displaying and printing, line by line. If everything you want is on the screen, use Shift-PrtSc; it's faster. But if you want to print something longer than one screenful, use Ctrl-PrtSc.

Ctrl-PrtSc is better for printing long displays, because you press it once to tell DOS to start simultaneous displaying and printing, enter a command—such as the Directory command—to create the display, and then press Ctrl-PrtSc again when you want to stop printing. If you use Shift-PrtSc for printing displays more than one screen long, you have to display the first screen, print it, then display the second screen, print it, and so forth until everything you want has been printed.

Repeating Commands with Doskey

Beginning with version 5, DOS includes the Doskey command you saw in Chapter 2. Doskey makes your work with DOS easier and more efficient by letting you repeat DOS commands you've used recently without retyping them.

To help you minimize keystrokes (and the chance of mistyping a command), Doskey lets you use several special keys, among them the arrow and function keys shown in Figures 3-6 and 3-7.

Figure 3-6. *Keys on the IBM PC and PC/XT keyboards that have special meaning to Doskey.*

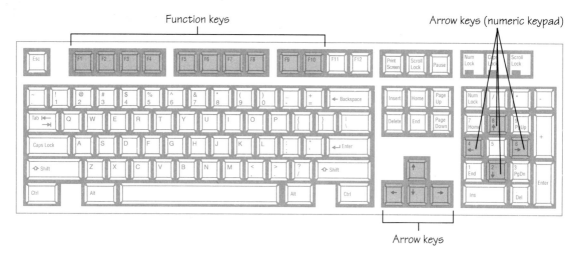

Figure 3-7. *Keys on the enhanced IBM PC/AT keyboard that have special meaning to Doskey.*

Note: If you're using version 5 of DOS from diskettes and saw the message Bad command or file name *the last time you tried to start Doskey, it's because you need the diskette that contains the DOSKEY file. Now that you're familiar with the Directory command, check your Support diskette (and others, if necessary) for this file by typing* dir *or* dir /p. *When you see DOSKEY in the directory list, leave the diskette containing the file in drive A.*

The following examples show you some of Doskey's basic features. Recall that you start Doskey simply by typing its name and pressing Enter:

`C:\DOS>`doskey

DOS responds:

DOSKey installed.

As you've seen, Doskey lets you repeat your last DOS command in a simple two-step procedure: Press Up arrow to redisplay the command, and then press Enter to carry it out. But you won't always want to repeat the last command you typed. You might want to repeat one you used several commands ago. Doskey lets you do that, too. To try it, first type the following DOS commands (just press Enter when DOS prompts for the date and time):

```
C:\DOS>date
C:\DOS>time
C:\DOS>ver
C:\DOS>dir
C:\DOS>cls
```

Now you've entered some commands Doskey can help you find and reuse.

Although you probably wouldn't have much trouble remembering five commands, Doskey can help you keep track of dozens. But when you've typed a number of commands, you can't always remember which ones you typed or in what order. Once you've started Doskey, you can simply press the F7 function key to see a list of your previous commands, in sequence. Try it now. Press F7, and Doskey displays:

```
C:\DOS>
1: date
2: time
3: ver
4: dir
5: cls
C:\DOS>_
```

The commands are numbered and in the same order you typed them. Press the Up arrow key. Doskey displays the last command:

```
C:\DOS>cls_
```

Press the Up arrow key again, and Doskey replaces *cls* with *dir*, the next-to-last command. Whenever you press the Up arrow key, Doskey recalls and displays the previous command.

Now try some other keys. Press the Down arrow key. The display changes back to:

```
C:\DOS>cls_
```

The Down arrow key does the opposite of the Up arrow key: It tells Doskey to retrieve the next command (as opposed to the previous command) in the list.

You can take bigger leaps through the list, too, with the Page Up and Page Down keys. Press the Page Up key, and the display changes to:

```
C:\DOS>date_
```

Page Up tells Doskey to recall the first command in the current list. And, predictably, when you press the Page Down key, the display changes to:

```
C:\DOS>cls_
```

which is the last command in the current list.

You can also request a specific command by entering its line number. Press the F9 key. Doskey displays:

```
C:\DOS>Line number: _
```

This time, request the Ver command, which is number 3 in the list. Type:

```
C:\DOS>Line number: 3
```

and press Enter, and this appears:

```
C:\DOS>ver_
```

Press Enter. DOS carries out the Ver command and displays the system prompt.

Doskey has many uses for everyone from beginners to advanced users of DOS. These examples showed a few quick ways to use it; later chapters show you how to use Doskey to tailor DOS to the way you work.

RESTARTING THE SYSTEM

Suppose you find yourself in a situation where your computer is not responding as you think it should, or it complains about something you don't know how to handle, or you decide it would be best to scrap what you're doing and start over from the beginning. You don't have to turn the power switch off and on to restart your system; you can do it by pressing Ctrl-Alt-Del.

Try it. If you are using DOS from diskettes, check that your normal Startup diskette is in drive A. If you have a fixed disk, be sure drive A is open.

Now hold down both Ctrl and Alt and press Del.

The screen clears, the drive lights blink, the system beeps, and DOS is loaded just as it was when you turned the power on. Restarting with Ctrl-Alt-Del takes less time, though, because the computer doesn't test all its devices and memory as it does whenever you switch the power off and on. If the DOS Shell appears, press F3 to leave it.

A SHORT DIVERSION

The system prompt is an economical way for DOS to show you the current drive and directory and to let you know that you can enter a command. But the combination of the current drive and directory and the greater-than sign (>) is only one possible system prompt. The DOS Prompt command lets you change the system prompt to almost anything you want.

For example, you might prefer a more courteous machine. Type the following and press Enter (<space> means press the Spacebar):

```
C:\DOS>prompt May I help you?<space><Enter>
```

Now the system prompt isn't quite so cryptic:

```
May I help you? _
```

Each time DOS returns to the command level, it displays this polite phrase. Try it by pressing the Enter key once or twice to cause DOS to display the system prompt again. Although your new prompt looks quite different from C:\> or C:\DOS> (and actually conveys less information), the meaning is the same: DOS is at the command level, ready for you to enter a command.

To see just how much you can cram into the system prompt, type the following example as a single line (as before, <space> means press the Spacebar). Although the example is shown on two separate lines and won't fit on a single line on screen either, don't press the Enter key until you come to <Enter> at the end of the second line:

May I help you? prompt The time is<space>t_The date is<space>
d_The current disk is<space>n_Your command:<space><Enter>

Now the system prompt is three lines of data followed by a request for a command:

    The time is 16:26:03.54
    The date is Wed 10-16-1991
    The current disk is C
    Your command: _

You would probably quickly tire of all this, but the exercise shows how much flexibility DOS gives you. You don't have to take advantage of it all, but the possibilities are there if you want them.

To return the system prompt to a more normal form, simply type the following Prompt command:

    The time is 16:26:03.54
    The date is Wed 10-16-1991
    The current disk is C
    Your command: prompt pg

Your system prompt changes to the familiar C:\> or C:\DOS>.

CHAPTER SUMMARY

Each disk has a directory that lists the name, extension, and size of each file, and the date and time the file was created or last changed. You can see the directory by typing *dir* and pressing Enter.

▶ The Escape key cancels a line you have typed.

▶ Pause or Ctrl-Num Lock freezes the display. Ctrl-S has the same effect.

▶ Ctrl-Break cancels a command. Ctrl-C has the same effect.

▶ Ctrl-PrtSc turns simultaneous displaying and printing on and off. Ctrl-P has the same effect.

▶ Ctrl-Alt-Del restarts DOS.

▶ The version 5 Doskey command helps you display, choose from, and repeat commands you've already used.

Now that you're more familiar with the keyboard, the next chapter gives you a closer look at diskettes and files.

CHAPTER 4

A LOOK AT FILES AND DISKETTES

The computer's memory is temporary; it is cleared each time you turn off the computer. The only way you can save data permanently is to store the data in a file on a disk. When DOS needs data that is stored in a file, it reads the data from the disk into memory. If you change the data and want to keep the changed version, you must store the revised version on disk before turning off the system.

TYPES OF FILES

In general, a file contains either a program or data. A *program* is a set of instructions for the computer. *Data* is the text and numbers, such as a project proposal, a table of tax rates, or a list of customers, that the program needs to do your work.

Two types of files are important to your work: text files and command files. They are quite different, so it's important to look more closely at the kind of information these files contain and at how the files are used.

Text Files

Text files are data files that contain characters you can read (everyday letters, numbers, and symbols). Word processing programs store their documents in text files, as do the version 5 MS-DOS Editor and (in all versions) the Edlin text editor. Many files you use in your work with the computer—and all the files that you will create and use in this book—are text files.

The definition of a text file may seem self-evident at first, but it actually introduces you to an important characteristic of computer information storage. Your computer keeps information in two very different forms: One is text, the characters contained in text files; the other is machine-readable code, which looks meaningless to most people but is quite meaningful to computers.

Command Files

Command files contain the instructions DOS needs to carry out commands. DOS command files can be programs, such as DISKCOPY.COM, or, as you will see in Chapter 14, "Creating Your Own Commands," they can be a series of commands that you put together to perform a specific task and store in a file.

Not all DOS commands are stored in separate command files, however. Some commands, such as the Directory command, are built into the main body of DOS. When you load DOS into memory, you load these commands with it. When you want to use these commands, DOS has them on tap for immediate use—it does not need to look up a separate command file to carry them out.

These built-in commands are called *permanent,* or *internal,* commands. In contrast, the commands that are kept in command files until they are requested by you are called *temporary,* or *external,* commands. When you use a permanent command, you simply request the command, and DOS carries it out. When you use a temporary command, DOS must load the command file from disk into memory before it can carry out the command.

An application program, such as a word processor, is also stored in a command file; it stores your work, such as documents, in data files.

HOW FILES ARE NAMED

No matter the type of file, each file must have a file name. Recall that a file name can be up to eight characters long. You can use almost any character on the keyboard when you name your files, but it's a good idea to give your files names, such as BUDGET or SALESRPT, that describe their contents.

To identify a file more completely, a three-character suffix called the file *extension* can be added to the file name; this suffix is separated from the file name by a period. So that you and DOS can tell your files apart, each file on a disk must have either a different name or a different extension; REPORT.JAN and REPORT.FEB, for example, are different files to DOS, even though their file names are the same.

Specifying the Drive

When you name a file in a command, DOS needs to know which drive contains the disk with the file on it. If you don't specify a drive, DOS looks on the disk in the current drive (the drive letter shown in the system prompt). If the disk containing the file is not in the current drive, you can precede the file name with the letter of the drive and a colon. For example, if you specify the file as *b:report.doc*, DOS looks for it on the disk in drive B.

PREPARING FOR THE EXAMPLES

The following pages show a number of examples to help you become more comfortable with files and diskettes. With DOS, as with most other computer applications, doing is often the easiest and most effective way of learning.

If you have a fixed disk, make sure the latch on drive A is open, turn on or restart the computer, and go through the startup routine until you see the system prompt (C:\> or C:\DOS>). (If the DOS Shell starts automatically, startup instructions from here on assume that you press F3 to leave the Shell.) You'll be working with files in the DOS subdirectory, so change to it if necessary by typing:

```
C:\>cd \dos
```

Go on to the next heading.

If your system doesn't have a fixed disk, start or restart your computer and go through the startup routine until you see the A:\> prompt. The examples use several external DOS commands, beginning with DISKCOPY.COM. Use the Directory command to check your DOS diskettes for this file, and start with the diskette containing DISKCOPY.COM in drive A. Use the Directory command whenever DOS responds *Bad command or file name* because it cannot find the command file it needs for a particular example.

Don't Worry About Memorizing

You'll use several commands in this chapter, but you needn't remember exactly how to use each one; all the commands are described in more detail in the remaining chapters of the book. The purpose of this chapter is to introduce you to files and diskettes.

QUALIFYING A COMMAND

Up to now, most commands you have entered have consisted of a single word or abbreviation, such as *time* or *dir*. Many commands, however, let you add one or more qualifiers to make the action more specific. These qualifiers are called *parameters*.

Some commands require parameters; others allow you to add parameters if you want. The Directory command, for example, does not require parameters, but it lets you tailor a command with such specifications as the name of a particular file you want to see. You'll use some parameters in the following examples; descriptions of commands in later chapters show their parameters, both required and optional.

DISPLAYING SPECIFIC DIRECTORY ENTRIES

In the previous chapter you used the Directory command to display the directory entries of the files in your DOS subdirectory or on your startup diskette. You can display the directory entry of a single file, or the directory entries of a set of files, by adding a parameter to the Directory command.

Displaying the Directory Entry of a Single File

To display the directory entry of a specific file, you simply type the file name (and its extension, if there is one) after the command name. For example, the command to copy the contents of one diskette to another is called Diskcopy. Its command file is DISKCOPY.COM. To display the directory entry for only DISKCOPY.COM, type the following command. (If you're not using a fixed disk, the diskette with DISKCOPY.COM should be in drive A; remember that your system prompt is A:\>, not C:\DOS.)

```
C:\DOS>dir diskcopy.com
```

DOS displays only the directory entry of the file you specified (don't worry if you see a different size, date, or time):

```
 Volume in drive C is FIXED DISK
 Volume Serial Number is 1608-5A30
 Directory of C:\DOS

DISKCOPY COM      11697 03-01-91  12:00a
        1 file(s)      11697 bytes
                    36333568 bytes free
```

```
C:\DOS>
```

If the file you name isn't on the disk, or if you don't type the file name exactly as it is stored, DOS responds *File not found.*

Displaying the Directory Entries of a Set of Files

What if you remember most of a file name, or the file name but not the extension? DOS helps you out by giving you two wildcard characters, ∗ and ?, that you can substitute for actual characters in a file name. Like wild cards in a poker game, the wildcard characters can represent any other character. They differ only in that ? can substitute for one character, while ∗ can substitute for more than one character.

Suppose you remember only that a file's name begins with the letter F. It takes only a moment to check all the files that begin with F.

Use the DOS directory as an example. Type the following command:

```
C:\DOS>dir f*
```

DOS displays the directory entries of all file names that begin with F:

```
 Volume in drive C is FIXED DISK
 Volume Serial Number is 1608-5A30
 Directory of C:\DOS

FORMAT    COM     32833 03-01-91  12:00a
FASTOPEN  EXE     11890 03-01-91  12:00a
FDISK     EXE     57192 03-01-91  12:00a
FC        EXE     18138 03-01-91  12:00a
FIND      EXE      6642 03-01-91  12:00a
        5 file(s)     126695 bytes
                    36333568 bytes free
```

```
C:\DOS>
```

(This listing shows the names of all the DOS files that begin with F. If you're using DOS from diskettes, your list might differ, but you should see FORMAT.COM or FORMAT.EXE.)

Wildcard characters can simplify the task of keeping track of your files. Chapter 5, "Managing Your Files," includes several examples of using wildcard characters. Now it's time to stop practicing and to create some files of your own.

PREPARING A DISKETTE FOR USE

Before DOS can store a file on a new diskette, it must prepare the diskette for use. This preparation, in which DOS writes certain information for its own use on the diskette, is called *formatting*. You tell DOS to do this formatting with the Format command. You'll need two formatted diskettes for the examples in this book. Now is a good time to format them, so get out two blank diskettes and two blank labels before proceeding.

Type the following:

```
C:\DOS>format b:
```

This command tells DOS to format the diskette in drive B.

Formatting a diskette effectively deletes any files that may be stored on it, so DOS gives you a chance to make sure you haven't put the wrong diskette in the specified drive by displaying a message, then waiting for you to type something:

```
Insert new diskette for drive B:
and press ENTER when ready..._
```

If you discover that you put in the wrong diskette, no problem: Just take out the wrong one and put in the right one before you press the Enter key.

If you can't find a diskette to format, and you want to cancel the command, again, no problem: You don't have to turn the system off; just press Ctrl-Break.

But you do want to format the diskette now. If you have one diskette drive, place a blank diskette in drive A and close the drive latch if necessary. If you have two diskette drives, place a blank diskette in drive B and close the latch.

Press Enter. If you have version 5, DOS begins by displaying a message telling you it is *Checking existing disk format*. The message then becomes a constantly changing display that looks like this:

```
Formatting 1.2M
   8 percent completed
```

Version 4 of DOS tells you x *percent of disk formatted.* In earlier versions, the message might look like this:

```
Head:    0 Cylinder:    1
```

or it might simply read *Formatting....* In any case, the light on the drive goes on, and DOS begins writing on the diskette. When DOS is finished, it tells you *Format complete.* If you have version 4 or 5, it then displays the message:

```
Volume label (11 characters, ENTER for none)? _
```

A volume label is a name you give a formatted disk to help identify it and the files it contains. The name can be up to 11 characters long, including blanks, but cannot include certain characters DOS reserves for special uses—characters such as a period (used between a file name and an extension), an asterisk or a question mark (used as wildcard characters), or a forward slash (used when typing command parameters).

You don't have to assign a volume label to a disk, but because DOS displays the volume label at the beginning of any directory listing you request, the few seconds you spend thinking up and typing a volume label when you format a disk can, in the long run, save you time by helping to identify what the disk contains. (If you don't have version 4 or 5, you can assign a volume label after formatting with the /V option of the Format command; you'll find out about this in Chapter 6, ''Managing Your Diskettes.'')

If DOS is requesting a volume label, assign one to the disk you just formatted. Type a simple but descriptive name, such as:

```
Volume label (11 characters, ENTER for none)? examples 1
```

and press Enter.

DOS then displays some information about the diskette, followed by a final message:

```
   1213952 bytes total disk space
   1213952 bytes available on disk

       512 bytes in each allocation unit
      2371 allocation units available on disk

Volume Serial Number is 1A2C-13F5

Format another (Y/N)?_
```

The numbers shown are for the 1.2 MB diskette drive on the IBM PC/AT and compatible machines. Depending on the type of diskette drives you have and the version of DOS you're using, the total disk space in your report might differ—for example, 1,457,664, 730,112, or 362,496.

The messages about allocation units and the volume serial number are provided by DOS beginning with version 4. Allocation units are groups of bytes used by DOS in storing information; the volume serial number is assigned as part of the formatting procedure. Neither is likely to be significant in your day-to-day use of DOS.

The final message, *Format another (Y/N)?*, means that DOS is now waiting for you to say whether you want to format another diskette. Type *y* and press Enter. The message asking you to put the diskette in drive B and press Enter is repeated, so go through the same process to format the second diskette; name it EXAMPLES 2. When DOS finishes, it asks you again whether you want to format another.

Now type *n* and press Enter. DOS displays the system prompt (C:\DOS>), telling you that the Format command is complete and that DOS is waiting for you to type another command.

You now have two formatted diskettes. It's time to put one of them to use by creating a file; if you removed the diskette you just formatted, put it in your diskette drive (drive B if you have two diskette drives).

CREATING A TEXT FILE

An easy way to create a text file is by using the DOS Copy command. As you might guess from its name, the Copy command can be used to make a copy of a file. It can also be used to copy characters from the keyboard into a file.

DOS refers to the parts of your computer, such as the keyboard, display, and printer, as *devices*. To DOS, devices, like files, have names. The keyboard is known to DOS as CON (for CONsole).

You are going to create a file by telling DOS to copy what you type from the keyboard onto the blank diskette in drive B.

To create a file named NOTE.DOC on the diskette in drive B, type the following example. End each line by pressing Enter; where you see a blank line, press Enter to tell DOS to insert an extra line:

```
C:\DOS>copy con b:note.doc
October 16, 1991

Dear Fred,
Just a note to remind you
that our meeting is at 9.

Jack
```

That's the end of the file. To tell DOS that it's the end of the file, press Ctrl-Z (hold down the Control key and press Z), then press Enter:

```
<Ctrl-Z><Enter>
```

When you press Ctrl-Z, DOS displays ^Z (the ^, remember, represents the Control key). After you press Enter, DOS acknowledges that it copied a file:

```
        1 file(s) copied
```

```
C:\DOS>_
```

To verify that the file is there, display the directory of the diskette in drive B:

```
    C:\DOS>dir b:
```

Sure enough, NOTE.DOC is on the diskette:

```
Volume in drive B is EXAMPLES 2
Volume Serial Number is 1839-10EE
Directory of B:\

NOTE        DOC         94 10-16-91    2:03p
        1 file(s)              94 bytes
                        1213440 bytes free
```

C:\DOS>_

This method of creating a text file is quick and convenient and is used in examples throughout the book.

Displaying a Text File

Because you can read the characters in text files, you'll often want to display a text file on the screen. It's even easier to display one than it is to create it. Just use the DOS Type command. To display your file, type the following:

C:\DOS>type b:note.doc

DOS displays each line and returns to the command level:

```
October 16, 1991

Dear Fred,
Just a note to remind you
that our meeting is at 9.

Jack
```

C:\DOS>_

This is the quickest way to see what's in a file; you'll probably use the Type command frequently. Displaying a file isn't always helpful, though, because not all files are text files; they don't all contain readable characters. See for yourself. (If you're using DOS from diskettes, place the diskette with MORE.COM in drive A.) Type:

C:\DOS>type more.com

Yes, the display is correct. It's hard to tell from that jumble what is in the file because the file contains a program stored in machine code, not text.

Printing a Text File

One of the main reasons you write documents, of course, is to have a printed copy. You can print your file by copying it to the printer. You've already copied from the keyboard to a disk. Now, copy from the disk to the printer. The printer is known to DOS as PRN. Make certain the printer is turned on, and type the following:

C:\DOS>copy b:note.doc prn

The file is printed. When you print a file, you'll probably want to position the paper by hand before you enter the command so that the printing will begin where you want it to on the page.

There's an easier way, however, to print a file: the Print command.

Note: If you're using DOS from diskettes, you need the diskette containing the file PRINT.COM. Remember, if DOS cannot find a file, it displays the message Bad command or file name *and waits for you to try again. When necessary, remember to check your DOS diskettes for appropriate command files. Examples from here on assume that DOS can find the files it needs to carry out your commands.*

To print your file with the Print command, type the following:

```
C:\DOS>print b:note.doc
```

If DOS responds:

```
Name of list device [PRN]: _
```

press the Enter key. DOS displays one or both of the following messages and prints the file you specified:

```
Resident part of PRINT installed


 B:\NOTE.DOC is currently being printed

C:\DOS>_
```

These messages are explained in more detail in Chapter 5, "Managing Your Files."

The Print command makes most printers advance to the next page after printing. Although this file is too short to show it, you can continue to use the system to do other work while the Print command is printing a file.

Copying a Text File

The Copy command is one of the more versatile DOS commands. You have already used it to create and print a text file. The Copy command also duplicates files.

To copy the file named NOTE.DOC into another file named LETTER.DOC, type:

```
C:\DOS>copy b:note.doc b:letter.doc
```

When you press Enter, DOS copies the file; then it acknowledges that it did so:

```
 1 file(s) copied

C:\DOS>_
```

Display the directory of the diskette in drive B again to verify the copy:

```
C:\DOS>dir b:
```

Now you have two text files:

```
 Volume in drive B is EXAMPLES 2
 Volume Serial Number is 1839-10EE
 Directory of B:\

NOTE      DOC         94 10-16-91   2:03p
LETTER    DOC         94 10-16-91   2:03p
        2 file(s)          188 bytes
                    1212928 bytes free
```

```
C:\DOS>
```

If you wanted, you could make changes to one file and still have a copy of the original version on disk. You'll find the Copy command quite useful when you need several files that differ only slightly or when you have several small files that can be combined in different ways to create other files: often-used paragraphs, for example, that can be recombined in different letters, contracts, or other documents.

Deleting a Text File

Just as you get rid of paper files, you can get rid of disk files. To delete NOTE.DOC from the diskette in drive B, type:

```
C:\DOS>del b:note.doc
```

```
C:\DOS>_
```

Now check the directory one more time:

```
C:\DOS>dir b:
```

```
 Volume in drive B is EXAMPLES 2
 Volume Serial Number is 1839-10EE
 Directory of B:\

LETTER    DOC         94 10-16-91   2:03p
        1 file(s)           94 bytes
                    1213440 bytes free
```

```
C:\DOS>_
```

It's gone.

SOME ADVANCED FEATURES

Several commands and features give you much greater control over the way DOS does its work. You can:

▶ Sort lines of data—for example, sort alphabetically the list of directory entries produced by the Directory command.

▶ View a long display one screenful at a time, without having to freeze the display by pressing Ctrl-Num Lock or Pause.

▶ Tell DOS to send the results, or *output,* of a command to the printer instead of to the display, simply by adding a few characters to the command.

▶ Search lines of data for a series of characters.

The examples in this section give you a glimpse of these advanced features; the features are described in detail, with many additional examples, in later chapters.

Sorting Lines of Data

You have probably arranged card files or lists in some sequence, such as alphabetic or numeric order. The Sort command sorts, or arranges, lines of data such as a list of names. To see how this works, sort the lines of the text file LETTER.DOC.

Type the following:

```
C:\DOS>sort < b:letter.doc
```

The less-than symbol (<) tells DOS to send a copy of the file LETTER.DOC to the Sort command, which then displays the lines of the file after rearranging (sorting) them into alphabetic order:

```
Dear Fred,
Jack
Just a note to remind you
October 16, 1991
that our meeting is at 9.

C:\DOS>_
```

Although you probably don't want to sort the lines of your letters, you can put whatever you like in a text file—for example, a list of customers or employees. The Sort command is a powerful addition to your kit of computer tools.

Viewing a Long Display One Screenful at a Time

When you displayed a directory in Chapter 3, lines might have scrolled off the top of the screen because the display was too long to fit. You saw that you can freeze the display by pressing Ctrl-Num Lock or Pause or by using the /P parameter of the Directory command. There's another way to stop scrolling: The More command displays

50

one screenful, with -- *More* -- at the bottom of the screen, then waits for you to press any key to continue to the next screenful. Display the current directory again, this time using the More command. Type the vertical bar by holding down a Shift key and pressing the key labeled with a ¦ character:

    `C:\DOS>dir ¦ more`

DOS displays the first screenful, but the last lines aren't displayed yet (notice the -- *More* -- in the last line):

```
Volume in drive C is FIXED DISK
 Volume Serial Number is 1608-5A30
 Directory of C:\DOS

 .              <DIR>       09-01-91    9:04a
 ..             <DIR>       09-01-91    9:04a
EGA       SYS      4885 03-01-91   12:00a
FORMAT    COM     32833 03-01-91   12:00a
DISPLAY   SYS     15723 03-01-91   12:00a
COUNTRY   SYS     16944 03-01-91   12:00a
HIMEM     SYS     11424 03-01-91   12:00a
KEYB      COM     14442 03-01-91   12:00a
KEYBOARD  SYS     33776 03-01-91   12:00a
MODE      COM     23313 03-01-91   12:00a
SETVER    EXE     11821 03-01-91   12:00a
EGA       CPI     58848 03-01-91   12:00a
ANSI      SYS      8934 03-01-91   12:00a
DEBUG     EXE     20522 03-01-91   12:00a
DOSKEY    COM      5751 03-01-91   12:00a
EDLIN     EXE     12578 03-01-91   12:00a
EMM386    EXE     91210 03-01-91   12:00a
FASTOPEN  EXE     11890 03-01-91   12:00a
FDISK     EXE     57192 03-01-91   12:00a
-- More --
```

To see the rest of the directory, press any key. If DOS once again displays -- *More* -- at the bottom of the screen, press Ctrl-Break to end the command.

The More command displays long output one screenful at a time, giving you a chance to view it all at your convenience.

Note: When you use More and certain other commands that require DOS to manipulate files, you might see directory entries for files with odd names, such as ALCJDEAO, 1106002B, or %PIPE1.$$$. These are temporary files that DOS creates, then erases when it no longer needs them.

Sending Command Output to the Printer

In earlier examples, you printed the output of the Directory command by using the Print Screen key. There's a more direct way to print the output of a command: Simply follow the command with a greater-than symbol (>) and the name of the printer, PRN. To print the current directory, make sure the printer is turned on and type:

```
C:\DOS>dir > prn
```

If you don't want to wait for the whole directory to be printed, cancel the printing by pressing Ctrl-Break. This same technique can be used to send the output of a command to some other device or to a file, by substituting the device name or file name for PRN.

Note: If you're using DOS from diskettes, try using this command to print a list of the command files on each diskette. Such lists are useful for reference.

Finding a Series of Characters in a File

How many times have you searched through a pile of letters or notes, looking for a particular item or reference? If you have to look through DOS files or the output of DOS commands, the Find command will do the looking for you. For example, suppose you want to see the directory entries of all DOS files with SK in their names. Try the following (the quotation marks tell DOS which letters—known technically as a *character string,* or just *string*—to look for).

(If you don't have a fixed disk, check to see which of your DOS diskettes contains a few command files with the letters SK in their names.)

Type:

```
C:\DOS>dir | find "SK"
```

DOS displays only the entries with SK in their names (your list might differ):

```
Volume in drive C is FIXED DISK
DOSKEY    COM     5751 03-01-91  12:00a
FDISK     EXE    57192 03-01-91  12:00a
CHKDSK    EXE    16360 03-01-91  12:00a
DISKCOMP COM    10604 03-01-91  12:00a
DISKCOPY COM    11697 03-01-91  12:00a

C:\DOS>
```

The Find command is even more useful when you search for a series of characters in a text file. If a file contains a list of names and telephone numbers, for example, you can quickly display one particular entry, or all entries that contain a particular series of characters (such as an area code), or you can even display all entries that *don't* contain a particular series of characters. Chapter 13, ''Taking Control of Your System,'' shows you how to create such an automated index of names and telephone numbers with nothing but DOS commands.

Combining Features

These advanced features of DOS can also be used together in a single command, giving you even more flexibility in controlling DOS. Combining these features makes it possible to do a great deal with just one command. For example, suppose you want to print the directory entries of all files in the current directory whose names include the letter F; further, you want the entries sorted alphabetically. Type the following:

```
C:\DOS>dir | find "F" | sort > prn
```

This whole command translates easily into: Look at the directory, find all files with the letter F in their names, sort those files alphabetically, and send the results to the printer. DOS does as it is told:

```
Volume in drive C is FIXED DISK
FASTOPEN EXE     11890 03-01-91  12:00a
FC       EXE     18138 03-01-91  12:00a
FDISK    EXE     57192 03-01-91  12:00a
FIND     EXE      6642 03-01-91  12:00a
FORMAT   COM     32833 03-01-91  12:00a
GRAFTABL COM     11125 03-01-91  12:00a
LOADFIX  COM      1063 03-01-91  12:00a
NLSFUNC  EXE      6924 03-01-91  12:00a
UNFORMAT COM     18304 03-01-91  12:00a
```

(Your list might differ, and you might see the name of a temporary file whose size is 0, but the files should still be sorted alphabetically.)

You may rarely search your directories this carefully, but such combinations make DOS a powerful tool for handling text files.

CHAPTER SUMMARY

This chapter concludes the portion of the book designed to give you a feel for running DOS, including some of its advanced features. The key points to remember include:

▶ The computer's memory is cleared each time you turn the system off. To save your work permanently, you must store it in a file on a disk.

▶ A text file contains ordinary characters you can read.

▶ A command file contains instructions that DOS uses to carry out a command.

▶ A file name can be up to eight characters long; you can add an extension of up to three characters, separated from the file name by a period.

▶ Each file on a disk must have a different name or a different extension.

The remainder of the book shows you how to use DOS to manage your files, disks, and devices; use the DOS text editors; and create your own commands.

PART II

~~~~~~~~~~

LEARNING TO USE DOS

Part II shows you how to use DOS to manage your work with the computer. The chapters in Part II include extensive examples that use real-life situations to illustrate each DOS command, but the information is organized so that you can quickly find a particular topic to refresh your memory.

These chapters present many different features, and much of the material is relevant to all versions of DOS. Chapter 9 covers the use of a fixed disk in detail. Chapter 10 introduces the DOS Shell. Chapters 11 and 12 describe the DOS text editors, Chapters 13 through 17 show you how to use advanced features, and Chapter 18 describes DOS as an international system.

CHAPTER 5

MANAGING YOUR FILES

he previous chapters defined a file as a named collection of related information stored on a disk, and showed you several ways to create, copy, display, print, and otherwise work with your computer files. This chapter describes the DOS filing system in detail, showing you more about how files are named and how you can use DOS to manage your computer files.

Note: A few of the examples in the remaining chapters of this book may look familiar, because they repeat some of the examples in Chapters 2, 3, and 4. This repetition is intentional, so that Chapters 5 through 18 present a complete guide to DOS commands. You won't have to refer back to Chapters 2, 3, or 4 for command descriptions.

THE DOS FILE COMMANDS

To be useful, a filing system—whether it contains disk files or paper files—must be kept orderly and up to date. Using the DOS file commands, you can manage your disk files much as you manage your paper files. This chapter covers the DOS commands you use most often on a day-to-day basis. It shows you how to:

▶ Display directory entries in different ways with the Directory command.

▶ Display a file with the Type command.

▶ Copy and combine files with the Copy command.

▶ Send a copy of a file to a device with the Copy command.

▶ Remove a file from a disk with the Delete command.

▶ Track deleted files with the Mirror command.

▶ Recover deleted files with the Undelete command.

▶ Change the name of a file with the Rename command.

▶ Compare two files with the Compare command.

▶ Print a file with the Print command.

▶ Control access to a file with the Attribute command.

FILE NAMES AND EXTENSIONS

As Chapter 4 pointed out, files are named so that you (and DOS) can tell them apart; each file on a disk must have a different name. You know that a file name can be up to eight characters long, made up of any letters or numbers; you can also use the following symbols:

    `~ ! @ # $ % ^ & ( ) _ - { }´

You can add a suffix—called an *extension*—to the file name to describe its contents more precisely. The extension can be up to three characters long and can include any of the characters that are valid for the file name. It must be separated from the name by a period. The extension distinguishes one file from another just as the name does: REPORT and REPORT.JAN, for example, are two different files, as are REPORT.JAN and REPORT.FEB. Figure 5-1 shows some valid and invalid file names.

These File Names Are Valid	These Are Invalid...	Because
B	1991BUDGET	Name too long
90BUDGET	BUDGET.1991	Extension too long
BUDGET.90	.91	No file name
BUDGET.91	SALES 90.DAT	Blank not allowed
BDGT(91)	$1,300.45	Comma not allowed

Figure 5-1. *Some valid and invalid file names.*

Try to make file names and extensions as descriptive as possible. A short name might be easy to type, but you can have difficulty remembering what the file contains if you haven't used it for a while. The more descriptive the name, the more easily you can identify the contents of the file.

Special Names and File Name Extensions

Some names and file name extensions have special meanings to DOS. As you'll see in Chapter 7, "Managing Your Devices," DOS refers to the parts of your computer system by certain reserved names known as *device names*. The keyboard and screen, for example, are named CON, and the system clock is called CLOCK$. You cannot use any of these device names as file names.

Similarly, certain file name extensions have special meanings to DOS. These extensions either are created by DOS or cause DOS to assume the file contains a particular type of program or data. You should avoid giving files any of these extensions. A number of the most important ones are listed in Figure 5-2 on the following page.

Application programs also usually recognize special extensions. For example, Microsoft Word, the Microsoft word processor, uses DOC to identify a document, BAK to identify a backup version of a document, and STY to identify a file that contains a style sheet of print specifications. Again, avoid using extensions that have special meaning for your application programs; these extensions are usually listed in the documentation that comes with each program.

Name	Meaning to DOS
BAS	Short for *Basic*. Contains a program written in the Basic programming language. You run the program while using Basic.
BAT	Short for *batch*. Identifies a text file you create that contains a set of DOS commands that are run when you type the name of the file.
COM	Short for *Command*. Identifies a command file that contains a program DOS runs when you type the file name.
EXE	Short for *Executable*. Like COM, identifies a command file that contains a program DOS runs when you type the file name.
HLP	Short for *Help*. Contains a file of help text displayed by certain programs, including the DOS Shell and the version 5 Editor and Basic programs.
SYS	Short for *System*. Identifies a file that can be used only by DOS.

Figure 5-2. *Some special DOS file name extensions.*

Specifying the Drives

You can tell DOS to look for a file in a specific drive by typing the drive letter and a colon before the file name. If you specify a file as *b:report*, for example, DOS looks in drive B for a file named REPORT; if you specify the file as *report*, DOS looks for the file in the current drive.

PREPARING FOR THE EXAMPLES

If your system isn't running, start it. If you don't have a fixed disk, replace your DOS diskette with a blank, formatted diskette. Now, whether you use a fixed disk or diskettes, type the lines shown below to create a file named SAMPLE.NEW. Where you see ^Z, either hold down the Ctrl key and press Z or press the function key labeled F6:

```
C:\>copy con sample.new
This is a sample file.
^Z
```

(If you don't have a fixed disk, put the diskette with SAMPLE.NEW on it aside for now. If you have two diskette drives, place your DOS diskette back in drive A.)

Place a blank, formatted diskette in your diskette drive (drive B if you have two diskette drives). Whether you have a fixed disk or not, type the following to change the current drive to B:

```
C:\>b:
```

If you have one diskette drive, DOS asks that you make sure the correct diskette is in the drive:

Insert diskette for drive B: and press any key when ready

The correct diskette is in the drive, so just press the Spacebar or any other key. DOS acknowledges by changing the system prompt:

`B:\>_`

Now you're ready to create a set of sample files on this diskette. Type the following, again pressing Ctrl-Z or F6 where you see ^Z:

```
B:\>copy con report.doc
This is a dummy file.
^Z
```

DOS responds:

```
        1 file(s) copied
B:\>_
```

Now that you've created this file, you can use it and the DOS Copy command to create some more.

Creating the Remaining Sample Files

Type the following Copy commands (described in detail later in this chapter) to create some other sample files.

```
B:\>copy report.doc report.bak
        1 file(s) copied

B:\>copy report.doc bank.doc
        1 file(s) copied

B:\>copy report.doc budget.jan
        1 file(s) copied

B:\>copy report.doc budget.feb
        1 file(s) copied

B:\>copy report.doc budget.mar
        1 file(s) copied
```

Now check the directory.

```
B:\>dir
```

It should list six files:

```
Volume in drive B is EXAMPLES 1
Volume Serial Number is 1A2C-13F5
Directory of B:\

REPORT    DOC          23 10-16-91     9:16a
REPORT    BAK          23 10-16-91     9:16a
BANK      DOC          23 10-16-91     9:16a
BUDGET    JAN          23 10-16-91     9:16a
BUDGET    FEB          23 10-16-91     9:16a
BUDGET    MAR          23 10-16-91     9:16a
          6 file(s)          138 bytes
                         1210880 bytes free
```

Remember, the time and date in your list will be different, but the file names and sizes (23 bytes) should be the same.

WILDCARD CHARACTERS

To make it easier to manage your disk files, most file commands let you use wildcard characters to handle several files at once. That way, when you want to do the same thing to several files—change their names, perhaps, or erase them—you don't have to enter a separate command for each file. You can use wildcard characters to tell DOS you mean a set of files with similar names or extensions. Just as a wild card in a poker game can represent any other card in the deck, a wildcard character can represent any other character in a file name or extension.

There are two wildcard characters, the asterisk (*) and the question mark (?). The following examples use the Directory command to illustrate ways you can use wildcard characters to specify groups of files.

Using the Asterisk Wildcard Character: *

The asterisk makes it easy to carry out commands on sets of files with similar names or extensions; it can represent up to all eight characters in a file name or up to all three characters in an extension. If you use the asterisk to represent the entire name or extension, you are specifying all file names or all extensions.

The following examples illustrate several ways to use the asterisk to find selected directory entries. You can use the asterisk with other DOS commands as well.

To specify all files named BUDGET, regardless of extension, type the following:

```
B:\>dir budget.*
```

DOS displays the directory entry of each sample file named BUDGET, regardless of its extension:

```
Volume in drive B is EXAMPLES 1
Volume Serial Number is 1A2C-13F5
Directory of B:\

BUDGET    JAN          23 10-16-91    9:16a
BUDGET    FEB          23 10-16-91    9:16a
BUDGET    MAR          23 10-16-91    9:16a
          3 file(s)             69 bytes
                     1210880 bytes free
```

To specify all file names beginning with B, type the following:

```
B:\>dir b*
```

If you don't specify an extension, the Directory command displays the entry for each file that matches the name, regardless of extension (it's the equivalent of specifying the extension as *). There are four such files:

```
Volume in drive B is EXAMPLES 1
Volume Serial Number is 1A2C-13F5
Directory of B:\

BANK      DOC          23 10-16-91    9:16a
BUDGET    JAN          23 10-16-91    9:16a
BUDGET    FEB          23 10-16-91    9:16a
BUDGET    MAR          23 10-16-91    9:16a
          4 file(s)             92 bytes
                     1210880 bytes free
```

To specify all files with the same extension, regardless of name, you replace the name with *. For example, to specify each file with the extension DOC, type:

```
B:\>dir *.doc
```

DOS displays just those entries:

```
Volume in drive B is EXAMPLES 1
Volume Serial Number is 1A2C-13F5
Directory of B:\

REPORT    DOC          23 10-16-91    9:16a
BANK      DOC          23 10-16-91    9:16a
          2 file(s)             46 bytes
                     1210880 bytes free
```

Using the Question Mark Wildcard Character: ?

The question mark replaces only one character in a file name or extension. You'll probably use the asterisk more frequently, using the question mark only when one or two characters in the middle of a name or extension vary.

To see how the question mark works, type the following:

```
B:\>dir budget.?a?
```

PART II: LEARNING TO USE DOS

This command specifies all files named BUDGET that have extensions beginning with any character, followed by the letter *a*, and ending with any character. DOS displays two entries:

```
Volume in drive B is EXAMPLES 1
Volume Serial Number is 1A2C-13F5
Directory of B:\

BUDGET    JAN        23 10-16-91    9:16a
BUDGET    MAR        23 10-16-91    9:16a
        2 file(s)           46 bytes
                      1210880 bytes free
```

A Warning About Wildcard Characters

Be careful using wildcard characters with commands that can change files. Suppose you spent several days entering a year's worth of budget data into 12 files named BUDGET.JAN, BUDGET.FEB, BUDGET.MAR, and so on. On the same disk you also have three files you don't need named BUDGET.OLD, BUDGET.TST, and BUDGET.BAD. The disk is getting full, so you decide to delete the three unneeded files. It's 2 A.M., you're tired, and you're in a hurry, so you quickly type *del budget.** and press Enter. You have told DOS to do more than you wanted.

You may realize immediately what you have done, or it may not dawn on you until you try to use one of the 12 good budget files and DOS replies *File not found.* You display the directory; there isn't a single file named BUDGET, because you told DOS to delete them all.

With commands that can change or delete a file, use wildcard characters with extreme caution.

This warning applies even—perhaps especially—if you have version 5 of DOS, which includes a command named Undelete that can help you recover deleted files. Bear this in mind: *Undelete cannot always recover files completely.* As you'll see later in this chapter, Undelete can be valuable. But don't let it lull you into a false sense of security.

HELP WHEN YOU NEED IT

NOTE: If you don't have version 5 of DOS, your version of DOS doesn't include the help feature described here. Skip to the heading "Displaying Directory Entries."

As you work with DOS, you'll find that some commands become so familiar you type them without thinking. Others, less often needed, will linger in your mind, but you'll need to refresh your memory to use them correctly. If you have version 5 of DOS, you have a feature called *online help* that you can call on whenever you want help with a command.

To see a list of the commands for which you can request help, you simply type *help* and press Enter. For help with a specific command, you can type either the name of the command followed by a slash and a question mark or *help* followed by the name of the command. Which you use is up to you, although typing the command name, a slash, and a question mark is probably simpler.

When you request help, DOS displays a screen of information that resembles the descriptions you see in this book. Online help is not intended to teach you how to use DOS, but it is a handy guide that can remind you of the form of a command you haven't used in a while. Because this help is so easy to use and understand, two brief examples are enough to illustrate it. (If you have two diskette drives and you're using DOS from diskettes, change the current drive to A: and check that the diskette in drive A contains the file named HELP.EXE.)

To request a list of the commands for which you can get help, type:

    B:\>help

DOS responds with the first of several screenfuls of information (note the *--- More ---* at the bottom of the screen). The first line tells you that *For more information on a specific command,* you type *help* (uppercase or lowercase doesn't matter) followed by the name of the command. Below this is a list of the commands for which you can request help, along with a brief description of what each command does. The first few lines (several are shortened here) look like this:

    APPEND   **Allows applications to open data files in...**
                  they were in the current directory.
    ASSIGN   **Redirects requests for disk operations...**
                  drive
    ATTRIB   **Displays or changes file attributes.**
    BACKUP   **Backs up one or more files from one disk...**

To see the rest of the list, press any key. To cancel the display, press Ctrl-Break.

Now to request help on a specific command. You've used the Date command in an earlier chapter. It's compact and familiar, so use it to see what type of help DOS can provide. Type:

    B:\>help date

or

    B:\>date /?

Both commands produce the same result:

    Displays or sets the date.

    DATE [date]

    Type DATE without parameters to display the current date setting and
    a prompt for a new one. Press ENTER to keep the same date.

Now on to the DOS file-management commands. (If you're using DOS from diskettes, change the current drive back to B: before continuing.)

DISPLAYING DIRECTORY ENTRIES

As you have seen, the Directory command (dir) displays entries from the directory that DOS keeps on each disk. Each entry includes the name and extension of the file, its size in bytes, and the date and time it was created or last updated. You can use the Directory command to display all entries or just the entries of selected files.

In the descriptions of the commands here and throughout the remaining chapters, you are shown the general form of the command—the name of the command and most or all of its parameters—before you try the examples. If a parameter has an exact form, such as /W, the form is shown. If a parameter is something you specify, such as a file name, it is named and shown enclosed in angle brackets: for example, <filename>.

The Directory Command and Its Parameters

Depending on your version of DOS, the Directory command has either three or seven parameters. All versions allow you to specify a file name and two parameters typed as /W and /P. Version 5 adds a number of parameters, among them one that allows you to display only the file name and extension of the directory entries, and another that arranges directory entries by name, extension, size, or date and time.

Written out, the format of the Directory command and its above-mentioned parameters looks like this:

dir <filename> /W /P /O:sortorder /B

Other parameters of the Directory command are described later, and a complete summary appears in Appendix C, ''DOS Command Reference.'')

If you include <filename>, DOS searches the current directory for the file you specify. You can also:

▶ Precede <filename> with a drive letter. For example, *dir b:report.doc* tells DOS to look on the drive you specify rather than on the current drive.

▶ Use wildcard characters to specify a group of files. For example, *dir budget.** tells DOS to display the entries for all files named *budget* regardless of extension.

▶ Omit <filename> to tell DOS to display the entries for all files in the current directory. For example, *dir* displays all entries for the current directory in the current drive; *dir b:* displays all entries for the current directory in drive B.

The /W (Wide) parameter tells DOS to display only the file names and extensions in five columns across the screen. This display contains less information than does a complete directory listing because it omits file sizes, dates, and times, but is useful when a directory listing is quite long and you only want to see what files are in the directory.

The /P (Pause) parameter tells DOS to display the entries one screenful at a time; a message at the bottom of the screen tells you to press any key to continue. The /P parameter provides complete file information, including size, date, and time, so it is useful when you want a detailed look at a long directory listing.

The /O:<sortorder> parameter in version 5 tells DOS to sort (arrange) a directory listing by name, extension, size, or date and time:

▶ Typing *dir /o:n* sorts the files alphabetically by file name.

▶ Typing *dir /o:e* sorts the files alphabetically by extension.

▶ Typing *dir /o:s* sorts the files by size, smallest to largest.

▶ Typing *dir /o:d* sorts the files by date (earliest to latest) and, within the same date, sorts by the time (morning to evening) the file was created or last changed. You cannot sort by time only; that is, you cannot type *dir /o:t* to sort by time but not by date.

▶ Combining the /O:<sortorder> and /P parameters displays the files in the order you specify, with a pause after each screenful.

The /B parameter, also new in version 5, tells DOS to display only the names and extensions of the files you specify.

Examples of Displaying Directory Entries

Because you have already used the Directory command several times, only the options are shown here. First, use the /W parameter to see a wide directory display showing the files on your sample diskette. Type:

```
B:\>dir /w
```

DOS arranges just the name and extension of each file in five columns across the screen. If you have version 5, the display looks something like this (only three of the five columns are shown):

```
Volume in drive B is EXAMPLES 1
Volume Serial Number is 1A2C-13F5
Directory of B:\

REPORT.DOC        REPORT.BAK        BANK.DOC ...
BUDGET.MAR
          6 file(s)          138 bytes
                        1210880 bytes free
```

If you have version 4 or earlier, your display is similar, but doesn't include quite as much detail.

Your sample diskette doesn't contain enough files to show how many file names a wide directory display can contain, so the following illustration shows a wide listing for part of a much longer directory. (This directory shows some DOS version 5 files as they are stored on a fixed disk; again, only three of the five columns are shown.)

```
Volume in drive C is FIXED DISK
Volume Serial Number is 1608-5A30
Directory of C:\DOS

[.]                [..]               EGA.SYS             .  .  .
COUNTRY.SYS        HIMEM.SYS          KEYB.COM            .  .  .
SETVER.EXE         EGA.CPI            ANSI.SYS            .  .  .
EDLIN.EXE          EMM386.EXE         FASTOPEN.EXE        .  .  .
MIRROR.COM         MORE.COM           RAMDRIVE.SYS        .  .  .
SYS.COM            UNDELETE.EXE       UNFORMAT.COM        .  .  .
DOSSHELL.INI       DOSSHELL.COM       DOSSHELL.EXE        .  .  .
PRINT.EXE          DOSSHELL.HLP       EDIT.HLP            .  .  .
HELP.EXE           QBASIC.HLP         EDIT.COM            .  .  .
.
.
.
        86 file(s)     2151468 bytes
                       2093056 bytes free
```

Such a display doesn't contain as much information as the standard directory display, but it packs a lot of entries onto the screen. The wide format is particularly handy when all you want is a quick look at the names of the files on a crowded disk.

Pausing the Directory Display

To display the directory of a disk one screenful at a time, you use the /P option. DOS displays the first screenful of entries, followed by either *Press any key to continue...* or *Strike a key when ready...*, depending on your version of DOS. To see the next screenful, press any key. This option lets you view the entire directory without using Pause or Ctrl-Num Lock to freeze the display periodically.

Your sample disk contains less than one screenful of file names, but you can try using the /P parameter to list your DOS files.

If you are using DOS from a fixed disk, try either of these commands (they differ only in specifying the two likeliest locations for your DOS files):

    B:\>dir c: /p

or:

    B:\>dir c:\dos /p

If you have two diskette drives and are using DOS from diskettes, try typing:

    B:\>dir a: /p

Depending on your version of DOS, your DOS diskette may or may not contain more than a screenful of files; if it does, you see the pause message described above and can continue the display by pressing any key. If you do not see the message, keep this parameter in mind for a later time when you need to see a listing of all the files on a crowded disk, one screenful at a time.

If DOS is waiting for you to continue, press a key to see more of the display, or press Ctrl-Break to cancel.

Sorting the Directory Display

As described earlier, version 5 of DOS adds new ways for you to display a directory. Suppose you have a diskette full of files with different extensions, and you want to group them to get a better idea of what the diskette contains. The /O parameter of the Directory command does the job. If you have version 5, try it. Type:

B:\>dir /o:e

DOS responds:

```
Volume in drive B is EXAMPLES 1
Volume Serial Number is 1A2C-13F5
Directory of B:\

REPORT    BAK        23 10-16-91    9:16a
REPORT    DOC        23 10-16-91    9:16a
BANK      DOC        23 10-16-91    9:16a
BUDGET    FEB        23 10-16-91    9:16a
BUDGET    JAN        23 10-16-91    9:16a
BUDGET    MAR        23 10-16-91    9:16a
        6 file(s)          138 bytes
                       1210880 bytes free
```

The files are arranged alphabetically by extension. Remember that you can also group files by size or by date and time. The latter is particularly useful when you have more than one version of a file and you want to look at them in chronological order.

Listing Only Files

If you simply want to see what files are on a disk, the /B parameter gives you a bare-bones look at its contents. With the sample files, for instance, typing:

B:\>dir /b

produces this display:

```
REPORT.DOC
REPORT.BAK
BANK.DOC
BUDGET.JAN
BUDGET.FEB
BUDGET.MAR
```

Finally—and this applies to any DOS command—remember that you can type *help* or use the universal /? parameter to refresh your memory about a command and its parameters.

DISPLAYING A FILE

Many of the files you use are text files, and there will be times when you want to check the contents of a file but don't need a printed copy. DOS gives you a quick way to see what's in a file: the Type command. (The name Type is a carryover from the days when most computers had only typewriter-like consoles.)

When you use the Type command, DOS displays the file without stopping; if the file is longer than one screenful and you want to read the entire file, freeze the display by pressing Pause or Ctrl-Num Lock.

The Type command has one parameter:

type <filename>

<filename> is the name of the file to be displayed. The Type command displays just one file at a time, so you can't use wildcard characters in the file name. If you do use a wildcard character, DOS displays *Invalid filename or file not found* and returns to command level. If the file you name doesn't exist, DOS displays *File not found* followed by the file name you typed and, again, returns to command level.

An Example of Displaying a File

To display the file named REPORT.DOC on the diskette in the current drive, verify that your sample disk is in drive B and type:

```
B:\>type report.doc
```

DOS displays the file:

```
This is a dummy file.
```

You'll probably use the Type command frequently to check your text files.

MAKING COPIES OF FILES

Just as you sometimes make copies of your paper files, you'll find yourself needing copies of your disk files.

You may want to share a file with a colleague who has a computer, you may want to alter the copy slightly to produce a different version, or you may want to copy a file from your fixed disk to a diskette you can carry with you. The Copy command can make a copy of a file on the same disk (with a different file name) or on a different disk (with any valid file name).

When used to make copies of files, the Copy command has two major parameters, <file1> and <file2>. The format of the Copy command is:

copy <file1> <file2>

<file1> is the name of the file to be copied (the *source* file), and <file2> is the name of the copy to be made (the *target* file). You can use wildcard characters to copy a set of files.

Note: Three additional, seldom-used parameters (/A, /B, and /V) are described in Appendix C, "DOS Command Reference."

When copying files, if you:

▶ Specify a <file1> (including the drive letter) that is not on the disk in the current drive and omit <file2>, DOS copies <file1> to the disk in the current drive and gives the copy the same name as the original. Example (if the current drive is B): *copy a:report.mar.*

▶ Specify only a drive letter as <file2>, the file is copied from the disk in the current drive to the disk in the drive you specify and is given the same name as <file1>. Example: *copy report.feb a:.*

▶ Specify a <file1> that doesn't exist, DOS responds *File not found*, followed by the name you typed for <file1> and *0 file(s) copied*, and it returns to command level.

▶ Specify a <file2> that doesn't exist, DOS creates it.

▶ Specify a <file2> that does exist, DOS replaces its contents with <file1>. This is the same as deleting the existing target file, so be careful not to give the target the same name as an existing file you want to keep.

The following practice session illustrates different ways to copy files; it also indicates the type of situation in which you might want to use each form of the command.

Examples of Copying Files

You want to change a document you already have on disk, but you want to keep the original as well as the changed version. For example, to make a copy of the file REPORT.DOC on the same diskette and to name the copy RESULTS, type:

```
B:\>copy report.doc results
```

DOS acknowledges *1 file(s) copied.*

To verify that both files, REPORT.DOC and RESULTS, are on the diskette, display the directory by typing:

```
B:\>dir
```

DOS now shows seven files on the diskette:

```
Volume in drive B is EXAMPLES 1
Volume Serial Number is 1A2C-13F5
Directory of B:\

REPORT    DOC      23 10-16-91    9:16a
REPORT    BAK      23 10-16-91    9:16a
BANK      DOC      23 10-16-91    9:16a
BUDGET    JAN      23 10-16-91    9:16a
BUDGET    FEB      23 10-16-91    9:16a
BUDGET    MAR      23 10-16-91    9:16a
RESULTS            23 10-16-91    9:16a
        7 file(s)           161 bytes
                      1210368 bytes free
```

Any time you want to verify the results of an example, use the Directory command to see what files are on the diskette.

Suppose you want to copy a file from another disk and store it, under the same file name, on the disk in the current drive.

For example, your current drive is drive B. To copy a file from a different drive to the diskette in drive B, all you need to specify is the drive letter and name of the source file, because DOS assumes you want to copy the source file to the disk in the current drive and give the target file the same name.

If you have a fixed disk, there's no preparation for the next example. If you don't have a fixed disk, however, recall that you created a file named SAMPLE.NEW on a separate diskette when preparing for the examples in this chapter. You're going to use that diskette now, so place it in drive A.

To copy a file (SAMPLE.NEW) from a different drive to the disk in the current drive, type the following (substitute *a:* for *c:* if you don't have a fixed disk):

```
B:\>copy c:sample.new
```

DOS responds *1 file(s) copied.*

Next, suppose you want to change a file and store the new version under the same file name and on the same disk as the original, but you want to be able to distinguish between the two versions. Simply make a copy of the file on the same disk, with the same file name but a different extension. You can use the asterisk wildcard character to tell DOS to use the same file name. For example, to make a copy of BUDGET.MAR and call it BUDGET.APR, type the following:

```
B:\>copy budget.mar *.apr
```

DOS acknowledges that it copied one file.

You have several files named REPORT stored on disk. Suppose you want to keep the originals, but make copies of them all for a new project; to avoid confusion, you want to give the copies a new file name but keep the same extension. For example, to make a copy of each file named REPORT, giving each copy the name FORECAST, type the following:

```
B:\>copy report.* forecast.*
```

DOS displays the name of each source file as it makes the copies:

```
REPORT.DOC
REPORT.BAK
        2 file(s) copied
```

You can copy all the files on a diskette by specifying the source file as *.* and specifying the target as just a drive letter. This procedure is not the same as copying the diskette with the Diskcopy command; the difference is explained under the heading ''Copying a Complete Diskette'' in Chapter 6, ''Managing Your Diskettes.''

In addition to the Copy command, DOS versions 3.2 and later include two additional commands for copying files selectively: Replace, which lets you copy only files that already exist on the target disk; and Xcopy, which lets you copy only files that haven't been backed up. Both of these commands are described in Chapter 9, ''Managing Your Fixed Disk.''

SENDING FILES TO DEVICES

In Chapter 4, you printed a file by using the Copy command to send a copy of the file to the printer. You can also send a copy of a file to any other output device. If, for example, you copy a file to a communications connection, or *port,* on the computer, the file goes to whatever device is attached to the port—such as a telecommunications line to another computer.

When it is used to send a copy of a file to an output device, the Copy command has two parameters:

copy <filename> <device>

<filename> is the name of the file to be sent; <device> is the name of the device to which the file is to be sent.

Be sure <device> exists. If you try to send a file to a device that doesn't exist or isn't ready, DOS might stop running. You won't hurt anything, but you'll have to restart the system.

An Example of Sending Files to a Device

To send a copy of each sample file with the extension DOC to the printer, make certain your printer is turned on and type:

```
B:\>copy *.doc prn
```

DOS displays the name of each file as it sends the file to the printer:

```
REPORT.DOC
BANK.DOC
FORECAST.DOC
        1 file(s) copied
```

The files are printed with no separation between them. DOS reports only one file copied because, in effect, only one output file was created: the printed copy of the three files.

COMBINING FILES

Sometimes, it's useful to combine several files. Perhaps you have several short documents, and you decide it would be easier and more convenient to work with a single document that includes all the shorter ones. If you have several sets of files with similar names or extensions, you can combine each set into a new file, creating several new files. The Copy command lets you copy several files into a new file without destroying the original versions.

When it is used to combine files, the Copy command has two parameters:

copy <source> <target>

<source> represents the files to be combined. You can use wildcard characters to name the source files to be combined, or you can list several file names, separating them with a plus sign (+). If any file in the list doesn't exist, DOS goes on to the next name without telling you the file doesn't exist.

<target> represents the file that results from combining the source files. If you specify a target, DOS combines the source files into the target file. If you don't specify a target but do specify individual source files, DOS combines all the source files into the first file in the <source> list, changing its contents.

Examples of Combining Files

Suppose you have two files you want to use as the basis for a single new file, but you want to keep the originals intact. For example, to combine the files BANK.DOC and REPORT.DOC into a new file named BANKRPT.DOC, type:

```
B:\>copy bank.doc+report.doc bankrpt.doc
```

DOS displays the names of the source files as it copies them:

```
BANK.DOC
REPORT.DOC
        1 file(s) copied
```

Again, DOS reports one file copied because the command created only one file.

You can copy several files into an existing file. To combine BUDGET.JAN, BUDGET.FEB, and BUDGET.MAR into the first file, BUDGET.JAN, type:

B:\>copy budget.jan+budget.feb+budget.mar

DOS displays the name of each source file as it copies:

```
BUDGET.JAN
BUDGET.FEB
BUDGET.MAR
        1 file(s) copied
```

Now, suppose you've been keeping monthly budget files. It's the end of the year. You still need separate monthly files for comparison with next year's figures, but right now, you want to work with all the files together. To combine all the files named BUDGET into a file named ANNUAL.BGT, type:

B:\>copy budget.* annual.bgt

DOS responds:

```
BUDGET.JAN
BUDGET.FEB
BUDGET.MAR
BUDGET.APR
        1 file(s) copied
```

Or, suppose you want to combine pairs of files with the same file names, but different extensions. You can combine them under the same file names, with new extensions, and end up with both the original and combined versions.

If you have entered all the examples, among the files on the diskette in drive B are REPORT.DOC and REPORT.BAK, FORECAST.DOC and FORECAST.BAK. To combine each pair of files with the same name and the extensions DOC and BAK into a single file with the same name and the extension MIX, type:

B:\>copy *.bak+*.doc *.mix

DOS displays the names of the files as it copies them:

```
REPORT.BAK
REPORT.DOC
FORECAST.BAK
FORECAST.DOC
        2 file(s) copied
```

This time DOS reports two files copied because the command created two files: REPORT.MIX and FORECAST.MIX.

DELETING FILES

Just as you have to clean out a file drawer once in a while, you'll occasionally have to clear your disks of files you no longer need. The Delete command (you can type it either as *del* or as *erase*) deletes one or more files from a disk.

The Delete command has two parameters:

delete <filename> /P

<filename> is the name of the file to be deleted. If you use wildcard characters, DOS deletes all files that match <filename>. If the file doesn't exist, DOS displays *File not found* and returns to command level.

/P, in versions 4 and 5 only, tells DOS to prompt you for verification before deleting the file. If you use wildcard characters to delete more than one file, DOS prompts you to verify deletion of each file.

Safeguards

When you delete files, DOS assumes you know what you're doing—that you know exactly which files you're eliminating, and that you really don't want them anymore. But being human, you sometimes make mistakes, so you need ways to protect your files.

One good safeguard is the Copy command. DOS doesn't limit the number of times you can copy a data file, so think of the Copy command as the computer-based equivalent of your photocopy machine. Copy a file, preferably onto a different disk, whenever its value outweighs the minimal time and effort required for duplication. (Chapter 9, ''Managing Your Fixed Disk,'' describes additional commands that can help you copy sets of files selectively.)

When you delete files, use the /P parameter, especially if you use wildcard characters to specify a set of files. If you don't use this parameter to tell DOS to prompt for confirmation, the only time it hesitates before carrying out a Delete command is when you type *del *.**. Because this form of the Delete command removes all files in a directory, DOS tells you *All files in directory will be deleted! Are you sure (Y/N)?*

If your version of DOS doesn't include the /P parameter, double-check the command on the screen before pressing Enter. Verify the drive letter (if necessary), the file name, and the extension you typed. If you used wildcard characters, either be certain you know exactly which files will be deleted or consider using this safety check: Press Esc to cancel the Delete command, and then use the same wildcard characters with a Directory command. The Directory command lists all the files that match the wildcard characters. If the file names you see match the ones you expected to see, you can reenter the original Delete command with confidence.

Delete Tracking and the Undelete Command

Note: The following information applies only to version 5 of DOS. If you do not have version 5, skip to the heading "Examples of Deleting Files."

Beginning with version 5, DOS includes an Undelete command that can some-times help you recover a file you've deleted. When you delete a file, DOS marks its storage space as available for reuse, but it doesn't physically remove the information contained in that space. Because DOS manages storage space in this way, it's possible to recover a deleted file until (and only until) DOS reuses part or all of the file's disk space for another file.

Undelete works by reinstating the information about the disk locations where the deleted file was stored. Bear in mind, however, that DOS does not necessarily store an entire file in a single location on disk. Sometimes, especially on much-used disks, it tucks sections of a file into widely separated storage areas in order to make the best possible use of available space. As you save files, even small ones, DOS assigns and reassigns these storage areas. Because disk storage is so changeable, Undelete is suc-cessful only if it can follow a file's chain of storage locations from beginning to end. If, as often happens, DOS uses a "link" in this chain for storing part of another file, Undelete reaches a dead end and cannot recover the entire file.

If you need Undelete, use it as soon as possible after realizing that you need to recover a deleted file. Each time DOS saves other information on that disk, your chances of recovering the file are reduced.

You can use Undelete either on its own or with a feature called *delete tracking*. De-lete tracking is activated by the Mirror command, which creates a special file named PCTRACKR.DEL for holding disk-storage information about the files you delete. Once you start delete tracking for a disk drive, the Mirror command records storage information for all subsequent deleted files. Undelete can then use this information to try to recover one or more deleted files. Because delete tracking tends to be more effective than using DOS-based information in recovering files, the following ex-amples show you how to start this feature and use it to restore deleted files.

When used for tracking deleted files, the Mirror command has the form:

mirror /T<drive>-<files>

<drive> is the letter (without a colon) of the drive for which you want to start delete tracking. You must include this parameter.

<files> is the number of deleted files you want to track. If you include <files>, you can specify from 1 through 999, separating it from <drive> with a hyphen. If you omit <files>, the delete tracker assumes a generous number based on the size of the disk: 25 for a 360 K diskette, 50 for a 720 K diskette, 75 for a 1.2 MB or a 1.44 MB diskette, and about 100 to 300 for fixed disks with capacities ranging from 20 MB to 32 MB or more.

To start delete tracking for the sample diskette in drive B, type:

B:\>mirror /tb

Mirror responds with a set of messages, among them *Drive B being processed* and, when all goes well, *The MIRROR process was successful* and *Installation complete.*

Examples of Deleting Files

Cautionary statements aside, Delete itself is one of the easiest DOS commands to use. For example, to delete the file named BUDGET.APR on the diskette in the current drive, type:

B:\>del budget.apr

Press the Enter key, and the file's gone.

The next example deletes all files on the sample diskette whose extension is BAK.

If you have version 4 or 5, use the /P parameter to ask DOS to prompt you for verification; type the following:

B:\>del *.bak /p

If you have an earlier version of DOS, the /P parameter is unavailable, so type:

B:\>del *.bak

With the /P parameter, DOS responds by displaying the name of the first file whose extension is BAK and asking you whether to delete it:

B:\REPORT.BAK, Delete (Y/N)?_

Type *y* to delete it. Now DOS shows you the name of the next file and again asks:

B:\FORECAST.BAK, Delete (Y/N)?_

Type *y* again to delete the file. If you had typed *n* in response to either prompt, DOS would have left the file alone and moved on to the next file (if any) that matched the file name you typed as part of the Delete command. The /P option is thus handy when you want to delete several—but not all—files that have similar names or extensions. The prompt lets you avoid the work of entering a separate command for each file.

But what if your version of DOS doesn't have the /P option? If you typed the Delete command as *del *.bak*, your disk drive became active for a brief time after you pressed the Enter key, and then the system prompt returned to the screen. In that short time, DOS deleted the two sample files whose extension was BAK without telling you the names of the files. This example underscores the need for you to be sure you have typed the correct file name and the correct drive letter or extension (if necessary) whenever you use wildcard characters with the Delete command.

Whether or not you use the /P parameter, be particularly careful when you use the question mark in a file extension. To see why, create two additional test files by typing the following:

```
B:\>copy results *.1
      1 file(s) copied

B:\>copy results *.12
      1 file(s) copied
```

This gives you three files with the same name but different extensions: RESULTS, RESULTS.1, and RESULTS.12. Now type a Directory command, using a single question mark as the extension. Before you press Enter, decide which files you believe DOS will list.

```
B:\>dir results.?
```

DOS lists two files:

```
Volume in drive B is EXAMPLES 1
Volume Serial Number is 1A2C-13F5
Directory of B:\

RESULTS   1          23 10-16-91    9:46a
RESULTS              23 10-16-91    9:46a
         2 file(s)          46 bytes
                       1180160 bytes free
```

If you expected to see only RESULTS.1, the response to this Directory command is a surprise. If you had typed a Delete command, instead of a Directory command, the files you see listed are the files DOS would have erased. An unexpected directory listing can be momentarily confusing, but unintentionally deleting files is definitely an unpleasant surprise.

To delete both of the files you just created but leave your original RESULTS file untouched, type the following command:

```
B:\>del results.1?
```

Typing *1* as the first character of the extension ensures that the file RESULTS isn't affected. Note, however, that even though you included a question mark (which takes the place of a single character) after the 1, DOS deleted RESULTS.1 as well as RESULTS.12. Be careful whenever you use wildcard characters with commands that change or delete files.

Undeleting Files

Now that you've deleted some files, you can try out the Undelete command if you have version 5. (If you don't have version 5, skip to the heading ''Changing File Names.'')

The Undelete command has the following parameters:

undelete <filename> /dt /dos /all /list

<filename> is the name of the file or files you want to restore. You can specify a drive and path, and you can use wildcards to specify a set of files. If you don't include <filename>, Undelete assumes you want to recover all deleted files in the current directory of the current drive.

/dt tells Undelete to use the delete-tracking file recorded by the Mirror command. The */dt* parameter causes Undelete to prompt for confirmation before undeleting each file. Undelete assumes */dt* if a delete-tracking file exists, even if you don't include this parameter.

/dos tells Undelete to use information recorded by DOS. Like the */dt* parameter, */dos* causes Undelete to prompt for confirmation. Because of the way DOS deletes files, the */dos* parameter also causes Undelete to ask you to provide the first character in the name of the file. Undelete assumes */dos* if a delete-tracking file does not exist, even if you omit this parameter.

/all causes Undelete to recover all possible deleted files without stopping to prompt for confirmation.

/list causes Undelete to display a list of files it can recover, without actually undeleting them.

You just deleted several files from the disk in drive B. To request a list of these files, type:

    B:\>undelete /list

The Undelete command responds with a display like this:

```
Directory: B:\
File Specifications: *.*
   Searching deletion-tracking file...
   Deletion-tracking file contains    5 deleted files.
   Of those,    5 files have all clusters available,
                0 files have some clusters available,
                0 files have no clusters available.

   MS-DOS directory contains    3 deleted files.
   Of those,    3 files may be recovered.

Using the deletion-tracking file.

       RESULTS  12        23 10/16/91  9:46a  ...A  Deleted: 10/17/91  3:24p
       RESULTS  1         23 10/16/91  9:46a  ...A  Deleted: 10/17/91  3:24p
       FORECAST BAK       23 10/16/91  9:16a  ...A  Deleted: 10/17/91  3:18p
       REPORT   BAK       23 10/16/91  9:16a  ...A  Deleted: 10/17/91  3:18p
       BUDGET   APR       23 10/16/91  9:16a  ...A  Deleted: 10/17/91  3:17p
```

Although longer and more detailed than most DOS reports, this display is not difficult to interpret. First, Undelete tells you that it is checking the disk in drive B for all deleted files (*File Specifications: *.**).

The middle section of the report tells you what Undelete has found. If you use the delete-tracking file, Undelete can completely restore five deleted files. (The message *all clusters available* means that Undelete can find all storage units allotted to each file.) On the other hand, if you use the information recorded by DOS (by specifying the */dos* parameter), Undelete can find and recover three of the deleted files.

Because you started delete tracking, Undelete gives precedence to the delete-tracking file, so the bottom section of the report lists the five deleted files, giving their names, sizes, and dates and times of creation. The ...*A* tells you that the files have not been backed up (archived), and the remainder of each line tells you the date and time the file was deleted.

Note: The delete-tracking file can help you recover files deleted after you have started delete tracking with the Mirror command. If you delete a file when this feature is not turned on, the delete-tracking file cannot help you recover it. However, because DOS also records deletions, you might still be able to use the /dos parameter of the Undelete command instead.

Suppose you want to recover one of the deleted files, BUDGET.APR, on the disk in drive B. Type:

```
B:\>undelete budget.apr
```

You see some preliminary messages telling you the recovery process has been started, and then Undelete displays:

```
Using the deletion-tracking file.

   BUDGET   APR      23 10/16/91  9:16a  ...A  Deleted: 10/17/91  3:17p
All of the clusters for this file are available. Undelete (Y/N)?
```

Type *y*, and in a moment the recovery process ends:

```
    File successfully undeleted.
```

To recover all deleted files on this disk, or to search through the deleted files and recover those you wanted, you would type *undelete*. For each file that Undelete could recover, it would display a message and prompt similar to those you just saw. In each case, you would type *y* or *n* to tell Undelete whether to recover or ignore the file.

Before continuing, delete BUDGET.APR once again to return your sample disk to its earlier state.

CHANGING FILE NAMES

There will be times when you want to change the name of a file. You might simply change your mind, or perhaps you'll have changed the contents of a file so much that you want to give it a name that more closely describes its new contents. If your application program automatically makes a backup copy whenever you edit and save a file, the Rename command is also valuable when (as can happen) your working copy is inadvertently lost or damaged—perhaps the power fails, you have a problem with the application itself, or you've mangled the file with editing changes and want to start all over from scratch.

The Rename command changes a file's name or extension, or both. You can use wildcard characters to rename a set of files.

The Rename command has two parameters:

rename <oldname> <newname>

<oldname> is the name of an existing file. If the file doesn't exist, DOS displays *Duplicate file name or file not found* and returns to command level.

<newname> is the name you want to give to the file specified by <oldname>. If there is already a file with the new name, DOS displays *Duplicate file name or file not found* and returns to command level. Two files on the same disk can't have the same name, and DOS would have to erase the existing file to carry out the command, so this built-in safeguard keeps you from inadvertently erasing one file in the process of renaming another.

You can abbreviate the Rename command as *ren.*

The Rename command simply changes the name of a file; it doesn't copy a file to a different disk. Both the old name and the new name must refer to the same drive. If you specify a drive letter with the new name, DOS responds *Invalid parameter.*

Examples of Changing File Names

To change the name of the file ANNUAL.BGT to FINAL on the disk in the current drive, type:

```
B:\>ren annual.bgt final
```

DOS changes the name and displays the system prompt.

To change the extension of the file BUDGET.MAR from MAR to 003 on the disk in the current drive, you can use the * wildcard character for the new file name. Type the following:

```
B:\>ren budget.mar *.003
```

The file is now named BUDGET.003.

To change the extension DOC to TXT for all files on the disk in the current drive, use the * for both the old and new file names. Type the following:

B:\>ren *.doc *.txt

Verify this change with the Directory command by typing:

B:\>dir *.txt

DOS shows four files, all of which used to have the extension DOC:

```
Volume in drive B is EXAMPLES 1
Volume Serial Number is 1A2C-13F5
Directory of B:\

REPORT    TXT        23 10-16-91    9:16a
BANK      TXT        23 10-16-91    9:16a
FORECAST  TXT        23 10-16-91    9:16a
BANKRPT   TXT        47 10-16-91   10:51a
        4 file(s)           116 bytes
                        1181184 bytes free
```

If you use the Directory command now to display the entries of all files with the extension DOC, DOS responds *File not found.*

PREPARING FOR THE REMAINING EXAMPLES

The remaining examples in this chapter show you how to use some external DOS commands. These commands are on your fixed disk or on your DOS diskettes.

If you're using a fixed disk, DOS can find the files it needs, but to ensure that the following examples work on any type of system, change the current drive to C:

B:\>c:

and leave your practice diskette in drive B.

If you're not using a fixed disk, change the current drive to A:

B:\>a:

and leave your practice diskette in drive B. The examples use the command files named ATTRIB, COMP, and PRINT. Use the Directory command to check the DOS diskette in drive A for these files. If DOS responds *File not found*, check your other DOS diskette(s) for the files you need. Begin the examples with the diskette containing ATTRIB.EXE in drive A.

Now the current drive is the one containing some or all of the command files DOS will need to carry out your requests, and drive B contains the diskette with the files on which DOS will act. To tell DOS where to find the practice files, you'll preface their file names with the drive letter, *b:*.

CONTROLLING ACCESS TO YOUR FILES

Your fixed disk and diskettes will contain many files. Some, such as program files (including DOS and application programs), you will never change and seldom, if ever, erase. Although you probably have backup copies, some of these files might exist only on your working disks. Deleting or modifying them could represent a serious loss.

You will have other files, too. Some, such as spreadsheets for periodic calculations or reports and word processing style sheets or form letters, will seldom change in their basic form. Because these files can represent a significant investment of time and information, inadvertently changing them would also be a serious loss.

Similarly, you will probably have some files that you prefer to keep out of view. You might, for example, want to keep your most recent word processing backup files (those with a BAK extension) on disk, but would also like an easy way to keep them from cluttering up your directory listings. Or you might have some personal files — your résumé, perhaps, or an idea you're developing — on disk and would appreciate a way to keep them out of plain sight.

While DOS is not designed for high-security conditions, it does offer some ways to keep control over your files. You can, for example, make files *read-only*, so that you and others don't inadvertently change or delete them. With version 5, you can also mark files as *hidden* from casual browsing. Within the DOS Shell, you can assign *passwords* to programs so they can be used only by yourself and others who know the passwords. The next examples show you ways to make your files read-only and hidden from view. Chapter 10 describes the use of passwords.

To make a file read-only or hidden, you use the Attribute (attrib) command. A read-only file can be read but cannot be deleted or changed. A hidden file, in contrast, can be read or changed, but its name is not displayed by the Directory command.

Controlling Whether a File Can Be Changed

Because you can affect the read-only status of a file with only one command, it's easy to temporarily protect files that may change later—the most recent version of a text file or spreadsheet, for example. This protection can be particularly useful if someone else is going to use the same disk or computer that you use. When you decide modifications can be made to the file, another command removes the read-only protection and makes the file available for change.

When used to control the read-only status of a file, the Attribute command has three parameters:

attrib +R −R <filename>

+R tells DOS to make <filename> read-only—that is, to deny all attempts to change or erase <filename>.

−R tells DOS to let <filename> be changed or erased.

<filename> is the name of the file whose read-only status is to be affected. If you enter the command with <filename> only, DOS displays the name of the file and, if the file is read-only, displays an *R* to the left of the file name. You can check or change the read-only status of a series of files by using wildcard characters.

The display of the Directory command doesn't show whether a file is read-only; you must use the Attribute command.

Example of Controlling Whether a File Can Be Changed

Type the following command to tell DOS to display the status of the files with the extension TXT on the disk in drive B:

```
C:\>attrib b:*.txt
```

DOS responds:

```
A            B:\REPORT.TXT
A            B:\BANK.TXT
A            B:\FORECAST.TXT
A            B:\BANKRPT.TXT
```

None of the file names is preceded by an R; this tells you none is read-only. The A shows that the file's archive status is on; this means that the file has not been backed up since it was created or last changed. The importance and use of a file's archive status is described in Chapter 9, ''Managing Your Fixed Disk.''

To make BANK.TXT read-only, type:

```
C:\>attrib +r b:bank.txt
```

DOS responds by displaying the system prompt. Now, when you check the status again, DOS shows that BANK.TXT is read-only. Type the following:

```
C:\>attrib b:*.txt
A            B:\REPORT.TXT
A      R     B:\BANK.TXT
A            B:\FORECAST.TXT
A            B:\BANKRPT.TXT
```

If you try to delete BANK.TXT, DOS displays an error message:

```
C:\>del b:bank.txt
Access denied
```

The result would be the same if you edited the file with a word processor; when you tried to store the revised version, DOS or the word processor would issue an error message. You could, however, save the revised version with a different name.

Remove the read-only protection and verify that it is gone by typing:

```
C:\>attrib -r b:bank.txt

C:\>attrib b:bank.txt
A            B:\BANK.TXT
```

Controlling Whether a File Can Be Seen

The following examples apply only to version 5 of DOS. If you have an earlier version, skip ahead to the heading ''Comparing Files.''

When you decide to hide a file or restore it to full view, you use the same form of the Attribute command you've just seen but, instead of +R or −R, you use +H or −H to indicate the hidden attribute. As in making files read-only, you can use wildcard characters to apply the command to groups of files.

Example of Controlling Whether a File Can Be Seen

If you've entered all the examples in this chapter, you have three sample files named BUDGET: BUDGET.JAN, BUDGET.FEB, and BUDGET.003. Suppose they contain information—salary increases or sales projections—that you'd prefer to keep out of full view for awhile. Before you hide the files, use the Directory command to see a list of all the sample files:

```
C:\>dir b:
```

Notice that DOS reports 13 files that take up 12,800 bytes of storage. Type the following Attribute command to hide all three budget files from casual view:

```
C:\>attrib +h b:budget.*
```

Now try listing them with the Directory command:

```
C:\>dir b:
```

DOS responds:

```
Volume in drive B is EXAMPLES 1
Volume Serial Number is 1A2C-13F5
Directory of B:\

REPORT   TXT        23 10-16-91    9:16a
BANK     TXT        23 10-16-91    9:16a
RESULTS            23 10-16-91    9:16a
SAMPLE   NEW        24 10-16-91    9:14a
FORECAST TXT        23 10-16-91    9:16a
BANKRPT  TXT        47 10-16-91   10:51a
FINAL             139 10-16-91   10:54a
REPORT   MIX        47 10-16-91   10:54a
FORECAST MIX        47 10-16-91   10:54a
MIRROR   FIL     12288 10-16-91   11:01a
       10 file(s)        12684 bytes
                       1181184 bytes free
```

Notice that no budget files appear in the list and that DOS adjusts the directory report to show 10 files taking 12,684 bytes of storage. It's as if your budget files no longer exist.

But if a directory list doesn't show hidden files, what if you forget where they are? You'll have to devise some means of keeping track of hidden files, especially if they're on a fixed disk, but the version 5 Directory command also includes a parameter to help you check for them: the /A parameter. In this form, the Directory command is:

dir /A:<attribute>

where <attribute> can be any of the following: R or –R (read-only); H or –H (hidden); A or –A (archive); D or –D (directory); and S or –S (system). As mentioned earlier, the archive attribute shows whether or not the file has been backed up; the directory attribute applies to entire directories, such as your DOS directory; the system attribute applies to program files and is not needed in your day-to-day work with DOS.

When you use the /A parameter of the Directory command, DOS displays only the names of files with the attribute you specify. You can try it with the budget files you've just hidden. Type:

```
C:\>dir b: /a:h
```

DOS responds:

```
Volume in drive B is EXAMPLES 1
Volume Serial Number is 1A2C-13F5
Directory of B:\

BUDGET    JAN        70 10-16-91   10:53a
BUDGET    FEB        23 10-16-91    9:16a
BUDGET    003        23 10-16-91    9:16a
MIRORSAV  FIL        41 10-16-91   11:01a
          4 file(s)          157 bytes
                         1181184 bytes free
```

(MIRORSAV.FIL is a file created by the Mirror command, which you used for tracking deleted files on this disk.)

Before continuing with the rest of the chapter, remove the hidden attribute from your sample files. Type:

```
C:\>attrib -h b:budget.*
```

If you use the hidden attribute to keep files from full view, bear in mind the ease with which you just found some. If you can, so can others. Remember that the hidden attribute is more of a convenience than a security measure.

COMPARING FILES

Note: Some versions of DOS prior to version 3 do not include the Compare command. If you're not sure whether you have this command, check your DOS diskettes. If you don't have the Compare command, you have a similar command named FC (for File Compare); it is described in Appendix C.

Sometimes you'll want to know whether two files are exactly the same. Suppose you have two files named BUDGET on different disks. They're the same length, but are they different budgets, or two copies of the same one? You could display or print both files and compare them, but that could take quite a while and you still might miss some small difference. It's quicker and more accurate to use Compare (comp).

The Compare command has two parameters:

comp <file1> <file2>

<file1> and <file2> are the file names of the files to be compared. If you omit <file2>, DOS prompts you for it. If you omit both <file1> and <file2>, DOS prompts you for both.

If the files are different lengths, DOS displays *Files are different sizes* and asks you if you want to compare any more files. If the files are the same length, the Compare command compares them byte by byte. If the files are identical, DOS tells you so by displaying *Files compare OK*.

If the files are the same length but DOS finds a difference, DOS displays a message that shows the characters that differ and how far each is from the beginning of the file. If DOS finds 10 mismatches, it displays *10 Mismatches - ending compare*, and asks if you want to compare any more files.

The following examples show the DOS prompts and responses as they appear in version 5. If you have an earlier version of DOS, your messages differ, but the command works as described. Type the commands as shown, but bear in mind that you won't see exactly what is shown here.

To compare REPORT.TXT with BUDGET.FEB, type:

```
C:\>comp b:report.txt b:budget.feb
```

The files are identical, so DOS replies as follows:

```
Comparing B:REPORT.TXT and B:BUDGET.FEB...
Files compare OK

Compare more files (Y/N) ? _
```

Type *y* and press Enter to tell DOS you want to compare more files. DOS prompts you for the names of the files. To compare REPORT.TXT with REPORT.MIX, type the file names as shown, and press Enter when DOS prompts for an option:

```
Name of first file to compare: b:report.txt
Name of second file to compare: b:report.mix
Option : <Enter>
```

(If you don't have version 5, DOS asks for the *primary filename* and then requests the *2nd filename or drive id*. It does not prompt for an option.)

This time, DOS determines that the two files are different lengths, and it doesn't even begin to compare them:

```
Comparing B:REPORT.TXT and B:REPORT.MIX...
Files are different sizes

Compare more files (Y/N) ? _
```

Type *n* and press Enter, and DOS returns to command level.

You can use wildcard characters to compare two sets of files with one command. To compare all files with the extension TXT and all files with the same file name but the extension MIX, type the following:

```
C:\>comp b:*.txt b:*.mix
```

There are four files with the extension TXT, but only two (REPORT.MIX and FORECAST.MIX) with the extension MIX. DOS tells you which files it can find and which ones it tried to compare:

```
Comparing B:REPORT.TXT and B:REPORT.MIX...
Files are different sizes

Comparing B:BANK.TXT and B:BANK.MIX...
Can't find/open file:   B:BANK.MIX

Comparing B:FORECAST.TXT and B:FORECAST.MIX...
Files are different sizes

Comparing B:BANKRPT.TXT and B:BANKRPT.MIX...
Can't find/open file:   B:BANKRPT.MIX

Compare more files (Y/N) ? _
```

Type *n* and press Enter to return DOS to command level.

Because all the sample files contain the same words, you'll have to create one that is different, but still the same length (23 bytes), to see how DOS notifies you of differences. To create a different file and name it DIFF, type the following:

```
C:\>copy con b:diff
This is not the same.
^Z
        1 file(s) copied
```

Now compare REPORT.TXT with DIFF. Type:

```
C:\>comp b:report.txt b:diff
```

89

DOS quickly finds and reports 10 errors (your display might differ slightly):

```
Comparing B:REPORT.TXT and B:DIFF...
Compare error at OFFSET 8
file1 = 61
file2 = 6E
Compare error at OFFSET 9
file1 = 20
file2 = 6F
Compare error at OFFSET A
file1 = 64
file2 = 74
Compare error at OFFSET B
file1 = 75
file2 = 20
Compare error at OFFSET C
file1 = 6D
file2 = 74
Compare error at OFFSET D
file1 = 6D
file2 = 68
Compare error at OFFSET E
file1 = 79
file2 = 65
Compare error at OFFSET 10
file1 = 66
file2 = 73
Compare error at OFFSET 11
file1 = 69
file2 = 61
Compare error at OFFSET 12
file1 = 6C
file2 = 6D

10 Mismatches - ending compare
Compare more files (Y/N) ? _
```

Type *n* to return DOS to command level.

The messages that show the differing characters and their locations use numbers that are combinations of the digits 0 through 9 and the letters A through F. These characters are from the base-16 number system, usually called *hexadecimal,* in which A through F are used to represent the decimal numbers 10 through 15. If you must know what the differing characters are, the /A parameter described in Appendix C can help if you have version 5 of DOS. If you have an earlier verson, or you must calculate exact locations, you need a chart of the American Standard Code for Information Interchange (ASCII), which shows how characters are encoded, and you need a guide to hexadecimal arithmetic. The manuals that came with your computer might contain both. In addition, the book *Supercharging MS-DOS* (Microsoft Press) describes both the ASCII code and hexadecimal numbers.

PRINTING FILES

You can print files at the same time you're using the computer to do other things. The Print command keeps a list—called the *print queue*—of files to be printed, and it prints the files in the order in which they appear in the queue. The print queue normally can hold up to 10 files.

In addition to printing files, the Print command lets you change some characteristics of its operation—notably, the size of the print queue and the printer that DOS uses. For a description of these uses of the Print command, see ''Changing Operation of the Print Command'' later in this chapter.

Because the computer can really do only one thing at a time, DOS prints when nothing else is happening, such as when you pause to think between keystrokes. You'll notice that printing slows and sometimes even stops when something else is going on—especially when DOS is using a disk drive.

You use the Print command to add a file to the print queue, delete a file from the queue, cancel all printing, and display the names of the files in the queue. When used to print a file, the Print command has four parameters:

print <filename> /P /C /T

<filename> is the name of the file to be added to or deleted from the print queue. You can enter more than one file name with a Print command; just type the list of file names, separating each from the next with a blank.

/P (Print) tells DOS to add <filename> to the print queue. DOS assumes this parameter if all you specify is <filename>.

/C (Cancel) tells DOS to remove <filename> from the print queue. If the file is being printed, printing stops.

/T (Terminate) stops all printing. If a file is being printed, printing stops and all files are removed from the print queue.

If you enter the Print command with no parameters, DOS displays the list of files in the print queue.

Examples of Printing a File

The following examples work best with a dot-matrix printer equipped with a tractor feed that uses fanfold paper. If you don't have such a printer, or if you use a network printer, you might prefer to read through these examples rather than try them for yourself. Some examples might not work as described, and several can cause a fast printer to use many sheets of paper.

DOS advances the paper to the next page each time it prints a new file, so check what each example does before you try it. You can then be ready to stop the printing process, and you'll save both time and paper. First, a bit of preparation.

Most of the sample files you created in this chapter consist of a single line and would print too quickly for you to try using all the Print parameters in the following examples. Increase the size of the file REPORT.TXT using Edlin, the text editor that comes with all versions of DOS. It's described in Chapter 11.

Note: If you're using DOS from diskettes, you'll need the files named EDLIN and PRINT for these examples. Check your DOS diskette(s) for these files, and place the appropriate diskette in drive A before requesting either Edlin or the Print command. Begin with the diskette that contains EDLIN.COM (or EDLIN.EXE) in drive A.

To increase the size of the file REPORT.TXT, type the following lines:

```
C:\>edlin b:report.txt
End of input file
*1,1,2,199c
*e
```

The Edlin command copies the first (and only) line 199 times, so REPORT.TXT now consists of 200 identical lines. (If you're using DOS from diskettes, you don't need Edlin anymore. If necessary, replace the DOS diskette in drive A with the diskette that contains PRINT.COM or PRINT.EXE.)

Now make sure that the printer is turned on and that the paper is adjusted to the top of a page. This completes the preparation for the Print command examples.

To print the file REPORT.TXT, type:

```
C:\>print b:report.txt
```

The first time you enter the Print command after starting the system, DOS might prompt you for the name of the printer to use:

```
Name of list device [PRN]: _
```

The brackets around PRN mean that DOS will use the device named PRN if you press the Enter key. Unless you have more than one printer attached to your system, or you are using a printer with a serial interface, just press the Enter key. If you have never printed with your printer, press the Enter key.

When you respond to the prompt, DOS loads the Print command file from the system disk and keeps it in memory until you either turn the system off or restart DOS. DOS reports that the program is loaded:

```
Resident part of PRINT installed
```

When DOS begins to carry out your Print command, it displays the names and print status of the files in the print queue:

```
        B:\REPORT.TXT is currently being printed
```

There is one file in the print queue (REPORT.TXT), and it's now being printed.

When you printed a file in Chapter 4 by copying it to the printer, DOS didn't display the system prompt—and you couldn't use the system—until the file had been printed. This time, the system prompt returned as soon as printing started. As soon as DOS starts printing a file with the Print command, DOS is ready to accept another command from you.

If you decide you don't want to print a file after all, you can remove it from the print queue with the /C parameter; type the following command while REPORT.TXT is being printed:

```
C:\>print b:report.txt /c
```

DOS displays a terse acknowledgment of your command:

PRINT queue is empty

and stops sending lines to your printer, even though your printer will probably continue to operate until it finishes printing the characters it has already received. At that point, the printer stops and advances the paper to a new page. If you check the last line of the printout, you see a message like this:

```
This is a dummy file.
This is a dummy file.
This is a dumm
File B:\REPORT.TXT canceled by operator
```

You can put more than one file into the print queue with a single Print command. To tell DOS to print both REPORT.TXT and BUDGET.JAN, type:

```
C:\>print b:report.txt b:budget.jan
```

DOS starts printing REPORT.TXT and displays the print queue:

```
        B:\REPORT.TXT is currently being printed
        B:\BUDGET.JAN is in queue
```

If you want to stop printing, you can remove all files from the print queue with the /T parameter. Type the following, again while REPORT.TXT is being printed:

```
C:\>print /t
```

Again, DOS displays the acknowledgment *PRINT queue is empty*. This time, it prints the message *All files canceled by operator* at the point where it stopped printing and, again, advances the paper and removes all remaining files from the queue.

You can also put several files in the print queue at once by using wildcard characters. To print all the files whose extension is TXT, type:

```
C:\>print b:*.txt
```

Now DOS tells you that there are four files in the queue (the order might vary):

```
B:\BANK.TXT is currently being printed
B:\REPORT.TXT is in queue
B:\FORECAST.TXT is in queue
B:\BANKRPT.TXT is in queue
```

DOS prints the files in the order shown. Stop all printing again by typing:

```
C:\>print /t
```

Again, DOS stops printing the current file, prints the cancellation message, advances the paper, removes all remaining files from the queue, and acknowledges on the screen *PRINT queue is empty.*

The following example uses several sheets of paper. If you're not using continuous form paper or an automatic sheet feeder, you shouldn't try this example because it might print on the platen of your printer. Skip to the heading ''Changing Operation of the Print Command.''

The print queue normally holds up to 10 files. To fill it, tell DOS to print all the files on the diskette in drive B; there are 14 text files, of which DOS puts the first 10 in the queue. Type the following:

```
C:\>print b:*.*
```

DOS tells you the queue is full and displays the list of files in the queue (again, the order might vary):

```
PRINT queue is full

        B:\REPORT.BAK is currently being printed
        B:\DIFF is in queue
        B:\BANK.TXT is in queue
        B:\BUDGET.JAN is in queue
        B:\BUDGET.FEB is in queue
        B:\BUDGET.003 is in queue
        B:\RESULTS is in queue
        B:\SAMPLE.NEW is in queue
        B:\REPORT.TXT is in queue
        B:\FORECAST.TXT is in queue
```

You really don't need to print all these files. Stop all printing by typing:

```
C:\>print /t
```

DOS empties the queue and alerts you as before:

```
PRINT queue is empty
```

Changing Operation of the Print Command

DOS initially limits the print queue to 10 files, but you can increase the size of the queue and can also tell DOS to use a printer other than the standard printer, PRN (more details on printers are in Chapter 7, "Managing Your Devices").

You can change Print command operations only the first time you use the Print command during a session at your computer; if you try to use these options again before restarting DOS or turning the computer off, DOS displays the message *Invalid switch* and ignores the command.

When used to change the size of the print queue or the name of the printer, the Print command has two parameters:

print   /D:<printer>   /Q:<size>

/D:<printer> tells DOS to use the printer named <printer>. If you omit /D:<printer>, DOS uses the standard printer named PRN.

/Q:<size> tells DOS the number of files the print queue can hold; the minimum number is 4 and the maximum number is 32. If you omit /Q:<size>, the print queue holds 10 files.

If you wanted to increase the size of the print queue to 15 files, you would type *print /q:15* the first time you used the Print command. If you wanted to tell DOS to use the printer named LPT2, you would type *print /d:lpt2*. You can combine these parameters in the same Print command, but you cannot combine them with other parameters unless you are entering the Print command for the first time since starting DOS.

The Print command lets you print text files without losing the use of your system during printing; it can make both you and your system more productive.

Several infrequently used parameters that give you more precise control over how the print program interacts with DOS are described in Appendix C.

CHAPTER 6

MANAGING YOUR DISKETTES

Diskettes are the computer's filing cabinets. Managing your computer filing system includes not only keeping track of your files, as described in the previous chapter, but also taking care of your diskettes. There are many ways to prepare and store information on diskettes; the concepts underlying diskette handling, however, apply to all microcomputers.

Several DOS commands deal with entire diskettes, not with individual files. For example, you must prepare a new diskette for use; this process is called formatting (or, less commonly, initializing). Or, if you need an exact copy of a diskette, you don't copy each file separately; you copy the entire diskette with one command.

This chapter suggests ways to handle your diskettes, briefly describes how DOS stores files on diskettes, and shows you how to do the following:

▶ Prepare a diskette for use with the Format command.

▶ Save information about the condition of a disk with the Mirror command.

▶ Reverse an inadvertent format with the Unformat command.

▶ Duplicate a diskette with the Diskcopy command.

▶ Compare the contents of two diskettes with the Diskcomp command.

▶ Analyze and report on the use of diskette storage space with the Check Disk command.

▶ Assign, change, or delete the volume label (identifying name) of a disk with the Label command.

▶ Display the volume label of a disk with the Volume command.

The Diskcopy and Diskcomp commands are for diskettes only. A number of other DOS commands, such as Format, Check Disk, Label, and Volume, are used with both diskettes and fixed disks. Additional commands, such as Backup and Restore, are used exclusively or primarily with fixed disks. Depending on which chapter is more appropriate, these disk-management commands are described either in this chapter or in Chapter 9, "Managing Your Fixed Disk."

HANDLING DISKETTES

Diskettes are remarkably durable, especially the 3.5-inch type in a hard plastic shell. The useful life of diskettes depends on how often you use them, of course, but even more important is how you treat them. Handle your diskettes with the same care you use when handling valuable recording tapes or photographs:

▶ Avoid touching the diskette surfaces that show through the openings in the protective jacket. Dirt, fingerprints, or dust can shorten the life of a diskette and can damage or destroy the data.

▶ Keep diskettes away from magnets and other sources of magnetic influence, such as telephones, electric motors, and television sets.

▶ Keep food and drinks away from diskettes. The same goes for cigarettes, cigars, pipes, and ashtrays.

▶ Don't fold, spindle, or mutilate diskettes. Don't pile other objects on them.

▶ Don't write on diskette labels with a pencil, ballpoint pen, or other sharp instrument; use a felt-tipped marker.

▶ Store your diskettes in a safe place when you're not using them. Protect them from extreme heat and cold, humidity, and contact with other objects.

Many products are available for storing diskettes, including plastic boxes, vinyl pockets that fit a three-ring binder, and hanging file folders. All offer good protection; they aren't necessary, but they make it easier for you to organize your diskettes and store them safely, rather than leaving them scattered around your desk.

Although an office is a mild environment compared to a factory or a shop floor, data on a diskette can be damaged by such innocuous objects as a paper clip that has been stored in a magnetic paper-clip holder, a magnetized letter opener, an electric pencil sharpener, or a telephone-answering machine. If you put a letter down on top of a diskette lying on your desk, it's all too easy to put a hot coffee cup or a heavy object on the letter without realizing that the diskette is underneath.

The safest places for a diskette are in the computer and in protective storage. Information and time are two of your most valuable assets. A damaged diskette can cost you both, so protect your diskettes accordingly.

BACK UP YOUR DISKETTES

Even though you treat your diskettes with care, they can still be mislaid or damaged by accident. Files can be inadvertently changed or erased, and eventually diskettes simply wear out. Making backup copies of your diskettes limits the amount of information and time you lose if something goes wrong. The time it takes to make these copies could be one of your better investments.

Unless a program diskette is copy protected so that you cannot duplicate the original, make a copy of the program before you ever use it—even if you plan to install the program on your fixed disk. Store the original diskette in a safe place, and use the copy. If something happens to the copy, make another copy from the original. Always keep the original stored safely.

Your collection of data files will grow as you use application programs, such as a word processor or spreadsheet. Back up a data diskette whenever the value of the information it contains—or the time it would take to re-create it—is greater than the value of a blank diskette and the few minutes it takes to make a copy. Keep your backup copies in a safe place and use your computer with the comforting thought that, should something unforeseen happen, you're protected.

HOW INFORMATION IS STORED ON A DISKETTE

Information is stored on a diskette much as music or video is recorded on tape. A description of how DOS uses a diskette helps you understand the commands you use to manage your diskettes.

What Is a Diskette?

What we call a diskette actually consists of two parts: a disk of thin plastic coated with magnetic material, and a protective plastic jacket or hard shell. Figure 6-1 shows a 5.25-inch diskette in its flexible jacket, and Figure 6-2 shows both the front and back of a 3.5-inch diskette in its hard shell.

The dashed lines in Figures 6-1 and 6-2 show how the coated disk lies inside the protective jacket. The magnetic coating itself is visible through the openings in the jacket of a 5.25-inch diskette (the dark areas in Figure 6-1). The spring-loaded shutter that normally covers the opening in a 3.5-inch diskette is moved aside by the diskette drive to provide access to the magnetic coating. The hole in the center of the disk goes around the drive motor, which spins the disk so that data can be written (recorded) or read (played back).

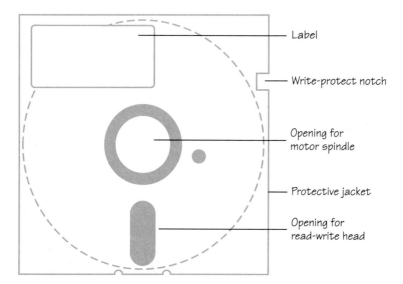

Figure 6-1. *A 5.25-inch diskette.*

The write-protect notch or slide lets you protect all the files on a diskette from being erased or changed. To protect a 5.25-inch diskette, cover the write-protect notch with one of the small tabs of tape included with the box of diskettes. To protect a 3.5-inch diskette, move the write-protect slide down (toward the edge of the diskette) until the hole through the diskette shell is open. To permit files on the diskette to be changed or erased, remove the tape or move the slide up until the hole is closed. Protect your DOS diskettes in this way; protect each of your application program diskettes, too, unless the application program manual tells you otherwise.

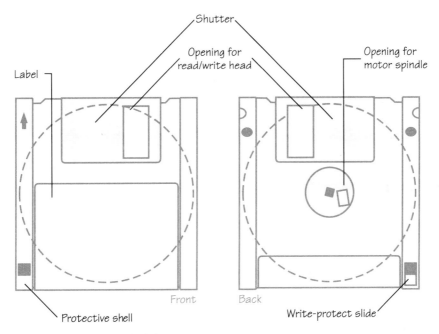

Figure 6-2. *A 3.5-inch diskette.*

How Does DOS Keep Track of Files?

Information is recorded on a diskette in narrow concentric circles called *tracks;* there are 40 such tracks on a standard 360-kilobyte (360 K) diskette and 80 tracks on the high-density 5.25-inch and 3.5-inch diskettes used on such systems as the IBM PC/AT and IBM PS/2 and PS/1 models. A track is divided into smaller areas called *sectors,* each of which can hold 512 bytes. Figure 6-3 shows how tracks and sectors are laid out on a diskette. For simplicity, the illustration shows only four tracks.

The side, track, and sector numbers of the beginning of a file are stored as part of its directory entry. You don't see this information when you use the Directory command, but DOS can find any sector on a diskette by its side, track, and sector numbers, just as you can find any seat in a theater by its section, row, and seat numbers.

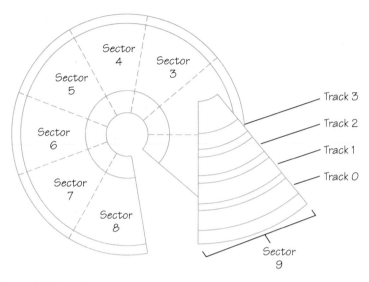

Figure 6-3. *Tracks and sectors on a diskette.*

Diskette Capacity

Tracks on a standard diskette are numbered 0 through 39 (making 40 in all); sectors are numbered 1 through 9, for a total of 360 sectors (40 tracks times 9 sectors per track) on each side. Most personal computers that run DOS have double-sided drives, which use both sides of a diskette, but some earlier models had single-sided drives that used only one side. A standard double-sided (or 360 K) diskette has an actual capacity of 368,640 bytes (though not all of it is available for files).

The high-density 5.25-inch diskettes used on the IBM PC/AT and compatible systems have 80 tracks (numbered 0 through 79), each of which has 15 sectors. A sector still stores 512 bytes, so the two sides of a high-capacity (or 1.2 MB) diskette can hold 1,228,800 bytes.

The 3.5-inch diskettes used on the IBM PS/2 computers and similar systems are also double-sided diskettes with 80 tracks per side. Depending on disk capacity, however, they have 9, 18, or 36 sectors per track—again with 512 bytes per sector. The 9-sectored (or 720 K) diskettes can hold 737,280 bytes; the 18-sectored (or 1.44 MB) diskettes can hold 1,474,560 bytes. The 36-sectored diskettes supported by version 5 of DOS hold 2.88 MB.

Volume Label

Any disk can be assigned a name, or *volume label,* to identify its contents. The volume label can be up to 11 characters long, and you can use the same characters allowed in a file name, plus a space. You can assign a volume label when you format a disk or at any time later on. DOS stores the volume label on the disk and displays it when you use the

Directory, Check Disk, Label, or Volume command. The volume label is for identification only; you can't use it in a command to specify a disk.

PREPARING FOR THE EXAMPLES

The examples in this chapter require one diskette. If you have version 5 of DOS, the Format command is more sophisticated than in earlier versions, so use a new diskette that's never been formatted. If you have an earlier version of DOS, use any diskette that doesn't contain any files you want to keep (the examples erase any data on the diskette). Put the diskette in your diskette drive; if you have two diskette drives, put the diskette in drive B. If you're using DOS on diskettes, be sure the DOS disk in drive A contains the file named FORMAT.COM.

PREPARING A DISKETTE FOR USE

As you've seen, the Format command prepares a diskette for use. The diskette can be either new or previously formatted. However, formatting means you can no longer use existing files, so don't format a diskette that contains files you need.

In carrying out the Format command, DOS normally checks for flaws on the recording surface of the diskette and marks any bad sectors so they won't be used. After formatting, DOS displays a message that tells you the maximum number of bytes the diskette can hold, how many bytes (if any) are defective, and how many bytes are available for storing files. Beginning with version 4, DOS also tells you how much storage space the diskette has in terms of *allocation units* (a term for packages of bytes DOS uses instead of reading from or writing to disk one byte at a time), and it displays the diskette's *volume serial number* (a disk identifier DOS assigns during formatting). As mentioned earlier, this information is unlikely to be of any concern to you.

DOS knows the type of diskette drive you have and formats the diskette accordingly. That is, it can tell whether the drive uses 3.5-inch or 5.25-inch, standard or high-density diskettes, and it formats the diskette to match the drive's maximum capabilities unless you specify otherwise.

This does not mean, however, that you can simply put any diskette in any drive and leave all the details to DOS. It is up to you to provide the appropriate diskette for formatting. You cannot expect a half-gallon bucket to hold a gallon of water, nor can you expect DOS to format a standard 360 K or 720 K diskette to reliably hold 1.2 MB or 1.44 MB of information.

You can, however, format and use low-capacity diskettes in a high-capacity drive. For example, if you have a high-capacity 3.5-inch drive and run out of 1.44 MB diskettes, you can format 720 K diskettes in the drive and use them reliably in a 720 K or a 1.44 MB drive. If you have a 5.25-inch drive, you can format, read, and write standard 360 K diskettes in it. In this case, though, you should expect to use your 360 K diskettes only in another high-capacity drive because a standard 360 K drive cannot read these diskettes reliably.

The Format command reserves space on the diskette for the directory, thus reducing the amount of storage available for files. Because the size of the directory varies, depending on whether the diskette is standard or high capacity, the storage capacity of your diskettes depends on the type of diskette you use. Figure 6-4 shows diskette sizes, tracks per side, number of sectors per track, and total disk capacity for standard two-sided diskette drives.

Size	Tracks per Side	Sectors per Track	Total Capacity in Bytes	System Where Used
3.5"	80	36	2,949,120 (2.88 MB)	DOS version 5
3.5"	80	18	1,474,560 (1.44 MB)	IBM PS/2 (except Models 25 and 30); DOS versions 3.3 and later
5.25"	80	15	1,228,800 (1.2 MB)	IBM PC/AT and compatibles; DOS versions 3 and later
3.5"	80	9	737,280 (720 K)	IBM PS/2 Model 30, IBM PC Convertible, and compatibles; DOS versions 3.2 and later
5.25"	40	9	368,640 (360 K)	IBM PC, PC/XT, and compatibles; DOS versions 2 and later

Figure 6-4. *Storage capacity of different diskettes.*

Format Command Parameters

When used to prepare a data diskette, the Format command has six main parameters:

format <drive> /4 /F:<size> /V:<label> /Q /U

<drive> is the letter, followed by a colon, of the drive that contains the diskette to be formatted (such as *b:*). With version 3.1 or earlier, if you omit <drive>, DOS formats the diskette in the current drive. If you omit <drive> with later versions, DOS responds either *Drive letter must be specified* or *Required parameter missing* and returns to the system prompt.

/4 formats a 360 K diskette in a high-capacity, 5.25-inch drive.

/F:<size>, in versions 4 and 5, formats a diskette for the capacity indicated by <size>. You can specify any appropriate diskette capacity from 160 K to 2.88 MB, and you can type <size> in any of the forms shown in Figure 6-5. If you are using version 3.2 or 3.3, two alternative parameters, /N:<sectors> and /T:<tracks>, enable you to specify diskette capacity by giving DOS the number of sectors and tracks to format; examples are given in Appendix C, "DOS Command Reference."

Disk Capacity	Type In Any of the Following Forms (No Blank Preceding K, KB, M, or MB)					
360 K	360	360K	360KB			
720 K	720	720K	720KB			
1.2 MB	1200	1200K	1200KB	1.2	1.2M	1.2MB
1.44 MB	1440	1440K	1440KB	1.44	1.44M	1.44MB
2.88 MB*	2880	2880K	2880KB	2.88	2.88M	2.88MB

* Version 5 only.

Figure 6-5. *Ways to type <size> as part of the /F:<size> parameter of the Format command in versions 4 and 5.*

/V:<label>, in versions 4 and 5, assigns the diskette the volume label <label>. This parameter speeds formatting by letting you specify the volume label ahead of time and thus skip the usual request for a volume label that DOS otherwise displays at the end of the format procedure. If you have an earlier version of DOS, your equivalent parameter is typed as /V (without <label>) and works in reverse, telling DOS to request a volume label at the end of the format procedure.

/Q, in version 5 only, tells DOS to perform a quick format. You can perform a quick format only on a previously formatted disk. During the procedure, DOS clears the records on the disk that tell it where files are stored, but it doesn't prepare the disk for use in any other way, nor does it check the disk for bad sectors. A quick format is very fast, and even though it isn't as thorough as a normal format, it does make all of the usable disk space available for storing new files.

/U, also in version 5 only, tells DOS to perform an unconditional format—one that clears the disk completely and cannot be reversed with the Unformat command.

Warning: If you're not using version 3.2 or later and you type a Format command without specifying a drive letter, DOS formats the disk in the current drive. If the current drive is a diskette drive that contains your system disk and you haven't covered the write-protect notch, DOS erases every file on your system diskette. If the current drive is a fixed disk, formatting erases every file on it: not just the DOS files, but every program and data file you have stored. Be certain you know which disk is going to be formatted before you press the Enter key after a Format command.

Examples of Preparing a Diskette

If you're not using a fixed disk, your system prompt is A>, not C:\>, as shown in the examples. This difference has no effect on what you type or how DOS responds, so follow the examples as printed; just remember the difference in the system prompt.

Format the diskette in drive B and give it a volume label. If you have version 4 or 5, type the following:

```
C:\>format b: /v:dosdisk
```

If you have an earlier version, type:

```
C:\>format b: /v
```

DOS asks you to put the diskette in drive B:

```
Insert new diskette for drive B:
and press ENTER when ready..._
```

Make sure the right diskette is in the drive, then press Enter.

If you're using version 5, DOS first displays a message telling you it's checking the existing format (if any) of the disk. Then it begins the format and tells the size disk it's formatting. Both versions 4 and 5 then report on their progress with a message that *xx percent* of the disk has been formatted.

If you're using version 3.1 or an earlier version, DOS displays *Formatting...* while it formats the disk. If you're using version 3.2 or 3.3, DOS displays *Head: 0 Cylinder: 0* and changes the head and cylinder numbers to show you its progress (*cylinder* is another way of referring to a track).

When DOS has formatted the diskette, it displays *Format complete.* If you have version 4 or 5, this message is followed by a report on available storage space and, on a separate line, the DOS-assigned volume serial number (which, if you're curious, is based on the current date and time). As you'll see in a moment, DOS has also used the parameter */v:dosdisk* to name the diskette DOSDISK. At the end of the report, DOS asks if you want to format another diskette:

```
Format another (Y/N)?_
```

Type *n* and press Enter.

If you have an earlier version of DOS, the *Format complete* message is followed by a prompt for the volume label:

```
Volume label (11 characters, ENTER for none)? _
```

Name the diskette DOSDISK by typing the following:

```
dosdisk
```

DOS displays the report of available storage on the diskette and asks if you want to format another. Reply *n*.

Now, regardless of your version of DOS, display the directory of the disk: It's empty, but you can see the volume label on the first line.

```
C:\>dir b:

 Volume in drive B is DOSDISK
 Volume Serial Number is 2F49-1AFF
 Directory of B:\

File not found
```

(If you don't have version 4 or 5, you don't see the volume serial number.)

Reformatting and Unformatting with Version 5

If you have version 5 of DOS, you can use the diskette you just formatted to experiment with the Mirror and Unformat commands. If you don't have version 5, go on to the heading "Copying a Complete Diskette."

Although you should try to be careful about formatting disks that already contain program or data files, version 5 of DOS can help you recover from an inadvertent format. As you saw in Chapter 5, the Mirror command can keep track of files you delete, and the Undelete command can often help you restore those files you delete and later need to recover. In much the same way, the Mirror command can also record the condition of a disk—its directory and the files on it—and the Unformat command can help you restore the disk to its earlier state after you've mistakenly formatted it. The following examples show you how to save the condition of a disk, reformat it with the /Q (quick) parameter of the version 5 Format command, and then reverse the format with the version 5 Unformat command.

Now that you've formatted the diskette in drive B, create a file on it so that you can see a change when you reformat the diskette. The file needn't be a large one, so copy from the console as you did in Chapter 5. Type:

```
C:\>copy con b:myfile.doc
This is my sample file.
^Z
```

Type the Dir command to verify that MYFILE.DOC is on the diskette in drive B. While you're looking at the display, also make a note of the volume serial number.

Saving the Disk Record

Now you can use the Mirror command to record the current status of the sample diskette. When used in this way, the Mirror command has two parameters:

mirror <drive> /1

<drive> is the letter of the drive whose current status you want to record. When you record the status of a disk, Mirror saves the information in a special file named MIRROR.FIL. It can use this file to restore the disk after an accidental format.

/1 (one, not the lowercase letter L) tells Mirror to save only one copy of the disk's status. If you don't specify /1 and Mirror finds an earlier record, the earlier version is saved as a backup copy.

For this example, type:

```
C:\>mirror b:
```

DOS responds with some copyright information telling you the name (Central Point Software, Inc.) of Mirror's original developer, followed by the message:

```
Creates an image of the system area.

Drive B being processed.

The MIRROR process was successful.
```

If you look at the directory now, you see two files listed: MYFILE.DOC and MIRROR.FIL. Mirror has recorded the information it needs to restore the diskette if necessary.

Reformatting the Diskette

Now try reformatting the diskette. This time, try the /Q parameter of the Format command. Type:

```
C:\>format b: /q
```

DOS responds much as it did before. First, it asks you to insert a diskette in drive B. The diskette is in the drive, so press Enter. Next, DOS checks the existing disk format and, because the diskette has already been formatted, it tells you it's *Saving UNFOR-MAT information*. This message appears whenever you reformat a disk, whether or not you've used the Mirror command, because DOS itself saves disk-storage information. Together, DOS and Mirror give you two safety nets, either of which you can use in recovering from a hasty or ill-advised Format command. Of the two, however, Mirror offers more accurate restoration of the files on a disk.

When the quick format starts, your diskette drive becomes active for a short time, and DOS tells you the size disk it's quick formatting. This message is followed almost immediately by:

```
Format complete
```

It's done, in much less time than your first Format command required.

DOS should now be asking you for a volume label:

```
Volume label (11 characters, ENTER for none)? _
```

Name the disk DOSDISK again and type *n* when DOS asks:

```
QuickFormat another (Y/N)?
```

If you try the Dir command again, you'll notice two changes: MYFILE.DOC and MIRROR.FIL no longer appear in the directory, and the volume serial number is now different. Both changes show that the diskette has, indeed, been reformatted.

Unformatting the Diskette

Note: This example shows how you can try to rebuild a diskette after mistakenly formatting it. Do not assume that you can reformat and rebuild diskettes whenever you want. As you'll see shortly from some of the messages DOS displays, rebuilding a disk can cause loss of stored data. The example is included here to help you in emergencies. Copying and careful handling are still your best methods of protecting the information on your diskettes.

Suppose now that you've just realized you formatted the wrong diskette. The one in drive B used to contain some valuable files, and you must try to recover them. You protected the disk with the Mirror command, so DOS should be able to use that information to restore the disk to its condition at the time MIRROR.FIL was created.

You can use the Unformat command to rebuild a disk, as long as you didn't use the /U parameter of the Format command in formatting the disk. Unformat has a number of parameters, some of which apply only to a fixed disk. This example uses only one parameter, the letter of the drive containing the disk to be unformatted. Other parameters are described in Chapter 9, ''Managing Your Fixed Disk,'' and in Appendix C, ''DOS Command Reference.''

To unformat the sample diskette in drive B, type:

```
C:\>unformat b:
```

DOS responds with the message asking you to insert the diskette to rebuild. The diskette is in the drive, so press Enter to begin unformatting.

Now you see a rather wordy response from DOS, but read through it all. The message tells you that MIRROR.FIL exists and that DOS will use the file in attempting to unformat the disk. You also see a message telling you that rebuilding the disk could cause loss of information. Keep this message in mind; rely on this command to rebuild a disk, but don't make it part of your everyday work with DOS. That's not how it's meant to be used.

DOS next tells you the last time Mirror or Format was used and asks you to press *l* (lowercase L) if you want to use this file to rebuild the disk, *p* if you want to use the prior file (you rarely will), or Esc to end the command. You want to continue, so press *l*. DOS then checks the Mirror file and gives you one more chance to change your mind (the following message appears on one line on your screen):

```
Are you sure you want to update the system area
of your drive B (Y/N)? _
```

This time you're sure, so press *y*. The drive becomes busy for a few moments, and DOS finishes up with the message:

The system area of drive B has been rebuilt.

You may need to restart the system.

(You don't have to restart the system with this disk.)

It's done. If you check the directory of drive B, you'll find that Unformat has not only recovered MYFILE.DOC and two Mirror files, it has even restored the original volume serial number of the disk.

COPYING A COMPLETE DISKETTE

The Diskcopy command makes an exact duplicate of any diskette. If the target diskette isn't formatted, recent versions of DOS format it before copying; Diskcopy in other versions may require formatted diskettes. Diskcopy works only with diskettes of the same size and capacity. For example, you cannot use it to copy from a 360 K diskette to a formatted 1.2 MB, 5.25-inch diskette, nor can you use it to copy from a fixed disk to any diskette.

The Diskcopy command has three parameters:

diskcopy <source> <target> /V

<source> is the letter, followed by a colon, of the drive that contains the diskette to be copied (such as *a:*).

<target> is the letter, followed by a colon, of the drive that contains the diskette that is to receive the copy (such as *b:*). If you have only one diskette drive, <source> and <target> can be the same letter (for example, *diskcopy a: a:*).

/V (*verify*) ensures that the diskette is copied correctly.

If you omit <target>, DOS copies from the diskette in <source> to the diskette in the current drive; if you omit <target> and you specify the current drive as <source>, DOS assumes you want to use only the current drive and prompts you to switch diskettes during the copy. If you don't specify <source> or <target>, DOS assumes you want to use only the current drive and prompts you to switch diskettes during the copy.

Examples of Copying a Diskette

This example copies an existing diskette, duplicating information from the source on the target diskette. If you are using DOS from a fixed disk, use one of your DOS diskettes as the source. If your DOS diskettes are not close at hand, use a diskette for one of your application programs or use a data diskette—the one you used for the examples in Chapter 5 will do. Place your source diskette in drive A (replace the diskette you just formatted if you have one diskette drive).

If you do not have a fixed disk, check that the DOS diskette in drive A contains the file DISKCOPY.COM. The diskette will serve the dual purpose of ensuring that DOS can find the command file it needs and that you have a disk to copy.

Before proceeding, be sure that your target diskette is either unformatted or formatted for the same capacity as the source diskette. Remember, Diskcopy works only if the target diskette is or can be formatted for the same capacity as the source.

If You Have One Diskette Drive

Because you have only one diskette drive, DOS must use it for both the source and target diskettes, prompting you to exchange diskettes as required. Check that the source diskette is in the diskette drive.

To copy the diskette, type:

```
C:\>diskcopy a: a:
```

DOS prompts you to put in the source diskette:

```
Insert SOURCE diskette in drive A:

Press any key to continue . . .
```

You put the diskette in already, so press any key. DOS tells you how many tracks, sectors, and sides it's copying, then prompts you to put the target diskette in the drive:

```
Insert TARGET diskette in drive A:

Press any key to continue . . .
```

Remove the source diskette, put in the target diskette, and press a key. If the diskette is unformatted and you have a version of DOS that formats as it copies, you see a message telling you what is happening. During the copy, DOS might also prompt you to exchange diskettes until it has finished copying the original. When DOS has finished, it asks if you want to copy another:

```
Copy another diskette (Y/N)? _
```

Reply *n*.

If You Have Two Diskette Drives

If you're using DOS on a system with two diskette drives, your source diskette should be in drive A. If you don't have a fixed disk, verify that the diskette containing DISKCOPY.COM is in drive A.

To copy the diskette in drive A to the target diskette, type:

```
A>diskcopy a: b:
```

DOS prompts you to put in the diskettes. The correct diskettes are in the two drives, so just press a key. DOS tells you how many tracks, sectors, and sides it's copying, then asks if you want to copy another; reply *n*.

COMPARING TWO DISKETTES

Note: The command for comparing two diskettes might not be included in your version of DOS. You can check for it in your DOS manual, or you can check your DOS diskette for the file named DISKCOMP.COM. If you don't have the Diskcomp command, skip to the heading "Checking the Condition of a Disk."

Sometimes you'll want to know whether two diskettes are identical. Diskcomp compares two diskettes track by track. The Diskcomp command can only be used with diskettes of the same size and capacity; you cannot use it to compare a fixed disk with a diskette.

Note: Just because two diskettes contain the same files, they're not necessarily identical, because the files might be stored in different sectors. If you want to compare all the files on two diskettes, rather than the diskettes themselves, use the Compare (comp) command described in Chapter 5 and specify all files (*.*).

The Diskcomp command has two parameters:

diskcomp <drive1> <drive2>

<drive1> and <drive2> are the drive letters, each followed by a colon, of the drives containing the diskettes to be compared (such as *a:* and *b:*).

If DOS finds any differences, it displays the side and track of each—for example:

```
Compare error on
side 0, track 33
```

Examples of Comparing Two Diskettes

Follow the instructions under the heading that describes your system.

If You Have One Diskette Drive

To compare the source diskette to the copy you just made, type:

```
C:\>diskcomp a: a:
```

DOS prompts you to put in the first diskette:

```
Insert FIRST diskette in drive A:

Press any key to continue . . .
```

Make sure the copy you just made is in the drive, then press a key:

```
Comparing 40 tracks
9 sectors per track, 2 side(s)
```

DOS prompts you to put in the second diskette:

```
Insert SECOND diskette in drive A:

Press any key to continue . . .
```

Remove the diskette, put in the source diskette you used for the Diskcopy example, and then press a key. If necessary, DOS continues to prompt you to exchange diskettes until it finally tells you it's done and asks if you want to compare more diskettes:

```
Compare OK

Compare another diskette (Y/N) ?_
```

Reply *n*.

If You Have Two Diskette Drives

To compare the diskette in drive B (the copy you just made) to the diskette in drive A (the diskette you used as your source), type:

```
A>diskcomp a: b:
```

DOS prompts you to put in the diskettes:

```
Insert FIRST diskette in drive A:

Insert SECOND diskette in drive B:

Press any key to continue . . .
```

The diskettes are already in the drives, so press a key. DOS reports how many tracks, sectors, and sides it is comparing, then reports the results of the comparison and asks if you want to compare more diskettes:

```
Comparing 40 tracks
9 sectors per track, 2 side(s)

Compare OK

Compare another diskette (Y/N) ?_
```

Reply *n*.

CHECKING THE CONDITION OF A DISK

Computers aren't infallible; malfunctions can produce errors in the directory of a disk. Such errors are rare, but the Check Disk (chkdsk) command helps by making sure that all files are recorded properly.

Check Disk analyzes the directory on a disk, comparing the directory entries with the locations and lengths of the files, and reports any errors it finds. The Check Disk report includes the items in the list on the next page.

▶ The total amount of space on the disk.

▶ The number of files and directories and how much space they take up.

▶ How much space on the disk remains available for files.

▶ In versions 4 and 5, the size of each allocation unit, the number of such units on the disk, and the number available for storage.

▶ The size of the computer's memory (up to 640 K) and how many bytes remain free for use.

You can also ask the command to display the name of each file on the disk and to check whether any files are stored inefficiently.

If possible, DOS stores files in adjacent, or *contiguous,* sectors. As files are deleted and new files are stored, however, they can become fragmented (stored in nonadjacent sectors). A fragmented file isn't a cause for worry; the worst that can happen is that DOS will take slightly longer to read the file. If several files on a diskette are fragmented, you can restore them to contiguous sectors by copying all the files to an empty, formatted diskette with the Copy command. (Remember, don't use the Diskcopy command, because it makes a faithful sector-by-sector copy of the diskette, storing the files in exactly the same—nonadjacent—sectors in which they are stored on the original diskette.)

The Check Disk command has four parameters:

chkdsk <drive><filename> /V /F

<drive> is the letter, followed by a colon, of the drive that contains the disk to be checked. If you omit <drive>, DOS checks the disk in the current drive.

<filename> is the name of the file whose storage you want DOS to check. DOS displays a message if the file is stored in noncontiguous sectors. You can use wildcard characters to check a set of files.

/V displays the name of each directory and file on the disk.

/F tells DOS to correct any errors it finds in the directory if you so specify when the error is found.

Examples of Checking a Disk

Whether you have one or two diskette drives, check the diskette in drive B by typing:

```
C:\>chkdsk b:
```

Press any key if DOS prompts you to insert a diskette in drive B.

DOS displays its report. (The report you see might be somewhat different. This is for a sample DOS diskette.)

```
Volume DISK      1 created on 03-01-1991 12:00a
Volume Serial Number is 1BC6-425F

   362496 bytes total disk space
   350208 bytes in 10 user files
    12288 bytes available on disk

     1024 bytes in each allocation unit
      354 total allocation units on disk
       12 available allocation units on disk

   655360 total bytes memory
   562384 bytes free
```

To check the diskette in drive B, and to check whether all files on it are stored in contiguous sectors, type:

C:\\>chkdsk b:*.*

DOS displays the same report as the preceding, but adds the following message:

All specified file(s) are contiguous

If any files were stored in noncontiguous sectors, DOS would display their names and the number of noncontiguous blocks of storage in place of this message.

To check the diskette in drive B and, at the same time, display the name of each file on it, type:

C:\\>chkdsk b: /v

DOS displays the name of each file on the diskette, then appends its usual report of disk space and memory available. If the list of files scrolls off the top of the screen, remember that, to view it all, you can freeze the display by pressing the Pause key or Ctrl-Num Lock.

Note: If you had organized the files on a diskette into directories, the /V parameter of the Check Disk command would list the directories, as well as the files grouped within them. Directories are covered in Chapter 8, "A Tree of Files."

You can combine the Check Disk parameters in one command; for example, *chkdsk b:*.* /v* would check the diskette in drive B, check all files on it for fragmentation, and display the names of all files.

If the Check Disk command finds an error, it displays a message such as xx *lost allocation units found in yy chains. Convert lost chains to files (Y/N)?* Although this message might look confusing, it simply means that Check Disk has found some storage units on the disk that have been used but, because of a program or system problem, aren't linked with any particular files. If you type the Check Disk command with the /F parameter and then type *y* when the *Convert lost chains...* message appears, DOS turns these ''lost'' units into files with the file name and extension FILE*nnnn*.CHK (where *nnnn* is a number such as 0001). Depending on the type of error that caused these units to be lost, DOS may or may not be able to recover the data in them. When the Check Disk command is complete, you can look at the contents of these files with the Type command and determine whether or not they contain information you want to save. If you don't want to save the information, delete the files to make the storage space available for new files.

ASSIGNING OR CHANGING A DISK'S VOLUME LABEL

The Label command assigns, changes, or deletes the volume label of a diskette or a fixed disk. It has two parameters:

label <drive><newlabel>

<drive> is the letter, followed by a colon, of the drive (such as *b:*) that contains the disk whose volume label is to be altered.

<newlabel> is the volume label to be assigned to the disk in <drive>.

If you omit <drive>, DOS assumes you want to alter the label of the disk in the current drive. If you omit <newlabel>, DOS prompts you to enter the new label.

Examples of Changing a Disk's Volume Label

At the beginning of this chapter, you used the /V option of the Format command to assign the volume label DOSDISK to your practice diskette. Sometimes you'll want to change or modify a volume label. You can do so with the Label command. Check that your original sample diskette is in drive B and then type the Label command:

```
C:\>label b:
```

DOS responds with something like this:

```
Volume in drive B is DOSDISK
Volume Serial Number is 2F49-1AFF
Volume label (11 characters, ENTER for none)? _
```

The sample disk isn't really a DOS disk, so change its name to MYDISK. Type:

```
mydisk
```

and press Enter.

If the diskette had a volume label and you wanted to delete it, you would reply to the prompt by pressing the Enter key without typing a name. DOS would then ask *Delete current volume label (Y/N)?* You would reply *y* to delete the volume label.

DISPLAYING A DISK'S VOLUME LABEL

The Volume (vol) command also displays the volume label and volume serial number of a fixed disk or a diskette but doesn't ask for a new label as the Label command does. If you assign descriptive volume labels to your diskettes when you format them, you can use the Volume command to make sure that you're using the correct diskettes. It's faster and easier than checking the directory.

The Volume command has one parameter:

vol <drive>

<drive> is the letter, followed by a colon, of the drive (such as *b:*) that contains the diskette whose volume label is to be displayed. If you omit <drive>, DOS displays the volume label of the disk in the current drive.

To display the volume label of the diskette in drive B, type:

```
C:\>vol b:
```

DOS displays the volume label:

```
Volume in drive B is MYDISK
Volume Serial Number is 2F49-1AFF
```

If the diskette had no volume label, DOS would respond *Volume in drive B has no label.*

CHAPTER 7

MANAGING
YOUR DEVICES

Data flows into and out of a computer system through pieces of equipment called *devices*. Devices are categorized by whether they handle data coming in (input) or going out (output) or both. The keyboard, for example, is an input device; the computer gets information from it. A printer is an output device; the computer sends information to it. A disk drive is both an input device and an output device; the computer can either read a file from a disk or write a file onto a disk.

Some devices, such as the keyboard, don't usually need much attention from you because DOS requires no special instructions to operate them. Beginning with version 4, however, you can fine-tune their performance, as you'll see later in this chapter. Other devices can be operated in different ways and so allow you to tell DOS how you want to use them. For example, modems follow certain rules in transferring information, and some displays allow you to change the number of lines shown on the screen. With DOS, you can set up a modem to work as it should and just as easily alter your display to work as you want.

Displays, keyboards, printers, and the computer's communications channels, called *ports,* can all be used in a variety of ways. This chapter shows you how to do the following with the DOS commands that help you manage your system:

▶ Check on system memory with the Mem command.

▶ Clear the screen with the Clear Screen command.

▶ Set the speed at which your keyboard repeats a key that is held down with the Mode command.

▶ Specify the number of characters and lines on the screen with the Mode command.

▶ Control the width and line spacing of your printer with the Mode command.

▶ Define the settings of the communications ports with the Mode command.

▶ Copy from a device to a file or to another device with the Copy command.

▶ Enable DOS to print and display graphics with the Graphics and Load Graphics Table (Graftabl) commands.

▶ Change your keyboard layout for use with a different language with the keyboard (Keyb) command.

DOS also includes a group of commands that let you change available characters and certain operating characteristics of your system to match the requirements of other languages and countries. If you need to use your computer with more than one language, Chapter 18, "DOS Is an International System," shows you how to use these commands.

DEVICE NAMES

Just as files have names, so do devices. You can use a device name in many DOS commands just as you would use a file name. DOS assigns all device names, however. You can't name a device yourself. Figure 7-1 shows the devices that make up a typical system, with the names assigned to them by DOS.

CON is short for *Console*. It is both an input device and an output device and refers to both the keyboard (input) and the display (output). Because the keyboard is input only and the display is output only, DOS can tell which one to use by the way you use the name CON in a command.

PRN is short for *Printer*. It is an output device and refers to the parallel printer that DOS uses unless you specify otherwise (much as DOS looks for files on the current drive unless you specify otherwise). You can attach as many as three parallel printers (named LPT1, LPT2, and LPT3); PRN usually means LPT1.

AUX is short for *Auxiliary*. It is for both input and output and refers to the communications port that DOS uses unless you instruct otherwise. You can attach one or two communications ports, named COM1 and COM2, with any version of DOS; if you're using version 3.3 or later, you can attach up to four communications ports (COM1 through COM4). Unless you or a program specifies otherwise, DOS assumes that AUX means COM1. On a typical system, COM1 could be used for a modem, and COM2 could be used for a serial printer—or vice versa.

DOS reserves these names for use with devices only; you cannot give any of these names to a file.

PREPARING FOR THE EXAMPLES

Note: Devices on a network are shared resources set up to respond to requests from more than one authorized user. If your computer is part of a network, check with your network administrator before attempting to manipulate or change the settings of shared printers or other devices.

Devices often need very specific setup instructions and operating parameters. The examples in this chapter work with IBM and IBM-compatible personal computers, displays, and printers. If you're not using one of these machines, you might need to use different instructions to manage your devices. Refer to your documentation for specific information.

When you try the examples, make sure the devices you name are attached to the system and are turned on. You won't hurt anything by entering a command naming a device that isn't present or isn't ready, but the command may cause an error that requires you to restart DOS.

If you're using DOS from diskettes, you'll need the command files MEM.EXE (versions 4 and 5 only), MODE.COM, GRAPHICS.COM, and GRAFTABL.COM. Before using the Mem, Mode, Graphics, or Graftabl commands, check that the appropriate DOS diskette is in drive A.

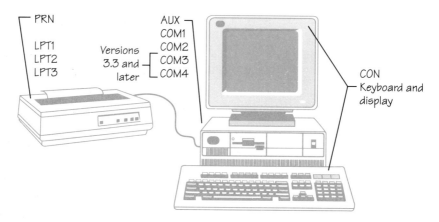

Figure 7-1. *DOS device names.*

CHECKING SYSTEM MEMORY WITH THE MEM COMMAND

Even though computer memory isn't a device as you would normally think of the term, it can be both useful and reassuring to know how much memory a system contains, what programs have been loaded into memory, and how much can be used by another program. Beginning with version 4 of DOS, you can use the Mem command to request a report on memory and memory usage. Type:

```
C:\>mem
```

DOS quickly produces a report like this one:

```
       655360 bytes total conventional memory
       655360 bytes available to MS-DOS
       617600 largest executable program size

      2097152 bytes total contiguous extended memory
            0 bytes available contiguous extended memory
      2031616 bytes available XMS memory
              MS-DOS resident in High Memory Area
```

This is the type of report you see with version 5 on an IBM or compatible that has 640 K (655,360 bytes) of regular, or conventional, memory plus 2 MB of extended memory.

The first two lines tell how much conventional memory is in the computer and available to DOS. The third line of the report tells how much of this memory an application program, such as your word processor, can use. This figure varies with the amount of memory a computer has, the version of DOS it runs, and the types of programs you use.

The second part of this report refers to the extra 2 MB of memory in the computer used for this example. Extra memory can be installed in two forms, *extended* (as here) or *expanded*. If such memory is installed so that DOS can find and use it, the Mem command also reports on its availability. In this instance, the report shows that the computer has 2 MB (2,097,152 bytes) of extended memory, of which 2,031,616 bytes are available for use as XMS memory, a form in which application programs can use it. The last line of the report tells you that DOS is *resident in High Memory Area*. The High Memory Area, or HMA, is a special portion of extended memory, and this line tells you that DOS has placed a large part of itself outside the computer's 640 K of conventional memory in order to give application programs more room to work. The ability to use high memory is a significant feature available only in version 5 of DOS. More details on extended memory and high memory are in Chapter 17, "Tailoring Your System."

The Mem command also includes three parameters, /*classify* (version 5 only), /*program*, and /debug. All three cause DOS to produce a more detailed report that shows both the names of programs you've loaded and the amount of memory they occupy. The /*classify* parameter, described in Chapter 17 and Appendix C, is useful if you want to use two version 5 commands, Loadhigh and Devicehigh, to place programs in a special portion of memory known as the upper memory area. The /*program* and /*debug* parameters, which tell you exactly where in memory your programs are located, probably won't seem very meaningful unless you're interested in programming or in learning about the inner workings of your computer.

CLEARING THE SCREEN

Sometimes you might want to erase distracting clutter from the screen: old directory listings, perhaps, or the display of commands DOS has already completed for you. You can clean things up with the Clear Screen (cls) command, which erases everything on the screen and then displays the system prompt in the upper left corner.

The Clear Screen command has one form:

cls

To test it, type its name:

`C:\>cls`

The screen is cleared, except for the system prompt.

FINE-TUNING THE KEYBOARD

Beginning with version 4 of DOS, you can control how quickly a keystroke repeats when you press and hold a key. To change the way your keyboard operates, you use the Mode command, an all-purpose device-control command that lets you tell DOS not only about your keyboard but about many other parts of your computer system, including your display and printer.

To refine the use of your keyboard, the Mode command has three parameters:

mode con rate=<speed> delay=<pause>

con is the name of the console device (here, the keyboard).

rate=<speed> specifies the speed at which DOS is to repeat the same keystroke. You can specify any number from 1 through 32.

delay=<pause> specifies how long DOS is to wait before starting to repeat the keystroke. You can specify 1 for a 0.25-second delay; 2 for a 0.5-second delay; 3 for a 0.75-second delay; or 4 for a 1-second delay.

You must specify both a rate and a delay. For example, the average keyboard repeats about 20 times per second with a delay of 0.5 second before repeating begins. To see the effect of this version of the Mode command, slow the keyboard considerably. Type:

```
C:\>mode con rate=1 delay=4
```

and try pressing the X key to see the result.

If you are a fast typist, impatient with a too-slow keyboard, set the rate for a high value, such as 32, and set the delay to a low number, such as 1. To slow keyboard repetition, lower the rate and, if you want, increase the delay time.

CONTROLLING THE DISPLAY

A number of different displays and display adapters (the printed-circuit cards that operate the display) are used with IBM personal computers and compatible machines. Figure 7-2 describes the most commonly used types of displays and display adapters.

The Mode command has several display-related options. Which one you use depends on the type of display you have and how much you want to see on the screen.

Normally, a computer screen displays 80 columns (characters) across and 25 lines down. If you have an EGA or a VGA display you can, beginning with version 4, change the size of the characters on your display and the number of lines on the screen. When used in this way, the Mode command has three parameters:

mode con cols=<columns> lines=<lines>

Short Name	IBM Product Name	Description
MDA	Monochrome Display Adapter	Text only, medium resolution, one color (usually green on a dark background). Introduced with the IBM PC.
CGA	Color/Graphics Adapter	Text and graphics, low resolution, up to 16 colors. Introduced with the IBM PC.
Hercules	None (works with mono-chrome display)	Displays graphics on monochrome display. (Not compatible with CGA. An application program must specifically support the Hercules board, but most major applications do because of its popularity.)
EGA	Enhanced Graphics Adapter	Text and graphics, medium resolution, up to 16 colors. Introduced with the IBM PC/AT.
MCGA	Multicolor Graphics Array	Text and graphics, low to medium resolution, up to 256 colors. Introduced with the IBM PS/2 models.
VGA	Video Graphics Array	Text and graphics, medium to high resolution, up to 256 colors. Introduced with the IBM PS/2 models.
—	Photo Graphic color	Text and graphics, medium to high resolution, up to 256 colors. Introduced with the IBM PS/1 models.

Figure 7-2. *IBM and IBM-compatible displays and adapters.*

con is the name of the console device (here, it means the display).

cols=<columns> sets the number of characters displayed on each line.

<columns> can be either 40 (for extra-large characters) or 80 (for normal-sized characters).

lines=<lines> sets the number of lines on the screen. <lines> can be 25, 43, or 50, but not all display adapters can handle all three choices.

To set the screen to display 40 characters per line, type:

```
C:\>mode con cols=40
```

To display 80 characters per line and 43 lines per screen, type:

```
C:\>mode con cols=80 lines=43
```

125

Note: If you try this command and DOS displays the message Function not supported on this computer, *the command does not work on your computer system. If you see the message* ANSI.SYS must be installed to perform requested function, *you need to identify a program named ANSI.SYS to DOS, in a startup file named CONFIG.SYS. Chapter 17, "Tailoring Your System," tells you how to do this.*

In all versions of DOS, you can also use another form of the Mode command to control the number of characters per line. When used to control the number of columns, the Mode command has one form:

mode <characters>

<characters> is either 40 or 80.
To display 40 columns with this command, type:

`C:\>mode 40`

DOS clears the screen and displays the system prompt in large characters in the upper left corner of the screen.

CONTROLLING THE PRINTER WIDTH AND SPACING

A dot-matrix printer normally prints a maximum of 80 characters per line and 6 lines per inch. It can also print in a smaller type, called *condensed,* that fits 132 characters on a line. This ability to change widths can be useful for printing documents wider than 80 characters. The printer can also print 8 lines per inch, to fit more lines on a page.

Note: If you have a laser printer, the documentation that came with the printer tells you how to define the printer to DOS and how to control the printer's characteristics, such as line and character spacing. The examples here most likely won't work, unless your laser printer can emulate an IBM or an Epson dot-matrix printer.

If your printer is attached to a parallel port, you can use the Mode command to specify the line width (80 or 132) and spacing (6 or 8).

When used to control a dot-matrix printer attached to a parallel port, the Mode command has three parameters, which you type in one of the following two forms. The first form applies to versions 4 and 5; the second applies to any version of DOS:

mode <printer> cols=<width> lines=<spacing>

or:

mode <printer> <width>,<spacing>

<printer> is the name of the printer, followed by a colon (*lpt1:*, *lpt2:*, or *lpt3:*).
<width> is either 80 or 132.

<spacing> is either 6 or 8. Notice the comma preceding <spacing> in the second form of the command.

You must always include <printer>. You can omit either <width> or <spacing>, and DOS will leave the current width or spacing unchanged. In the second form of the command, however, if you omit <width> you must still type the comma before <spacing> to tell DOS you omitted <width>.

Examples of Controlling a Dot-Matrix Printer

The following examples work with a dot-matrix printer connected to the computer's first parallel printer port (LPT1:). If this describes your equipment, make sure your printer is turned on before proceeding with the following examples. If you have a different type of printer or printer setup, you might prefer to read through the examples or skip ahead to the next section, "Controlling the Serial Communications Port."

Note: Because different versions of DOS accept different forms of the command, the examples first show the command used with versions 4 and 5, and then show the command form for 4, 5, and earlier versions of DOS.

To cause a printer attached to LPT1 to print in small type (up to 132 characters per line if the printer can do so), use the following command.

If you have version 4 or 5, type:

```
C:\>mode lpt1: cols=132
```

If you have an earlier version of DOS, type:

```
C:\>mode lpt1: 132
```

DOS replies with a display like this one:

```
LPT1: not rerouted

LPT1: set for 132

No retry on parallel printer time-out
```

The second line of this message, which you see with any version of DOS, tells you the command worked correctly and your printer is now set for small characters. If you have version 4 or 5, the other lines are additional messages telling you that DOS will, indeed, use your parallel printer for output and that, if the printer is busy or turned off, it will not keep trying to send data to it.

To test the new printer setting, print the contents of the screen by pressing Shift-PrtSc. (If you have an IBM PS/2 keyboard, press Print Screen, not Shift-PrtSc.)

To set the spacing of the same printer to 8 lines per inch, but leave the width unchanged, use the following command.

If you have version 4 or 5, type:

```
C:\>mode lpt1: lines=8
```

If you have an earlier version of DOS, type:

```
C:\>mode lpt1: ,8
```

DOS replies with a message like this:

LPT1: not rerouted

Printer lines per inch set

No retry on parallel printer time-out

(Again, if you don't have version 4 or 5, your message is shorter.)

To see the effect of this setting, print the contents of the screen again by pressing Shift-PrtSc. This time the text is printed both in small type (from the previous example) and with closer line spacing.

To restore the printer to normal width and line spacing with version 4 or 5, type:

```
C:\>mode lpt1: cols=80 lines=6
```

If you have an earlier version of DOS, type:

```
C:\>mode lpt1: 80,6
```

DOS displays a message similar to those you've already seen:

LPT1: not rerouted

LPT1: set for 80

Printer lines per inch set

No retry on parallel printer time-out

CONTROLLING THE
SERIAL COMMUNICATIONS PORT

Serial communications is controlled by several characteristics, or communications parameters, that define how fast and in what form data is transmitted. Different devices often require different parameter settings. The parameters of your serial port must match those of the device or computer service with which you want to communicate. Before you can use a communications port, you must set these parameters with the Mode command.

The communications parameters you can set include:

▶ *Baud,* how quickly characters are sent or received.

▶ *Parity,* the kind of error-checking technique used.

▶ *Data bits,* the number of electrical signals required to define a character.

▶ *Stop bits,* the number of electrical signals that mark the end of a character.

A more complete definition of these parameters is beyond the scope of this book. Figure 7-3 lists the parameters you can set with the Mode command. The documentation of the device or computer service you want to use shows the required setting; compare these settings with those shown in Figure 7-3 to see which, if any, parameters you must change.

When used to set the parameters of a serial communications port, the Mode command has the following form in versions 4 and 5:

mode <port> baud=<baud> parity=<parity> data=<databits> stop=<stopbits>

In earlier versions, the command is:

mode <port> <baud>,<parity>,<databits>,<stopbits>

<port> is the name, followed by a colon, of the communications port—*coml:* through *com4:* (*coml:* or *com2:* if you're using a version earlier than 3.3). The remaining parameters, separated by commas, are those described in Figure 7-3.

Name	Valid Settings	How You Specify	Value DOS Assumes
Baud	110, 150, 300, 600, 1200, 2400, 4800, 9600, 19,200*	You can abbreviate to the first two digits (11 for 110, 24 for 2400)	None (you must set a value)
Parity	None, Odd, Even, Mark†, or Space†	N, O, E, M, or S	Even (E)
Databits	5†, 6†, 7, or 8	5, 6, 7, or 8	7
Stopbits	1, 1.5†, or 2	1, 1.5, or 2	2 if baud = 110, 1 otherwise

* 19,200 is available from version 3.3 onward and can be used only with a computer capable of that speed, such as some IBM PS/2 models.

† Versions 4 and 5 only.

Figure 7-3. *Serial communications parameters.*

You must specify a value for <baud> each time you enter this form of the Mode command. DOS assumes the values for the other parameters listed in the last column of Figure 7-3 unless you specifically change them; you needn't specify these parameters unless the device or service with which you want to communicate requires values different from those that DOS assumes.

If you omit any parameter from the second form of the Mode command shown above, you must still type the comma that precedes it, to show DOS that you omitted the parameter.

Examples of Controlling the Serial Port for Communications

These examples show you different uses of the Mode command. Don't enter them unless you have a serial communications port and you want to change the settings.

To set the baud rate for COM1 to 1200 and let DOS assume values for the other parameters, you would type the following command.

If you have version 4 or 5:

```
C:\>mode com1: baud=1200
```

If you have an earlier version of DOS:

```
C:\>mode com1: 1200
```

DOS would reply by reporting the current setting of each parameter:

```
COM1: 1200,e,7,1,-
```

This report shows that <baud> is 1200, <parity> is even, <databits> is 7, and <stopbits> is 1. The hyphen at the end tells you DOS will not keep trying to send to a device that isn't ready, but will stop after a brief time.

To set <baud> for COM1 to 2400, <parity> to none, leave <databits> set to 7, and set <stopbits> to 2, you would type the following command.

If you have version 4 or 5:

```
C:\>mode com1: baud=2400 parity=n stop=2
```

If you have an earlier version of DOS:

```
C:\>mode com1: 2400,n,,2
```

(Note the two commas before the 2, telling DOS that you omitted <databits>.)

DOS confirms the settings:

```
COM1: 2400,n,7,2,-
```

130

CONNECTING A SERIAL PRINTER

If you want to use a serial printer attached to a communications port, you must use the Mode command to tell DOS to send printer output to the communications port instead of to the regular (parallel) printer port. This is called *redirecting* or *rerouting* the printer output. (You might recall from the earlier examples of controlling a dot-matrix printer that the DOS responses to the Mode command included the line *LPT1: not rerouted*. Here, you can see the meaning of that message: DOS was reporting that output to the regular printer port was not redirected to a serial port.)

Before you redirect the printer output, you must first set the parameters of the serial communications port to the values required by the printer, as described in the preceding topic.

When used to redirect printer output to a serial communications port, the Mode command has one form:

mode   <printer>=<port>

<printer> is the name of the printer (*lpt1:, lpt2:,* or *lpt3:*) whose output is to be redirected.

<port> is the name of the serial communications port (*com1:* or *com2:* in all versions of DOS, *com1:* through *com4:* in 3.3 and later versions). You must enter both parameters.

Example of Connecting a Serial Printer

To redirect printer output from LPT1 to serial port COM1, you would first set the serial port to match the communications parameters of your printer, then type:

```
C:\>mode lpt1:=com1:
```

DOS would acknowledge:

```
LPT1: rerouted to COM1:
```

Now all output that would normally go to LPT1: would be sent to COM1: instead. To cancel the redirection and restore the printer output to LPT1:, you would type:

```
C:\>mode lpt1:
```

FINDING OUT ABOUT YOUR SYSTEM

You have, up to this point, seen a number of ways to use the Mode command to control the devices on your system. But just as it's useful to know how to control your devices, it's also helpful to know what devices DOS is prepared to use and how it "sees" them.

Beginning with version 4, you can use the Mode command not only to describe devices to DOS but to find out about them.

To check on the status of any or all devices on your system, you use the command:

mode <device> /status

<device> is the name of a particular device you want to check on. If you omit <device>, DOS reports on all the devices it recognizes.

/status, which you can abbreviate as */sta*, is needed only when you want to check the status of a parallel printer you've redirected. (The */sta* is needed because simply typing *mode lptl:* would cancel the redirection.)

To check on the status of a single device, you type *mode* and the name of the device. For example, if the display were set to show 80 characters per line and 43 lines per screen, the command:

```
C:\>mode con
```

would produce a report like this:

```
Status for device CON:
----------------------
Columns=80
Lines=43

Code page operation not supported on this device
```

(The message *Code page operation not supported on this device* simply means that DOS, on this computer, has not been told to recognize international language, date, decimal, and currency conventions. If you need this capability, refer to Chapter 18, ''DOS Is an International System.'')

To check on all the devices on your system, you would type:

```
C:\>mode
```

and DOS would respond with a report like this:

```
Status for device LPT1:
----------------------
LPT1: not rerouted
Retry=NONE

Code page operation not supported on this device

Status for device LPT2:
----------------------
LPT2: not rerouted

Status for device LPT3:
----------------------
LPT3: not rerouted
```

```
Status for device CON:
-----------------------
Columns=80
Lines=25

Code page operation not supported on this device

Status for device COM1:
-----------------------
Retry=NONE
```

Although parts of the report might look unfamiliar, here's what it means:

▶ The report covers five devices: three parallel ports (LPT1, LPT2, and LPT3), the display (CON), and a serial port (COM1).

▶ The message *LPTx: not rerouted* simply means that information sent to any of these output channels has not been diverted to another port.

▶ The message *Retry=NONE* means that, if the device connected to a port is busy, DOS will not keep trying to send information to the device (a printer or modem, for example).

▶ The *Code page...* message is explained earlier.

COPYING FROM A DEVICE TO A FILE OR ANOTHER DEVICE

As you saw in earlier examples, you can use the Copy command to copy from a device to a file. You have used this technique several times to create sample files by copying from the keyboard to a file, and you will find it handy for creating short text files.

You can also copy from one device to another. Copying from the keyboard to the printer, for example, is a quick and convenient way to print short notes or lists.

When you copy from one device to a file or another device, DOS continues to copy until it encounters the character (Ctrl-Z) that marks the end of a file. Whenever you copy from the keyboard, you can send this end-of-file character by pressing the key labeled F6 and then pressing the Enter key (or, as you've done before, by pressing Ctrl-Z and Enter).

When used to copy from a device to a file or another device, the Copy command has two parameters:

copy <source> <target>

<source> is the name of the source device.
<target> is the name of the target file or device.

Examples of Copying from a Device to a File or Another Device

To copy from the keyboard (CON) to the printer (PRN), make certain the printer is turned on and type:

```
C:\>copy con prn
```

Now everything you type will be both displayed and sent to the printer. Type a few lines, and then end the copy by pressing F6 or Ctrl-Z (shown as ^Z in the example because that's how DOS displays it):

```
These lines are being
copied from the
keyboard to the printer.
^Z
        1 file(s) copied

C:\>_
```

Note: If this command doesn't produce a printed copy, you may need to tell the printer to eject the printed page and move to a new page. Try taking your printer off line and pressing the formfeed button.

PRINTING GRAPHICS IMAGES

Pressing Shift-PrtSc prints the text displayed on either a monochrome or a color display, but it does not print graphics images from a display that is attached to a graphics adapter. The Graphics command enables DOS to print these graphics images on any of several different printers.

You need enter the Graphics command only once. After you enter it, pressing Shift-PrtSc prints everything on the screen of the active display, including graphics images, accented characters, lines, and boxes. Color on noncolor printers is simulated with shading. Depending on the resolution of the display, the graphics image itself may be printed across the page (as you see it on-screen), or it may be printed sideways (rotated 90 degrees) and enlarged.

The Graphics command loads a program that increases the amount of memory that DOS uses. The command has four main parameters:

graphics <printer> /R /B /LCD

<printer> can be any of the IBM and non-IBM printers listed in Figure 7-4.

/R (Reverse) tells DOS to print the screen as you see it—in other words, light characters on a dark background.

Specify as:	For printer model:
color1	IBM Personal Computer Color Printer with a black ribbon or the black band of a color ribbon
color4	IBM Personal Computer Color Printer with a red-green-blue ribbon
color8	IBM Personal Computer Color Printer with a cyan-magenta-yellow ribbon
compact	IBM Personal Computer Compact Printer (versions prior to 4)
graphics	IBM Graphics Printer, Proprinter, Pageprinter, or Quietwriter
graphicswide	IBM Quietwriter or Proprinter with an 11-inch carriage (versions 4 and 5 only)
thermal	IBM PC Convertible Printers (versions 3.3 and later)
hpdefault	Any Hewlett-Packard PCL printer (version 5 only)
deskjet	Hewlett-Packard DeskJet (version 5 only)
laserjet	Hewlett-Packard LaserJet (version 5 only)
laserjetII	Hewlett-Packard LaserJet Series II (version 5 only)
paintjet	Hewlett-Packard PaintJet (version 5 only)
quietjet	Hewlett-Packard Quietjet (version 5 only)
quietjetplus	Hewlett-Packard Quietjet Plus (version 5 only)
ruggedwriter	Hewlett-Packard Rugged Writer (version 5 only)
ruggedwriterwide	Hewlett-Packard Rugged Writer with wide carriage (version 5 only)
thinkjet	Hewlett-Packard ThinkJet (version 5 only)

Figure 7-4. *Printers supported by the Graphics command.*

/B tells DOS to print the background color if you have specified *color4* or *color8* for <printer>. If you don't specify /B, DOS doesn't print the background color.

/LCD tells DOS to print the contents of the liquid crystal display of the IBM PC Convertible computer.

When you enter the Graphics command, DOS loads the program, adds it to the parts of the system kept in memory, and displays the system prompt. You needn't enter the command again until the next time you start DOS.

If you're using a color display and have a printer that can print graphics, you can test the Graphics command by entering the command and appropriate parameters, then displaying a graphics image and pressing Shift-PrtSc.

DISPLAYING GRAPHICS CHARACTERS

A color/graphics (CGA) adapter normally cannot reproduce the 128 special characters that include accented characters, Greek letters, box-drawing graphics, and others, even when it's in graphics mode. By providing the adapter with descriptions of how these characters are drawn, however, the Graftabl command enables DOS to display these graphics characters when the display adapter is in graphics mode.

When you enter the Graftabl command, DOS loads a small table into memory. The table describes the graphics characters to DOS so that DOS, in turn, can display them on the screen.

You don't need the Graftabl command in normal DOS operation, nor do you need it if you have an EGA, VGA, or MCGA adapter. But if you have a CGA adapter, there are certain times the Graftabl command can come in handy—for example, in reproducing lines, boxes, or accented letters on the screen. To tell DOS to display such characters, you would simply type *graftabl*.

DOS acknowledges with a message like the following:

```
Previous Code Page: None
Active Code Page: 437
```

Or, if you have a version of DOS earlier than 3.3, it might simply display a message telling you that the graphics characters are loaded. In either case, all 128 special graphics characters would be available until you reset or turned off your computer.

Note: The 128 characters that Graftabl makes available to DOS can be varied to suit different purposes, such as the need for unique characters in some languages. To handle different sets of characters, versions 3.3 and later include special tables known as code pages *that enable DOS to display and print international characters. You can use the Graftabl command to specify particular code pages for languages such as Norwegian and Portuguese. Chapter 18, "DOS Is an International System," describes code pages and the commands, including Graftabl, that you use with them.*

CHANGING THE KEYBOARD LAYOUT

Whenever you start DOS, it assumes the language and keyboard layout of the country for which your computer was manufactured. Since the mid-1980s, however, successive releases of DOS have offered increasing amounts of support for languages other than its original American English. As part of this international support, DOS versions 3 and later include a Keyboard (keyb) command that changes the keyboard layout to accommodate the special characters of different languages and to match the arrangement of keys used in different countries.

The first time the Keyboard command is carried out, it loads a small program that increases the size of DOS in memory by about 6000 bytes. Subsequent Keyboard commands then tell DOS to use different sets of characters that correspond to different country-specific keyboard layouts.

Keyboard Layouts

When you use the Keyb command, you tell DOS which keyboard layout you want by adding a two-letter country code to the command. If you're using either IBM releases 3.0 through 3.2 of DOS or Microsoft's version 3.2, you can choose from six layouts by typing the command as shown in the center column:

Code	Command	Country
dv	keybdv	Dvorak (an alternative English-language layout)
fr	keybfr	France
gr	keybgr	Germany
it	keybit	Italy
sp	keybsp	Spain
uk	keybuk	United Kingdom

If you're using version 3.3 or later, you have a significantly expanded group of keyboard codes to choose from because these versions of DOS offer much more international support. The following table shows the keyboard codes readily available for IBM and compatible computers in most countries.

Code	Command	Country
be	keyb be	Belgium
br	keyb br	Brazil (version 5 only)
cf	keyb cf	French-speaking Canada
cz	keyb cz	Czechoslovakia—Czech (version 5 only)
dk	keyb dk	Denmark
fr	keyb fr	France
gr	keyb gr	Germany
hu	keyb hu	Hungary (version 5 only)
it	keyb it	Italy
la	keyb la	Latin America
nl	keyb nl	Netherlands
no	keyb no	Norway
pl	keyb pl	Poland (version 5 only)

(continued)

137

Continued

Code	Command	Country
po	keyb po	Portugal
sf	keyb sf	French-speaking Switzerland
sg	keyb sg	German-speaking Switzerland
sl	keyb sl	Czechoslovakia—Slovak (version 5 only)
sp	keyb sp	Spain
su	keyb su	Finland
sv	keyb sv	Sweden
uk	keyb uk	United Kingdom
us	keyb us	United States, Australia, English-speaking Canada
yu	keyb yu	Yugoslavia (version 5 only)

Because entering a Keyboard command changes the location of common keys (especially punctuation marks), the character that results from pressing a key doesn't always match the label on the key, as you'll see shortly.

Typing Accented Characters with Dead Keys

Many languages use *accented characters* that combine an accent mark and a common character (such as Å or ñ). Some of these accented characters are assigned locations on the keyboard; on the French keyboard, for example, you type è by pressing the 7 key in the top row of the keyboard (to type the number 7, you press Shift-7).

Often, there aren't enough available keys to provide all the accented characters, however, so DOS also uses *dead keys* to combine accent marks and characters. Some typewriters use this same technique, so dead keys might be familiar to you.

A dead key is one that represents just an accent mark. Pressing a dead key doesn't produce any apparent result, but it tells DOS to combine the accent mark with the next key you press. On the French keyboard, for example, you type ô by pressing the key labeled with a { and a [, which is the dead key for the circumflex (ˆ), then pressing the key labeled O.

If you press a dead key, then press a character that cannot be combined with the accent mark represented by the dead key, DOS beeps and displays the accent mark, followed by the key you pressed, to show you it can't combine them as an accented character. For example, ˆp indicates DOS cannot put a circumflex over the letter p. If the dead key represents the diaeresis (¨), DOS displays a small dot (·) or a filled-in square (■) followed by the second key you pressed.

To correct the error, backspace to erase the two characters and type the correct dead-key sequence.

138

Example of Using the Keyboard Command

If you're using DOS version 3.0 through 3.2, type:

```
C>keybfr
```

If you're using DOS version 3.3 or later, type the following to change the keyboard arrangement to French:

```
C:\>keyb fr
```

If you're using DOS from a fixed disk and DOS responds *Bad or missing Keyboard Definition File*, you need to expand the command to tell DOS where to find the command file it needs. The file is named KEYBOARD.SYS, and it should be in your DOS directory. Retype the command as follows, substituting the name of your DOS directory if it is not C:\DOS:

```
C:\>keyb fr,,c:\dos\keyboard.sys
```

If you are accustomed to the United States layout, here are the most obvious changes with the French layout: You must hold down the Shift key to type a number; the locations of two pairs of letter keys are reversed (Q-A and W-Z); M is to the right of L; and most symbols and punctuation marks are in different places.

Now that you have switched keyboards, you must follow the new layout. For example, the command to display a directory in wide format is *dir /w*. If you don't follow the French keyboard layout, you'll type something like *dir =z* because the equal sign or another character is where the forward slash used to be, and the W and Z have also changed places.

Suppose you wanted to type the sentence *L'hôtel célèbre est grand* (The famous hotel is big). Both the é and the è are on the keyboard (2 and 7, respectively), but the ô is not, so you must use the dead key for the circumflex (to the right of P). And remember, the Q and the A keys have changed places. Here, step by step, is how you would type the phrase:

```
C>L
```

For the apostrophe, press the 4 key in the top row. After the apostrophe, type *h*:

```
C>L'h
```

Now, you have to use the circumflex dead key, which is to the right of the P. Press the circumflex dead key ([). Nothing happens yet. Now type *o*; DOS displays *ô*. Continue by typing *tel c*:

```
C>L'hôtel c
```

For é, press the 2 key in the top row; then type *l*:

```
C>L'hôtel cél
```

For è, press the 7 key in the top row; then type *bre est gr*:

C>L'hôtel célebre est gr

And finally, press Q to get the French a, and type *nd*:

C>L'hôtel célèbre est grand

Although that's a painfully long list of instructions just to type a simple sentence, in fact it goes quite quickly after a bit of practice. Press Esc to clear the line and type *keyb us* to return to the United States layout.

If your computer was manufactured for use in the United States and you have an IBM keyboard or a strict compatible, you can switch back and forth between the United States configuration and a different layout by pressing Ctrl-Alt-F1 (hold down both the Ctrl and Alt keys and press the F1 function key) for the United States layout, and Ctrl-Alt-F2 for the other layout.

CHAPTER 8

A TREE
OF FILES

A s you have seen, when DOS formats a disk it creates a directory that describes each of the files on the disk. The directory holds a fixed number of entries: 112 on a 360 K or 720 K diskette, 224 on a 1.2 MB or 1.44 MB diskette, and 512 or more on a fixed disk (the number varies with the size of the disk).

To make your computer filing system more flexible, DOS lets you create additional directories, called *subdirectories*, on a disk. The subdirectories divide the disk into different storage areas, each of which you can use as if it were a different disk.

To distinguish the main directory that DOS creates from the subdirectories that you create, the main directory is known as the *root directory*. *Root* because a multilevel directory structure can grow from it.

As you add levels to your file structure, a block diagram would show it spreading from the root directory and branching to other directories, like a tree branching from its root. This type of file structure is often called a *tree-structured* file system.

DEFINING A SUBDIRECTORY

To DOS, a subdirectory is simply a file that contains directory entries; these entries are identical in form to the entries in the main directory, but there is no limit to the number of entries you can put in a subdirectory.

You name a subdirectory as you name any other file, but because the subdirectory defines other files, you cannot use the normal file commands to copy or erase a subdirectory. This chapter shows you how to use several commands that enable you to do the following:

▶ Create a subdirectory with the Make Directory command.

▶ Change or display the name of the current directory with the Change Directory command.

▶ Delete a subdirectory with the Remove Directory command.

▶ Display a list of files and the directories on a disk with the Directory and Tree commands.

▶ Tell DOS where to look for a command file, if it's not in the current directory, with the Path command.

▶ Tell DOS where to look for a data file, if it's not in the current directory, with the Append command (3.3 and later versions).

Using these features of DOS, you can create and manage a computer filing system that is tailored to the way you work.

142

PREPARING FOR THE EXAMPLES

The examples in this chapter require one formatted diskette. If you're using a fixed disk or have a one-drive system, put the diskette in the diskette drive. If you're using two diskette drives, put the formatted diskette in drive B. If any files from earlier examples are stored on the diskette, delete them by typing the following; be sure to include the *b:* in the command:

```
C:\>del b:*.*
```

If you have only one diskette drive, DOS asks you to make sure the correct diskette is in the drive:

Insert diskette for drive B: and press any key when ready

Press any key.

DOS asks you to confirm that you want to erase all the files:

All files in directory will be deleted!
Are you sure (Y/N)?_

Before you respond, check the command you entered and be certain that you typed the drive letter (*b:*). If you didn't, press Ctrl-Break to cancel the Delete command, and retype the command correctly. If you did type the drive letter, respond *y*. Because a mistake in using the Delete command in this way could cause the loss of valuable files, you must also press the Enter key after typing *y* before DOS will carry out the command.

After you have deleted the files, change the current drive to B by typing:

```
C:\>b:
```

This completes the preparation.

CREATING A MULTILEVEL FILE STRUCTURE

Suppose you work at a small company and provide services to two departments, Marketing and Engineering. You keep all your papers in a file drawer. You keep miscellaneous items in the front of the drawer, and dividers labeled MKT and ENG separate the parts where you store papers that relate to each department.

Now that you're going to be using a computer, you can set up your computer filing system to match your paper files by creating two subdirectories named MKT and ENG. You can store miscellaneous computer files in the main, or root, directory of the disk, and you can store the files relating to each department in separate subdirectories. Figure 8-1 on the following page shows the filing cabinet and a block diagram of this corresponding DOS file structure.

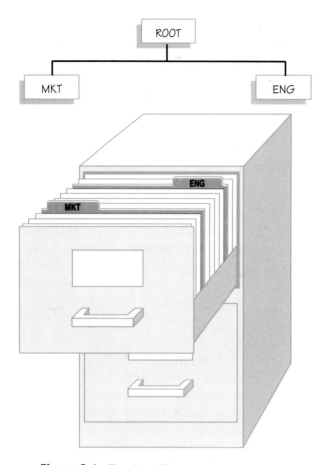

Figure 8-1. *Two-level file system.*

Creating a Subdirectory

The Make Directory (md, or mkdir) command creates a subdirectory. The only parameter that you must include is the name of the subdirectory you want to create. The command is described later in more detail; for now, type the following to create two subdirectories named MKT and ENG:

```
B:\>md mkt
```

```
B:\>md eng
```

You can see the subdirectories you just created by displaying the entries in the root directory. Type:

```
B:\>dir
```

DOS shows two files named MKT and ENG:

```
Volume in drive B is EXAMPLES 2
Volume Serial Number is 1839-10EE
Directory of B:\

MKT            <DIR>       10-16-91  10:54a
ENG            <DIR>       10-16-91  10:54a
        2 file(s)             0 bytes
                      1212928 bytes free
```

Note that the directory identifies the files as subdirectories by displaying <DIR> after their names. The backslash (\) in the third line of the display is the character that DOS uses to refer to the root directory of a disk. You've seen the backslash as part of the system prompt throughout this book; you'll see more of it and its uses in later examples.

Because MKT is a subdirectory, you can display its contents with the Directory command, just as you can display the contents of the root directory. Type the following command:

```
B:\>dir mkt
```

DOS displays the contents of MKT:

```
Volume in drive B is EXAMPLES 2
Volume Serial Number is 1839-10EE
Directory of B:\MKT

.              <DIR>       10-16-91  10:54a
..             <DIR>       10-16-91  10:54a
        2 file(s)             0 bytes
                      1212928 bytes free
```

Even though you just created it, MKT seems to contain subdirectories named . (one period) and .. (two periods). These really aren't subdirectories; they're abbreviations you use to refer to other directories. You'll see how these abbreviations are used a bit later.

The Path to a Directory

The third line of the preceding directory display tells you that you're looking at the directory of B:\MKT. The \ (backslash) refers to the root directory, and MKT is the name of the subdirectory whose contents you're displaying. Together, they are called the *path name* of the directory, or just the *path*, because they describe the path DOS follows to find the directory. The path names of the two subdirectories you created, \MKT and \ENG, tell DOS that the subdirectories are in the root directory.

You can also include a path name with a file name, to tell DOS where to find a file. The path name goes just before the file name (after the drive letter, if one is included) and is separated from the file name by a backslash. For example, if the subdirectory \MKT contained a file named BUDGET.JAN, the full path and file name would be \MKT\BUDGET.JAN.

The Current Directory

Just as DOS keeps track of the current drive, it also keeps track of the current directory. If you use DOS from a fixed disk, the current directory when you start up is usually either the root directory (C:\) or your DOS directory (C:\DOS). If you use DOS from diskettes, the current directory when you start up is normally the root directory of the startup drive (A:\).

Just as you can change the current drive, you can change the current directory, so that you don't have to type the path name each time you want to work with a directory other than the current directory.

The Change Directory (cd, or chdir) command changes or displays the name of the current directory. If you enter the command with no parameter, it displays the name of the current directory. To see what the current directory is, type:

`B:\>cd`

The current directory is the root directory, so the response is short:

`B:\`

It tells you that any command you enter will apply to the root directory of the diskette in drive B, unless you specify a different path name. Change the current directory to the subdirectory named MKT by typing:

`B:\>cd mkt`

If your system prompt normally shows the current directory, DOS acknowledges:

`B:\MKT>`

as soon as it carries out the Change Directory command.

If your system prompt doesn't display the current directory, DOS acknowledges merely by displaying the system prompt. But if you display the current directory again by typing:

`B>cd`

DOS responds:

`B:\MKT`

Note: Whenever you work with subdirectories, it's useful to have the current directory displayed as part of the system prompt. If your system prompt does not include the current directory, change it by typing prompt pg. Chapter 14, "Creating Your Own Commands," tells you how to make this command a normal part of your system's startup routine. Chapter 17, "Tailoring Your System," shows you many other types of information you can include in the system prompt.

You've changed the current directory to \MKT, so any command you enter applies to the subdirectory MKT in the root directory. Type the Directory command again:

```
B:\MKT>dir
```

DOS displays the entries in the subdirectory \MKT:

```
Volume in drive B is EXAMPLES 2
Volume Serial Number is 1839-10EE
Directory of B:\MKT

.            <DIR>        10-16-91  10:54a
..           <DIR>        10-16-91  10:54a
        2 file(s)              0 bytes
                        1212928 bytes free
```

This display is the same as the one you saw earlier when you typed *dir mkt*, but this time you didn't have to name the subdirectory because you had changed the current directory to \MKT.

Using Subdirectories

Your diskette now has the directory structure shown in Figure 8-1. You can use each of these directories as if it were a separate disk. The current directory is \MKT. Create a file named SAMPLE.TXT in the root directory by typing the following lines:

```
B:\MKT>copy con \sample.txt
This is a sample file.
^Z
        1 file(s) copied
```

Notice that you included the backslash to tell DOS to put the file in the root directory. You also use the backslash to display the contents of the root directory when it's not the current directory. Type the following:

```
B:\MKT>dir \
```

Again DOS displays the entries in the root directory:

```
Volume in drive B is EXAMPLES 2
Volume Serial Number is 1839-10EE
Directory of B:\

MKT          <DIR>        10-16-91  10:54a
ENG          <DIR>        10-16-91  10:54a
SAMPLE   TXT         24   10-16-91  11:13a
        3 file(s)             24 bytes
                        1212416 bytes free
```

The root directory contains two subdirectories and the file you just created.

Copying from One Directory to Another

Because you can treat directories as if they were separate disks, you can copy a file from one directory to another. Copy SAMPLE.TXT from the root directory of drive B to a file named ACCOUNT in the current directory (\MKT) by typing:

```
B:\MKT>copy \sample.txt account
         1 file(s) copied
```

You included the path (the backslash, meaning the root directory) in front of SAMPLE.TXT to tell DOS where to find the file; you didn't have to include a path for ACCOUNT because you were putting it in the current directory. Now display the current directory by typing the following:

```
B:\MKT>dir

 Volume in drive B is EXAMPLES 2
 Volume Serial Number is 1839-10EE
 Directory of B:\MKT

 .            <DIR>       10-16-91   10:54a
 ..           <DIR>       10-16-91   10:54a
 ACCOUNT               24 10-16-91   11:13a
         3 file(s)           24 bytes
                       1211904 bytes free
```

The file is there. You can copy files from one directory to another as easily as you can copy them from one disk to another.

Just as DOS doesn't confuse two files with the same name on different disks, it doesn't confuse two files with the same name in different directories. DOS can tell the latter apart because their paths are different. You can demonstrate this by copying the file named ACCOUNT from \MKT to the subdirectory \ENG, giving it the same file name. Type the following:

```
B:\MKT>copy account \eng
         1 file(s) copied
```

You didn't include the file name after the path name of the target directory because you wanted to give the copy the same name as the original. Assure yourself that the file was copied correctly by displaying the directory of \ENG:

```
B:\MKT>dir \eng

 Volume in drive B is EXAMPLES 2
 Volume Serial Number is 1839-10EE
 Directory of B:\ENG

 .            <DIR>       10-16-91   10:54a
 ..           <DIR>       10-16-91   10:54a
 ACCOUNT               24 10-16-91   11:13a
         3 file(s)           24 bytes
                       1211392 bytes free
```

You now have two files named ACCOUNT on the same disk; but they are in different subdirectories, and their different path names make them as different to DOS as if you had given them different file names.

Time Out for a Quick Review

Before completing your multilevel file structure, take a few minutes to review the following definitions. They summarize the terms and concepts introduced in the preceding examples.

Directory entry: A description of a file that includes the name, extension, and size of the file, and the date and time it was created or last updated.

Directory: A list of directory entries. You'll also see it used with a sense of place: "Which directory am I in?"

Root directory: The list of directory entries that DOS creates and maintains on each disk. It is called the root directory (or simply the root) because the entire directory structure on the disk grows from it. Because the root has no name to DOS, it is represented by a backslash (\).

Subdirectory: A file that contains directory entries. Like the term *directory,* it is also sometimes used with a sense of place: "Which subdirectory is that file in?"

Path name: The list of directory names that defines the path to a subdirectory. The directory names are separated by backslashes (\). The root directory is represented by a backslash at the beginning of the path. If a file name is included at the end of the path, it is separated from the last directory name by a backslash.

Current directory: The directory that DOS assumes you want to use unless you specify another in a command. The current directory is similar in concept and effect to the current drive.

ADDING MORE LEVELS TO YOUR FILE STRUCTURE

The subdirectories you create can contain any type of file, including other subdirectories. Like putting dividers between other dividers in a file drawer, this further structuring narrows the subject of a storage area. Suppose you do the following type of work for the Marketing and Engineering departments:

MARKETING	ENGINEERING
Word processing	Word processing
Budgets	Budgets
Customer lists	Project scheduling
Sales forecasts	

You decide to set up your file structure to match your work.

The following list shows the subdirectories you could create to match your computer files to the work you do (MKT and ENG are the departmental subdirectories you created). You would then have created the file structure shown in Figure 8-2:

In MKT:	In ENG:
WP	WP
BUDGET	BUDGET
CUSTOMER	SCHEDULE
SALES	

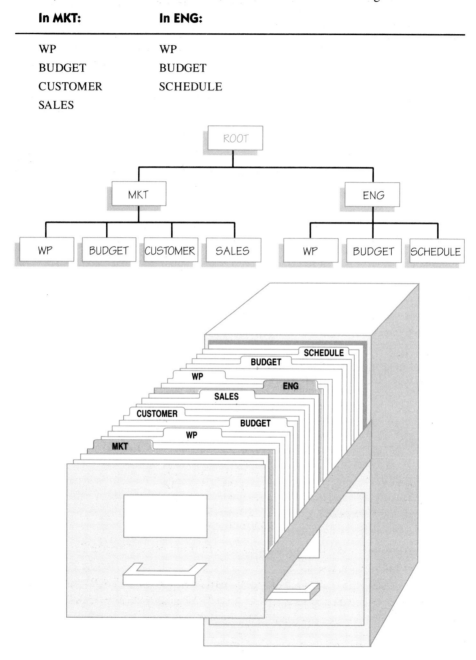

Figure 8-2. *Three-level file systems.*

Making a Subdirectory: The MD Command

As you saw earlier, the Make Directory (md, or mkdir) command creates a subdirectory. The Make Directory command has three parameters:

md   <drive><path><directory>

<drive> is the letter, followed by a colon, of the drive (such as *b:*) that contains the disk on which the subdirectory is to be created. If you omit <drive>, DOS creates the subdirectory on the disk in the current drive.

<path> is the path name of the directory in which the subdirectory is to be created. If you omit <path>, the subdirectory is created in the current directory.

<directory> is the name of the new directory.

The current directory is \MKT. For the example in this chapter, you want four subdirectories in \MKT named WP, BUDGET, CUSTOMER, and SALES. Type the following Make Directory commands to create the subdirectories:

B:\MKT>md wp

B:\MKT>md budget

B:\MKT>md customer

B:\MKT>md sales

Display the directory of \MKT by typing:

B:\MKT>dir

```
Volume in drive B is EXAMPLES 2
Volume Serial Number is 1839-10EE
Directory of B:\MKT

.              <DIR>      10-16-91   10:54a
..             <DIR>      10-16-91   10:54a
ACCOUNT            24     10-16-91   11:13a
WP             <DIR>      10-16-91   11:22a
BUDGET         <DIR>      10-16-91   11:22a
CUSTOMER       <DIR>      10-16-91   11:23a
SALES          <DIR>      10-16-91   11:23a
       7 file(s)            24 bytes
                       1209344 bytes free
```

The directory shows the file you copied a few minutes ago (ACCOUNT) and the four subdirectories you just created.

Your file structure calls for subdirectories named WP and BUDGET in \ENG also. Remember, DOS can distinguish between \MKT\WP and \ENG\WP, \MKT\BUDGET and \ENG\BUDGET, because their paths are different.

To create the subdirectory \ENG\WP, type:

B:\MKT>md \eng\wp

You included the path (\ENG) because the current directory is \MKT. The Make Directory command doesn't change the current directory, so it's still \MKT, but you can verify that the subdirectory \ENG\WP was created by displaying the contents of \ENG. Include the path here, too, by typing:

B:\MKT>dir \eng

```
Volume in drive B is EXAMPLES 2
Volume Serial Number is 1839-10EE
Directory of B:\ENG

.                <DIR>       10-16-91   10:54a
..               <DIR>       10-16-91   10:54a
ACCOUNT                   24 10-16-91   11:13a
WP               <DIR>       10-16-91   11:25a
        4 file(s)              24 bytes
                        1208832 bytes free
```

Now you're going to start moving around from subdirectory to subdirectory, so before creating the last two subdirectories in \ENG, here's a closer look at your navigator, the Change Directory command.

Changing the Current Directory: The CD Command

You have already used the Change Directory (cd, or chdir) command to change and display the current directory. The Change Directory command has two parameters:

cd   <drive><path>

<drive> is the letter, followed by a colon, of the drive (such as *b:*) that contains the disk on which the current directory is to be changed. If you omit <drive>, DOS changes the current directory of the disk in the current drive.

<path> is the path name of the directory that is to become the current directory. If you omit <path>, DOS displays the current directory on <drive>.

If you omit both <drive> and <path> (enter the command with no parameters), DOS displays the current directory of the disk in the current drive.

Keeping Track of Where You Are

As a note earlier in this chapter showed, you can change the system prompt to display not only the current drive but other information, such as the current directory.

Up to this point, the system prompt has shown the current drive and directory in abbreviated form (for example, *B:\MKT>*). In the remainder of the chapter, you'll be changing directories fairly often, so change the prompt to one that helps you identify the current directory at a glance. Type the following, including a blank at the end of the line, just before you press the Enter key:

B:\MKT>prompt Current Directory is p_Command: <Enter>

Now the system prompt becomes:

```
Current Directory is B:\MKT
Command: _
```

You could restore the system prompt to its more familiar form by typing the Prompt command with no parameters (*prompt*) or by typing *prompt pg*, but leave it this way for the rest of the chapter. The prompt takes up a bit more space, but it helps you keep track of where you are—a useful feature, especially if you are still adjusting to the idea of moving from one directory to another.

Using the Subdirectory Markers

Remember those markers (. and ..) listed in each subdirectory? They're designed to let you move quickly up and down a directory structure, particularly when several levels make the path names long.

The .. represents the directory that contains the current directory (sometimes called the *parent* of the current directory). The current directory is \MKT; to move the current directory up (toward the root directory) one level, type:

```
Current Directory is B:\MKT
Command: cd ..

Current Directory is B:\
Command: _
```

The system prompt still shows you the current directory but, as you can see, the current directory has changed to the root directory, which is one level above \MKT.

To complete your file structure, you need two more subdirectories in \ENG. Change the current directory to \ENG, and then create \ENG\BUDGET and \ENG\SCHEDULE by typing the following:

```
Current Directory is B:\
Command: cd eng

Current Directory is B:\ENG
Command: md budget

Current Directory is B:\ENG
Command: md schedule
```

This completes the structure of your multilevel file system.

You have nine subdirectories, plus the root directory, any of which you can use as if it were a separate disk. To show you how easy this is, the next few examples have you put sample files in several of the subdirectories. Figure 8-3 shows how your final file system will look, including the path names of all directories (above the boxes) and the names of the files you'll add (inside the shaded boxes).

To create the sample files in \ENG\WP, first change the current directory to \ENG\WP and copy the file named ACCOUNT from \ENG, naming it LET1.DOC, by typing the following:

```
Current Directory is B:\ENG
Command: cd wp

Current Directory is B:\ENG\WP
Command: copy \eng\account let1.doc
         1 file(s) copied
```

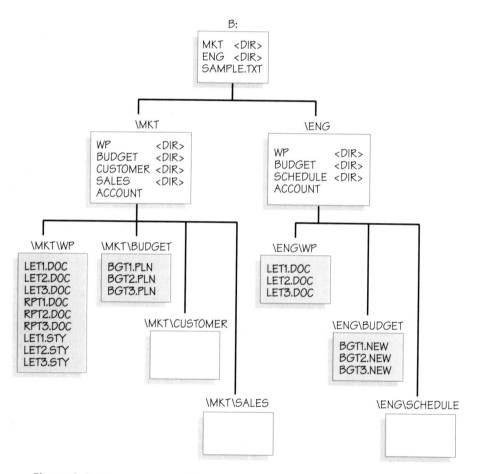

Figure 8-3. *Two-department file structure.*

Note that you must use \ENG in the command, even though \ENG\WP is a subdirectory of \ENG.

Now copy LET1.DOC twice, to create LET2.DOC and LET3.DOC, and display the directory by typing:

```
Current Directory is B:\ENG\WP
Command: copy let1.doc let2.doc
        1 file(s) copied

Current Directory is B:\ENG\WP
Command: copy let1.doc let3.doc
        1 file(s) copied

Current Directory is B:\ENG\WP
Command: dir

 Volume in drive B is EXAMPLES 2
 Volume Serial Number is 1839-10EE
 Directory of B:\ENG\WP

 .              <DIR>      10-16-91   11:25a
 . .            <DIR>      10-16-91   11:25a
 LET1     DOC        24 10-16-91   11:13a
 LET2     DOC        24 10-16-91   11:13a
 LET3     DOC        24 10-16-91   11:13a
        5 file(s)            72 bytes
                       1206272 bytes free
```

From this subdirectory, you can copy all three of these files to \MKT\WP with one command. Type the following:

```
Current Directory is B:\ENG\WP
Command: copy *.* \mkt\wp
```

DOS lists the source files as it copies them:

```
LET1 .DOC
LET2 .DOC
LET3 .DOC
        3 file(s) copied
```

These files could be word processing files that contain letters. Now create three more files in \MKT\WP that could represent word processing files that contain reports. First, change the directory to \MKT\WP, then copy the three files whose names begin with LET, changing their names so they begin with RPT. Type:

```
Current Directory is B:\ENG\WP
Command: cd \mkt\wp

Current Directory is B:\MKT\WP
Command: copy let?.doc rpt?.doc
```

DOS again lists the source files as it makes the copies:

```
LET1.DOC
LET2.DOC
LET3.DOC
        3 file(s) copied
```

To complete the files in this subdirectory, copy the same three files again, this time changing their extension to STY, which could identify word processing files that contain style sheets for formatting and printing documents. Type the following:

```
Current Directory is B:\MKT\WP
Command: copy let?.doc let?.sty
```

Now display the directory to verify that all nine files are there by typing:

```
Current Directory is B:\MKT\WP
Command: dir

 Volume in drive B is EXAMPLES 2
 Volume Serial Number is 1839-10EE
 Directory of B:\MKT\WP

 .              <DIR>        10-16-91   11:22a
 ..             <DIR>        10-16-91   11:22a
 LET1     DOC        24 10-16-91   11:13a
 LET2     DOC        24 10-16-91   11:13a
 LET3     DOC        24 10-16-91   11:13a
 RPT1     DOC        24 10-16-91   11:13a
 RPT2     DOC        24 10-16-91   11:13a
 RPT3     DOC        24 10-16-91   11:13a
 LET1     STY        24 10-16-91   11:13a
 LET2     STY        24 10-16-91   11:13a
 LET3     STY        24 10-16-91   11:13a
        11 file(s)          216 bytes
                        1201664 bytes free
```

To complete the file system, you need three files in \MKT\BUDGET named BGT1.PLN, BGT2.PLN, and BGT3.PLN, and three files in \ENG\BUDGET named BGT1.NEW, BGT2.NEW, and BGT3.NEW. First, use the Copy command to create the files in \MKT\BUDGET by typing:

```
Current Directory is B:\MKT\WP
Command: copy let?.doc \mkt\budget\bgt?.pln
```

DOS lists three source files as it makes the copies, and then displays the prompt.

To finish, you could create the files in \ENG\BUDGET from the current directory, but that would mean typing the full path and file name. To save some keystrokes, change to the \MKT\BUDGET directory by typing:

```
Current Directory is B:\MKT\WP
Command: cd ..\budget
```

The .. marker tells DOS to move up to the parent (\MKT) of the current directory and, from there, move down to the \BUDGET directory. The prompt changes to:

```
Current Directory is B:\MKT\BUDGET
Command: _
```

Now you can finish creating the sample files by typing:

```
Current Directory is B:\MKT\BUDGET
Command: copy *.pln \eng\budget\*.new
```

DOS lists three source files copied: BGT1.PLN, BGT2.PLN, and BGT3.PLN. Your file system now has the directories and files shown in Figure 8-3.

MANAGING YOUR SUBDIRECTORIES

Once subdirectories become part of your work with DOS, they quickly become essential for organizing your programs and data files, especially on a fixed disk. But the more subdirectories and files you create, the harder it is to keep track of where they are and what they contain. Giving descriptive names to your subdirectories and files is one way to maintain order. Another way is to group your files—especially data files—logically. At times, however, you'll still find yourself wondering what an old subdirectory contains and whether you still need it. And even if you're tremendously well organized, you'll also sometimes forget just where you saved *that* file (usually when you're in a desperate hurry to find it).

As you would expect, DOS includes several commands that help you manage your subdirectories and the files they contain. You've already seen the Directory and Change Directory commands, which allow you to move around through your directory structure. The remainder of this chapter describes other commands that help you:

▶ Eliminate unneeded subdirectories (the Remove Directory command).

▶ Use command files from any subdirectory (the Path command).

▶ Search for particular files by name or attribute (the /S parameter of the Directory command).

▶ View the directory structure of a disk (the Tree and Checkdisk commands).

▶ Help DOS find data files in different subdirectories (the Append command).

Removing a Subdirectory: The RD Command

As you work with a multilevel filing system, you might find that you no longer need a particular subdirectory, or that you want to combine the files from several subdirectories into one and then delete the unneeded subdirectories from your file structure. The

Remove Directory (rd, or rmdir) command removes a subdirectory. A subdirectory cannot be removed if it contains any files or subdirectories.

The Remove Directory command has two parameters:

rd   <drive><path>

<drive> is the letter, followed by a colon, of the drive that contains the disk with the subdirectory to be removed. You can omit <drive> if the subdirectory is on the disk in the current drive.

<path> is the path name of the subdirectory to be removed. You must specify <path> because DOS will not remove the current directory.

Suppose you decide you don't need the subdirectory \ENG\WP. Tell DOS to remove it by typing:

```
Current Directory is B:\MKT\BUDGET
Command: rd \eng\wp
```

DOS responds *Invalid path, not directory, or directory not empty* because \ENG\WP isn't empty: You put three files, LET1.DOC, LET2.DOC, and LET3.DOC, in it.

This example points out the difference in the ways you handle files and subdirectories. As you saw in earlier chapters, you use the Delete command to delete a file from a disk. To remove a directory, however, you use the Remove Directory command.

In the next example, you will delete three files with the Delete command and then remove a directory with the Remove Directory command. First, change the current directory to \ENG, and then delete the files with the Delete command by typing:

```
Current Directory is B:\MKT\WP
Command: cd \eng
```

```
Current Directory is B:\ENG
Command: del wp\*.doc
```

You changed the current directory to \ENG, rather than to \ENG\WP, because DOS won't remove the current directory. Now that \ENG\WP is empty, type the Remove Directory command and verify the change by displaying the directory.

```
Current Directory is B:\ENG
Command: rd wp
```

```
Current Directory is B:\ENG
Command: dir
```

```
 Volume in drive B is EXAMPLES 2
 Volume Serial Number is 1839-10EE
 Directory of B:\ENG
```

```
    .               <DIR>        10-16-91   10:54a
    . .             <DIR>        10-16-91   10:54a
ACCOUNT                       24 10-16-91   11:13a
BUDGET              <DIR>        10-16-91   11:30a
SCHEDULE            <DIR>        10-16-91   11:30a
        5 file(s)                 24 bytes
                             1200640 bytes free
```

The subdirectory \ENG\WP is gone.

If you want to remove a directory but need some of the files it contains, copy the files you need to another subdirectory, then erase all the files and remove the unneeded directory.

Note: The next few topics cover features in verson 5 of DOS. If you don't have version 5, skip ahead to the section "The Path to a Command."

Viewing Files in More than One Subdirectory

If you have version 5 of DOS, you can display the contents of the current subdirectory and all subdirectories below it by using the /S parameter of the Directory command. When used to display the contents of more than one subdirectory, the command is:

dir   <filename>   /S

If you include <filename>, DOS searches for the file in the current subdirectory and all subdirectories below it. You can use wildcards to specify a group of files. If you do not include <filename>, DOS displays the names of all files in all the subdirectories.

You can also combine /S with other parameters of the Directory command. For example, you can include /P to halt the display after each screenful, and you can include the /A parameter to limit the search to files to which you've assigned a particular attribute, such as hidden or read-only.

To see how the /S parameter works, begin by changing to the root directory of the disk in drive B to start at the highest level of your directory tree. Type the following Change Directory command (remember, \ means the root directory):

```
Current Directory is B:\ENG
Command: cd \
```

Now request a listing of all subdirectories and files stored in the root directory. The list is long, so use the /P parameter as well as /S so that DOS will pause after each screenful. Type:

```
Current Directory is B:\
Command: dir /s /p
```

The first screenful looks like the following:

```
Volume in drive B is EXAMPLES 2
Volume Serial Number is 1839-10EE

Directory of B:\

MKT          <DIR>      10-16-91   10:54a
ENG          <DIR>      10-16-91   10:54a
SAMPLE   TXT         24 10-16-91   11:13a
         3 file(s)         24 bytes

Directory of B:\ENG

.            <DIR>      10-16-91   10:54a
..           <DIR>      10-16-91   10:54a
ACCOUNT              24 10-16-91   11:13a
BUDGET       <DIR>      10-16-91   11:30a
SCHEDULE     <DIR>      10-16-91   11:30a
         5 file(s)         24 bytes

Directory of B:\ENG\BUDGET

.            <DIR>      10-16-91   11:30a
..           <DIR>      10-16-91   11:30a
Press any key to continue . . .
```

Notice that DOS displays the name of each subdirectory on a separate line above the list of subdirectory entries. If you want to display another screenful, press any key. If you want to cancel, press Ctrl-Break.

Viewing Specified Files in More Than One Subdirectory

A listing of every file in every subdirectory on a disk can be very long. You can limit the display by telling DOS to show only the names of files that you specify. For example, use the asterisk wildcard to tell DOS to list any file in any subdirectory whose extension is DOC. Type:

```
Current Directory is B:\
Command: dir *.doc /s
```

DOS responds:

```
Volume in drive B is EXAMPLES 2
Volume Serial Number is 1839-10EE

Directory of B:\MKT\WP
```

```
LET1      DOC           24 10-16-91   11:13a
LET2      DOC           24 10-16-91   11:13a
LET3      DOC           24 10-16-91   11:13a
RPT1      DOC           24 10-16-91   11:13a
RPT2      DOC           24 10-16-91   11:13a
RPT3      DOC           24 10-16-91   11:13a
          6 file(s)          144 bytes


Total files listed:
          6 file(s)          144 bytes
                         1200640 bytes free
```

Only the subdirectory \MKT\WP contains files with the extension DOC.

Now try limiting the display to files with a particular attribute. To do this, you combine the /A and /S parameters of the Directory command. For example, you have six budget files in two subdirectories, \MKT\BUDGET and \ENG\BUDGET. Suppose you want to ensure that these files are not accidentally changed. Like the Directory command, the Attribute command includes a parameter, /S, that allows you to affect files in more than one directory.

To see how this works, type the following Attribute command to make the files read-only:

```
Current directory is B:\
Command: attrib +r bgt?.* /s
```

This command tells DOS to give the read-only attribute to all sample files whose names begin with BGT, regardless of extension, in all subdirectories below the root directory. DOS responds by displaying the prompt:

```
Current directory is B:\
Command:
```

Now use the /A and /S parameters of the Directory command. Type:

```
Current directory is B:\
Command: dir /a:r /s
```

Written out, this command tells DOS, ''Show me the directory entries of all files with the read-only attribute (*dir /a:r*) in the current directory and all subdirectories it contains (*/s*).'' DOS responds:

```
Volume in drive B is EXAMPLES 2
Volume Serial Number is 1839-10EE

Directory of B:\ENG\BUDGET

BGT1      NEW           24 10-16-91   11:13a
BGT2      NEW           24 10-16-91   11:13a
BGT3      NEW           24 10-16-91   11:13a
          3 file(s)           72 bytes
```

```
Directory of B:\MKT\BUDGET

BGT1      PLN          24 10-16-91   11:13a
BGT2      PLN          24 10-16-91   11:13a
BGT3      PLN          24 10-16-91   11:13a
          3 file(s)            72 bytes

Total files listed:
          6 file(s)           144 bytes
                          1200640 bytes free
```

Only the read-only files are listed. Type the following Attribute command to remove the read-only attribute from the budget files:

```
Current Directory is B:\
Command: attrib -r bgt?.* /s
```

The /S parameter can be particularly useful if you remember the name of a file, but you can't remember where you put it. Change to the root directory of the disk and use the /S parameter to search every subdirectory. Use wildcards, if needed, to search for a group of files or for a file whose name you're not sure of.

The Path to a Command: The PATH Command

In a multilevel filing system, you'll probably change the current directory as you use data files in different subdirectories. But you'll use command files too, such as the external DOS commands and application programs. When you type a command, DOS looks for the command file in the current directory. If you have changed directories, chances are the current directory doesn't contain the command file you need.

The Path command lets you tell DOS where to look for a command file if it's not in the current directory. You can name one or more directories—the root directory or any subdirectory on the disk in any disk drive. This command lets you work in any subdirectory you want and still be able to use any command file.

The Path command has three parameters:

path <drive><path> ;

<drive> is the letter, followed by a colon, of the drive (such as *b:*) with the disk that contains the command file. If you omit <drive>, DOS looks on the disk in the current drive.

<path> is the path name of the directory that contains the command file.

You can specify several command paths in one command, separating them with semicolons. If you enter a Path command with no parameters (just type *path*), DOS displays the command paths you have defined. If you type *path* followed only by a semicolon, DOS cancels any command paths you have defined.

If you have a fixed disk, the root directory probably contains a special file named AUTOEXEC.BAT that DOS reads each time you start or restart your computer.

AUTOEXEC.BAT contains instructions that help DOS work well for you. One of those instructions is probably a Path command that enables you to use application programs, as well as external DOS commands, no matter what the current directory is. For example, suppose you use Microsoft Word, Lotus 1-2-3, R:BASE, and MaxThink, and your DOS files are in a directory named \DOS. Your Path command probably looks something like this:

```
path c:\dos;c:\word;c:\123;c:\rbfiles;c:\max
```

The order in which the directory names are specified determines the order in which DOS searches for the command file. Because the drive letter and root-directory symbol (\) precede each subdirectory name, DOS knows where to find each program, and you can use any program in any of these directories even if the current drive isn't C.

If you have a fixed disk and DOS has no trouble starting application programs or carrying out external commands when drive B is the current drive, you can be sure you have an AUTOEXEC.BAT file with a Path command in it. You can check on your own command path by typing *path* with no parameters. Type:

```
Current Directory is B:\
Command: path
```

If you do have any problems starting programs from another drive, Chapter 14, "Creating Your Own Commands," describes how you can create or modify an AUTOEXEC.BAT file.

And what if you don't have a fixed disk? You use the Path command to tell DOS to look on drive A for its command files. The following few examples use external command files. The current drive is B, so use the Path command to tell DOS where to find its external commands. Type:

```
Current Directory is B:\
Command: path a:\
```

Displaying the Directory Structure: The Tree and Check Disk commands

As described in Chapter 10, "The DOS Shell," the Shell lets you quickly display a diagram of the directory structure of any disk and use that diagram to move from one directory to another. Tree and Checkdisk are commands that allow you to view your directory structure from the system prompt.

The Tree command has two main parameters:

tree <drive> /F

<drive> is the letter of the drive, followed by a colon, that contains the disk whose directory structure is to be displayed.

/F displays a list of the files in each directory.

Checking the Directory Structure of a Disk

Note: The following two examples use the Tree command. If your version of DOS does not include this command, a later example shows you how to use the Check Disk command to see a list of directories and files on a disk.

Suppose you're about to create a new file and you want to check on the most appropriate subdirectory for it. As its name implies, the Tree command shows you the structure of the directory tree on whichever disk you specify. For example, check the directories on your sample disk. To be sure you see the entire structure, first check that the current directory is the root directory. If it isn't, change directories by typing *cd*.

Now ask DOS to show you the names and relative levels of the directories on the disk. (If you're not using a fixed disk, place the diskette with the file TREE.COM in drive A.) Type:

```
Current Directory is B:\
Command: tree
```

If you're using version 4 or 5 of DOS, you see a report like this:

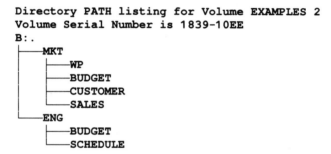

```
Directory PATH listing for Volume EXAMPLES 2
Volume Serial Number is 1839-10EE
B:.
├───MKT
│       ├───WP
│       ├───BUDGET
│       ├───CUSTOMER
│       └───SALES
└───ENG
        ├───BUDGET
        └───SCHEDULE
```

If you're using an earlier version of DOS, you see a report like the following (some blank lines that appear on the screen have been removed to condense the display):

```
DIRECTORY PATH LISTING
Path: \MKT
Sub-directories:   WP
                   BUDGET
                   CUSTOMER
                   SALES
Path: \MKT\WP
Sub-directories:   None
Path: \MKT\BUDGET
Sub-directories:   None
Path: \MKT\CUSTOMER
Sub-directories:   None
Path: \MKT\SALES
Sub-directories:   None
Path: \ENG
```

```
Sub-directories:   BUDGET
                   SCHEDULE
Path: \ENG\BUDGET
Sub-directories:   None
Path: \ENG\SCHEDULE
Sub-directories:   None
```

But suppose a report on the directory structure isn't detailed enough. You want to know the name of each file in each subdirectory—perhaps because there is one file in particular you need. To do this, you use the /F parameter, which shows not only the directory structure of the disk but the names of the files in each directory. For example, versions 4 and 5 of DOS produce a report like this when you type *tree /f*:

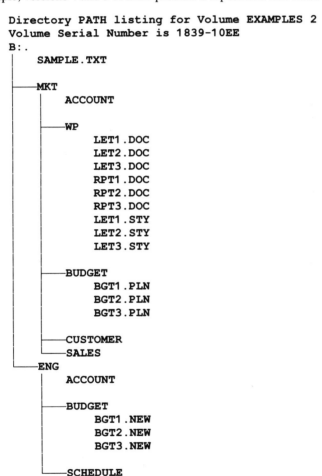

```
Directory PATH listing for Volume EXAMPLES 2
Volume Serial Number is 1839-10EE
B:.
    │    SAMPLE.TXT
    │
    ├────MKT
    │        ACCOUNT
    │
    │    ┌────WP
    │    │        LET1.DOC
    │    │        LET2.DOC
    │    │        LET3.DOC
    │    │        RPT1.DOC
    │    │        RPT2.DOC
    │    │        RPT3.DOC
    │    │        LET1.STY
    │    │        LET2.STY
    │    │        LET3.STY
    │    │
    │    ├────BUDGET
    │    │        BGT1.PLN
    │    │        BGT2.PLN
    │    │        BGT3.PLN
    │    │
    │    ├────CUSTOMER
    │    └────SALES
    └────ENG
             ACCOUNT

         ┌────BUDGET
         │        BGT1.NEW
         │        BGT2.NEW
         │        BGT3.NEW
         └────SCHEDULE
```

Now the tree shows the names of your files beneath the names of the subdirectories that contain them.

If your version of the Tree command doesn't produce the graphic type of report shown above, or if your version of DOS doesn't include a Tree command, you can use the /V parameter of the Check Disk command to see a list of files and directories. (If you're not using a fixed disk, check that the file CHKDSK.COM or CHKDSK.EXE is on the disk in drive A.) Type:

```
Current Directory is B:\
Command: chkdsk /v
```

DOS responds with a report like this:

```
Volume EXAMPLES 2   created 10-16-1991 10:46a
Volume Serial Number is 1839-10EE
Directory B:\
Directory B:\MKT
B:\MKT\ACCOUNT
Directory B:\MKT\WP
B:\MKT\WP\LET1.DOC
B:\MKT\WP\LET2.DOC
B:\MKT\WP\LET3.DOC
B:\MKT\WP\RPT1.DOC
B:\MKT\WP\RPT2.DOC
B:\MKT\WP\RPT3.DOC
B:\MKT\WP\LET1.STY
B:\MKT\WP\LET2.STY
B:\MKT\WP\LET3.STY
Directory B:\MKT\BUDGET
B:\MKT\BUDGET\BGT1.PLN
B:\MKT\BUDGET\BGT2.PLN
B:\MKT\BUDGET\BGT3.PLN
Directory B:\MKT\CUSTOMER
Directory B:\MKT\SALES
Directory B:\ENG
B:\ENG\ACCOUNT
Directory B:\ENG\BUDGET
B:\ENG\BUDGET\BGT1.NEW
B:\ENG\BUDGET\BGT2.NEW
B:\ENG\BUDGET\BGT3.NEW
Directory B:\ENG\SCHEDULE
B:\SAMPLE.TXT

   1213952 bytes total disk space
      4096 bytes in 8 directories
      9216 bytes in 18 user files
   1200640 bytes available on disk

       512 bytes in each allocation unit
      2371 total allocation units on disk
      2345 available allocation units on disk

    655360 total bytes memory
    528688 bytes free
```

Here, the directories are identified by *Directory* preceding the path and file name. The file in the root directory (SAMPLE.TXT) is listed at the end, above the usual Check Disk reports on disk space and memory.

A printed copy of either of these reports can be helpful, especially if your filing system has several levels. For a fixed disk with several hundred files, however, bear in mind that either a Tree or a Check Disk report showing both directories and files could be several pages long. Here are some ways you can print the reports of either or both the Tree and Check Disk commands.

If you want to print a list of both directories and files, use the Tree command with the /F parameter or the Check Disk command with the /V parameter. If you have version 4 or 5 and your printer is not an IBM or IBM-compatible printer, either use the Check Disk command or use the /A parameter of the Tree command, which tells DOS to use hyphens, backslashes, and other common characters to print the diagram. Without the /A parameter, your printout might include accented letters, small open circles, or other such characters in place of the horizontal and vertical lines showing the branches of your directory tree.

For example, to print a complete report for the disk in drive B, type:

```
Current Directory is B:\
Command: tree /f > prn
```

or:

```
Current Directory is B:\
Command: tree /f /a > prn
```

or:

```
Current Directory is B:\
Command: chkdsk /v > prn
```

To print only a list of directories on the disk in drive B, you can use either of the following commands.

With the Tree command, type:

```
Current Directory is B:\
Command: tree > prn
```

With the Check Disk command, you use techniques described in Chapter 13, "Taking Control of Your System" to filter out all the file names from the output of the Check Disk command, leaving just the subdirectory names, which are then sent to the printer. Try it. (Notice that a slash, not a backslash, precedes the *v*.) Type:

```
Current Directory is B:\
Command: chkdsk /v | find "Di" > prn
```

The printed output of this command shows only the names of the directories (the lines that contain *Di*).

Any of these guides to your filing system can help you keep track of both files and subdirectories and can help you use your system more efficiently.

Another Type of Path: The APPEND Command

If you're using 3.3 or a later version of DOS, you can use the Append command as well as the Path command to tell DOS where to look for a file if it's not in the current directory. Although it seems redundant to have two commands that can set a search path, there's a significant difference between Path and Append: Path sets the path to *command* files; Append sets the path to *data* files too. Just as with the Path command, you can name one or more directories on any disk drive.

The Append command has three main parameters related to helping DOS find data files (and program files):

append   <drive ><path>   ;

<drive> is the letter, followed by a colon, of the drive (such as *c:*) with the disk that contains the files. If you omit <drive>, DOS looks on the current drive.

<path> is the path name of the directory that contains the files.

You can specify several appended paths in one command, separating them with semicolons. If you enter an Append command with no parameters (just type *append*), DOS displays the paths you have defined. If you type *append* followed only by a semicolon, DOS cancels any paths you have defined.

It's easy to try the Append command. The root directory is the current directory, and the file RPT1.DOC is in the directory \MKT\WP. First, try to display the file by using the Type command:

```
Current Directory is B:\
Command: type rpt1.doc
```

DOS replies *File not found* because RPT1.DOC isn't in the current directory. Now type two Append commands to set the data path to \MKT\WP and display the data path:

```
Current Directory is B:\
Command: append \mkt\wp

Current Directory is B:\
Command: append
APPEND=\MKT\WP
```

Now try the Type command again:

```
Current Directory is B:\
Command: type rpt1.doc
This is a sample file.
```

This time DOS finds the file because you told it where to look. Cancel the appended path by typing *append* with just a semicolon, then check again:

```
Current Directory is B:\
Command: append ;

Current Directory is B:\
Command: append
No Append
```

The Path and Append commands are valuable tools for improving the efficiency and convenience of using a fixed disk. Appendix C, the DOS command reference, includes a complete description of each.

If you're going to continue using your system, restart your computer or type the following to restore the system prompt:

```
Current Directory is B:\
Command: prompt $p$g

B:\>
```

CHAPTER SUMMARY

Although this chapter introduced several new terms and concepts, it doesn't take many commands to set up a multilevel file system. The structure shown in Figure 8-3, for example, required only the following 11 commands (don't enter them; this list is just to show you the commands you entered):

md mkt	md sales
md eng	md\eng\wp
cd mkt	cd\eng
md wp	md budget
md budget	md schedule
md customer	

You might not create a file structure with this many levels on a diskette, although it's certainly possible if you use high-capacity diskettes. As you noticed, subdirectories require a great deal of work from the diskette drive. But you might find that two or three subdirectories reduce the number of diskettes you use, or that they let you use your system more efficiently. The examples in this chapter showed you how to use all the commands you need to create and manage a multilevel filing system.

If you're using a fixed disk, save the diskette that contains the file system you created in this chapter. You'll use it to copy sample files in the next chapter, ''Managing Your Fixed Disk.''

CHAPTER 9

MANAGING YOUR FIXED DISK

A fixed disk holds far more data than a diskette does, and DOS can use it much more quickly. As its name implies, you don't remove the disk; it is permanently fixed in the drive. Like a diskette, a fixed disk stores data in tracks and sectors; unlike a diskette, however, a fixed disk stores data on magnetically coated, rigid metal—not plastic—disks that are enclosed in a nonremovable case.

A typical fixed-disk drive contains two or more separate disks that give it a total storage capacity of 20 to 40 megabytes, but fixed disks with even higher capacities are becoming common. Several computers offer a fixed disk that can hold 300 megabytes or more. This chapter focuses on how to use your fixed disk efficiently. If you don't have a fixed disk, you can skip to Chapter 10, ''The DOS Shell.'' (Go on to Chapter 11, ''Creating and Editing Files of Text,'' if you don't have version 4 or 5 of DOS.)

Managing your fixed disk requires more thought and planning than managing your diskettes, simply because of the sheer number of files involved. But properly organized and managed, your fixed disk is a fast and effective tool you use with a minimum of fuss. Two tasks are more important than any others in managing your fixed disk efficiently. One is setting up a filing system that lets you take advantage of the disk's capacity without losing track of all your files. The other is backing up the files periodically, both to protect your data in the event your fixed disk is inadvertently erased or damaged, and to clear out old files you no longer use regularly.

The previous chapter covered setting up and using a multilevel filing system. Everything you learned there applies to managing your fixed disk properly. This chapter covers the additional tasks of organizing directories and files on your fixed disk, managing large numbers of files, backing up files to diskettes and restoring them to the fixed disk, and protecting the integrity of the disk itself.

In most ways, you treat a fixed disk as if it were a large diskette, using the DOS directory commands to create, change, and remove directories, and the DOS file commands to copy, erase, rename, and otherwise work with your files. The Volume and Label commands described in Chapter 6, ''Managing Your Diskettes,'' can also be used with a fixed disk. But two commands—Diskcopy and Diskcomp—don't work with the fixed disk because they are designed to work only with entire diskettes.

This chapter suggests some guidelines to simplify the job of managing your fixed disk; it shows you how to:

▷ Control the archive attribute of a file with the Attribute command.

▷ Copy files selectively with the Replace and Xcopy commands.

▷ Back up files from one disk to another with the Backup command.

▷ Restore files from a backup disk with the Restore command.

▷ Record information on file storage and the condition of the fixed disk with the Mirror command (version 5 only).

172

▶ Recover from inadvertently formatting a fixed disk with the Unformat command (version 5 only).

PUTTING APPLICATION PROGRAMS ON THE FIXED DISK

When you actually set up a directory structure of your own, you'll undoubtedly want to copy the command and data files of your application programs onto the fixed disk. Some application programs suggest installing themselves in their own subdirectories on a fixed disk. It's wise to accept the suggestion unless you have strong feelings about organizing your fixed disk in another way. In general, however, you shouldn't put all your programs in the root directory or in a single large program directory. You'll have difficulty telling one program file from another, and you'll end up with as much disorganization as you would if you tossed all your program diskettes into a big drawer.

Remember, too, that DOS itself is a collection of command (program) files. Like application-program files, the DOS files can be stored in a variety of places on your fixed disk, including the root directory. As mentioned early in the book, versions 4 and 5 of DOS suggest that you install them in a \DOS subdirectory. This approach has been used for years in installing any version of DOS on a fixed disk. If, for some reason, your DOS files are in the root directory, you should consider moving them to a subdirectory so they'll be easy to find and won't clutter up either your root directory or your directory displays. Instructions for doing this are in Appendix A, "Installing DOS."

PREPARING FOR THE EXAMPLES

The examples in this chapter rely on the information presented in the previous chapter, "A Tree of Files," and use the directory structure and files you created there. If you haven't completed those examples, do so before continuing.

The examples in this chapter require the sample subdirectories and files in Figure 9-1 on the next page. You will create these on the fixed disk in a subdirectory named \RUNDOS, which will keep all your examples in one place for easy removal.

If your system prompt doesn't show the current directory, change it to an abbreviated version of the *Current Directory is...* prompt you used in the last chapter. Type:

```
C>prompt $p$g<Enter>

c:\>
```

Now your system prompt shows both the current drive and the current directory and will help you keep track of where you are in your directory structure.

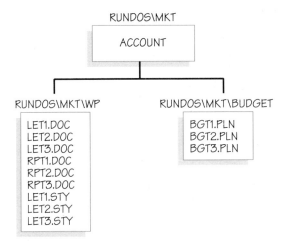

Figure 9-1. *Subdirectories and files for fixed-disk examples.*

To create the \RUNDOS subdirectory, type:

```
C:\>md \rundos
```

Now change the current directory to \RUNDOS by typing:

```
C:\>cd \rundos
```

Moving Files to Your Fixed Disk

The remainder of your preparation depends on which version of DOS you're using. If you have version 3.2 or later, follow the instructions under the heading ''Moving Files with the Xcopy Command.'' If you have a version of DOS prior to 3.2, follow the instructions under the heading ''Moving Files with the Copy Command.''

Moving Files with the Xcopy Command

If you're using version 3.2 or later of DOS, moving everything from your practice diskette to the \RUNDOS directory is simple. All you need is one Xcopy command, which copies subdirectories and files from the source disk to the target disk. The Xcopy parameter you use here, /S, copies all subdirectories as well as all files. Xcopy is described in more detail later. For now, put the diskette that contains your sample files in drive A and type:

```
C:\RUNDOS>xcopy a: /s
```

DOS responds:

```
Reading source file(s)...
A:SAMPLE.TXT
A:MKT\ACCOUNT
```

```
A:MKT\WP\LET1.DOC
A:MKT\WP\LET2.DOC
A:MKT\WP\LET3.DOC
A:MKT\WP\RPT1.DOC
A:MKT\WP\RPT2.DOC
A:MKT\WP\RPT3.DOC
A:MKT\WP\LET1.STY
A:MKT\WP\LET2.STY
A:MKT\WP\LET3.STY
A:MKT\BUDGET\BGT1.PLN
A:MKT\BUDGET\BGT2.PLN
A:MKT\BUDGET\BGT3.PLN
A:ENG\ACCOUNT
A:ENG\BUDGET\BGT1.NEW
A:ENG\BUDGET\BGT2.NEW
A:ENG\BUDGET\BGT3.NEW
        18 File(s) copied
```

You don't need the file named SAMPLE.TXT, the directories named \ENG and \ENG\BUDGET, or the files they contain, so remove them by typing:

```
C:\RUNDOS>del sample.txt
C:\RUNDOS>del eng\account
C:\RUNDOS>del eng\budget\*.new
C:\RUNDOS>rd eng\budget
C:\RUNDOS>rd eng
```

You're through.

Moving Files with the Copy Command

Put the diskette that contains your sample files in drive A and type the following commands to duplicate the diskette's directory structure on your fixed disk:

```
C:\RUNDOS>md mkt
C:\RUNDOS>md mkt\wp
C:\RUNDOS>md mkt\budget
```

Now type the following to copy the files from the diskette to the fixed disk:

```
C:\RUNDOS>copy a:\mkt\account mkt
        1 File(s) copied

C:\RUNDOS>copy a:\mkt\wp\*.* mkt\wp
A:\MKT\WP\LET1.DOC
A:\MKT\WP\LET2.DOC
A:\MKT\WP\LET3.DOC
A:\MKT\WP\RPT1.DOC
A:\MKT\WP\RPT2.DOC
A:\MKT\WP\RPT3.DOC
A:\MKT\WP\LET1.STY
A:\MKT\WP\LET2.STY
A:\MKT\WP\LET3.STY
        9 File(s) copied
```

```
C\RUNDOS>copy a:\mkt\budget\*.* mkt\budget
A:\MKT\BUDGET\BGT1.PLN
A:\MKT\BUDGET\BGT2.PLN
A:\MKT\BUDGET\BGT3.PLN
        3 File(s) copied
```

This completes the preparation.

CHANGING THE ATTRIBUTES OF A FILE OR A DIRECTORY

In Chapter 5, you saw how to use the Attribute command to control access to a file or a group of files by using read-only and hidden attributes. If you're using 3.2 or a later version of DOS, you can also use the Attribute command to control the *archive attribute* of a file, which tells DOS (or any other program that checks it) whether the file has been changed since the last time it was backed up for archival storage. If you're using version 5 of DOS, the Attribute command offers even more flexibility because it allows you to control more than the read-only and archive attributes available in earlier versions, and it lets you assign attributes to directories as well as to files.

The hidden attribute is particularly useful with directories, both because it can help reduce screen clutter by omitting hidden directories from directory listings, and because it can also help you hide directories and the files they contain from casual view. This chapter describes the Attribute command in more detail and shows other examples of its use.

In all, the Attribute command lets you control the following attributes: read-only, archive, hidden, and system. It has these parameters:

attrib +R -R +A -A +H -H +S -S <filename> /S

+R turns on the read-only attribute, as you saw in Chapter 5; -R turns it off.

+A turns on the archive attribute (sometimes called the *archive bit*); -A turns it off.

+H turns on the hidden attribute; -H turns it off. If you have version 5 of DOS, you can use the hidden attribute.

+S turns on the system attribute, which tells DOS to treat a file as a system (program) file; -S turns it off. The system attribute is in version 5 only and is normally used by programmers.

<filename> is the drive, path, and name of the file or directory whose attributes are to be changed or displayed. You can use wildcard characters to specify a group of files. In version 5, you can omit <filename> to view or change the attributes of all files in the current directory. In effect, omitting <filename> in version 5 is the same as specifying <filename> as *.*.

/S, which is in 3.3 and later versions of DOS, applies the Attribute command to each subdirectory contained in <filename>. If you specify <filename> as the root directory of a disk and include /S, the Attribute command is applied to every subdirectory on the disk.

Through version 4 of DOS, if you omit all parameters except <filename>, DOS displays the name or names of the files preceded by an A if the file has the archive attribute, an R if the file has the read-only attribute, or both if the file has both attributes set.

In version 5 of DOS, omitting all parameters, including <filename> if you choose, causes DOS to display the name or names of all files in the current directory. It precedes the file names with A and R for archive and read-only as it does in earlier versions, and uses H and S to indicate the hidden and system attributes.

Examples of Changing the Archive Attribute

The archive attribute, like the read-only and hidden attributes, is a part of the directory entry that isn't displayed by the Directory command but that can be examined or changed by DOS or another program that checks it. This attribute is used by the Backup and Xcopy commands described later in this chapter, and by some programs that back up files from a fixed disk. The archive attribute is turned on by the DOS editors, by Microsoft Word, and by most other programs that change a file. Because the archive attribute tells DOS or another program whether a file has been changed since the last time (if ever) it was backed up, it is used principally by Backup, Xcopy, and other programs to determine which files must be backed up.

To try the following examples, change the current directory to \RUNDOS-\MKT\WP. Type:

```
C:\RUNDOS>cd mkt\wp
```

As a first step, check the attributes of the files in the current directory. Type the following command if you have version 5 of DOS:

```
C:\RUNDOS\MKT\WP>attrib
```

Type this command if you have an earlier version:

```
C:\RUNDOS\MKT\WP>attrib *.*
```

DOS responds with a display like the following:

```
A          C:\RUNDOS\MKT\WP\LET1.DOC
A          C:\RUNDOS\MKT\WP\LET2.DOC
A          C:\RUNDOS\MKT\WP\LET3.DOC
A          C:\RUNDOS\MKT\WP\RPT1.DOC
A          C:\RUNDOS\MKT\WP\RPT2.DOC
A          C:\RUNDOS\MKT\WP\RPT3.DOC
A          C:\RUNDOS\MKT\WP\LET1.STY
A          C:\RUNDOS\MKT\WP\LET2.STY
A          C:\RUNDOS\MKT\WP\LET3.STY
```

DOS displays the name of each file with an A in column 3 because the files have never been backed up.

To turn off the archive attribute of all files with the extension DOC and check the result, type:

```
C:\RUNDOS\MKT\WP>attrib -a *.doc

C:\RUNDOS\MKT\WP>attrib *.*
                    C:\RUNDOS\MKT\WP\LET1.DOC
                    C:\RUNDOS\MKT\WP\LET2.DOC
                    C:\RUNDOS\MKT\WP\LET3.DOC
                    C:\RUNDOS\MKT\WP\RPT1.DOC
                    C:\RUNDOS\MKT\WP\RPT2.DOC
                    C:\RUNDOS\MKT\WP\RPT3.DOC
      A             C:\RUNDOS\MKT\WP\LET1.STY
      A             C:\RUNDOS\MKT\WP\LET2.STY
      A             C:\RUNDOS\MKT\WP\LET3.STY
```

Now only those files whose extension is STY have the archive attribute.

If you're using 3.3 or a later version of DOS, you can use the /S parameter to apply the Attribute command to all subdirectories. To turn off the archive attribute of all files in \RUNDOS\MKT, \RUNDOS\MKT\WP, and \RUNDOS\MKT\BUDGET and then check the results in all three directories, type the following commands to change the directory to \RUNDOS\MKT, turn off the archive attribute of all files in all subdirectories, and check the attributes of all files in all subdirectories:

```
C:\RUNDOS\MKT\WP>cd ..

C:\RUNDOS\MKT>attrib -a *.* /s

C:\RUNDOS\MKT>attrib *.* /s
                    C:\RUNDOS\MKT\WP\LET1.DOC
                    C:\RUNDOS\MKT\WP\LET2.DOC
                    C:\RUNDOS\MKT\WP\LET3.DOC
                    C:\RUNDOS\MKT\WP\RPT1.DOC
                    C:\RUNDOS\MKT\WP\RPT2.DOC
                    C:\RUNDOS\MKT\WP\RPT3.DOC
                    C:\RUNDOS\MKT\WP\LET1.STY
                    C:\RUNDOS\MKT\WP\LET2.STY
                    C:\RUNDOS\MKT\WP\LET3.STY
                    C:\RUNDOS\MKT\BUDGET\BGT1.PLN
                    C:\RUNDOS\MKT\BUDGET\BGT2.PLN
                    C:\RUNDOS\MKT\BUDGET\BGT3.PLN
                    C:\RUNDOS\MKT\ACCOUNT
```

The response to the second Attribute command shows that you turned off the archive attribute of all the files in \RUNDOS\MKT\WP, \RUNDOS\MKT\BUDGET, and \RUNDOS\MKT.

If you don't have version 5, type the following command to turn on the archive attributes of all files in all subdirectories in \RUNDOS\MKT. (Examples later in the chapter expect them to be on.)

```
C:\RUNDOS\MKT>attrib +a *.* /s
```

Go on to the heading "Copying Selected Files."

If you do have version 5, the following examples give you practice with other file attributes.

Examples of Changing Other Attributes

As already mentioned, the hidden attribute can be useful in minimizing screen clutter and, to some extent, in hiding files and directories from casual view. Because an experienced user of DOS would know how to search for hidden files and directories, however, consider this attribute more of a convenience than a security measure.

To apply and change the hidden attribute with both directories and files, begin by hiding the \RUNDOS\MKT\BUDGET directory. Type:

```
C:\RUNDOS\MKT>attrib +h budget
```

Now tell DOS to show the directory for \RUNDOS and all its subdirectories, pausing after each screenful:

```
C:\RUNDOS\MKT>dir \rundos /s /p
```

DOS lists \RUNDOS, \RUNDOS\MKT, and \RUNDOS\MKT\WP and the files they contain, but it does not list the BUDGET directory or any of its files. However, if you use the /A parameter of the Dir command to tell DOS to list all hidden files and directories in \RUNDOS and its subdirectories:

```
C:\RUNDOS\MKT>dir /a:h \rundos /s
```

DOS displays:

```
    Volume in drive C is FIXED DISK
    Volume Serial Number is 1608-5A30

 Directory of C:\RUNDOS\MKT

BUDGET        <DIR>       10-16-91    8:21a
        1 file(s)            0 bytes

Total files listed:
        1 file(s)              0 bytes
                     15159296 bytes free
```

And if you check the attributes of \RUNDOS\MKT\BUDGET:

```
C:\RUNDOS\MKT>attrib budget
```

You see:

      H   **C:\RUNDOS\MKT\BUDGET**

Next, to see how hiding files differs from hiding a directory, first remove the hidden attribute from \RUNDOS\MKT\BUDGET:

   C:\RUNDOS\MKT>attrib -h budget

To reduce your typing chores, change to the \RUNDOS\MKT\BUDGET directory:

   C:\RUNDOS\MKT>cd budget

Now apply the hidden attribute to the three files in the directory:

   C:\RUNDOS\MKT\BUDGET>attrib +h *.pln

Type the command *dir \rundos /s /p* to again display the directory for \RUNDOS and all its subdirectories. This time, DOS shows that \RUNDOS\MKT\BUDGET exists, but notice that the directory doesn't seem to contain any files. You removed the hidden attribute from the directory, so DOS has no trouble including it in the listing, but you added the hidden attribute to the files in the directory, so now DOS refuses to report on the contents of the directory. Even when you display the directory itself, DOS does not show the hidden files:

   C:\RUNDOS\MKT\BUDGET>dir

```
Volume in drive C is FIXED DISK
Volume Serial Number is 1608-5A30
Directory of C:\RUNDOS\MKT\BUDGET

.             <DIR>      10-16-91     8:21a
..            <DIR>      10-16-91     8:21a
     2 file(s)              0 bytes
                    15159296 bytes free
```

Check the attributes of the files in this directory, however, and DOS responds:

   C:\RUNDOS\MKT\BUDGET>attrib *.pln
      H   **C:\RUNDOS\MKT\BUDGET\BGT1.PLN**
      H   **C:\RUNDOS\MKT\BUDGET\BGT2.PLN**
      H   **C:\RUNDOS\MKT\BUDGET\BGT3.PLN**

When files are hidden, you can't change their other attributes. For example, suppose you decide to make the files read-only; try it by typing:

   C:\RUNDOS\MKT\BUDGET>attrib +r *.pln

DOS refuses:

```
Not resetting hidden file C:\RUNDOS\MKT\BUDGET\BGT1.PLN
Not resetting hidden file C:\RUNDOS\MKT\BUDGET\BGT2.PLN
Not resetting hidden file C:\RUNDOS\MKT\BUDGET\BGT3.PLN
```

You can, however, change other attributes if you also specify the hidden attribute. Make the files both read-only and hidden with one Attribute command:

C:\RUNDOS\MKT\BUDGET>attrib +r +h *.pln

Check the attributes again:

```
C:\RUNDOS\MKT\BUDGET>attrib *.pln
        HR        C:\RUNDOS\MKT\BUDGET\BGT1.PLN
        HR        C:\RUNDOS\MKT\BUDGET\BGT2.PLN
        HR        C:\RUNDOS\MKT\BUDGET\BGT3.PLN
```

DOS reports the files are now both hidden (H) and read-only (R).

To return all the files in RUNDOS and its subdirectories to their original state, first remove the hidden and read-only attributes from the budget files:

C:\RUNDOS\MKT\BUDGET>attrib -r -h *.pln

Now change the current directory to C:\RUNDOS\MKT and turn on the archive attribute of all files in C:\RUNDOS\MKT and all its subdirectories:

C:\RUNDOS\MKT\BUDGET>cd ..
C:\RUNDOS\MKT>attrib +a *.* /s

COPYING SELECTED FILES

In earlier chapters, you saw that you can copy files with similar names or extensions by using the Copy command and wildcard characters. If you're using 3.2 or a later version of DOS, you have even more flexibility in copying files:

▶ The Replace command lets you replace all files in every subdirectory of a target disk that have the same name as the files on a source disk. The Replace command also lets you copy only the files on a source disk that *don't* exist on the target disk or in a target directory. Beginning with version 4, the Replace command also lets you update files by replacing only those on the target disk that are *older* than those of the same name on the source disk.

▶ The Xcopy command, as you saw in preparing for this chapter's examples, lets you copy whole subdirectories and the files in them. It also lets you copy only files that have changed since they were last backed up, or those that have changed since a particular date.

Replacing Files on a Disk

The Replace command, like the Copy command, copies files from one disk or directory to another. The Replace command, however, is more selective:

▶ If used without the /A or /U parameter, the Replace command copies only source files that also exist on the target; it *replaces* files, hence its name.

▶ If used with the /A parameter, it lets you reverse the operation of the Replace command and tell it to copy only source files that *don't* exist on the target; with this option, it only *adds* files.

▶ If used with the /U parameter, the Replace command lets you copy only source files that are newer than files of the same name on the target; with this option, it *updates* files.

As a further refinement, the Replace command also lets you copy files not only from the source directory, but also from all the subdirectories the source contains.

The Replace command has eight parameters:

replace <source> <target> /A /S /R /P /U /W

<source> is the name of the file to be copied. You can use wildcard characters to replace a set of files that have similar file names or extensions.

<target> specifies where <source> is to be copied. You can include a drive letter and a path name.

/A (for *add*) copies only the files specified in <source> that don't exist in <target>. This lets you add files to <target> without replacing files that already exist. If you don't specify /A, only files specified in <source> that also exist in <target> are copied. If you specify /A, you cannot specify /S or /U.

/S applies the Replace command to all subdirectories contained in <target>. If you specify <target> as the root directory of a disk, the command is applied to every subdirectory on the disk. If you specify /S, you cannot specify /A.

/R replaces files in <target> that are read-only.

/P prompts you for confirmation before it replaces or adds each file.

/U (for *update*) replaces only those files on the target disk that are older than the corresponding files on the source disk. If you specify /U, you cannot specify /A.

/W prompts you to press a key before the Replace command begins. This lets you put in the correct diskette before starting to replace or add files.

To see how the Replace command works, copy the file named LET1.DOC from \RUNDOS\MKT\WP to \RUNDOS\MKT\BUDGET and then check the directory by typing:

```
C:\RUNDOS\MKT>copy wp\let1.doc budget
        1 file(s) copied

C:\RUNDOS\MKT>dir budget

 Volume in drive C is FIXED DISK
 Volume Serial Number is 1608-5A30
 Directory of C:\RUNDOS\MKT\BUDGET

 .            <DIR>      10-16-91    8:21a
 ..           <DIR>      10-16-91    8:21a
```

```
BGT1      PLN          24 10-16-91    8:17a
BGT2      PLN          24 10-16-91    8:17a
BGT3      PLN          24 10-16-91    8:17a
LET1      DOC          24 10-16-91    8:17a
          6 file(s)              96 bytes
                      15157248 bytes free
```

Now use the Replace command with no parameters to replace every file in the directory \RUNDOS\MKT\BUDGET whose name begins with LET and whose extension is DOC that also exists in \RUNDOS\MKT\WP. Type:

```
C:\RUNDOS\MKT>replace wp\let*.doc budget
```

DOS responds:

```
Replacing C:\RUNDOS\MKT\BUDGET\LET1.DOC

1 file(s) replaced
```

The Replace command copied only the file—the one you copied at the beginning of this example—that already existed in \RUNDOS\MKT\BUDGET. The message tells you that DOS *replaced* one existing file.

Now type the Replace command again, but this time include the /A parameter, which tells DOS to copy only those files that do *not* exist in the target; you're doing the opposite of what you did with the previous Replace command:

```
C:\RUNDOS\MKT>replace wp\let*.doc budget /a
```

DOS responds:

```
Adding C:\RUNDOS\MKT\BUDGET\LET2.DOC

Adding C:\RUNDOS\MKT\BUDGET\LET3.DOC

2 file(s) added
```

This time the Replace command copied the files that it didn't copy in the previous example. The message tells you that DOS *added* files to the target directory.

Finally, if you have version 4 or 5 of DOS, see how you can update files. Begin by creating a newer version of LET1.DOC in the directory \RUNDOS\MKT\WP:

```
C:\RUNDOS\MKT>copy con wp\let1.doc
This is a newer file.
^Z
          1 file(s) copied
```

Now you have one version of the file in \RUNDOS\MKT\BUDGET and a newer version with the same file name in \RUNDOS\MKT\WP. Update all files in the BUDGET subdirectory by typing:

```
C:\RUNDOS\MKT>replace wp\let*.doc budget /u
```

DOS responds:

```
Replacing C:\RUNDOS\MKT\BUDGET\LET1.DOC

1 file(s) replaced
```

This time, DOS compared matching file names and updated only the one, LET1.DOC, that had a more recent version in the source directory than in the target.

Copying Files with the Xcopy Command

In preparing for this chapter, you used the Xcopy command to move an entire directory structure from one disk to another. If the corresponding subdirectories don't exist on the target disk or directory, the Xcopy command creates them.

Unlike Copy and Replace, Xcopy can be used to copy only files whose archive attribute is on, or to copy only files that have been changed since a date you specify.

The Xcopy command has 10 parameters:

xcopy <source> <target> /A /M /D:<date> /E /P /S /V /W

<source> is the name of the file to be copied. You can include a path name, and you can use wildcard characters to copy a set of files with similar file names or extensions.

<target> specifies where <source> is to be copied. You can include any combination of drive letter, path name, and file name. If you specify different drives, the target directory does not have to have the same name as the source directory.

/A copies only those files whose archive attribute is on, and leaves the archive attribute of the source unchanged.

/M copies only those files whose archive attribute is on, and turns off the archive attribute of the source. This tells DOS (or any other program) that the file hasn't been changed since it was last backed up and therefore doesn't need to be backed up again.

/D:<date> copies only files created or changed on or after <date>. (The date of creation or last change is the date shown in the directory entry for any file. Enter <date> just as you would for the Date command.)

/E creates subdirectories in <target> even if they're empty in <source>.

/P prompts for confirmation before each file specified in <source> is copied.

/S applies the Xcopy command to all subdirectories contained in <source> that are not empty. If you specify <source> as the root directory of a disk, the Xcopy command is applied to every non-empty subdirectory on the disk.

/V verifies that the copy of the file on <target> was stored correctly. This can slow the operation of the Xcopy command somewhat, but it's good insurance if you're copying critical data and must be certain that it was copied correctly.

/W prompts you to press a key before the Xcopy command begins. This wait gives you a chance to put in the correct diskette before starting to copy files.

For this example, you create a temporary subdirectory named FRED in the root directory and dispose of it at the end of the example. First, change the current directory to \RUNDOS:

```
C:\RUNDOS\MKT>cd ..
```

Now type the following Make Directory command:

```
C:\RUNDOS>md \fred
```

and add the following sample file to \RUNDOS:

```
C:\RUNDOS>copy con test.doc
This is a test file.
^Z
        1 file(s) copied
```

All the files in \RUNDOS and its subdirectories have the archive attribute turned on. For the first Xcopy command, use the /A parameter to copy all the files in \RUNDOS whose extension is DOC and whose archive attribute is turned on:

```
C:\RUNDOS>xcopy *.doc \fred /a
```

DOS responds by displaying the name of each source file as it is copied:

```
Reading source file(s)...
TEST.DOC
        1 File(s) copied
```

DOS copied TEST.DOC, the only file in \RUNDOS whose extension is DOC. Verify this by displaying the directory of \FRED:

```
C:\RUNDOS>dir \fred

 Volume in drive C is FIXED DISK
 Volume Serial Number is 1608-5A30
 Directory of C:\FRED

 .              <DIR>      10-16-91   12:28p
 ..             <DIR>      10-16-91   12:28p
 TEST     DOC        22    10-16-91   12:35p
        3 file(s)             22 bytes
                       14096384 bytes free
```

Now type the same Xcopy command, but add the /S parameter to copy all files whose extension is DOC and whose archive attribute is turned on, not only in \RUNDOS but also in all its subdirectories:

```
C:\RUNDOS>xcopy *.doc \fred /a /s
Reading source file(s)...
TEST.DOC
MKT\WP\LET1.DOC
MKT\WP\LET2.DOC
MKT\WP\LET3.DOC
```

```
MKT\WP\RPT1.DOC
MKT\WP\RPT2.DOC
MKT\WP\RPT3.DOC
MKT\BUDGET\LET1.DOC
MKT\BUDGET\LET2.DOC
MKT\BUDGET\LET3.DOC
        10 File(s) copied
```

This time DOS copied 10 files; it also copied the subdirectories named MKT\WP and MKT\BUDGET. Verify this by displaying the directory of \FRED\MKT:

C:\RUNDOS>dir \fred\mkt

```
Volume in drive C is FIXED DISK
Volume Serial Number is 1608-5A30
Directory of C:\FRED\MKT

.               <DIR>       10-12-91   12:28p
..              <DIR>       10-12-91   12:28p
WP              <DIR>       10-12-91   12:39p
BUDGET          <DIR>       10-12-91   12:39p
        4 file(s)              0 bytes
                        14071808 bytes free
```

The Xcopy command created the subdirectories named WP and BUDGET in \FRED, then copied the files whose extension is DOC and whose archive attribute is on from \RUNDOS\MKT\WP to \FRED\MKT\WP and from \RUNDOS\MKT\BUDGET to \FRED\MKT\BUDGET.

The value of the archive attribute, however, is that it can tell you which files have changed since they were last backed up, if the archive attribute is turned off when a file is backed up and it is turned on when a file is changed. The /M parameter, like the /A parameter, tells Xcopy to copy only those files whose archive attribute is on; but it also turns the archive attribute off on the source file, so that you can mark the files as backed up. Type another Xcopy command to copy the files whose extension is DOC, but this time use /M instead of /A:

C:\RUNDOS>xcopy *.doc \fred /m /s

DOS responds just as it did to the previous Xcopy command, because it copied the same 10 files, but this time it turned their archive attributes off. It's easy to check this; retype the last Xcopy command:

C:\RUNDOS>xcopy *.doc \fred /m /s
```
        0 File(s) copied
```

This time no files were copied because the previous command turned off the archive attributes of the files.

Now suppose you change one of the files. A new file's archive attribute is on, just as if it were an existing file you changed with the DOS editors or with a word processor, so type the following to create a different version of \RUNDOS\TEST.DOC:

```
C:\RUNDOS>copy con test.doc
A new version of TEST.DOC.
^Z
        1 file(s) copied
```

Type the same Xcopy command you typed twice before; the first time Xcopy copied 10 files, the second time it copied no files, and this time it should copy one file:

```
C:\RUNDOS>xcopy *.doc \fred /m /s
Reading source file(s)...
TEST.DOC
        1 file(s) copied
```

Xcopy copied only the file whose archive attribute was on.

Type the following commands to dispose of the files and directories you added for this example:

```
C:\RUNDOS>del \fred\mkt\wp\*.doc
C:\RUNDOS>rd \fred\mkt\wp
C:\RUNDOS>del \fred\mkt\budget\*.doc
C:\RUNDOS>rd \fred\mkt\budget
C:\RUNDOS>rd \fred\mkt
C:\RUNDOS>del \fred\test.doc
C:\RUNDOS>rd \fred
```

Change the current directory back to \RUNDOS\MKT:

```
C:\RUNDOS>cd mkt
```

and, finally, clean up your \RUNDOS\MKT\BUDGET directory for later examples:

```
C:\RUNDOS\MKT>del budget\let*.doc
```

DEVELOPING A BACKUP PROCEDURE

It could take a drawerful of diskettes to back up all the files on a fixed disk. If your average file were 10,000 bytes long (about 6½ double-spaced typed pages), a full 20 MB fixed disk would have more than 2000 files, and you'd need almost sixty 360 K diskettes to back them all up. A full 40 MB fixed disk could require about one hundred fifteen 360 K diskettes, or about thirty-five high-density (1.2 MB) diskettes.

But you don't have to back up all your files. You needn't back up program files, for example, because you've already got the original DOS and application-program diskettes. Some data files, such as a spelling dictionary, don't usually change, so it isn't necessary to back them up either.

How often you back up your other data files, such as word processing documents or spreadsheets, depends on how often they change. For example, spreadsheets might change often while the budget is being prepared but remain unchanged the rest of the year. The backup procedures you use depend on how you use your computer. But no matter how you decide to back up your files, be certain to do so regularly. A system failure can happen, but if you back up your files regularly, such a failure will be more of an inconvenience than a disaster.

BACKING UP FILES

The Backup command lets you select files on the basis of their path name, their file name, whether they have been changed since the last backup, or whether they have been changed since a particular date. The options can be combined, so you can back up files in just about any way you like.

The Backup command can have as many as nine parameters:

backup <source> <drive> /A /S /M /F /D:<date> /T:<time> /L:<logfile>

<source> is the file or set of files you want to back up. You can specify a drive (such as *b:*), a path (such as *b:\myfiles*), a file name with or without wildcards (such as *b:*.doc*), or a combination of these elements (such as *b:\myfiles\report.doc*).

<drive> is the letter, followed by a colon, of the drive (such as *a:*) that contains the disk that receives the backup files. You must specify <drive>.

/A adds the backup files to the backup disk, rather than erasing all files on the backup disk as the command usually does before making the backup copies.

/S backs up files from all subdirectories.

/M backs up only the files that have been modified since the last backup.

/F, in versions prior to 4, formats the target disk if it isn't already formatted. The /F option of the Backup command uses the Format command file (FORMAT.COM) to format the target disk, so FORMAT.COM must be in either the current directory or a directory that is in the command path. The /F parameter isn't required in versions 4 and 5. If you haven't already done so, DOS automatically formats the diskette for the normal capacity of the drive, again assuming that it can find FORMAT.COM. You can, however, use the /F parameter either to format a set of diskettes or to format one or more diskettes with a capacity other than the one DOS assumes for the diskette drive (for example, specify */f:360* to format 360 K diskettes in a 1.2 MB drive). When DOS finishes whatever formatting you choose, it moves on to the backup procedure you've requested in your Backup command.

/D:<date> backs up all files that have changed since <date>. Enter <date> just as you would for the Date command.

/T:<time> backs up all files that have changed since <time> on <date>. Enter <time> just as you would for the Time command.

/L:<logfile> creates a log file on the disk in the source drive. The log file contains the date and time of the backup procedure and, for each file that is backed up, the path name, the file name, and the number (assigned by DOS) of the diskette that contains the file. If a log file already exists, the backup information is added at the end, creating a history of backups for the source drive. If you include /L but omit the colon and <logfile>, DOS names the log file BACKUP.LOG and stores it in the root directory of the source drive.

You can combine parameters in one Backup command.

Note: Although the Backup command exists in versions of DOS numbered 2.0 and later, not all the versions include all the parameters described here, nor are all the versions and releases of DOS compatible with one another. For a list of the options available to you, check the documentation that came with your version of DOS. You should use the same version of DOS both to back up and to restore files.

Backing Up All the Files in a Directory

The simplest way to back up files is by directory. You back up all files in a directory by specifying just the path of the directory and the letter of the diskette drive that contains the backup diskette. To ensure that the examples proceed smoothly, have ready either a formatted blank diskette or a new diskette that matches the capacity of your diskette drive. (Remember, if you have version 3 or earlier, the diskette must be formatted before you back up any files.)

To back up all the files in the directory named \RUNDOS\MKT\BUDGET, type the following:

```
C:\RUNDOS\MKT>backup budget a:
```

DOS displays a warning:

```
Insert backup diskette 01 in drive A:

WARNING! Files in the target drive
A:\ root directory will be erased
Press any key to continue . . .
```

If you don't use the /A option, DOS erases any files on the backup diskette before it makes the backup copies. This warning gives you a chance to make certain the correct diskette is in the drive. Put your blank diskette in drive A and press any key.

If you have version 4 or 5 and are using an unformatted diskette, DOS begins the backup procedure by formatting the diskette. When the backup procedure begins, DOS displays the name of each file as it makes the copies:

```
*** Backing up files to drive A: ***
Diskette Number: 01

\RUNDOS\MKT\BUDGET\BGT1.PLN
\RUNDOS\MKT\BUDGET\BGT2.PLN
\RUNDOS\MKT\BUDGET\BGT3.PLN
```

The directory of the backup diskette shows one or two files you might not expect. Type the following:

```
C:\RUNDOS\MKT>dir a:
```

If you're using 3.3 or a later version, the DOS response to your directory command looks something like this:

```
Volume in drive A is BACKUP   001
Volume Serial Number is 2543-14F7
Directory of A:\

BACKUP    001         72 10-16-91    1:48p
CONTROL   001        311 10-16-91    1:48p
         2 file(s)          383 bytes
                        1212928 bytes free
```

DOS has stored all the backed-up files in the file named BACKUP.001 and all the path names in the file named CONTROL.001. (On a second backup diskette, the extensions would be 002; on a third backup diskette, they would be 003.) Note that the size of BACKUP.001 corresponds to the total number of bytes in the three files it contains; CONTROL.001 contains all the extra information DOS needs to restore those files. This difference in the way backup files are stored is one reason you should use the Backup and Restore commands from the same version of DOS.

If you're using 3.2 or an earlier version, DOS responds:

```
Volume in drive A has no label
Directory of  A:\

BACKUPID @@@        128  10-16-91   1:48p
BGT1     PLN        152  10-16-91   8:17a
BGT2     PLN        152  10-16-91   8:17a
BGT3     PLN        152  10-16-91   8:17a
         4 File(s)     358400 bytes free
```

BACKUPID.@@@ is a small file that DOS stores on a backup diskette to identify it. Also, note that the files you backed up are larger than the originals on the fixed disk.

If you're using 3.2 or an earlier version, DOS adds 128 bytes at the beginning of each backup file. This addition contains the path and file name of the file that was backed up and is used by the Restore command when it restores files to the fixed disk. The Restore command deletes the path and file name information, so the restored version of the file is identical to the one you originally backed up. You'll work with the Restore command later in the chapter.

If a Backup command fills the diskette before backing up all the files you specified, DOS prompts you to put in another diskette. It displays the same warning, but refers to the second diskette as Diskette Number 02.

If another diskette is required, DOS prompts again, increasing the diskette number each time. If you were actually backing up files, you would label the diskette you just used with the contents and date and store it in a safe place.

Backing Up All Subdirectories

You can back up the files in the current directory and all its subdirectories with the /S option. For example, the current directory is \RUNDOS\MKT. To back up all the files in it and its subdirectories, you can either type the entire path (\RUNDOS\MKT) or you can use the . (single period) shorthand symbol for the current directory. Follow either one with the /S parameter as follows. Type either:

    C:\RUNDOS\MKT>backup . a: /s

or:

    C:\RUNDOS\MKT>backup \rundos\mkt a: /s

Again, DOS displays the warning; press any key to start the backup. DOS displays the file names as it makes the copies:

```
*** Backing up files to drive A: ***
Diskette Number: 01

\RUNDOS\MKT\ACCOUNT
\RUNDOS\MKT\WP\LET1.DOC
\RUNDOS\MKT\WP\LET2.DOC
\RUNDOS\MKT\WP\LET3.DOC
\RUNDOS\MKT\WP\RPT1.DOC
\RUNDOS\MKT\WP\RPT2.DOC
\RUNDOS\MKT\WP\RPT3.DOC
\RUNDOS\MKT\WP\LET1.STY
\RUNDOS\MKT\WP\LET2.STY
\RUNDOS\MKT\WP\LET3.STY
\RUNDOS\MKT\BUDGET\BGT1.PLN
\RUNDOS\MKT\BUDGET\BGT2.PLN
\RUNDOS\MKT\BUDGET\BGT3.PLN
```

This backup diskette contains all your marketing files, not just the files from one of the subdirectories. Note that you again backed up BGT1.PLN, BGT2.PLN, and BGT3.PLN. As the warning indicated, your prior backups were erased.

Backing Up Specific Files

You can back up specific files by including a file name with the Backup command. A word processing directory, for example, might contain both documents, which can change frequently, and style sheets, which seldom change. You would back up the documents much more frequently than you would the style sheets. Type the following to change the current directory to \RUNDOS\MKT\WP and back up only the documents (files whose extension is DOC):

```
C:\RUNDOS\MKT>cd wp
```

```
C:\RUNDOS\MKT\WP>backup *.doc a:
```

DOS displays its usual warning, but wait a moment before you press any key to back up the files. It's good practice to store a printed list of the files on a backup diskette along with the diskette itself. That's easy; make sure your printer is on, and press Ctrl-PrtSc to start simultaneous printing. Now press any key. As usual, DOS displays the file names as it backs them up, but this time it prints them too:

```
*** Backing up files to drive A: ***
Diskette Number: 01

\RUNDOS\MKT\WP\LET1.DOC
\RUNDOS\MKT\WP\LET2.DOC
\RUNDOS\MKT\WP\LET3.DOC
\RUNDOS\MKT\WP\RPT1.DOC
\RUNDOS\MKT\WP\RPT2.DOC
\RUNDOS\MKT\WP\RPT3.DOC
```

The files whose extension is STY were not backed up because you specified only those whose extension is DOC. You can store the printed list with the backup diskette. Remember to press Ctrl-PrtSc again to stop simultaneous printing.

Backing Up Only Files That Have Changed

As your files increase, you might want to be even more selective about the ones you back up. For example, a word processing directory might contain hundreds of documents; backing them all up could take a lot of time and several diskettes. Two options of the Backup command let you back up only the files that have changed since a directory was backed up, or only the files that have changed since a particular date.

Selecting Files That Have Changed Since the Last Backup

The /M (Modify) option of the Backup command backs up only those files that have changed since the directory was last backed up. To see this option, you need a file that has changed since you backed up \RUNDOS\MKT\WP in the last example. Create a short file by copying from the console:

```
C:\RUNDOS\MKT\WP>copy con new.doc
This file has changed
since the last backup.
^Z
        1 file(s) copied
```

Now tell DOS to back up only the files whose extension is DOC that have changed since the directory was last backed up:

```
C:\RUNDOS\MKT\WP>backup *.doc a: /m
```

DOS displays its warning and, when you press a key, it displays the files backed up:

```
*** Backing up files to drive A: ***
Diskette Number: 01

\RUNDOS\MKT\WP\NEW.DOC
```

Only the new file is backed up.

Selecting Files That Have Changed Since a Particular Date

The /D:<date> option backs up only those files that have changed since a particular date. To see this, you'll need a file with a different date. Change the system date with the Date command. Type the following, using the date shown below or any other, as long as it is later than 12-31-91.

```
C:\RUNDOS\MKT\WP>date
Current date is Wed 10-16-1991
Enter new date (mm-dd-yy): 1-1-92
```

Now create a file named DATE.DOC by copying from the console:

```
C:\RUNDOS\MKT\WP>copy con date.doc
This file was changed
after the last backup.
^Z
        1 file(s) copied
```

Use the /D:<date> option to back up the files that have changed since December 31, 1991, by typing the following. Use whatever date format DOS used in response to your Date command:

```
C:\RUNDOS\MKT\WP>backup *.doc a: /d:12-31-91
```

After the warning, DOS displays the file it backs up:

```
*** Backing up files to drive A: ***
Diskette Number: 01

\RUNDOS\MKT\WP\DATE.DOC
```

Only the file changed after the date you specified is backed up. You can use the /T:<time> option to specify a time in addition to using the /D:<date> option to specify the date.

Adding Files to a Backup Diskette

Each form of the Backup command you have used so far starts by erasing any files on the backup diskette. There might be times, however, when you want to back up files from several different directories on one diskette or add a file or two to an existing backup diskette. The /A option adds a file to a backup diskette.

Your backup diskette now contains \RUNDOS\MKT\WP\DATE.DOC. To back up the files in \RUNDOS\MKT\BUDGET, adding them to the backup diskette, type the following command:

```
C:\RUNDOS\MKT\WP>backup \rundos\mkt\budget a: /a
```

This time DOS doesn't need to warn you that it's going to erase any files from the backup diskette. If you're using 3.3 or a later version, DOS prompts with a message like this:

```
Insert last backup diskette in drive A:
Press any key to continue . . .
```

Press a key to start the backup.

With all versions, DOS then starts backing up the files and displaying their names on the screen:

```
*** Backing up files to drive A: ***
Diskette Number: 01

\RUNDOS\MKT\BUDGET\BGT1.PLN
\RUNDOS\MKT\BUDGET\BGT2.PLN
\RUNDOS\MKT\BUDGET\BGT3.PLN
```

If your backup procedure involves periodically backing up a few files from several different directories, you can use the /A option to put all the backup files on one diskette. A word of caution about this technique: With versions of DOS through 3.2, if a file you add to a backup diskette has the same name and extension as a file already on the diskette, DOS changes the extension of the added file to @01, regardless of what it was before.

RESTORING FILES TO THE FIXED DISK

It's easy to restore a file from a backup diskette to the fixed disk. Simply put the backup diskette in the diskette drive and type the Restore command, specifying the name of the file to be restored. The Restore command needs the path and file name information added to files by the Backup command, so you can restore only files that were backed up with the Backup command. The Restore command in version 5 of DOS can restore files backed up with the Backup command in any prior version of DOS. If you don't have version 5, however, you should try to use the same version of DOS for both the Backup and Restore commands.

The Restore command can have as many as 12 parameters:

restore <drive> <path><filename> /S /P /M /N /D /B:<date>
/A:<date> /E:<time> /L:<time>

<drive> is the letter, followed by a colon, of the drive (such as *a:*) that contains the backup diskette. You must include <drive>.

<path> is the path name, preceded by a drive letter and a colon, if appropriate, of the directory to which the file is to be restored. If you omit <path>, the file is restored to the current directory.

<filename> is the name of the file to be restored. You can use wildcard characters to restore a set of files. You must specify either <path> or <filename>.

/S restores files to all subdirectories.

/P tells DOS to prompt you for confirmation before restoring read-only files or files that have changed since they were last backed up.

/M restores files that were *modified* since they were backed up.

/N restores files that have been deleted from the original source disk since they were backed up.

/D doesn't restore any files; it displays a list of the files stored on the backup diskette that match the path and file names you specified as part of the Restore command (version 5 only).

/B:<date> restores only those files that were changed on or *before* <date>. Enter <date> just as you would for the Date command.

/A:<date> restores only those files that were changed on or *after* <date>. Enter <date> just as you would for the Date command.

/E:<time> restores only those files that were changed at or *earlier than* <time> on <date>. Enter <time> just as you would for the Time command.

/L:<time> restores only those files that were changed at or *later than* <time> on <date>. Enter <time> just as you would for the Time command.

Note: Although the Restore command exists in versions of DOS numbered 2.0 and later, not all the versions include all the parameters described here. For a list of the options available to you, check the documentation that came with your version of DOS.

Warning: Don't use the Backup or Restore command if you have entered an Assign, Join, or Substitute command to alter the way DOS interprets drive letters. Because these commands can mask the type of drive, DOS could damage or delete the files you specify in the commands or other files on the disk. For more information on Assign, Join, and Substitute, see "Commands for Occasional Use" in Chapter 17.

Preparing for the Restore Command Examples

Type the following command to change the date back from 1/1/92. You can type either the real date or, as shown here, use 10-16-91. Either will work with the examples:

```
C:\RUNDOS\MKT\WP>date
Current date is Wed 01-01-1992
Enter new date: 10-16-91
```

Now type the following commands. The first command backs up all the files in \RUNDOS\MKT\WP, creating a log file with the /l (lowercase L) parameter in the root directory of drive C; the second deletes all the files in the \RUNDOS\MKT\WP:

```
C:\RUNDOS\MKT\WP>backup *.* a: /l

Insert backup diskette 01 in drive A:

WARNING! Files in the target drive
A:\ root directory will be erased
Press any key to continue . . .

*** Backing up files to drive A: ***
Diskette Number: 01

Logging to file C:\BACKUP.LOG

\RUNDOS\MKT\WP\LET1.DOC
\RUNDOS\MKT\WP\LET2.DOC
\RUNDOS\MKT\WP\LET3.DOC
\RUNDOS\MKT\WP\RPT1.DOC
\RUNDOS\MKT\WP\RPT2.DOC
\RUNDOS\MKT\WP\RPT3.DOC
\RUNDOS\MKT\WP\LET1.STY
\RUNDOS\MKT\WP\LET2.STY
\RUNDOS\MKT\WP\LET3.STY
\RUNDOS\MKT\WP\NEW.DOC
\RUNDOS\MKT\WP\DATE.DOC

C:\RUNDOS\MKT\WP>del *.*
All files in directory will be deleted!
Are you sure (Y/N)?y
```

Finding Out What's on a Backup Diskette

It's always a good idea to keep a record of the files you back up, by printing a list as you did earlier or, as you did in preparing for these examples, by using the /L parameter of the Backup command to create a log file on the disk from which you back up the files. A printed list is easy enough to store and check, but suppose you decide to let DOS do the listing and checking for you. If you have version 5 of DOS, you can use the /D parameter of the Restore command to list the files on a backup diskette. In this and earlier versions of DOS, you can also use the Type command to list the contents of your Backup log file. To view the contents of the log file BACKUP.LOG, type:

C:\RUNDOS\MKT\WP>type c:\backup.log

DOS responds with a report like this, showing the date and time of backup and the number of the diskette on which the files were backed up:

```
10-16-1991  16:59:28
001    \RUNDOS\MKT\WP\LET1.DOC
001    \RUNDOS\MKT\WP\LET2.DOC
001    \RUNDOS\MKT\WP\LET3.DOC
001    \RUNDOS\MKT\WP\RPT1.DOC
001    \RUNDOS\MKT\WP\RPT2.DOC
001    \RUNDOS\MKT\WP\RPT3.DOC
001    \RUNDOS\MKT\WP\LET1.STY
001    \RUNDOS\MKT\WP\LET2.STY
001    \RUNDOS\MKT\WP\LET3.STY
001    \RUNDOS\MKT\WP\NEW.DOC
001    \RUNDOS\MKT\WP\DATE.DOC
```

But suppose you forgot to use the /L parameter, or you just want to check the files on a particular backup diskette. If you have version 5, try the following command to list the names of the files stored on your sample backup diskette:

C:\RUNDOS\MKT\WP>restore a: *.* /d

DOS first asks you for the backup diskette:

```
Insert backup diskette 01 in drive A:
Press any key to continue...
```

Verify that the correct diskette is in the drive and press a key. DOS now responds:

```
*** Files were backed up 10-16-1991 ***

*** Listing files on drive A: ***
Diskette: 01
\RUNDOS\MKT\WP\LET1.DOC
\RUNDOS\MKT\WP\LET2.DOC
\RUNDOS\MKT\WP\LET3.DOC
\RUNDOS\MKT\WP\RPT1.DOC
\RUNDOS\MKT\WP\RPT2.DOC
\RUNDOS\MKT\WP\RPT3.DOC
\RUNDOS\MKT\WP\LET1.STY
\RUNDOS\MKT\WP\LET2.STY
\RUNDOS\MKT\WP\LET3.STY
\RUNDOS\MKT\WP\NEW.DOC
\RUNDOS\MKT\WP\DATE.DOC
```

There's your list. If you want to find a particular file or set of files, limit the file specification in your command. For example, to check the backup diskette for all files with the extension STY, you'd type *restore a: *.sty /d.*

Restoring One File

Inadvertently erasing or changing a file is probably the most common reason for restoring a file. You restore a file by specifying the source drive and the target drive, path name, and file name with the Restore command. (You must include the path if you are restoring a file to a directory other than the current directory, and the path you specify must be the same as the path from which the file was originally backed up.)

For example, to restore \RUNDOS\MKT\WP\LET1.STY, type:

```
C:\RUNDOS\MKT\WP>restore a: let1.sty
```

Note that the drive and path can be omitted because the file is being restored to the current directory.

DOS prompts you for the backup diskette:

```
Insert backup diskette 01 in drive A:
Press any key to continue . . .
```

The correct diskette is in the drive, so press any key. DOS displays the name of the restored file:

```
*** Files were backed up 10-16-1991 ***

*** Restoring files from drive A: ***
Diskette: 01
\RUNDOS\MKT\WP\LET1.STY
```

You can display the directory to verify that it's back.

Restoring a Set of Files

You can use wildcard characters to restore a set of files. For example, to restore all the files whose extension is DOC that you backed up from the current directory (\RUNDOS\MKT\WP), type the following:

```
C:\RUNDOS\MKT\WP>restore a: *.doc
```

When DOS prompts you for the backup diskette, press any key. DOS displays the names of the files it restores.

Restoring All the Files in a Directory

If you enter the Restore command with a path name and the wildcard specification *.*, DOS restores all files belonging in that directory. For example, to restore all the files you backed up from \RUNDOS\MKT\WP, type:

```
C:\RUNDOS\MKT\WP>restore a: \rundos\mkt\wp\*.*
```

Again, press any key when DOS prompts for the diskette. DOS restores all the files you backed up from \RUNDOS\MKT\WP, not just those whose extension is DOC.

Restoring All Subdirectories

Just as the /S option of the Backup command backs up the files in a directory and all its subdirectories, the /S option of the Restore command restores the files in a directory and all its subdirectories. To restore the files in \RUNDOS and all its subdirectories, you would type *restore a: \rundos*.* /s.*

Selecting Files to Be Restored

A file you restore replaces a file with the same name on the fixed disk. You might not want this replacement, especially if you have changed the file on the fixed disk since the backup diskette was made. You can protect yourself from unwanted changes by using the /P (*prompt*) option of the Restore command, which tells DOS to prompt for confirmation if the file on the fixed disk has changed since the backup was made.

Warning: If you're using version 3.2 or earlier and are restoring files that were backed up with a previous version of DOS, be sure to use the /P parameter. If DOS asks whether to restore files named MSDOS.SYS, IO.SYS, IBMBIO.COM, or IBMDOS.COM, reply n (no). Otherwise, you would replace parts of your DOS program with portions of an earlier version, and DOS wouldn't start from your fixed disk.

To see how the /P parameter works, change LET3.DOC and LET1.STY. First, copy from the console to create a new version of LET3.DOC:

```
C:\RUNDOS\MKT\WP>copy con let3.doc
The new version of let3.doc.
^Z
        1 file(s) copied
```

Copy this file to LET1.STY, making it a new file too:

```
C:\RUNDOS\MKT\WP>copy let3.doc let1.sty
        1 file(s) copied
```

Now restore the entire directory with the /P option:

```
C:\RUNDOS\MKT\WP>restore a: \rundos\mkt\wp\*.* /p
```

DOS asks for the diskette and begins restoring files in the usual way, but finds a file on the fixed disk that has changed since its backup copy was made.

```
*** Files were backed up 10-16-1991 ***

*** Restoring files from drive A: ***
Diskette: 01
\RUNDOS\MKT\WP\LET1.DOC
\RUNDOS\MKT\WP\LET2.DOC

WARNING! File LET3.DOC
was changed after it was backed up
Replace the file (Y/N)?
```

This message (yours might vary) gives you a chance to decide whether you want to restore the file. Suppose you don't want to restore this file; type *n* (and press Enter if you don't have version 4 or 5). DOS resumes displaying the names of the files it restores, starting with the one that follows LET3.DOC:

```
n
\RUNDOS\MKT\WP\RPT1.DOC
\RUNDOS\MKT\WP\RPT2.DOC
\RUNDOS\MKT\WP\RPT3.DOC

WARNING! File LET1.STY
was changed after it was backed up
Replace the file (Y/N)?
```

Now suppose you do want to replace the version on the fixed disk with the backup version; type *y*. DOS again resumes displaying the names of the files it restores, starting with LET1.STY:

```
y
\RUNDOS\MKT\WP\LET1.STY
\RUNDOS\MKT\WP\LET2.STY
\RUNDOS\MKT\WP\LET3.STY
\RUNDOS\MKT\WP\NEW.DOC
\RUNDOS\MKT\WP\DATE.DOC
```

This completes the examples for backing up and restoring files.

DELETING THE SAMPLE FILES AND DIRECTORIES

If you don't want to keep the files and subdirectories you created for these examples, the following commands delete the files and remove the directories. Be certain to type the Delete commands exactly as shown to avoid the possibility of erasing other files. If you created a temporary subdirectory with a name other than \RUNDOS, don't forget to type its name in place of \RUNDOS.

Change the current directory to \RUNDOS\MKT:

```
C:\RUNDOS\MKT\WP>cd ..
```

Delete the file ACCOUNT in \RUNDOS\MKT:

```
C:\RUNDOS\MKT>del account
```

Delete the files in \MKT\WP:

```
C:\RUNDOS\MKT>del wp\*.*
All files in directory will be deleted!
Are you sure (Y/N)?y
```

Remove \RUNDOS\MKT\WP:

`C:\RUNDOS\MKT>`rd wp

Delete the files in \RUNDOS\MKT\BUDGET:

`C:\RUNDOS\MKT>`del budget*.*

Remove \RUNDOS\MKT\BUDGET:

`C:\RUNDOS\MKT>`rd budget

Change the current directory to \RUNDOS:

`C:\RUNDOS\MKT>`cd ..

Delete the file TEST.DOC:

`C:\RUNDOS>`del test.doc

Remove \MKT:

`C:\RUNDOS>`rd mkt

The fixed disk now contains an empty \RUNDOS directory (which you'll use in later chapters) and the directories and files it had before you started this chapter.

DOS AND YOUR FIXED DISK

Now that you're familiar with directories and the commands you use to manage them, you can look at your own system and put some of your knowledge to work.

Because a fixed disk can hold so many files, it's important to create a directory structure that lets you keep track of your files and programs. You can set up your subdirectories to match the way you use your computer, organizing them by department, application program, people's names, or any other way that's comfortable. The topic ''Setting Up a Filing System'' in Chapter 17 suggests several ways you might want to set up your directories.

Until you get a directory structure established, however, files have a tendency to collect in the root directory, making it difficult to find a file you need. If you reserve the root directory for nothing but subdirectories and files that must be there, finding your way around your fixed disk becomes much easier.

If you've been using your fixed disk for some time and haven't known about or paid much attention to the idea of creating a directory structure on it, it's possible that the root directory of your fixed disk contains many files that need not be there: DOS files, for example, if DOS is not in a subdirectory of its own; program files; data files; perhaps files inherited from a former user of the computer. Some of these files, such as the DOS command files, are essential, but need not all be in the root directory;

others, such as files you've inherited, might be unnecessary to your work; still others, such as application program files and data files, might be much easier to find and keep track of in directories of their own.

Few people, and certainly no book, can tell you the best way to organize your directories and files. If your root directory contains many files that should be in sub-directories of their own, the Make Directory, Copy, Xcopy, and (when you've moved files to new subdirectories) Delete commands can help you with your housekeeping. Ultimately, you are the best judge of your own work and work habits, but there are some general guidelines you can follow, either in setting up a new fixed disk or in organizing one you've been using:

▶ Keep your DOS command files in a subdirectory of their own. The only files that DOS requires to be in the root directory are named COMMAND.COM, CONFIG.SYS, and AUTOEXEC.BAT. Versions 4 and 5 of DOS automatically offer to install themselves so that these files are in the root directory but all other DOS files are in a separate subdirectory. If you have an earlier version of DOS and all of the DOS files are in your root directory, Appendix A, "In-stalling DOS," tells you how to set up and move files to a DOS subdirectory.

▶ Some application programs also require files in the root directory; the docu-mentation that came with the program should tell you about this, and the pro-gram itself might create the necessary files when you install it. When in doubt, follow the advice given in the documentation.

▶ If your fixed disk has been used by someone else, print a listing of the root directory before you try reorganizing or deleting the files in it. Be par-ticularly careful about removing any files with the extensions COM, SYS, or EXE; remember, they are program files. If you don't know what a particular command file is supposed to do, ask someone who does know.

▶ When you install a new program, put it in its own subdirectory if you can. Some programs propose this during the installation procedure. If yours doesn't, you might still be able to put it in a subdirectory, provided it can be installed on a fixed disk and has the ability to work with different drives and subdirectories. Check the program's documentation for instructions. After a program is installed in a subdirectory, all you need do is add the subdirectory name to the command path in order to make the program's command files available at any time.

▶ Think about the data files you create. These are generally the files that take up the most room on a fixed disk. They are also the ones that can become the most confusing as file names begin to proliferate and come close to duplicat-ing one another. Although this book uses files with the names LET1.DOC,

LET2.DOC, and so on, real data files with such names would mean little in a root directory cluttered with a hundred other letters. On the other hand, such names might mean a great deal in subdirectories named for clients, projects, proposals, and the like. In short, pay as much attention to organizing your fixed disk as you would to organizing a large set of files in a file cabinet.

Safeguarding Your Fixed Disk

There's no doubt that a fixed disk is faster and more convenient to use than diskettes, even high-capacity diskettes that can hold more than a megabyte of information. But the same features that make a fixed disk so valuable can also make loss of the disk or the information it holds more distressing. It's bad enough to discover that DOS either can't find or can't use information you stored on a diskette. It's worse when the same thing happens to your fixed disk.

Taking Care of Your Data

As you've seen in this chapter, DOS helps you safeguard valuable files by providing the Backup and Restore commands with which you can copy and store files on another disk for safekeeping.

When you're working with your data files, DOS also helps out by requesting confirmation before it carries out a Delete command that would remove all files in a directory. And recent versions of DOS protect you from accidental formats by requiring you to type a drive letter and, if you specify a fixed disk, by prompting you to verify the command. In these various ways, DOS helps you safeguard the integrity of your data, either by duplicating the information or asking you to think twice before carrying out a potentially destructive command.

Despite these safeguards, you can still lose information accidentally, so beginning with version 5, DOS provides some security here, too. Chapter 5 showed you how to use the Mirror command's delete tracking feature to maintain an on-disk record of the files you delete. For those times you're really not paying attention, Chapter 5 also described the Undelete command, which can help recover deleted files.

There's more to the Mirror command than delete tracking, however. And version 5 of DOS also includes the Unformat command, which can rebuild a disk after it's been formatted and can also preserve information (called a *partition table*) that DOS needs in order to recognize and use a fixed disk.

Note: If you don't have version 5 of DOS, the following two sections don't apply to your system. Skip ahead to the heading "Taking Care of Your Fixed Disk."

More About Mirror

Through version 4, formatting a disk meant that any files on it became inaccessible to DOS. In effect, you wiped the disk clean when you formatted it. With version 5, however, DOS normally performs a safe format, which is one that can be reversed with the Unformat command. In addition, you can use the Mirror command to record file-storage information about a diskette or a fixed disk, and that information can also help you recover files and directories or rebuild the disk after an inadvertent format. If you use the Mirror command to save the partition table for a fixed disk, you can use this information to gain access to the disk if the original partition table is damaged and DOS is unable to recognize the drive. Including the parameters described in Chapters 5 and 6, the Mirror command has the following form:

mirror <drive> /1 /T<drive>-<files> /partn /U

<drive:> is the letter, followed by a colon, of the drive whose file and directory information you want to record. For each drive you specify, Mirror creates a read-only file named MIRROR.FIL in the root directory.

/1 tells Mirror to keep only one copy of MIRROR.FIL. If you don't specify /1 and Mirror finds an earlier version of MIRROR.FIL, it renames the old file MIRROR.BAK before creating a new MIRROR.FIL.

/T<drive>-<files> tells Mirror to start delete tracking, as described in Chapter 5. <drive> is the letter of the drive on which Mirror is to track deleted files; <files> is optional and is the number (1 through 999) of deleted files to track.

/partn tells Mirror to save partition information about a fixed disk. If you use this parameter, Mirror saves the information on diskette in a file named PARTNSAV.FIL. Before carrying out the command, Mirror prompts you for the letter of a diskette drive. Unless you specify otherwise, it uses drive A.

/U (for *unload*) removes the delete-tracking program from your computer's memory. When you unload this program, Mirror stops tracking deleted files, so its record does not include any files you later delete.

Chapter 5 showed how to use the delete-tracking feature of the Mirror command. The following examples show some ways in which you can use Mirror to safeguard your fixed disk and the information on it. The current directory should be C:\RUNDOS. For simplicity, change to the root directory by typing:

```
C:\RUNDOS>cd ..
```

To record up-to-date disk storage information for your fixed disk, type:

```
C:\>mirror
```

Because you didn't specify a drive, Mirror assumes you meant the current drive and responds:

Creates an image of the system area.

Drive C being processed.

The MIRROR process was successful.

(The system area is the portion of your fixed disk that contains directory and file-storage information.) Although nothing special seems to have happened, a Dir command will show that Mirror has created a file named MIRROR.FIL in the root directory.

Note: Storage on your fixed disk changes each time you save or delete a file. To ensure that your MIRROR.FIL file is complete and up to date, you can include the Mirror command in the special startup file named AUTOEXEC.BAT. This file is described in more detail in Chapter 14, "Creating Your Own Commands."

A damaged partition table means that DOS can't find (and therefore start from) your fixed disk. You can, however, use the */partn* parameter of the Mirror command to save a backup copy of the table. To do this, begin by placing a formatted diskette in drive A. Next, type:

C:\>mirror /partn

Mirror responds with a message like this (the copyright line has been shortened to fit on the page):

MIRROR...Copyright (C) 1987-1991 Central Point Software, Inc.

Disk Partition Table saver.

The partition information from your hard drive(s) has been read.

Next, the file PARTNSAV.FIL will be written to a floppy disk. Please insert a formatted diskette and type the name of the diskette drive. What drive? A

Notice that Mirror proposes to save the partition information on a diskette in drive A. The diskette is already in drive A, so just press Enter. Mirror responds:

Successful.

Rebuilding a Fixed Disk

Because of the extent of potential loss in terms of programs and data, recent versions of DOS require deliberate effort on your part to format a fixed disk. It's not a step to be taken lightly, and the most experienced computer user feels at least a small twinge after pressing Enter to start the process. Beginning with version 5, the Unformat command provides a means for you to undo the format of either a diskette or a fixed disk. In restoring a disk, Unformat can work either with the files created by the Mirror command or with the file-storage information recorded on the disk by DOS itself.

Chapter 6 showed you how to use the Unformat command with diskettes. This section briefly describes other parameters that help you with a fixed disk; a more complete description is in Appendix C, ''DOS Command Reference.''

Note: Files stored on a fixed disk become unavailable after the disk has been formatted. In order for Unformat to work on a system with, for example, one fixed disk and one diskette drive, you need a startup diskette with which you can start DOS from drive A. You can create such a diskette with the Format /S command. Copy to this diskette both the DOS file UNFORMAT.COM and an accurate copy of the file named CONFIG.SYS, which is in the root directory of your startup disk.

The complete form of the Unformat command is:

unformat <drive> /J /L /test /partn /P /U

<drive> is the letter, followed by a colon, of the drive containing the disk to be unformatted.

/J checks the disk in <drive> to verify system information against the disk-storage information recorded by the Mirror command, but it does not unformat the disk at the same time.

/L produces either of two results, depending on whether you also specify the /*partn* parameter:

▶ /L without the /*partn* parameter causes Unformat to assume there is no Mirror file on the disk and to search the disk directly, listing all the files and directories it finds.

▶ /L with the /*partn* parameter causes Unformat to display the disk's current partition table.

/*test* tells Unformat to show how it will rebuild the disk without actually doing so. It is similar in effect to /J, but does not use files recorded by the Mirror command.

/*partn*, used without the /L parameter, restores the partition table of a fixed disk. For this parameter to work, you need the partition-information file recorded on a diskette by the /*partn* parameter of the Mirror command.

/P tells Unformat to send its display messages to the printer attached to LPT1.

/U tells Unformat to rebuild the disk using information saved by DOS instead of the Mirror command.

To avoid risking any inadvertent change to your fixed disk, the following examples are not tutorial. Although they show how you would use the Unformat command, do not enter them. They are meant for reference only, in the event you one day need to rebuild your fixed disk. Because Unformat needs the command file

UNFORMAT.COM and might also need information in the file named CONFIG.SYS to rebuild a fixed disk properly, the examples assume a DOS startup diskette to which these files have been copied. Note that the system prompt is A>, not C>.

To check that Unformat could rebuild a fixed disk with files created by the Mirror command, but without actually rebuilding the disk, the command would be:

```
A>unformat c: /j
```

To actually unformat the fixed disk, using the Mirror file:

```
A>unformat c:
```

And to rebuild the partition table of the fixed disk:

```
A>unformat c: /partn
```

Note: The file named CONFIG.SYS is described in more detail in Chapter 17, "Tailoring Your System."

Taking Care of Your Fixed Disk

Although DOS can't help you physically protect your fixed disk, there are common-sense approaches you can use. Dire warnings aside, a fixed disk is neither fragile nor temperamental. Many people use the same fixed disk for years without encountering any problems. In fact, considering the close tolerances involved—the read/write heads literally float on air a tiny fraction of an inch above the disk itself—a fixed disk is remarkably sturdy and reliable. All it normally needs is a little help from you. For example:

▶ Don't turn your system off and on repeatedly during the day. Leaving the system on minimizes wear on the mechanical parts of your fixed disk.

▶ Don't turn the system off while the fixed disk is active. By the same token, avoid bumping or jostling the system at those times too. You'll help preserve both disk and data.

▶ Keep the system and its surroundings reasonably clean. You don't have to sterilize anything; just clean and relatively dust-free will do.

▶ Save your work and turn off your system during windstorms and at other times when the power is likely to surge or be interrupted. A sudden loss of electricity or a sudden surge of excess power can cause problems, especially if the computer is reading from or writing to the fixed disk at the time.

▶ If you have extra memory on your system, consider using some of it for a RAM disk. Not only will you reduce stress on your fixed disk, you'll find that file access becomes noticeably quicker.

▶ Shut the system down before moving it. Don't worry about sliding it across your desk, but do be careful not to drop it or bang it into walls or furniture. If you're planning to move the system some distance or ship it, use a program that parks the read/write heads so that they (and the data on your disk) are protected.

Barring equipment failure, about all it takes to keep your fixed disk running smoothly are a little common sense and the same type of care you'd give your VCR or stereo system.

CHAPTER SUMMARY

If you organize your file structure to match your work, a fixed disk quickly becomes an essential part of your computer system. If, in addition, you develop a backup procedure that protects only those files whose loss would cost you time or data, backing up your fixed disk takes just a little time and a few diskettes. The relatively small investments required to organize and safeguard your data will be returned many times over in ease of use and peace of mind, especially the first time an error—by the system, by a program, or by you—causes the loss of a valuable file.

You can also create your own commands to back up the fixed disk. With the techniques described in Chapters 14, 15, and 16, backing up the fixed disk can become a routine part of using your computer, simplifying the job and guaranteeing consistency no matter who backs up the files on the fixed disk.

CHAPTER 10

THE DOS SHELL

Versions 4 and 5 of DOS include a program called the DOS Shell that lets you use menus and small on-screen images to manage your files and disks without typing DOS commands or file names at the system prompt. With the Shell, you can see your directory structure outlined on-screen, and you can navigate from one directory to another with the keyboard or with a mouse. You can also set up your application programs so you can run them simply by selecting from a list. If you have version 5 of DOS, you can even switch among multiple programs without having to quit one before you start another.

This program is called a *shell* because it surrounds DOS. When you use it, you see the Shell and its menus rather than DOS itself or its system prompt. The Shell even adds some capabilities that DOS commands don't offer. For example, you can rename a directory, move one or more files without having to copy and erase them, and view the contents of two disks or directories at the same time.

This chapter gives you a quick tour of the version 5 Shell. It shows you how to use the Shell's major capabilities with either the keyboard or the mouse. If you have version 4 of DOS, your Shell is visually similar, but differs in some significant respects. You can use this chapter as a general guide to the Shell, but you'll need to refer to your documentation and to the online Help facility in your Shell for specifics.

STARTING THE SHELL

DOS can be installed so that it runs the Shell whenever you start or restart your computer, or so that it waits until you give the command to run the Shell. If DOS runs the Shell automatically, the Shell appears as soon as DOS finishes its startup routine. If DOS does not run the Shell automatically, you see the normal DOS startup, ending with the system prompt. In this case, you start the Shell by typing its name:

`C:\>dosshell`

When you start the Shell, the program begins by reading the name of each directory and file from the disk in the current drive. If the disk contains many directories and files, the process can take a short while, so the Shell reports on its progress in a box headed *Reading Disk Information*. The Shell then displays its opening screen, which looks like the illustration at the top of the next page. For simplicity, the illustration shows only the files most likely to be in the root directory of a fixed disk. You might see others.

Note: If your opening Shell screen doesn't show areas headed Directory Tree *and* Main, *you can change the display by choosing Program/File Lists from the View menu at the top of the screen. If you don't know how to do this, refer to the illustrations and disregard your display for a few minutes.*

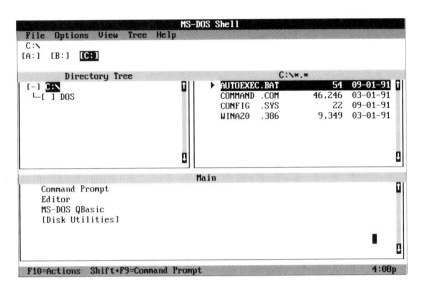

The Shell operates either in *text mode,* as shown in the preceding illustration, or in *graphics mode.* Text mode uses text characters only—no pictures—to create the display you see. Graphics mode, which you can use on EGA, VGA, and similar displays, combines text characters and some graphic images. Figure 10-1 on the next page shows how the screen in the preceding illustration looks in graphics mode. Notice that the mouse pointer is arrow-shaped instead of rectangular and that small images of disk drives and file folders replace the square brackets used in text mode.

The rest of this chapter shows screens in graphics mode.

Parts of the Shell Window

The opening Shell screen shows a large *window* containing a number of different elements. This window also shows two major parts of the Shell, the *File List* at the top and the *Program List* below it. From top to bottom, these are the principal elements in the Shell's opening window (they're labeled in Figure 10-1):

▶ The top line of the screen (title bar) identifies the DOS Shell.

▶ The second line (menu bar) displays the names of the available menus: File, Options, View, Tree, and Help. You choose commands from these menus.

▶ The next two lines identify the current drive and directory (probably C:\, as shown earlier) and show the disk drives attached to your system.

▶ The next one-third to one-half of the window comprises the File List area, which is divided vertically into two smaller sections.

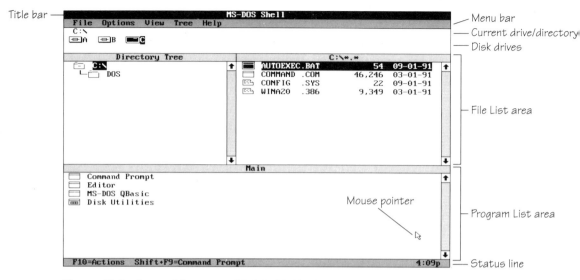

Figure 10-1. *Parts of the version 5 MS-DOS Shell window.*

The left-hand portion, titled *Directory Tree*, shows all the directories on the current disk, arranged with subdirectories indented to the right and connected by lines that show the directory structure. This display is like the output of the Tree command. A minus sign inside the symbol that represents a directory (for example, the symbol to the left of *C:*) means the directory contains one or more subdirectories that are currently displayed in the directory tree. A plus sign inside the symbol that represents a directory means that the directory contains one or more subdirectories that are not currently displayed.

The right-hand portion lists the files in the current drive and directory (C:*.* in the preceding illustration). Like a directory listing, these entries list the name, size, and date of creation or last change of each file in the selected directory.

▶ The lower section of the Shell window, titled *Main*, is the Program List area. It displays a list of programs you can run. Until you add your own programs to this window, it contains at least two basic choices, Command Prompt and Disk Utilities.

▶ Finally, the bottom line of the screen (status line) shows you the time of day and the effect of using two shortcut keystrokes, F10 and Shift-F9 (produced by pressing Shift and F9 at the same time). The F10 key activates the menus in the menu bar; Shift-F9 lets you temporarily leave the Shell and work at the DOS system prompt.

Using the Keyboard and Mouse

Before you begin to explore the Shell, it's useful to know how to get around in it with a mouse or with the keyboard.

If you have a mouse, you already know that using one is easy and relatively standard among different application programs. In the Shell, maneuvering is as simple as you'd expect: Just roll the mouse on your desktop until the pointer is wherever you want it to be. Once you've pointed to the item or the part of the window you want, you can select it by clicking the left mouse button. (The right button is inactive in the Shell.) For certain tasks, you double-click on an item by pressing the left button twice in rapid succession. In addition, you sometimes drag an item, as when you move a file from one directory to another, by pressing and holding the left button and moving the mouse pointer to a new location before releasing the button.

With the keyboard, you use the Tab key to move from one area of the Shell to another—for example, to move from the list of drives to the Directory Tree, and then to the list of files in the current directory. To reverse direction, press Shift-Tab.

Figure 10-2 describes basic techniques you can use to perform the most common Shell operations with the keyboard or a mouse.

Keyboard	Mouse
To select a menu:	
Press either Alt or F10 to activate the menu bar; press the key letter of the menu name (underlined in graphics mode, highlighted in text mode).	Click on the menu name.
To select a menu command:	
Select the menu; press the key letter of the command you want (underlined in the command name).	Click on the command.
To select a file:	
Highlight the file name by using the arrow keys.	Click on the file name.
To choose (carry out) a command:	
Highlight the command by using the arrow keys; press the Enter key.	Double-click on the command name.

Figure 10-2. *Basic keyboard and mouse techniques.*

If you're a keyboard user who is unfamiliar with menu-based programs, don't be concerned if the techniques don't have much meaning as yet; they soon will. For both mouse and keyboard, the hands-on examples in this chapter also help you along when necessary.

Note: For the sake of standardization, this chapter assumes a computer with a fixed disk (drive C) and at least one subdirectory (C:\DOS). If your system differs, the examples are still appropriate but might not work exactly as described.

HELP IS A KEYSTROKE AWAY

The Shell includes on-screen help information that can guide you through most of its features. You can request either general information or direct help with a specific situation. General help is a good way of finding out about the Shell and how it works—which keys you use, what procedures are available, and so on. Direct help provides details about whatever task you're working on at the time you request help. To request general help, you use the Help menu at the top of the screen. To request direct help, you choose the item or command you want and then press F1. You'll try both types of help in the following examples.

Start by choosing the Help menu:

▶ With the keyboard, press Alt or F10 to activate the menus, and then press H.

▶ With the mouse, click on Help.

The Help menu opens, showing a list of choices with Index highlighted. Press Enter, and the Shell displays a window headed *MS-DOS Shell Help*:

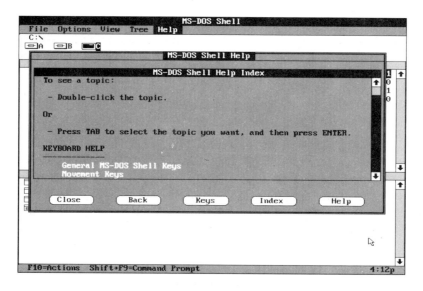

The top line of the Help window contains the title of the screen. The main part of the Help window, titled *MS-DOS Shell Help Index*, describes what you can do next. The bottom line of the Help window—no matter what Help information is displayed—offers you five choices:

▶ Close ends Help, removes the Help window, and returns you to whatever you were doing.

▶ Back returns to the previous Help display if you've moved from one topic to another within Help.

▶ Keys displays a list of topics related to using the keyboard with the Shell.

▶ Index displays the Help index you're looking at now.

▶ Help displays help on Help.

Right now, notice that the box labeled *MS-DOS Shell Help Index* starts with a few lines that tell you how to choose an index topic. Just below this is the heading *Keyboard Help,* which is followed by a group of topics beginning with *General MS-DOS Shell Keys.* The index breaks Help information into broad categories with related topics grouped under them. To see what help is available, press the PgDn key a few times, stopping when you see the heading *MS-DOS SHELL BASICS HELP* and the topic *Welcome to MS-DOS Shell.* Now try requesting some help:

▶ With the keyboard, press the Tab key as many times as necessary to move the highlight or the small arrow at the left edge of the window to *Welcome to MS-DOS Shell*; press Enter.

▶ With the mouse, double-click on *Welcome to MS-DOS Shell.*

The title at the top of the window changes to *Welcome to MS-DOS Shell*, and the old display is quickly replaced by a description of the Shell. Press the PgDn key several times. At the end of the description, you see the the words *Next topic* followed by Scroll Bars. Press the Tab key to select this new topic and press Enter, or double-click on it with the mouse. The window changes again, this time to one that tells you how to use the scroll bar the Shell displays along the right edge of certain windows.

Instead of moving deeper into Help, now try moving back the way you came. Choose the button marked Back at the bottom of the window. Either press the Tab key until the "cursor" is on Back and press Enter, or click on Back with the mouse. The Help display changes to the previous screenful of information, *Welcome to MS-DOS Shell.* Choose Back again, and you see the original index screen.

If you want, experiment with other Help topics or with the other buttons at the bottom of the window. When you're ready to stop, either press Escape or use the Close button by tabbing to it and pressing Enter or by clicking on the button with the mouse.

Before leaving Help entirely, try requesting some direct help. First, choose the File menu (press Alt-F or click on File). Notice that the Open command is highlighted. Ask Help what this command does. Press the F1 key, and a Help window appears, this one telling you not only about the File Open command, but also referring you to additional information if you need it. Press Esc to close the Help window.

If you plan to use the Shell frequently, consider browsing through Help as you just did. It's a good way to learn to use the Shell. And remember the F1 key; it's all you need to request help on a particular task.

THE FILE LIST

If you're using the keyboard to operate the Shell, you use the Tab key to activate the screen area you want to work in. If you're using a mouse, clicking in an area is enough to activate that portion of the window.

The current drive—probably drive C—should be highlighted. To prepare for the next examples, select the Directory Tree by pressing the Tab key or by clicking the mouse anywhere in that area. If the highlight is on the root directory (for example, C:\), use the Down arrow key or the mouse to highlight a different directory.

If you're using the Shell with a monochrome display and you see only two colors, one dark and one light, you can make your screen more closely match the shading in the illustrations in this chapter by changing to four-color monochrome. To do this, press the Alt key and then press the letter O twice. When a box labeled *Color Scheme* appears, press the Down arrow key until the dark highlight is on Monochrome-4 Colors. Press Enter, and your screen will change to shades of light and dark.

The File Menu

The Shell menus are lists of choices. Although they are menus like those in a restaurant, they show you both what items you can choose and whether the Shell will ask for more information when you make a choice. To see this, select the File menu again. The screen should look like this:

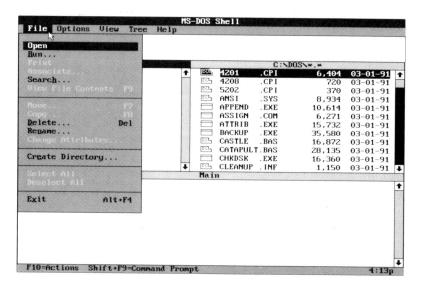

Notice that the menu items are displayed in both light (dimmed) and dark characters. The Shell uses dimmed characters to let you know which menu options you can't choose because they're not appropriate for what you're doing at the time.

Right now, the File menu tells you that you can open a file (to work with), run a program file, search for a file, delete (careful!) or rename the current directory, create a directory, or exit the Shell. Until you select one or more files, these are the only actions you can perform from the File menu. You can't print, for example, because you haven't selected a file to print.

The ellipsis (...) following certain choices, such as Run, means that the Shell needs a little more information before it can carry out the command. When you see an ellipsis following a command name, you can expect the Shell to prompt you for more information before it carries out the command. You'll see how this works a bit later. Keys and key combinations, such as *F8* and *Alt+F4* along the right edge of the menu, represent shortcut keys you can press instead of using the menu to choose the commands they carry out.

Press Esc to close the File menu.

Selecting a Directory

The Directory Tree outlines the directory structure of the disk in the current drive. If it's not already highlighted, select your \DOS directory. There are faster ways to move through a list, but for now, press an arrow key until DOS or the name of your DOS directory is highlighted and press Enter, or click on DOS (press the PgDn key, if necessary, to bring the directory into view). The area to the right should show the DOS files.

(If you don't have a fixed disk, substitute the root directory of your startup disk for the \DOS directory unless the instructions here tell you otherwise.)

Select the files area to the right of the Directory Tree by pressing the Tab key or by clicking anywhere in that portion of the screen.

Scrolling Through the Directories

The list of files in \DOS is probably too long to fit on the screen, so to see it all you need to *scroll* through the directory. Using the keyboard, you can scroll through this or any other long list of files or directories in any of several ways:

▶ By pressing the Down (or Up) arrow key to move a line at a time.

▶ By pressing the PgDn (or PgUp) key to move a screen at a time.

▶ By pressing a letter key to move directly to the first entry that begins with that letter.

▶ By pressing Home to move to the first entry in the list, or by pressing End to move to the last entry.

If you're using a mouse, the Shell includes a mechanism that makes scrolling even easier: the *scroll bar*, for which you saw Help earlier. The scroll bar is the vertical bar at the right margin of each window. It has an arrow at the top and at the bottom, and it contains a shaded box or rectangle called the *scroll box*. Clicking on one of the arrows moves a list one line in the direction of the arrow. Clicking in the blank part of the scroll bar moves a screenful, and dragging the scroll box to any position between the top and bottom moves you the same relative distance in the list.

To try scrolling through a list, use one of the techniques described to view different parts of the \DOS directory.

Selecting Files

In order to work with your files, both DOS and the Shell require you to indicate which files you want to affect with any particular command. From the DOS command prompt, you type a file name, with or without wildcards, to specify files. Within the Shell, you literally mark the names of the files you want to affect.

With the mouse, a file is selected as soon as you point to it and click the left button. With the keyboard, you tab to the list of file names and use the arrow keys to highlight the file name you want. In graphics mode, the symbol to the left of the file name is highlighted as soon as you select the file. In text mode, an arrow and a triangle appear before the file name. Your next file-oriented action will affect that particular file.

With a file selected, open the File menu again. Notice that all of the choices except Create Directory are now available. That's because all the other commands on the menu can be applied to a selected file. Press Esc to close the menu.

You can select more than one file at a time—for copying, perhaps, or moving to another directory:

▶ To select a series of files with the keyboard, move the highlight to the name of the first file, press and hold the Shift key, and extend the selection with the arrow keys.

▶ To use the mouse, click on the first file, press and hold the Shift key, and click on the last file in the group you want to select.

▶ To use the keyboard to select files scattered throughout a list, press and release Shift and the F8 key. When you do this, the word *ADD* appears near the right edge of the status line at the bottom of the screen. Using the arrow keys to highlight file names, press the Spacebar to select each file you want.

▶ To use the mouse to select discontinuous files, hold down the Ctrl key instead of the Shift key as you click on each file name you want.

If you've practiced selecting groups of files, reduce the selection to one file by choosing Deselect All from the File menu. (Press Alt, then F, then L, or click on File and then on Deselect All.)

The next few topics show you some of the File menu items; you can explore the rest. Most of the items are self-explanatory, but a few might not seem obvious. *Associate*, for example, lets you tell the Shell to run an application program when you select a file with a particular file extension. You might associate your word processing program, for example, with files whose extension is DOC. If you need explanations you don't find here, remember that Help is always available.

Copying a File

To see how the Shell prompts you for additional information, move to the files area and select ASSIGN.COM from your DOS directory. Now press F8 or select Copy from the File menu:

The screen should look like this:

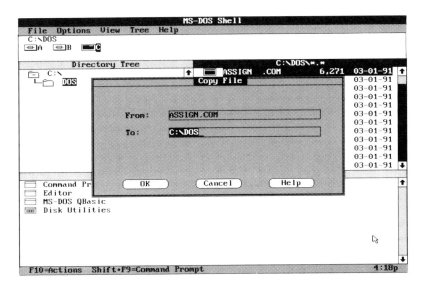

The Shell displays a box titled *Copy File* in the middle of the screen. The box, called a *dialog box,* is what the Shell uses to ask for any additional information it needs in order to carry out a menu command. As you can see, the Shell makes some assumptions. Here, for example, the From field is already filled in with ASSIGN.COM, the file you selected to copy.

Because you must include a drive letter and path name when you copy files, the Shell tries to help here too by suggesting the current directory, placing the cursor at the end and highlighting its guess. To add to this drive and path, you would press the Right arrow or the End key and start typing. To replace the suggested drive and path, you would simply start typing; the characters you typed would replace what the Shell displayed.

You're going to copy ASSIGN.COM to a file named ASSIGN.NEW in the current directory, so press End, type \assign.new (don't forget the backslash), and press Enter. The dialog box disappears, and ASSIGN.NEW is added to the list of files. It's as if you had typed the command copy assign.com assign.new at the system prompt.

Moving a file works just like copying a file, but the Shell deletes the original file after making the new copy. If you used the Shell to move ASSIGN.NEW from the current directory (\DOS) to the root directory, for example, it would be as if you typed copy assign.new \ and del assign.new.

Note: If you're using a mouse with the Shell, you can move files easily by selecting them and dragging to the name of a different directory on the Directory Tree of the current drive. When you do this, the Shell asks if you're sure you want to move the files. If you are, click Yes or press Enter. The files are moved. No need to copy and delete; no need even to choose the File Move command.

Viewing a File

Viewing a file is a quick way to see what's in it; you can't change the file—you can only look at it. DOSSHELL.INI is a text file created when you install DOS. Among other things, this file tells the Shell about your system and the way it should look when it starts. Select DOSSHELL.INI from the list of files, then select View File Contents from the File menu. The screen should look like this:

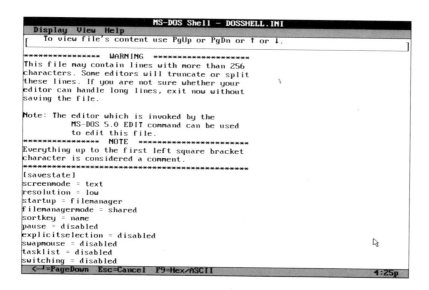

The top line identifies the file, the next line lists the menus available, and the third line tells you which keys you can press to scroll through the file. (If you're using a mouse, you can also scroll by clicking on the PgUp, PgDn, and arrow symbols.) The main part of the screen shows part of DOSSHELL.INI.

The Shell can display files in either of two modes, ASCII or hexadecimal. As you see it now, the file is displayed as an ASCII file, so called because it is translated into readable text characters according to the American Standard Code for Information Interchange, or ASCII. In hexadecimal format, the characters in a file are translated into the mathematical language of computers—specifically, the base-16 numbering system often used by programmers. To see the hexadecimal view, press F9.

It's certainly different. Each line of the hexadecimal view shows 16 characters. The first column of numbers at the left margin is the address—in hexadecimal, of course—of the beginning of each line, starting at 0 at the beginning of the file. Each of the middle four columns of numbers is the hexadecimal representation of four characters, two digits per character. The 16 columns at the right show the ASCII characters that correspond to the hexadecimal digits in the line.

Press F9 again, and the display returns to the ASCII view. Press Esc to return to the File List display.

Deleting a File

Using the Shell, you can delete one file, several files, all files in a directory, or any directory except the root (\) simply by selecting the file, files, or empty directory you want to delete, and then pressing Del or selecting Delete from the File menu. Because it's so easy to change directories and select files in the Shell, using the Shell to delete files you no longer need is a snap compared to typing comparable commands at the DOS system prompt.

Simply because the Shell makes it so quick and easy to delete files, however, it's a good idea to give yourself some protection by making sure that the Shell asks you to confirm each deletion. With the Shell, in fact, you can protect yourself not only from inadvertently deleting a file with the Delete command, but also against inadvertently replacing a file by copying another in its place.

Protecting Yourself

To protect yourself against inadvertently deleting a file, select the Options menu, then select Confirmation. The Shell displays the dialog box at the top of the next page.

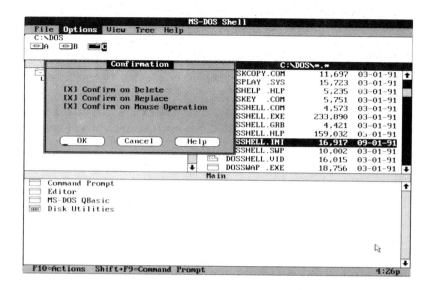

The brackets to the left of each option contain an X if the option is active. Selecting an active option turns it off; selecting an inactive option turns it on.

Confirm On Delete determines whether the Shell prompts you for confirmation before deleting a file. Confirm On Replace protects you against a less obvious way of losing a file: It determines whether the Shell prompts you for confirmation before copying over an existing file. Confirm On Mouse Operation determines whether the Shell warns you before carrying out a mouse operation that moves or copies a file.

All three options should be on (contain an X between the brackets). If one is off, tab to it and press the Spacebar to turn it on. Otherwise, press Esc to clear the dialog box.

Now to delete a file. A while ago you created ASSIGN.NEW by copying ASSIGN.COM. You don't need ASSIGN.NEW, so select it (don't select ASSIGN.COM by mistake), then press Del or choose Delete from the File menu. The Shell displays a dialog box headed *Delete File Confirmation*.

This is how the Shell gives you a second chance. The dialog box shows the name of the file to be deleted, and the buttons at the bottom ask you to choose Yes, No, or Cancel. Press Enter to choose Yes. The Shell deletes ASSIGN.NEW and returns you to the File List display.

You can delete an entire directory and its contents in two quick steps with the Shell. Because the Shell refuses to delete a directory that contains files, you first select the directory in the Directory Tree, and then select and delete all files in it with the Select All and Delete commands on the File menu. Once the files are gone, you can use Delete again, this time to remove the directory itself. Because it's so easy, make sure you do, indeed, want to erase both the directory and everything in it—a few valuable files might be hidden in a welter of unnecessary ones.

Whether or not you have set Confirm On Delete, you must delete all files in a directory before you can delete the directory, just as when you use the DOS Remove Directory command. Likewise, you cannot delete any directory that contains subdirectories, nor can you delete (or rename) the root directory, because each disk must contain this directory.

Using the Options and Arrange Menus

You just used the Confirmation command from the Options menu to protect against inadvertently deleting or copying over a file. Other choices on the Options and View menus let you specify the order in which file names are listed; display information about the selected file, directory, and disk; display the files in two directories at once; display all the files on the selected disk; display only the File List; or display the Program List and File List at the same time, as the Shell is doing now.

Controlling the Order in Which File Names Are Displayed

When you first start the Shell, the File List displays the file names in alphabetic order. You can change this order to display the files arranged by extension, date, size, or even the order in which they are stored on the disk. To display the files arranged by extension, choose File Display Options from the Options menu. The Shell displays the Display Options dialog box, which looks like this:

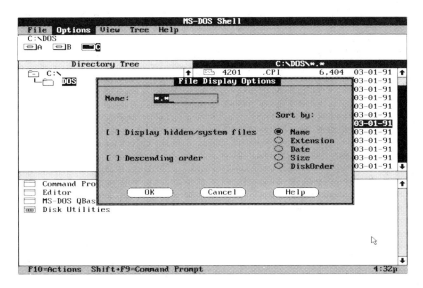

223

In addition to specifying the order in which files are to be displayed, this dialog box lets you tell the Shell whether to display hidden and system files and whether to display files in ascending (A to Z) or descending (Z to A) order.

To change Display Hidden/System Files or Descending Order with the keyboard, you would tab to the option and press the Spacebar. With the mouse, you would simply click anywhere on the option. Either way, if the option is turned on, an X appears in the brackets; if the option is off, as it should be now, the brackets are empty.

The different ways you can sort files are in the list at the right side of the dialog box. These options are mutually exclusive, so only one can be active at any time. The active choice is indicated by a dark dot inside the circle (a dot between parentheses in text mode).

To try changing one of the settings, select Extension and press Enter or click on OK to close the dialog box. When the full window reappears, the files are listed alphabetically by extension—BAS files, then COM files, and so on—rather than by name as they were before. Finding files arranged alphabetically by name is generally easier than sorting through them by extension, so use the File Display Options command again and return to sorting by name.

Displaying File, Directory, and Disk Information

The Show Information command on the Options menu displays information about the currently selected file, directory, and disk. Select FORMAT.COM, then choose the Show Information command. The screen should look like this:

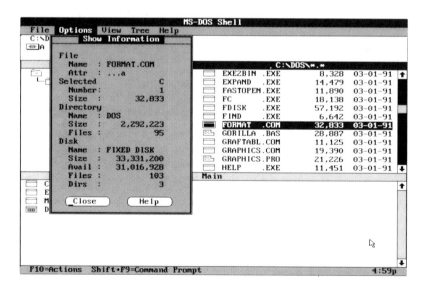

There's nothing in this window for you to type or select; it simply shows you the following information:

▶ *File* shows the name and attributes of the selected file (the first file selected if you've selected more than one).

▶ *Selected* shows the letter of the selected disk drive and the number and total size of all selected files. If you're displaying directories from two disks, it shows both disk letters and the number and total size of all selected files on both disks.

▶ *Directory* shows the name of the directory that contains the file named under *File*, the number of bytes taken up by all the files in the directory, and the number of files in the directory. Knowing the size of a directory can be quite useful in certain operations, such as copying a directory from a fixed disk to a diskette.

▶ *Disk* shows the name (volume label), capacity, available space, number of files, and number of directories on the disk that contains *File*.

Press Esc or click Close to remove the Show Information window from the screen.

Changing the View

The Shell lets you display the File List, the Program List, or both (as you're doing now). You choose what you want to see with the View menu. To change the view, open the View menu. The screen should look like this:

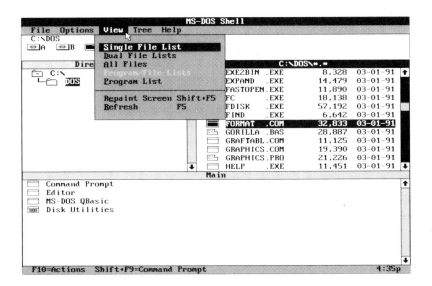

The first choice (Single File List) is highlighted; the item Program/File Lists is dimmer than the other choices because that's what the Shell is displaying now. Press Enter to select the highlighted choice. Now the File List takes up the entire window:

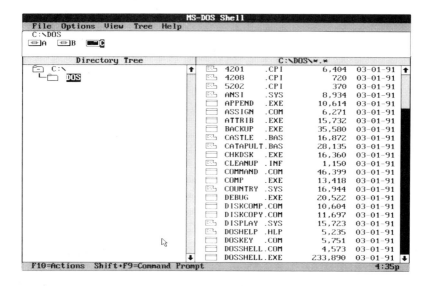

Displaying Two Directories at Once

The Shell lets you display the files in two directories, on the same or on different drives. To see this, choose Dual File Lists from the View menu. The Shell divides the middle portion of the screen horizontally into two areas, one above the other. The areas are nearly identical: Each includes the disk-drive list, the Directory Tree, and the names of the files in the selected directory. The only difference between them is that the name of the current directory appears above the top row of disk drives.

In the example shown on the next page, the upper file area lists the names of the files in the directory \DOS on the system disk (usually drive C), and the lower file area lists the names of the files in the root directory.

When you're viewing a dual file list, you can select files in either list for copying, deleting, moving, and so on. You can select files in more than one directory by displaying two directories and activating Select Across Directories on the Options menu, and you can even view directories on two disks by selecting different drives for the two areas.

Choose Single File List again to return the display to one directory.

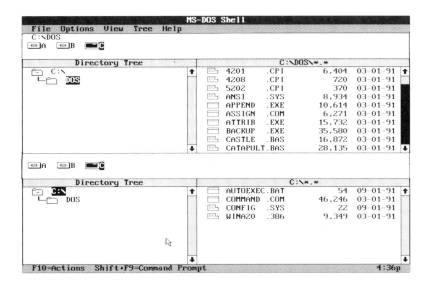

Finding That File

The bigger the disk, the more you can store on it. That's the good part. The more you store, the harder it can be to find a particular file. That's the bad part. Eventually, everyone who uses a computer for a while confronts the same frustrating question: Where did I save that file?

If you use version 5, that question becomes, if not negligible, at least less irritating. Rather than search through each directory, you can tell the Shell to do the work with the Search command on the File menu much as you can use the /S parameter of the Directory command from the system prompt. Suppose, for example, you use a fixed disk with many directories on it. Last year, you wrote a bid proposal, and you think you saved it as PROPOSAL.DOC. You're pretty sure the proposal is still on your fixed disk somewhere, and now you'd like to resurrect the document, change it a bit, and submit it as a different bid. With one command, you can tell the Shell to go look for what you want. When you choose Search from the File menu, you see a dialog box like the one on the next page.

Notice that the Shell initially proposes to search the entire disk for all files (*.*). That can be useful in some situations, particularly because the Shell's report on what it finds includes the path to each file. In this example, however, you're interested in a particular file name and extension, so you'd type *proposal.doc* in the field labeled Search For. (To find a set of files, you could use wildcard characters—for example, *.doc* to see a list of all files on the disk with the extension DOC.) To search the entire disk, leave the X next to Search entire disk. To limit the search to a path you specify, you turn this option off.

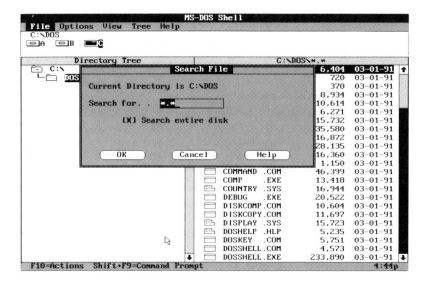

To try this command, tell the Shell to search the entire disk for COM-MAND.COM. When you press Enter or click OK to start the search, the Shell might become still for a short time. Don't be concerned; it's working, just as DOS is working when you use Check Disk or a similar command. When the search is complete, a new window appears, displaying a list of all files that match the path (if any), file name, and extension you specified. Press Esc to clear the window.

Displaying All the File Names on a Disk

Whereas the Search command gives you a way to find one or more needles in a haystack, the All Files command on the View menu lets you see the whole pile of hay—every file in every subdirectory on a disk.

When you choose the All Files command, the Shell combines two types of display in one. At the right side of the screen, it lists the names of all files on the disk, showing the same directory information it normally shows in the File List area. Along the left side of the screen, it provides the same information you see when you choose the Show Information command from the Options menu. This combined display not only lets you see the directory information for each file on the disk, it also provides you with the directory name, attributes, directory size, and other details displayed by the Show Information command. As you select different file names, the Shell updates the information on the left side of the screen to tell you about the currently selected file.

If you've used the All Files command, return to displaying the directory tree. Choose Program/File Lists from the View menu.

228

Viewing the Directory Tree

When you use directories and subdirectories to organize your files, you can eventually create a directory tree of many levels. In the Shell, the Tree menu lets you control how many directory levels are displayed in the Directory Tree area of the File List. If you want, you can choose to see only the root directory of a disk. On the other hand, you can tell the Shell to outline the entire tree, including every subdirectory of every directory on the disk. Between these extremes, you can selectively collapse and expand single directories or subdirectories according to the level of detail that interests you at the time.

You can use the various commands on the Tree menu to expand and collapse directories, but the Shell also recognizes certain keys that make your work much easier. Here are the commands and what they do, as well as the keys you use:

▶ Expand One Level expands the selected directory to display the next directory level. Speed key: plus (+).

▶ Expand Branch expands the selected directory to show all directory levels under it. Speed key: asterisk (∗).

▶ Expand All expands the entire directory tree to show all subdirectories under all directories. Speed keys: Ctrl-∗ (Control plus the asterisk).

▶ Collapse Branch collapses the selected directory. Speed key: minus (–).

The Tree menu does not include a command or a key combination that collapses the entire directory tree once you've expanded all levels. You don't have to collapse the branches one by one, however. To return to the Shell's normal display of the directory tree, select the root directory and press the minus key to collapse the entire tree. Once that's done, press the plus key to expand the root directory one level.

Beyond this description, all you need is a little bit of experimentation with your own directory tree in order to become comfortable with the Shell's ability to show you different levels of your directory structure from the root directory to the entire tree. Notice, as you select different directories, that the file list at the right side of the File List area changes to show the files in the selected directory.

Although the Shell isn't suited for everything you'll do with DOS, you can see that it makes many routine file-management tasks much simpler and quicker.

The next part of this chapter deals with a different side of the Shell, the Program List. If you want to stop temporarily, you can leave the Shell and return to DOS by pressing F3 or choosing Exit from the File menu.

PROGRAM LIST

If you think of the File List area as the part of the Shell window that provides information, you can think of the Program List area as the part that provides functionality. The Program List area can contain two different types of items: programs and program groups. Although both represent applications and other programs you can run directly from the Shell, programs are stand-alone items that run as soon as you activate them. Program groups are umbrella items that cover a group of related programs. (In text mode, a program group is enclosed in square brackets [ ].)

When you start the Shell, the Program List area displays a list of programs and the name of one program group. Typically, the programs and the program group are:

▶ Command Prompt, which temporarily stops the Shell and displays the DOS system prompt so that you can type DOS commands. You return to the Shell by typing *exit*.

▶ Editor, which starts the version 5 MS-DOS Editor program that you meet briefly here and learn about in more detail in the next chapter.

▶ MS-DOS QBasic, which starts the QBasic program, a version of the Microsoft QuickBasic programming language.

▶ Disk Utilities, which is a program group that displays another list of choices when you select it. In this case, Disk Utilities groups a set of commonly used DOS disk and file operations.

You'll experiment with these and add programs and a group of your own. Before you start, however, prepare for one of the later examples by copying one file to a diskette in drive B. Put a formatted diskette in drive B (your diskette drive if you have only one), and then go through your DOS directory and find the file named DOSSHELL.INI, which you viewed earlier. Once you've found the file, highlight it and press F8 or use the Copy command on the File menu to copy DOSSHELL.INI to B:\. (Press a key if the Shell beeps and tells you to insert a diskette in drive B.) You won't need the File List area for now, so clear the window a bit by choosing Program List from the View menu.

Starting a Program

To start a program item or display the choices in a program group, you simply choose from the Program List. For example, Command Prompt should be highlighted now. Although you wouldn't necessarily consider this the name of a program, it does in fact start a program that causes DOS to temporarily leave the Shell and display the system prompt. Press Enter or double-click on Command Prompt, and in a few moments the screen clears, DOS displays an opening message, and you see the DOS prompt.

230

To return to the Shell, type:

```
exit
```

Unless you're running a program that has its own quit command, this is the command you use to return to the Shell.

Switching Among Programs

Have you ever been using a program (a word processor, for example) and needed to use another program (a spreadsheet, say, or a graphics program)? If so, you had to leave the first program, start the second, finish with the second program, leave it, and start the first program again. Sometimes this can happen fairly often, making you spend too much time just starting and stopping programs.

The Shell includes a feature called the Task Swapper, which lets you start one or more programs and switch from the Shell to each program with just a few keystrokes. You'll test this with the MS-DOS Editor and QBasic, both of which come with DOS.

Note: If you're interested in trying the Task Swapper with your own application programs, you can follow the instructions given here by substituting the names of your application programs when you're told to activate the Editor and QBasic. A word processing program, such as Microsoft Word, will do. You can even start another copy of the Shell if you want. But try not to use a memory-resident ("pop-up") program, such as Doskey; you might see a message telling you to quit the program before returning to the Shell.

To start the Task Swapper, display the Options menu. The fifth item is Enable Task Swapper, and this choice is either on or off. If it's on, it's preceded by a dot. If it's off, select it to turn it on. Otherwise, press Esc to clear the Options menu.

Now the Program List area should be divided into two parts: The left half should be titled Main; the right half should be titled Active Task List. The right side displays the names of all programs that you have started and left running; you haven't left any running, so the list should be blank.

Start the Editor by choosing Editor from the Main window. When the Editor dialog box asks you which file to edit, type *edfile* and press Enter or click OK. When the Editor starts, it displays a blank window. So that your applications will be easy to recognize, type the following line:

```
This is my Editor file.
```

Now return to the Shell without stopping the Editor. To do this, press Ctrl and the Esc key (Ctrl-Esc). In a few moments the Shell displays the Program List screen again. This time, Editor appears in the Active Task List to tell you that you can rejoin the Editor any time you like. To do so, you simply select it from the Active Task List.

Start a second program by selecting MS-DOS QBasic from the Main window. When the program asks you the name of the file to edit, type *basfile* and press Enter or click OK. When QBasic starts, type:

```
This is my QBasic file.
```

Again, press Ctrl-Esc to return to the Shell. Now the Active Task List shows two entries, MS-DOS QBasic and Editor.

To switch to the Editor, select it from the Active Task List. There's the Editor again, just as when you left it. Now suppose you were using the Editor and remembered that you wanted to check something with QBasic. Hold down the Alt key and tap Tab until the title bar at the top of the screen displays *MS-DOS QBasic*. Release the Alt key, and you're back to your other program. Press Ctrl-Esc to return to the Shell.

You can switch among your programs and the Shell at will with this Alt-Tab key combination. When you use Alt-Tab, the Shell displays its own name and the name of each active program, cycling through them in round-robin fashion. There are several other key combinations you can also use with the Task Swapper. While using one program you can, for example, press Alt-Esc to switch to the next application in the Active Task List, or you can press Shift-Alt-Esc to move to the previous application. To familiarize yourself with these keys, choose Keyboard from the Help menu and choose Active Task List Keys from the list of topics the Shell displays.

One particular key combination to remember is Shift-Enter, which starts a program and adds it to the Active Task List without leaving the Shell. To try this, move the highlight to Command Prompt in the Main window and then press Shift-Enter. Although the Shell remains on-screen, Command Prompt is added to the Active Task List, and you can switch to it anytime you want simply by selecting it from the list.

When you're through using a program, just end it as you normally would; the Shell displays the Program List screen again, but now the name of the program you left doesn't appear in the Active Task List.

To stop the three tasks you've started, choose Command Prompt from the Active Task List and type *exit* when DOS displays the system prompt. When the Shell reappears, Command Prompt is gone from the list of tasks. Next, switch to QBasic and choose Exit from the File menu. Choose No when QBasic asks if you want to save the sample file. When you return to the Shell, switch to the Editor, choose Exit from the File menu, and again choose No when asked if you want to save the file. This time when you return to the Shell there are no entries in the Active Task List.

You'll find that switching among programs like this lets you make much better use of your time at the computer.

Selecting a Program Group

The symbol or brackets associated with Disk Utilities in the Main area tells you that selecting this item displays a different list of choices. To see the list, choose Disk Utilities.

The screen is now titled Disk Utilities—the name of the program group you selected—rather than Main, and you see a different list of choices. With a fixed disk, they are: Main (which returns you to the main Program List screen), Disk Copy, Backup Fixed Disk, Restore Fixed Disk, Quick Format, Format, and Undelete. As you'll see shortly, you can customize this list of choices by adding your own program items and program groups. Choose Main to return to the Main screen.

When the Program List area is active, the menu bar at the top of the screen undergoes a rather subtle change. If you look, you can see that the Tree menu disappears because it's inappropriate here. The Options and Help menus remain the same. The View menu remains almost the same (Refresh is not available from the Program List area), but the File menu contains a number of different choices.

The Program List File Menu

Rather than offering choices that deal with files, the Program List's File menu lets you manage its list of program items and program groups. The choices include:

▶ New, which adds a new program item or program group to the Program List.

▶ Open, which starts the highlighted program item or displays the items in a selected program group. (It has the same effect as pressing Enter.)

▶ Copy, which copies a program item to a program group you specify.

▶ Delete, which deletes a program item or a program group (from which you've already deleted all program items).

▶ Properties, which lets you specify the title, startup command, and other definitions of a program item or program group.

▶ Reorder, which lets you change the order in which the program items and program groups are displayed.

▶ Run, which lets you start any program, whether or not it is displayed in the list of program items and program groups.

▶ Exit, which leaves the Shell.

Adding a Program Item

Adding a program item to the Shell can be fairly simple. You can even add a program that requires more than one command simply by separating the commands, up to a maximum of 500 characters, with semicolons.

Suppose you wanted to add an entry called Memory Check that would carry out the DOS Mem command. Choose New from the File menu. The Shell displays a dialog box that gives you the choice of adding a Program Group or a Program Item. The Shell assumes you want to add a Program Item, which you do, so press Enter or click on OK.

Now the Shell displays the Add Program dialog box:

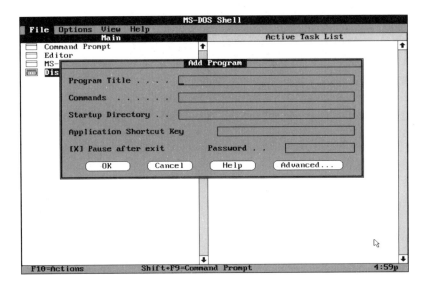

The Shell requires that you fill out only the Program Title and Commands fields to define a new entry. The Program Title field specifies how the Program List item will be displayed; type *Memory Check*. Press Tab to move to the Commands field, which specifies the command (or commands) to be carried out; type *mem* and press Enter. The Add Program dialog box disappears, and the item Memory Check is added to the list of programs.

Choose the new item by highlighting and pressing Enter or by double-clicking on it; the screen clears, and in a few moments DOS displays the report of the Mem command, followed by the message *Press any key to return to MS-DOS Shell*. Press any key to return to the Shell.

Changing a Program Item

You can change any of the characteristics of a program item—the title, commands to be carried out, and so forth. The Shell refers to these characteristics as *properties;* to change them, you highlight the program item to be changed and select Properties from the File menu. Highlight Memory Check and then select Properties from the File menu. The Shell displays the Program Item Properties dialog box:

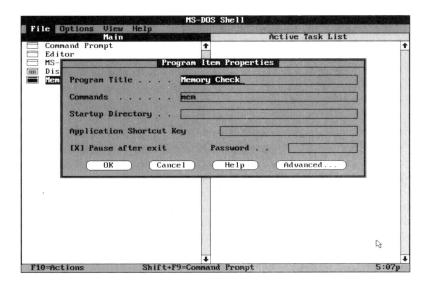

This dialog box contains the same fields as the Add Program dialog box. Because it lets you change an existing definition, however, fields to which values have been assigned—in this case, Program Title and Commands—are filled in.

To change one of the properties or add a new one, you simply enter the new value in the appropriate field. Suppose, for example, you decide that you want the program item to be named Mem Command instead of Memory Check. You also want to assign it the password IQ.

Type *Mem Command* in the Program Title field, type *IQ* (notice the capitals) in the Password field, and press Enter to carry out the change. Try the command again. This time, a dialog box appears, asking for the password. Type *IQ*, and be sure to type in capital letters; the Shell can tell the difference. Once you've entered the password, the dialog box disappears, the screen clears, and the memory report is displayed. Your program item is the same command, but you've now given it a new definition.

Deleting a Program Item

This Mem Command example has served its purpose, so you'll delete it. Make sure that Mem Command is highlighted and select Delete from the File menu. The Shell displays the Delete Item dialog box shown on the next page.

Like the Delete File dialog box, the Delete Item dialog box lets you confirm the name of the item to be deleted. Because you've assigned a password to Mem Command, the dialog box reminds you of the fact. The dialog box offers two choices, Delete and Do not delete, highlighting Delete and asking you to choose OK, Cancel, or Help. You want to delete the item, so press Enter. The dialog box disappears, and the Shell continues to display the Program List Main screen, but Mem Command is gone.

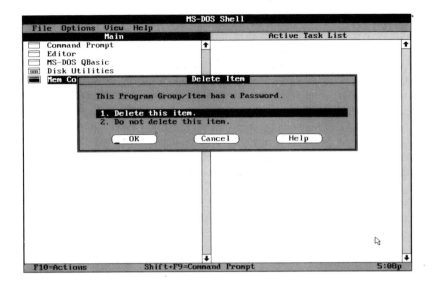

Customizing the Program List

You can customize the list of program items and program groups that the Shell displays, tailoring the Shell to reflect the programs you use. You might add a program group named Word Processing, for example, to include your word processor and associated programs, or you might add a program group named Financial for your spreadsheet or accounting programs. Once you created the groups, you would add program items to them. The program items would run the programs themselves.

Adding a Program Group

Suppose you wanted to create a separate program group named Text Files that would let you edit, display, and print files from the Shell. You'll add the program group and then add the MS-DOS Editor to it.

Note: If you want, you can try adding your word processor as the program item. Assuming that your word processor accepts a file name as part of the startup command, the following instructions should work for you. Just remember to use the command that starts your program instead of the Edit command that starts the MS-DOS Editor.

To create the program group, select New from the File menu just as when you added the Memory Check program item. As before, the Shell displays the New Program Object dialog box. This time, however, you don't want to accept the Shell's assumption that you want to create a program item, so select Program Group and then press Enter (or click on OK). The Shell displays the Add Group dialog box:

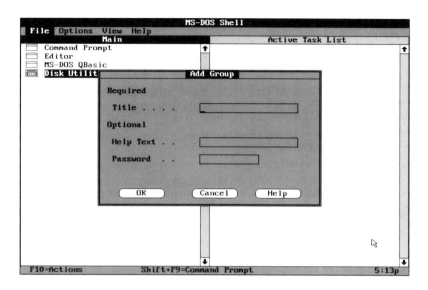

As the dialog box shows, the only field you must complete is Title, which specifies the group name you want on the Program List screen. If you wish, you can also specify the Help text that the Shell displays if F1 is pressed when the group name is highlighted, and (as before) a password that must be entered in order to use the group. For this program group, you'll enter a title and some help text.

First, type *Text Files* in the Title field, then tab to the Help Text field. Type *This group lets you edit text files*, and press Enter to save these entries; the Shell displays the Program List screen again, with the added group Text Files.

Now activate the Text Files group by highlighting it and pressing Enter or by double-clicking on it. The title line at the top of the display changes from *Main* to *Text Files*, and even though you haven't added any program items yet, the list contains one choice: Main. The Shell adds this program item for you so you can return to the Main Program List screen. (You can also return by pressing Esc.)

Specifying a Command Parameter

The first program item you'll add to the Text Files program group will run the MS-DOS Editor or the alternative you've chosen. (Yes, you can already run the Editor from the Main list, but it's used as an example here because most computer users have a text-handling program of some type.)

Select New from the File menu. The Shell displays the New Program Object dialog box, just as it did when you added Memory Check and Text Files. Press Enter or click OK to create a program item. The Shell displays the Add Program dialog box. Type *Text Editor* and tab to the Commands field.

When you specified the Memory command in the earlier example, you entered just the command name in the Commands field. A text editor, however, normally lets you specify the name of a file you want to work on. For example, if you include a file name with the command that starts the MS-DOS Editor, DOS opens the file if it exists or creates the file if it doesn't exist; if you don't include a file name, DOS starts the Editor without opening or creating a file.

To tell the Shell that you want a program item to accept a parameter, you include a percent sign followed by the numeral 1 (%1) in the Commands field. For the MS-DOS Editor, type *edit %1*. (For a different editor or a word processor, type the appropriate startup command. For example, type *word %1* if you're using Microsoft Word.) Now tab to the Startup Directory field.

Specifying a Path

If you routinely use directories in your work, you probably organize your data files in different directories, depending on what they contain or what type of application you use them with. Your word processing files, for example, might be categorized by type (letters, memos, reports), client, department, or in any of a number of other ways.

In setting up a program to run from the Shell, you can use the Startup Directory field in the Add Program dialog box to change to a particular drive or directory whenever you start the associated program. If you write a lot of letters, for example, you might change to your LETTERS directory when you start your word processor.

To see how the startup directory works, tell the Shell to use the root directory of drive B whenever it starts by typing *b:* in the Startup Directory field. Now tab to the Application Shortcut Key field.

Specifying a Shortcut Key

Just as some Shell menu selections have keyboard shortcuts—F8 for Copy in the File Menu of the File List, for example—you can specify a shortcut key combination for a program item or program group. The shortcut key must be Shift, Alt, or Ctrl, combined with another key on the keyboard. To make Alt-E the shortcut key for the Editor, press Alt plus the E key. *Alt+E* appears in the Application Shortcut Key field. Finally, tab to the Pause After Exit field.

Controlling the Pause Message

When you tried the Memory Check examples, you saw that the Shell displayed *Press any key to return to MS-DOS Shell* and waited to let you read the message and press a key. This pause isn't required, however, and you can control it with the Pause After Exit field. There's an X between the brackets now, to show that the option is turned on. Press the Spacebar (or click on the X) to turn the option off.

Chances are you won't want to keep anyone from using the Editor, so there's no need for a password. Besides, you've already seen how it works, so press Enter to tell the Shell you've finished with the dialog box. Instead of returning to the Program List, however, the Shell displays another dialog box titled Add Program.

Designing Your Own Dialog Box

The command you entered for the Editor was *edit %1*, telling the Shell that you wanted the command to accept one parameter, a file name, of your choice. The Shell will have to prompt for this parameter, and the dialog box you're looking at now lets you specify the contents of the dialog box that displays the prompt.

The cursor is at the beginning of the Window Title field; this field specifies the title displayed in the bar at the top of the dialog box (*Add Program* in the dialog box you're working with now). Type *File To Edit* and tab to the Program Information field.

The Program Information field specifies the explanatory text that appears below the title but still at the top of the dialog box. (In the box you're working in now, the text reads *Fill in information for %1 prompt dialog.*) Type *Enter the name of the file to be edited (or press Enter to start the Editor with no file).* Tab to the Prompt Message field.

The Prompt Message field specifies the text that appears to the left of the field to be filled in (here it's *Prompt Message* for the field you're working in now). The Edit command parameter must be a file name, so type *File name:* and tab to the Default Parameters field.

The Default Parameters field lets you specify a value that the Shell fills in for the command parameter. (You'll see how this works shortly.) Type *fred*, then press Enter to complete the definition of the Text Editor program item. The Shell displays the Text Files program list again, this time with two items: Main and Text Editor.

Testing the New Program Item

To try out your new program item, check that the diskette with DOSSHELL.INI is in drive B. Highlight Text Editor and press Enter to start the program. First, the Shell displays the File To Edit dialog box that you just designed:

Check the title of the dialog box, the instruction line at the top, and the prompt to the left of the entry field. They should match the text you entered in the Window Title, Program Information, and Prompt Message fields a moment ago.

The entry field contains *fred*, the default parameter you specified in the Default Parameters field. If you pressed Enter now, the Shell would tell DOS to run the Edit command, using FRED as the name of the file to edit. Because there is no such file, DOS would create it and the Editor would show you a blank screen.

Instead, request the DOSSHELL.INI file that you copied to the diskette in drive B earlier in the chapter. The Shell erases all of the default file name as soon as you start typing, so just type *dosshell.ini*.

Now press Enter. Drive B becomes active, and soon the screen fills with the lines of DOSSHELL.INI.

Right now, you're just verifying that the Text Editor program item works, so select Exit from the Editor's File menu (or use the appropriate Quit command if you're using a different program). The Editor quits, and the Shell screen returns, showing your Text Files group and its two choices.

The Disk Utilities Program Group

You can learn still more about defining program items and groups by selecting a program item from the Disk Utilities group and seeing how the fields are filled out. Just don't change anything. For example, return to the Main screen and select Format in the Disk Utilities group. The screen looks like this:

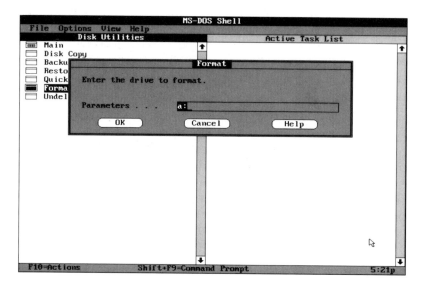

Notice that the Parameters field is filled in with *a:*, suggesting that the diskette in drive A should be formatted. Now press Esc (not Enter) to return to the Program List and, with Format still highlighted, select Properties from the File menu to see how the Format program item is defined. The screen should look like this:

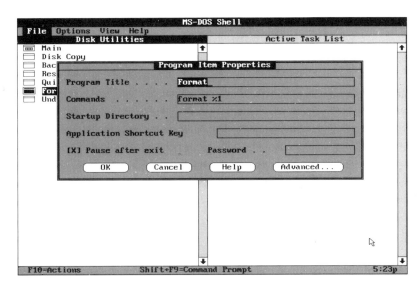

One parameter, %1, is specified in this dialog box. To see how this parameter is defined, press Enter or click on OK. The Shell displays the Program Item Properties dialog box for %1:

Compare the fields of this dialog box with the dialog box itself, as illustrated earlier; the text in the fields matches the text that defines the title, instructions, and prompt of the Format dialog box. Press Enter or click on OK to clear the screen.

The Editor example showed the degree to which you can tailor the Shell to your own use. Although the example prepared only one command for DOS to carry out (the Edit command with a file name as a parameter), remember that you can specify more than one command, if necessary, by separating the commands with a semicolon (surround each with blank spaces).

You've also seen how to specify and define a parameter for the Edit command. In your own work, you can specify more than one parameter, each of which has its own dialog box with separate instructions, prompts, and default values. Together, multiple commands and multiple parameters should let you add any program you like to the Shell Program List, providing all the startup information the program might need.

You added only one program item to the Text Files group, but you could add several more, using the same method you used to add the Editor. If you want, you can experiment with programs that are part of DOS. You could, for example, add an item named Display File that runs a Type command.

Using the same techniques, you could add program groups such as Desktop Publishing or Financial Management to run all the application programs you use. With the Task Swapper, you could then start several of your application programs and switch among them without having to exit from one to start another. With the help of the Associate command on the File List's File menu, you can even set up your system so that the Shell starts a particular program and opens the specified file whenever you choose a file name with a specified extension.

Just as you can structure your file system to match your work, you can structure the program choices of the Shell to run the programs that you use.

Deleting a Program Group

When you're through experimenting with the DOS Editor program item, you can delete the program item from the Text Files group, and you can delete the Text Files group itself. A short while ago, you deleted the Mem Command program item. Deleting a program group is just as easy; the only catch is that you cannot delete a group that contains any program items. In this respect, deleting a program group is like deleting a directory: It works only if the group or directory is empty.

To return the Program List to its original state, return to the Program List Main screen if necessary. Next, activate your Text Files group and highlight the Text Editor program item. Choose Delete from the File menu and press Enter or click on OK when the Shell displays the Delete Item dialog box. (If you've added other program items to this group, delete them too if you want to remove the Text Files group from the Program List area.)

Once you've deleted all of the program items in a group, you can delete the group itself. It's the same procedure you just followed. First, return to the Program List Main screen. Next, highlight Text Files, choose Delete from the File menu, and press Enter or click on OK to delete the group. When you're finished, the Shell displays the Program List Main screen again, this time without the Text Files group.

This chapter hasn't covered all the features of the Shell, but it has shown you the most common ones. Because the operating techniques are fairly consistent throughout the Shell and because the Help information is quite thorough, you should be able to learn what isn't covered by selecting the menu items and using the Help feature to guide you.

CHAPTER 11

CREATING AND EDITING FILES OF TEXT

Although computers were once thought of primarily as machines for mathematics—you still occasionally hear them referred to as number crunchers—word processing is the most common use of personal computers today. Word processing programs offer a stunning array of features, accommodating not only the usual memos and reports, but even book-length documents that include multiple columns, a table of contents, an index, and many graphics.

But this array of capabilities is a mixed blessing because a high-end word processor is a large program requiring a significant commitment from both the computer (memory and disk space) and the person using it (learning time).

Beginning with version 5, DOS includes a simple menu-based text editor that offers a good alternative to a word processor for smaller jobs. The official name for this program is the *MS-DOS Editor,* but this chapter will use the name *Edit* instead, both because it's simpler and because that's the name of the command that starts the MS-DOS Editor.

Edit lacks many of the capabilities of a word processor: You must press Enter at the end of each line, for example, and you can't control the capabilities of your printer much beyond the simple printing of text. These very limitations, however, make Edit small, fast, and easy to learn. It's admirably suited for writing short memos and lists and for creating sets of DOS commands known as batch files. If you have used a word processor, especially one with drop-down menus, Edit's basic operation should feel familiar.

This chapter shows you around Edit by using a situation that could occur in any office: You're in charge of a project, and your team has completed several spreadsheets, a 10-page proposal, and a cover letter. You've copied these files to a diskette and want the team to review the results one last time before the presentation. You're going to send copies of the diskette to the team members, and you need a short memo to tell them what's on it.

Note: If you don't have version 5 of DOS, you have a different editor named Edlin, which is described in Chapter 12. If you are considering upgrading to version 5, you might want to scan this chapter. Otherwise, go on to Chapter 12.

USING THE KEYBOARD AND THE MOUSE

Like many application programs, Edit responds to either the keyboard or a mouse for most operations. On-screen, the keyboard cursor is represented, as usual, by a flashing underline; the mouse is represented by a rectangular block (the mouse pointer). You use the keyboard and the mouse much as you do in the Shell, so if you haven't yet tried out the Shell, turn to the heading "Using the Keyboard and Mouse" near the beginning of Chapter 10 for a description of how to display a menu and select a menu item or a file name. The text you find there, plus Figure 10-2 on page 213, summarizes the techniques and defines possibly unfamiliar mouse terms, such as click, double-click, drag, and select. The first few examples in this chapter give instructions for both keyboard and mouse, but the remaining examples simply ask you to select a menu or a menu item.

In addition to choosing from menus, however, you'll frequently use two techniques with Edit that you don't need in the Shell: positioning the cursor where you want to edit text, and selecting a block of text. The following descriptions provide some needed background information. Examples later in the chapter provide specifics.

Positioning the Cursor

You can use either the keyboard or the mouse to position the cursor. You'll probably find yourself using both at different times, depending on where your hands are when you have to move the cursor. Figure 11-1 shows the main cursor-movement keys and their effect.

Key	Moves the cursor to
Right arrow	Next character
Left arrow	Previous character
Up arrow	Previous line
Down arrow	Next line
End	Last character in the line
Home	First nonblank character in the line
Ctrl-Right arrow	Beginning of the next word
Ctrl-Left arrow	Beginning of the previous word
Ctrl-Enter	Beginning of next line
Ctrl-End	End of the document
Ctrl-Home	Beginning of the document

Figure 11-1. *Edit's cursor-control keys.*

To position the cursor with the mouse, move the mouse pointer to the text location you want, and then press the left mouse button.

Selecting a Block of Text

Some edit operations, such as moving and copying text, require you to select the block of text to be affected. Other operations, such as printing, let you select a portion of the document if you wish; otherwise, the action applies to the entire document.

To select a block of text with the keyboard, position the cursor at the first character to be selected, hold down the Shift key, and then use any of the cursor-movement keys described in Figure 11-1 to select the text you want. Edit highlights the selected text as you move the cursor. When you release the Shift key, the block remains selected until you move the cursor.

To select a block of text with the mouse, position the mouse pointer on the first character to be selected, press and hold the left mouse button, and move the mouse pointer to the last character of the block. The selected text is highlighted as you move the mouse. Just as when you select text with the keyboard, the text remains selected until you move the cursor again or position the mouse pointer elsewhere and click the left mouse button.

STARTING EDIT

To use the Edit command, you need two files named EDIT.COM and QBASIC.EXE. If you're using DOS from a fixed disk, these files are in your DOS directory. If you're using DOS from diskettes, check that EDIT.COM and QBASIC.EXE are on the diskette in drive A. To keep the sample files from cluttering your system, put a formatted diskette in drive B.

All you do to start Edit from the DOS system prompt is type its name:

`C:\>edit`

DOS copies the Edit program into memory, and after a moment Edit displays its opening screen.

The screen looks substantially different from a normal DOS display and is noticeably different from the opening Shell screen, too. If you take a closer look, however, you can see that the Edit screen has the same essential features as the Shell: A large window in which you work, a menu bar across the top, scroll bars along the edges, and a bar across the bottom telling you how to carry out basic operations. For the most part, you can think of the differences between Edit and the Shell as comparable to the differences between a sedan and a station wagon: They don't look the same, but if you can drive one, you can drive the other. And, as you'll soon see, Edit is easy to work with.

HELP

Right now, you should be looking at a large dialog box in the middle of the screen. As in the Shell, dialog boxes are Edit's means of displaying and requesting information. The flashing cursor suggests that you *<Press Enter to see the Survival Guide>*, so press Enter. The screen changes to this:

```
 File  Edit  Search  Options                                    Help
┌──────────────────── HELP: Survival Guide ────────────────────────┐
│                                                                  ↑ │
│ Using the MS-DOS Editor:                                         │ │
│                                                                  │ │
│   ▪ To activate the MS-DOS Editor menu bar, press Alt.           │ │
│   ▪ To activate menus and commands, press the highlighted letter.│ │
│   ▪ To move between menus and commands, use the direction keys.  │ │
│   ▪ To get help on a selected menu, command, or dialog box, press F1. │
│   ▪ To exit Help, press Esc.                                     │ │
│                                                                  │ │
│ Browsing the MS-DOS Editor Help system:                          │ │
│                                                                  │ │
│   ▪ To select one of the following topics, press the Tab key or the first │
│     letter of the topic. Then press the Enter key to see information on: │
│                                                                  │ │
│     ◀Getting Started▶  Loading and using the MS-DOS Editor and the │ │
│                        MS-DOS Editor Help system                 │ │
│     ◀Keyboard▶         Editing and navigating text and MS-DOS Editor Help │
│                                                                  │ │
│ Tip: These topics are also available from the Help menu.         │ │
│                                                                  ↓ │
├─────────────────────────── Untitled ─────────────────────────────┤
│                                                                  │
└──────────────────────────────────────────────────────────────────┘
 <F1=Help> <F6=Window> <Esc=Cancel> <Ctrl+F1=Next> <Alt+F1=Back>
```

The Survival Guide is the introductory screen to Edit's online help. (*Online* is a venerable computer term meaning that a program or a device is available; hence, online help.) Most of the information you need to operate Edit is available from online help whenever Edit's running.

As in the Shell, Edit's help feature explains what you can do at any point in using the program. And, as in the Shell, you can request two types of help: general information and specific instructions (known as context-sensitive help) for using a particular command or dialog box. The examples in this chapter direct you to display both types of help, but you can also request assistance any time you want by pressing F1 or by choosing from the Help menu. Because Edit's Help differs substantially from the Shell's, the next few pages describe Edit's Help in some detail.

Some help screens include several topics you can choose among. These topics are enclosed in left-pointing and right-pointing arrowheads. The cursor right now, for example, is under the *G* in the topic *Getting Started*. To see Edit's own description of how to use it and its help feature, select this topic by pressing Enter or by moving the mouse pointer anywhere between the arrowheads and clicking the right mouse button. Edit responds by displaying a set of topics on *Getting Started*:

At the top of the Help window, Edit displays *HELP: Getting Started* to remind you of the topic you chose. Below this are three choices: *Getting Started*, *Keyboard*, and *Back*. *Getting Started* is highlighted to show that it is the current topic; its choices are displayed in the lower part of the Help window. *Keyboard* displays additional help, and *Back* returns you to the previous help screen.

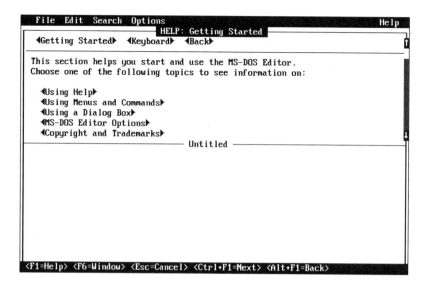

To see a little more help, select *Using Help*. Either press the Tab key until the cursor is under the *U* and then press Enter, or move the mouse pointer anywhere between the arrowheads and press the right mouse button. Edit now displays the *Using Help* screen:

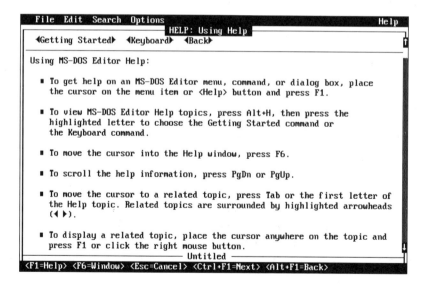

This screen describes the help capabilities and how you use them. After you have read the description, press Enter or select *Back* to return to the *Getting Started* screen.

The bottom line of the screen displays some additional help information—in this case, the effect of pressing function and other special keys. No matter what you're doing with Edit, the bottom line displays information specific to what you're doing. Right now, the bottom line tells you what happens if you press the following keys:

Key	Description	Effect of pressing
F1	Help	Display the help screen of the selected item.
F6	Window	Switch windows. In this case, move the cursor to the Edit window (now labeled *Untitled*); if the cursor were in the Edit window, F6 would move it to the Help window.
Esc	Cancel	Close the Help window and return to the Edit window.
Ctrl-F1	Next	Display the next help topic. (Steps through all the help topics, whether or not they apply to what you're doing right now.)
Alt-F1	Back	Display the previous help topic.

Customizing Help

Right now, the Edit window where you create documents is between the Help window and the bottom line. If you're using a color display, the background color of the Edit window probably isn't the same as that of the Help window. The Edit window is labeled *Untitled* because you didn't name a file when you started Edit.

When you're using Help, you can leave all or part of its current display visible and move between the Edit window and the Help window by pressing F6 or by placing the mouse pointer in the window you want and clicking the left button. That way, you can work on a file and yet refer to help whenever you need it. As you may already have noticed, however, the help screens vary in size. Some, like the one you're looking at now, take about half the screen. Others take only a line or two, and some, like the *Using Help* screen, take almost all the available space.

To help you control your workspace, Edit lets you increase or decrease the size of the active window—the one that contains the cursor. With the keyboard, press Alt-Plus (Alt and the plus sign) to make the active window larger; press Alt-Minus (Alt and the minus sign) to make the active window smaller. With the mouse, simply place the pointer at the top of the Edit window, hold down either mouse button, and move the window border up or down until the Help and Edit windows are the size you want.

If you resize windows and find that either window is too small to display an entire help topic or the file you're working on, you can either change the size again or use the PgUp, PgDown, and arrow keys to scroll through the text with the keyboard. You can also scroll with the mouse by using the scroll bar at the right edge of the active window.

Viewing both windows can be helpful when you're exploring Edit on your own, but for now press Esc to clear the help screen.

ENTERING LINES

It's time to enter the first few lines of the sample memo. If you make a typing error, you can backspace and correct it before pressing Enter. But don't worry if you press Enter before you realize a line contains errors; as you'll learn, it's easy to correct mistakes. Type the following lines, pressing Enter at the end of each line (press Enter without typing anything where there's a blank line):

```
This diskette has 5 files on it.
Please check the spreadsheets and print the
documents to make sure they agree with our
assumptions.

You can review the documents on the
screen. To check the proposal, type:

TYPE B:PROPOSAL.DOC | MORE

This displays one screen at a time.
Press the Spacebar to display the
next screen, or press Ctrl-Break to stop.

Let's do this quickly; it's due Thursday.

Tom
```

The screen shows the lines you have entered.

ADDING TEXT TO A FILE

You insert text in a file by positioning the cursor where the text is to be inserted and typing the new text. For example, to insert the words *and recommendations* following *assumptions*, use the arrow keys or the mouse to position the cursor under the period that follows *assumptions*, and type *and recommendations*.

Now suppose you also decide to add a title to your memo. Use the mouse or press Ctrl-Home to move the cursor to the beginning of the file, the *T* in the word *This*. Type the following lines (press Enter twice after *team* to add a blank line):

```
Final Project Review -- 10/16/91
To: Project team
```

Oops. You also wanted a blank line between the title lines. Move the cursor to the *T* in *To* and press Enter.

Now you decide you want to include a list of file names after the first sentence. Position the cursor at the beginning of the line that starts *Please check*. Press Enter to insert a blank line, press Tab to indent the line, then type the following (don't forget to press Enter at the end of the line):

```
FORECAST.PLN
```

Look at the cursor. It moved down to the next line, but it isn't at the left margin. It's indented so that it's directly below the beginning of the line you just inserted. What's going on?

WHERE'S THE MARGIN?

If you indent a line with spaces or tabs (which Edit converts to spaces), Edit assumes that you want the next line to start with the same indent. This assumption can be quite a convenience when you're writing an outline or other type of document that has many indented lines, and that's why pressing the Home key moves the cursor to the first non-blank character in a line, not to the left margin.

Type the following lines to enter four more file names in the indented list, pressing Enter at the end of each:

```
OPTION1.PLN
OPTION2.PLN
LETTER.DOC
PROPOSAL.DOC
```

The assumption that you want to continue an indent isn't always true, of course, so sometimes you'll have to erase the spaces Edit inserts at the beginning of a line. To reduce the inconvenience, Edit lets you erase all the spaces at the beginning of a line by pressing Backspace once when the cursor is under the first nonblank character in an indented line.

Try it. Press Enter once to put a blank line between the last file name in the list and the first line of the following paragraph. Check that the cursor is under the *P* in *Please*, which should be indented eight spaces. Press Backspace; Edit erases the indent and moves the cursor to the left margin.

This completes the first draft of the memo. The illustration on the next page shows how your screen should look.

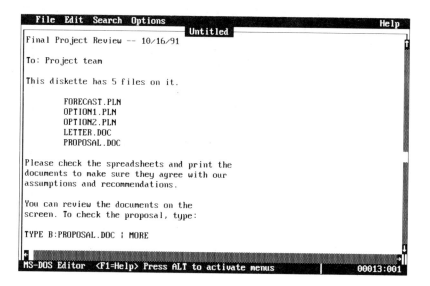

PRINTING A FILE

A file stored on disk is perfect for distribution but is otherwise of limited value. In most cases, you want a printed copy of the documents you create. To print this version of the memo, make sure your printer is turned on, and then select Print from Edit's File menu:

▶ Using the keyboard, press Alt, F, and then P.

▶ Using the mouse, click on File in the menu bar at the top of the screen, and then click on Print.

Note: From now on, use keystroke or mouse sequences like this whenever you're asked to select a command from a particular menu.

Edit responds with a dialog box asking whether you want to print the entire document or just the part that is selected. The small dot in parentheses tells you that Edit proposes to print the complete document. This is what you want, so press Enter or click on OK; Edit should print the file. If your printer isn't ready, Edit displays the message *Device fault.* Check the printer and try again by pressing Enter.

SAVING A FILE

Your memo so far is stored just in the computer's memory, not on disk. If you turned the computer off, the document would be lost. To save the file on disk, select Save As from the File menu. Edit displays a dialog box that asks you to name the file:

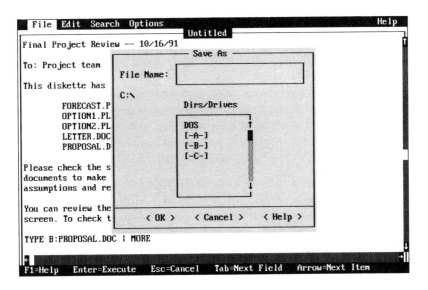

The cursor is in the text box titled File Name because Edit is waiting for you to type a file name. Below File Name is the name of the current directory (it should read either C:\ or A:\). The box that follows, titled Dirs/Drives, lets you save the file in a different directory or even on a disk in a different drive.

Edit can save a file to any directory or drive it can find on your system. For this example, you'll simply type a drive letter and a file name in the File Name text box. Check that a formatted diskette is in drive B and type:

```
b:memo.txt
```

Now press Enter or choose OK at the bottom of the dialog box. If Edit displays another dialog box saying *Insert Diskette for drive B:*, press Enter. The file is saved, as you can see from the title block at the top of the screen, which has changed from *Untitled* to *MEMO.TXT*.

More About Directories and Drives

As you saw in Chapters 8 and 9, directories are invaluable tools, especially if you use a fixed disk. Before you move on, choose the File Save As and File Open commands, and take a few moments to examine the dialog boxes they display a little more closely. (Press Esc or choose Cancel to clear the screen when you're through.)

To help you find and save files in any directory on any drive, File Save As and File Open both cause Edit to display a Dirs/Drives text box. In it is a list that begins with the names of all subdirectories of the current directory and ends with the names of all the drives on your system. The drives are easy to recognize because they are enclosed in square brackets like this: [-A-].

To use the Dirs/Drives text box, move the cursor with the Tab key, use the arrow keys to highlight the directory or drive you want, and press Enter, or double-click with the mouse to change the current drive/directory. Repeat the same steps if you want to move farther down the directory tree.

Once you've chosen a new drive or directory in the File Save As dialog box, the highlight returns to the File Name text box, so you can type the name you want to give the file. If you're using the File Open dialog box, you can either type a file name or choose a file from the list displayed in the Files box.

The Dirs/Drives text box is particularly useful when you want to scan your drives and directories, either to store a file or to load one whose location you're not sure of.

DELETING TEXT

To delete the character at the location of the cursor, press Del. To delete more than one character, select them and either press Del or use the Edit Clear command. Using either the keyboard or the mouse, you can select any amount of text, from a single character to the entire document, as described early in this chapter.

To practice deleting text, you'll begin by deleting the words *on it* at the end of the line that precedes the list of file names. Position the cursor under the period at the end of the line. Although it seems as if you're starting at the wrong end, remember that you can extend the selection either to the left or to the right. Hold down the Shift key and press the Left arrow key until *on it* and the preceding blank are highlighted. Now, simply press Del or choose Clear from the Edit menu. The words are gone.

To delete an entire line and not leave any odd line spacing in your document, you delete everything: text, blank spaces, even the invisible carriage return that Edit uses to mark the end of a line. Suppose, for example, you decide not to include the file named LETTER.DOC and want to delete the entire line from the memo. Simply highlighting the file name won't do the job because the carriage return will still be there, creating a blank line. Instead, start by positioning the cursor. If you're using the keyboard, hold down Ctrl and press Enter several times to move the cursor to the *L* in *LETTER*. Press Backspace to delete the indent. Now hold down the Shift key and press the Down arrow key once. The entire line is selected.

With the mouse it's even easier: Position the cursor at the left edge of the line, press and hold the left mouse button, and move the mouse slightly to drag the mouse pointer one row down.

When the line is selected, press Del or choose Edit Clear to delete the line.

ENDING AN EDITING SESSION

To leave Edit and return to DOS, select Exit from the File menu. You have changed the file since the last time you saved it, so Edit asks you whether it should save the file first; select Yes. Edit saves the file, then ends and returns to DOS, which displays the system prompt.

If you make some changes to a file, then decide you don't want to change the file after all, you can cancel the editing session without saving the changes by selecting No when Edit asks what you want to do.

EDITING AN EXISTING TEXT FILE

When you type *edit* followed by the name of a file, Edit checks to see if the file you named exists. If the file exists, Edit copies the file into memory; if the file doesn't exist, Edit shows you an empty window but uses the file name as a title and remembers the file name when you save the file.

To work with the file you just created, type the following:

```
C:\>edit b:memo.txt
```

Edit starts and displays the memo.

Copying and Moving Text

You can copy or move text from one place in a document to another by using a special area of Edit's memory called the Clipboard. Copying, of course, leaves the text in the original location unchanged, while moving erases the text from its original location.

To copy text, you first copy it to the Clipboard, then copy it from the Clipboard to the cursor location. (This is called *paste,* from cut and paste.) Suppose you wanted to copy the list of file names to the end of the memo, following the signature line. First, select the file names. To use the keyboard, position the cursor under the F in FORECAST.PLN, hold down either Shift key, and press the Down arrow key three times; to use the mouse, move the mouse pointer to the F, hold down the left mouse button, and move the mouse down until all four lines are highlighted.

Next, select the Edit menu. All the choices show a highlighted letter; the second choice is Copy, with a highlighted C (notice that the shortcut key for copying to the Clipboard is Ctrl-Ins); click on Copy or press C. The Edit menu disappears. There's no indication that anything has happened, but Edit has copied the four lines to the Clipboard.

Now move the cursor down to the line that follows *Tom* and select the Edit menu again. This time, only Paste shows a highlighted letter, meaning that it's the only valid choice from the menu (its shortcut key is Shift-Ins). Paste is an option only when something is on the Clipboard, so the dark characters and the highlighted P tell you that the lines were indeed copied to the Clipboard. Press P, and the four file names appear in the new location.

Moving text is almost the same as copying; the only difference is that you select Cut instead of Copy from the Edit menu. To move the new set of file names back immediately following the original list, select the lines you just pasted and select Cut from the Edit menu (the shortcut key for Cut is Shift-Del). The lines disappear from the screen, just as if you had deleted them. But move the cursor up to the blank line that follows the last file name in the original location and press Shift-Ins (the shortcut key for Paste). The second list of file names appears immediately below the first.

Pasting from the Clipboard doesn't erase its contents. Press Shift-Ins again, and the four lines of file names are inserted again. You should now see 12 file names.

Copying, cutting, and pasting make it easy to rearrange a document. You don't want to keep this version of the memo, so select Open from the File menu, type *b:memo.txt* in the File Name text box, and select No when Edit asks if you want to save the loaded file. The changed version of the file is replaced by the original.

SEARCHING FOR A GROUP OF CHARACTERS

As a file gets longer, it takes you longer to find a particular word or line, and there's more chance that you'll miss it. Edit eliminates this problem by searching for any character or group of characters you specify.

This memo isn't long enough to require that sort of help, but you can still see how it works. Suppose you wanted to check the names of all the files whose extension is DOC. Select Find from the Search menu. Edit asks you what you want to find and proposes whatever word the cursor is currently beneath. Type *doc* in the Find What text box and press Enter.

Almost immediately, Edit highlights *DOC* in *PROPOSAL.DOC*. Notice that although you typed *doc*, Edit found *DOC*, too. As you'll see in a moment, you can tell Edit whether to distinguish between uppercase and lowercase letters.

If you want to find the same characters again, you don't have to repeat the whole process: Just press F3, which tells Edit to repeat the last search. This time it highlights *doc* in *documents*. That's not quite what you had in mind, but it's perfectly normal behavior for Edit: It searches for the characters you specify in either uppercase or lowercase, anywhere within a word, unless you specify otherwise.

Select Find from the Search menu again (it should show *doc* in the Find What text box). First, type *DOC* to replace *doc*. Next, notice the option labeled Match Upper/Lowercase. Select the option by pressing Tab and then pressing the Spacebar, or by clicking the mouse anywhere in the option. An X appears inside the brackets.

Now press Enter or choose OK to search again. Edit jumps down and highlights *DOC* in the line beginning *TYPE B:PROPOSAL.DOC*. Press F3 to repeat the search, and the highlight moves up to the preceding PROPOSAL.DOC. Now press F3 again; instead of highlighting *doc* in *documents*, Edit again highlights DOC in the line beginning *TYPE*. You told Edit you didn't want to find *doc*, just *DOC*.

REPLACING ONE GROUP OF CHARACTERS WITH ANOTHER

One of the most common reasons you'll want to find a particular word or group of characters in a document is so that you can change it. Edit will not only find the characters for you, as you just saw, it will also make the change for you. Suppose you want to change the file extension PLN to XLS wherever it occurs in the memo.

Select Change from the Search menu. Edit displays the Change dialog box:

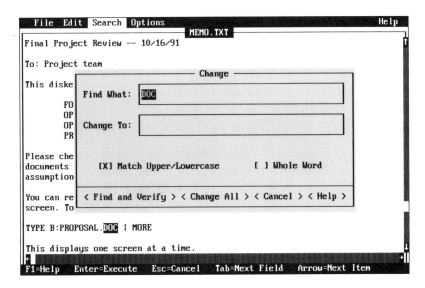

In addition to the Find What text box you saw in the Find dialog box, there's a Change To text box. The Find What text box should contain *DOC*; you want to change every occurrence of PLN to XLS, so type *PLN*. Move to the Change To text box and type *XLS*. Leave the Match Upper/Lowercase option turned on so that Edit will search only for PLN and not pln. Find and Verify is highlighted at the bottom of the dialog box as the action to take, so press Enter to start the search.

Edit highlights the first occurrence of PLN (in *FORECAST.PLN*) and asks you whether to change or skip this occurrence. Press Enter (or click on Change) to change it; Edit displays the next occurrence and repeats the question. Change this occurrence, too. When Edit displays the last occurrence of PLN (in *OPTION2.PLN*), change it as well. Press Enter or click OK when Edit tells you *Change complete*. The screen shows that all three file extensions have changed from PLN to XLS.

To tell Edit to change all occurrences without prompting for verification, you would select Change All instead of Find and Verify.

INSERTING AND OVERSTRIKING TEXT

You probably used the Backspace key to correct typing errors while you were entering the memo. After writing a memo or a report, however, you'll usually want to make some changes after you read through the first draft. To change text after you have entered it, you start by positioning the cursor where you want to make the change. At that point you can delete incorrect characters, insert new ones, or type correct characters in place of the incorrect ones (the latter is called *overstrike*). The next few examples show you how to make typical changes in a document.

To change the word *Project* to *Product* in the first line, move the cursor to the *j* and press the Insert key. The cursor changes from an underline to a flashing block. When you press Insert, you alternate back and forth between inserting characters (signified by the flashing underline) and replacing characters (signified by the flashing block). Now whatever you type won't be inserted; it will replace what is on the screen. Type *du*; the new characters replace the old, changing *Project* to *Product*.

Press Insert again to change the cursor back to an underline, so that characters you type are inserted.

Insert the word *New* before *Project* in the second title line by moving the cursor to the *P* and typing *New* followed by a space (but don't press Enter, because you don't want to enter a carriage return character). The remainder of the line moves over to make room for the new characters.

Next, change the 5 to a 4 in the third line and change the period at the end of the third line to a colon. Position the cursor under the 5, press Ins to change to overstrike, and type *4*. Then move the flashing block to the period and type a colon. Press Ins to return to inserting rather than overstriking characters.

Finally, add a file description to the second file name (OPTION1.XLS). Move the cursor to the space after *XLS*, press the Spacebar three times, and type *Higher sales*. Do the same to add the file description *No staff increase* three spaces after the third file name (OPTION2.XLS).

COPYING FROM ANOTHER FILE

Suppose you had another file that contained the mailing address of the project team members, and you wanted to include that list at the beginning of the memo. You wouldn't have to type the list; you could simply copy it from the other file. You can try this feature by creating another file of addresses and copying it into MEMO.TXT.

You'll create a file named ADDRESS.TXT that contains six dummy address lines. First, save MEMO.TXT by selecting Save from the File menu, and then erase the file from memory by selecting New from the File menu. Edit clears the screen to show you that you're starting a new file.

Next, type the following line:

```
XXX ADDRESS LIST XXX
```

Now make five more copies of the line: Select the line (make sure that the entire line, from the left margin to the right edge of the screen, is highlighted), press Ctrl-Ins to copy it to the Clipboard, press Home to shrink the highlight, and press Shift-Ins five times to copy the lines. You should see six identical lines. Copy all six of the lines to the Clipboard, and then save the file by selecting Save As from the File menu, typing *b:address.txt*, and pressing Enter.

Now copy the lines from the Clipboard into a different file. Load MEMO.TXT by selecting Open from the File menu and typing *b:memo.txt* in the File Name box. You want to paste the address list just after *To: New Project team*, so position the cursor at the beginning of the blank line below *To*. Press Enter to add an extra blank line for spacing. Now press Shift-Ins to insert the six lines from the Clipboard. This is the final version of the memo; the screen should look like this:

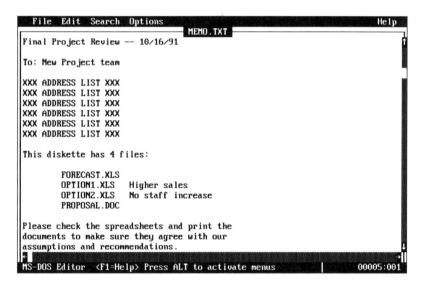

Save this final version of the memo. Now for something a bit less tedious before you leave Edit.

CHANGING THE SCREEN DISPLAY

If you have a color monitor, Edit probably displayed white text against a blue background when you first started it. You can change this color scheme to any combination of foreground (text) and background (screen) color your display is capable of showing. Select Display from the Options menu. The screen should look like this:

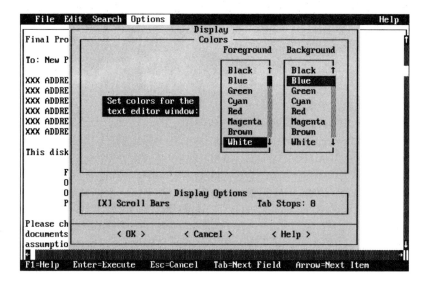

Before you start customizing your display, turn to Edit's Help again, this time to see how Edit can advise you on whatever you happen to be doing when you request Help. Press F1, and Edit displays the Help box that tells you how to use the Display dialog box. Read the explanation, and then press Esc to remove the Help box.

The cursor is now in the text box that lists possible foreground colors. Using the arrow keys or the mouse, select different colors (you can move the cursor between the foreground and background color boxes by pressing Tab and Shift-Tab). The text block to the left of the color boxes changes to show the effect of each color.

When you find a combination you like, press Enter to return to Edit. It will use these colors the next time you start it. (If you prefer the standard combination, press Esc to cancel the dialog box; Edit leaves the colors unchanged.) Leave Edit by choosing Exit from the File menu.

CHAPTER SUMMARY

This chapter showed you the basics of using Edit. You're ready to use it for many of the short text-editing jobs that don't require a word processor.

There's more to Edit, such as different methods of cutting and pasting text and shortcut keys based on the WordStar word processor. You can explore further on your own, using Help as your guide: Display a help screen—the Keyboard help screens are a good place to start—and use the F6 key to switch back and forth between the Help and Edit windows as you try out new features. You'll find Help the most patient instructor you've ever had.

CHAPTER 12

THE EDLIN
TEXT EDITOR

E dlin is the text editor included with all versions of DOS. If you're using version 5 of DOS, you'll probably prefer the MS-DOS Editor, described in Chapter 11. But Edlin remains in the book because it's still part of DOS. Over the years, it has been a quick and easy DOS alternative to starting and using a word processing program for short editing jobs.

In this chapter, you'll learn the basics of using Edlin for creating and editing short text files, including batch files, which you'll encounter two chapters from now. If you have version 5 of DOS, skip ahead to Chapter 13, ''Taking Control of Your System.''

The example here assumes a fairly common situation: You're a project leader. Your team has completed several spreadsheets, a proposal, and a cover letter. You have copied these files to a diskette and want the team to review them before the big presentation. You're going to send copies of the diskette to the team members, and you need a short memo to tell them what's on it.

The example requires one formatted diskette. If you have one diskette drive, put the diskette in it. If you have two diskette drives, put the diskette in drive B.

Edlin is an external command file. Whenever you use Edlin, DOS must be able to find the command program on disk. If you aren't using a fixed disk, verify that EDLIN.COM is on the system disk in drive A.

CREATING A NEW TEXT FILE

Each time you start Edlin, you must give it the name of a file to work on. If the file already exists, Edlin copies it into memory; if the file doesn't exist, Edlin creates a file with the name you specified.

To start Edlin, you simply type its name, so start the program and create a file named MEMO.TXT on the disk in drive B by typing the following (press any key if DOS prompts for a diskette in drive B):

```
C:\>edlin b:memo.txt
```

Edlin tells you that MEMO.TXT is a new file and waits for a command:

```
New file
*_
```

The asterisk (*) is the Edlin command prompt; it tells you that Edlin is ready for you to type an Edlin command. All you can do with a new file is insert lines. Most Edlin commands are abbreviated as single letters, so type the abbreviation for the Insert command:

```
*i
```

Edlin responds with:

```
1:*_
```

When you use Edlin, you work with a file line by line. To help you keep track of where you are, Edlin displays a line number at the beginning of each line. You use these line numbers with many Edlin commands to tell the program what line or lines you want to work on. Because this is a new file, the first line number is 1. The asterisk following the line number isn't part of the line; it shows you the *current line,* and it is no more a part of your document than the system prompt or the cursor.

As you type lines, you end each by pressing Enter. Edlin then adds the line to the file and moves to the beginning of the next line, where it displays the new line number, an asterisk, and the cursor. To stop inserting, you press Ctrl-Break or Ctrl-C.

ENTERING LINES

It's time to enter the first few lines of the sample memo. If you make a typing error, you can backspace and correct it before pressing Enter. But don't worry if you enter a line with errors; you can correct them later. Type the following lines, but not the line numbers. <Ctrl-Break> means hold down Ctrl and press Break; <Enter> means press Enter without typing anything:

```
 1:*This diskette has 5 files on it.
 2:*FORECAST.PLN
 3:*OPTION1.PLN
 4:*OPTION2.PLN
 5:*LETTER.DOC
 6:*PROPOSAL.DOC
 7:*<Enter>
 8:*Please check the spreadsheets and print the
 9:*documents to make sure they agree with our
10:*assumptions.
11:*<Enter>
12:*You can review the documents on the screen.
13:*To check the proposal, type:
14:*<Enter>
15:*TYPE B:PROPOSAL.DOC | MORE
16:*<Enter>
17:*This displays one screen at a time. Press
18:*the Spacebar to display the next screen,
19:*or press Ctrl-Break to stop.
20:*<Enter>
21:*Let's do this quickly; it's due Thursday.
22:*<Ctrl-Break>

  *_
```

Ctrl-Break shows on your screen as ^C. It tells Edlin you don't want to insert any more lines, so Edlin moves the cursor to the edge of the screen and displays its prompt, *, telling you it's waiting for another command.

DISPLAYING LINES

Although the memo is on the screen now, you want to display your file at other times, too: to see if you have included everything you meant to include; to check what you have done; or to edit your file.

The List command (l) displays one line or a range of lines. If you type a line number followed by l (lowercase L), Edlin displays a maximum of 23 lines (one screenful), starting with the line you specify. For example, use the List command to display the document you just typed, starting at line 1. Type:

```
*1l
```

Edlin responds by displaying the lines you just entered.

To display a range of lines, you precede the l with the numbers, separated by a comma, of the first and last lines you want to see. For example, to display only lines 2 through 6, type:

```
*2,6l
```

Edlin shows you:

```
            2: FORECAST.PLN
            3: OPTION1.PLN
            4: OPTION2.PLN
            5: LETTER.DOC
            6: PROPOSAL.DOC
     *_
```

ADDING LINES TO A FILE

You can insert lines anywhere in an existing file by preceding the Insert command with a line number. Edlin inserts the new line or lines before the line you specify, renumbering the lines that follow the insertion.

For example, to insert a blank line before the list of file names, type:

```
*2i
        2:*<Enter>
        3:*<Ctrl-Break>

     *_
```

To insert lines at the end of a document, use the Insert command and either specify a line number larger than the last line number or use the symbol #, which means "the line after the last line." To use # to add a signature line, type:

```
*#i
     23:*<Enter>
     24:*Tom
     25:*<Ctrl-Break>

*_
```

Now suppose you decide to add a title to your memo. The beginning is line 1, so specify line 1 with the Insert command:

```
*1i
     1:*Final Project Review -- 10/16/91
     2:*<Enter>
     3:*To: Project team
     4:*<Enter>
     5:*<Ctrl-Break>

*_
```

PAGING THROUGH A FILE

Earlier, you displayed the file by including line numbers with the List command. Your file contains 28 lines now and is longer than one screenful, so try the Page command (p) to display it. The Page command lets you page through a file without worrying about line numbers. Start with line 1 and page through the practice memo by typing *1p*. Edlin displays the first 23 lines. Now simply type *p* (and press Enter) to see the rest of the memo.

If you don't specify a line number, the Page command displays the line after the current line and the following 22 lines. The Page command changes the current line to the last line displayed, so you can page through a file just by typing p for each screenful.

ENDING AN EDITING SESSION

When you end an editing session with e (the End Edit command), Edlin stores your file on disk and returns you to DOS. After the file has been stored, DOS displays the system prompt (C:\>). Type the End Edit command:

```
*e.
```

DOS stores the file on the disk and displays the system prompt.

PRINTING A FILE

Edlin doesn't include a print command, but DOS makes it easy to print a file. First, make sure the printer is turned on. Next, use the DOS Copy command to copy the practice file to the printer. Type the following:

```
C:\>copy b:memo.txt prn
```

DOS prints the file and tells you:

1 file(s) copied

Your memo is ready for distribution. For many short jobs, that's all there is to it. Using Edlin, you can create and print a file in only a few minutes.

EDITING AN EXISTING TEXT FILE

There will be times you'll want to change an existing text file—perhaps to add items to a list, delete a sentence or two, or change some wording. Use Edlin now to edit your practice file. Type *edlin*, followed by the name of the file:

```
C:\>edlin b:memo.txt
End of input file
*_
```

This time you're not creating a new file, so Edlin tells you that it has copied your file (the *input* file) into memory. Display the file by typing *p*.

DELETING LINES

You can use Edlin to delete a line by typing the number of the line followed by d (the Delete command). For example, suppose you decide not to include line 10 (LETTER.DOC) in your memo. To delete the line, type:

```
*10d
```

Edlin acknowledges by displaying the * prompt. Use the Page command again to display the first 23 lines. Type:

```
*1p
```

To delete several lines, precede the d with the numbers of the first and last lines to be deleted, separating the numbers with a comma (*number,number* represents a *range* of lines). To delete the heading (lines 1 through 4), type:

```
*1,4d
```

To verify that the lines have been deleted, display the memo again by typing:

```
*1p
```

Edlin responds by displaying the memo without the heading or the file name LET-TER.DOC. Notice that Edlin has renumbered the lines.

CANCELING AN EDITING SESSION

If you change a file, then decide you really don't want the changes, you can cancel the editing session with q (the Quit command) and return to DOS. The revised version of your file won't be stored on disk.

So that you don't inadvertently cancel an editing session and lose your work, Edlin prompts you to confirm the Quit command. Cancel this session by typing:

    *q

Edlin responds:

    Abort edit (Y/N)? _

Type *y*, and Edlin returns you to DOS.

Edit the file again:

```
C:\>edlin b:memo.txt
End of input file
*_
```

Now display the memo by typing *p* to verify that the lines you deleted earlier are still in the version stored on disk.

SEARCHING FOR A GROUP OF CHARACTERS

As a file gets longer, the List and Page commands become less and less efficient ways to display specific parts of a document. If your sample memo were 80 or 90 lines long, for example, it would take several List or Page commands to display it all, because the screen normally displays only 23 lines at a time.

When you want to locate a particular line, you can do so quickly, even if you don't know the line number, by telling Edlin to search for a group of characters (called a *string*) that the line contains. To do this, you type the number of the line where Edlin should begin searching, then type *s* (for the Search command) and the string.

Suppose the sample memo were several pages long and you wanted to delete a file name ending with the extension PLN. Use the Search command and specify PLN as the string to search for. To start searching at the beginning of the file for PLN (note the capitalization), type:

    *1 sPLN

Edlin displays the first line that contains PLN:

        7: FORECAST.PLN
    *_

The line Edlin finds (7 in this case) becomes the current line. If no line contains the string you specified, Edlin responds *Not found.*

Suppose you know that several lines contain the same string. You can broaden the Search command so Edlin shows you each line it finds and asks if it is the one you want. The search continues until you type *y* for *yes* or until Edlin finds no other lines containing the string.

You tell Edlin to prompt in this way by typing a question mark before the s. For example, suppose you know that several lines contain PLN, and you want Edlin to find OPTION2.PLN. Type the following:

```
*1?sPLN
```

Edlin responds as follows. Type *n* or *y* as shown here:

```
        7:*FORECAST.PLN
O.K.? n
        8: OPTION1.PLN
O.K.? n
        9: OPTION2.PLN
O.K.? y
*_
```

As with most Edlin commands, you can also specify a range of lines to search. Later examples show you how to indicate a range, as does the description of the Search command in Appendix C, ''DOS Command Reference.''

EDITING A LINE

Up to this point, you have been editing the memo by inserting and deleting entire lines. You can also edit individual lines with either the Replace command or some special editing keys.

Replacing One String with Another

The Replace command (r), like the Search command, tells Edlin to look for a string of characters. The format of the Replace command is much like the format of the Search command, except that the command ends with the new string that is to replace the old one. If you don't specify a replacement string, Edlin deletes the original string (replaces it with nothing). If you do specify a new string, you must separate the two strings by pressing F6 or Ctrl-Z.

Note: When you press F6 or Ctrl-Z, Edlin displays the keystroke as ^Z. When you see ^Z in the following examples, remember to press F6 or Ctrl-Z.

In the sample memo, suppose you remember that the extension of your document files should be TXT, not DOC. You can use the Replace command to change all occurrences of DOC with one command. If you don't specify an ending line, Edlin assumes you mean the entire file. Type:

```
*1 rDOC^ZTXT
```

Edlin displays each line it changes:

```
        10: LETTER.TXT
        11: PROPOSAL.TXT
        20: TYPE B:PROPOSAL.TXT ¦ MORE
*_
```

As with the Search command, the last line changed (line 20 in the example) becomes the current line. If no line contains the string, Edlin responds *Not found.*

What if you want to change some, but not all, occurrences of the first string? Again, as with the Search command, you can tell Edlin to prompt you for confirmation. When Edlin prompts you for confirmation, it shows the changed version, but the change isn't permanent yet; you can still decide whether to make the change. If you type *n*, Edlin keeps the original. You ask Edlin to display the prompt by typing *?* before the command name.

Suppose you want to change PLN to DIF, except in the line that refers to the file OPTION1. Because one occurrence of PLN is going to stay the same, tell Edlin to prompt for confirmation by typing:

```
*1 ?rPLN^ZDIF
         7: FORECAST.DIF
O.K.? y
         8: OPTION1.DIF
O.K.? n
         9: OPTION2.DIF
O.K.? y
*_
```

To see the results, type *1p*. The memo should look the same except for the file names in lines 7 through 11 and 20. Restore all the lines you changed by typing:

```
*1 rDIF^ZPLN
        7: FORECAST.PLN
        9: OPTION2.PLN
```

and:

```
*1 rTXT^ZDOC
        10: LETTER.DOC
        11: PROPOSAL.DOC
        20: TYPE B:PROPOSAL.DOC ¦ MORE
*_
```

The Replace command is powerful, so use it with some care. You could change every occurrence of a string of characters in the entire file with one command—including some occurrences you didn't intend to change. For safety's sake, either tell Edlin to prompt for verification or check ahead of time to make certain there aren't any occurrences that you don't want to change.

Using the Editing Keys

Using the editing keys is usually the fastest way to make specific changes in a line. These keys and their functions are listed in Figure 12-1.

Key	Function
Right arrow	Copies one character.
Left arrow	Erases the last character you copied.
Ins	Causes characters you type to be inserted in the new line. Pressing Ins again stops the insert.
Del	Skips one character in the old line (effectively deleting it from the new line).
Backspace	Same as Left arrow.
F1	Same as Right arrow.
F2	Copies to a certain character in the old line. (Type the character after pressing F2.)
F3	Copies the remaining characters in the line.
F4	Skips to a certain character in the old line. (Type the character after pressing F4.)

Figure 12-1. *Edlin editing-key functions.*

Changing a Line

To tell Edlin you want to change a line, you type the line number and press Enter. Edlin displays the line, moves the cursor down a line, displays the line number again, and waits for instructions. You can then use the editing keys to edit the line. To edit line 3 of the sample memo, first type the line number (3) and press Enter:

```
*3
```

Edlin responds:

```
3:*To: Project team
3:*_
```

Think of the displayed line as the old line, and the row underneath, with the cursor at the beginning, as the new line. You edit a line by copying the characters you want to keep from the old line to the new line, and by inserting any new characters in the new line. The editing keys tell Edlin which characters to copy. Press the Right arrow key a few times. Notice that each press copies one character from the old line to the new. The Left arrow key reverses the action, so use it to erase all the characters you copied.

The F(unction) Keys

As shown in Figure 12-1, the F3 key copies all the characters from the cursor location to the end of the original line, and the F2 key copies all the characters in the original line up to a particular character you specify.

To see how these keys work, suppose you want to change the word *Project* to *Product* in the example. To do this, press F2 and *j*. This copies all the characters up to the *j*:

```
3:*To: Project team
3:*To: Pro_
```

Now type *du*:

```
3:*To: Project team
3:*To: Produ_
```

Finally, press F3 to copy the rest of the line:

```
3:*To: Project team
3:*To: Product team_
```

Use the Left arrow key to move the cursor back to the beginning of the line.

As you just saw, characters you type replace the corresponding characters from the old line. If you press the Insert key before typing the characters, however, Edlin inserts the characters into the new line without replacing any characters in the old line. To insert the word *New* after the word *To:* in line 3, for example, first copy *To:* by pressing the Right arrow key four times:

```
3:*To: Project team
3:*To: _
```

Now press the Insert key, type *New* (don't forget to add a space after it), and press F3 to copy the rest of the old line:

```
3:*To: Project team
3:*To: New Project team_
```

Use the Left arrow key to move the cursor back to the left margin again.

Now suppose you want to delete one or more characters in your original line. You use the Delete key (Del), which tells Edlin to skip over the next character in the old

273

line. For example, to delete *To:* from line 3, press Del four times (once for each character, plus the blank). Nothing seems to happen, but when you press F3 to copy the rest of the line, you see:

```
3:*To: Project team
3:*Project team_
```

Move the cursor back to the left margin again.

But suppose you want to delete a number of characters. The F4 key skips to a specified character in the old line, deleting the characters it skips.

To delete *To: Project* in line 3, for example, press F4, then *t* to skip *To: Projec*. Press Del twice to delete the *t* and the blank. Now press F3 to copy the rest of the line:

```
3:*To: Project team
3:*team_
```

Remember, no matter how many changes you make, you can always cancel them by pressing Ctrl-Break before you press Enter. If you press Enter, the line is changed. Press Ctrl-Break to cancel the editing of line 3.

For future reference, here is a quick way to confirm your editing changes. Type the line number and press Enter. Edlin assumes you want to edit the line again and displays the line for you. Press Enter again. The second Enter tells Edlin to save the line without any further changes.

Moving Lines

You can move one or more lines from one place to another in the file with the Move command (m). You specify the starting and ending numbers of the range of lines to be moved, then the number of the line before which the range should be placed, separating the numbers with commas.

For example, suppose you want to move lines 5 through 12 from where they are to just before the last sentence (line 26). To move the lines and to verify the move, type the following. Notice that you are giving Edlin two commands on one line. When you do this, you separate the commands with a semicolon:

```
*5,12,26m;1p
```

You see:

```
1: Final Project Review -- 10/16/91
2:
3: To: Project team
4:
5: Please check the spreadsheets and print the
6: documents to make sure they agree with our
7: assumptions.
8:
9: You can review the documents on the screen.
```

```
10: To check the proposal, type:
11:
12: TYPE B:PROPOSAL.DOC | MORE
13:
14: This displays one screen at a time. Press
15: the Spacebar to display the next screen,
16: or press Ctrl-Break to stop.
17:
18: This diskette has 5 files on it.
19:
20: FORECAST.PLN
21: OPTION1.PLN
22: OPTION2.PLN
23:*LETTER.DOC
*_
```

Note that Edlin renumbers the lines, just as when you insert or delete lines.

If you omit either the starting or ending line number, Edlin assumes you mean the current line. To move one line that is not the current line, specify it as both the beginning and end of the block. (For example, to move line 26 to just before line 5, the command would be 26,26,5m.) After the lines are moved, the first line that was moved becomes the current line.

COPYING LINES

You can copy a range of lines to another place in the file with the Copy command (c). To do so, specify the beginning and ending line numbers of the range and the number of the line before which the range is to be copied, just as you did with the Move command. Copy differs from Move in that the range you specify remains in its original location and is repeated in the new location.

For example, suppose you want to copy the line that begins with *This diskette has* plus the list of files (lines 18 through 24) to the end of the document so that you can use these lines as a label. Type the following Copy and Page commands to copy the lines and verify the copy (remember that # means the line that follows the last line):

```
*18,24,#c;18p
```

You see:

```
18: This diskette has 5 files on it:
19:
20: FORECAST.PLN
21: OPTION1.PLN
22: OPTION2.PLN
23: LETTER.DOC
24: PROPOSAL.DOC
25:
26: Let's do this quickly; it's due Thursday.
27:
```

```
       28:  Tom
       29:  This diskette has 5 files on it.
       30:
       31:  FORECAST.PLN
       32:  OPTION1.PLN
       33:  OPTION2.PLN
       34:  LETTER.DOC
       35:*PROPOSAL.DOC
*_
```

You can make several copies of a range of lines with one Copy command by adding a comma and the number of copies just before the *c*. For example, to make five more copies of the same range of lines, you would type 16,22,#,5c.

If you omit the starting or ending line number, Edlin assumes the omitted line number is the current line. To copy one line other than the current line, specify it as both the beginning and end of the block. After the lines are copied, the last line that was copied becomes the current line.

COPYING ANOTHER FILE

You can copy another file into the file you're editing. Suppose you have a file that contains the name and address of each member of the project team. If you want to include the address list in this memo, you don't have to type it again; you can merge the two files with the Transfer command (t).

To see how this works, quit the edit of this file, use Edlin to create a small file named ADDRESS on the diskette in drive B, then return to editing MEMO.TXT and display the first 23 lines of the file. To do this, type:

```
*q
Abort edit (Y/N)? y
C:\>edlin b:address
New file
*i
       1:*XXX ADDRESS LIST XXX
       2:*<Ctrl-Break>

*1,1,2,3c;1p
       1: XXX ADDRESS LIST XXX
       2: XXX ADDRESS LIST XXX
       3: XXX ADDRESS LIST XXX
       4:*XXX ADDRESS LIST XXX
*e

C:\>edlin b:memo.txt
End of input file
*p
```

The first 23 lines of MEMO.TXT are on the screen.

To copy another file with the Transfer command, you specify the line before which the file is to be placed, then type *t* and the name of the file. Do not use commas.

To copy the file named ADDRESS to just before line 5, type:

```
•5tb:address
```

Type *lp* to see the result. The first 11 lines look like this:

```
 1: Final Project Review -- 10/16/91
 2:
 3: To: Project team
 4:
 5: XXX ADDRESS LIST XXX
 6: XXX ADDRESS LIST XXX
 7: XXX ADDRESS LIST XXX
 8: XXX ADDRESS LIST XXX
 9: This diskette has 5 files on it.
10:
11: FORECAST.PLN
```

If you don't specify the line number, Edlin copies the file to just above the current line, and the first line of the copied file becomes the current line.

CHAPTER SUMMARY

Although Edlin is a simple text editor and lacks most of the features required of a word processor, its speed and simplicity make it a useful tool for creating and revising short text files. The examples in this chapter showed you how you can use Edlin to write a short memo. The remaining chapters of this book describe some of the advanced features of DOS, many of which require short files of text. If you're using a version of DOS that doesn't include the MS-DOS Editor, you'll find that Edlin is a convenient way to take advantage of these features.

CHAPTER 13

TAKING CONTROL
OF YOUR SYSTEM

U p to now, you have used the DOS commands in their standard form. DOS, however, gives you a great deal of flexibility in controlling the way some commands do their work for you. This chapter describes two ways in which you can take control of your system.

The first part of the chapter introduces the concept of input and output *redirection*. Essentially, redirection is a form of traffic control that allows you to route input and output between devices and files you specify. You'll also see how to use redirection with DOS commands that let you control both the form and content of command input and output.

If you have version 5 of DOS, the second part of this chapter takes you further into the Doskey program introduced in Chapter 3. Using Doskey, you'll see not only how to edit commands you've already used, but how to enter and carry out more than one command at a time.

REDIRECTING COMMAND OUTPUT

It is easy to visualize what happens with command output, so even though it might seem odd to discuss results before discussing causes, this section on command output gives you a foundation for understanding command input as well.

The result, or output, of most commands is some action, such as copying a file (with the Copy command) or controlling the operation of a device (with the Mode command). The output of some commands, however, such as Directory, Check Disk, and Tree, is a report. Up to now, you have used these reports primarily as displays—DOS has sent them to the *standard output* device, the console. (Recall from Chapter 7 that DOS uses the name CON, or console, for both the keyboard, which is input only, and the display, which is output only.)

As you'll see in this chapter, DOS lets you send reports and other output to a different device, such as a printer, or to a file. This is called *redirecting* the output of the command; you did it a few times in previous chapters with such commands as *dir > prn*. The technique is simple: To redirect the output of a command that normally sends its results to standard output (the display), you type the command name followed by > and the name of the device or file to which the output is to be sent. The > looks something like an arrowhead pointing toward the alternate output device or file.

Using redirection it's easy, for example, to print a copy of the directory as you did in Chapter 4. To repeat that example, but this time with an understanding of what happens, be sure the printer is turned on and type the following:

```
C:\>dir > prn
```

The > tells DOS to redirect the output of the Directory command, and PRN tells DOS where to send it: to the printer. The directory should be printing now. If it's long and you want to cancel the printing, press Ctrl-Break.

REDIRECTING COMMAND INPUT

You've seen how quickly and easily you can redirect output to a device or a file. You can just as easily redirect input, in effect telling certain DOS commands to get their data from a source other than the one (often called *standard input*) they would normally use.

Together, redirected input and output are known as redirection. Although redirection might sound complicated, it is easy to understand, as the examples in this chapter show.

Three DOS commands, known collectively as *filter commands,* make particularly effective use of redirection.

FILTER COMMANDS

Filter commands take input from a device or a file, change the input in some way, and send the result to an output device or file. They are called filter commands because they work much like a filter in a water system, which takes incoming water, changes it in some way, and sends it along the system.

DOS includes three filter commands that allow you to:

▶ Arrange lines in ascending or descending order with the Sort command.

▶ Search for a string of characters with the Find command.

▶ Temporarily halt the display after one screenful (to give you a chance to read the lines) with the More command.

You can redirect both the input and the output of a filter command. The filter commands aren't really intended to be used with keyboard input. Rather, they are designed to get their input from a file or even from the output of another command. This chapter shows you how to use and combine the filter commands to create your own powerful, specialized commands.

PREPARING FOR THE EXAMPLES

Redirection and filter commands give you the elements of a simple file-management program. While they won't replace a file manager, they let you use DOS to search and sort simple lists without spending extra money or time on another program.

The examples in this chapter use a sample file that almost everyone needs: a list of names and telephone numbers. Too often, files of telephone numbers and business cards are out of date, incomplete, or in the other office. Questions arise: ''Was that number in the telephone index or the business-card file?'' Or ''Did I file the number under Jones or under Accountants?'' This example shows you how to let DOS keep track of your phone list and eliminate these questions.

If you're using a fixed disk, change the current directory to \RUNDOS by typing the following:

```
C:\>cd \rundos
```

If you don't have a fixed disk, put a formatted diskette that has room for a few small files in drive B. You also need the DOS diskette(s) containing, in order, the command files EDIT.COM or EDLIN.COM, FIND.EXE, SORT.EXE, and MORE.COM. If you have version 5, begin with the diskette containing EDIT.COM in drive A. If you have any other version of DOS, begin with the diskette containing EDLIN.COM in drive A. Change the current drive to B by typing:

```
A:\>b:
```

Finally, tell DOS where to find the command files it needs by setting the command path to the root directory of the system diskette:

```
B:\>path a:\
```

ENTERING THE SAMPLE FILE

The sample file is named PH.TXT. You can use either Edit or Edlin to create it from DOS, or you can use your own word processor if it is capable of saving documents as unformatted or text files—that is, files that don't contain any of the program's own formatting codes.

Each line of the file contains six items of data: last name, first name, area code, telephone number, a key word that identifies a category, and a short description. The key words are: *cust* for customer, *cons* for consultant, and *vend* for vendor. You'll enter the items in specific columns so you can sort the list by any item.

If you're using Edit to create the file, start the editor and name the file in a single command by typing the following:

```
C:\RUNDOS>edit ph.txt
```

If you're using Edlin to create the file, type:

```
C:\RUNDOS>edlin ph.txt
New file
*i
        1:*_
```

Now, regardless of the editor you're using, you can begin to enter the items in the file. To help you get the items in the correct columns, the following entry shows the first line, with a period marking each space. Type the line as shown, pressing the Spacebar once for each period shown:

```
Jones.....Michele...(747).429-6360..cons.chemist
```

End the line by pressing Enter.

282

Now enter the remaining lines in the sample file, shown in Figure 13-1. Remember, you already typed the first line.

When you've typed all the lines, save the file and quit the editor. DOS should return to the system prompt.

```
Jones      Michele    (747) 429-6360    cons chemist
Smith      John       (747) 926-2945    vend furniture
White      Alice      (747) 425-7692    cust Accountant
Green      Fred       (541) 926-4921    cust math teach
Black      John       (747) 426-3385    cons mech eng pkg
Smith      Ed         (541) 835-8747    vend caterer
Jones      Alison     (747) 429-5584    cons Chem engineer
IBM        sales      (747) 463-2000    vend Dave Hill
Jones      James      (747) 636-3541    cust architect
Black      Alice      (747) 426-7145    cust Elec eng
```

Figure 13-1. *Telephone and business-card list.*

Now you're ready to use the file. To see the entry for Alice White, type the following (notice the capital W):

```
C:\RUNDOS>find "Wh" ph.txt

---------- PH.TXT
White      Alice      (747) 425-7692    cust Accountant
```

That's fast, but it's just the beginning.

THE SORT FILTER COMMAND

The Sort filter command arranges, or sorts, lines of input and sends them to standard output (the display) unless you redirect the output—for example, to the printer. If you enter the command with no options, it sorts the lines of input in ascending order (alphabetically from A to Z, or numerically from lowest to highest number), starting the sort on the character in the first column.

The Sort command has two parameters:

sort /R /+<column>

/R (*Reverse*) sorts the lines in reverse order (Z to A, or highest to lowest number).

/+<column> sorts the lines starting at the specified column, rather than starting in the first column.

To sort a particular file, you can redirect the input of the Sort command by following the command name with < and the name of the file to be sorted; use a space both before and after the <. If you don't redirect the input, the Sort command sorts lines that you type at the keyboard (standard input).

283

Sort Command Examples

Figure 13-2 shows the column number of each of the six items in the telephone list: last name, first name, area code, telephone number, key word, and description. You'll use these column numbers to sort the file in different ways.

```
1           11          21    27          37    42
Jones       Michele     (747) 429-6360    cons  chemist
```

Figure 13-2. *Column numbers of items in the telephone list.*

The simplest way to sort the file is in ascending order, starting in the first column. (In the sample file, this sorts the entries by last name.) Type:

```
C:\RUNDOS>sort < ph.txt
```

DOS quickly displays the sorted result:

```
Black       Alice       (747) 426-7145    cust Elec eng
Black       John        (747) 426-3385    cons mech eng pkg
Green       Fred        (541) 926-4921    cust math teach
IBM         sales       (747) 463-2000    vend Dave Hill
Jones       Alison      (747) 429-5584    cons Chem engineer
Jones       James       (747) 636-3541    cust architect
Jones       Michele     (747) 429-6360    cons chemist
Smith       Ed          (541) 835-8747    vend caterer
Smith       John        (747) 926-2945    vend furniture
White       Alice       (747) 425-7692    cust Accountant
```

The file itself isn't changed; what you see is simply the result of DOS reading, sorting, and displaying the lines of the file.

To sort the file in reverse order, use the /R option:

```
C:\RUNDOS>sort /r < ph.txt
```

It doesn't take DOS any longer to sort backward:

```
White       Alice       (747) 425-7692    cust Accountant
Smith       John        (747) 926-2945    vend furniture
Smith       Ed          (541) 835-8747    vend caterer
Jones       Michele     (747) 429-6360    cons chemist
Jones       James       (747) 636-3541    cust architect
Jones       Alison      (747) 429-5584    cons Chem engineer
IBM         sales       (747) 463-2000    vend Dave Hill
Green       Fred        (541) 926-4921    cust math teach
Black       John        (747) 426-3385    cons mech eng pkg
Black       Alice       (747) 426-7145    cust Elec eng
```

Suppose you wanted to arrange the list by the key word—first the consultants, then the customers, then the vendors. The first letter of the key word is in column 37, so use the column option:

`C:\RUNDOS>`sort /+37 < ph.txt

Now it's easy to pick out the different categories:

```
Jones      Alison      (747) 429-5584   cons Chem engineer
Jones      Michele     (747) 429-6360   cons chemist
Black      John        (747) 426-3385   cons mech eng pkg
White      Alice       (747) 425-7692   cust Accountant
Jones      James       (747) 636-3541   cust architect
Black      Alice       (747) 426-7145   cust Elec eng
Green      Fred        (541) 926-4921   cust math teach
Smith      Ed          (541) 835-8747   vend caterer
IBM        sales       (747) 463-2000   vend Dave Hill
Smith      John        (747) 926-2945   vend furniture
```

Sorting is fast, easy, and useful.

THE FIND FILTER COMMAND

The Find filter command searches lines of input for a string of characters you specify. If you enter the command with no parameters other than the string and the file name, the Find command displays all lines that contain the string.

The Find command has five parameters:

find /V /C /N /I "<string>" <filename>

/V displays all lines that do not contain the string.

/C (*Count*) displays just the number of lines found, not the lines themselves.

/N (*Number*) displays the input line number with each line found.

/I (*Ignore*), in version 5 only, causes the Find command to ignore differences between uppercase and lowercase—for example, to treat *a* and *A* as the same letter.

"<string>" is the string of characters you want to find; it must be enclosed in quotation marks. Except in version 5, the Find command distinguishes between uppercase and lowercase letters, so ''cons'' and ''CONS'', for example, are different strings.

<filename> is the name of the file to be searched. If you omit <filename>, the Find command searches standard input. You can include several different file names in a single Find command simply by separating the file names with blanks. If some of the files are in a different directory or on a disk in a different drive, precede the file name with the appropriate path name or drive letter.

Find Command Examples

To display the entries for all consultants in the file named PH.TXT, type the following:

```
C:\RUNDOS>find "cons" ph.txt
```

The first line of output identifies the input file, PH. Each line that contains the string *cons* is displayed immediately after:

```
---------- PH.TXT
Jones      Michele      (747) 429-6360   cons chemist
Black      John         (747) 426-3385   cons mech eng pkg
Jones      Alison       (747) 429-5584   cons Chem engineer
```

To see how the Find command works with more than one file, type the following to make a duplicate copy of the phone list:

```
C:\RUNDOS>copy ph.txt ph1.txt
```

Now type the Find command you used in the preceding example, but this time include both files:

```
C:\RUNDOS>find "cons" ph.txt ph1.txt
```

DOS displays the name of each file as it finds ''cons'' in PH.TXT and PH1.TXT:

```
---------- PH.TXT
Jones      Michele      (747) 429-6360   cons chemist
Black      John         (747) 426-3385   cons mech eng pkg
Jones      Alison       (747) 429-5584   cons Chem engineer

---------- PH1.TXT
Jones      Michele      (747) 429-6360   cons chemist
Black      John         (747) 426-3385   cons mech eng pkg
Jones      Alison       (747) 429-5584   cons Chem engineer
```

Obviously, using the Find command to search for a character string in several files is more productive when the contents of the files differ, but this example shows the method, if not the full capability, of the command. You don't need PH1.TXT anymore, so type *del phl.txt* to keep your disk uncluttered.

Return now to the original phone list, PH.TXT. If you just want to know how many consultants are in the list, use the /C option:

```
C:\RUNDOS>find /c "cons" ph.txt
```

This time, the line that identifies the input file also shows the number of lines that contain the string:

```
---------- PH.TXT: 3
```

Three lines in the file contain *cons*.

As often happens in a real telephone index, the sample file uses different words or abbreviations to mean the same thing. Both *engineer* and *eng* are used, for example, to

286

describe an engineer. Both words contain *eng*, however, so you can find all the engineers by typing the following:

```
C:\RUNDOS>find "eng" ph.txt

---------- PH.TXT
Black      John       (747)  426-3385   cons mech eng pkg
Jones      Alison     (747)  429-5584   cons Chem engineer
Black      Alice      (747)  426-7145   cust Elec eng
```

As also happens in real life, capitalization in the sample file is not consistent. One entry, for example, contains the notation *Chem engineer* and another contains the all-lowercase *chemist*. You could avoid the inconsistency by specifying the string as *hem* rather than as *chem* or *Chem*. But if you have version 5, you can use the /I parameter instead, to tell the Find command to ignore uppercase/lowercase differences. If you have version 5, type:

```
C:\RUNDOS>find /i "chem" ph.txt
```

DOS quickly responds:

```
---------- PH.TXT
Jones      Michele    (747)  429-6360   cons chemist
Jones      Alison     (747)  429-5584   cons Chem engineer
```

Finding Lines That Don't Contain the String

With any version of DOS, you can also use the /V parameter to display lines that *don't* contain a string. For example, to display the entries *not* in the 747 area code, type:

```
C:\RUNDOS>find /v "(747" ph.txt

---------- PH.TXT
Green      Fred       (541)  926-4921   cust math teach
Smith      Ed         (541)  835-8747   vend caterer
```

Including the left parenthesis with 747 distinguishes between entries with an area code of 747 and entries that might contain 747 in the phone number. Try the example without the left parenthesis:

```
C:\RUNDOS>find /v "747" ph.txt

---------- PH.TXT
Green      Fred       (541)  926-4921   cust math teach
```

Ed Smith's telephone number is 835-8747, so his entry wasn't displayed even though his area code is 541. When you specify the characters to find, be sure to include enough to specify what you're looking for. In the sample file, for example, typing *"(7"* would be enough to specify the 747 area code; it wouldn't be enough, however, if the file contained another area code beginning with 7. And, as you saw, you must include the left parenthesis to distinguish an area code from some other set of numbers.

Including Line Numbers with the Output

To display the entries for people named Smith and to include the line numbers of the entries, use the /N option:

```
C:\RUNDOS>find /n "Smith" ph.txt


---------- PH.TXT
[2]Smith      John       (747) 926-2945   vend furniture
[6]Smith      Ed         (541) 835-8747   vend caterer
```

The two entries displayed are the second and sixth lines of the sample file.

Combining Find Command Options

You can combine Find command options. For example, to display the entries not in the 747 area code and to include their line numbers, use both the /V and /N options:

```
C:\RUNDOS>find /v /n "(7" ph.txt


---------- PH.TXT
[4]Green      Fred       (541) 926-4921   cust math teach
[6]Smith      Ed         (541) 835-8747   vend caterer
```

(If you used Edit to create the sample file, you might also see *[11]* appear at the end of this report. That's probably because you pressed Enter when you finished typing the last entry and, in doing so, created a blank line that Find has included in its search. The blank line is listed because you told Find to show the *numbers* of all lines that *don't* contain the 747 area code.)

MORE ON REDIRECTING

Earlier in this chapter, you redirected input to the Sort command by specifying the file PH.TXT. You can also redirect the output of a filter command. To print the entries for all vendors (that is, redirect output from the display to the printer), type the following:

```
C:\RUNDOS>find "vend" ph.txt > prn
```

The entries are printed. If your phone list has two or three hundred entries, this technique of using options and redirecting output is a quick way to print a copy showing a selected group of entries.

Redirecting Both Input and Output

You can redirect both input and output by following the command name with < and the name of the input file or device and then > and the name of the output file or device. (Be sure to include blanks before and after both < and > if you don't have version 4 or 5 of DOS).

For example, to print the alphabetized version of PH.TXT, check that your printer is on and then type:

```
C:\RUNDOS>sort < ph.txt > prn
```

The input for the Sort command comes from PH.TXT, and the output is redirected to the printer.

DOS allows you to redirect both the input and output of a single command from and to the same file. That is, DOS does not report any error if, for example, you type the command *sort < ph.txt > ph.txt*. Doing this, however, can make a large file unusable. If you want to sort a file and keep the same file name, do the following:

▶ Redirect the output to a temporary file, such as PH-TMP. For example, to sort PH in reverse order, you would type *sort /r < ph.txt > ph-tmp.txt*.

▶ If you're certain you no longer need it, delete the original file (*del ph.txt*). If you want to keep the original, give it a different name, such as OLDPH.TXT, with the Rename command (*ren ph.txt oldph.txt*).

▶ Then use the Rename command to give the temporary file the original file name (*ren ph-tmp.txt ph.txt*).

▶ The new version of PH.TXT would contain the telephone list sorted in reverse order. You could verify the contents by displaying PH.TXT with the Type command.

Adding Redirected Output to a File

When you redirect output to an existing file, the redirected output replaces the original file. But you can also *add* redirected output to the end of an existing file by using >>, instead of >. If the file doesn't exist, it is created, just as when you use >.

CONNECTING COMMANDS WITH A PIPE

A powerful way of using a filter command is to redirect the output of some other command to the input of the filter command. In effect, the two commands are connected, with the output of the first command feeding directly into the filter command. Continuing the analogy to a water system, this connection is called a *pipe*.

You tell DOS to pipe the output of one command to the input of another by typing ¦ between the names of the two commands; the ¦ provides the connection between the two commands. The More filter command provides a simple example.

The More Filter Command

The More filter command displays one screenful (24 lines unless you've specified otherwise with the Mode command) followed by the line -- *More* --, and then it pauses.

When you press any key, More displays the next screenful and pauses again if necessary, continuing in the same way until all the input has been displayed.

For the following example, you need a disk or directory that contains more than one screenful of files. If you're using a fixed disk, your \DOS directory will do. If you're not using a fixed disk, use the Dir command to find a diskette whose directory listing is longer than one screenful.

If you have a fixed disk, type:

```
C:\RUNDOS>dir \dos | more
```

If you don't have a fixed disk, place the diskette you'll use in drive B and type:

```
B>dir | more
```

Either of these commands tells DOS to redirect the output of the Directory command to the input of the More command. The More command displays the first screenful of the directory and -- *More* -- at the bottom of the screen. Press any key to see the rest of the directory, or press Ctrl-Break to cancel the More command and return to the system prompt. The More command lets you review a long output sequence or file without having to press Ctrl-Num Lock or Pause to start and stop the display.

Combining Filter Commands

You can pipe the output of one Find command to the input of another Find command to make a more specific search. A real-life list like the sample phone list, for example, might include several dozen customers. Suppose you want to display the names of customers in the 747 area code only. To do this, pipe the output of a Find command that searches for *cust* to another Find command that searches for *(7*. If you don't have a fixed disk, check that the diskette in drive A contains the command file FIND.EXE and that the diskette in drive B contains PH.TXT.

Type:

```
C:\RUNDOS>find "cust" ph.txt | find "(7"
White      Alice      (747) 425-7692   cust Accountant
Jones      James      (747) 636-3541   cust architect
Black      Alice      (747) 426-7145   cust Elec eng
```

If you check an earlier list of the file, you'll see that Fred Green is a customer, but his area code is 541, so the second Find command eliminated the entry for his name. Notice that the line that identifies the file (---------- *PH.TXT*) isn't displayed. The first Find command pipes ---------- *PH.TXT* as part of its output to the second Find command, but because the line does not contain the string *(7*, it is not included as part of the output of the second Find command.

You can also pipe the output of the Find command to the Sort command. To see all the consultants sorted by last name, type the following:

```
C:\RUNDOS>find "cons" ph.txt : sort


---------- PH.TXT
Black     John      (747)  426-3385   cons mech eng pkg
Jones     Alison    (747)  429-5584   cons Chem engineer
Jones     Michele   (747)  429-6360   cons chemist
```

You can combine as many commands as you like. Suppose you want to print a list of all customers in the 747 area code, sorted by telephone number. You can search PH.TXT for *cust*, pipe that output to a Find command that searches for *(7*, pipe that output to a Sort command that sorts at column 27 (the telephone number), and redirect the output to the printer. Type the following:

```
C:\RUNDOS>find "cust" ph.txt : find "(7" : sort /+27 > prn
```

The printed output includes:

```
White     Alice     (747)  425-7692   cust Accountant
Black     Alice     (747)  426-7145   cust Elec eng
Jones     James     (747)  636-3541   cust architect
```

If your list included several dozen customers, this could be a handy way to organize a calling campaign.

The Difference Between > and :

Sometimes the distinction between > and : isn't readily apparent, but the difference is easy to demonstrate. Sort is a filter command. To make the output of the Directory command the input to the Sort command, type the following (substitute *a:* if you don't have a fixed disk):

```
C:\RUNDOS>dir c:\ : sort
```

As you would expect, DOS displays the directory sorted in alphabetic order. (If the directory includes two files whose names look like 072F2321 or %PIPE1.$$$, don't be alarmed. These are temporary files DOS creates in order to pipe the output of one command to the input of another; DOS deletes the files automatically.)

Now type:

```
C:\RUNDOS>dir c:\ > sort
```

This time you don't see anything on the screen because you told DOS to redirect the output of the Directory command to a file named SORT. Confirm this by displaying the file with the Type command:

```
C:\RUNDOS>type sort
```

The file contains the directory, which is not sorted. You created the file when you redirected the output of the Directory command. You don't need this file, so delete it by typing *del sort*.

EDITING A DOS COMMAND

As you've seen, commands that redirect and filter input, output, or both can become long and complex, especially if you also include subdirectory names, file names, and extensions. By now you've also used many DOS commands over and over again—to the point where you probably have no idea, other than "a lot," of the number of times you've typed *dir* followed by a drive letter, path, or file name.

With any version of DOS, you can save typing time by using the DOS editing keys, especially F2, F3, and F4, to edit the last command you carried out. DOS saves your last command in a small portion of memory, so you can use the DOS editing keys to retrieve, modify, and carry out the command again.

F2 copies the last command up to a character you specify; F3 copies the entire command; and F4 skips to the character you specify. To change or delete characters, use Backspace to delete characters to the left of the cursor; Del to delete the character at the location of the cursor; and Ins to add characters you type, again at the location of the cursor.

Start by entering a fairly long command so you can see how editing works. Type:

```
C:\RUNDOS>find "Jones" ph.txt | sort /+11
```

Press Enter to carry out the command, which tells DOS to search for *Jones* in the file named PH.TXT and sort the entries it finds at column 11 (where the first name starts).

Now see how DOS can help you reuse your last command. Start by pressing F2 and capital J to copy all characters up to, but not including, the *J* in *Jones*:

```
C:\RUNDOS>find "_
```

Type *Smith* (note the capitalization) and press F3 to copy the rest of the command:

```
C:\RUNDOS>find "Smith" ph.txt | sort /+11
```

With just a few keystrokes, you've changed your last command to search for and alphabetize the entries for Smith instead of Jones. Carry out the command and try another example. This time, press F4 followed by lowercase s to tell DOS to skip to the *s* in *sort*. Now press F3 to copy the rest of the command:

```
C:\RUNDOS>sort /+11_
```

Press the Spacebar and type < *ph.txt*:

```
C:\RUNDOS>sort /+11 < ph.txt
```

Again, with a few keystrokes you've used the editing keys to change one command into another. Although it's often easier to simply retype a short command, the editing keys can be useful time-savers.

EDITING COMMANDS WITH DOSKEY

The DOS editing keys are useful, but they do have one restriction: They work only on the last command you entered and carried out. Sometimes you don't want to repeat the last command, you want to repeat (or edit) a command you used a while ago. If you have version 5, you can repeat (or edit) any recent command by using the small program named Doskey that you first encountered in Chapter 3. (If you don't have version 5, you must retype the command; skip ahead to Chapter 14.)

If you recall, typing *doskey* for the first time during a session with your computer causes DOS to load the Doskey program into memory. Once in memory, Doskey keeps track of the commands you type and allows you to go back and review or repeat them by pressing the arrow and function keys.

But even though Doskey allows you to choose among earlier commands, you still might not want to repeat a command exactly. As in the editing example in the previous section, you might want to specify a different drive, path, or file name. Doskey responds to F2, F3, and F4 as described earlier, but when you've recalled a previous command you can also use the keys described in Figure 13-3, which allow much more flexibility in editing the command.

Key	Action
Home	Moves the cursor to the beginning of the command
Ctrl-Home	Deletes from the cursor location to the beginning of the command
End	Moves the cursor to the end of the command
Ctrl-End	Deletes from the cursor location to the end of the command
Left arrow	Moves the cursor one character left
Ctrl-Left arrow	Moves the cursor one ''word'' (string of characters without blanks) left
Right arrow	Moves the cursor one character right
Ctrl-Right arrow	Moves the cursor one ''word'' (string of characters without blanks) right
Ins	Adds typed characters at the location of the cursor; does not overstrike existing characters
Del	Deletes the character at the location of the cursor; does not move the cursor
Esc	Erases the displayed command

Figure 13-3. *The Doskey editing keys.*

To see how to edit commands with Doskey, start by loading the program into memory. Type:

```
C:\RUNDOS>doskey
DOSKey installed.
```

Now type a command and press Enter to carry it out:

```
C:\RUNDOS>find "Smith" ph.txt | sort /+11
```

Press the Up arrow key to redisplay the command. Your first edit will change *Smith* to *Black*. Press Home to move the cursor to the beginning of the command. Press Ctrl-Right arrow once to move the cursor to the quotation mark preceding *Smith*, and then press the Right arrow to move the cursor under the *S* in *Smith*:

```
C:\RUNDOS>find "Smith" ph.txt | sort /+11
```

Now type *Black*. Notice that the characters you type replace the characters that were there. To insert characters rather than replace them, you would press Ins before beginning to type. To delete characters, you would press Del once for each character you wanted to remove.

Your command should look like this:

```
C:\RUNDOS>find "Black" ph.txt | sort /+11
```

Press Enter, and this time DOS lists all people named Black, alphabetizing them by their first names. Press the Up arrow key again to display the last command. Now try moving the cursor around.

Press Home to move the cursor to the beginning of the command. Next, press Ctrl-Right arrow three times to move the cursor right three words:

```
C:\RUNDOS>find "Black" ph.txt | sort /+11
```

As a final exercise, try deleting parts of the command. Press Ctrl-End, and all characters from the cursor to the end of the line vanish:

```
C:\RUNDOS>find "Black" ph.txt _
```

Press Ctrl-Left arrow to move the cursor to the *p* in *ph*:

```
C:\RUNDOS>find "Black" ph.txt
```

Press Ctrl-Home. This time, you delete all characters between the cursor and the beginning of the command:

```
C:\RUNDOS>ph.txt
```

What's left isn't very meaningful, so clean up by pressing Esc to erase the entire line:

```
C:\RUNDOS>_
```

ENTERING MULTIPLE COMMANDS WITH DOSKEY

In this chapter, you've seen many ways to use the redirection (< and >) and filter (¦) symbols to carry out more than one command at the same time. But what about other commands? While using DOS you might sometimes have thought it would be nice to type two or more related (or unrelated) commands and have DOS carry them out one after the other. With Doskey, you can type as many commands as you want, up to a maximum of 128 characters. To tell Doskey where one command ends and the next begins, you press Ctrl-T, which is displayed as a paragraph mark (¶).

To see how this feature works, try the following example, which clears the screen, creates a new directory named TEST, makes TEST the current directory, and displays the directory listing. You'll enter all four commands on the same line, separating them by pressing Ctrl-T:

```
C:\RUNDOS>cls <Ctrl-T> md test <Ctrl-T> cd test <Ctrl-T> dir
```

When you press Enter, the screen clears and the commands are carried out one at a time. It happens quickly, but each command is displayed as it is carried out, so you can see the results:

```
C:\RUNDOS> md test

C:\RUNDOS> cd test

C:\RUNDOS\TEST> dir

 Volume in drive C is FIXED DISK
 Volume Serial Number is 1608-5A30
 Directory of C:\RUNDOS\TEST

.           <DIR>     10-16-91  11:27a
..          <DIR>     10-16-91  11:27a
        2 file(s)          0 bytes
                    14069807 bytes free
```

The next example uses the Copy command to create a sample file by copying from the console (CON). Type:

```
C:\RUNDOS\TEST>copy con example <Ctrl-T> type example
```

When you press Enter this time, the system pauses after the first command is displayed. DOS is waiting for you to create the sample file, so type the following:

```
This is a sample file named EXAMPLE.
<Ctrl-Z>
```

When you press Enter, you see the familiar *1 file(s) copied* message followed by your second command:

```
C:\RUNDOS\TEST> type example
This is a sample file named EXAMPLE.
```

This time, you created a file and displayed it.

Finally, clean up your directory by typing the following set of commands:

```
C:\RUNDOS\TEST>del example <Ctrl-T> cd .. <Ctrl-T> rd test
```

CHAPTER SUMMARY

As you've seen, redirection, filter commands, and pipes let you create powerful, specific commands. When you consider these—and all the other DOS commands you've encountered—you can begin to see ways in which you can adapt DOS to your own needs and circumstances.

This chapter ends the part of the book that deals with DOS as it is provided on disk. The next three chapters show you how to combine DOS commands in sets known as batch files to put more of the power of DOS to work. You have the building blocks. Now it's time to use them to customize DOS.

CHAPTER 14

CREATING YOUR OWN COMMANDS

As the preceding chapters show, DOS gives you a great deal of control over your computer system. But DOS is necessarily general purpose, because many people use it for many different tasks. So that you can adapt the computer to your work, DOS lets you combine existing DOS commands to create your own special-purpose commands.

The technique is simple: To make your own command, you create a text file that contains DOS commands. You can give such a file—called a *batch file*—any valid name except the name of an existing command; the extension of the file must be BAT. To use your command, simply type the name of the batch file; DOS carries out the commands contained in the file as if you had typed each of them separately. Commands you create this way are called *batch commands*.

This chapter describes how to create batch files and batch commands. It also describes the Remark command, which is intended for batch files, and it shows you how to modify the DOS startup procedure if there are certain commands you always want DOS to carry out when you start your system.

A BATCH OF WHAT?

The term *batch* has its origins in the early days of large computers, when most work was done by submitting a deck of punched cards to the data-processing department. The punched cards had to contain all the instructions required for the program to run correctly. There was no chance to interact with the system. The data-processing personnel ran these jobs in batches and delivered the output.

In effect, you do the same thing when you use a batch command, because a batch file contains all the instructions needed to carry out a job. *Batch,* then, is used to describe a computer job that runs without interruption, as opposed to an interactive job—such as word processing—that consists of an exchange of instructions and responses between you and the computer.

You can use batch files to automate frequently used command sequences and to make the system more accessible to colleagues who use application programs but might not know DOS as well as you do.

HOW DOS SEARCHES FOR A COMMAND

If you type something when DOS is displaying the system prompt, DOS assumes you have typed a command name. It then follows a particular sequence in trying to carry out the command:

1. It checks to see if you typed the name of a built-in command, such as *dir* or *copy.* If you did, DOS carries out that command.

2. If what you typed isn't the name of a built-in command, DOS checks to see if you typed the name of a file with the extension COM or EXE (a command file). If you did, DOS loads the program contained in the file and runs it.

3. If what you typed isn't the name of a command file, DOS checks to see if you typed the name of a file with the extension BAT (a batch file). If you did, DOS carries out the commands in the batch file.

The sequence is important, because it explains why DOS won't carry out a command file with the same name as a built-in command, and why it won't carry out a batch file that has the same name as either a built-in command or a command file.

PREPARING FOR THE EXAMPLES

If you're using a fixed disk, change to the \RUNDOS directory:

```
C:\>cd \rundos
```

Because you'll be creating your own commands in this chapter, the system prompt is shown as a simple C> to keep it unobtrusive. If your system prompt normally shows the current directory, you can simplify it temporarily by typing:

```
C:\RUNDOS>prompt
```

When you next start or restart your computer, the system prompt will revert to showing both the current drive and the current directory. Go on to the heading ''Creating the Sample Files.''

If you're not using a fixed disk, leave your system diskette in drive A and put a formatted diskette in drive B. Type the following to change the current drive to B:

```
A>b:

B>_
```

The system prompt in the examples will be B>, not C>.

Creating the Sample Files

You will use three sample files in this chapter: LETR1.DOC, LETR2.DOC, and LETR3.DOC. Type the following to create the sample files (remember, press either F6 or Ctrl-Z, and then press Enter, where you see ^Z):

```
C>copy con letr1.doc
This is the sample file.
^Z
        1 file(s) copied

C>copy letr1.doc letr2.*
        1 file(s) copied
```

```
C>copy letr1.doc letr3.*
        1 file(s) copied


C>_
```

CREATING A BATCH FILE

A batch file is simply a text file, whose extension is BAT, that contains DOS commands. There are several ways to create a batch file. If the batch file is short and you are confident that it will work correctly, you can simply copy from the console to a file. If you think you might want to tinker with the file before saving it, you can use Edit, Edlin, or a word processor that can store files without inserting its own formatting codes. If want to see how the commands work together, you can use Doskey for a test-as-you-go approach as described later in this chapter.

Because the examples in this chapter are short and have already been checked for usability, you'll copy from the console to create your first batch files. You can't go back to correct an error after you press Enter at the end of a line, but if you make a typing error you can recover easily by pressing Ctrl-Break and reentering the batch file.

Suppose one of the application programs you use is a word processor, and you name the files that contain letters LETR1.DOC, LETR2.DOC, LETR3.DOC, and so forth. You use the Directory command fairly often to display the names of those particular files. Instead of typing *dir letr*.doc* each time, you could put the Directory command in a batch file named DIRLET.BAT.

Type the following to create the batch file:

```
C>copy con dirlet.bat
dir letr*.doc
^Z
        1 file(s) copied


C>_
```

The first line you typed names the batch file; the second line contains the command DOS carries out. Test your batch command by typing its name:

```
C>dirlet

C>dir letr*.doc

  Volume in drive C is FIXED DISK
  Volume Serial Number is 1608-5A30
  Directory of C:\RUNDOS

LETR1      DOC        26 10-16-91    3:13p
LETR2      DOC        26 10-16-91    3:13p
LETR3      DOC        26 10-16-91    3:13p
        3 file(s)          78 bytes
                    13277184 bytes free
```

It's possible that you'll see a double prompt, like this:

```
C>
C>_
```

when your batch file finishes running. Don't worry about it.

The first line displayed after you type your batch command is the Directory command that you entered into your batch file. DOS displays the commands in a batch file as they are carried out; it's as if you typed the command itself.

You could make the batch command even easier to type by naming the batch file just LDIR.BAT. In the long run, however, it's usually better to make the name long enough to give a good hint of what the command does, especially if you create a large number of batch files.

Displaying Messages from a Batch File

The Remark (rem) command doesn't cause DOS to do anything, but it is a valid command. You can include a message with the Remark command. The command form is:

rem <message>

Although this command isn't especially useful at the DOS command level, it lets you display a message from a batch file. To see how the Remark command works, create another version of DIRLET.BAT that displays a descriptive message; type the following:

```
C>copy con dirlet.bat
rem DIRECTORY OF LETTERS
dir letr*.doc
^Z
        1 file(s) copied
```

The new version of DIRLET.BAT replaces the first version you created a few minutes ago. Test this new version by typing:

```
C>dirlet
```

The Remark command you included causes DOS to display the message before it displays the directory:

```
C>rem DIRECTORY OF LETTERS

C>dir letr*.doc

 Volume in drive C is FIXED DISK
 Volume Serial Number is 1608-5A30
 Directory of C:\RUNDOS
```

```
LETR1     DOC         26 10-16-91    3:13p
LETR2     DOC         26 10-16-91    3:13p
LETR3     DOC         26 10-16-91    3:13p
          3 file(s)             78 bytes
                        13277184 bytes free

C>_
```

Carrying Out the Same Batch Command with Different Data

You have seen that most DOS commands include one or more parameters that you can use to make your instructions more specific. When you enter a Directory command, for example, you can specify a file name to display some portion of the files on a disk and the /W option to display the wide form of the directory. The Copy command is another example. It requires two parameters: the name of the file to be copied, and the name to be given to the new copy.

Parameters let you use the same DOS command with different data. You can give a batch file the same capability with a feature called a *replaceable parameter.*

A replaceable parameter is a special symbol you put in a batch file. When you use the batch file, DOS replaces the symbol with a parameter you include when you type the batch command. The symbol consists of a percent sign followed by a one-digit number, such as %1. You can use the numbers 1 through 9 in replaceable parameters, and you can include more than one replaceable parameter in a batch file. (DOS also recognizes %0 as a replaceable parameter but reserves this parameter to mean the drive, path, and file name of the batch file itself.)

The number of the symbol identifies which parameter replaces the symbol. If a batch command takes two parameters, for example, DOS replaces %1, wherever it occurs in the batch file, with the first parameter you type with the batch command, and it replaces %2 with the second parameter you type. Replaceable parameters can be used anywhere in a batch command.

For example, suppose you wanted a batch command that would print a file by copying it to the printer. (You already have a DOS Print command, but go through the example anyway; it illustrates the use of replaceable parameters.) All the batch file needs is a Copy command and one replaceable parameter that identifies the file to be printed. The batch command is called *Prnt* to avoid confusion with the Print command. Type the following:

```
C>copy con prnt.bat
copy %1 prn
^Z
          1 file(s) copied
```

To test your Prnt batch command, make certain the printer is turned on and type the following:

```
C>prnt letr1.doc
```

DOS displays the command after replacing %1 with the batch-command parameter, LETR1.DOC, and prints the file:

```
C>copy letr1.doc prn
        1 file(s) copied
```

Figure 14-1 shows several versions of PRNT.BAT that you might create for printing other documents. Each version contains at least one replaceable parameter; the last version contains two. To the left of each version is an example of how the batch command would be typed, and to the right are the corresponding commands that would be carried out after DOS replaced the replaceable parameters. The batch-command parameters, the replaceable parameters in each version of the batch file, and the result after DOS replaces them with the batch-command parameters, are in *italics*.

Batch Command You Would Type	Contents of PRNT.BAT	Commands That Would Be Carried Out
C>prnt *memo.doc*	copy *%1* prn	copy *memo.doc* prn
C>prnt *memo*	copy *%1*.doc prn	copy *memo*.doc prn
C>prnt *memo rept*	copy *%1*.doc prn	copy *memo*.doc prn
	copy *%2*.doc prn	copy *rept*.doc prn

Figure 14-1. *Replaceable parameters in a batch file.*

Replaceable parameters make batch files much more flexible. Your batch commands needn't be limited to handling the same files or devices all the time—they can be used just like DOS commands to operate with any file or device.

Canceling a Batch Command

As with other DOS commands, you press Ctrl-Break to cancel a batch command. But when you cancel a batch command, DOS prompts you to confirm. To see this, create a short new batch file named DIRS.BAT that first displays the entries in your \DOS directory (or on your DOS diskette) and then displays the entries in the current directory (\RUNDOS).

If you're using a fixed disk, create the DIRS.BAT file shown on the next page. (Replace *c:\dos* in the second line with the name of your DOS directory if your DOS command files are not in a directory named \DOS.)

```
C>copy con dirs.bat
dir \dos
dir
^Z
```
1 file(s) copied

If you're not using a fixed disk, type:

```
B>copy con dirs.bat
dir a:
dir
^Z
```
1 file(s) copied

The directory displays should be long enough to give you time to press Ctrl-Break. Type the name of the Dirs batch command, then press Ctrl-Break as soon as DOS starts displaying the file names:

```
C>dirs
```

C>dir \dos

```
 Volume in drive C is FIXED DISK
 Volume Serial Number is 1608-5A30
 Directory of C:\DOS

 .              <DIR>      10-10-90    6:05p
 ..             <DIR>      10-10-90    6:05p
 EGA      SYS     4885 03-01-91   12:00a
 DISPLAY  SYS    15682 03-01-91   12:00a
 FORMAT   COM    32285 03-01-91   12:00a
 PACKING  LST     3492 03-01-91^C
```

Terminate batch job (Y/N)?_

If you respond *n*, the command being carried out is canceled, but DOS continues with the next command in the batch file. Type *n*; DOS carries out the next command, which displays the current directory:

C>dir

```
 Volume in drive C is FIXED DISK
 Volume Serial Number is 1608-5A30
 Directory of C:\RUNDOS

 .              <DIR>      10-16-91    8:21a
 ..             <DIR>      10-16-91    8:21a
 PH       TXT      526 10-16-91    1:43p
 LETR1    DOC       26 10-16-91    3:13p
 LETR2    DOC       26 10-16-91    3:13p
 LETR3    DOC       26 10-16-91    3:13p
```

```
DIRLET    BAT        41 10-16-91   3:17p
PRNT      BAT        13 10-16-91   3:24p
DIRS      BAT        15 10-16-91   3:30p
          9 file(s)           673 bytes
                      13265422 bytes free
```

If you respond *y* to the "Terminate?" question, DOS cancels the entire batch command and displays the system prompt. Type the Dirs batch command and cancel it again, but this time respond *y*:

```
C>dirs

C>dir \dos

 Volume in drive C is FIXED DISK
 Volume Serial Number is 1608-5A30
 Directory of C:\DOS

 .               <DIR>      10-10-90    6:05p
 ..              <DIR>      10-10-90    6:05p
 EGA      SYS      4885 03-01-91   12:00a
 DISPLAY  SYS     15682 03-01-91   12:00a
 FORMAT   COM     32285 03-01-91   12:00a
 PACKING  LST      3492 03-01-91   12:00a
 ANSI     SYS      8868 03-01-91^C

Terminate batch job (Y/N)? y
```

DOS returns to command level without completing the batch command.

DEVELOPING YOUR OWN STARTUP PROCEDURE

Each time you start or restart the system, DOS goes through a startup procedure that includes searching the root directory of the startup disk for a special batch file named AUTOEXEC.BAT. If it finds the file, DOS carries out whatever commands the file contains. Typically, AUTOEXEC.BAT is used to hold the commands you don't want to have to type each time you start or restart the system—a Path command, for example, that tells DOS where to find command files on a fixed disk, and a Prompt command that sets the system prompt to show the current directory.

Versions 4 and 5 of DOS create AUTOEXEC.BAT (or modify the existing version) as part of the installation procedure. Earlier versions of DOS don't create the file automatically, but because AUTOEXEC.BAT is so useful, individuals responsible for installing all versions from 2.1 through 3.3 have usually included an AUTOEXEC.BAT file on systems with fixed disks.

Although DOS gives special treatment to AUTOEXEC.BAT, that doesn't mean the file is untouchable. You can add commands to it at any time, but you should always be careful not to change or delete any existing commands, especially those you don't clearly understand. (You *can* encounter such commands in AUTOEXEC.BAT, particularly on systems that connect to a network and those that have been set up by someone else for maximum performance.)

The following examples show you some commands you might want to include in AUTOEXEC.BAT to tailor DOS and your computer more closely to your needs or preferences. Following these examples replaces any AUTOEXEC.BAT file you might have now, however, so before you start, you'll check for, and protect, your existing file. You'd be unhappy to lose a familiar startup procedure you're using now.

A Safety Check

Whether you use DOS from a fixed disk or from a DOS diskette, it's easy to check for AUTOEXEC.BAT. Remember, it must always be in the root directory of the system disk, so a simple Dir command does the job.

If you use a fixed disk, the current directory should still be C:\RUNDOS, so type the following command to check the root directory:

```
C>dir \autoexec.bat
```

If you use DOS from diskettes, the current drive should be B, so check the system disk for AUTOEXEC.BAT by typing:

```
B>dir a:autoexec.bat
```

If DOS responds *File not found*, you don't have an AUTOEXEC.BAT file and you won't hurt a thing by trying the following examples. If, however, DOS responds by showing an entry for AUTOEXEC.BAT, type one of the following commands to protect your existing file from inadvertent loss.

If you have a fixed disk, type:

```
C>ren \autoexec.bat \autoexec.sav
```

If you use DOS from diskettes, type:

```
B>ren a:autoexec.bat autoexec.sav
```

Type the Dir command again. This time, DOS should respond *File not found*.

You'll restore your original AUTOEXEC.BAT later.

Creating an AUTOEXEC.BAT File

Depending on how your system is set up and what you want to do with it, an AUTOEXEC.BAT file can contain anywhere from a few to many commands. As mentioned earlier, however, two that are usually included are a Path command that tells

DOS where to find command files and a Prompt command that sets the system prompt to display the current directory.

Although your normal AUTOEXEC.BAT file might well include more than these two commands, the following example shows you how to create just such a simple AUTOEXEC.BAT file. The file is short, so copy from the console to create it.

If you have a fixed disk, type the following, substituting the name of your DOS directory if it isn't C:\DOS:

```
C>copy con \autoexec.bat
rem SAMPLE STARTUP PROCEDURE
path c:\;c:\dos;c:\rundos
prompt $p$g
^Z
```

If you don't have a fixed disk, type:

```
B>copy con a:autoexec.bat
rem SAMPLE STARTUP PROCEDURE
path a:\
prompt $p$g
^Z
```

You created the file in the root directory of the system disk because that's where DOS always looks for AUTOEXEC.BAT. To test your startup procedure, you must restart the system.

Note: If you're using a fixed disk, be sure to open the latch or remove any diskette in the diskette drive so that DOS restarts from the fixed disk.

Now restart the system by pressing Ctrl-Alt-Del. DOS might display some messages before carrying out the commands in your new AUTOEXEC.BAT file, but regardless of your version of DOS, at least part of the startup screen looks like this:

```
C>rem SAMPLE STARTUP PROCEDURE

C>path c:\;c:\dos;c:\rundos

C>prompt $p$g

c:\>_
```

So far so good, but as you've probably realized, a simple batch file like this just begins to tap the power of AUTOEXEC.BAT. Suppose, now, that you want DOS to display its version number each time you start your computer. You also want DOS to clear the screen, change to a particular directory (to a different drive if you don't have a fixed disk), and display a directory listing. Here's a new AUTOEXEC.BAT file that does what you want. You can use Edit, Edlin, or a word processor if you want to try your editing skills. Otherwise, simply copy from the console again (as shown in the example) to replace the sample AUTOEXEC.BAT file with a new version.

If you have a fixed disk, type the following:

```
C:\>copy con autoexec.bat
rem SAMPLE STARTUP PROCEDURE
path c:\;c:\dos;c:\rundos
prompt $p$g
cls
ver
cd \rundos
dir
^Z
```

If you're not using a fixed disk, type the following:

```
A:\>copy con autoexec.bat
rem SAMPLE STARTUP PROCEDURE
path a:\
prompt $p$g
cls
ver
b:
dir
^Z
```

Again, restart the system to test your new AUTOEXEC.BAT file. This time, you see (though briefly):

```
C>rem SAMPLE STARTUP PROCEDURE

C>path c:\;c:\dos;c:\rundos

C>prompt $p$g
```

The screen clears, and then DOS displays:

```
C:\>ver

MS-DOS Version 5.0

C:\>cd rundos

C:\RUNDOS>dir

 Volume in drive C is FIXED DISK
 Volume Serial Number is 1608-5A30
 Directory of C:\RUNDOS

 .            <DIR>      10-16-91    8:21a
 ..           <DIR>      10-16-91    8:21a
 PH       TXT      526 10-16-91    1:43p
 LETR1    DOC       26 10-16-91    3:13p
 LETR2    DOC       26 10-16-91    3:13p
 LETR3    DOC       26 10-16-91    3:13p
```

```
DIRLET    BAT        41 10-16-91    3:17p
PRNT      BAT        13 10-16-91    3:24p
DIRS      BAT        15 10-16-91    3:30p
          9 file(s)           673 bytes
                       13265422 bytes free
```

Your new startup procedure not only tells DOS where to find the files it needs, it also displays the version number, clears the screen, changes the current directory or drive and tells you what it is, and then displays the entries in the current directory.

You can also use AUTOEXEC.BAT to handle special startup requirements. For example, if your system has equipment options that require special setup instructions with the Mode command, put the commands in AUTOEXEC.BAT so that you needn't type them each time you start or restart the system. Or, if your system has an electronic clock and calendar that require you to run a program to set the date and time, you can put the command in AUTOEXEC.BAT so that you don't have to enter the command each time you start the system.

If other people use the system to run an application program, you can make a copy of the system diskette for them that includes an AUTOEXEC.BAT file ending with the command to start the application program automatically.

If you renamed your existing AUTOEXEC.BAT file at the beginning of this example, type the following to save the example and restore the original:

C:\RUNDOS>ren \autoexec.bat autoexec.run

C:\RUNDOS>ren \autoexec.sav autoexec.bat

Now your real AUTOEXEC.BAT will be executed the next time you start up your system. The version you created in the example is still in the root directory as AUTOEXEC.RUN, in case you want to experiment with it further.

If you didn't have an AUTOEXEC.BAT file to begin with, type the following so DOS will not carry out your example file the next time you start your system:

C:\RUNDOS>ren autoexec.bat autoexec.run

Finally, to rid your system of a possibly invalid Path command, restart your computer by pressing Ctrl-Alt-Del.

SOME USEFUL COMMANDS

The following examples describe a few batch commands you might find useful; they might also give you some ideas for other commands you could create. Each topic includes a description of what the command does, the contents of the batch file, and one or two examples of its use.

These examples are illustrative; they are not hands-on exercises because you might not have the necessary files or devices to use them. But remember that they're here; you'll probably find a situation in which they can be helpful.

Printing a File

Earlier in the chapter you created the Prnt batch command, which prints a file by copying it to the printer. PRNT.BAT contains *copy %1 prn*. To use it, you type the name of the batch file followed by the name of the file to be printed. (For example, to print a file named REPORT.DOC, you would type *prnt report.doc*.)

As the examples in Figure 14-1 showed, you can make batch commands more specific by including common parts of a file name or extension in the batch file. For example, if you frequently print files that have the extension DOC, you could enter the command in the batch file as *copy %1.doc*; to print the file named REPORT.DOC, you would only have to type *prnt report*.

Printing a File in Small Type

If your printer is compatible with Epson or IBM dot-matrix printers, you can use the Mode command to print 132 characters on a line. This type is handy for wide reports or spreadsheets, and putting the Mode and Copy commands in a batch file named SMALL.BAT makes them easy to use. SMALL.BAT contains:

```
mode lpt1: 132
copy %1 lpt1:
mode lpt1: 80
```

If your printer is attached to a different port, change *lpt1* to *lpt2* or *lpt3*, as necessary. The Small command takes one parameter, the name of the file to be printed in small type. To use the Small command to print the file REPORT.DOC, you would type:

```
C:\>small report.doc
```

DOS would display the Mode and Copy commands and print the file in small type:

```
C:\>mode lpt1: 132

LPT1: not rerouted

LPT1: set for 132

No retry on parallel printer time-out

C:\>copy report.doc lpt1:
        1 file(s) copied

C:\>mode lpt1: 80

LPT1: not rerouted

LPT1: set for 80

No retry on parallel printer time-out
```

The second Mode command resets the printer to normal type.

Eliminating Old BAK Files

Because many word processors create a backup file with an extension of BAK each time you edit a file, your disks can get crowded with files you might not need. The CLEANUP.BAT batch file described here would erase all the files in the current directory whose extension is BAK. CLEANUP.BAT contains:

```
del %1*.bak
```

The Cleanup command takes one parameter, the directory name followed by a backslash. If you omit the parameter, the command cleans up the current directory. You can clean up the disk in a different drive by preceding the path name with the drive letter and a colon. For example, to erase all files whose extension is BAK in the current directory, you would simply type *cleanup*. To erase all BAK files in the directory \MKT\WP, you would type *cleanup \mkt\wp*. Similarly, to erase all BAK files in the directory \LASTYEAR\RPT on the disk in drive A, you would type *cleanup a:\lastyear\rpt*. Finally, to erase all files whose extension is BAK in the current directory of the disk in drive B, you would type *C:\>cleanup b:*.

CREATING COMMANDS WITH DOSKEY

Note: Doskey is included with version 5 of DOS. If you have an earlier version and are thinking of upgrading, this section can help you evaluate version 5. If you're content with the version of DOS you use, skip ahead to the next chapter.

You've seen how batch files can help you customize DOS by combining commands to perform those special tasks you want done. To create a batch file, you can copy from the console, as in the preceding examples, or can use a text editor or a word processor. If you have version 5, you can also use Doskey.

Chapters 3 and 13 showed how Doskey can help you edit and repeat DOS commands you've already used. This section introduces you to several Doskey parameters that help you not only view but save commands in either of two forms: as batch files or as keyboard shortcuts called *macros*.

Batch Files and Macros

You know that batch files are sets of DOS commands that you save in a text file and carry out by typing the name of the batch file. A macro is a similar type of work-saver. You create a macro by assigning a descriptive name to one or more commands. Once you've defined a macro in this way, you simply type the name to carry out the commands. You benefit by saving time and keystrokes, especially with often-used, long, or complicated sets of commands.

In some respects, macros are very much like batch files. Both are your creations; both cause DOS to carry out one or more commands to do a specific job; and both let you start the command sequence by typing a short, descriptive name.

Doskey Command Parameters

In earlier chapters, you've typed *doskey* to start the Doskey program, and you've used function and editing keys to retrieve, display, and edit commands. Doskey also includes several parameters you can use to create and view commands and macros. Three important ones are:

doskey /history <macro>=<command> /macros

doskey is the name of the program. When you type *doskey* by itself, DOS loads the program into memory, where it remains until you turn the system off or restart DOS.

/history, which you can abbreviate as /h, tells Doskey to show you a list of all commands currently in memory. You can use the /history parameter to create a batch file, by redirecting the commands from memory to a file.

<macro>=<command> tells Doskey to create a macro. As already mentioned, you assign a name (shown here as *macro*) to one or more commands (*command*). An equal sign must follow the macro name.

/macros, which you can abbreviate as /m, tells Doskey to display the macros currently in memory. You can use the /macros parameter to save macros by redirecting them from the computer's memory, where they will be lost when you shut down the system, to a file.

Doskey includes a few other parameters you can use to control its behavior. You don't need these parameters here; the details are in Appendix C, ''DOS Command Reference.''

Using Doskey to Create a Batch File

When you use DOS, you can retrieve and edit the last command you entered. When you use Doskey, you can retrieve and edit many more because the commands remain in a special portion of your computer's memory until you turn off the computer or restart Doskey, or until you've typed so many commands that the oldest ones are discarded to make room for newer ones.

Because commands remain in memory, you can use Doskey as an alternative to a text editor for creating some batch files. The following example shows how to redirect Doskey's list of commands to a batch file. Begin by starting Doskey. Type:

```
C:\>doskey
```

(If Doskey is already running, press Alt-F7. This clears the list of commands Doskey has recorded and assures you of a fresh start.)

Now type some commands:

`C:\>cd \rundos`

`C:\RUNDOS>dir /o:e > prn`

`C:\RUNDOS>cd \`

These three commands change the current directory, print a directory listing sorted by extension, and return to the root directory of drive C. These commands could form a small but useful batch file for keeping track of the files you create with your applications, especially if you can specify the directory you want to list and print. You can create the file in a two-step process.

First, use the Doskey /history parameter to redirect the commands to a file. This example uses the extension BAT, but you could just as easily save the commands as a standard text file with an extension such as TXT or DOC. Type:

`C:\>doskey /h > list.bat`

That's really all there is to using Doskey to save a sequence of commands you've typed. If you want to save the commands as a usable batch file, however, your work isn't quite done, so use Edit to add a few finishing touches. Type:

`C:\>edit list.bat`

When Edit displays the file, change \RUNDOS to a replaceable parameter so you can specify any directory you choose. Change:

cd \rundos

to:

cd %1

Notice, too, that Doskey has included the command you typed to create the batch file. You have to omit this command to avoid accidentally redirecting some future list of unrelated Doskey commands to your batch file, so delete the line that contains *doskey /h > list.bat*. Save the file, and you're done. From now on, whenever you want to print the directory entries of the files in a particular directory, sorted by extension, just type *list* followed by the name of the directory.

Using Doskey in this way can be especially useful when you're developing a batch file and aren't certain the commands you're putting together will do the job you have in mind. Start Doskey and type each command you intend to use. Because each command is carried out immediately, you can see exactly what it does, and you can see how all the commands work together before you save them as a batch file.

Using Doskey to Create a Macro

Creating a macro with Doskey is just as easy as creating a batch file, perhaps even easier. To define a macro to Doskey, you type a macro name, an equal sign, and the command or commands you want the macro to carry out. You can use replaceable parameters as you do in batch files, but instead of %1, %2, %3, and so on, you use $1, $2, $3, and so on through $9.

The following examples use the Directory and Mode commands to create some macros you might want to use.

In version 5, the /O parameter of the Directory command allows you to sort a directory in a number of ways: by name, extension, size, or date and time, or with subdirectories grouped together. Depending on what you're doing, you might choose to look at a directory in any of these ways. To keep typing to a minimum, you can create a macro for each type of listing and add the /P parameter so that DOS will pause after each screenful.

If you haven't turned off or restarted your computer, clear Doskey's memory by pressing Alt-F7. If you have turned off your computer, turn it back on and type *doskey* to load the program. Now create the macros by typing or editing the following:

```
C:\>doskey dname=dir $1 /o:n /p

C:\>doskey dext=dir $1 /o:e /p

C:\>doskey dsize=dir $1 /o:s /p

C:\>doskey ddate=dir $1 /o:d /p

C:\>doskey dsubs=dir $1 /o:g /p
```

Now try them out. Using your \DOS directory as an example, type *dname \dos* to list the entries alphabetically by file name, *dext \dos* to list them by extension, *dsize \dos* to list them by size, and *ddate \dos* to list them by date and time. If you want, type *dsubs c:* to group directories on drive C.

If you have a monitor that can change between a normal display (25 lines) and a condensed display (43 or 50 lines) with the Mode command, you can create macros that switch you quickly back and forth. You might, for example, prefer a condensed display for directory listings but a regular 25-line display for most other work. Type the following:

```
C:\>doskey big=mode con lines=25

C:\>doskey little=mode con lines=43
```

Now, when you want a condensed display, simply type *little*. To switch back to 25 lines, type *big*. (If you try these examples and DOS responds *ANSI.SYS must be installed to perform requested function*, you need to identify a file named ANSI.SYS to DOS as part of your startup procedure. Chapter 17, ''Tailoring Your System,'' tells you how.)

You can also combine the screen macros with the directory-display macros by taking advantage of Doskey's ability to accept more than one command on a line. At the system prompt, you separate commands by pressing Ctrl-T. In a macro, you do the same thing by typing *$T* (or *$t*). For example, the following macro changes the screen to a condensed display, lists by size the entries in the directory you specify, waits for you to press a key, and then returns to a 25-line display. Note the *$t* separating the Mode, Pause, and Dir commands. Although the macro is shown on two lines here, don't press Enter until you reach the end:

```
doskey dir43=mode con lines=43 $t dir $1 /o:s /p
$t pause $t mode con lines=25<enter>
```

To see a condensed listing of your \DOS directory, you would type *dir43 \ dos*.

Saving Macros for Later Use

Although macros act much like batch files, they are stored in your computer's memory, not on disk, so they are not automatically saved when you turn off or restart the computer. You can save the macros you create, however, by using either the /history or /macros parameter to redirect the macros into a file. The difference between the two parameters is an important one:

▶ If the macro-definition commands are in the list of commands Doskey can retrieve, /history saves the *commands* that create the macros.

▶ If the macros are currently in your computer's memory, /macros saves the macros themselves.

To see how these parameters work, first use the /history parameter to save the macro definitions currently in your computer's memory. Type:

```
C:\>doskey /h > macros1.txt
```

Now, save the macros themselves by typing:

```
C:\>doskey /m > macros2.txt
```

Use the DOS Type command to view the two files you just saved. The commands saved with /history look something like this (you probably won't see them all if you've been trying out the macros):

```
doskey dname=dir $1 /o:n /p
doskey dext=dir $1 /o:n /p
doskey dsize=dir $1 /o:n /p
doskey ddate=dir $1 /o:n /p
doskey big=mode con lines=25
doskey little=mode con lines=43
doskey dir43=mode con lines=43 $t dir $1 /o:s /p
  $t pause $t mode con lines=25
doskey /h > macros1.txt
```

The file saved with /macros looks like this:

```
DNAME=dir $1 /o:n /p
DEXT=dir $1 /o:n /p
DSIZE=dir $1 /o:n /p
DDATE=dir $1 /o:n /p
BIG=mode con lines=25
LITTLE=mode con lines=43
DIR43=mode con lines=43 $t dir $1 /o:s /p
  $t pause $t mode con lines=25
```

The first file contains the *commands* that created the macros. You can easily turn such a file into a batch file by entering the macro-definition commands, giving the file a BAT extension, and deleting the last line (for example, *doskey /h > macrosl.txt*).

The second file contains the *macros* you created. They form a useful record of your macros, but in order to run them again in your next session with DOS, you must edit the file, adding *doskey* in front of each one to turn the macro into the command that creates it.

Thus, although the /macros parameter might appear to be more useful because it saves the actual macros, the reverse is actually true. Each time you start DOS, you must also define any macros you want to use. If you're going to save a macro, you want to save the macro definition because you must run the command that creates the macro before you can use the macro itself. You can, if you want, put a macro-definition command in a batch file and run it without any problems. You cannot, however, run the macro itself from a batch file, even if you first define it in the same batch file. Macro names can be typed only at the DOS system prompt.

CHAPTER 15

CREATING SMART COMMANDS

The previous two chapters showed how redirection, pipes, filter commands, batch files, and macros let you build your own commands or change the way that DOS commands work. This chapter shows how DOS gives you more control over the way it carries out the commands you build into a batch file. The techniques in this chapter help you create powerful commands tailored to your needs.

You can make your commands display their own instructions or warning messages. Or you can specify the circumstances under which DOS carries out one command—or a different sequence of commands altogether. You can even make the system pause until you tell it to proceed.

This chapter shows you how to develop a batch file that uses most of these capabilities. The next chapter extends the example, describes two additional batch commands, and shows several useful commands you can create. When you complete these two chapters, you'll be ready to apply the full power of DOS to your needs.

PREPARING FOR THE EXAMPLES

For these examples, you'll need one or two formatted diskettes and some sample files. If you completed the examples in Chapter 13, ''Taking Control of Your System,'' use the diskette or directory that contains the phone-list file.

If You're Using a Fixed Disk

If you're using a fixed disk, you need one formatted diskette; put it in drive A. Change the current directory to \RUNDOS by typing:

```
C:\>cd \rundos
```

All the DOS commands you need are on the fixed disk. If you want, change the prompt to C>, as shown in the following examples, by typing *prompt*.

If You're Not Using a Fixed Disk

If you're not using a fixed disk, you need two formatted diskettes because the examples copy files from drive B to drive A. You'll take the DOS diskette out of drive A and replace it with the second formatted diskette, but before you do, note that DOS will need this diskette, plus the three command files FIND.EXE, SORT.EXE, and MORE.COM in the next chapter.

To make these command files available to DOS, you can either copy the files to the diskette in drive B, or you can set the command path to A:, keep your DOS diskettes close at hand, and swap the sample diskette with the appropriate DOS diskette in drive A as required. If you decide to use your DOS diskettes, try not to copy sample files to them inadvertently. You can always delete the files, but the examples might not work as you expect. Besides, it's a good idea to keep your DOS diskettes DOS-only.

You'll also edit a batch file in this chapter. Because both Edit and Edlin are in external command files, the easiest way to make changes on a diskette-only system is to copy from the console. If you want to use a text editor, however, Edlin is a better choice than Edit for these examples because it is a simpler program and makes fewer demands on your system.

With all this in mind, prepare for the examples by placing the diskette with the phone list in drive B and replacing the system diskette in drive A with the second formatted diskette. Change the current drive to B by typing:

```
A>b:

B>_
```

As you follow the examples, remember that your system prompt will be B>, not C>.

Creating the Sample Files

You will use six sample files in the next two chapters:

P.DOC	Q.DOC
P.BAK	Q.BAK
P.OLD	Q.OLD

Type the following to create the files (as usual, press F6 or Ctrl-Z and Enter where you see ^Z):

```
C>copy con p.doc
This is a sample file.
^Z
        1 file(s) copied

C>copy p.doc p.bak
        1 file(s) copied

C>copy p.doc p.old
        1 file(s) copied

C>copy p.* q.*
P.DOC
P.BAK
P.OLD
        3 file(s) copied
```

If you're creating these files on a diskette, you'll need this diskette in the next chapter, so title it BATCH COMMANDS. (If it's already labeled for the phone-list file, just add the new words.) This completes the preparation for the examples.

CREATING AN ARCHIVE COMMAND

Disk files proliferate as you use your computer. You'll probably archive files from time to time, copying them to long-term storage diskettes and then erasing them from your working disks, just as you occasionally remove documents from your paper files and put them in long-term storage.

Although DOS includes the Backup and Restore commands to help you archive old files, this chapter shows you how to use the DOS batch commands to develop an Archive command that everyone can use, whether or not they're comfortable using DOS commands.

Starting with just a Copy command, you expand the batch file to display instructions, provide a safeguard against inadvertently erasing a previously archived file, and erase the file after it is archived.

The diskette in drive A represents the archive diskette, the one you store in a safe place. Your fixed disk or the diskette in drive B represents the working disk that contains files you want to archive.

Your Archive command will be a file named ARCHIVE.BAT. The initial version contains only a Copy command. To create the file, type the following:

```
C>copy con archive.bat
copy %1 a:%1
^Z
        1 file(s) copied
```

This file is the starting point for your Archive command. It requires only one parameter, the name of the file to be archived. The Copy command copies this file (*%1* in the Copy command) to the diskette in drive A, giving it the same name (*a:%1*) as the original. To see how the batch file works, make certain the archive diskette is in drive A; archive P.DOC by typing:

```
C>archive p.doc
```

DOS responds by displaying and carrying out the Copy command in the batch file:

```
C>copy p.doc a:p.doc
        1 file(s) copied
```

This isn't much, but then it's only a starting point. You'll add significantly to this simple command as you go through the examples in this chapter.

MODIFYING THE SAMPLE BATCH FILE

This chapter describes four batch commands: Echo, Pause, If, and Goto. Each command description explains the purpose of the batch command, then adds it to ARCHIVE.BAT. The modified version of the batch file is shown with the changed or added lines shaded. Either use your text editor (Edit or Edlin) to make the indicated changes or enter the updated version by copying from the console.

CONTROLLING SYSTEM MESSAGES

The Echo command controls whether commands in a batch file are displayed, and it lets you display your own messages. It has three parameters:

echo on off <message>

on causes commands to be displayed as they are carried out (this is called "turning echo on"). Echo is on unless you turn it off.

off causes commands not to be displayed as they are carried out (this is called "turning echo off"). Eliminating the commands from the display can make a batch file easier to use by reducing clutter on the screen.

<message> is a string of characters, such as a reminder or a warning, that you want to display. <message> is displayed whether echo is turned on or off.

You can include only one parameter with an Echo command. If you omit all parameters (just type *echo*), DOS displays the status of echo (either *ECHO is on* or *ECHO is off*).

The first changes to your Archive command add an Echo command at the beginning to turn echo off and another Echo command after it to display a title message.

Here is the modified version of ARCHIVE.BAT (the line numbers are for reference only):

```
1. echo off
2. echo Archive Procedure
3. copy %1 a:%1
```

To archive P.DOC with your new Archive command, type the name of the batch file and the name of the file to be archived:

```
C>archive p.doc
```

Because echo is always on when DOS starts carrying out the commands in a batch file, DOS displays the first Echo command, which turns echo off. Then it carries out the second Echo command, which displays the title *Archive Procedure*. Finally, it carries out the Copy command from the original ARCHIVE.BAT and copies the file:

```
C>echo off
Archive Procedure
        1 file(s) copied
```

Messages produced by a command itself (such as *1 file(s) copied* in the preceding example) are displayed whether echo is on or off.

Starting with version 3.3, you can prevent any command from being echoed by preceding it with the @ symbol. This means that you can eliminate even that first *echo off* message by changing the first line of ARCHIVE.BAT to *@echo off*. If you're using 3.3 or a later version, edit the file again to add the @ symbol at the beginning of line 1. From now on, all the examples will show the @ symbol; if you're not using 3.3 or a later version, simply ignore it.

Your Archive command is starting to take shape. It's time to add some instructions for the person who uses it.

MAKING THE SYSTEM PAUSE

Some DOS commands, such as Format and Diskcopy, display a message and wait for you to respond, giving you a chance to confirm your intention, or to complete preparation by inserting a diskette or by turning on the printer. You can have your batch files do the same by using the Pause command, which displays the message *Press any key to continue...* and makes the system wait until you press any key. (The message is *Strike a key when ready...* in versions prior to 4.0.)

The Pause command has one parameter:

pause <message>

<message> is a string of characters, such as a reminder or a warning, that you want the Pause command to display. <message> is displayed only if echo is on.

You'll add a Pause command to ARCHIVE.BAT now. You'll also add a message—a reminder to make certain that the archive diskette is in drive A before the file is copied.

But wait: Any message you include as a parameter with the Pause command is displayed only if echo is on, and you have turned echo off in line 1 of ARCHIVE.BAT.

You can still use the Pause command, however. Instead of using the message capability of the Pause command, just use an Echo command to display the reminder, then add a Pause command without a message. This approach is a bit more work than simply adding a message after the Pause command, but the result is a command that's easier to use because you avoid cluttering the display with all the commands that DOS would display if you were to turn echo on.

The modified version of ARCHIVE.BAT is:

```
1. @echo off
2. echo Archive Procedure
3. echo Make sure archive diskette is in drive A
4. pause
5. copy %1 a:%1
```

Remember, if you're not using version 3.3 or later, ignore the @ in line 1. Test this version by typing:

```
C>archive p.doc
Archive Procedure
Make sure archive diskette is in drive A
Press any key to continue . . .
_
```

The Echo command displays the reminder, the Pause command displays its message telling you to press a key, and the system waits. Complete the command by pressing any key. DOS copies the file and acknowledges:

```
1 file(s) copied
```

CONTROLLING WHICH COMMANDS ARE CARRIED OUT

Besides carrying out DOS commands as though you had typed them individually, batch files let you specify that a command should be carried out only if some condition (such as whether a file exists) is true. This capability makes your batch files more flexible, letting you adapt them to a variety of situations.

The If command specifies the condition to be checked and the DOS command to be carried out. It has three parameters:

if not <condition> <command>

not reverses the meaning of the If command so that <command> is carried out only if <condition> is not true.

<condition> is the condition to check. It has two commonly used forms:

▶ *exist* <filename> checks whether the named file exists. You can include a path name, if necessary. If <filename> exists, the condition is true.

▶ <string1>==<string2> compares the two character strings you specify. If they are identical, the condition is true. Note that there are two equal signs.

<command> is any DOS command.

You'll add an If command to ARCHIVE.BAT to control when a warning message is displayed.

Adding Protection to Your Archive Command

When you copy a file with the Copy command, you tell DOS the name of the original and the name to be given to the new copy. DOS checks to see whether there is already a file with the same name as the copy on the target disk; if there is, DOS replaces the existing file with the copy. What if you didn't realize that a file with the same name existed on the disk? You might inadvertently lose a valuable file.

To protect yourself against such an oversight, you'll include two more commands in ARCHIVE.BAT. First, you'll add an If command that checks to see whether the file to be archived already exists on the archive diskette in drive A. If it does, an Echo command in the second part of the If command displays a warning message telling you that you can cancel the command by pressing Ctrl-Break. You'll also add a Pause command to give you time to read the warning message and, if necessary, cancel the Archive command by pressing Ctrl-Break.

Here is the modified version of ARCHIVE.BAT. Type line 5 on one line, even though it is shown on two lines in the text:

```
1.  @echo off
2.  echo Archive Procedure
3.  echo Make sure archive diskette is in drive A
4.  pause
5.  if exist a:%1 echo a:%1 exists. Press
    CTRL-BREAK to cancel, or
6.  pause
7.  copy %1 a:%1
```

Test this version of your Archive command by typing:

```
C>archive p.doc
Archive Procedure
Make sure archive diskette is in drive A
Press any key to continue . . .
_
```

Press any key to continue the command:

```
a:p.doc exists. Press CTRL-BREAK to cancel, or
Press any key to continue . . .
_
```

Don't press any key yet.

You might not want to replace the copy of the file in drive A. Press Ctrl-Break to cancel the command. DOS asks whether you really mean it:

```
Terminate batch job (Y/N)?_
```

Type *y* to confirm. DOS cancels the rest of your Archive command and displays the system prompt without copying the file. If you had not pressed Ctrl-Break, the file would have been copied as before, erasing the previously archived version of P.DOC.

Smoothing a Rough Edge

Your Archive command is getting more useful; you've protected yourself from inadvertently erasing an existing file. But there's a problem now. See what happens if the name of the file to be archived isn't the name of a file already on the diskette in drive A. Delete P.DOC from drive A and archive it again:

```
C>del a:p.doc

C>archive p.doc
Archive Procedure
Make sure archive diskette is in drive A
Press any key to continue . . .
_
```

324

Fine so far. Press the Spacebar to continue:

Press any key to continue . . .

—

That's not too good. The system comes right back and pauses again, even though everything is OK, because the Pause command that follows the If command is always carried out. Press the Spacebar again:

1 file(s) copied

DOS copies the file as it should. Your Archive command is working properly, but the two pauses could be confusing, especially if someone else uses your batch command. How can you fix this?

You could delete the first Pause command, but if you did, you wouldn't have a chance to make certain that the correct diskette has been placed in drive A. That's not a very good solution.

Or you could delete the second Pause command and change the If command, making the "file exists" warning a Pause message instead of an Echo message, as it is now. But then, recall that you would have to delete the command *echo off* at the beginning of the batch file so that the message following the new Pause command would be displayed. And that would mean all your commands in the file would be displayed. This solution would make the response to your Archive command cluttered and confusing, so it isn't very good either.

There is, however, a way to change your Archive command so that the second Pause command is carried out only if the file to be archived is already on the diskette in drive A. This solution requires using another command for batch files, the Goto command.

CHANGING THE SEQUENCE OF COMMANDS

The batch files you have created up to now carry out the DOS commands they contain in the order in which the commands appear. Your batch commands would be more flexible if you could control the order in which the commands are carried out. The Goto command gives you this control by telling DOS to go to a specific line in the command file, rather than to the next command in the sequence.

You tell DOS where to go in the batch file by specifying a *label*. A label identifies a line in a batch file; it consists of a colon (:) immediately followed by a string of characters (such as *start*). A label is not a command. It merely identifies a location in a batch file. When DOS goes to a label, it carries out whatever commands follow the line on which the label appears.

The Goto command has one parameter:

goto <label>

<label> is the label that identifies the line in the batch file where DOS is to go.

The Goto command is often used as part of an If command. For example, the If command checks some condition. If the condition is not true, DOS carries out the next command; if the condition is true, DOS carries out the Goto command and moves to some other part of the batch file.

Remember the problem with your Archive command? If the file to be archived is already on the diskette in drive A, you want to display a warning message and pause; otherwise, you just want to copy the file. This situation is tailor-made for an If command that includes a Goto command.

The modified version of ARCHIVE.BAT is:

```
1. @echo off
2. echo Archive Procedure
3. echo Make sure archive diskette is in drive A
4. pause
5. if not exist a:%1 goto safe
6. echo a:%1 exists. Press CTRL-BREAK to cancel, or
7. pause
8. :safe
9. copy %1 a:%1
```

These changes warrant a bit more explanation:

▷ The If command still checks whether the file to be archived exists on the diskette in drive A. Now, however, the command includes the parameter *not*, which means that the command in the second part of the If command is carried out only if the reverse of the condition is true (that is, if the file does *not* exist on the diskette in drive A).

▷ The second part of the If command—the command to be carried out if the condition is true—is changed to a Goto command that tells DOS to skip to a label called *:safe*.

▷ If the file to be archived doesn't exist on the diskette in drive A, the Goto command is carried out and DOS jumps to the label *:safe*, skipping the Echo and Pause commands. The Copy command following *:safe* copies the file.

▷ If the file to be archived does exist on the diskette in drive A, the Goto command is not carried out and DOS continues with the Echo and Pause commands. If you don't cancel by pressing Ctrl-Break, DOS carries out the Copy command. In this instance, DOS ignores the line that contains the label *:safe* because the only purpose of the label is to identify a location in a batch file.

P. DOC is on the diskette in drive A (you archived it again a bit earlier), so first see if this version of your Archive command warns you that the file exists. Type the following:

```
C>archive p.doc
Archive Procedure
Make sure archive diskette is in drive A
Press any key to continue . . .

_
```

Press any key to continue the command:

```
a:p.doc exists. Press CTRL-BREAK to cancel, or
Press any key to continue . . .

_
```

There's the warning. Press any key to complete the command:

```
              1 file(s) copied
```

But the problem came up when the file wasn't on the archive diskette: You got the second pause anyway. Test your revised Archive command in this situation by archiving P.BAK, which hasn't yet been archived:

```
C>archive p.bak
Archive Procedure
Make sure archive diskette is in drive A
Press any key to continue . . .

_
```

Press a key:

```
              1 file(s) copied
```

Problem solved. Because P.BAK wasn't on the archive diskette in drive A, the Goto command was carried out; it caused DOS to skip over the intervening Echo and Pause commands and to copy the file.

Your Archive command works properly. You had to do a little more work to avoid the double pause, but now the command is less confusing and easier to use. You'll probably encounter this kind of circumstance fairly often as you create batch commands. Just remember: It takes a little more time to make a command easy to use, but the investment is usually worthwhile, especially if someone other than you will use the command.

Using Wildcard Characters with a Batch File

You can use wildcard characters to archive a series of files with your Archive command. Type the following command to archive all the files named P:

327

```
C>archive p.*
Archive Procedure
Make sure archive diskette is in drive A
Press any key to continue . . .
_
```

Press any key:

```
a:p.* exists. Press CTRL-BREAK to cancel, or
Press any key to continue . . .
_
```

You archived P.DOC and P.BAK in earlier examples, so they're on the archive diskette. The Archive command doesn't identify the specific file that exists, but it does give you a chance to cancel if you don't want to overwrite a file.

Press Ctrl-Break to cancel the rest of the command, and respond to the DOS prompt for confirmation with *y*:

```
Terminate batch job (Y/N)?y
```

If you had pressed any key other than Ctrl-Break, all the files named P would have been copied to the diskette in drive A, replacing any that were already there.

Erasing the Original of an Archived File

Archiving not only involves copying a file to an archive diskette, it also means deleting the original. Your Archive command only copies; now it's time to make it delete too. But just as it's prudent to check whether the file exists on the archive diskette before you make the copy, it's also prudent to check again before deleting the original, just to be sure the file was copied to the archive diskette.

You need only one additional If command to check whether the file to be archived is on the archive diskette and, if it is, to delete the original from the working disk. Here is this modified version of ARCHIVE.BAT:

```
 1. @echo off
 2. echo Archive Procedure
 3. echo Make sure archive diskette is in drive A
 4. pause
 5. if not exist a:%1 goto safe
 6. echo a:%1 exists. Press CTRL-BREAK to cancel, or
 7. pause
 8. :safe
 9. copy %1 a:%1
10. if exist a:%1 del %1
```

The screen responses of this version of your Archive command are the same as in the previous version, but the new command deletes the original file after copying it. Test it by archiving P.DOC again:

```
C>archive p.doc
Archive Procedure
Make sure archive diskette is in drive A
Press any key to continue . . .
_
```

Press any key:

```
a:p.doc exists. Press CTRL-BREAK to cancel, or
Press any key to continue . . .
_
```

You want to copy the file to the archive diskette, so press any key:

```
        1 file(s) copied
```

See if the original version of P.DOC still exists by typing:

```
C>dir p.doc

Volume in drive C is FIXED DISK
Volume Serial Number is 1608-5A30
Directory of C:\RUNDOS

File not found
```

The original is gone. Your Archive command does copy the specified file to the archive diskette and then deletes the original.

Functionally, the command is complete.

DRESSING UP YOUR ARCHIVE COMMAND

The value of your batch files depends not only on what they do, but also on how easy it is to use them correctly. This ease of use is particularly important if you use a batch file only occasionally, or if someone else uses it; it's vital if the batch file deletes other files, as your Archive command does.

That's why, for example, your Archive command starts by turning echo off: An uncluttered screen helps to make the responses less confusing. You can also do some other things to make a batch file easy to use:

▶ Clear the screen.

▶ Use the Echo command to display messages that report on progress or results.

▶ Use spaces or insert tabs so you can position messages displayed by the Echo command where they are prominent on the screen.

▶ Use the Echo command to include blank lines that further improve the readability of the screen.

You can also use the Remark command to put notes to yourself in the batch file. As long as echo is off, these remarks aren't displayed. Remarks can help you remember how a batch file works, in case you have to change it or you want to create a similar command using the same technique. Remarks are especially useful if the batch file is long or if it's one you may not look at very often.

Echoing a Blank Line

Up to now, you have used the Echo command either to turn echo off or to display a message. You can also use the Echo command to display a blank line—something you'll probably want to do fairly often to improve the appearance of the display.

You've seen that you turn echo on or off by following *echo* with either *on* or *off*. If you follow *echo* with some other words, they are displayed as a message, and if you simply type *echo*, DOS tells you whether echo is on or off. How do you tell DOS to echo a blank line? Beginning with version 3.1, typing *echo.* (echo and a period, with no space between) causes DOS to display a blank line. If this does not work with your version of DOS, you can also type *echo*, press the Spacebar once, hold down the Alt key, and press 255 on the numeric keypad (not the numbers in the top row of the keyboard). When you release the Alt key, the cursor moves over one column. You don't see any characters displayed, but when DOS carries out your Echo command, it will echo a blank line on the screen.

The following example modifies ARCHIVE.BAT. If your version of DOS doesn't respond to *echo.*, substitute Alt-255 in the appropriate lines. The changes in this batch file don't add any capability to your Archive command, but they do make it easier for someone to understand what's happening. The changes are described in more detail in a moment. Here is the modified version of ARCHIVE.BAT:

```
 1. @echo off
 2. cls
 3. REM THREE TABS IN FOLLOWING ECHO COMMAND
 4. echo<tab><tab><tab>***ARCHIVE PROCEDURE***
 5. echo.
 6. echo Make sure archive diskette is in drive A
 7. pause
 8. REM BRANCH AROUND WARNING IF FILE NOT ARCHIVED
 9. if not exist a:%1 goto safe
10. echo.
11. echo a:%1 exists. Press CTRL-BREAK to cancel, or
12. pause
13. :safe
14. copy %1 a:%1
15. if exist a:%1 del %1
16. echo.
17. echo %1 archived
```

The purpose of each change is as follows:

▶ In line 2, the Clear Screen command starts your Archive command off with a blank screen, giving you complete control over what is displayed.

▶ In line 3, the Remark command reminds you that the space at the beginning of the Echo command in line 4 is created by pressing the Tab key three times.

▶ In line 4, the title (***ARCHIVE PROCEDURE***) is made more prominent and is displayed in the center of the screen by the insertion of three tabs.

▶ In line 5, an Echo command displays a blank line below the title.

▶ In line 8, the Remark command explains the purpose of the Goto command included in line 9.

▶ In line 10, another Echo command displays a blank line to make the warning message in line 11 more visible.

▶ In line 16, the Echo command displays another blank line to make the message in line 17 more visible.

▶ In line 17, the Echo command's message tells which file has been archived.

Make the necessary changes and compare your display with the modified form of ARCHIVE.BAT shown earlier. If there are any differences, correct them before saving the revised version.

Although you haven't changed anything your Archive command does, its screen responses are quite different now. Test the new version by archiving P.OLD (which isn't on the archive diskette):

```
C>archive p.old
```

Because ARCHIVE.BAT now starts by clearing the screen, everything you see from this point on is displayed by your Archive command. When the command prompts you to check the diskette in drive A, press any key. The screen now looks like this:

```
              ***ARCHIVE PROCEDURE***

Make sure archive diskette is in drive A
Press any key to continue . . .

              1 file(s) copied

p.old archived
```

Test ARCHIVE.BAT again to see how it responds when the file already exists on the archive diskette. P.DOC and P.OLD are no longer on the disk in drive C (you archived them after making the change that erases the file), so archive P.BAK. Type the following, pressing any key to continue the command after each pause:

```
C>archive p.bak
```

The screen looks like this:

```
          ***ARCHIVE PROCEDURE***

Make sure archive diskette is in drive A
Press any key to continue . . .

a:p.bak exists. Press CTRL-BREAK to cancel, or
Press any key to continue . . .

          1 file(s) copied

p.bak archived
```

ARCHIVE.BAT is quite a bit longer than when you began, but your Archive command doesn't look much like a homemade command any more. Although you needn't always go to such lengths when you create a command, it's nice to know that a little extra effort can make your work look professional. If others will use the batch files you create, the investment of your effort can quickly pay off in shorter training time, more efficient use of the system, and fewer mistakes.

CHAPTER SUMMARY

This chapter covered a lot of ground. Experimenting is the best way to put what you learned here into practice. Just be certain to use diskettes that don't contain files you need until you're sure your batch commands are working properly.

The next chapter describes two additional batch commands that let you create even more flexible batch files, and it shows you several useful batch commands you can use to start your personal collection. You need the archive diskette in drive A. Remove this diskette and label it ARCHIVED FILES.

CHAPTER 16

CREATING MORE SMART COMMANDS

The previous chapter showed you how to use the advanced capability of batch files. Knowing how to create batch files is only half the job, however; the other half is finding uses for them. This chapter shows you how to create some commands to search through the phone-list file you created in Chapter 13; it also describes two advanced batch commands and shows several useful batch files to give you some ideas for your own use.

PREPARING FOR THE EXAMPLES

For the first examples in this chapter, you need the phone-list file (PH.TXT) that you created in Chapter 13, "Taking Control of Your System." If you haven't gone through the examples in Chapters 13, 14, and 15, you should do so before proceeding.

If you're using a fixed disk, PH.TXT should already be in the directory named \RUNDOS. Change the current directory to \RUNDOS by typing:

```
C:\>cd \rundos
```

If your system prompt shows the current directory, type *prompt* if you want to change it to C>, as in the following examples.

If you're using diskettes, remember that DOS will need the files FIND.EXE, SORT.EXE, and MORE.COM. Either make sure that the diskette with the PH.TXT file also contains these command files, or set the command path to A: and place the DOS diskette(s) with the Find, Sort, and More command files in drive A. Put the sample diskette in drive B and change the current drive to B. The system prompt will be B> instead of C>, as in the examples.

COMMANDS TO SEARCH THROUGH A FILE

In Chapter 13, you created a file of names, addresses, and telephone numbers, and you used the Find and Sort commands to display entries. You can also put the Find and Sort commands in batch files to create your own search commands and achieve some of the capabilities of a simple record-management program.

For example, the simplest search uses the Find command to display all records that contain a particular string. Create a batch file named SHOW.BAT by typing the following (ignore the @ symbol at the beginning of the Echo command if you're not using 3.3 or a later version):

```
C>copy con show.bat
@echo off
find "%1" ph.txt
^Z
        1 file(s) copied
```

This batch file gives you a Show command that displays all records from PH.TXT that contain the string you specify as the parameter to your Show command. To search the phone list, type *show* followed by the string. For example, to display the entries for all consultants (entries that contain the string *cons*), type:

```
C>show cons
```

DOS displays all entries for consultants:

```
---------- PH.TXT
Jones      Michele    (747) 429-6360   cons chemist
Black      John       (747) 426-3385   cons mech eng pkg
Jones      Alison     (747) 429-5584   cons Chem engineer
```

Note: As it stands, your Show command requires that you specify the string in the same combination of uppercase and lowercase letters that appear in the file. If you have version 5 of DOS, remember that you can include the /I parameter to tell the Find command to ignore differences in case. For example, if you entered the Find command as find /i "%1" ph.txt, *you could type the Show command in the preceding example as* show cons, show Cons, *or* show CONS *and still be assured of finding the entries you wanted. For simplicity, the following examples omit the /I parameter of the Find command. If you want, however, you can include it to make your batch files even more flexible.*

As you've seen, typing *show cons* is easier than typing *find "cons" ph.txt*. Read on, and you'll find that you can use similar batch files to conduct even more powerful searches just as easily.

Compound Searches

As the examples in Chapter 13 showed, you can also combine Find commands to search for records that contain various combinations of character strings—for example, all consultants named Jones or all entries that are outside the 747 area code. Putting these Find commands in a batch file saves even more typing than the Show command you just created.

For example, suppose you want to create a command to show all entries that contain both one string and another. This requires two Find commands, with the output of the first piped to the second. You could call such a command Showand; create a file named SHOWAND.BAT by typing:

```
C>copy con showand.bat
@echo off
find "%1" ph.txt | find "%2"
^Z
        1 file(s) copied
```

335

This batch command takes two parameters: the two strings the Find command searches for. Now you can search the phone list for entries that contain two strings as easily as you can search it for entries containing one string; just type *showand* followed by the two strings. For example, to display all consultants named Jones, type:

```
C>showand cons Jones
```

DOS displays the records that contain both strings:

```
Jones     Michele    (747) 429-6360   cons chemist
Jones     Alison     (747) 429-5584   cons Chem engineer
```

This is definitely easier than typing *find "cons" ph.txt ¦ find "Jones"*.

What if you want to create a command that shows all entries except those that contain a particular string? Use a Find command with the /V parameter. You could call this command Showxcpt; create SHOWXCPT.BAT by typing the following:

```
C>copy con showxcpt.bat
@echo off
find /v "%1" ph.txt
^Z
        1 file(s) copied
```

This batch command requires one parameter, the string you don't want to see. For example, to display all entries not in the 747 area code, type the following:

```
C>showxcpt (7
```

DOS displays all lines from PH.TXT that don't contain *(7*:

```
---------- PH.TXT
Green     Fred       (541) 926-4921   cust math teach
Smith     Ed         (541) 835-8747   vend caterer
```

These three batch files—SHOW, SHOWAND, and SHOWXCPT—let you search a file quickly in several ways. You can combine all three searches into a single command just by changing SHOW.BAT.

Chaining Batch Files to Create Powerful Commands

As your skill in creating batch files grows, you'll sometimes find that you want to use one batch file to carry out the commands in another batch file. One way to do this is to *chain* the batch files. Another, described later in this chapter, is to use the Call command available in versions 3.3 and later of DOS.

When you chain batch files, you use the name of one batch file as a command in another. DOS then carries out the commands in the second batch file as if you had typed its name; if the second batch file contains the name of a third batch file, DOS carries out its commands, and so on. When the commands in the last chained batch file have been carried out, DOS returns to the system prompt.

To see how this works, modify SHOW.BAT to cover all three types of searches you just performed by chaining it to either SHOWAND.BAT or SHOWXCPT.BAT. When you do this, the parameters you type with the revised Show command must specify the type of search as well as the string or strings to search for.

You're creating your own Show command with the following parameters:

show xcpt and <string1> <string2>

xcpt searches for entries that don't contain the specified string.

and searches for entries that contain two specified strings.

<string1> and <string2> are the strings to search for. If you include *and*, you must include both <string1> and <string2>; otherwise just include <string1>.

If you don't specify either *xcpt* or *and*, your Show command searches for all entries that contain <string1>.

This more powerful version of SHOW.BAT is still fairly short; type the following:

```
C>copy con show.bat
@echo off
if %1==xcpt showxcpt %2
if %1==and showand %2 %3
find "%1" ph.txt
^Z
        1 file(s) copied
```

The first If command checks whether the first parameter (%1) typed with the Show command is *xcpt* (recall that the == compares two strings to see if they are identical). If %1 is the same as *xcpt*, SHOWXCPT.BAT is carried out. The second parameter (%2) you type with the Show command is the string to search for; it is the single parameter that SHOWXCPT.BAT requires.

The second If command checks whether the first parameter typed with the Show command is *and*. If it is, SHOWAND.BAT is carried out. The second and third parameters (%2 and %3) typed with the Show command are the two strings to search for; they are the two parameters that SHOWAND.BAT requires.

If the first parameter (%1) typed with the Show command is neither *xcpt* nor *and*, the Find command is carried out to perform a simple search.

Except for the Echo command, only one of the commands in SHOW.BAT is carried out in any particular search. Figure 16-1 shows the contents of SHOW.BAT and an example of each type of search you can make. For each example, the figure lists the Show command as you would type it, and substitutes values for the replaceable parameters in SHOW.BAT. The command in SHOW.BAT that is carried out is not shaded. An arrow to the right represents chaining to SHOWXCPT or SHOWAND; the contents of each chained batch file, with values substituted for its replaceable parameters, are shown below the chained batch file.

Now you can perform any of the three types of searches with the Show command. The simple search works as it did in the earlier Show command. For example, to display all entries that contain *Jones*, type:

```
C>show Jones

---------- PH.TXT
Jones     Michele    (747) 429-6360   cons chemist
Jones     Alison     (747) 429-5584   cons Chem engineer
Jones     James      (747) 636-3541   cust architect
```

To display all entries that don't contain a particular string, type *xcpt* as the first parameter. For example, to display all entries outside the 747 area code, type:

```
C>show xcpt (7

---------- PH.TXT
Green     Fred       (541) 926-4921   cust math teach
Smith     Ed         (541) 835-8747   vend caterer
```

Or, to search for two strings, type *and* as the first parameter. For example, to see all engineers named Jones, type:

```
C>show and Jones eng
Jones     Alison     (747) 429-5584   cons Chem engineer
```

If you put your telephone numbers and business cards in a text file like this, these three batch files put the contents of the file at your fingertips. Not only can you search for an entry quickly, you can easily display groups of related entries.

You can use this same technique with other data files that might not justify a full database program, but whose contents are a constant part of your work; some more examples are shown in Chapter 17, "Tailoring Your System." This application, like the use of Edit or Edlin, is another example of how DOS can make your computer more useful without additional software.

Contents of SHOW.BAT:

```
@echo off
if %1==xcpt showxcpt %2
if %1==and showand %2 %3
find "%1" ph.txt
```

```
C>show cust

@echo off
if cust==xcpt showxcpt
if cust==and showand
find "cust" ph.txt
```

Figure 16-1. *Chaining batch files.*   *(continued)*

Figure 16-1. *continued*

```
C>show xcpt cust

@echo off
if xcpt==xcpt showxcpt cust  -----> showxcpt cust
if xcpt==and showand cust
find "xcpt" ph.txt                   @echo off
                                     find /v "cust" ph.txt


C>show and cust Jones

@echo off
if and==xcpt showxcpt cust
if and==and showand cust Jones  --> showand cust Jones
find "and" ph.txt
                                     @echo off
                                     find "cust" ph.txt ¦ find
                                        "Jones"
```

SOME USEFUL BATCH FILES

To give you some ideas about the sort of batch commands that might help you from day to day, several useful batch files are shown here. These are not step-by-step examples; each description gives the purpose of the batch file, shows its contents, explains how it works, and describes how you would use it.

An effective way to become familiar with batch commands is to experiment. You could enter the following batch files, for example, then experiment with them, making changes and seeing the effects of the changes. If your batch files include commands that can modify or delete files, be sure to test your batch files on disks that don't contain irreplaceable copies of files you need.

You can create the batch files by copying from the console to a file or by using a text editor. Where line numbers are shown, they're just for reference; don't enter them. Most of the batch files include one or more Echo commands to add a blank line to the display (for readability); they are shown as *echo* followed by a period (*echo.*). If you don't have version 3.1 or later, echo a blank line by typing *echo*, holding down the Alt key, and pressing 255 on the numeric keypad. If neither of these methods works, type *echo*, press the Spacebar, and then press Enter.

Viewing a Long Directory Listing

Even though you back up old files and clear out unneeded ones regularly, a directory can soon contain more files than DOS can list on one screen. And some often-used directories—word processing directories, for example, or collections of spreadsheets and charts—can become quite large.

If you have version 4 or 5 of DOS and an EGA or VGA display, you can use the LONGDIR.BAT file described here to change the display to 43 lines per screen, display a long directory one screenful at a time, and then change the display back to 25 lines.

LONGDIR.BAT contains:

```
1. @echo off
2. cls
3. mode con lines=43
4. dir %1 /p
5. pause
6. mode con lines=25
```

The Mode command in line 3 switches the display to 43 lines. The Dir command in line 4 finds the listings for the directory (%1) you specify as a parameter with the Longdir command, displays the entries 43 lines at a time, and waits for you to press a key. The Pause command in line 5 displays *Press any key to continue* when the directory listing is complete, and the Mode command in line 6 returns the screen display to 25 lines.

To use the command, you type *longdir*, followed by the directory listing you want to see. You can include a drive letter, followed by a colon, a path name, and a file name including wildcard characters. For example, you can type the command as *longdir a:*, *longdir \clients\wp*, or *longdir \clients\wp*.doc*. If you don't include a drive, path, or file name (type just *longdir*), the command displays the current directory.

(Depending on how your system is set up, LONGDIR.BAT might list the directory you specify but refuse to change to 43 lines per screen after telling you that *ANSI.SYS must be installed to perform requested function.* If this happens, you need to identify a file named ANSI.SYS to DOS. Chapter 17 tells you how to do this.)

Cleaning Up Disk Storage

Because Edlin and many word processors create a backup file with the extension BAK each time you edit a file, your disks can get crowded with backup files you don't need. The CLEANUP.BAT batch file described here replaces one you created earlier; it displays the directory entries of all files with an extension of BAK and then pauses. At that point, you can cancel the command by pressing Ctrl-Break; if you press any key to proceed, the command erases the files.

CLEANUP.BAT contains:

```
1. @echo off
2. cls
3. echo *** Will erase the following files: ***
4. dir %1*.bak
5. echo.
6. echo Press CTRL-BREAK to cancel, or
7. pause
8. del %1*.bak
```

Notice that there is no blank between *%1* and *∗.bak* in lines 4 and 8; this lets you specify a drive letter or a path name as a parameter with the file name, but be sure to end a path name with a backslash (\ ).

To erase all BAK files from the current directory on the disk in the current drive, type *cleanup* and press any key when the Pause command prompts you.

To erase all BAK files from another directory, type the path name followed by \ as a parameter; you can also precede the path name with a drive letter and colon (for example, *cleanup a:* or *cleanup \mkt\wp*).

Directory of Subdirectories

The Directory command displays *<DIR>* instead of the file size to identify a subdirectory. If a directory contains many directories and files, viewing only the subdirectories can be awkward, even with the /0 parameter, which lets you group subdirectories at the beginning or end of the version 5 display. The DIRSUB batch file described here lets you display only the entries for subdirectories.

DIRSUB.BAT contains:

```
1. @echo off
2. echo *** Subdirectories in %1 ***
3. echo.
4. dir %1 | find "<"
```

In this file, the output of the Directory command is piped to a Find command that displays all directory lines that contain a less-than sign (<).

You can type one parameter (%1) with the Dirsub command to specify the directory whose entries are to be displayed. The parameter can include a drive letter and colon, a path name, or both. If you don't include a parameter, this Dirsub command displays the subdirectories in the current directory (but doesn't display the directory name because you didn't type any characters to replace %1 in the message line).

To see the subdirectories in the current directory, you would type *dirsub*. To see those in the current directory of drive B, you would type *dirsub b:*, and to see the subdirectories in \MKT\WP, you would type *dirsub \mkt\wp*.

The special entries **.** and **..** are in all directories except the root. You can modify DIRSUB.BAT so that it doesn't display these entries by changing line 4 of the batch file to the following:

```
dir %1 | find "<" | find /v "."
```

Now the output of the Find command is piped to a second Find command that uses the /V parameter to eliminate all lines that contain a period. You would use this version of the Dirsub command just as you would use the earlier version.

Moving Files from One Directory to Another

In a tree-structured file system, you'll sometimes want to move files from one directory to another. You can do this by copying the file to the new directory with the Copy command, then erasing the original with the Delete command. MOVE.BAT combines these in one command.

MOVE.BAT contains:

```
 1. @echo off
 2. copy %1 %2
 3. cls
 4. echo Files in target directory:
 5. echo.
 6. dir %2 /p
 7. echo.
 8. echo If files to be moved are not in directory,
 9. echo press CTRL-BREAK to cancel. Otherwise
10. pause
11. del %1
```

Here is how the batch file works, line by line:

▶ In line 1, the Echo command turns echo off.

▶ In line 2, the Copy command copies the files to the target directory.

▶ In line 3, the Clear Screen command clears the screen.

▶ In lines 4 and 5, Echo commands display a message and a blank line.

▶ In line 6, the Directory command displays the contents of the target directory. The /P parameter is included to ensure time enough to view even a very long directory.

▶ In lines 7 through 9, Echo commands display a blank line and a warning message.

▶ In line 10, the Pause command makes the system pause to let you cancel the Delete command in line 11 if the files you moved are not displayed in the listing of the target directory.

You have created a command with two parameters:

move <source> <target>

<source> is the name of the file to be moved (copied and then deleted). You can include a drive letter and path name. If you use wildcard characters in the file name, DOS displays the name of each file it copies.

<target> is the name of the directory to which the <source> files are to be copied. If you omit <target>, the files are copied to the current directory.

For example, assume that the current directory is \MKT\WP. To move the file REPORT.DOC to the directory \ENG\WP, you would type *move report.doc \eng\wp*. To move the file BUDGET.JAN from \ENG\WP to \MKT\WP, you type the command as *move \eng\wp\budget.jan*. To move all files from \MKT\WP to \WORD\MKT, you would type *move *.* \word\mkt*.

THREE ADVANCED BATCH COMMANDS

Note: The batch commands you have worked with up to this point are sufficient for you to create useful batch files like the search commands for the phone-list file. Rather than continue with the rest of this chapter right now, you might want to put the book aside for a while and experiment, and then return to learn the last three batch commands this book discusses.

The three remaining batch commands, Shift, For, and Call, give you even more control over how your batch files work. They're somewhat more complicated than the other batch commands, but the examples should make their use clear.

Preparing for the Advanced Examples

The remaining examples in the chapter require the P files you archived in Chapter 15. Put the diskette you labeled ARCHIVED FILES in drive A.

Shifting the List of Parameters

The Shift command moves the list of parameters you type with a batch command one position to the left. For example, suppose you type a Shift command with three parameters. After the Shift command is carried out once, what was %3 becomes %2 and what was %2 becomes %1; what was %1 is gone. After a second Shift command, what started out as %3 is %1; what started as %2 and %1 are both gone.

This command lets a short batch file handle any number of parameters; the following sample batch file illustrates the technique. ARCH1.BAT archives any number of files. Here are its contents; remember, the line numbers are just for reference:

```
1. @echo off
2. :start
3. if "%1"=="" goto done
4. echo *** Archiving %1 ***
5. if not exist a:%1 copy %1 a:
6. shift
7. goto start
8. :done
```

Here's a line-by-line description of how it works:

▶ As usual, the first line is an Echo command to turn echo off.

▶ In line 2, the label *:start* marks the beginning of the commands that will be repeated for each parameter.

▶ In line 3, the If command checks to see whether a parameter was entered for %1. It does this by comparing "%1" with two quotation marks enclosing nothing at all (""). You're telling DOS to compare the first parameter (if one was typed) with nothing, or no parameter. When the comparison is true, meaning that there are no more parameters, the Goto command sends DOS to the label *:done* in line 8.

▶ In line 4, the Echo command displays the name of the file that is being archived.

▶ In line 5, the If command checks whether the file to be archived exists on drive A; if it doesn't, the Copy command copies the file from the current drive to drive A.

▶ In line 6, the Shift command moves the list of parameters one position left.

▶ In line 7, the Goto command sends DOS back to the label *:start*.

▶ In line 8, the label *:done* marks the end of the command file.

To use this batch file you type *arch1* followed by the names of the files to be archived. The command stops when "%1" equals ""—in other words, when there are no more file names to be substituted for %1.

To test the command, copy the file named P.OLD, which you archived in Chapter 15, from the diskette in drive A to the current drive by typing:

```
C>copy a:p.old
```

Now archive P.OLD, Q.DOC, and Q.OLD by typing:

```
C>arch1 p.old q.doc q.old
*** Archiving p.old ***
*** Archiving q.doc ***
        1 file(s) copied
*** Archiving q.old ***
        1 file(s) copied
```

The confirming messages show that DOS did not copy the file that was already on the diskette in drive A (P.OLD), but that it did copy the files that weren't on the diskette (both Q.DOC and Q.OLD).

This short Archive command doesn't display instructions or warnings like the batch file you created in Chapter 15, but it does show how you can use the Shift command to write a batch file that handles any number of parameters. The technique is simple: Do something with %1, shift the parameters, then use a Goto command to send DOS back to the beginning to do it all over again. Just make sure you define a way to stop the process, or DOS will carry out the command forever.

Carrying Out a Command More than Once

Sometimes you might want DOS to carry out a command more than once in a batch file—for instance, once for each file that matches a file name with wildcard characters. The For command does just that. Like the If command, the For command has two parts: The first part defines how often a command is to be carried out, and the second part is the command to be carried out.

The For command is somewhat more complex than the other batch commands. If you don't fully understand the description of its parameters, read on and try the examples. As with many other aspects of using a computer, it's easier to use the For command than it is to read about it.

The For command has three parameters:

for %%p in (<set>) do <command>

The words *in* and *do* are required in the command; they are not parameters.

%%p is a replaceable parameter used inside the For command. DOS assigns to it, in turn, each value included in (<set>).

(<set>) is the list of possible values that can be given to %%p. You separate the values with blanks, and you must enclose the entire list in parentheses—for example, *(1 2 3)*. You can also specify a set of values with a file name that includes wildcard characters—for example, *(b:*.doc)*.

<command> is any DOS command other than another For command. You can use both batch-command parameters (such as %1) and the For command replaceable parameter (%%p) in <command>.

It's all less complicated than it sounds. When DOS carries out a For command, it assigns to %%p, in turn, each value that you specify in (<set>), then it carries out <command>. Each time it carries out <command>, DOS first substitutes for %%p the current value taken from (<set>).

A brief example shows how the For command works. The following batch command carries out an Echo command three times, displaying each of the three words enclosed in parentheses. Create FOR1.BAT by typing:

```
C>copy con for1.bat
for %%p in (able baker charlie) do echo %%p
^Z
        1 file(s) copied
```

In this For command, *(able baker charlie)* is (<set>) and *echo %%p* is <command>. The For command tells DOS to carry out the Echo command once for each word in parentheses, substituting, in turn, *able*, *baker*, and *charlie* for %%p. Test it by typing:

```
C>for1
```

For a change, this batch file doesn't begin by turning echo off, so DOS displays each command it carries out, starting with the For command:

```
C>for %p in (able baker charlie) do echo %p
```

DOS then displays and carries out the Echo command once for each value in the set, each time substituting the next value from the set for the replaceable parameter in the Echo command:

```
C>echo able
able

C>echo baker
baker

C>echo charlie
charlie
```

Instead of specifying actual values in the set, you can use replaceable parameters, such as %1. This technique works just like any other batch command, but can be confusing because now you can have %1 and %%p in the same command. Here's the difference: %1 refers to the first parameter typed with the batch command, %2 refers to the second parameter typed with the batch command, and so forth; %%p refers to the value selected from the set enclosed in parentheses within the For command.

The next example shows you the difference. Here, the words to be displayed are typed as parameters of the batch command, instead of being included as part of the For command. Create FOR2.BAT by typing:

```
C>copy con for2.bat
for %%p in (%1 %2 %3) do echo %%p
^Z
        1 file(s) copied
```

This For command tells DOS to carry out the Echo command (*echo %%p*) once for each value in parentheses, substituting for %%p the first, then the second, and finally the third parameter you type with the For 2 command. Test it by typing:

```
C>for2 dog easy fox
```

DOS displays each command it carries out. First it displays the For command:

```
C>for %p in (dog easy fox) do echo %p
```

Note that DOS has substituted values for all replaceable parameters. The set in parentheses is now *(dog easy fox)* because those are the three parameters you typed; they have replaced *(%1 %2 %3)*. As you may have noticed in the preceding display, DOS has also dropped one of the percent signs from %%p. DOS removes the first percent sign when it substitutes the parameters you type with the command for %1, %2, and so forth. It does, however, leave one percent sign to show that a value must still be substituted for %p.

DOS then displays and carries out three Echo commands, each time substituting one value from the set in parentheses for %p:

```
C>echo dog
dog

C>echo easy
easy

C>echo fox
fox
```

If you wish, you can specify the set in a For command with a file name and wildcard characters. DOS then assigns to %%p, in turn, each file name that matches the wildcard characters. You can use this technique to create a simple Archive batch file using only a For command. The following command doesn't display instructions and warnings, but it does show you how much can be done with a single batch command.

Create a batch file named ARCH2.BAT by typing the following:

```
C>copy con arch2.bat
for %%p in (%1) do if not exist a:%%p copy %%p a:
^Z
        1 file(s) copied
```

Q.DOC and Q.OLD are on the diskette in drive A (you copied them in the example of the Shift command). Use them to test ARCH2.BAT by archiving all Q files:

```
C>arch2 q.*
```

DOS displays each command it carries out, starting with the For command (remember, you have not turned echo off):

```
C>for %p in (q.*) do if not exist a:%p copy %p a:
```

DOS then displays and carries out three If commands, each time substituting a file name that matches the set enclosed in parentheses for the replaceable parameter in the If command:

```
C>if not exist a:Q.DOC copy Q.DOC a:

C>if not exist a:Q.BAK copy Q.BAK a:
        1 file(s) copied

C>if not exist a:Q.OLD copy Q.OLD a:
```

The messages displayed by the Copy command confirm that DOS did not copy either Q.DOC or Q.OLD because they were already on the archive diskette, but did copy Q.BAK, which hadn't been archived.

The For command gives you a quick way to carry out a DOS command several times. As shown in some of the sample batch files that conclude this chapter, the For command makes it possible to create powerful batch commands.

Using a Batch Command in a Batch File

Earlier in this chapter, in the final version of SHOW.BAT, you used batch commands (Showand and Showxcpt) in a batch file. DOS returned to the system prompt after carrying out these batch commands, even though neither was actually the last command in SHOW.BAT; the last command was Find. You can use this capability, called chaining, with any version of DOS.

If you're using 3.3 or a later version, however, you can also use the Call command in a batch file to tell DOS to carry out the commands in another batch file. Unlike chaining, the Call command causes DOS to come back and continue with the next command in the original batch file instead of returning to the system prompt. This lets you use a batch command of your own making in a batch file, just as you would use a DOS command.

The Call command has two parameters:

call <batchfile> <parameters>

<batchfile> is the name of a batch command that you want DOS to carry out from within the calling batch file.

<parameters> represents any parameters that <batchfile> requires.

Two short batch files demonstrate the usefulness of the Call command. First, create a batch file named ECHOIT.BAT by typing the following:

```
C>copy con echoit.bat
@echo off
echo %1
^Z
        1 file(s) copied
```

ECHOIT.BAT simply echoes the parameter you enter with it. For example, to echo *fred*, type the following:

```
C>echoit fred
fred
C>_
```

Now create another batch file named ECHOALL.BAT that uses a For command to carry out ECHOIT.BAT for each of up to three parameters, pauses until you press a key, and displays an ending message:

```
C>copy con echoall.bat
@echo off
for %%p in (%1 %2 %3) do call echoit %%p
pause
echo End of ECHOALL.BAT
^Z
        1 file(s) copied
```

The For command carries out the Call command for each of up to three parameters that can be entered with the Echoall batch command. The Call command carries out the batch command ECHOIT.BAT, specifying, in turn, each parameter entered with the Echoall batch command.

Now type the following to echo the words *xray*, *yankee*, and *zulu*:

```
C>echoall xray yankee zulu
xray
yankee
zulu
Press any key to continue . . .
_
```

Press a key, and DOS displays the final message in ECHOALL.BAT:

End of ECHOALL.BAT

If you hadn't included the Call command, DOS would have carried out ECHOIT.BAT once to display the first parameter (*xray*) and then would have returned to the system prompt. Because you did use the Call command, DOS carried out ECHOIT.BAT three times, once for each parameter, and then returned to the final lines of ECHOALL.BAT before displaying the system prompt.

SOME MORE USEFUL BATCH FILES

The following batch files use the advanced batch commands. Again, they aren't step-by-step examples; they're working samples to give you an idea of what can be done with the full set of batch commands. You can enter the batch files by copying from the console or by using a text editor. The line numbers shown are for reference only.

Displaying a Series of Small Text Files

If you work with many small text files, such as batch files or boilerplate paragraphs for word processor documents, it's handy to be able to review several files with one command, rather than having to print or display them one at a time. The batch file shown here, REVIEW.BAT, uses the Shift, Type, and Pause commands to display any number of files one at a time. Remember, *echo.* (or *echo* Alt-255) echoes a blank line. REVIEW.BAT contains:

```
 1. @echo off
 2. :start
 3. if "%1"=="" goto done
 4. cls
 5. echo<spacebar><tab><tab>••• FILENAME: %1 •••
 6. echo.
 7. type %1
 8. echo.
 9. echo.
10. pause
```

```
11. shift
12. goto start
13. :done
```

This batch file uses the same technique as the earlier examples of the Shift command. The Echo command in line 5 displays the file name (moved toward the center of the screen with two tabs), so that you'll know what file is displayed. Lines 8 and 9 display two blank lines to separate the file from the Pause command message.

With this Review command, you type the names of the files as parameters. To display several files with the extension DOC, for example, you type *review 1.doc 2.doc 3.doc*. DOS clears the screen and displays the first file, then displays the Pause command message and waits for you to press any key before clearing the screen and displaying the next file. When the If command in line 3 finds the first null parameter (""), DOS returns to command level.

Searching Files for a String of Characters

Have you ever searched through your paper files to find a specific letter or reference? Or wondered how many letters you wrote about a particular subject or how often you use a particular word? These three short batch files give you several ways to scan a file or set of files for lines that contain a string of characters.

Displaying All Lines That Contain a String

To help you find all lines that contain a particular string, SCAN.BAT lets you specify the file to be searched and one string to search for. It displays each line in the file that contains the string. You can also use wildcard characters to search a set of files. Here are the contents of SCAN.BAT:

```
1. @echo off
2. cls
3. echo<space><tab><tab>***LINES IN %1 THAT CONTAIN %2***
4. echo.
5. for %%p in (%1) do find " %2 " %%p
```

All the work here is done in the last line of the batch file. The earlier lines clear the screen and display a title. The For command in line 5 actually carries out the Find command for each file name that matches the first parameter you type with the Scan command; the Find command is the one that searches for the string that you type as the second parameter.

As mentioned earlier in the chapter, remember that if you have version 5 of DOS, you can use the /I parameter to tell the Find command to ignore differences between uppercase and lowercase characters (*for %%p in (%1) do find /i " %2 " %%p*).

To display each line that contained the word *sales* in all files with an extension of DOC, you would type *scan *.doc sales*. DOS would clear the screen and display each line that contained the word *sales* preceded and followed by a blank (" %2 ").

Displaying the Number of Lines Containing the String

COUNT.BAT is a slightly modified version of SCAN.BAT that displays the number of lines in the file that contain the string, but doesn't display the lines themselves.

Here are the contents of COUNT.BAT. Type line 3 on one line even though it is shown on two here. Note that changes from SCAN.BAT are shaded:

```
1. @echo off
2. cls
3. echo<space><tab><tab>•••NUMBER OF LINES IN %1 THAT
   CONTAIN %2•••
4. echo.
5. for %%p in (%1) do find /c " %2 " %%p
```

The only two changes are in the title displayed by the Echo command (line 3) and the addition of the /C parameter to the Find command (line 5).

As an example, to see how many lines in all files with an extension of DOC in the current directory contained the word *night*, you would type *count *.doc night*. The Count command would clear the screen and display the file name and the number of lines in each file that contained the word *night*.

Searching for Several Strings

Another batch file, SCANALL.BAT, again gives a count of lines, but it uses a different approach. The file or set of files to be searched is named in the batch file, but you can type however many strings you want as parameters to search for. This approach is particularly useful if you frequently search the same set of files, such as your word processing files. SCANALL.BAT contains:

```
 1. @echo off
 2. :start
 3. if "%1"=="" goto done
 4. cls
 5. echo<space><tab><tab>••• LINES IN *.DOC THAT CONTAIN %1 •••
 6. echo.
 7. for %%p in (*.doc) do find /c " %1 " %%p
 8. echo.
 9. pause
10. shift
11. goto start
12. :done
```

This batch file uses both the For and Shift commands to search several files for several strings. A line-by-line description is in order:

▶ Line 1 turns echo off.

▶ The label *:start* identifies the beginning of the commands to be repeated (it is the destination of the Goto command in line 11).

▶ The If command checks whether the parameter is null. If it is, the Goto command sends DOS to the end of the batch file (line 12).

▶ Line 4 clears the screen.

▶ The Echo commands in lines 5 and 6 display a title and a blank line.

▶ The For command in line 7 searches each file with an extension of DOC and displays the number of lines that contain the string (" %1 ") specified in the first parameter you type when you use the Scanall command.

▶ Like line 6, line 8 displays a blank line.

▶ The Pause command displays its message and waits for a key to be pressed.

▶ Line 10 shifts the parameters one position to the left.

▶ The Goto command sends DOS to the label :start to begin the search for the next parameter.

▶ The label :done identifies the end of the batch file (the destination of the Goto command in line 3).

To use the Scanall command, type the words to be searched for as parameters. Remember, if you don't use the /I parameter in your Find command, you must match uppercase and lowercase letters. If, for example, you wanted to search for the words *sales*, *January*, and *region*, you would type *scanall sales January region*.

The Scanall command would clear the screen, search all the files whose extension is DOC for the word *sales*, display the number of lines, and then pause. When you pressed any key, it would scan all the files for the word *January*, would again display the results, and so on for each word you specified. Try it with your own words and several dozen word processor files; you'll be surprised at how quickly this command searches all the files.

If you wanted to display the lines containing the strings, rather than just the count, you could simply omit the /C parameter from the Find command in the batch file. This command could produce a lot of output. To print a record of it, you could press Ctrl-PrtSc after you entered the command, but before you pressed the Enter key, to start simultaneously printing and displaying the results.

Displaying a Sorted Directory

Beginning with version 5, you can use the /O parameter of the Directory command to sort a directory by name, extension, size, or date and time. If you don't have version 5, you can create four small batch files to sort a directory by name, extension, or size.

Because the items in a directory entry always begin in the same column, you can sort the directory entries by extension or size by using the column parameter (/+<number>) of the Sort command. (Sorting by name doesn't require the column parameter because the file name starts in column 1.) These are the columns where the information begins:

▶ Name—column 1 (doesn't need to be specified).

▶ Extension—column 10.

▶ Size—column 16.

Although directory entries include the date and time, batch files that sort by date (column 24) or time (column 34) aren't really useful, so no examples are included here. Sorting by date, for example, would cause January of one year to appear in the list before December of the preceding year (that is, 1-1-92 would *precede* 12-31-91). If you sorted by time, a file created at 9 in the morning on October 16, 1991, would appear in the list *before* a file created at 11 in the morning a month earlier. Then, too, if you're using version 4 of DOS, which displays time based on a 12-hour clock rather than a 24-hour clock, a file created at 5 in the evening would be listed before a file created at 9 that morning.

Without being able to take both date and time of day into account, sorting by date or time is not particularly useful. On the other hand, the benefits of sorting a directory alphabetically by file name or by extension are obvious. Furthermore, if you need to delete some files to make space on a disk, or if you're just interested in the relative sizes of files, sorting by size is useful.

To create a command that displays a directory sorted by name, extension, or size, you create three batch files that actually sort and display the directory, and you create a fourth batch file that chains to the correct one of the other three.

First, copy from the console, as you have done before, to create the following one-line batch files; their names tell how they sort the directory:

DIRNAME.BAT:

```
dir %1 | sort | find "-" | more
```

DIREXT.BAT:

```
dir %1 | sort /+10 | find "-" | more
```

DIRSIZE.BAT:

```
dir %1 | sort /+16 | find "-" | more
```

Each of these batch files sorts and displays the directory specified in the parameter %1 and pipes the output of the Sort command to a Find command that selects only the lines that contain a hyphen. The output of the Find command is then piped to the More command to handle directories more than one screen long. If no parameter is specified, the batch command sorts and displays the current directory. The only difference among the batch files is the column in which sorting begins.

You now need the batch file that chains to the correct one of the previous three. Name the file DIRSORT.BAT; it contains:

```
1. @echo off
2. for %%p in (name ext size) do if "%1"=="%%p" dir%%p %2
3. echo First parameter must be name, ext, or size
```

Be sure *not* to put a blank between dir and %%p in line 2, or the result won't be a valid file name for any of the chained batch files. The quotation marks around %1 and %%p prevent DOS from displaying an error message if no parameter is typed with the command.

In the DIRSORT batch file, the For command sets %%p, in turn, to each of the words in the set in parentheses, then carries out the If command, which compares %%p to the first parameter typed with the Dirsort command. If there is a match, the If command adds the value of %%p to *dir* to produce the name of one of the three sort batch files, and chains to that file (for example, *dir* + *name* would become *dirname*). The second parameter (%2), if any, typed with the Dirsort command is the %1 parameter (the directory name) needed by the chained batch file.

If the first parameter you type with the Dirsort command isn't one of the three words in the set in parentheses, the condition in the If command is not true. Then the Echo command in the next line is carried out, displaying a message that lists the correct parameters, and the Dirsort batch command ends without chaining to one of the files that display a sorted directory.

To display a sorted directory, you would type the Dirsort command with one or two parameters: The first, which is required, would specify how to sort and would have to be *name*, *ext*, or *size*; the second parameter, which is optional, would be the drive letter, path name, or name of the directory to be displayed. If you didn't include the second parameter, the command would display the current directory of the disk in the current drive.

For example, to display the current directory of the disk in the current drive, sorted by size, you would type *dirsort size*. To display the root directory, sorted by name, of the disk in drive A, you would type *dirsort name a:*.

CHAPTER SUMMARY

These batch files should give you a good start on a collection of special-purpose commands, and they might give you some ideas for creating more of your own. This is where the flexibility of DOS really becomes apparent: The wide range of DOS commands and capabilities is only the starting point for putting DOS to work. With redirection, filter commands, batch files, and macros, you can combine all the other DOS commands into a set of custom-tailored commands, to make your personal computer truly personal.

CHAPTER 17

TAILORING YOUR SYSTEM

I f you have tried the examples in the book, you have used all the major features of DOS. Although it may sometimes seem that DOS offers more options than you need, those options give you flexibility in tailoring DOS; they let you adapt the computer to yourself rather than adapt yourself to the computer.

This chapter shows several ways you can tailor DOS to your needs or preferences. Not only does this tailoring make DOS fit your work needs better, but some of the techniques described here can also make your system immediately useful without your having to buy an application program. Some of these techniques can also make the system more accessible to people who may need to use the computer but who don't have your experience with DOS. And tailoring can also make it easier to achieve consistency in such procedures as backing up a fixed disk when several people use the computer.

This chapter describes:

▶ Ways to set up a filing system that matches the way the computer is used.

▶ Batch commands that simplify using a multilevel filing system.

▶ Batch commands that automate backing up a fixed disk.

▶ Several simple record-management schemes similar to the telephone index described in Chapters 13 and 16.

▶ Commands that help you tailor your system hardware with the DOS file named CONFIG.SYS.

▶ Some less frequently used DOS commands.

Examples are included, but they are not step-by-step exercises. The intent of this chapter is to give you some ideas about how to tailor DOS by applying what you have learned in previous chapters.

SETTING UP A FILING SYSTEM

The multilevel file system described in Chapter 8, "A Tree of Files," lets you organize your files to match your work. A file structure is affected by such factors as the application programs that are used, how many people use the computer, and how many departments are involved. This section shows several different file structures, each organized to focus on a different approach to using the computer. Because every real-life situation is different, these are guides, not exact models.

It doesn't take long to set up a file system—all you need are a few Make Directory commands—but changing a file structure once it contains dozens or hundreds of files can be time-consuming. A few minutes' thought ahead of time can result in a file structure that suits the way the computer will be used.

In the following examples, the computer system is assumed to have a fixed disk, on which a directory named DOS contains the DOS command files. The root directory is assumed to contain an AUTOEXEC.BAT file with a Path command that sets the command path at startup to \DOS and to all other program directories in the file structure. General-purpose batch files and any other files that are needed by anyone using the system regardless of the current directory are also assumed to be in the root directory, although they, too, could be in directories of their own, with appropriate command paths added to AUTOEXEC.BAT.

An Application-based File System

If a computer is used for several applications—as it would be by an independent professional or a small business—a natural approach to organizing the file structure is by application program. Figure 17-1 shows how such a file system might be set up by an independent professional who uses the machine with a word processor, a spreadsheet program, and a database manager.

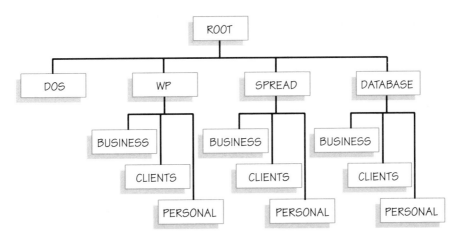

Figure 17-1. *Application-based file structure for an independent professional.*

The first level of directories contains the DOS directory and three others (WP, SPREAD, and DATABASE) for the application programs. The next level (BUSINESS, CLIENTS, and PERSONAL) holds the data files for the applications.

With this file structure, document files are grouped into directories beneath the application programs with which they (the documents) are created. Thus, even though the directory structure includes three sets of subdirectories named BUSINESS, CLIENTS, and PERSONAL, it's easy to see which type of document belongs in each. The Path command in AUTOEXEC.BAT provides access to the root directory (for general-purpose batch files), \DOS (for external DOS commands), and \WP, \SPREAD, and \DATABASE (for the application programs).

On the other hand, the file system for a computer used in a small business might define the second and subsequent directory levels to correspond to departments, rather than to data files for the applications. Figure 17-2 shows how such a file system might be set up. Once again, it's easy to see how files are organized by taking a quick look at the directory structure.

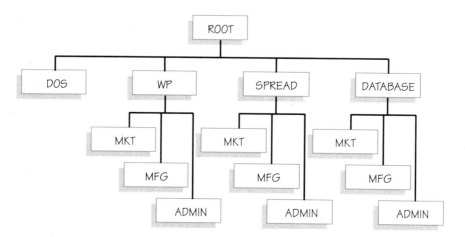

Figure 17-2. *Application-based file structure for a small business.*

A Department-based File System

Rather than beginning with the application program, as the preceding examples do, you can also organize files to emphasize the departments for which files are created. Figure 17-3 shows a file system for a computer used to do work for the Marketing,

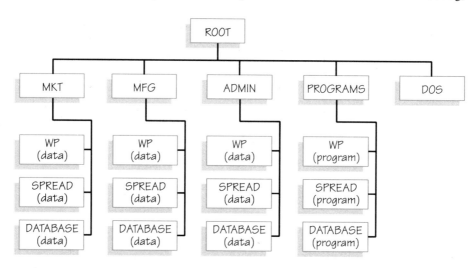

Figure 17-3. *Department-based file structure.*

358

Manufacturing, and Administration departments of a company. The application programs are the same as in the previous examples, but they are stored in subdirectories under \PROGRAMS. They are used for all three departments. Because each program is in a subdirectory of its own, and because the Path command in AUTOEXEC.BAT sets the command path to the \PROGRAMS directory, work for any department can be done by any program.

As much as anything else, the choice of how to organize files depends on how you view your work. If you think primarily in terms of what you do ("I do mostly word processing"), the application-based structure might be the most comfortable. If you think in terms of whom you do it for ("I do most of my work for Marketing"), a department-based structure might be more appropriate. Neither structure is more efficient than the other; each simply reflects a different way of looking at the file system.

A User-based File System

If several people use the computer (share one, perhaps, or use the main computer on a network), a file structure that emphasizes the users might be most appropriate, especially if the people use the machine for different applications. Figure 17-4 outlines a directory structure for a system used by three people.

Again, directories are defined for the same applications used in the other sample file structures. If the computer is used by people with varying degrees of familiarity with DOS, and if not all users need each application, this type of file structure can make use of the system seem more natural, especially if some batch commands simplify using the directories.

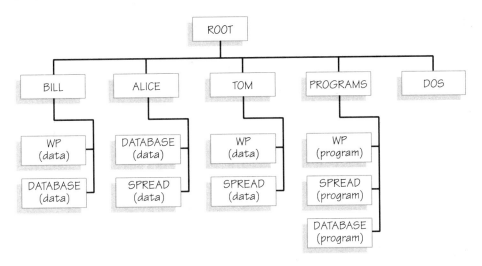

Figure 17-4. *User-based file structure.*

Batch Files and Macros for Your File System

Once you've designed a file structure that's right for your computer and the way it will be used, you can experiment with batch files and macros to simplify matters and make the system more accessible, especially to others who might not be as familiar with DOS as you are.

Batch files (and macros) can be simple or elaborate, depending on who will use them and how much time you want to invest in creating them. Even simple batch files and macros can hide directory changes and other details from beginning users. More elaborate ones can make ease of use a byword on your system.

Suppose, for example, that you've created the file structure shown in Figure 17-3. You have a number of subdirectories named WP, SPREAD, and DATABASE, and you want to be certain that you or anyone else who uses the system can easily find the correct directory for any given word processing, spreadsheet, or database document. You can automate the task with a few short batch files. If you make certain the command search path always includes the directory in which they're stored, the batch files for using directories can be accessible from any directory or subdirectory. Switching from one directory and application program to another is always just a matter of typing a single command.

In its simplest form, a batch file to use a directory simply changes the current directory. For the sample file structure shown in Figure 17-3, a batch file called WORDMKT.BAT in the root directory can help manage word processing documents for the Marketing department.

A basic, but functional, version of WORDMKT.BAT could look like the following example (line numbers here and throughout the chapter are for reference only):

```
1. @echo off
2. cd \mkt\wp
```

The Change Directory command sets the current directory to \MKT\WP, which contains the word processing documents for the Marketing department. Whenever you wanted to work with the files in this directory (perhaps to display, copy, or archive them), you would just type *wordmkt*. You could create a similar batch file for each of the other data directories and then use any directory just by typing the name of the appropriate batch file.

If you wanted to change directories and then immediately start your word processor, you could expand the batch file slightly, substituting the name of your word processor for <myprog> in line 3:

```
1. @echo off
2. cd \mkt\wp
3. <myprog>
4. cd \
```

This version of the batch file would change to the \MKT\WP directory, start the word processor and, when you quit the program, take you to the root directory (a good base from which to work).

If you have version 5 of DOS, you could put the Change Directory and program-startup routines into macros instead of batch files. For simple, short sequences of commands like these, macros have the advantage of being slightly faster to run because you can keep them in your computer's memory rather than on disk.

To create macros to perform the same tasks as the preceding batch files, you would type the following commands. Recall that the $t separates multiple commands in a macro. To change directories without starting the word processor, you might create a macro like this:

```
doskey dirmkt=cd \mkt\wp
```

To change directories and start the word processor, you might create a macro like this:

```
doskey wpmkt=cd \mkt\wp $t <myprog> $t cd \
```

If you put the commands to create these and other macros into a batch file—for example, MACROS.BAT—you could simply type *macros* to put all of your macros at your fingertips throughout a session with DOS. Then, to change to the \MKT\WP directory, you could simply type *dirmkt*. To change directories and start your word processor, the command would be *wpmkt*. Streamlining your work with DOS, directories, and applications can be as simple as that.

Dressing Up the Batch Files

To dress up the appearance of the batch files for using directories, you could clear the screen and display the directory one screenful at a time. The Change Directory command would be unchanged; the modified version of WORDMKT.BAT, for example, would look like the following:

```
1. @echo off
2. cd \mkt\wp
3. cls
4. dir /w /p
```

The /W parameter of the Directory command is used here in case the directory is long; the /P parameter is used in case the directory is *very* long.

If you have the time and the inclination, you can also do more by...

Creating Your Own Menu System

If someone unfamiliar with DOS will be using the system, you can use batch files to create a menu system that quickly moves the less-experienced user to the correct directory. For example, suppose again that you have the file structure shown in Figure 17-3;

the batch files described here let someone turn on the system and, by typing *mkt*, see the following display:

```
                    *** MARKETING ***

Applications: Word processing
              Spreadsheet
              Database

Enter W, S, or D
_
```

If the user types *w*, this screen is displayed (the entries are hypothetical):

```
              *** MARKETING--WORD PROCESSING ***
Document files:

  Volume in drive C is FIXED DISK
  Volume Serial Number is 1608-5A30
  Directory of C:\MKT\WP

  [.]            [..]           THP0315.DOC     SLSLTR.DOC ...
  INVEN04.DOC    LETR06.DOC     BUDGET.DOC      THP0311.DOC ...
  INVEN02.DOC    TAXMEMO.DOC    INVEN01.DOC     CONFNOT.DOC ...
  SVCREC.DOC
          16 file(s)        21897 bytes
                         17162384 bytes free
C>_
```

Displays of this kind would require four batch files for each department: For the Marketing department, there would be one (MKT.BAT) in the root directory and three (W.BAT, S.BAT, and D.BAT) in \MKT. First, here are the contents of MKT.BAT:

```
 1. @echo off
 2. cd \mkt
 3. cls
 4. REM FOUR TABS AT BEGINNING OF FOLLOWING ECHO COMMAND
 5. echo <tab><tab><tab><tab>*** MARKETING ***
 6. echo.
 7. echo Applications: Word processing
 8. echo               Spreadsheet
 9. echo               Database
10. echo.
11. echo Enter W, S, or D
12. prompt $a
```

As you can see, most of the commands are Echo commands. The batch file is straightforward: It turns off echo, changes the directory to \MKT, clears the screen, and displays the menu and choices. Then the Prompt command (described later in this chapter) makes the system prompt invisible, so the user sees only the cursor, and the system returns to command level. MKT.BAT has ended even though, as the sample screen showed, it appears to be waiting for a reply to the prompt *Enter W, S, or D*.

If the user types *w* (for word processing), DOS carries out the batch file W.BAT in \MKT. Its contents are:

```
1. @echo off
2. cls
3. cd wp
4. REM THREE TABS IN FOLLOWING ECHO COMMAND
5. echo <tab><tab><tab>*** MARKETING--WORD PROCESSING ***
6. echo Document files:
7. prompt $p$g
8. dir *.doc /w /p
```

This batch file produces the second sample display (the response to the menu selection). It, too, is straightforward. It turns echo off, clears the screen, changes the directory to \MKT\WP, displays the titles, resets the system prompt, and displays in wide format the directory entries of all files with the extension DOC.

Note: If you have version 5 of DOS, remember that you have a number of options for displaying a sorted directory: by name, extension, size, attribute, and so on. The batch files here and in the remainder of this chapter are structured so they can be used with several different versions of DOS. Bear the capabilities of version 5 in mind, however, and use them whenever appropriate. In the preceding batch file, for example, you could change line 8 to dir *.doc /w /o:n /p to enhance readability by displaying a wide directory sorted alphabetically by name.

To complete the menu system in \MKT, you need two additional batch files similar to W.BAT, one for your spreadsheet and one for your database program. The contents of S.BAT for the spreadsheet are:

```
1. @echo off
2. cls
3. cd spread
4. REM THREE TABS IN FOLLOWING ECHO COMMAND
5. echo <tab><tab><tab>*** MARKETING--SPREADSHEET ***
6. echo Spreadsheet files:
7. prompt $p$g
8. dir *.pln /w /p
```

In the preceding and following lists, the changes from W.BAT are shaded. You can see that the format is the same. In this example, spreadsheet files are given the extension PLN. To complete the menu system, here are the contents of D.BAT:

```
1. @echo off
2. cls
3. cd database
4. REM THREE TABS IN FOLLOWING ECHO COMMAND
5. echo <tab><tab><tab>*** MARKETING--DATABASE ***
6. echo Database files:
7. prompt $p$g
8. dir *.dat /w /p
```

By clearing the screen, displaying your own titles, displaying directory entries, and otherwise controlling the appearance of the system, you can use batch files like these to make the system appear custom-tailored for your own company or department, or even for an individual user. One person who understands how to use the flexibility and power of DOS can make the system easier to use and more productive for everyone else. Batch commands are the key.

AUTOMATING BACKUP OF A FIXED DISK

Chapter 9, "Managing Your Fixed Disk," described how to decide which files need backing up, and when, in order to reduce the number of backup diskettes you need. You can also reduce the amount of time required to back up files.

Suppose you have the file structure shown in Figure 17-3. You decide that each month you should back up all the marketing and manufacturing files (all files in \MKT and \MFG and their subdirectories), and each week you should back up all marketing word processing documents (files with an extension of DOC) and manufacturing spreadsheets (files with an extension of PLN) that have changed since the previous week. You can create two batch files—MNTHBKUP.BAT and WEEKBKUP.BAT—that contain the required Backup commands.

The contents of MNTHBKUP.BAT are:

```
1. @echo off
2. cls
3. echo *** MONTHLY FILE BACKUP ***
4. echo.
5. echo Put a formatted diskette in drive A
6. pause
7. backup \mkt a: /s
8. backup \mfg a: /s /a
9. echo LABEL DISKETTE "BACKUP" AND THE MONTH
```

The batch file starts by clearing the screen, displaying a title, and instructing the user to put the backup diskette in drive A. The first Backup command backs up all files from \MKT and all its subdirectories. Any previously existing files on the backup diskette are erased. The second Backup command backs up all files from \MFG and all its subdirectories, adding them to the files backed up from \MKT.

The form of WEEKBKUP.BAT is similar:

```
1. @echo off
2. cls
3. echo *** WEEKLY DOCUMENT BACKUP ***
4. echo.
5. echo Put a formatted diskette in drive A
6. pause
7. backup \mkt\wp\*.doc a: /m
8. backup \mfg\spread\*.pln a: /m /a
9. echo LABEL DISKETTE "BACKUP" AND MONDAY'S DATE
```

364

Like MNTHBKUP.BAT, WEEKBKUP.BAT starts by clearing the screen, displaying a title, and making sure the correct diskette goes in drive A. The first Backup command backs up all files with the extension DOC from \MKT\WP that have been modified since the last backup. Any previously existing files on the backup diskette are erased. The second Backup command backs up all files with the extension PLN from \MFG\SPREAD.

Unless your system is heavily used, only one or two high-capacity backup diskettes per week are likely to be required to back up the changed files of both departments. Because the monthly backup backs up all files, you can reuse the weekly backup diskettes in the following month.

With batch files like these, anyone who uses the system can back up files. Even people who don't know how to use the Backup command can simply type *weekbkup* once a week and *mnthbkup* once a month and follow the instructions on the screen. If your AUTOEXEC.BAT file sets the command search path to the directory containing the batch files, you or anyone else can use these batch files no matter what the current directory is.

USING DOS AS A RECORD-MANAGEMENT PROGRAM

Chapters 13 and 16 showed you how to use filter commands and batch files to search a telephone list. This procedure can also be used to keep track of any small or medium-sized file—say, from 50 to 200 entries. Although this technique doesn't replace a record-management or file-management program, it's simple and quick, and the price is right: You don't need anything except DOS.

The following topics describe other types of information you can keep track of in the same way. Using the same sort of batch files you created in Chapter 16, you can quickly locate any entry or group of entries in your record files.

The descriptions here don't include examples; they simply describe the information included in each line and the columns in which the items of information begin (so you can sort them). As with any batch files, the best way to get comfortable with this technique and apply it to your own needs is to experiment. These examples give you a starting point.

Keeping Track of Your Computer Files

As you use the computer, your collection of computer files will grow and grow. If you use a word processor, for example, keeping track of all the letters and other documents you create can be a problem. Using wildcard characters with the Directory command makes a particular file easier to find, but you still might have to do some searching to answer such questions as "How many letters did I write in October to the regional sales office?" or "When did we respond to that request from the National Science Foundation?"

You can solve this problem by creating an index file that describes all your word processing files. You could use the same technique to keep track of any large collection of files.

Figure 17-5 shows the items of information and the columns in which they begin, to give you the format for an index file that keeps track of word processing files.

Columns 1 through 3 contain the initials of the originator of the document (THP).

Columns 5 through 12 contain the file name (MFGLET31). All files are assumed to have the same extension.

Columns 14 through 21 contain the date the document was created (10/16/90).

Columns 23 through 79 contain a brief description of the document.

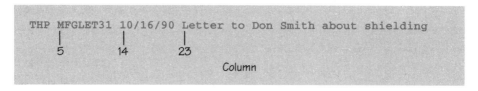

Figure 17-5. *Word processing index file.*

Keep this index file up to date as you create word processing files, and you can quickly locate files and answer questions with batch files like SHOW.BAT, SHOWAND.BAT, and SHOWXCPT.BAT, which you created in Chapter 16.

To Answer:	Type:
When did we respond to that request from the National Science Foundation?	show NSF
What letters did I write to the regional sales office in October?	show and sales 10/

Want a list of all the documents about the new inventory system, or a list of all letters sent in March? If you keep your index up to date, the answers are no more than a command away.

Simple Bibliographic Index

If your work requires a lot of reading, you're probably frustrated at times by how easy it is to forget where you saw something. If research is important to your job, but it is not significant enough to justify purchasing and learning to use a database manager or a bibliographic retrieval program, this simple technique might be the answer.

Again, the answer is to create an index file and search it with batch commands. Figure 17-6 shows the items of information and the columns in which they begin, to give you the format for an index file that keeps track of magazine articles, books, and other sources of reference material.

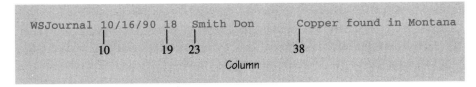

Figure 17-6. *Bibliographic index file.*

Columns 1 through 8 contain the abbreviated title of the reference source.
Columns 10 through 17 contain the date of the reference.
Columns 19 through 21 contain the page number.
Columns 23 through 36 contain the author's name.
Columns 38 through 79 contain the title or description of the reference.

Again, with batch files like the ones you created in Chapter 16, you can find bibliographic references with one command:

To Answer:	Type:
Where did I see that article on kinesthesia?	show kine
I remember an article last June about laser surgery.	show and 6/ laser

The time it takes to keep this index up to date pays off in the ability to find valuable information much more quickly.

Capital Inventory

If you're an independent professional or you operate a small business, you could easily have a much larger investment in capital goods than you realize. Your accountant and your insurance agent probably emphasize the importance of keeping an up-to-date inventory of capital goods, but it's easy to put off this sort of record keeping.

Figure 17-7 shows a simple index file that lets you keep track of your capital goods. It's no substitute for a complete inventory system, but it's a start, and one that lets you quickly search and sort your inventory.

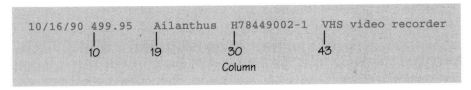

Figure 17-7. *Capital inventory index file.*

Columns 1 through 8 contain the date of the acquisition.

Columns 10 through 17 contain the cost of acquisition.

Columns 19 through 28 contain the manufacturer's name.

Columns 30 through 41 contain the serial number.

Columns 43 through 79 contain the description.

Here, too, with batch files like the ones you created in Chapter 16, you can keep track of your inventory with one command:

To Answer:	Type:
When did we get the copy machine?	show copy
What did we buy before 1991?	show xcpt /91

This technique can also be used to keep track of your personal inventory for insurance purposes; with a bit of modification, it could also be used for collections, such as coins, stamps, or first editions.

CHANGING YOUR SYSTEM CONFIGURATION

Unlike the other DOS commands, which tell DOS what to do, the configuration commands tell DOS *how* to do something, such as use a device or communicate with a disk drive. These commands help define the computer setup, or *configuration,* so that DOS can work well with your equipment. You don't type the configuration commands at the keyboard as you do other DOS commands. You put them in a special file called CONFIG.SYS, which must be in the root directory of your DOS disk. DOS carries out the commands in CONFIG.SYS only when you start or restart the system, so if you change a command in this file, you must restart DOS for the command to take effect.

If you purchase an application program or an accessory device that requires certain commands in CONFIG.SYS, either the installation program adds or modifies the needed commands, or the documentation provides step-by-step instructions. Most other times, however, the system configuration remains stable, so you don't change the configuration commands very often. But as you become more familiar with DOS and your computer, you might want to experiment with commands in CONFIG.SYS as a means of speeding up or refining the way your system works.

If you have version 5, DOS itself either creates a basic CONFIG.SYS (and an AUTOEXEC.BAT) for you, or it modifies the existing version of each file as part of its installation procedure. If you have version 4, DOS creates CONFIG.SYS and AUTOEXEC.BAT if they don't already exist; if they do exist, DOS creates versions named CONFIG.400 and AUTOEXEC.400, which you can later combine with your existing CONFIG.SYS and AUTOEXEC.BAT files. Earlier versions of DOS do not automatically create either CONFIG.SYS or AUTOEXEC.BAT.

If you want to create or edit CONFIG.SYS, you use a text editor just as you do when you create or edit a batch file. If the file is short, you can also copy from the console as you have done in earlier chapters, but remember that you cannot correct errors once you press Enter, so double-check your spelling and typing to avoid having to retype the file.

The following topics describe some of the configuration commands you might use on your system.

The Device Command and Device Drivers

The Device configuration command specifies a program (a special type of file whose extension is usually SYS) that tells DOS how to use a particular device. Such a program is called a *device driver*. The form of the Device command is:

device=<filename>

<filename> is the name of the file that contains the device driver. You can include a path name if the file is not in the root directory. If you have a mouse, for example, and the program that tells DOS how to use it is named MOUSE.SYS in the C:\MOUSE directory, the device command you put in your CONFIG.SYS file would be *device=c:\mouse\mouse.sys*.

Even though the word *device* brings hardware to mind, a Device command needn't always refer to a piece of equipment you can touch or carry. In certain instances, a "device" is actually a program that simulates hardware. DOS, for example, includes two special program files that enable it to use portions of memory on your system as if that memory were disk-based storage. One of these files, RAM-DRIVE.SYS, enables DOS to use memory as if it were an extremely fast disk drive instead; the other, SMARTDRV.SYS, lets you use extra memory as a rapid-access storage area for information DOS has read from disk.

RAMDRIVE.SYS and SMARTDRV.SYS are described shortly. First, though, a little information about your computer's memory will help you understand how and when to use these device drivers.

Types of Memory and How They Differ

You know that computers use random access memory, or RAM, for temporary storage of calculations, data, active programs, and other work in progress. You might not be aware, however, that a computer can have up to three types of RAM, known as *conventional, extended,* and *expanded* memory.

Conventional Memory

Conventional memory is the type most people refer to as RAM. Every computer that runs MS-DOS comes with a certain amount of conventional memory, normally between 256 K and 640 K. This memory can be used to hold DOS, application programs, and data. All computer programs can use conventional memory, but IBM and compatible computers running MS-DOS are limited to a maximum of 1 MB (1024 K) of this type of memory.

Even if your computer has 1 MB of conventional memory, however, not all of it is freely available for applications, data, or even DOS. In actuality, DOS normally uses only the first 640 K of conventional memory for applications and data. The remaining 384 K of conventional memory is known as *reserved* memory or the *upper memory area* and is set aside for special purposes such as hardware control and video memory. This reserved portion of memory is used by memory-management software in units called *upper memory blocks,* or UMBs. Beginning with version 5, DOS can load device drivers and programs such as Doskey into unused UMBs, thus helping you conserve as much as possible of your computer's first 640 K of memory for applications and data.

Extended Memory

Extended memory is additional memory that begins at the 1 MB boundary where conventional memory ends, so it literally extends the limits of conventional memory. You can add many megabytes' worth of extended memory to a computer, but that does not necessarily mean you can use it. Extended memory can be used for storage only by programs specifically designed to find and take advantage of it. If your programs cannot use extended memory, you might as well not have any. Extended memory is often managed by a program called an extended memory manager, which keeps two applications from trying to use the same portion of extended memory at the same time.

Expanded Memory

If you think of extended memory as "high" memory that a program can reach with the right tools, you can think of expanded memory as being like a separate reservoir that a program can draw on through a pipeline. Expanded memory must be handled by a program called an expanded memory manager. Only the manager can parcel the memory out to waiting programs, and it does so in 16 K blocks that it makes available through a memory section called a *page frame* in the computer's reserved memory area. An expanded memory manager should come with any expanded memory you install in your system. If the manager handles expanded memory according to the standard specifications devised by Lotus, Intel, and Microsoft for such programs, it is identified as LIM (Lotus-Intel-Microsoft) or LIM EMS (LIM Expanded Memory Specification).

Once your computer is set up with extended memory, expanded memory, or both, you really needn't worry about what type you have or how it's used. It's the job of the managing software to do all that for you. But you can use DOS, especially in version 5, to take advantage of extended, expanded, and reserved memory to make your system run faster and more efficiently.

Note: If you don't have version 5 of DOS, the following few sections don't apply to your system. Skip to the heading "Creating a Disk Cache with SMARTDRV.SYS" if you have the Microsoft release of version 4. Skip to the heading "Simulating a Disk Drive in memory with RAMDRIVE.SYS" if you have version 3 or IBM's version 4 of DOS.

Managing Memory

Your computer needs nothing more than DOS to manage conventional memory, but when you add extended or expanded memory to a system, DOS needs some extra help. In version 5, that help appears in the form of two device drivers named HIMEM.SYS and EMM386.EXE.

HIMEM.SYS is an extended memory manager. If extended memory is installed in your system when DOS version 5 is installed, DOS finds the memory and adds an appropriate Device command naming this device driver to CONFIG.SYS. If you install extended memory after installing DOS, you can add your own Device command to CONFIG.SYS. For example, if HIMEM.SYS is in the C:\DOS directory, the command would be:

device=c:\dos\himem.sys

Once you've identified HIMEM.SYS (or another extended memory manager) in CONFIG.SYS, you can turn some of the extended memory into a fast-access storage area, a simulated disk drive, or a home for DOS itself.

On a computer with an 80386 or 80486 microprocessor, you can also manage memory with EMM386.EXE. This memory manager performs two tasks:

▶ If your system has extended memory, but your applications require expanded memory, EMM386.EXE can help DOS treat a specified amount of that extended memory as if it were expanded memory.

▶ If your system has unused portions of the upper memory area available after all necessary amounts have been parceled out for hardware control, video, and other special purposes, EMM386.EXE can make those unused portions of memory available to DOS for loading device drivers and programs.

EMM386.EXE includes a number of parameters, most of which are needed only by programmers. Three that you might use, however, are described here. Assuming that EMM386.EXE is in the C:\DOS directory, the Device command and the three parameters look like this:

device=c:\dos\emm386.exe <memory> ram noems

<memory> tells DOS how much extended memory, in kilobytes, to treat as expanded memory. You can specify 16 to 32768. If you don't include <memory>, DOS assumes 256 K, rounding down to the nearest multiple of 16 if necessary. When you use this parameter, DOS sets aside the required amount of extended memory for use as

expanded memory. It also sets up your system's upper memory area so that part can be used to make the expanded memory available to programs, and the remainder can, if requested, be used for loading device drivers and programs.

ram tells DOS to provide access to both expanded memory and reserved memory (UMBs).

noems tells DOS to set aside all available reserved memory for loading device drivers and programs. If you use this parameter, you cannot use any expanded memory.

Include either *ram* or *noems* in the Device command that names EMM386.EXE. For example, a basic Device command in CONFIG.SYS would be:

device=c:\dos\emm386.exe

To treat 640 K of extended memory as expanded memory and make UMBs available, the command would be:

device=c:\dos\emm386.exe 640 ram

To set aside all available reserved memory for loading programs and device drivers, the command would be:

device=c:\dos\emm386.exe noems

Once you give DOS access to reserved memory, you can use this memory with either the Loadhigh command or the Devicehigh configuration command described in the section headed ''Using Reserved Memory.''

Running DOS in High Memory

In all versions through version 4, DOS has always loaded itself into conventional memory, reducing the amount of memory available for applications and data by the amount of space it needed. Beginning with version 5, DOS includes a simple configuration command named Dos that can help you conserve conventional memory on a system with extended memory, reserved memory, or both.

If your system has at least 64 K of extended memory, you can use the Dos command to tell DOS to position itself in a portion of extended memory called the *high memory area* (HMA). If your system has at least 350 K of extended memory (typical of 80386 systems with 1 MB of RAM), you can use the Dos command to make part or all of the upper memory area available for use by device drivers and programs. By moving DOS, device drivers, and utility programs such as Doskey and other memory-resident software out of conventional memory, you leave as much of that valuable storage space as possible for your applications and data to use.

The Dos configuration command is:

dos=high/low,umb/noumb

high tells DOS to load itself into the high memory area if it can. *low* tells DOS to load itself into conventional memory. If you don't specify *high,* or if DOS can't load itself into high memory, DOS automatically moves into conventional memory.

umb (short for upper memory blocks) tells DOS to use the upper memory area for device drivers and programs. *noumb* tells DOS not to use the upper memory area. If you don't specify *umb,* DOS does not use the upper memory area.

You can put this command anywhere in CONFIG.SYS, and you can specify both parameters in one command by separating them with a comma. If you use the *high* parameter, however, also include a Device command that names HIMEM.SYS so that you can be sure DOS can find and use extended memory. If you use the *umb* parameter, also include a Device command that names EMM386.EXE or another manager that makes the upper memory area available for use. The following two examples show different ways to use these commands in CONFIG.SYS.

To load DOS into high memory on a system with at least 64 K of extended memory, you would include these commands in CONFIG.SYS:

```
dos=high
device=c:\dos\himem.sys
```

To load DOS into high memory and provide access to all of the available upper memory area on an 80386 or 80486 system with at least 350 K of extended memory, you would include the following commands in CONFIG.SYS:

```
dos=high,umb
device=c:\dos\himem.sys
device=c:\dos\emm386.exe noems
```

Note: The Device command naming HIMEM.SYS must precede the Device command naming EMM386.EXE.

If you tell DOS to load itself into extended memory, you can check its position with the Mem command. DOS should respond *MS-DOS resident in High Memory Area.* If DOS cannot find the High Memory Area and load itself in extended memory, you don't have to worry. It will load into conventional memory just as it always has.

Creating a Disk Cache with SMARTDRV.SYS

If your computer has a fixed disk, either extended or expanded memory, and version 5 or Microsoft's version 4 of DOS, you can use the Device command and a "smart drive" device driver named SMARTDRV.SYS to turn part of this additional memory into a rapid-access storage area known as a *disk cache.* A disk cache speeds up your system because information that your computer reads from disk into memory remains in the cache. It's much faster for your computer to read information that's already in memory, so a disk cache can substantially reduce the amount of time your computer spends going out to disk, finding the information you need, and reading it into memory.

The form of the Device command to create a disk cache with SMARTDRV.SYS is:

device=smartdrv.sys <size> <minsize> /A

SMARTDRV.SYS is the name of the file that contains the device-driver program. If the program is not in the root directory of the current disk, precede the name with a drive and path—for example, *c:\dos\smartdrv.sys*.

<size> is the size you want the cache to be, in kilobytes. It can be any value from 128 to 8192 (8 MB). If you don't specify <size>, SMARTDRV.SYS sets the cache size to 256 K. When the cache is created, DOS rounds <size> to the nearest multiple of 16. If there is too little memory to create the size cache you specify, SMARTDRV.SYS creates a smaller one, using what memory is available.

<minsize> is the smallest you want the cache to be, again in kilobytes. You don't have to specify <minsize>, but if you don't, and you use Microsoft Windows version 3.0 or later, the other program might be able to reduce the size of your cache to suit its own purposes. In some cases, this might mean reducing the cache to 0.

/A creates the cache in *expanded* memory. If you don't include /A, the cache is created in *extended* memory. If you have both extended and expanded memory, choose the type that is more abundant on your system. If you have plenty of both, omit /A and create the cache in extended memory.

Because the disk cache is created in extended or expanded memory, the Device command specifying SMARTDRV.SYS must appear in your CONFIG.SYS file *after* the command that identifies your extended or expanded memory manager.

Also, when you specify the size, leave enough memory for other programs that also run in extended or expanded memory. If you're not certain how much of this memory you have (or have available), use the Mem command to ask DOS to report on memory usage for you.

The following examples create a 1 MB (1024 K) disk cache with a minimum size of 256 K. The examples assume that SMARTDRV.SYS is in the C:\DOS directory. Note that the command identifying the memory manager precedes the command that creates the disk cache. For extended memory, the commands would be:

```
device=c:\dos\himem.sys
device=c:\dos\smartdrv.sys 1024 256
```

For expanded memory, the commands would be:

```
device=<manager>
device=c:\dos\smartdrv.sys 1024 256 /a
```

In the first Device command, you would replace *manager* with the drive, directory, and name of your own expanded memory manager.

Simulating a Disk Drive in Memory with RAMDRIVE.SYS

Disk drives are mechanical and quite slow compared to the computer's memory. Starting with some versions numbered 3.0, DOS lets you set aside a portion of the computer's memory for use as a simulated disk, making it possible for disk operations to be performed at memory speeds.

This simulated disk is called a *RAM disk* or *RAM drive* because it exists in your computer's memory (RAM) rather than as a solid piece of hardware. It's also known as a *virtual disk* because having a RAM disk is virtually the same as having another disk drive. A RAM disk is particularly useful on a system with extended or expanded memory because DOS can create the RAM disk in either of these types of memory, leaving the computer's conventional memory for other uses.

On the surface, a RAM disk might not seem much different from a disk cache, as described in the preceding section. It is different, though. You can think of a disk cache—one created either by SMARTDRV.SYS or by a separate disk-caching program—as a warehousing area for information you've already used. In contrast, creating a RAM disk is like adding an extremely fast disk drive to your system.

A RAM disk behaves like any other disk: It has a drive letter and a directory, and you can specify it in any command that refers to a disk. It is much faster than a real disk drive, however, and the difference is especially noticeable when you use commands, such as Copy, that work with disk drives, or when you use application programs that access the disk frequently, as many word processors and database programs do. To use a RAM disk, you copy the files you need from a physical disk to the RAM disk after DOS has started, then copy them back to the disk after you have completed the work. Copying them back is particularly important because any changes you make to the files are recorded only in memory when you are using a RAM disk, and the contents of memory disappear whenever you turn off your computer.

DOS assigns the next available drive letter to the RAM disk. On a system with one or two diskette drives and a fixed disk, the next available letter is usually D.

Although a real disk drive has a fixed capacity, such as 360 K or 1.44 MB, a RAM disk can have whatever capacity you want, within the limits described below for the command parameters. If your computer has enough memory, you can define more than one RAM disk by including more than one RAM-disk Device command in CONFIG.SYS.

If your computer is equipped with expanded or extended memory, you should tell DOS to use this additional memory for your RAM disk, leaving your computer's conventional memory space for programs to use. If you have version 5 of DOS and an 80386 or 80486 computer, you can also use the Devicehigh configuration command described later to load the program that creates the RAM disk into the upper memory area. (You can check on available upper memory blocks with the /C parameter of the Mem command.)

As efficient as it is, the remarkable speedup offered by RAM disks can have some drawbacks. If your computer doesn't have expanded or extended memory (or if you don't tell DOS to use it) the memory used for a RAM disk reduces the amount of memory available to programs. Furthermore, the contents of a RAM disk are lost each time you turn the computer off.

If the RAM disk is large enough, you can speed operations by copying both programs and data files to it. Otherwise, make certain that your RAM disk leaves enough memory for the programs you use. In either case, be sure to copy the files you want to keep onto a real disk before you turn the computer off. You can automate this process by using a batch file to copy your working files to the RAM disk, start the application program, and then copy the revised working files back to the real disk after you leave the application program.

Depending on your version of DOS, the file that creates a RAM disk is called either RAMDRIVE.SYS or VDISK.SYS. To avoid excessive detail, the following description applies to RAMDRIVE.SYS as it can be used with version 5 of DOS. Differences in earlier versions and in VDISK.SYS are not major, but they do exist. If you need exact values, refer to Appendix C, "DOS Command Reference."

To define a RAM disk, the Device command is:

device=ramdrive.sys <size> <sector> <directory> /E /A

RAMDRIVE.SYS (or VDISK.SYS) is the name of the device-driver program. If it isn't in the root directory of the DOS disk, you must include the drive letter and path name of its directory—for example, *c:\dos\ramdrive.sys*.

<size> is the size, in kilobytes, of the RAM disk. The minimum is 16 K, and the maximum is 4096 K (4 MB). If you omit <size> or specify an incorrect value, RAM-DRIVE.SYS sets <size> to 64.

<sector> is the size, in bytes, of each sector on the RAM disk. You can specify 128, 256, or 512. If you omit <sector> or specify an incorrect value, RAMDRIVE.SYS sets <sector> to 512.

<directory> is the number of directory entries allowed in the root directory of the RAM disk. You can specify any value from 2 to 1024. Each directory entry takes up 32 bytes of the RAM disk. If you omit <directory> or specify an incorrect value, RAMDRIVE.SYS sets <directory> to 64.

/E puts the RAM disk in extended memory. It is valid only if the computer contains extended memory. Using extended memory for a RAM disk leaves the maximum amount of conventional memory for programs. If you use /E, you cannot use /A.

/A puts the RAM disk in expanded memory. Like the /E option, it leaves the maximum amount of conventional memory available for programs. If you use /A, you cannot use /E.

If there isn't enough memory to create the RAM disk as you specify it, RAM-DRIVE.SYS doesn't create the disk.

The following examples show the commands that would create RAM disks in conventional, extended, and expanded memory. All three examples assume that RAMDRIVE.SYS is in the C:\DOS directory.

To create a small (64 K) RAM disk in conventional memory, accepting the values DOS assumes for <sector> and <directory>, you would place either of the following commands in CONFIG.SYS:

```
device=c:\dos\ramdrive.sys 64
```

or:

```
device=c:\dos\ramdrive.sys
```

To create a much larger (720 K) RAM disk in extended memory, again accepting the values DOS assumes for <sector> and <directory>, you would need two commands: first, a Device command to identify the extended memory manager to DOS, and then a second Device command to create the RAM disk in extended memory. The commands would look like this:

```
device=c:\dos\himem.sys
device=c:\dos\ramdrive.sys 720 /e
```

Finally, to create the RAM disk described in the preceding example, but in expanded rather than extended memory, the commands would be:

```
device=<manager>
device=c:\dos\ramdrive.sys 720 /a
```

When you created this RAM disk on your own system, you would replace *manager* with the drive, path, and file name of your expanded memory manager.

A Word of Advice

If your computer does not have extended or expanded memory, or if it has less than 640 K of conventional memory, you probably should not try creating a RAM disk. Unless it is very small (64 K or thereabouts), a RAM disk in conventional memory will take a considerable amount of the memory you need for programs. DOS might then either refuse to start or present you with *Out of memory* messages. If you decide to create a RAM disk anyway, start with a small one and check to see whether your programs run. If you have version 4 or 5, you can also use the Mem command to see how large a program you can run after the RAM disk is created.

Using the Upper Memory Area

If you have an 80386 or 80486 computer, chances are your system has 1 MB of memory, and you can use the version 5 Loadhigh and Devicehigh commands to load programs and certain device drivers into upper memory blocks (UMBs). Both commands can help you conserve regular memory for applications and data.

Loadhigh is an internal DOS command like the Directory command. Devicehigh is a configuration command that you include in your CONFIG.SYS file. Because DOS does not normally treat the upper memory area as part of your computer's available RAM, you use the Loadhigh and Devicehigh commands with:

▶ The Dos configuration command, which tells DOS whether to use available upper memory blocks (UMBs).

▶ The HIMEM.SYS device driver, which enables DOS to use high memory.

▶ The EMM386.EXE device driver or a similar device driver that makes unused blocks of the upper memory area available.

Once you've used the Dos command and have identified the appropriate memory managers to DOS with Device configuration commands, you can use the Loadhigh and Devicehigh commands to tell DOS what to load into the upper memory area. To see if you have enough memory for a particular program or device driver, compare the file's size with available memory reported by the Mem /C command.

The following sample CONFIG.SYS file shows the Dos and Device commands you need to use Loadhigh and Devicehigh. Files are assumed to be in the C:\DOS directory. In this example, the Dos command also tells DOS to run in high memory; the *noems* parameter of the Device command naming EMM386.EXE indicates that the system has no need for expanded memory:

```
dos=high,umb
device=c:\dos\himem.sys
device=c:\dos\emm386.exe noems
```

Loading Programs with Loadhigh

The Loadhigh command can be used either from the system prompt or, for programs you want to load regularly into reserved memory, from your AUTOEXEC.BAT file. Loadhigh, which can be abbreviated lh, is particularly well suited for use with the type of program known as a TSR (Terminate and Stay Resident). Such programs sit in memory, but usually reside quietly in the background, as opposed to word processors and other application programs that remain in control of the system as long as they are active. DOS includes a number of TSRs, among them Doskey, Graphics, Mode, and Append.

To load a program into reserved memory, the form of the Loadhigh command is:

loadhigh <filename> <parameters>

<filename> is the name of the program you want to load, including a drive and path if necessary.

<parameters> represents any parameters you type when starting the program.

For example, after starting with the CONFIG.SYS file described earlier, you would load Doskey into reserved memory with the command:

```
loadhigh doskey
```

DOS would then attempt to load the program into the upper memory area. If there weren't enough room, DOS would load Doskey into conventional memory instead.

Loading Device Drivers with Devicehigh

The Devicehigh command enables you to tell DOS to load device drivers, such as RAMDRIVE.SYS, into the upper memory area and thus conserve as much of your computer's conventional memory as possible. Device drivers that are included with DOS and can be loaded into the upper memory area are EGA.SYS, DISPLAY.SYS, ANSI.SYS, RAMDRIVE.SYS, DRIVER.SYS, and PRINTER.SYS.

You can also load non-DOS device drivers into reserved memory. Some, however, change size when they're loaded and might cause your system to halt. If this happens, you might be able to use the *size* parameter of the Devicehigh command to specify the amount of memory the driver needs.

Note: Before experimenting, create a startup diskette (use the /S parameter of the Format command) and copy your CONFIG.SYS and AUTOEXEC.BAT files to it. Then, if you experience difficulties with a device driver, you have an alternative means of starting your computer so you can correct the situation.

The form of the Devicehigh command is:

devicehigh size=<memsize> <filename>

size=<memsize> is the amount of memory, given as a hexadecimal value, required by the device driver. Use *size* if you experience problems loading a device driver into the upper memory area. Although the value must be in hexadecimal (base 16) notation, you don't have to try and figure it out. Edit your CONFIG.SYS file (if necessary) to load the device driver into regular memory, and then use the Mem /C command to see how big the driver is. The second column of the Mem command report gives the size of the device driver in decimal; the third column gives the size in hexadecimal notation. If hexadecimal is new to you, by the way, don't be disconcerted if you see a combination of letters and numerals; both 0004A0 and 0038E0, for example, are valid hexadecimal numbers.

<filename> is the name, including extension, of the device driver you want to load. Include a path if the driver is not in the root directory of the disk from which you start DOS. You can also include parameters required by the device driver.

When you use Devicehigh, DOS attempts to load the specified device driver in the upper memory area. If there is not enough room, DOS loads the driver into conventional memory instead.

The following sample CONFIG.SYS file includes the commands shown earlier, plus a Devicehigh command that loads RAMDRIVE.SYS into the upper memory area and creates a 640 K RAM disk in extended memory:

```
dos=high,umb
device=c:\dos\himem.sys
device=c:\dos\emm386.exe noems
devicehigh=c:\dos\ramdrive.sys 640
```

Controlling the Display with ANSI.SYS

DOS includes a device driver called ANSI.SYS. (ANSI is an acronym for American National Standards Institute.) ANSI.SYS defines a standard set of methods for managing a display, including how to display and erase characters, move the cursor, and select colors. Some programs, including parts of the DOS Mode command, require your system disk to have a CONFIG.SYS file that contains the command *device= c:\dos\ansi.sys* (assuming the file is in your C:\DOS directory).

OTHER CONFIGURATION COMMANDS

Several configuration commands control internal operating characteristics of your system and usually deal with how DOS handles files or reads disks. Some application programs or devices include detailed instructions for adding or changing configuration commands. These configuration commands are described in more detail in Appendix C.

Defining Temporary Work Areas

The Buffers configuration command defines the number of work areas in memory (*buffers*) that DOS uses to handle reading from and writing to a disk. The effect of this configuration command on system performance depends on the type of disk drive you use and the types of programs you use. The form of the Buffers command is:

buffers=<number>

Unless otherwise instructed, versions of DOS through 3.2 use two or three buffers, depending on your system and the amount of memory it has. If you're using version 3.3, DOS sets the number of buffers primarily according to the amount of memory your system has. You can, of course, override these values by including or changing the Buffers configuration command in CONFIG.SYS. For optimum performance, some programs require you to set buffers to a higher number than DOS assumes. Fastback, for example, needs 40. For a list of values that DOS uses, see the description of the Buffers command in Appendix C.

Specifying the Number of Open Files

The Files configuration command tells DOS how many files it can use at one time. Unless otherwise instructed, DOS can use a maximum of eight files at a time. The form of the Files command is:

files=<number>

<number> can be any number from 8 to 255.

Setting the Highest Drive Letter

The Lastdrive configuration command specifies the highest drive letter that DOS recognizes as valid. If CONFIG.SYS doesn't contain a Lastdrive command, the highest drive letter DOS recognizes is E. This command is usually used to specify a higher letter (up to Z) if DOS needs more than five drive letters. This might happen because the computer is part of a network, because it uses many RAM disks, or because a large fixed disk is divided into sections, each of which is referred to by a different drive letter. The form of the Lastdrive command is:

lastdrive=<letter>

<letter> is any letter from A to Z.

COMMANDS FOR OCCASIONAL USE

This book has described all the commands you routinely use to operate DOS. There are a few remaining commands you might occasionally need, and there are several commands that you won't need unless you plan to do some programming or to use some of the advanced capabilities of DOS. The less commonly used commands are described briefly here, and in more detail in Appendix C.

Displaying the DOS Version Number

The Version command displays the number of the version of DOS you're using. If you use more than one version, or if you are using someone else's machine, this gives you a quick way to check the version.

The Version command has no parameters:

ver

If you're using version 5, for example, DOS replies *MS-DOS Version 5.0* in response to the command.

Changing the System Prompt

As shown in examples in earlier chapters, you can change the system prompt with the Prompt command to display much more than just the current drive letter. The change takes effect as soon as you enter the command.

The Prompt command has one parameter:

prompt <string>

<string> is a string of characters that defines the new system prompt. You can use any characters you want. You can also cause the new prompt to include one or more items of useful information by including a dollar sign and one of the following characters, to specify what you want the prompt to contain.

Character	Produces
d	The current date
p	The current drive and directory
n	The current drive
t	The current time
v	The DOS version number
g	A greater-than sign (>)
l	A less-than sign (<)
b	A vertical bar (¦)
q	An equal sign (=)
e	An Escape character
h	A backspace
$	A dollar sign ($)
_	A signal to end the current line and start a new one. (The character is an underscore, not a hyphen.)

You can include as many combinations of $, followed by a character, as you wish. DOS ignores any combination of $ followed by a character that is not in the preceding list. You saw an example of this earlier in this chapter: In the batch file MKT.BAT, the system prompt was set to nothing (made invisible) with the command *prompt $a*.

If you enter the Prompt command with no parameter (just type *prompt*), DOS restores the prompt to the standard DOS version: the letter of the current drive followed by a greater-than sign (for example, C>).

The Prompt command takes effect immediately, so it's easy to experiment. You saw how to change the system prompt to a courteous request (*May I help you?*) in Chapter 3, and you've changed it to suit your needs in other chapters. To restore the system prompt to its standard form is type *prompt pg* (for earlier versions, *prompt $g*).

Several examples follow. Notice how the system prompt changes each time to show the effect of the previous Prompt command. Press the Spacebar before pressing the Enter key to end each command, to leave a blank space between the end of the system prompt and the beginning of the command that you type next.

To define the system prompt as the current drive and directory, type:

```
C:\>prompt $p

C:\MKT\WP _
```

The example assumes that the current drive is C and that the directory is \MKT \WP. To define the system prompt as two lines that show the date and time, type:

```
C:\MKT\WP prompt $d$_$t

Wed 10-16-1991
14:57:10.11 _
```

The time and date will vary, depending on how you have set them in your system. Press the Enter key several times to see that DOS keeps the time current.

Finally, combining several of the options shows just how much you can include in a prompt:

```
Wed 10-16-1991
15:02:10.11 prompt $v$_$d $t$_Current directory $q $p$_Command:

MS-DOS Version 5.0
Wed 10-16-1991 15:02:57.68
Current directory = C:\MKT\WP
Command: _
```

The Prompt command lets you easily tailor the system prompt to the balance of brevity and information that you prefer. When you design a system prompt that you like, put it in AUTOEXEC.BAT and you'll never have to type it again; DOS will carry out the command every time you start the system.

Speeding Up File Access

Note: The Fastopen command described here was introduced in version 3.3 of DOS. If you have an earlier version of DOS, skip to the next section, "Altering the Way DOS Interprets Drive Letters."

Each time you (or an application program) need a file, DOS might first need to search for the subdirectory that contains the file, then search the directory entries for the file itself. On a fixed disk with hundreds or thousands of files, all this searching can take some time.

The Fastopen command tells DOS to keep track (in memory) of the locations of subdirectories and files as it uses them; the next time it's asked for a file or subdirectory, DOS checks in memory before it searches the disk. If it finds the location of the file or subdirectory in memory, DOS can go directly to it on the disk instead of searching for it.

If you or your application programs tend to use the same files or directories over and over, the Fastopen command can make DOS visibly faster. The Fastopen command works only with fixed disks. It has three parameters:

fastopen <drive>=<files> /X

<drive> is the drive letter, followed by a colon, of the fixed disk whose files and subdirectories you want DOS to keep track of (for example, *c:*).

<files> is the number of files and subdirectories whose location DOS is to keep in memory; it must be preceded by an equal sign. You can specify a value for <files> from 10 to 999. For example, if you had one fixed disk, drive C, and wanted DOS to keep track of the last 75 files and subdirectories used, you would type *fastopen c:=75*.

/X tells DOS to keep track of the locations in expanded memory. If you use /X, check to be sure your expanded memory conforms to the current standard, which is LIM EMS 4.0.

If you're using DOS from a fixed disk, the installation program might have set up a Fastopen command telling DOS to keep track of the last *x* files and subdirectories you used. This command will have been placed in your configuration file in a form like this: *install=c:\dos\fastopen.exe c:=(50,25)*. Although the command looks a bit more complicated than *fastopen c:=50*, its purpose is the same. The *install* part of the command (described in Appendix C) simply tells DOS to use your computer's memory as efficiently as it can. If you want to change the number of files, change the command in CONFIG.SYS. For example, to keep track of the last 75 files and sub-directories, change the command to *install=c:\dos\fastopen.exe c:=(75, 25)*.

Altering the Way DOS Interprets Drive Letters

Warning: The following three commands (Assign, Substitute, and Join) let you change the way DOS interprets drive letters. These commands restrict your use of other DOS commands, such as Backup, Restore, and Print, that deal with disks and files. Use the next three commands sparingly, and check the descriptions of the other disk and file commands in your DOS manual to make certain you understand the restrictions. The Substitute and Join commands must not be used on a network.

Assigning a Drive Letter to a Different Drive

Some application programs require that you put the diskettes with your data files in one particular drive. This can be inconvenient if you're using a fixed disk and prefer to use it for your data files. The Assign command gives you a solution: It lets you tell DOS to make a drive letter refer to a different drive (for example, to tell DOS to use the fixed disk, drive C, whenever it receives a request for drive B).

Because the Assign command affects all requests for a drive, you should use it with caution—especially if you are using a fixed disk. Always bear in mind that some DOS commands, such as Delete, erase existing files from the disk in the specified drive. If you use one of these commands after you have used Assign, you could in-advertently lose valuable programs or data files. Only two commands, Format and Diskcopy, ignore drive reassignments specified with Assign.

The Assign command has two parameters:

assign <drive1>=<drive2>

<drive1> is the letter of the drive to be assigned to a different drive.

<drive2> is the letter of the drive that is to be used in place of <drive1>.

If you omit both <drive1> and <drive2>, DOS cancels any assignments.

For example, suppose you have a graphics program that requires all data files to be on drive B, but you want to use your fixed disk (drive C) for data files. To tell DOS to assign all requests for drive B to drive C instead, you would type *assign b=c*.

The assignment affects all requests for the drive, including any commands you enter other than Format and Diskcopy. If you assign drive B to drive C as in the previous example, and then type *dir b:*, DOS displays the directory of the fixed disk. The assignment remains in effect until you restart DOS or cancel the assignment by typing *assign.*

Treating a Directory As If It Were a Disk

The Substitute (subst) command lets you treat a directory as if it were a separate disk. If your directory structure includes long path names, or if you use application programs that accept a drive letter but not a path name, you can use the Substitute command to tell DOS to treat all future references to a particular drive as references to a directory on the disk in a different drive.

After naming a drive letter in a Substitute command or in a Join command (described next), you cannot refer to that drive letter in any other command, so you will probably want to use a drive letter that doesn't refer to an existing drive. In order to do this, you must tell DOS to accept more drive letters than there are disk drives. You do this by putting a Lastdrive command in the CONFIG.SYS file in the root directory of your DOS system disk. The Substitute command has two parameters:

subst <drive> <pathname> /D

<drive> is the letter, followed by a colon, to be used to refer to <pathname>.

<pathname> is the path name of the directory to be referred to by <drive>.

/D deletes any substitutions that involve <drive>. If you include /D, you cannot include <pathname>.

If you omit all parameters (just type *subst*), DOS displays a list of any substitutions in effect.

For example, suppose you find yourself frequently referring to a directory whose path name is C:\SPREAD\SALES\FORECAST, and you would like to use a shorter synonym. To substitute *x:* for the path name, you would make certain that your CONFIG.SYS file contained a Lastdrive command that specified the letter *x*, then type *subst x: c:\spread\sales\forecast*. The substitution would remain in effect until you restarted DOS or canceled the substitution by typing *subst x: /d*.

Treating a Disk As If It Were a Directory

The Join command lets you treat a disk drive as a directory on the disk in a different drive. If you use an application program that stores its data files on the program disk, you can use the Join command to tell DOS to treat another drive as if it were a directory on the program disk. The Join command has three parameters:

join <drive> <pathname> /D

<drive> is the letter, followed by a colon, of the drive to be connected to the directory specified by <pathname>. It cannot be the current drive.

<pathname> is the path name of the directory to which <drive> is to be joined. It must be an empty subdirectory on the disk to which <drive> is to be joined.

/D deletes any joins that involve <drive>. If you include /D, you cannot include <pathname>.

If you omit all parameters (just type *join*), DOS displays a list of any joins in effect. Once you specify a drive letter as <drive> in a Join command, you cannot use that letter to refer to a drive.

For example, suppose you have an application program that takes up most of a diskette and you need a lot of disk space for data files. If you put the application program diskette in drive A and a blank diskette in drive B, you could tell DOS to treat the blank diskette in drive B as a directory named \DATA on the diskette in drive A by typing *join b: a:\data*. The join would remain in effect until you restarted DOS or canceled the join by typing *join b: /d*.

CHAPTER 18

DOS IS AN INTERNATIONAL SYSTEM

Many languages share the basic Latin alphabet, but some add accented Latin characters, such as é, è, ë, or ê, and some use characters that are altogether different, such as ¿ or £. Other languages, such as Arabic, Chinese, Hebrew, Japanese, and Korean, don't use the Latin alphabet at all.

Different countries, regardless of language, also represent the numeric form of a date in different ways. In most North American and European countries, the numeric form of a date is shown in a day-month-year sequence (for example, 16-10-91 for October 16, 1991). In the United States, however, the sequence is month-day-year (10-16-91), and in Japan it is year-month-day (91-10-16). Different countries with different traditions also use different currency symbols and different ways of separating large numbers or decimal fractions.

Depending on the country for which your computer was manufactured, DOS assumes a certain keyboard arrangement and a country code that determines how the date, currency symbols, and decimals are handled. Many versions of DOS, however, let you change these characteristics. The language that DOS itself uses — its command names and the messages it displays — remains unchanged, but you can tailor its operating qualities to the linguistic and monetary traditions of a particular country. This capability can be particularly useful if you use your computer for work with different languages or currencies, or if persons with different language requirements use the same computer.

This type of international support has been a part of DOS since Microsoft's version 2.1 and IBM's version 3.0. The amount of support, fairly restricted in all versions through 3.2, was expanded in version 3.3 as a feature known as *national language support.* The first part of this chapter covers international support in all relevant versions of DOS. Later sections, beginning with the heading "National Language Support," are for versions 3.3 and later.

Note: If you don't need international capability, you can skip this chapter completely. For your purposes, you've come to the end of the book. You have the knowledge you need to use DOS productively. If, at times, you need to refresh your memory, turn to Appendix C, "DOS Command Reference," for command descriptions and references to the chapters in which commands are introduced.

COUNTRY CONVENTIONS AND KEYBOARD LAYOUTS

In any version offering international support, you have two ways to internationalize DOS: You can change to the date, time, and other conventions of a different country, and you can change your keyboard layout to match that used in another country.

▶ To change country-specific formats, you use the Country command. This command must be in your CONFIG.SYS file; you cannot type it at the system prompt.

▶ To change the keyboard layout, as you saw in Chapter 7, "Managing Your Devices," you use the Keyboard command. You can use it at any time by typing the command at the system prompt, or you can set the keyboard layout whenever you start or restart the system by putting a Keyboard command in AUTOEXEC.BAT.

The following examples show how the Country and Keyboard commands work in versions of DOS through 3.2. If you have a later version of DOS, these same commands are available to you, but in expanded form. They are described later in the chapter.

Using the Conventions of a Different Country

Normally, DOS displays the date and time in the format typically used in the United States, but you can change to the conventions of another country by placing a Country command in your CONFIG.SYS file.

In versions of DOS through 3.2, the Country command has one parameter:

country=<code>

<code> can be any of the three-digit numbers (the same as the international dialing prefix) listed in the following table:

Country	Code	Country	Code
Australia	061	Netherlands	031
Belgium	032	Norway	047
Denmark	045	Spain	034
Finland	358	Sweden	046
France	033	Switzerland	041
Germany	049	United Kingdom	044
Israel	972	United States	001
Italy	039		

Suppose your computer was built for use in the United States, but someone also uses it for writing in French. To tell DOS to follow French conventions for date, time, currency, and decimals, include the following Country command in CONFIG.SYS:

```
country=033
```

Once the Country command is in CONFIG.SYS, DOS will use French conventions until you either delete or edit the command.

Choosing a Keyboard Layout

Keyboards used with different languages accommodate different characters and often use a different arrangement of keys. As shown by the Keyboard example in Chapter 7, you can change the keyboard to match the layout used in another country or with another language.

You can type the Keyboard command as follows in versions 3.0 through 3.2:

Command	Keyboard
keybfr	French
keybgr	German
keybit	Italian
keybsp	European Spanish
keybuk	United Kingdom English

Typing one of these Keyboard commands changes the keyboard layout and also enables you to use dead keys—keys that, in combination with the letter produced by another key (such as *a*, *e*, or *i*), produce accented characters not otherwise available on the keyboard. Figure 18-1 shows the dead keys and the characters they produce on the French, German, and Spanish keyboards. (Dead keys are not supported for the United Kingdom or Italy.)

Keyboard	Dead Key	Characters Produced
French	[	â ê î ô û
	{	ä ë ï ö ü Ä Ë Ï Ö Ü
German	=	á é í ó ú É
	+	à è ì ò ù
Spanish	[	á é í ó ú É
	]	à è ì ò ù
	{	ä ë ï ö ü ÿ Ä Ö Ü
	}	â ê î ô û

Figure 18-1. *Accented characters produced with dead keys with the French, German, and Spanish keyboard layouts.*

Suppose, for example, that you want to switch your keyboard from the United States to the French layout, on which, among other differences, the *q* and *a* keys are reversed and you can use the dead keys in Figure 18-1 to type accented characters.

If your version of DOS is 3.2 or earlier, you can type the following command at the system prompt:

```
keybfr
```

Once you've changed to the French keyboard, you can quickly switch to the United States layout by pressing Ctrl-Alt-F1. To switch back to the French layout, you would press Ctrl-Alt-F2.

Bear in mind that, unlike the Country command, the Keyboard command can be typed at the system prompt. If you switch keyboards often, you can also put the command in a batch file. If you want to start up your system with the alternate layout, put the Keyboard command in your AUTOEXEC.BAT file. Or, as described next, create a system diskette that starts DOS with the keyboard layout and conventions of a particular country.

Creating a Language-Specific DOS System Diskette

Note: This section describes the use of the Select command in version 3 of DOS. If you're using version 4 or 5, go on to the heading "National Language Support."

If you use more than one language, or if several users with different languages share the computer, DOS offers a simple way to handle multilingual operation: the Select command, which creates a system diskette tailored to the language and conventions of a particular country.

The Select command makes a copy of the DOS system disk that contains files that configure DOS for a specific country, including CONFIG.SYS and AUTOEXEC.BAT files. If you create several country-specific diskettes, you can change languages simply by restarting DOS after putting the appropriate system diskette in drive A.

The Select command has four parameters:

select <source> <target> <country> <keyboard>

<source> is the letter, followed by a colon, of the drive that contains the DOS system diskette. You can specify either *a:* or *b:*. If you don't specify <source>, DOS assumes drive A.

<target> is the drive letter, followed by a colon, and the path name of the directory on the diskette to which the DOS files are to be copied. If you omit the drive letter, DOS assumes drive B; if you omit the path name, DOS assumes the root directory. <target> and <source> must specify different drives. If you specify only one drive letter, DOS assumes it is <target>.

<country> is the three-digit country code you want set on the new DOS diskette. You must include all three digits of the country code, including any zeros at the beginning. <country> corresponds to the country's long-distance telephone prefix.

<keyboard> is the two-letter abbreviation of the country whose keyboard layout is to be selected for the new DOS diskette. (These are the last two letters of the corresponding Keyboard command.)

Warning: The Select command formats the target disk, erasing all files on it, so either use a new diskette or make sure that the diskette or fixed disk you use as the target contains no files that you must keep.

Figure 18-2 shows the country code and keyboard values allowed with the Select command in version 3 of DOS. Countries marked with an asterisk (*) are the only ones available in versions 3.0 through 3.2; the others are available starting with version 3.3. You can enter the keyboard code in either uppercase or lowercase.

Country	Country Code	Keyboard Code
Arab countries	785	—
Australia	061	US
Belgium	032	BE
Canada (English)	001	US
Canada (French)	002	CF
Denmark	045	DK
Finland	358	SU
France*	033	FR
Germany*	049	GR
Israel	972	—
Italy*	039	IT
Latin America	003	LA
Netherlands	031	NL
Norway	047	NO
Portugal	351	PO
Spain*	034	SP
Sweden	046	SV
Switzerland (French)	041	SF
Switzerland (German)	041	SG
United Kingdom*	044	UK
United States*	001	US

Figure 18-2. *Country and keyboard codes for the Select command.*

NATIONAL LANGUAGE SUPPORT

In versions 3.3 and later, *national language support* is the term used to describe the way in which DOS carries out the tasks of displaying and printing characters in your own and other languages. The basis of national language support is a table of characters known as a *code page*. With national language support and code pages, you can gain the ability to display and print language-specific characters that your computer, printer, or both are normally unable to reproduce.

As shown in Figure 18-3, a code page contains 256 characters. These are the characters needed for displaying or printing a particular language or group of languages. DOS keeps a code page in memory and refers to it whenever you press a key on the

	<space>	@	`	Ç	á	└	α
☺	!	A	a	ü	í	┴	β
☻	"	B	b	é	ó	┬	Γ
♥	#	C	c	â	ú	├	π
♦	$	D	d	ä	ñ	─	Σ
♣	%	E	e	à	Ñ	┼	σ
♠	&	F	f	å	ª	╞	µ
•	'	G	g	ç	º	╟	τ
◘	(	H	h	ê	¿	╚	Φ
○	)	I	i	ë	⌐	╔	Θ
◙	*	J	j	è	¬	╩	Ω
♂	+	K	k	ï	½	╦	δ
♀	,	L	l	î	¼	╠	∞
♪	-	M	m	ì	¡	═	φ
♫	.	N	n	Ä	«	╬	ε
☼	/	O	o	Å	»	╧	∩
►	0	P	p	É	░	╨	≡
◄	1	Q	q	æ	▒	╤	±
↕	2	R	r	Æ	▓	╥	≥
‼	3	S	s	ô	│	╙	≤
¶	4	T	t	ö	┤	╘	⌠
§	5	U	u	ò	╡	╒	⌡
▬	6	V	v	û	╢	╓	÷
↨	7	W	w	ù	╖	╫	≈
↑	8	X	x	ÿ	╕	╪	°
↓	9	Y	y	Ö	╣	┘	∙
→	:	Z	z	Ü	║	┌	·
←	;	[	{	¢	╗	█	√
∟	<	\	¦	£	╝	▄	η
↔	=	]	}	¥	╜	▌	²
▲	>	^	~	₧	╛	▐	■
▼	?	_	⌂	ƒ	┐	▀	

Figure 18-3. *Characters in a code page.*

keyboard or tell DOS to print a document. Because keys and the characters in a document are represented by code numbers rather than actual characters, DOS can check the code numbers against the code page in memory to find the characters it is to display or print.

To give you the ability to use your computer with more than one language, national language support provides DOS with the ability to change from one code page to a different one. This is called *code-page switching,* and when you use it, you load a different table of characters into your computer's memory. If your display and printer have the ability to reproduce the characters—monochrome and CGA displays and many printers cannot—you can then see and print the characters in the new table.

Currently, DOS can use up to six code pages: United States (as shown in Figure 18-3), multilingual (Latin I), Slavic (Latin II), Portuguese, French Canadian, and Nordic. Each of these code pages is identified by a three-digit number:

▶ Code page 437, the United States code page, is the character table used in previous versions of DOS. It supports United States English and, as shown in Figure 18-3, includes many accented characters used in other languages. It also includes various symbols and straight lines, corners, and other characters that can be used to draw boxes.

▶ Code pages 850 and 852 include the various characters and accent marks required by groups of languages based on the Latin alphabet. Code page 850, the so-called multilingual or Latin I code page, includes the characters common to languages such as French, German, Italian, Norwegian, and Portuguese. Code page 852, the Slavic or Latin II code page, is included with DOS 5 and provides the characters and accents used in Slavic languages such as Polish, Czech, and Hungarian.

▶ Code pages 860 (Portuguese), 863 (French Canadian), and 865 (Nordic) include the characters required by Portuguese (ª and º), Canadian French (Ê, Á, and others), and Nordic languages (ø and Ø).

Notice that the code-page number bears no relationship to the country code used by the Country configuration command.

To see how code pages are organized and what they contain, compare the United States code page in Figure 18-3 with the Nordic code page (865) in Figure 18-4. Note that most characters are the same in both, but that ø and Ø appear in code page 865 where ¢ and ¥ appear in code page 437. With code page 865, you could therefore display and print *Tromsø,* but not *95¢*; with code page 437, you could display and print *95¢*, but not *Tromsø.*

A computer uses the language of the country for which it was manufactured, and so it comes with a built-in code page that defines the characters in that language. This code page is called a *hardware code page* and is the code page that DOS uses unless you specify another. For many countries, the hardware code page is 437.

	<space>	@	`	Ç	á	└	α
☺	!	A	a	ü	í	┴	β
●	"	B	b	é	ó	┬	Γ
♥	#	C	c	â	ú	├	π
♦	$	D	d	ä	ñ	─	Σ
♣	%	E	e	à	Ñ	┼	σ
♠	&	F	f	å	ª	╟	µ
•	'	G	g	ç	º	╚	τ
◘	(	H	h	ê	¿	╔	Φ
○	)	I	i	ë	⌐	╩	Θ
◙	*	J	j	è	¬	╦	Ω
♂	+	K	k	ï	½	╠	δ
♀	,	L	l	î	¼	║	∞
♪	−	M	m	ì	¡	═	φ
♫	.	N	n	Ä	«	╬	ε
☼	/	O	o	Å	¤	╧	∩
►	0	P	p	É	░	╨	≡
◄	1	Q	q	æ	▓	╤	±
↕	2	R	r	Æ	█	╥	≥
‼	3	S	s	ô	│	╙	≤
¶	4	T	t	ö	┤	╘	⌠
§	5	U	u	ò	╡	╒	⌡
▬	6	V	v	û	╢	╓	÷
↨	7	W	w	ù	╖	╫	≈
↑	8	X	x	ÿ	╕	╪	°
↓	9	Y	y	Ö	╣	┘	•
→	:	Z	z	Ü	║	┌	·
←	;	[	{	ø	╗	█	√
∟	<	\	|	£	╝	▄	η
↔	=	]	}	ø	╜	▌	2
▲	>	^	~	Pt	╛	▐	■
▼	?	_	△	ƒ	┐	▀	

Figure 18-4. *Characters in the Nordic code page (865).*

When you need a different language that uses characters your hardware code page does not include, you switch to an alternate set of characters, a *prepared code page*. Unlike hardware code pages, prepared code pages are stored on disk, in your \DOS directory, in files with the extension CPI (for code-page information). You prepare such a code page for use with an option of the Mode command called cp prepare.

Although code-page switching requires some setup work, it is not difficult to use. Once you have defined the devices and code pages you'll use on your system, the only commands you deal with are those that switch from one code page to another— hence the term code-page switching.

Because the devices on your system must work in harmony—speak the same language, if you will—DOS recognizes certain combinations of country, keyboard, and code page as valid. When you use code-page switching, DOS verifies that you are not trying to use conflicting codes or code pages. If you do, you see a message telling you that one or more code pages you've specified are not compatible with one another. Figure 18-5 lists the countries/languages, keyboards, and code pages DOS recognizes.

Setting Up Your System for Code-Page Switching

National language support involves your keyboard, display, and printer, as well as whatever code pages you need to use, so you prepare for code-page switching by identifying the devices that use code pages and by setting up DOS to handle more than one code page. Doing this involves several commands, which DOS must find in certain files and must encounter in a certain sequence.

Typing commands in a particular sequence is not new to you. After all, you copy a file before deleting it, and you create a subdirectory before putting files in it. If your computer has extended or expanded memory, you identify that memory to DOS before you try to use it. Preparing for code-page switching is a little more detailed but no more complicated. The following list includes the commands you need and the files in which DOS looks for them:

▶ One or more Device (or, with version 5, Devicehigh) configuration commands in CONFIG.SYS.

▶ A National Language Support Function (nlsfunc) command in CONFIG.SYS or AUTOEXEC.BAT.

▶ One or more Mode Code Page Prepare (mode cp prepare) commands in AUTOEXEC.BAT.

▶ A Keyboard (keyb) command in AUTOEXEC.BAT.

The following topics describe these and supporting commands in detail, including examples of their use. Complete examples of how to set up a system follow the command descriptions. The descriptions and examples assume a computer system with no more than 640 K of memory. If you have version 5 of DOS and a computer with an 80386 or 80486 microprocessor and extended memory, you might be able to conserve regular system memory by using the Devicehigh and Loadhigh commands to load device drivers and commands such as Nlsfunc into the upper memory area (between 640 K and 1 MB). For more information on using this type of memory, refer to Chapter 17, "Tailoring Your System," and Appendix C, "DOS Command Reference."

National Language Support Commands

National language support can involve the use of up to seven commands—Device, National Language Support Function (nlsfunc), Change Code Page (chcp), Keyboard (keyb), Mode, Load Graphics Table (graftabl), and Country—and two system files, DISPLAY.SYS and PRINTER.SYS.

Country or Language	Country Code	Keyboard Code	Code Pages
Arabic*	785	—	437 (864 and 850 in version 4)
Belgium	032	be	437, 850
Brazil	055	br	850, 437
Canada (French)	002	cf	863, 850
Czechoslovakia (Czech)	042	cz	852, 850
Czechoslovakia (Slovak)	042	sl	852, 850
Denmark	045	dk	865, 850
Finland	358	su	437, 850
France	033	fr	437, 850
Germany	049	gr	437, 850
Hebrew*	972	—	437 (862 and 850 in version 4)
Hungary	036	hu	852, 850
International English	061	—	437, 850
Italy	039	it	437, 850
Japan*	081	—	932, 850, 437
Korea*	082	—	934, 850, 437
Latin America	003	la	437, 850
Netherlands	031	nl	437, 850
Norway	047	no	865, 850
People's Republic of China*	086	—	936, 850, 437
Poland	048	pl	852, 850
Portugal	351	po	860, 850
Spain	034	sp	437, 850
Sweden	046	sv	437, 850
Switzerland (French)	041	sf	437, 850
Switzerland (German)	041	sg	437, 850
Taiwan*	088	—	938, 850, 437
United Kingdom	044	uk	437, 850
United States	001	us	437, 850
Yugoslavia	038	yu	852, 850

*Special versions of DOS only.

Figure 18-5. *Valid combinations of country code, keyboard code, and code pages.*

The Device Configuration Command

Chapter 17, "Tailoring Your System," described the Device configuration command and showed ways you use it to identify various devices so that DOS can use them. To prepare your display and printer for code-page switching, you add one or more Device commands to your CONFIG.SYS file. These commands tell DOS where to find the device drivers DISPLAY.SYS and PRINTER.SYS, which it needs in order to make use of prepared code pages.

Specifying the Display Driver—DISPLAY.SYS

DISPLAY.SYS is the file that controls code-page switching for the display. This file supports IBM and compatible EGA, VGA, and LCD (liquid crystal display) adapters. The IBM Monochrome Display Adapter (MDA) and the Color Graphics Adapter (CGA) use their own hardware code pages, so you cannot use code-page switching with these displays. If you use the ANSI.SYS display driver, the Device command that defines it must precede the Device command that defines DISPLAY.SYS.

Assuming that DISPLAY.SYS is in the C:\DOS directory, the Device command to prepare an EGA, VGA, or LCD display for code-page switching is:

device=c:\dos\display.sys con=(<type>,<hwcp>,<prepcp>)

<type> is the type of display adapter connected to your computer. Use *ega* for either an EGA or a VGA display adapter; use *lcd* for a liquid crystal display.

<hwcp> is the name of the hardware code page for your display. Often it is the United States code page, 437, but you can check on yours by typing the Change Code Page command, chcp. DOS responds with the message *Active code page:* followed by the number of the hardware code page for your display. If you don't want to use the hardware code page, you can omit this parameter, but remember to include the commas that precede and follow it.

<prepcp> is the number of additional code pages you want to use. <prepcp> can be from 0 through 6 for EGA and VGA displays but must be 1 for an LCD display.

For example, the following configuration command in CONFIG.SYS specifies one extra (prepared) code page for an EGA display with a hardware code page of 437:

```
device=c:\dos\display.sys con=(ega,437,1)
```

Specifying the Printer Driver—PRINTER.SYS

PRINTER.SYS is the file that controls code-page switching for certain IBM printers and compatible models. The printers are the IBM 4201 Proprinter and 4202 Proprinter XL, the IBM 4207 Proprinter X24 and 4208 Proprinter XL24, and the IBM 5202 Quietwriter III.

Assuming that PRINTER.SYS is in the C:\DOS directory, the Device command to prepare a supported printer for code-page switching is:

device=c:\dos\printer.sys <printer>=(<type>,<hwcp>,<prepcp>)

<printer> is the DOS device name for the port the printer is connected to. <printer> can be LPT1 (or PRN), LPT2, or LPT3.

<type> is the type of printer attached to the system. <type> can be one of the following:

▶ *4201* for the IBM 4201 Proprinter, the 4202 Proprinter XL, or a compatible model.

▶ *4208* for the IBM 4207 Proprinter X24, the 4208 Proprinter XL24, or a compatible model.

▶ *5202* for the IBM 5202 Quietwriter III or a compatible model.

<hwcp> is the hardware code page for your printer. It is often 437, but you can check your printer's documentation to find out. If you can't find the hardware code page or you don't want to use it, you can omit this parameter. Remember, however, to include the commas that precede and follow it.

<prepcp> is the number of additional (prepared) code pages you want to use, usually 1 if the hardware code page is 437, and 2 otherwise.

For example, the following configuration command in CONFIG.SYS specifies one extra (prepared) code page for an IBM 4201 Proprinter that has a hardware code page of 437 and is attached to LPT1:

```
device=c:\dos\printer.sys lpt1=(4201,437,1)
```

National Language Support Function Command—Nlsfunc

The National Language Support Function (nlsfunc) command is the command that enables DOS to use code pages and code-page switching. If there is no Country configuration command in CONFIG.SYS, the Nlsfunc command also names the file that contains country-specific information such as date format and currency symbol. You must enter the Nlsfunc command before you can switch code pages with the Change Code Page (chcp) command.

You can type the Nlsfunc command directly, at the system prompt, or you can put it in AUTOEXEC.BAT or CONFIG.SYS if you use national language support whenever you start the system. The command has one parameter:

nlsfunc <countryfile>

<countryfile> is the name of the country-information file, which is usually COUNTRY.SYS. If you omit <countryfile>, DOS assumes there is a Country configuration command in CONFIG.SYS that names the file. If there is no Country command, DOS looks for a file named COUNTRY.SYS in the root directory of the current drive.

For example, the following command, typed at the system prompt, prepares DOS for code-page switching and specifies COUNTRY.SYS in the C:\DOS directory:

```
C:\>nlsfunc c:\dos\country.sys
```

You could place the same Nlsfunc command in AUTOEXEC.BAT to prepare DOS for code-page switching whenever you start or restart the system.

If you have version 4 or 5 of DOS, you can also use the Install configuration command to load the Nlsfunc program from your CONFIG.SYS file instead of including the command in AUTOEXEC.BAT. For example, assuming that the Nlsfunc program (NLSFUNC.EXE) is in C:\DOS and that CONFIG.SYS does not include a Country command specifying C:\DOS\COUNTRY.SYS, the Install command for the preceding example would be:

```
install=c:\dos\nlsfunc.exe c:\dos\country.sys
```

Preparing a Code Page

The Device and Nlsfunc commands prepare your system and DOS for code-page switching. Once this has been done (mostly or entirely in your CONFIG.SYS and AUTOEXEC.BAT files), you prepare the code pages themselves by moving them into the computer's memory. You do this with a Mode command in the form:

mode <device> cp prep=((<codepage>) <filename>)

<device> is the name of the device for which the code page or code pages are to be prepared. You use *con* to prepare code pages for the display, and you use *prn*, *lptl*, *lpt2*, or *lpt3* to prepare code pages for the printer.

<codepage> is the number of the code page you want to prepare for use. It is one of the following: 437, 850, 852, 860, 863, or 865. Valid code pages for various countries are listed in Figure 18-5.

<filename> is the name of the code-page information file DOS needs in order to load code pages into RAM. <filename> can be one of the following:

▶ EGA.CPI if you're preparing code pages for use with either an EGA or a VGA display adapter.

▶ LCD.CPI if you're preparing code pages for use with a liquid crystal display.

▶ 4201.CPI if you're preparing code pages for use with the IBM 4201 Proprinter, the 4202 Proprinter XL, or a compatible model.

▶ 4208.CPI if you're preparing code pages for use with the IBM 4207 Proprinter X24, the 4208 Proprinter XL24, or a compatible model.

▶ 5202.CPI if you're preparing code pages for use with the IBM 5202 Quietwriter III or a compatible model.

For example, suppose you wanted to prepare code page 850 for use with an EGA display and an IBM 4201 Proprinter attached to LPT1. Assuming that the code-page information files were in your \DOS directory, the Mode command for the display would be:

```
mode con cp prep=((850) c:\dos\ega.cpi)
```

The Mode command for the printer would be:

```
mode lpt1 cp prep=((850) c:\dos\4201.cpi)
```

When you are setting up code-page switching, be sure that the Mode cp prepare command follows an Nlsfunc command. Remember, DOS must encounter some of these commands in a certain order. In this case, bear in mind that you cannot prepare code pages before you've prepared DOS to use them. Thus, Nlsfunc must come before Mode cp prepare, whether you type the commands at the system prompt or put them in your AUTOEXEC.BAT file.

Device, Nlsfunc, and Mode cp prepare are the core commands in setting up your system for code-page switching. Others help you select or change code pages, check on their status, and restore those that are erased from memory. The next few topics describe these commands, as well as two others that you can use with or without code-page switching: Country and Keyboard.

Country Configuration Command

The Country configuration command, like the similar command in earlier versions of DOS, lets you change country-specific conventions, such as the way the date and time are displayed. In versions 3.3 and later, the Country command includes a parameter that lets you specify the code page to be used by DOS. You don't necessarily need a Country command in CONFIG.SYS, nor do you always need to specify a code page if you do use the command.

If you don't include a Country command in CONFIG.SYS, DOS assumes country 001 (United States) and code page 437. It also assumes there is a country-information file named COUNTRY.SYS in the root directory of the system disk.

The Country configuration command has three parameters:

country=<code>,<codepage>,<countryfile>

<code> is one of the three-digit country codes, such as 039 and 044, listed in Figure 18-5.

<codepage> is one of the three-digit code pages listed in Figure 18-5 for the country you specify.

<countryfile> is the name of the file that contains the country information. If you don't specify <countryfile>, DOS assumes the file is named COUNTRY.SYS and is in the root directory of the system disk. Because DOS looks only in the root directory, you must specify <countryfile> if COUNTRY.SYS is in your \DOS directory.

You put a Country command in CONFIG.SYS if you want to start your system with the conventions of a different country—for example, French rather than United States conventions. You can omit the <codepage> parameter in your command if the country you specify uses the same hardware code page as in your country. For example, assuming that COUNTRY.SYS is in the \DOS directory, the following command in CONFIG.SYS causes a United States system to use French conventions:

```
country=033,,c:\dos\country.sys
```

Note the two commas, which tell DOS that the code-page parameter is omitted. The code page does not need to be included if the hardware code page for the country you specify is the same as the hardware code page for your system.

If you want or need to change code pages, you include the <codepage> parameter. To specify the multilingual code page in the preceding example, the command would be:

```
country=033,850,c:\dos\country.sys
```

Keyboard Command—Keyb

The Keyboard (keyb) command selects a keyboard layout. It replaces the Keyb*xx* commands used through version 3.2 to select keyboard layouts.

The Keyb command has four parameters:

keyb <code>,<codepage>,<keybfile> /ID:<kbdid>

<code> is one of the two-letter keyboard codes listed in Figure 18-5.

<codepage> is one of the three-digit code pages listed in Figure 18-5 for the country whose keyboard code you want to use.

<keybfile> is the name of the system file that contains the keyboard layouts. If you don't specify <keybfile>, DOS assumes that the file is named KEYBOARD.SYS and is stored in the root directory of the system disk. Because DOS looks only in the root directory, you must specify <keybfile> if KEYBOARD.SYS is in your \DOS directory.

/ID: <kbdid> is a three-digit code in versions 4 and 5 of DOS that specifies a keyboard layout to be used when a country has more than one keyboard ID. These countries are:

Country	Keyboard IDs
France	120, 189
Italy	141, 142
United Kingdom	166, 168

For these countries, if you don't specify a keyboard ID, DOS assumes the first ID listed above.

When changing keyboard layouts, you don't have to specify a code page if the language to which you are switching uses the code page currently recognized by your system. For example, the United States, France, Germany, Italy, Latin America, the

Netherlands, Spain, and the United Kingdom all use code page 437. If this is the current code page, you can switch to the keyboard layout for any of these countries simply by specifying the keyboard code and, if necessary, the path to KEYBOARD.SYS. Thus, to change from the United States layout to the German layout, the command would be:

```
c:\>keyb gr,,c:\dos\keyboard.sys
```

To change both the keyboard layout and the code page used by the keyboard, you would specify both. For example, to switch to the German layout and use the multilingual code page, the command would be:

```
c:\>keyb gr,850,c:\dos\keyboard.sys
```

If you type the Keyboard command without any parameters, DOS displays the current keyboard code, keyboard ID, keyboard code page, and display (CON) code page in a message like the following:

```
Current keyboard code: GR   code page: 850
Current CON code page: 437
```

Another way to specify a different code page is to use the Change Code Page command described later. Using Change Code Page ensures that all devices with a currently selected code page will end up using the same one.

Using Code-Page Switching

Once you've set up your system for code-page switching, you can use commands that change the code page used by all devices, select code pages for specific devices, check on the status of your devices, and restore code pages that have been erased from memory:

▶ To change the current code page on all devices that support code-page switching, you use the Change Code Page command (chcp).

▶ To select a code page for a particular device, such as the printer, you use the codepage select option of the Mode command (mode cp select).

▶ To check on the code pages that are available and active, you use the Mode command with no parameters (mode) to check on all devices for which you've prepared code pages. You use the device option of the Mode command (mode <device>) to check on single devices.

▶ To restore a code page that was erased from memory after you selected it, you use the codepage refresh option of the Mode command (mode cp refresh).

Change Code Page Command—Chcp

The Change Code Page (chcp) command tells DOS which code page to use for all devices that support code-page switching. You use it to make a code page active throughout the system and to change to a new code page when you change character sets.

You can type the Change Code Page command when you need it at the system prompt. To activate a particular code page whenever you start or restart the system, you can also include the command in AUTOEXEC.BAT.

The Change Code Page command has one parameter:

chcp <codepage>

<codepage> is one of the three-digit code pages listed in Figure 18-5. The code page you specify must be one that you've already prepared with the Mode cp prepare command. If the code page you specify was not activated for one or more devices, DOS responds *Code page* nnn *not prepared for all devices.*

If you type the Change Code Page command with no parameter, DOS displays the number of the current code page for the system.

For example, the following command would change the system code page to 850:

```
C:\>chcp 850
```

If you checked on the code page by typing:

```
C:\>chcp
```

DOS would respond:

```
Active code page: 850
```

Selecting a Code Page—Mode Codepage Select

To select a code page for a single device, you use the cp select option of the Mode command. When used for selecting a code page, the Mode command has two parameters:

mode <device> cp select=<codepage>

<device> is the name of the device for which the code page is to be selected. It can be CON, PRN, LPT1, LPT2, or LPT3.

<codepage> is one of the three-digit codes listed in Figure 18-5. If you specify a code page that has not been prepared with the cp prepare option of the Mode command, DOS responds *Code page not prepared.*

For example, the following command would select code page 850 for the printer attached to LPT1:

```
C:\>mode lpt1 cp select=850
```

Displaying the Code-Page Status

To see a report on active and available code pages, you use one of two forms of the Mode command. When used to report on all devices, the Mode command has no parameters:

mode

When used to report on a particular device, the mode command has three parameters:

mode <device> cp /sta

<device> is the name of the device for which you want a report. It can be CON, PRN, LPT1, LPT2, or LPT3.

cp limits the report to code-page information only (as opposed to device status, such as printer redirection, as well).

/sta (short for status) is usually optional, but you can use it with Mode and a device name to check on redirected printers.

For example, to see a report on active and available code pages for all devices with code-page switching, type:

```
C:\>mode
```

To see a report on a particular device, such as the printer attached to LPT1, type the command as:

```
C:\>mode lpt1 cp
```

Restoring a Code Page That Was Lost

Some circumstances can cause a code page to be erased from memory. For example, if you prepare and select a code page for the printer, then turn the printer off and turn it back on again, the code page in the printer's memory may be different from the one you selected. The codepage refresh option of the Mode command restores the code page you selected without your having to specify the code-page number.

mode <device> cp refresh

<device> is the name of the device whose most recently selected code page is to be restored. It can be CON, PRN, LPT1, LPT2, or LPT3.

For example, the following command would restore the most recently selected code page for the printer attached to the LPT2 port:

```
C:\>mode lpt2 cp refresh
```

405

Graftabl Command

The Load Graphics Table (graftabl) command includes a parameter that loads a code page for the Color Graphics Adapter (CGA) so that its character set matches the code page used by DOS and other devices when displaying accented and other special characters in graphics mode.

The first time a Graftabl command is executed, the size of DOS in memory is increased by about 1200 bytes.

The Graftabl command has two parameters:

graftabl <codepage> /status

<codepage> is the three-digit number that specifies the code page that Graftabl is to load into memory and use.

/status displays the name of the code page that Graftabl is using. You can abbreviate it as /sta.

Setting Up Code-Page Switching for an EGA or VGA Display

Figure 18-6 shows the commands needed to set up national language support for a system whose only code-page switching device is a display attached to an EGA or a VGA adapter. The hardware code page of the display is 437 (United States English), and the system is set up to handle one additional code page, 850.

All DOS files are assumed to be in the directory C:\DOS. If you don't use the ANSI.SYS device driver, omit the configuration command *device=c:\dos\ansi.sys* from CONFIG.SYS; if you do use ANSI.SYS, however, be sure that its Device configuration command precedes the Device configuration command that defines DISPLAY.SYS, as in Figure 18-6.

Put these commands in CONFIG.SYS:

```
country=001,,c:\dos\country.sys
device=c:\dos\ansi.sys
device=c:\dos\display.sys con=(ega,437,1)
```

Put these commands in AUTOEXEC.BAT:

```
nlsfunc c:\dos\country.sys
mode con cp prepare=((850) c:\dos\ega.cpi)
mode con cp select=437
keyb us,,c:\dos\keyboard.sys
```

Figure 18-6. *Setup commands for a system with EGA or VGA only.*

When you start the system, code page 437 is selected for DOS, the display, and the keyboard. To change to code page 850, type *chcp 850.*

Setting Up Code-Page Switching for an IBM PS/2 and Printer

Figure 18-7 shows the commands required to set up national language support for an IBM PS/2 or compatible system that includes both a VGA (or compatible) display and an IBM Proprinter Model 4201 printer. The hardware code page of both devices is 437 (United States English), and the system is set up to handle one additional code page, 850. (Note that the *ega* in the Device configuration command that specifies DIS-PLAY.SYS means both EGA and VGA.)

Again, all DOS files are assumed to be in the directory C:\DOS. If you don't use the ANSI.SYS driver, omit the configuration command *device=c:\dos\ansi.sys* from CONFIG.SYS; if you do use ANSI.SYS, however, be sure that its Device configuration command precedes the Device configuration command that defines DISPLAY.SYS, as shown in Figure 18-7.

When you start the system, code page 437 is selected for DOS, the display, the keyboard, and the printer. To change to code page 850 during the session, type *chcp 850.* To switch back to code page 437, type *chcp 437.*

Put these commands in CONFIG.SYS:

```
country=001,,c:\dos\country.sys
device=c:\dos\ansi.sys
device=c:\dos\display.sys con=(ega,437,1)
device=c:\dos\printer.sys prn=(4201,437,1)
```

Put these commands in AUTOEXEC.BAT:

```
nlsfunc c:\dos\country.sys
mode con cp prepare=((850) c:\dos\ega.cpi)
mode prn cp prepare=((850) c:\dos\4201.cpi)
chcp 437
keyb us,,c:\dos\keyboard.sys
```

Figure 18-7. *Setup commands for a PS/2 with display and printer.*

PART III
APPENDIXES

Three appendixes are included in Part III. Appendixes A and B contain reference material for occasional use or background information. Appendix A, "Installing DOS," is a guide to installing and upgrading to versions 3, 4, and 5 of DOS. It supplements the step-by-step instructions you receive with a new version of DOS. Appendix B, the Glossary, contributes to your background knowledge by defining commonly used terms and those presented in the main portions of the book. Appendix C, a comprehensive reference to DOS commands and their parameters, provides easy-to-find answers to questions about the form or use of a command. Cross-references to Part II guide you to the discussions in Chapters 5 through 18.

APPENDIX A

INSTALLING DOS

This appendix tells you how to install different versions of DOS. Although computer buyers seldom need to install DOS themselves, you might someday need to reinstall DOS, or you might want to upgrade to a newer, more powerful version. To help you orient yourself, this appendix offers details for versions 3 through 5. If you are installing DOS or upgrading to a newer version, refer to the appropriate section. If you need more background or specific instructions, refer to the documentation that comes with your version of DOS.

INSTALLING OR
UPGRADING TO VERSION 5

Although DOS has grown in capability over the years, it has also become easier to install. Of all DOS versions, 5 is the easiest to set up, whether you're putting it on a brand-new system or upgrading from an earlier version of DOS. The first of the diskettes on which version 5 is supplied contains a setup program (SETUP.EXE) that does practically all the work for you.

Whether you're installing or upgrading to version 5, *use the Setup program.* Even if you've installed earlier versions of DOS by copying files from the DOS diskettes, you cannot install version 5 in this way. Many of the DOS files are shipped in a special condensed format that Setup expands during the installation procedure. In addition, this program checks the memory and devices on your system (so you don't have to), offers help at each stage, prompts whenever it needs a response from you, displays an indicator showing how much of the installation is complete, and even tells you what it's doing as it prepares DOS to work on your computer.

Installing Version 5 for the First Time

If your system is new, chances are that DOS has already been installed for you, especially if your computer has a fixed disk. If DOS is not installed, start by placing the diskette labeled *Disk 1* in drive A. Then start or restart your computer.

Your first encounter with Setup is a message telling you that it is checking the devices on your system. This is quickly replaced by a full-screen welcoming message telling you that help is available at the press of the F1 key (located at the top or along the left side of your keyboard). The welcoming screen also tells you which keys to press to continue or quit. If you press Enter to continue the process, Setup guides you through each succeeding step.

During installation, you are asked to provide some responses and to make a few choices (for example, whether you want the DOS Shell to appear whenever you start or restart the system). DOS proposes a response whenever it asks you to make a choice. This proposed response is highlighted, and it is either the one most people choose or the one DOS has determined suits your system best. If you need further information before deciding to accept or change a proposed response, press the F1 key. Accepting all of the choices DOS proposes will set up a basic working system for you. Once you're comfortable with this system, you can make any necessary modifications by tailoring the files AUTOEXEC.BAT and CONFIG.SYS to suit your own preferences. These files, and the commands they can contain, are described in Chapter 17, "Tailoring Your System," and Appendix C, "DOS Command Reference."

Upgrading to Version 5

If you have a fixed disk and are upgrading from an earlier version of DOS, Setup asks whether you want to back up your fixed disk before continuing with the installation. This is a personal choice and depends, in part, on the value and number of files on your fixed disk. If you have a backup system, such as a tape unit, you might want to use it for the backup before installing DOS.

This backup procedure is new with version 5 and is included as a safety feature to protect you in the (unlikely) event something goes wrong with the installation procedure. Another safety feature is a built-in recovery program that lets you restore your earlier version of DOS if the installation fails or if you find that some of your programs cannot work with version 5.

To upgrade to version 5 of DOS, have ready a blank diskette labeled *Recovery*. Place the diskette labeled *Disk 1* in drive A and start or restart the system. After checking your system, Setup displays a welcoming message and tells you which keys to press to request help, continue with the installation, or quit. From this point on, follow the on-screen instructions. If you are uncertain about any responses, press the F1 key for help and further information.

Once the installation is complete, place the *Recovery* diskette in a safe place while you try out version 5. It's unlikely that you'll need to return to your old version of DOS, but if you do, place the *Recovery* diskette in drive A, restart the system, and follow the instructions that appear on the screen.

INSTALLING OR UPGRADING TO VERSION 4

Like version 5, version 4 of DOS comes with an installation program. The program differs in several respects, however, and although it is thorough, it is not as completely self-contained as the Setup program in version 5.

The installation program prompts you through the process and includes online help that explains most of the choices. The manual that comes with DOS also includes detailed instructions for using the installation program with different types of disk drives: fixed disk, 5.25-inch diskette, and 3.5-inch diskette.

Essentially, all you do is place the diskette labeled *Install* in drive A, start or restart your computer, and then press the Enter key to begin. From that point on, the program, named Select, asks you questions about your computer system and tells you which of the original DOS diskettes it needs, and when. Before you start, however, there are a few things you should know or prepare for, to make the procedure as easy as possible.

Your Computer

Find out (roughly) how much memory your system has. The Select program doesn't ask you for the exact amount, but during installation it asks you to choose how you want to balance the memory used by DOS and by your programs.

If your system contains less than 512 K of memory, choose the first option (*Minimum DOS function; maximum program workspace*) to give your programs as much working room as possible. If your system has 512 K of memory, choose the option Select proposes (*Balance DOS function with program workspace*). If your system has more than 512 K of memory, choose the third option (*Maximum DOS function; minimum program workspace*) so that both DOS and your programs have plenty of room to work in.

Check the make and model of printer you use. Also, find out whether it is a serial or a parallel printer, and find out the number of the port it is connected to (for example, LPT1: for a parallel printer or COM1: for a serial printer). The Select program will ask you to choose your printer from a list. It will also propose a printer port, so it is up to you to know whether Select is correct.

In most instances, Select finds out about your computer system by offering you a list of options to choose from, one of which is highlighted. If you already know about your computer's memory and your printer, you shouldn't have any problems. If, for some reason, you don't understand what to do, request help by pressing the F1 key.

The Installation/Upgrade Process

Note: If you are using a fixed disk and are upgrading to version 4 from an earlier version of DOS, do not try to install IBM's release of DOS if your computer is currently running a version of DOS released by another manufacturer. There is a small but significant difference between IBM's release and others that prevents successful installation. You can install the IBM release, but to do so you must back up your fixed disk, reformat it, and then install DOS. If you are not sure of your version of DOS, start your computer; if the manufacturer's name and the version number are not displayed, type ver *to check.*

Whether you install DOS on a fixed disk or on diskettes, Select needs one or more blank diskettes for the installation. One of the first things Select does is display a list showing the number and capacity of diskettes it needs for installing DOS on various types of disk drives. You can find the diskettes during the installation, when Select provides a list or prompts for a blank diskette, but you'll probably be more comfortable having them on hand and labeled ahead of time. (This is especially important if you're installing DOS on diskettes.)

The diskettes don't have to be formatted; Select will do that for you. In fact, if your computer has a 1.2 MB 5.25-inch diskette drive, notice that Select requests 360 K diskettes; avoid using 1.2 MB diskettes, especially if they're preformatted by the manufacturer.

Finally, if you're installing DOS on diskettes, make sure you label your blank diskettes *exactly* the way the program suggests. The instructions for inserting diskettes can be confusing, especially if you're installing on 360 K diskettes. The program asks for diskettes by name; it does not give you messages such as "Insert the diskette you labeled Working 1." So keep your stack of DOS diskettes separate from your blank diskettes. The program asks for some diskettes more than once, and sometimes it asks for more than one DOS diskette before it asks for one of your blank diskettes. And don't be dismayed if your disk drive seems to continue working for quite some time. Select will tell you if it has any problems.

AUTOEXEC.BAT and CONFIG.SYS

When Select finishes putting DOS on a fixed disk that contains an earlier version of DOS, its final message might tell you that Select has saved information about your computer, printer, display, screen, and the DOS Shell in two files that it named AUTOEXEC.400 and CONFIG.400. You'll want DOS to be able to find this information whenever you start or restart your computer, and in order for that to happen, you'll have to rename the files AUTOEXEC.BAT and CONFIG.SYS. Only then will DOS automatically search for the information saved by the Select program.

The reason Select does not simply name these files AUTOEXEC.BAT and CONFIG.SYS to begin with is that you already have startup files by those names on your fixed disk. Select protects you (and your startup files) by giving the AUTOEXEC and CONFIG files the extension 400, but in return it expects you to merge any information you want to keep from your existing AUTOEXEC.BAT and CONFIG.SYS files with the files it has created. Such information might include a Path command in AUTOEXEC.BAT that guides DOS to your program files, or it might include a Device command in CONFIG.SYS that tells DOS you have a mouse attached to your system.

You can transfer any existing commands you want to keep to AUTOEXEC.400 or CONFIG.400 with the DOS editor, Edlin, or with a word processor that allows you to save files in unformatted form. If you're new to DOS, however, there's a chance that you don't yet know what to keep and what to discard in your existing AUTOEXEC.BAT and CONFIG.SYS files. When in doubt, save. Type the following commands to rename your existing files and keep them safe until you know how to or can find out how to merge their contents with AUTOEXEC.400 and CONFIG.400:

```
C:\>ren autoexec.bat autoexec.sav
```

```
C:\>ren config.sys config.sav
```

Now you can safely change AUTOEXEC.400 to AUTOEXEC.BAT by typing:

```
C:\>ren autoexec.400 autoexec.bat
```

and you can change CONFIG.400 to CONFIG.SYS by typing:

```
C:\>ren config.400 config.sys
```

Start your computer again by pressing Ctrl-Alt-Del, and DOS will start up, tailored to the choices you made during the installation procedure. If you've saved an old AUTOEXEC.BAT or CONFIG.SYS file, Chapters 14 and 17 and Appendix C contain the information you need to understand and to edit the commands in these two files.

INSTALLING VERSION 3

Versions 3 and earlier of DOS do not include an installation program, so it's up to you to determine how you want to set up DOS to work on your system. If your computer doesn't have a fixed disk, all you really need to do is make copies of your DOS diskettes with the Diskcopy command described in Chapter 6, "Managing Your Diskettes." Diskcopy makes an exact duplicate of a diskette, so once you've copied your original DOS diskettes you can store them safely away and use the copies in your everyday work with DOS.

If you have a fixed disk, you use a two-step procedure to copy DOS from your DOS diskette(s) to the fixed disk. The first step uses the System (sys) command to copy two hidden files that DOS needs in order to start from your fixed disk. The second step uses the Copy command to copy the remaining DOS files to your fixed disk.

Note: The following instructions assume that your fixed disk has already been formatted (prepared for use). If it has not, or if you want to wipe it clean and start anew, you can use the command format c: /s *to prepare the disk and copy the system files. If you try this command, however, and DOS displays a* WARNING *message followed by a request for you to confirm the format, be very sure you want to continue. Once DOS begins formatting the fixed disk, you'll lose whatever files it contains—forever.*

Copying the System Files

Place your DOS startup diskette in drive A. Depending on the version you're installing, this diskette is labeled either *Startup* or *DOS*. Turn on the computer or restart it by simultaneously pressing the keys marked Ctrl, Alt, and Del.

If you're upgrading to a newer release of version 3, or if your fixed disk is already formatted, use the System command to move the hidden DOS files to your fixed disk.

Type the following:

A>sys c:

DOS responds *System transferred.*

Note: If you're installing version 3.3 on a system using version 3.1 or earlier, DOS might display the message Insufficient memory for system transfer. *If you see this, it means that DOS cannot transfer the files properly. You must back up all the files on your fixed disk, format it, and later restore all the files you've backed up.*

Whether you use Format or System, your next step is to copy the DOS files to your fixed disk. The question now is, Where do they go? If you're working with a new or newly formatted fixed disk, follow the instructions in the next section, "Copying DOS to a DOS Directory." If you're upgrading an existing DOS version from one release to another (for example, from 3.1 to 3.3), skip to the heading "Upgrading with Version 3."

Copying DOS to a DOS Directory

If you've just formatted your fixed disk, it's an empty storage area you can use as you like, so make your future work easier by copying DOS to a special section—a directory—of its own. Doing this keeps your DOS files separate from application and data files, and it generally helps keep your fixed disk neat and organized.

If you're new to DOS, the following commands probably won't mean much to you, but if you type them exactly as shown, you should be able to install any release of version 3 without problems.

First, check that your startup diskette is still in drive A and copy the DOS file named COMMAND.COM to the base (root) directory of your fixed disk, where it normally goes. Type:

A>copy command.com c:\

Now create the DOS directory by typing:

A>md c:\dos

Copy the files from your DOS diskette to the new DOS directory:

A>copy *.* c:\dos

If you have more than one DOS diskette, repeat the Copy command to copy the rest of your DOS files.

When you typed *.* (meaning "all files") in your Copy command, you recopied COMMAND.COM. You don't need two copies of this file, so delete the one in your DOS directory by typing:

A>del c:\dos\command.com

Finally, create a special file, again in the root directory of your fixed disk, that tells DOS where to find its own command files. Type the following. Press Enter at the end of each line and press—at the same time—the two keys marked Ctrl and Z where you see <Ctrl-Z>:

```
A>copy con c:\autoexec.bat
path=c:\dos
<Ctrl-Z>
```

If all goes well, DOS should respond *1 File(s) copied*. If it does not, retype the preceding lines.

Your new version of DOS should now be ready for use. Remove any diskette from drive A and restart the computer by pressing Ctrl, Alt, and Del. When DOS starts up, the system prompt should be *C>*. You can verify that DOS can find its own command files by typing:

```
C>chkdsk
```

If DOS produces a report on your fixed disk, you're all set. If it does not start from drive C, repeat the setup procedure. If DOS responds *File not found* to your Chkdsk command, retype the preceding commands that start with *copy con c:\autoexec.bat*.

Upgrading with Version 3

If you're upgrading from one version of DOS to another, your earlier version might be in a DOS directory or it might be in the main (root) directory of your fixed disk. It all depends on how your fixed disk was organized.

Checking on, and possibly reorganizing, your fixed disk assumes some knowledge of disks, directories, and directory commands. If this is familiar territory, the following instructions should help you out. If you and DOS are relative strangers and you have a currently functional system, you might prefer to work through the examples in this book or ask someone for advice before trying to organize your fixed disk.

If You Have a DOS Directory

If you already have a DOS directory, use the Replace command to replace all the old DOS files with those in the new version. Change the current drive to C by typing:

```
A>c:
```

Now, for each new DOS diskette you place in drive A, type the following two commands. If necessary, change *dos* to the name of your DOS directory:

```
C>replace a:\*.* c:\ /s
C>replace a:\*.* c:\dos /a
```

The first command replaces existing files; the second adds any files from the DOS diskette that don't exist on drive C. That's it. You're done.

If You Don't Have a DOS Directory

If you don't have a DOS directory and all your DOS files are in the root directory of the fixed disk, you have two tasks to perform: first, to upgrade your current version of DOS; second, to clear old DOS files out of the root directory.

You've already moved the new system files to your fixed disk. Now, to upgrade your current version and place your DOS files in a DOS directory, start by creating the new DOS directory:

```
A>md c:\dos
```

Next, copy the file named COMMAND.COM to the root directory of your Fixed disk:

```
A>copy command.com c:
```

Now copy the other DOS files from the DOS diskettes to the DOS directory:

```
A>copy *.* c:\dos
```

If you have another DOS diskette, repeat the preceding Copy command. Next, check for an AUTOEXEC.BAT file by typing:

```
A>type c:\autoexec.bat
```

If DOS displays a file and one of the lines is a Path command like this:

PATH=C:\;C:\WP;C:\SPREAD;C:\DB

use Edlin or your word processor (if it can save unformatted files) to add your new DOS directory to the Path command:

PATH=C:\;C:\DOS;**C:\WP;C:\SPREAD;C:\DB**

If DOS responds *File not found* to your Type command, you need to create a basic AUTOEXEC.BAT file with a Path command as follows (press Ctrl and Z together where you see <Ctrl-Z>):

```
A>copy con c:\autoexec.bat
path=c:\dos
<Ctrl-Z>
```

Use the Type command again, this time to check for a file named CONFIG.SYS. If DOS displays a file, use Edlin or your word processor to edit it, adding the name of the DOS directory to all references to DOS files. For example:

DEVICE=C:\DOS**ANSI.SYS**
DEVICE=C:\DOS**VDISK.SYS**

(If DOS responds *File not found* to this command, you don't have to create a *CON-FIG.SYS* file for it to use. You might want to at some point, but for now your system will work without such a file.)

Finally, for the second stage in reorganizing your fixed disk, turn on your printer and print a listing of the root directory with the command:

```
A>dir c:\ > prn
```

Using the files in your DOS directory or the files on the diskettes for your old version of DOS as a guide, carefully mark the printout, noting all DOS files in the root directory other than COMMAND.COM, AUTOEXEC.BAT, and CONFIG.SYS. That is, mark files such as FORMAT.COM, PRINT.COM, DISKCOPY.COM, and so on.

Once you've marked these file names (and double-checked them to be sure you didn't include any non-DOS files), type a Delete command for each to remove it from the *root* directory. For example, type:

```
A>del c:\format.com
A>del c:\print.com
A>del c:\diskcopy.com
```

When you're finished, the root directory should contain only COMMAND.COM, AUTOEXEC.BAT, and CONFIG.SYS, as well as the non-DOS files and directories it held before. The remainder of your DOS files should all be in C:\DOS.

APPENDIX B

GLOSSARY

A

Adapter: A term sometimes used to refer to printed-circuit cards that plug into a computer and control a device, such as a display or a printer.

Application program: A program, such as a word processor or spreadsheet, that performs a specific task; an application of the computer to a particular type of work.

Archive: To transfer files to a separate disk or a backup tape for safekeeping. The Backup command helps archive files; the Restore command can, if necessary, be used to return archived files to the disk from which they were backed up.

ASCII: A standardized coding scheme that uses numeric values to represent letters, digits, symbols, and so on. ASCII is an acronym for *American Standard Code for Information Interchange* and is widely used in coding information for computers.

AUTOEXEC.BAT: A name reserved for a batch file that contains commands that are carried out by DOS each time the system is started. An AUTOEXEC.BAT file can be used to perform a desired set of startup procedures without your having to type the commands each time.

AUX: Short for *auxiliary*. The communications port DOS uses unless instructed otherwise. AUX can be either COM1 or COM2 in versions of DOS through 3.2; it can be COM1, COM2, COM3, or COM4 in versions 3.3 and later.

B

Backspace key: The key labeled with a single, left-pointing arrow and, often, the word *Backspace*; erases characters you have typed, one at a time.

Back up: To copy one or more files to disks or tapes for safekeeping.

BAK: An extension assigned by Edlin and by many word processors to the next-most-recent (penultimate) version of a text file. If the working copy of a file is damaged, the BAK file can be used to salvage a near-current version of the document.

Basic: A programming language included with DOS. When originally developed, BASIC was an acronym for *Beginner's All-purpose Symbolic Instruction Code*. Through version 4, DOS includes either BASIC and BASICA (Advanced BASIC) or GW-BASIC. Version 5 includes a more sophisticated, visually oriented form called QBasic.

Batch file: A text file whose extension is BAT; contains DOS commands. When you type the name of a batch file while DOS is at the command level, DOS carries out the commands in the file.

Baud: Broadly, the rate at which data is transmitted over a communications link; more specifically, *baud* refers to the number of changes per second (representing coded data) carried by the signal. For commonly used modem rates, approximately one character per second is transmitted for each 10 baud.

Binary: The base-2 numbering system whose only digits are 0 and 1. The binary system is particularly well suited to use with computers because the two digits can be represented by the presence or absence of a voltage.

Bit: The smallest unit of information used with computers; corresponds to a binary digit (either 0 or 1). Eight bits make up one byte.

Boot: To start up a computer; derived from the saying ''pull yourself up by your own bootstraps.''

Byte: The unit of measure used for computer memory and data storage. One byte contains eight bits and can store one character (a letter, number, punctuation mark, or other symbol).

C

Character string: A group of characters that you tell DOS to treat as a set of letters or numbers, rather than as a command. The Find filter command searches for character strings enclosed in quotation marks (""). In other commands, such as Search and Replace, the quotation marks are not needed.

Chip: *See* Integrated circuit.

Color Graphics Adapter (CGA): A printed-circuit card in the system unit of a computer that controls the display. Shows both text and graphics at low resolution in up to 16 colors.

COM1, COM2, COM3, COM4: Short for *communications.* The names of the serial communications ports. All versions of DOS recognize COM1 and COM2; versions 3.3 and later also recognize COM3 and COM4.

Command: An instruction you give to control a computer program such as DOS or an application program.

Command file: A file that contains the program or instructions required to carry out a command. If the file's extension is COM or EXE, the command file contains machine instructions; if its extension is BAT, the command file is a batch file and contains DOS commands.

Communications: The transmission of data between computers; also called telecommunications.

Communications port: *See* Port.

CON: Short for *console.* The name by which DOS refers to the keyboard (input) and the display (output).

Control key: The key labeled Ctrl; use it as you do the Shift key by holding it down while pressing another key. Control in combination with another key usually causes something to happen, rather than displaying a character on the screen. If displayed, it is shown as ^, as in the end-of-file marker, ^Z (Ctrl-Z).

Conventional memory: The name used for the first megabyte of random access memory in an IBM or compatible computer. DOS and application programs can freely use the first 640 K of conventional memory. Memory between 640 K and 1 MB is usually reserved for special purposes.

CPU: Short for *central processing unit.* The part of a computer that performs calculations and processes information. In microcomputers that use DOS, the CPU is an 8086/8088, 80286, 80386, or 80486 microprocessor.

Ctrl: *See* Control key.

Ctrl-Break: The key combination that cancels a command; entered by holding down the Ctrl key and pressing the Break key.

Ctrl-C: Same as Ctrl-Break.

Ctrl-Num Lock: The key combination that stops DOS until you press any other key. On keyboards without a Pause key, Ctrl-Num Lock is used to freeze the display so you can view long displays. Entered by holding down the Ctrl key and pressing the Num Lock key.

Ctrl-P: Same as Ctrl-PrtSc.

Ctrl-PrtSc: The key combination that controls simultaneous printing and displaying. Pressing Ctrl-PrtSc once causes DOS to print everything that is displayed; pressing Ctrl-PrtSc again causes DOS to stop printing everything that is displayed. Entered by holding down the Ctrl key and pressing the PrtSc key.

Ctrl-S: Same as Ctrl-Num Lock.

Ctrl-Z: The key combination that creates the special character (displayed as ^Z) that DOS uses to mark the end of a file. Created by holding down the Ctrl key and pressing Z, or by pressing the function key labeled F6.

Current directory: The directory in which DOS looks for files unless otherwise instructed.

Current drive: The drive containing the disk on which DOS looks for and saves files unless otherwise instructed.

D

Data: The information processed by a computer in doing its work.

Data bit: A signal used in serial communications to represent part of a character; seven or eight data bits can be used to represent one transmitted character.

Data file: A file that contains the data needed by a program; can be numbers, text, graphics images, or a combination.

Device: A piece of computer equipment, such as a display or a printer, that performs a specific task; the program that controls a device is called a device driver.

Device name: The name by which DOS refers to a device (for example, PRN, LPT1, LPT2, or LPT3 for a printer). Device names are treated like file names by DOS.

Directory: The index of files that DOS maintains on a disk. The directory entry for each file includes the file's name, extension, size, date and time it was created or last changed, and the location of the beginning of the file. All but the last item are displayed by the Directory command.

Disk: A magnetically coated disk used to store information. The term is used when no distinction need be made between a diskette and a fixed disk.

Disk cache: A portion of memory set aside for use as a temporary, rapid-access storage area for information read from disk. A disk cache speeds operations by cutting down on the number of times the computer must perform relatively slow disk reads.

Disk drive: The device that rotates a disk in order to read (retrieve) and write (store) information.

Diskette: A disk for storing files, made of thin plastic and enclosed in a protective jacket.

Diskette drive: A disk drive used for diskettes.

Display: The screen on which the computer shows both what you type at the keyboard and the result of its work; assumed by DOS to be the standard output device unless a different device is specified.

Doskey: A program in version 5 of DOS that records commands and enables you to repeat, edit, or store them as batch files or keyboard macros.

Drive letter: The letter that identifies a disk drive; can be any letter from A to Z.

E

Edit: As a verb, to change the contents of a file, usually with a word processor or an editing program. As a noun, Edit is the name of the command that starts the MS-DOS Editor, the menu-based text editor included with version 5 of DOS.

Editor: A program used to create or change text files; also called a *text editor*.

Edlin: One of the two DOS text editors. (The other, new with version 5, is the MS-DOS Editor. *See* Edit.) Edlin numbers the lines in a file and uses those numbers as references in finding, changing, or deleting lines.

Enhanced Graphics Adapter (EGA): A printed-circuit card in the system unit of a computer that controls the display. Shows both text and graphics at medium resolution in up to 64 colors.

Enter key: The key you press to tell DOS that you have finished typing a line. Labeled *Return* on some keyboards.

Escape key: The key labeled Esc; cancels a line you have typed but have not yet entered by pressing the Enter key.

Expanded memory: Additional memory that can be installed on any IBM PC or compatible computer. A special program called an expanded memory manager is required to use this memory; programs must be written specifically to use such memory. Standardized use of expanded memory is governed by the Lotus-Intel-Microsoft (LIM) specification. Up to 32 MB of expanded memory can be installed.

Extended memory: Memory above 1 MB that can be installed on an IBM PC/AT; IBM PS/2 Models 50, 60, 70, or 80; or any computer compatible with those models that has an 80286 or 80386 microprocessor. Up to 15 MB of extended memory can be installed. Extended memory is often handled by a program called an extended memory manager.

Extension: A suffix of up to three characters that can be added to a file name to identify the contents of the file more precisely.

F

File: A named collection of information stored on a disk; usually contains data, graphics, or a program.

File name: A name of up to eight characters that you assign and that DOS uses to find a file on a disk; can be followed by a period and three additional characters called the file-name extension.

Filespec: The complete specification of a file; can include a drive letter, path name, file name, and extension.

Filter command: A DOS command that reads standard input, processes it in some way (for example, sorts it in alphabetic order), and writes the result to standard output.

Fixed disk: A disk of large capacity (10 MB or more) that cannot be removed from its drive. Also called a *hard disk*.

Floppy disk: *See* Diskette.

Format: To prepare a disk for use.

Function key: One of 10 or more keys, usually labeled F1, F2, and so on, that cause DOS (or an application program) to perform a certain function, such as copying characters in a line of text.

H

Hard disk: *See* Fixed disk.

Hardware: The equipment that makes up a computer system, as opposed to the programs, or software.

Hexadecimal: The base-16 numbering system whose digits are 0 through F (the letters A through F correspond to the decimal numbers 10 through 15); often used in computer programming because it is easily converted to and from binary, the base-2 numbering system the computer itself uses.

Hidden file: A file that is not normally listed when you display the directory. DOS uses two special, hidden files on any startup disk. They are hidden so that they cannot be altered or deleted under normal circumstances. Beginning with version 5, directories and data files can also be hidden for a certain amount of privacy.

Hierarchical filing system: *See* Multilevel filing system.

High Memory Area (HMA): The name given to the first 64 K of extended memory (additional memory starting at 1 MB). On a computer with extended memory, version 5 of DOS can run in the HMA, leaving more conventional memory available for applications and data.

I

Initialize: *See* Format.

Input: The data that a program reads.

Input/output: A term that refers to the devices and processes involved in the computer's reading (input) and writing (output) of data.

Integrated circuit: An electronic device that combines thousands of transistors on a small wafer of silicon. Such devices are the building blocks of computers. Also referred to as a *chip*.

Interface: The boundary between two systems or entities, such as a disk drive and the computer, or the user and a program.

I/O: Abbreviation for *input/output*.

I/O redirection: *See* Redirection.

K

Keyboard: The device consisting of alphabetic and other keys on which instructions and data are typed into the computer; assumed by DOS to be the standard input device unless a different device is specified.

L

LPT1, LPT2, LPT3: Short for *line printer*. The names that DOS uses to refer to the three ports to which parallel printers can be attached.

M

Macro: A set of keystrokes or commands that you assign a name and store either temporarily in memory or permanently on disk. A macro is a means of saving time by assigning a short name to a long or involved set of commands you use frequently. You can create macros with Doskey in version 5 of DOS.

Memory: A type of electronic circuitry that the computer uses to store programs and data. Unlike disk storage, which is permanent, a computer's working memory is temporary—its contents are lost when power is removed. Memory is usually measured in units of 1024 bytes, called kilobytes and abbreviated K or KB; a megabyte (M or MB) is 1024 kilobytes, or 1,048,576 bytes.

Microcomputer: A small computer system whose central processing unit is a microprocessor; usually used by only one person.

Microprocessor: An integrated circuit, or chip, that contains the circuits needed to carry out program instructions. The microprocessor performs calculations, briefly stores instructions and data, and transfers information to and from a computer's memory.

Modem: Contraction of *modulator-demodulator*. A device that enables transmission of computer data over telephone lines.

Monitor: A television-like device that displays computer input and output; often used synonymously with *display*.

Monochrome: A term used to describe a computer display capable of displaying one color (usually white, green, or amber).

Monochrome Display Adapter (MDA): A printed-circuit card, in the system unit of a computer, that controls the display. Shows text only, not graphics, at medium resolution in one color.

Multicolor Graphics Array (MCGA): A printed-circuit card, in the system unit of a computer, that controls the display. Shows both text and graphics at low to medium resolution in up to 256 colors; used in IBM PS/2 model computers.

Multilevel filing system: A computer filing system that lets you define directories within other directories, creating a structure with many levels. Also called a *tree-structured* or *hierarchical filing system*.

N

Network: A group of computers that are linked by printed-circuit cards, cables, and network software and can share resources, such as programs, data, disk drives, and printers.

O

Operating system: A program that coordinates the operation of all parts of a computer system.

Output: The result of a program's processing input data.

P

Parallel communications: A communications technique that uses multiple wires to send all eight bits of a byte at once (in parallel).

Parallel port: A port for parallel communications; the port to which the printer is usually attached.

Parameter: A qualifier that you include with a command to define more specifically what you want DOS to do; also called an *argument* or an *option*.

Parity: An error-detection technique that is used to ensure accuracy during data communication.

Path: The list of directory names that defines the location of a directory or file.

Path name: The portion of a file specification that defines the path to the file; can include a drive letter followed by a colon.

Pipe: To direct the output of one command for use as the input of another command. The pipe symbol DOS uses is the broken vertical bar (¦).

Port: The electrical connection through which the computer sends and receives data to and from devices or other computers.

Printed-circuit card: A thin, rectangular card or board, usually made of fiberglass or epoxy and coated with copper. Electrical circuits and connections are etched into

the copper, and electronic devices, such as integrated circuits, are soldered to the circuits. These cards are at the heart of a computer system, giving the machine its ability
to perform calculations, store and transfer data, and use the display, disk drives,
mouse, printer, modem, and other devices.

Printer: A device that produces images of text and graphics on paper.

Print queue: The list of files to be printed by DOS; you create, examine, and modify
the print queue with the Print command.

PRN: Short for *printer*. The printer DOS uses unless instructed otherwise. Can refer
to LPT1, LPT2, or LPT3.

Program: A set of instructions for a computer.

Prompt: A request displayed by the computer for you to provide some information or
perform an action.

Q

Queue: *See* Print queue.

R

RAM: Short for *random access memory*. The memory that DOS uses for programs and
data; RAM content changes often while you use the computer and is lost when the
computer is turned off.

RAM disk: A portion of the computer's random access memory reserved for use as a
simulated disk drive. Also called an *electronic* or *virtual disk*. Unless saved on a physical disk, the contents of a RAM disk are lost when the computer is turned off.

Read-only file: A file whose read-only attribute is set so that its contents can be displayed and read, but not changed.

Redirection: The process of causing a command or program to take its input from a
file or device other than the keyboard (standard input), or of causing the output of a
command or program to be sent to a file or device other than the display (standard
output). The DOS redirection symbols are the greater-than ($>$) and less-than ($<$)
signs.

Replaceable parameter: A symbolic reference, consisting of a percent sign followed
by a one-digit number (such as %1), that can be included with commands in a batch
file to refer to the parameters entered with the batch command. In version 5, replaceable parameters can also be used with Doskey; they are represented by a dollar sign
followed by a one-digit number (such as $1).

Return key: The Enter key.

ROM: Short for *read-only memory.* A type of computer memory that is permanently recorded in hardware; contains instructions that help a computer carry out routine tasks, such as starting itself up. The contents of ROM cannot be changed and are not lost when the computer is turned off. On some computers, such as the IBM PS/1 series, DOS is contained in ROM.

Root directory: The main directory that DOS creates on each disk; the top directory in a multilevel filing system.

S

Serial communications: A communications technique that transfers information one bit at a time (serially) rather than one byte at a time (in parallel); used in modem communications and with some printers and other devices, such as mice.

Serial port: The communications port (COM1, COM2, COM3, or COM4) to which a device, such as a modem or a serial printer, can be attached.

Shell: A program that shows itself to the person using the computer, then passes commands to a different program to be carried out. It's called a shell because it effectively surrounds the other program, hiding it from view. Versions 4 and 5 of DOS include shell programs that let you use many DOS commands without having to type commands or file names at the system prompt. Other DOS shell programs are also available.

Software: The programs that are used with a computer system, as opposed to the equipment, or hardware.

Standard input: The device from which a program reads its input unless the input is redirected; in normal DOS operation, standard input is the keyboard.

Standard output: The device to which a program sends its output unless the output is redirected; in normal DOS operation, standard output is the display.

Stop bit: A signal used in serial communications that marks the end of a character.

Subdirectory: A file that contains directory entries; sometimes also used to refer to the group of files whose directory entries are in the same file.

System program: A program whose purpose is to control the operation of all or part of the computer system, such as managing the printer or interpreting commands.

System prompt: The characters DOS displays when it is at the command level (ready to accept a command). Unless you specify otherwise, the system prompt usually shows the current drive and directory followed by a greater-than sign (for example, C:\DOS>).

T

Telecommunications: *See* Communications.

Temporary file: A file that DOS or an application program creates for holding interim data. DOS, for example, creates temporary files when redirecting input or output. Temporary files are deleted by the program when they are no longer needed.

Text: Ordinary, readable characters, including the uppercase and lowercase letters of the alphabet, the numerals 0 through 9, and punctuation marks.

Text editor: A program that you use to create or change text files. Also called simply an *editor*.

Text file: A file that you can read (contains ordinary letters, numerals, and punctuation marks).

U

Update: To change a file, creating a new (or updated) version.

V

Video Graphics Array (VGA): A printed-circuit card, in the system unit of a computer, that controls the display. Shows both text and graphics at medium to high resolution in up to 256 colors; used in IBM PS/2 model computers.

Virtual disk: *See* RAM disk.

Volume label: An 11-character identifying name you can assign to a disk.

W

Wildcard character: A special character that, like the wild card in a poker game, can be used to represent any other character. DOS recognizes two wildcard characters: the question mark (?), which can represent any single character, and the asterisk (*), which can represent any number of characters.

Write protect: To cover the small notch on a 5.25-inch diskette or to uncover the opening on a 3.5-inch diskette so that new or changed information cannot be written onto the diskette.

APPENDIX C

DOS COMMAND REFERENCE

<COMMAND> /?
Command Help

See Help.

ANSI.SYS
Control Program for Screen and Keyboard
Versions 2.0 and later

Page 380

ANSI.SYS is a program that lets you control the console device. With it, you can manipulate the characters assigned to keys on the keyboard, and the color, position, and other attributes of the display. A program that controls a device is called a *device driver;* ANSI.SYS is a device driver that follows the conventions adopted by the American National Standards Institute (ANSI) for screen and keyboard control.

ANSI.SYS is widely used and offers many ways to extend your control over the console. It is used by a few DOS commands, such as Mode, but is not required in your everyday use of DOS. A full description is beyond the scope of this book. Details, explanations, and examples are in *Supercharging MS-DOS* by Van Wolverton and Dan Gookin (Microsoft Press, 1991) and might also be in your DOS manual.

APPEND
Define a Data Path
Versions 3.2 and later

Page 168

The Append command specifies one or more directories that DOS searches for a data file that isn't in the current directory. You can use the Append command on a network. The Append command is entered in either of the following two forms.

As the first use of Append after starting or restarting the system:

append /E /X

At any time during a session with DOS:

append <path> /X:on /X:off /path:on /path:off

/E makes the data path part of the DOS environment. You can specify /E only if you're using Append for the first time after starting the system. You cannot specify any search directories with this form of the command. Use Append a second time to define appended directories.

/X, beginning with version 3.3, enables DOS to search appended directories for command files (files with the extension COM, EXE, or BAT) as well as data files. The /X parameter lets Append act like the Path command, letting you use program files as if they were in the current directory. In versions 4 and 5 of DOS, this parameter can be typed as either /x or /x:on.

<path> is the name of the directory to be added to the search path. You can specify a directory on the same or a different drive, or you can specify only a drive letter (such as a:). If you specify more than one drive or directory, separate the path names with a semicolon (;).

/X:on and /X:off, in versions 4 and 5 only, turn the search path on and off. Using /X:off tells DOS not to search appended directories for command files. It has the reverse effect of /X:on (or /X). DOS assumes /X:off unless you specify otherwise.

/path:on and /path:off in versions 4 and 5 tell DOS whether to search the appended directories for data files in which the file name is preceded by a drive letter, a path, or both. The /path:on parameter tells DOS to include the drive letter or path name; /path:off tells DOS to ignore them. If you don't specify otherwise, DOS assumes /path:on.

If you type *append* without any parameters, DOS displays the current data path. If you type *append ;* (note the semicolon), DOS removes all appended directories from the data path.

Note: If you define a data path consisting of several directories, DOS doesn't tell you where it found a file you requested. Nor does DOS necessarily save a revised file in its original directory if the directory is part of the data path. It might instead save the file in the current directory. If you're not using versions 4 or 5, use the Append command with care. If you are using either of these versions, the /path:off parameter helps to overcome this problem.

Examples

To tell DOS to search the appended data path for command files as well as data files (versions 4 and 5):

```
C:\>append /x:on
```

To tell DOS to search for data files in \MKT\WP and \ENG\WP on drive C:

```
C:\>append \mkt\wp;\eng\wp
```

To display appended directories:

```
C:\>append
```

To remove all directories from the data path:

```
C:\>append ;
```

ASSIGN
Route Disk Operations to a Different Drive
Versions 3.0 and later, IBM releases 2.0 and later

Page 384

The Assign command routes requests for disk operations on one drive to a different drive. Its primary use is with application programs that look for files on a specific drive (such as B) and don't let you specify a different drive (such as C).

> **assign <drive1>=<drive2> /sta**

<drive1> is the letter of the drive to be assigned.

<drive2> is the letter of the drive that is to be used instead of <drive1>.

/sta (short for *status*) exists in version 5 only; it tells DOS to display a report on drives you've assigned.

Both <drive1> and <drive2> must refer to existing disk drives, including fixed disks and RAM drives. Do not, however, assign your fixed disk (such as C) to another drive. You can assign more than one drive in a single Assign command by separating the <drive1>=<drive2> pairs with blanks.

If you omit all parameters (just type *assign*), DOS deletes all drive assignments so that all drive letters refer to their original drives.

Note: The Assign command masks the actual type of disk drive from DOS, so use it only when necessary, and don't enter a Backup, Restore, Label, Join, Substitute, or Print command that uses an assigned drive. Two DOS commands—Format and Diskcopy—ignore any drive assignments made with the Assign command. If you have version 3.1 or later, use the Substitute command instead of the Assign command; for example, type subst b: c:<path> *instead of* assign b=c.

Examples

To assign drive B to drive C:

```
C:\>assign b=c
```

To assign drives A and B to drive D:

```
C:\>assign a=d b=d
```

To display a report of assigned drives:

```
C:\>assign /sta
Original A: set to D:
Original B: set to D:
```

To reset all drive letters to their original drives:

```
C:\>assign
```

ATTRIBUTE
Display or Change File Attributes
Versions 3.0 and later

Pages 84, 176

The Attribute command (attrib) displays or changes any of up to four attributes of a file: read-only, archive, hidden, and system.

If a file is read-only, you cannot change or delete the file. If a file's archive attribute is on, the Backup, Restore, and Xcopy commands can use the attribute's status to determine whether the file should be copied (archived) to another disk.

Beginning with version 5, you can also give a file the hidden and system attributes. Neither hidden nor system files appear in directory listings unless you specifically request them with the /A (attributes) parameter of the Directory command. These files are also unaffected by Rename and certain other commands.

The hidden attribute can be applied to data files you want to keep personal or keep from cluttering the screen. The system attribute is traditionally reserved for a command file used only by DOS. It's usually used only by programmers and is included here for completeness only.

attrib +R -R +A -A +H -H +S -S <filename> /S

+R assigns the read-only attribute; −R removes it.

+A (versions 3.2 and later) assigns the archive attribute; −A removes it.

+H (version 5 only) assigns the hidden attribute; −H removes it.

+S (version 5 only) assigns the system attribute; −S removes it.

You can set or change more than one attribute in a single command by separating the attributes with a blank.

<filename> is the name of the file whose attribute or attributes are to be displayed or changed. The file name can include a drive letter, followed by a colon, and a path name if appropriate.

/S applies the Attribute command to all subdirectories contained in <filename> (versions 3.3 and later).

If you type only *attrib <filename>*, DOS displays the attribute status of the file(s) to the left of the file name.

Examples

Assume that drive C includes a directory named C:\MKT. To make the file named REPORT.DOC in C:\MKT a read-only file:

```
C:\>attrib +r \mkt\report.doc
```

To make the file named BUDGET.PLN in C:\MKT both read-only and hidden:

```
C:\>attrib +r +h \mkt\budget.pln
```

To display the attributes of all files in C:\MKT:

`C:\>`attrib \mkt*.*

DOS responds:

```
A    R      C:\MKT\REPORT.DOC
A           C:\MKT\FORECAST.DOC
A           C:\MKT\SALESREP.DOC
A    HR     C:\MKT\BUDGET.PLN
            C:\MKT\FIRSTQTR.PLN
```

To remove the hidden attribute from BUDGET.PLN:

`C:\>`attrib -h \mkt\budget.pln

BACKUP
Make a Backup Copy of Files
Versions 2.0 and later

Page 188

The Backup command makes a backup copy of files so that you can safeguard data against damage or other loss. Files can be backed up from and to any type of source and target disk. Rather than making an exact copy of the file, as the Copy command does, the Backup command records the directory from which each file was backed up. The Restore command uses this data to reinstate files in the correct locations.

Although the Backup command is present in versions 2.0 and later, not all the parameters described here are in every release of DOS; refer to your DOS manual to find out which parameters are available to you.

backup <path><filename> <drive> /A /S /M /F:<size> /D:<date> /T:<time> /L:<logfile>

<path> and <filename> specify the file or files to be backed up. You must specify at least a drive letter, followed by a colon. You can include a path name or a file name, or both, and you can use wildcard characters.

<drive> is the letter, followed by a colon, of the drive that contains the backup disk (such as *a:*). In versions earlier than 3.3, the backup disk must be formatted.

/A adds the backup files to the backup disk. If you don't use /A, DOS displays a warning message and then erases any files on the target disk before copying the files. If you omit /A, be sure the backup diskette doesn't contain any files you want to keep.

/S backs up all files in all subdirectories contained in the current directory or the specified directory.

/M backs up only files that have been modified since they were last backed up.

/F:<size>, available in versions 3.3 and later, formats the target disk if it isn't already formatted. If you specify /F, the current command path must include the directory containing the file FORMAT.COM.

▶ In version 3.3, you cannot specify <size>. Backup formats the target diskette to match the capacity of the drive, so if you use /F, do not put a low-density diskette in a high-density drive; put a 1.2 MB diskette in a 1.2 MB drive, a 1.44 MB diskette in a 1.44 MB drive, and so on. Lower-capacity diskettes (such as 360 K diskettes) formatted for high capacity (such as 1.2 MB) cannot always be read reliably.

▶ In versions 4 and 5, Backup automatically formats an unformatted diskette to match the normal capacity of the diskette drive. Specify /F:<size> only if the capacity of the target diskette does not match that of the drive in which you put it—for example, a 360 K diskette in a 1.2 MB drive. <size> can be 160, 180, 320, 360, 720, 1.2, 1.44, or (in version 5) 2.88.

/D:<date> backs up only files that have been modified since the date specified in <date>. Specify <date> as you would for the Date command.

/T:<time> backs up all files that have changed since <time> on <date>. Specify <time> as you would for the Time command.

/L:<logfile> creates a log file on the source drive that contains the date and time of the backup, the path name and file name of each file that is backed up, and the backup number that DOS assigned to the diskette on which the file is backed up. If a log file already exists, the backup information is added at the end, creating a history of backups for the source drive. If you don't specify a name for the log file, DOS names it BACKUP.LOG and stores it in the root directory of the source drive.

DOS displays the name of each file as it is backed up. If the target disk is a diskette, the backup files are stored in its root directory. If the target disk is a fixed disk, the backup files are stored in a directory named \BACKUP.

If the files to be backed up require more than one diskette, DOS prompts you to insert another diskette; be sure to label these diskettes, because the Restore command asks for them by number. Files can't be backed up from a write-protected diskette.

When it finishes, the Backup command reports to DOS on the backup procedure by setting an internal value named *errorlevel* to one of the following:

▶ 0: Backup was completed successfully.

▶ 1: No files were found to back up.

▶ 2: Some files were not backed up because of conflicting file-sharing needs (networks only).

▶ 3: Ctrl-C was pressed to end the backup process before all files were backed up.

▶ 4: System problems stopped the backup process.

If you use batch files to help with your backup procedure, you can check this value with the *errorlevel* option of the If batch command and use the result to control which other commands are carried out in a batch file.

439

Note: Because the Backup command varies among different versions of DOS, it's advisable to use the same version both to back up and to restore files. In particular, do not try to use version 3.3 or later to restore files backed up with version 3.2 or earlier.

Do not back up files from a drive that is affected by an Assign, Substitute, or Join command; restoring the files with the Restore command can damage the directory structure of the disk to which the files are restored.

Examples

To back up all files with the extension DOC from the current drive and directory to the disk in drive A and create the log file named BACKUP.LOG:

```
C:\>backup c:*.doc a: /l
```

To back up to drive A all files in all subdirectories on drive C that have been modified since they were last backed up:

```
C:\>backup c:\ a: /s /m
```

(If the disk in drive A is filled before all the files are backed up, you are prompted to insert a new disk. If you're using a version earlier than 3.3 and you regularly back up large files from a fixed disk to diskettes, prepare an adequate supply of formatted diskettes before beginning a backup procedure. If you're using version 3.3 with unformatted diskettes, use the /F parameter.)

To back up all files whose extension is DOC from the current directory and all its subdirectories in drive D to the disk in drive A and add them to the backup disk:

```
C:\>backup d:*.doc a: /s /a
```

To back up all files whose extension is DOC that were changed on or after October 16, 1991, backing them up from the directory \WORD\MKT on the disk in drive C to the disk in drive A:

```
C:\>backup c:\word\mkt\*.doc a: /d:10-16-91
```

BATCH COMMANDS AND BATCH FILES
Executing a File of DOS Commands

Chapters 14 through 17

In addition to typing DOS commands at command level, you can put one or more commands in a batch file—a file with the extension BAT. When you create a batch file, you group commands in the order and combination in which you want them carried out. DOS carries out all the commands, in order, when you type the name of the batch file. Batch files can save typing time, tailor DOS to work with your equipment, and make DOS commands easy to use, even for people who know little about computers.

One widely used batch file is the special file named AUTOEXEC.BAT, which must be in the root directory of the startup disk. DOS carries out the commands in AUTOEXEC.BAT whenever you start or restart the system, so this file lets you set up DOS to match your system and preferences.

Batch Commands

Several DOS commands are intended primarily for use in batch files:

▶ Call carries out the commands in another batch file, then returns to complete the original batch file (versions 3.3 and later). *See* Call.

▶ Echo controls whether DOS displays (echoes) each command it carries out. You can also use the Echo command to display a message or to tell you whether the echo option is on or off. *See* Echo.

▶ For repeatedly carries out a DOS command according to limits that you set. *See* For.

▶ Goto tells DOS to skip to a different location in a batch file, rather than carry out the next sequential command. *See* Goto.

▶ If tests a condition and, if the condition is true, carries out a DOS command you specify. *See* If.

▶ Pause stops carrying out commands and waits for a key to be pressed before continuing with the next command in a batch file. *See* Pause.

▶ Rem lets you include comments (remarks) in a batch file. *See* Rem.

▶ Shift moves a series of command-line parameters entered with a batch command one position to the left. The first parameter is lost, the second parameter becomes the first, and so on. *See* Shift.

BREAK
Controlling When DOS Checks for Ctrl-C
Versions 2.0 and later

The Break command lets you control how often DOS checks to find out whether you typed Ctrl-C (or Ctrl-Break on some machines) to end a program. Normally, DOS checks for Ctrl-C only when it reads or writes characters from or to a standard character device, such as the display, a printer, or a communications port.

break on off

on tells DOS to extend its Ctrl-C checking—for example, to include each time it reads from or writes to a disk drive.

off tells DOS to check for Ctrl-C only when it reads from or writes to a standard character device.

If you enter *break* with no parameters, DOS displays the current break status: either *BREAK is on* or *BREAK is off*.

If break is off, your system runs somewhat faster than when break is on, but you have fewer opportunities to stop a program that spends a lot of time doing computations without using an input or output character device.

DOS starts with break off unless you specify otherwise. You can use the Break command described here to set break on any time after starting DOS, or you can tell DOS to start with break on by including the similar Break configuration command in your CONFIG.SYS file. For information on the Break configuration command, see the next entry.

Examples

To turn break on:

    C:\>break on

To turn break off:

    C:\>break off

To display the break status:

    C:\>break

BREAK (CONFIGURATION COMMAND)
Controlling When DOS Checks for Ctrl-C
Versions 2.0 and later

Like the DOS Break command, the Break configuration command controls how often DOS checks for Ctrl-C. DOS normally starts with break off, meaning that it checks for Ctrl-C whenever it reads from or writes to a character device, such as the keyboard or display. You can set the break status with the DOS Break command any time while you're using DOS. You can also start DOS with break on by placing a *break=on* configuration command in CONFIG.SYS. If you need more information on this command, refer to the documentation that came with your version of DOS.

BUFFERS (CONFIGURATION COMMAND)
Controlling the Number of Disk Buffers
Page 380

The Buffers configuration command specifies how many disk buffers DOS sets aside each time it starts. A disk buffer is an area of memory that DOS uses to hold data being read from or written to disk. DOS creates the buffers in a portion of the computer's memory. Each buffer holds one sector (about 530 bytes, or 0.5 K) of information, so the more buffers you use, the less memory is available for programs. If you have version 5 and are running DOS in the HMA portion of extended memory, the buffers are also placed in the HMA and thus leave more conventional memory for programs and data.

Unless you specify otherwise with a Buffers command in CONFIG.SYS, DOS uses the following number of buffers:

2	If the system has 360 K drives and less than 128 K of memory.
3	If the system has a diskette drive with a capacity greater than 360 K.
5	If the system has more than 128 K of conventional memory (versions 3.3 and later).
10	If the system has more than 256 K of conventional memory (versions 3.3 and later).
15	If the system has 512 K to 640 K of conventional memory (versions 3.3 and later).

The optimum number of buffers depends on several factors, among them:

▶ The type and size of disk drives you use. If you have a fixed disk, you can increase speed by setting the number of buffers to 20 for a fixed disk up to 40 MB; 30 for a disk of 40 to 79 MB; 40 for a disk of 80 to 119 MB; or 50 for a disk of 120 MB or more.

▶ The type of programs you use. If you use applications that normally access files sequentially rather than by jumping from one place to another, 10 to 20 buffers can increase speed by keeping information in memory and reducing the number of times DOS must go out to disk.

▶ The type of file structure you use. If you have a large, multilevel subdirectory structure, using 10 to 25 buffers can significantly speed disk operations.

Beginning with version 4, the Buffers command also includes a secondary-cache feature. This feature tells DOS that, whenever it reads one sector, it should also "look ahead" at following sectors and read them into memory as well. Using this look-ahead feature, especially with programs that access information sequentially, increases the store of information that DOS keeps in memory and can find quickly without resorting to relatively slow disk-read operations.

The Buffers command can have three parameters:

buffers=\<number>,\<look-ahead> /X

\<number> is the number of buffers to set aside. It is normally from 1 through 99. If you have version 4 and a system with expanded memory, you can place buffers in expanded memory with the /X parameter. In this case, \<number> can be from 1 through 10000.

\<look-ahead>, in versions 4 and 5 only, is the number of buffers for holding sectors you want DOS to read beyond the sector currently being used. \<look-ahead> can be from 1 through 8. Each look-ahead buffer takes about 530 bytes of additional memory. If you already use a disk-caching program, such as Smartdrive in versions 4 and 5, you can ignore this look-ahead feature because your program should work as well as, or better than, a secondary cache created with the Buffers command.

/X, in version 4 only, tells DOS to put the buffers in expanded memory.

Examples

To allocate 30 buffers, put the following Buffers command in CONFIG.SYS:

```
buffers=30
```

To allocate 30 regular buffers and allow 4 look-ahead buffers:

```
buffers=30,4
```

CALL (BATCH COMMAND)
Carry Out Another Batch File
Versions 3.3 and later

Page 348

You can use the Call batch command in a batch file to tell DOS to carry out the commands in a second batch file, then return to the original batch file and continue with the next command in it instead of returning to the system prompt. This lets you use a batch command of your own making in a batch file just as you would use any other DOS command.

call <batchfile> <parameters>

<batchfile> is the name of the file of commands you want DOS to carry out. Include a drive letter, path, or both if the batch file you call is not in the current directory.

<parameters> represents any parameters that <batchfile> requires. You can enter the parameters themselves, or you can use replaceable parameters so that parameters typed on the command line with the name of the first batch file are passed along to the batch file being called.

Example

Suppose you have two batch files. One, named SORTFILE.BAT, first uses the Sort command to sort the file whose name you type as a parameter with *sortfile,* then redirects the sorted output to the printer; the other, WEEKRPT.BAT, carries out several commands to print a series of sorted lists that make up a weekly report.

To use the SORTFILE batch command in WEEKRPT.BAT to print the sorted version of the file named REPORT.LST, include the following Call command in WEEKRPT.BAT:

```
call sortfile report.lst
```

DOS carries out the commands in SORTFILE.BAT—printing the sorted version of REPORT.LST—and continues with the command that follows the Call command in WEEKRPT.BAT.

CHANGE CODE PAGE (CHCP)
Display or Change System-Wide Code Page
Version 3.3

Page 403

The Change Code Page command (chcp) tells DOS which code page to use for all devices that have been prepared for code-page switching. You use it to display the current code page or to change code pages when you want to change the language or character set that DOS uses. The *codepage select* option of the Mode command changes the code page for individual devices.

> **chcp <codepage>**

<codepage> is the three-digit number from the list below that specifies a particular code page (852, Slavic, is in version 5 only).

Code-Page Number	Code Page
437	United States
850	Multilingual (Latin I)
852	Slavic (Latin II)
860	Portuguese
863	French Canadian
865	Nordic

If you omit <codepage>, DOS displays the number of the current code page. If you specify a code page, but it cannot be activated for all devices that support code-page switching, DOS responds *Code page* nnn *not prepared for all devices.*

You must execute the National Language Support Function (nlsfunc) command before you can use the Change Code Page command to change a code page.

Examples

To change the system code page to multilingual (850):

> `C:\>chcp 850`

To display the current code page (assume that it's 850):

> `C:\>chcp`

DOS responds *Active code page: 850.*

CHANGE DIRECTORY (CD)
Change Current Directory
Versions 2.0 and later

Page 152

The Change Directory command (cd or chdir) changes or displays the current directory.

cd <drive><path>

<drive> is the letter, followed by a colon, of the drive whose current directory is to be displayed or changed.

<path> is the path name of the directory that is to become the current directory.

If you omit <path>, DOS displays the current directory of the disk in <drive>. If you omit both <drive> and <path>, DOS displays the current directory of the disk in the current drive.

Examples

To change the current directory on the disk in the current drive to \MKT\WP:

    C:\>cd \mkt\wp

To change the current directory on the disk in drive A to \MKT\WP:

    C:\>cd a:\mkt\wp

To display the current directory of the disk in the current drive:

    C:\>cd

To display the current directory of the disk in drive D:

    C:\>cd d:

CHECK DISK (CHKDSK)
Check Disk Status
Versions 1.0 and later

Pages 113, 163

The Check Disk command (chkdsk) checks the allocation of storage on a disk and displays a report that shows the total amount of disk space, how much is used by directories and files, including hidden files, and how much is not available because of disk imperfections. Chkdsk also tells you how much memory is in the system and how much is free for use. Beginning with version 4, Chkdsk also reports on disk usage in terms of allocation units (storage units consisting of groups of bytes).

chkdsk <drive><filename> /V /F

<drive> is the letter, followed by a colon, of the drive that contains the disk to be checked (such as *a:*). If you omit <drive>, DOS checks the disk in the current drive.

<filename> specifies one or more files to be checked for fragmentation (stored in two or more nonadjacent locations on the disk). If you don't specify a drive, Chkdsk checks the disk in the current drive. If you don't specify a path, Chkdsk checks the current directory. If you omit <filename>, Chkdsk checks storage on the entire disk.

/V displays the full path name and file name of each file and directory on the disk being checked (versions 2.0 and later).

/F tells Chkdsk to correct allocation errors, if it finds any and if you respond *y* when it notifies you of the errors and asks whether to correct them. Correcting allocation errors requires changing the information on the disk and may cause loss of some data, so this parameter safeguards against disk changes unless you approve them (versions 2.0 and later).

If Chkdsk finds errors in the allocation of disk space, it refers to this space as *allocation units* (or *clusters*) and *chains* and asks whether you want to recover the space into a file. If you reply *y*, Chkdsk corrects the errors only if you included the /F parameter. The space is then recovered into a file named FILE*nnnn*.CHK in the root directory of the drive being checked (*nnnn* is a sequence number that starts with 0000).

If you specify a file name or a set of file names (by using wildcards) when you enter the Chkdsk command, the Chkdsk report tells you whether any of the files are fragmented by displaying the name of each file, followed by the message *Contains* n *non-contiguous blocks*. A badly fragmented disk can slow performance. If too many files on a diskette are fragmented, restore them to contiguous sectors by copying them all to another diskette with the Copy command (*copy *. **). If too many files on a fixed disk are fragmented, restore them to contiguous sectors with a disk-reorganizing program or by using DOS to back up all the files, reformat the fixed disk, and restore the files to the fixed disk.

Note: Chkdsk cannot be used with a drive created or affected by the Assign, Join, or Substitute command, nor can it be used with a network drive.

Examples

To check the disk in the current drive:

```
C:\>chkdsk
```

If there are no errors, Chkdsk displays a report like that on the next page.

```
Volume FIXED DISK   created 08-30-1990 3:31p
Volume Serial Number is 1608-5A30

  33462272 bytes total disk space
    112640 bytes in 5 hidden files
     86016 bytes in 34 directories
  25919488 bytes in 967 user files
     10240 bytes in bad sectors
   7333888 bytes available on disk

      2048 bytes in each allocation unit
     16339 total allocation units on disk
      3581 available allocation units on disk

    655360 total bytes memory
    513072 bytes free
```

To check the disk in drive A, checking all files in the directory \MKT\WP to see if they are fragmented:

    C:\>chkdsk a:\mkt\wp*.*

Chkdsk displays its usual report, followed by a list of any fragmented files:

    A:\MKT\WP\REPORT.DOC Contains 2 non-contiguous blocks
    A:\MKT\WP\FORECAST.DOC Contains 5 non-contiguous blocks
    A:\MKT\WP\SALESREP.DOC Contains 4 non-contiguous blocks

To check the disk in the current drive and tell Chkdsk you want to be able to recover any lost clusters:

    C:\>chkdsk /f

Chkdsk displays its usual report. If there are allocation errors, it displays a message similar to this:

    x lost allocation units found in y chains.
    Convert lost chains to files (Y/N)?

If you want to recover the lost units, reply *y*. When the command has completed, display the file named FILE*nnnn*.CHK; rename it if it contains data you want to keep, or delete it to make the disk space available to other files.

CLS
Clear the Screen
Versions 2.0 and later

Page 123

The Clear Screen command clears the screen and displays the system prompt in the top left-hand corner. Clear Screen has no parameters.

    cls

Example

To clear the screen:

```
C:\>cls
```

COMMAND
Start a New Command Processor
Versions 1.0 and later

The Command command loads another copy of the DOS command processor (COM-MAND.COM), the program that displays the system prompt and responds to the commands you type.

command /P /C <command>

/P makes the new copy of COMMAND.COM permanent. It displays the sign-on message and system prompt and waits for a command. There is no way to return to the previous command processor (versions 2.0 and later).

/C <command> loads the new copy of COMMAND.COM, carries out the command specified by <command>, and returns control to the previous command processor (versions 2.0 and later).

If you enter a Command command with no parameters, the new copy of COM-MAND.COM displays the sign-on message and system prompt and waits for a command. The new copy of COMMAND.COM remains in memory until you type *exit*. Control then returns to the previous command processor.

If you put a Command command with the /C parameter in a batch file and use it to carry out another batch file, DOS continues with the next statement in the first batch file when the second batch file completes. This allows a batch file to call another batch file, as well as to chain to another batch file. This technique is unnecessary in versions 3.3 and later because they include the Call command.

Examples

To load a new copy of COMMAND.COM that remains in control until you type *exit*:

```
C:\>command
```

To load a permanent new copy of COMMAND.COM:

```
C:\>command /p
```

To cause a batch file (BATCH1.BAT) to load a new copy of COMMAND.COM, carry out the commands in a second batch file (BATCH2.BAT), finish carrying out the commands in the first batch file, and return to the previous command processor, put the following command in BATCH1.BAT:

```
command /c batch2.bat
```

COMPARE (COMP)
Compare Two Files
Version 3.3, IBM releases 1.0 and later

Page 87

The Compare command (comp) compares two files or sets of files byte by byte and reports up to 10 differences for each comparison. If it finds any differences, Compare displays the location of each. In all versions of DOS in which it appears, Compare displays the hexadecimal (base-16) value of the differing bytes. Beginning with version 5, you can specify decimal values or ASCII characters instead, and you can also tell Compare to display line numbers, compare a specified number of lines, and ignore differences between uppercase and lowercase.

If the files are the same, Compare displays *Files compare OK*. If the files are different lengths, Compare displays *Files are different sizes* and quits comparing the files. If the files are the same length but their content differs, Compare displays the locations and values of up to 10 bytes that differ; if more than 10 bytes differ, it displays the message *10 Mismatches - ending compare*. After completing any comparison, Compare asks whether you want to compare more files. If you type *y*, Compare prompts for the names of the next files to compare and, if you have version 5, any options, such as decimal, ASCII, or line numbers, that you want to specify.

comp <file1> <file2> <option>

<file1> is the name of the first file to be compared. You can include a drive and path, and you can use wildcard characters to specify a group of files with similar names or extensions.

<file2> is the name of the second file to be compared. You can include a drive and path, and you can use wildcard characters. If you specify only a drive letter or path name, Compare compares <file1> to the file with the same name on the drive or in the directory you specified in <file2>. If you use wildcard characters in <file1>, Compare finds and compares all files in the second set that match the file specification.

If you omit <file2>, Compare prompts for it. If you omit both <file1> and <file2> by typing *comp* with no parameters, Compare prompts for both file names (and options in version 5).

<option> is the version 5 parameter that lets you specify the type of comparison you want. If you don't specify an option, Compare displays any differences it finds in hexadecimal, which, though invaluable to programmers, is generally indecipherable to other people. To help you make the report more understandable and to let you refine the comparison, version 5 offers these alternatives:

▶ /D to display decimal rather than hexadecimal numbers.

▶ /A to translate numbers into recognizable characters according to the widely used code called ASCII.

▶ /L to display the line number where a difference occurs.

▶ /N=*xxx* to compare only a specified (*xxx*) number of lines.

▶ /C to ignore the difference between uppercase and lowercase letters.

Examples

Suppose that the current directory (C:\) contains FILE1 and FILE2. FILE1 contains the words *This is a sample file*. FILE2 contains the words *This one is different*. The directory \DOCS on the same drive contains identical files—same names, same contents.

To compare the two files in the current directory:

```
C:\>comp file1 file2
```

Because the files are the same lengths but more than 10 bytes differ, Compare would display the locations and values of the differences followed by *10 Mismatches - ending compare*.

To compare FILE1 in the current directory with \DOCS\FILE1:

```
C:\>comp file1 \docs\file1
```

Because the files are the same, Compare would display *Files compare OK*.

To compare FILE1 in the current directory with \DOCS\FILE2 and display the characters that differ:

```
C:\>comp file1 \docs\file2 /a
```

Compare would display 10 characters that differ in each file and end the comparison.

Finally, suppose each file were 100 lines long. To compare the first 20 lines of FILE1 and FILE2 and display the line numbers where differences occur:

```
C:\>comp file1 file2 /n=20 /l
```

CONFIG.SYS
File of System Configuration Commands

Page 368

CONFIG.SYS is a file that contains configuration commands that define the hardware and software that make up your system. It must be in the root directory of the system disk. Each time DOS starts, it carries out the commands in CONFIG.SYS. If there is no file named CONFIG.SYS in the root directory of the system disk, DOS assumes certain configuration values.

The configuration commands include:

▶ Break, which controls how often DOS checks for Ctrl-C. *See* Break.

▶ Buffers, which specifies how many disk buffers DOS sets aside. *See* Buffers.

▶ Country, which specifies the country whose date and time format is to be used. *See* Country.

▶ Device, which identifies a file that contains a program to control a device (such a program is called a *device driver*). *See* Device.

▶ Devicehigh, which enables DOS to load device drivers into the upper memory area (the portion of memory between 640 K and 1 MB) on computers with an 80386 or 80486 microprocessor and extended memory. *See* Devicehigh.

▶ Dos, which serves two functions: telling DOS whether to load itself into conventional or extended memory, and maintaining access to the upper memory area so that programs can be loaded into it. *See* Dos.

▶ Drivparm, which defines the operating characteristics of a disk or a tape drive. *See* Drivparm.

▶ FCBS, which specifies the number of files controlled by File Control Blocks (FCBs) that can be open at the same time. *See* FCBS.

▶ Files, which specifies how many files controlled by handles can be open at the same time. *See* Files.

▶ Install, which loads a command file from CONFIG.SYS. *See* Install.

▶ Lastdrive, which sets the highest drive letter that DOS recognizes. *See* Lastdrive.

▶ Shell, which specifies the name of a command processor to be used instead of COMMAND.COM. *See* Shell.

▶ Stacks, which tells DOS how much memory to reserve for its temporary use. *See* Stacks.

▶ Switches, which blocks enhanced keyboard functions. *See* Switches.

CONFIG.SYS is a text file; you can create it or modify an existing version with a text editor, such as Edit or Edlin, or with a word processor that lets you store a file without formatting codes.

COPY

Copy a File or Device

Versions 1.0 and later

Copy is one of the most flexible and often-used DOS commands. It lets you duplicate, store, move, display, and even print files. Because Copy can be used in different ways, the command is described in four entries that cover:

▶ Copying one or more files from one location (drive or directory) to another.

▶ Copying one or more files to a device, such as a printer.

▶ Copying from a device, such as the keyboard, to a file or another device.

▶ Combining files.

COPY
Copy a File to Another File (Location)

Page 70

This form of the Copy command duplicates a file on the same or a different disk. You can give the copy the same file name if you're copying to another drive or directory. If you want to duplicate a file in the same directory (for example, to create a second copy for editing), you must give it a different name or extension because DOS doesn't allow two files with the same name in the same directory.

copy <file1> <file2> /A /B /V

<file1> is the file to be copied. You can include a drive letter, a path name, or both, and you can use wildcard characters to copy a set of files with similar names or extensions.

<file2> is the file to which <file1> is copied. If <file1> is not on the current drive or in the current directory and you omit <file2>, DOS copies <file1> to a file with the same name in the current directory of the current drive. If you specify <file2> as a drive letter, a path name, a file name (and extension), or all three, DOS copies <file1> as follows:

Target	Source File Is Copied To
Drive letter	A file with the same name in the current directory of the specified drive.
Path name	A file with the same name in the specified directory.
File name	A file with the specified name in the current directory.
All three	A file with the specified file name, in the specified drive and directory.

Note: Be very careful when you specify <file2>. If a file with the same name already exists in the drive and directory you specify, DOS replaces the existing file with the copy, deleting the original version without warning you.

/A (for *ASCII*) treats the file as a text file. You can include /A either before or after <file2>. If /A precedes <file2>, DOS copies up to the first Ctrl-Z character in each file specified by <file1>. The Ctrl-Z and any data that follows are not copied. If /A follows <file2>, DOS adds a Ctrl-Z character to the end of each file specified by <file2>. When DOS combines files or copies to or from a device, it uses the /A option.

/B (for *binary*) treats the file as a non-text file. If /B precedes <file2>, DOS copies everything, including the end-of-file mark, in each file specified by <file1>. If /B follows <file2>, DOS does not add a Ctrl-Z character at the end of each file it copies.

Both /A and /B affect the preceding file and all subsequent file names in the command up to, but not including, a file name followed by /A or /B.

/V verifies that the file was copied correctly. DOS turns verification on, copies the file, then turns verification off. You don't need this parameter if you've turned on the DOS verify option with the Verify command. Verification slows the copy process.

Examples

To copy the file named LETTER.DOC from the disk in drive A to the current directory (MKT\WP) of the current drive (C:):

```
C:\MKT\WP>copy a:letter.doc
```

To copy the file named FORECAST.DOC from the directory \MKT\BUDGET on the disk in drive A to the directory \MKT\WP on the disk in the current drive (C:):

```
C:\>copy a:\mkt\budget\forecast.doc \mkt\wp
```

To copy the file named REPORT.TXT from the root directory of drive A to a file named FINAL.RPT in the directory named \MKT\WP on the disk in the current drive:

```
C:\>copy a:\report.txt \mkt\wp\final.rpt
```

To copy all files with the extension TXT from the current directory of the disk in drive D to the current drive and directory (C:\MKT\WP), giving the copies the extension DOC:

```
C:\MKT\WP>copy d:*.txt *.doc
```

COPY
Copy a File to a Device

Page 73

This form of the Copy command copies one or more files from a disk to a device such as the printer.

copy <filename> <device> /A /B

<file> is the name of the file or files to copy. You can use wildcards to specify more than one file, and you can precede the file name with a drive letter (followed by a colon), a path name, or both.

<device> is the name of the device, usually CON or PRN, to which <file> is to be copied.

/A and /B specify ASCII and binary files, as described in the preceding entry.

Examples

To copy the file named REPORT.TXT to the screen (CON) from the current drive and directory:

`C:\WP>copy report.txt con`

The file is displayed, just as if you had entered *type report.txt*.

To copy the file named LETTER.DOC to the printer (PRN) from the directory \DOCS on the disk in drive A:

`C:\>copy a:\docs\letter.doc prn`

COPY
Copy from a Device to a File or Another Device

Page 133

This form of the Copy command copies from a device to a file or to a different device.

copy <source> <target>

<source> is the device to copy from.

<target> is the file or device to copy to. If you specify a file, you can include a drive and path, but you cannot use wildcards.

Examples

To copy from the keyboard (CON) to the printer (PRN), effectively treating your computer as if it were a typewriter:

`C:\>copy con prn`

To copy from the keyboard to a file named SAMPLE.TXT in the directory named \EXAMPLES on the disk in drive A:

`C:\>copy con a:\examples\sample.txt`

DOS copies all characters you type until you end the file by pressing Ctrl-Z or F6 and the Enter key.

COPY
Combine Files

Page 74

This form of the Copy command combines two or more source files into a destination file you specify.

copy <source>+<source>+... <target> /A /B /V

<source> is the name of each file to be combined. You can include a drive letter, a path name, or both, and you can use wildcards to specify a set of files. Use a plus sign (+) when you specify two or more file names. If a source file does not exist, DOS doesn't notify you. It simply goes on to the next file in the list.

<target> is the name of the file into which the source files are combined. If you don't specify <target>, the files are combined into the first source file in the series.

Note: When you use wildcards to combine one or more source files into a target file that already exists in the same directory, the original contents of the target file are replaced by the contents of the combined source files. DOS doesn't warn you that data will be lost, but does display the message Content of destination lost before copy *when the copy procedure is completed. If you want to add files to an existing file but keep the original information intact, use the plus sign between the names of the source files and specify the target file name first.*

/A and /B specify ASCII and binary files, as described in an earlier entry on the Copy command. /V tells DOS to verify the copy.

Examples

To combine the files named APR.DOC, MAY.DOC, and JUN.DOC in the current directory into a file named 2Q.DOC in the current directory:

C:\MKT\WP>copy apr.doc+may.doc+jun.doc 2q.doc

To add the files named MAY.DOC and JUN.DOC to the file in the current directory named APR.DOC:

C:\MKT\WP>copy apr.doc+may.doc+jun.doc

To combine all the files in the current directory whose extension is DOC, in the order in which their directory entries appear, into another file, named TOTAL.DOC, which is also in the current directory:

C:\MKT\WP>copy *.doc total.doc

COUNTRY (CONFIGURATION COMMAND)
Set the International Date and Currency Format
Versions 2.1 and later, IBM releases 3.0 and later

Pages 389, 401

The Country command specifies a country code that tells DOS to follow date, time, and other conventions for a particular country. If there is no Country command in CONFIG.SYS, DOS follows the conventions of the country for which it was manufactured.

DOS also uses the country code to choose the currency symbol and the character that separates the thousands and decimal fraction parts of a number. Although these characters aren't used in normal DOS operation, the country code is available to application programs so that they can use the proper conventions.

country=<code>,<codepage>,<countryfile>

<code> is the three-digit country code that specifies the country whose date format is to be followed; it is the same as the international telephone dialing prefix. DOS can recognize the country codes listed in Figure C-1. You must include all three digits, including any zeros at the beginning.

Country or Language	Country Code	Valid Code Pages	DOS Versions/Notes
Arabic			Special version 5 of DOS
		864, 850	Version 4 with country-specific supplement
Australia	061	437, 850	Versions 2.1 and later
Belgium	032	850, 437	Versions 2.1 and later
Brazil	055	850, 437	Version 5
Canada (French)	002	863, 850	Versions 3.3 and later
Czechoslovakia	042	852, 850	Version 5
Denmark	045	850, 865	Versions 2.1 and later
Finland	358	850, 437	Versions 2.1 and later
France	033	437, 850	Versions 2.1 and later
Germany	049	437, 850	Versions 2.1 and later
Hebrew			Special version 5 of DOS
		862, 850	Version 4 with country-specific supplement
Hungary	036	852, 850	Version 5
Italy	039	437, 850	Versions 2.1 and later
Japan			Special version 5 of DOS
		932, 437	Asian edition of version 4 on a computer manufactured for use in Asia
Korea			Special version 5 of DOS
		934, 437	Asian edition of version 4 on a computer manufactured for use in Asia
Latin America	003	850, 437	Versions 3.3 and later

Figure C-1. *Valid country codes and code pages for different versions of DOS.* *(continued)*

457

Figure C-1. *continued*

Country or Language	Country Code	Valid Code Pages	DOS Versions/Notes
Netherlands	031	437, 850	Versions 2.1 and later
Norway	047	850, 865	Versions 2.1 and later
People's Republic of China		936,437	Special version 5 of DOS Asian edition of version 4 on a computer manufactured for use in Asia
Poland	048	852, 850	Version 5
Portugal	351	850, 860	Versions 3.3 and later
Spain	034	850, 437	Versions 2.1 and later
Sweden	046	437, 850	Versions 2.1 and later
Switzerland	041	850, 437	Versions 2.1 and later
Taiwan		938, 437	Special version 5 of DOS Asian edition of version 4 on a computer manufactured for use in Asia
United Kingdom	044	437, 850	Versions 2.1 and later
United States	001	437, 850	Versions 2.1 and later
Yugoslavia	038	852, 850	Version 5

<codepage> is a three-digit number, also listed in Figure C-1, that specifies the code page that DOS is to use (versions 3.3 and later).

<countryfile> is the name of the DOS file that contains the country-specific information. If you omit <countryfile>, DOS assumes the file is COUNTRY.SYS and is stored in the root directory of the current drive (versions 3.3 and later).

Example

In Belgium, the date is formatted as dd/mm/yyyy; for example, 16/10/1991 for October 16, 1991. To specify the Belgian format, put the following Country command in CONFIG.SYS:

```
country=032
```

CTTY

Change the Console Device

Versions 2.0 and later

The CTTY command specifies the device that is to be used for standard input and standard output. You can assign standard input and output to a communications port, for example, to permit remote operation of the computer, or you can assign them to special devices supported by custom control programs.

Not all programs recognize the assignment of standard input and standard output. The Microsoft Basic interpreter, for example, does not, and so is unaffected by the Change Console command.

ctty <device>

<device> is the name of the device that is to be used for standard input and standard output; the device must be capable of both input and output. If <device> specifies a device other than CON, AUX, PRN, LPT*n*, or COM*n*, CONFIG.SYS must include a Device command that names the file that contains the control program (device driver), and DOS must have access to that file.

Examples

To assign standard input and standard output to communications port COM1:

```
C:\>ctty com1
```

To reassign standard input and standard output to the keyboard and display:

```
C:\>ctty con
```

DATE
Change or Display the System Date
Versions 1.0 and later

Page 17

The Date command displays the date kept by DOS and prompts you to enter a new date. The sequence of the day, month, and year depends on the country code set with the Country or Select command. The sequence here is for the United States.

date <mm-dd-yy>

<mm-dd-yy> is the new date to be set. <mm> is the month (1 through 12), <dd> is the day (1 through 31), and <yy> is the year (1980 through 2079—2099 if you type all four digits). You can separate the day, month, and year with hyphens, slashes, or periods: 10-16-91 or 10/16/91 or 10.16.91.

If you type just *date*, DOS displays the current date and prompts you to enter the new date. Type a new date or press the Enter key to leave the date unchanged.

Examples

To set the date to October 16, 1991:

```
C:\>date 10-16-91
```

To display the current system date and respond to the prompt for a new date:

```
C:\>date
```

DOS·responds:

```
Current date is Wed 10-16-1991
Enter new date (mm-dd-yy): _
```

Type the new date, or press the Enter key to leave the current date unchanged.

DELETE (DEL)
Delete (Erase) a File
Versions 1.0 and later

Page 76

The Delete command (del or erase) deletes a file or set of files.

del <filename> /P

<filename> is the name of the file to be deleted. You can use wildcard characters to delete a set of files with similar file names or extensions.

/P tells DOS to prompt for verification before deleting a file (versions 4 and 5).

If you don't use the /P parameter, DOS deletes the file or files you specified as soon as you press the Enter key. The only exception occurs when you use the wildcard specification *.* to indicate all files or when you specify only a directory name (which implies *.*). Because *.* deletes the contents of an entire disk or directory, DOS prompts for confirmation with a message like this: *All files in directory will be deleted! Are you sure (Y/N)?* You must press Y to carry out the command.

Beginning with version 5, DOS offers you some protection if you inadvertently delete one or more files you meant to keep. The Undelete command can help you recover lost files, but it can work effectively *only* if you use Undelete as soon as possible—preferably immediately after deleting needed files. Because DOS might save new information in the space formerly occupied by your deleted files, any delay in using the Undelete command can mean loss of some portion(s) of the files you want to recover. For more details, see the entry on the Undelete command.

Examples

To delete the file named REPORT.DOC in the current directory on the disk in the current drive:

```
C:\MKT\WP>del report.doc
```

To delete all files with the extension BAK in the directory named \MKT\WP on the disk in drive A, telling DOS to prompt for verification:

```
C>del a:\mkt\wp\*.bak /p
```

DEVICE (CONFIGURATION COMMAND)
Define a Device-Control Program
Versions 2.0 and later

Page 369

The Device configuration command identifies a file that contains a program to control a device. DOS automatically recognizes and works with certain devices, such as the keyboard and the display. But other devices, such as a mouse, can be added to a computer system. If you add a device that DOS doesn't already know about, you must tell DOS the name of the device's controlling program. Such a control program, called a *device driver,* usually has the extension SYS and comes with the device. You can put more than one Device command in CONFIG.SYS.

device=<filename>

<filename> is the name of the file that contains the device driver. You can include a drive and path if necessary.

The device drivers listed in Figure C-2 are included with DOS.

Driver Name	DOS Version(s)	Controls
ANSI.SYS	2.0 and later	Display and keyboard. This is an advanced use of DOS; details may be in your DOS manual and can also be found in the book *Supercharging MS-DOS.*
DISPLAY.SYS	3.3 and later	Code-page switching for the display; *see* Chapter 18.
DRIVER.SYS*	3.2 and later	Diskette drives. This device driver enables you to assign a drive letter to an internal or external diskette drive.
EGA.SYS	5.0	Screen restoration on an EGA display when the DOS Shell's Task Swapper is used.
EMM386.EXE	5.0	Extended memory. This device driver, for use on 80386 and 80486 systems only, allows you to treat extended memory as expanded memory and to gain access to the reserved portion of conventional memory known as upper memory blocks (the memory between 640 K and 1 MB); *see* Chapter 17 and the entries EMM386 and EMM386.EXE in this appendix.

Figure C-2. *Device drivers shipped with DOS.*   (continued)

Figure C-2. *continued*

Driver Name	DOS Version(s)	Controls
HIMEM.SYS	5.0	Extended memory and the High Memory Area (HMA). Among other features, this device driver enables DOS to load itself into extended memory and thus leave more conventional memory available for programs to use; *see* Chapter 17 and the entry HIMEM.SYS in this appendix.
PRINTER.SYS	3.3 and later	Code-page switching for the printer; *see* Chapter 18.
RAMDRIVE.SYS	3.2 and later	RAM drive; *see* Chapter 17 and the entry RAMDRIVE.SYS in this appendix.
SETVER.EXE	5.0	Table of DOS version numbers needed by applications and other programs; *see* the entry Set Version in this appendix.
SMARTDRV.SYS	4.0 and later	Disk cache in extended or expanded memory; *see* Chapter 17 and the entry SMARTDRV.SYS in this appendix.
VDISK.SYS	IBM releases 3.0 and later	RAM drive; *see* Chapter 17 and the entry RAMDRIVE.SYS in this appendix.
XMAEM.SYS*	IBM version 4	Extended/expanded memory.
XMA2EMS.SYS*	IBM version 4	Expanded memory.

*Use of these device drivers is beyond the scope of this book; for details, refer to your computer's manual(s) and to your DOS manual.

Example

To load (from the root directory) a mouse driver named MOUSE.SYS, put the following Device command in CONFIG.SYS:

```
device=mouse.sys
```

To manage extended memory and the High Memory Area (HMA), assuming a \DOS directory:

```
device=c:\dos\himem.sys
```

If used to load DOS into the HMA, this command must be accompanied by the *dos=high* command in CONFIG.SYS.

DEVICEHIGH (CONFIGURATION COMMAND)
Load Device Drivers into the Upper Memory Area
Version 5.0

Page 379

The Devicehigh command tells DOS to load a device driver into available upper memory blocks (UMBs) in the upper memory area (memory between 640 K and 1 MB). The Devicehigh command requires a computer with at least 350 K of extended memory. It also requires HIMEM.SYS and either EMM386.EXE or a comparable memory manager that provides access to UMBs. If you use EMM386.EXE, your computer must have either an 80386 or an 80486 microprocessor. Loading one or more device drivers into UMBs helps make more of your system's conventional memory available to programs.

You can load any of the following DOS device drivers into UMBs: ANSI.SYS, DISPLAY.SYS, DRIVER.SYS, EGA.SYS, PRINTER.SYS, RAMDRIVE.SYS, and SMARTDRV.SYS. If you normally load any of these drivers into conventional memory, you can place them in UMBs instead by adding the Dos and Device commands shown in the example for this entry and by changing the Device command for each driver to Devicehigh.

Note: Device drivers other than those listed here might cause problems with your system. Before using Devicehigh, consult your DOS documentation and refer to the section on Devicehigh in Chapter 17, "Tailoring Your System."

devicehigh size=<memsize> <driver> <dparameters>

size=<memsize> lets you specify the minimum amount of the upper memory area, given as a hexadecimal (base-16) value, needed by the device driver. If you don't include this parameter and the driver attempts to use more memory than is available, the system might halt. You can find <memsize> by using a Device configuration command to load the driver in conventional memory and then using the /*classify* parameter of the Mem command, which displays the names and sizes (in decimal and hexadecimal) of programs in memory.

<driver> is the name of the device driver. You can include a path name.

<dparameters> represents any parameters required by the device driver.

Example

To tell DOS to use the upper memory area, make it available to device drivers, and load RAMDRIVE.SYS in UMBs with instructions to create a 1024 K RAM disk in extended memory, put commands like the following in CONFIG.SYS:

```
dos=high,umb
device=c:\dos\himem.sys
device=c:\dos\emm386.exe noems
devicehigh=C:\dos\ramdrive.sys 1024 /e
```

DIRECTORY (DIR)
Display Directory Entries
Versions 1.0 and later

Pages 66, 87, 159

The Directory command (dir) displays the directory entry of one or more files. A Directory command display looks like the following:

```
Volume in drive C is FIXED DISK
Volume Serial Number is 1608-5A30
Directory of C:\MKT\WP

.               <DIR>      07-02-91    5:24p
..              <DIR>      07-02-91    5:24p
REPORT   DOC    60780 08-15-91    1:09a
FORECAST DOC    18256 10-10-91    7:46p
SALESREP DOC    25728 10-13-91    8:42a
LETTERS  <DIR>
FCST-APR DOC     4328 10-12-91    9:07a
FCST-MAY DOC    20982 09-24-91   10:09p
STYLE    <DIR>
FCST-MAR DOC      996 10-12-91    5:36p
WKRPT    STY     2688 10-12-91    5:50p
BUDGET   DOC     5888 10-11-91    9:28a
       12 file(s)       139646 bytes
                     23633152 bytes free
```

The first three lines show the volume label of the disk (FIXED DISK), the volume serial number (beginning with version 4), and the drive and path name of the directory whose entries are displayed (C:\MKT\WP). The last lines show the number of directory entries displayed (12), the number of bytes (139,646) used by the files (version 5 only), and the available space on the disk (23,633,152 bytes).

The directory entry for a file includes the file name and extension, size in bytes, and the date and time it was created or last changed. The directory entry for a subdirectory (LETTERS and STYLE in the preceding example) includes the file name and extension, followed by <DIR>.

The first two subdirectory entries in the preceding example are symbolic; the first (one period) represents the directory whose entries are displayed, and the second (two periods) represents the directory that contains the directory whose entries are displayed (sometimes referred to as the *parent* directory). The entries . and .. do not appear in the listing of the root directory of a disk.

dir <filename> /W /P /A:<attribute> /O:<sortorder> /S /B /L

<filename> is the name of the file whose directory entry is to be displayed. You can use wildcard characters to display the entries of a set of files with similar names or extensions. If you omit <filename>, DOS displays the directory entry of each file in

the specified or current directory. If you specify only a drive letter, DOS displays the directory entry of each file in the current directory of the specified drive. If you specify a filename but no extension, DOS displays the directory entry for each file with that file name, regardless of extension.

/W (for *wide*) displays only the file name and extension of each directory entry in five columns across the screen. Beginning with version 5, the names of subdirectories are enclosed in square brackets for readability—for example, *[DOS]* instead of *DOS*.

/P (for *pause*) displays the directory one screenful at a time, displaying *Press any key to continue...* (*Strike a key when ready...* in versions prior to 4) at the bottom of the screen. Pressing any key displays the next screenful of entries; pressing Ctrl-Break or Ctrl-C cancels the command. Beginning with version 5, DOS heads each new screenful of entries with the message *(continuing* <pathname>*)* to help you keep your bearings.

The following parameters are new in version 5 of DOS.

/A:<attribute> displays the entries for files with the attribute you specify. (The colon is optional; omit it if you want.) <attribute> can be any of the following:

▶ H displays hidden files—that is, files whose hidden attribute is on.

▶ S displays system files—that is, files normally used by DOS. These files are typically hidden as well to avoid inadvertent change or deletion. DOS requires two system files named MSDOS.SYS and IO.SYS (IBMDOS.COM and IBMBIO.COM in IBM releases) on any disk you use to start your system. Don't tamper with these.

▶ D displays only the names of directories.

▶ A displays files whose archive attribute is on—that is, files that have not been archived since they were created or last changed.

▶ R displays read-only files—that is, files that can be read but not changed.

You can precede any of these attributes with a hyphen (minus sign) to omit files or directories with the specified attribute.

/O:<sortorder> specifies the order in which directory entries are displayed. <sortorder> can be any of the following. As with attributes, you can use a hyphen to reverse the order:

▶ N sorts entries alphabetically by file name from A to Z.

▶ E sorts alphabetically by extension from A to Z.

▶ D sorts by date, oldest to newest.

▶ S sorts by size, smallest to largest.

▶ G groups directories ahead of files. (-G groups directories after files.)

/S displays every file in every subdirectory on the disk that matches <filename>. So that you know where the files are stored, DOS identifies each subdirectory with the words *Directory of* <path> before displaying the directory entries.

/B displays only the name and extension of each file in the specified directory that matches <filename>.

/L displays the directory entries in lowercase letters.

Note: Beginning with version 5, you can use the Set command with a variable named dircmd to tailor directory listings to your preferences. For an example, see the entry on the Set command.

Examples

To display the directory entry of each file with the extension DOC in the current directory on the disk in drive A:

```
C:\>dir a:*.doc
```

To display the directory entry of each file in the directory \MKT\WP on the disk in the current drive, in wide format:

```
C:\>dir \mkt\wp /w
```

To display the directory entry of each file in the parent directory (MKT) of the current directory on the disk in the current drive, pausing after each screenful:

```
C:\MKT>dir .. /p
```

To display the directory entry of each file without an extension in the current directory on the disk in the current drive:

```
C:\>dir *.
```

To display only subdirectories (not files) in the current directory:

```
C:\>dir /a:d
```

To display files (but not subdirectories) in the current directory:

```
C:\>dir /a:-d
```

To display the files in the current directory alphabetically by extension:

```
C:\>dir /o:e
```

To display the files in the current directory in order from newest to oldest, placing directories at the end of the listing:

```
C:\>dir /o:-d /o:-g
```

DISK COMPARE (DISKCOMP)
Compare Two Diskettes
Versions 3.2 and later, IBM releases 1.0 and later

Page 112

The Diskcomp command compares two diskettes of the same size and capacity track by track and reports the side and track of any sectors that differ. If the diskettes are identical, Diskcomp reports *Compare OK*. Because it compares the tracks of the diskettes without regard to the names of the files, Diskcomp does not report that two diskettes containing the same files are identical if the files are stored in different locations.

The Diskcomp command automatically determines the number of sides and sectors per track from the disk in the first drive specified (which it calls the source). You cannot compare a diskette in a double-sided drive to a diskette in a single-sided drive, nor can you compare two diskettes with different numbers of sectors per track. You can, however, use the Diskcomp parameters to compare just one side of diskettes in double-sided drives, or just the first 8 sectors of each track on diskettes written with 9 sectors per track.

Note: The Diskcomp command cannot be used with a fixed disk, with a drive created or affected by an Assign, Join, or Substitute command, or with a network drive.

diskcomp <drive1> <drive2> /1 /8

<drive1> is the letter of the diskette drive, followed by a colon, that contains the first diskette to be compared (such as *a:*).

<drive2> is the letter of the diskette drive, followed by a colon, that contains the second diskette to be compared.

If you have two diskette drives and one is the current drive, specifying only the second drive in the Diskcomp command causes DOS to compare the diskette in the second drive to the diskette in the current drive.

If you have one diskette drive and it is the current drive, Diskcomp prompts you through a one-drive comparison if you type the command in any of the following forms: *diskcomp, diskcomp a:, diskcomp a: a:, diskcomp b:,* or *diskcomp a: b:.*

If you have a fixed disk and it is the current drive, you must specify both <drive1> and <drive2> because Diskcomp is for diskettes only.

/1 compares only the first side of the diskettes, even if they are in double-sided diskette drives.

/8 compares only the first 8 sectors of each track, even if the diskettes have more sectors per track.

After it has compared the diskettes, the Diskcomp command prompts *Compare more diskettes (Y/N)?* If you reply *y*, it again prompts you to insert the source and target diskettes in the specified drives.

Examples

To compare the diskette in drive A to the diskette in drive B:

```
C:\>diskcomp a: b:
```

If you have only one diskette drive, Diskcomp tells you when to swap diskettes.

To compare the first side of the diskette in drive A to the first side of the diskette in the current drive (B):

```
B>diskcomp a: /1
```

To compare two diskettes using only the current drive (A):

```
A>diskcomp
```

DISKCOPY
Copy a Complete Diskette
Versions 2.0 and later

Page 110

The Diskcopy command makes a sector-by-sector copy of a diskette. If the target diskette isn't formatted to match the source diskette, Diskcopy formats the diskette for you in versions 4 and 5 and in all earlier IBM releases of DOS.

Because the Diskcopy command makes an identical copy, it does not consolidate fragmented files; to consolidate fragmented files, use the Copy command and specify *.* to copy all files from the source diskette to the target diskette.

Note: The Diskcopy command cannot be used with a fixed disk, with a drive created or affected by an Assign, Join, or Substitute command, or with a network drive. You cannot use Diskcopy with dissimilar diskette types—for example, a 720 K and a 1.2 MB diskette.

diskcopy <source> <target> /1 /V

<source> is the letter, followed by a colon, of the diskette drive that contains the diskette to be copied (such as *a:*). If you enter only one drive letter, DOS assumes it contains the source diskette.

<target> is the letter of the diskette drive, followed by a colon, that contains the diskette to which <source> is copied.

If you have two diskette drives and one is the current drive, specifying only the second drive in the Diskcopy command causes DOS to copy from the diskette in the second drive to the diskette in the current drive.

If you have one diskette drive and it is the current drive, Diskcopy prompts you through a one-drive copy if you type the command in any of the following forms: *diskcopy, diskcopy a:, diskcopy a: a:, diskcopy b:,* or *diskcopy a: b:.*

If you have a fixed disk and it is the current drive, you must specify both <source> and <target> because Diskcopy is for diskettes only.

/1 copies only the first side of <source>, even if <source> is a double-sided diskette.

/V verifies that the copy is indeed an exact copy of the source disk. Using this switch causes Diskcopy to take longer to complete the process (version 5 only).

After it has copied the diskette, DOS prompts *Copy another (Y/N)?* If you reply *y*, DOS prompts you to insert the source and target diskettes. After ending the Diskcopy command by replying *n* to the concluding prompt, you can verify the copy with the Diskcomp command.

The Diskcopy command reports the side, track, and sector of any disk errors it encounters. If these sectors contain valid data, the copy may not be usable.

Examples

To copy the diskette in drive A to the diskette in drive B:

```
C:\>diskcopy a: b:
```

If you have only one diskette drive, DOS prompts you through a one-drive copy.

On a system with two diskette drives, to copy the first side of the diskette in drive B to the first side of the diskette in the current drive (A):

```
A>diskcopy b: /1
```

To copy a diskette using only the current drive (A):

```
A>diskcopy
```

DOS (CONFIGURATION COMMAND)
Load DOS into High Memory

Version 5.0

Page 372

The Dos configuration command, new with version 5, tailors DOS to use memory above 640 K, the upper limit of conventional memory, and thus leave more room for programs and data. In order to function correctly, the Dos command requires a computer with extended memory (above 1 MB), reserved memory (the upper memory area between 640 K and 1 MB), or both. Depending on the parameters you use, your computer must also be based on an 80286, 80386, or 80486 microprocessor.

On an 80286, 80386, or 80486 machine with extended memory, the Dos command can be used with the *high* parameter to tell DOS to load part of itself into the first 64 K of extended memory—the region known as the high memory area, or HMA. On a computer with at least 350 K of extended memory, the Dos command can be used with the *umb* parameter to enable loading of device drivers and other programs into available portions of the upper memory area known as upper memory blocks (UMBs).

Because the Dos command deals with memory that is not normally accessible to DOS, it is used with the Device configuration command and two device drivers: HIMEM.SYS, which manages extended memory, and EMM386.EXE (or a comparable program), which manages extended/expanded memory and provides access to UMBs. The examples at the end of this entry show such commands. Like other configuration commands, the Dos command belongs in the file CONFIG.SYS.

dos=high/low,umb/noumb

high tells DOS to load part of itself into the HMA whenever you start or restart the computer. In order to succeed, this command must be accompanied in CONFIG.SYS by a Device command that tells DOS where to find HIMEM.SYS, the program that manages extended memory.

low tells DOS to load itself into conventional memory. If you don't use the Dos command, DOS assumes *low*. If you specify *high* but DOS can't find or use the HMA at startup, it loads itself into conventional memory instead.

umb (for *upper memory blocks*) tells DOS to allow device drivers and other programs to be loaded into the upper memory area. The actual loading of programs is done by the Devicehigh and Loadhigh commands described in Chapter 17 and elsewhere in this appendix.

noumb (for *no upper memory blocks*) tells DOS not to allow device drivers and other programs to be loaded into the upper memory area. If you don't use the Dos command, DOS assumes *noumb*.

You can use both the *high/low* and *umb/noumb* parameters in the same command.

Examples

To load DOS into the HMA on an 80286-based computer (such as an IBM PC/AT) with at least 64 K of extended memory, put the following commands in CONFIG.SYS:

```
device=c:\dos\himem.sys
dos=high
```

(The example assumes that HIMEM.SYS is in the C:\DOS directory.)

To load DOS into the HMA and allow device drivers and other programs to be loaded into the upper memory area on an 80386-based computer (such as an IBM PS/2 Model 80) with 350 K or more of extended memory, put the following commands in CONFIG.SYS:

```
device=c:\dos\himem.sys
device=c:\dos\emm386.exe noems
dos=high,umb
```

The example assumes that HIMEM.SYS, the extended memory manager, and EMM386.EXE, the program that manages upper memory blocks, are both in C:\DOS. The *noems* option used with EMM386.EXE tells DOS you don't need access to both the upper memory area and expanded memory. If you do need both, use the *ram* parameter described in the entry EMM386.EXE.

DOSKEY
Command History and Macro Recorder
Version 5.0

Pages 293, 311

Doskey, available with version 5 of DOS, performs two main tasks: It maintains a log of the commands that you type, and it records sequences of keystrokes for later playback as macros. Doskey is something like an editor, but one that works on commands rather than on documents or other files. Typing *doskey* causes DOS to load the program into memory, where it remains until you restart your system. As you work, you can then retrieve, edit, and carry out earlier commands without retyping them. In addition, you can create macros by assigning short, easy-to-remember names to long, complex, or often-used sequences of DOS commands.

doskey /insert /overstrike /reinstall /bufsize=<size> /macros /history <macro>=<commands>

doskey, typed with no parameters, tells DOS to install the Doskey program.

/insert causes Doskey to insert text rather than replace characters as you edit commands and macros.

/overstrike causes Doskey to type over (replace) existing characters with those you type. If you don't specify */insert* or */overstrike*, Doskey assumes */overstrike*.

/reinstall causes Doskey to load a new copy of the program into memory. When you reinstall Doskey, previously recorded commands and macros are no longer available for use. The old copy remains in memory, but the new copy takes over the tasks of recording commands and macros.

/bufsize=<size> is the size (in bytes) of the storage area (called the buffer) in which Doskey saves commands as you enter them. You can specify */bufsize* only when you start or reinstall Doskey. If you don't specify */bufsize*, Doskey assumes 512 bytes—enough for about 25 commands, each about 20 characters long. The smallest value you can use for <size> is 256.

/macros (or */m*) tells Doskey to display all macros currently in memory.

/history (or */h*) tells Doskey to display all commands currently in memory. If you've used Doskey to create macros, you can use the */history* parameter with the redirection symbol (>) to send the commands to a file—a batch file, for example, so that you can save and reuse the macros in a later session.

<macro>=<commands> tells Doskey to create the macro named <macro> and save it in memory. <macro> is the name you want to assign to a set of commands; <commands> are the DOS commands to be carried out whenever you type the macro name. To delete a macro, omit the <commands> part of the parameter; that is, type the macro name followed by an equal sign, and then press Enter.

You can include multiple commands in a macro by separating them with a dollar sign followed by the letter *t* ($t). You can also use replaceable parameters, which function just as they do in batch files but are typed with a dollar sign rather than a percent sign ($1 through $9 instead of %1 through %9).

Just as the Prompt command lets you include character combinations that begin with $ to represent characters you can't type, Doskey lets you include the combinations shown in Figure C-3. Doskey also uses special editing keys, described in Chapter 13, ''Taking Control of Your System,'' Figure 13-3.

Character	Use
$g	Redirect output; same function as >.
gg	Append output; same function as >>.
$l	Redirect input; same function as <.
$b	Pipe output to another command; same function as ¦.
$t	Separate commands.
$$	Dollar sign (for use in file names).
$1–$9	Replaceable parameters; same function as %1–%9 in batch files.
$*	Special-purpose replaceable parameter used to include everything typed after the macro name as part of the parameter.

Figure C-3. *Doskey special character combinations.*

Examples

To load the Doskey program:

```
C:\>doskey
```

To reinstall Doskey and specify a 256-byte buffer:

```
C:\>doskey /reinstall /bufsize=256
```

To save the commands currently in memory by redirecting them to a file named MINE.TXT:

```
C:\>doskey /h > mine.txt
```

To create a macro that formats a 360 K diskette in whatever diskette drive you specify on the command line:

```
C:\>doskey 360=format $1 /f:360
```

To format the diskette in drive A, you would type *360 a:*.
To display the macros currently in memory:

```
C:\>doskey /m
```

DOSSHELL
Start the DOS Shell
Versions 4 and 5

Page 209
Dosshell is the command that starts the DOS Shell, the program that provides a visual environment in which you use menus and graphics, rather than typed commands, to work with DOS, your applications, and your data files.

The Shell has been modified both functionally and in appearance between versions 4 and 5 of DOS. Both versions are easier to use than DOS commands; the version 5 Shell is faster and makes more use of graphics than its version 4 predecessor. Use of the Shell in its version 5 form is described in Chapter 10, ''The DOS Shell.''

The following command format and examples apply to the version 5 Shell.

dosshell /T:<res> /G:<res> /B

/T starts the Shell in text (character mode). <res> is an optional letter, such as L for low or H for high that specifies screen resolution. The values you can use depend on your display hardware. If you don't know what resolutions are available, start the Shell without any parameters and choose the Display command on the Options menu to see a list of display modes that can run on your system.

/G starts the Shell in graphics mode; as with /T, you can specify a particular resolution if you want.

/B starts the Shell in black-and-white rather than color.

Examples

To start the version 5 Shell in text mode on a system capable of graphics:

```
C:\>dosshell /t
```

To start the Shell in black and white on a color monitor:

```
C:\>dosshell /b
```

DRIVE PARAMETERS—DRIVPARM (CONFIGURATION COMMAND)
Define a Disk or Tape Drive
Versions 3.2 and later, non-IBM releases only

The Drive Parameters configuration command (drivparm) defines the operating characteristics of a disk drive or tape drive. If you don't specify device characteristics with Drivparm, DOS assumes standard characteristics for that type of device. In general, you need to use the Drivparm command only when you need to change the way DOS defines a disk or tape drive on your system. If you need more information, refer to the documentation that came with the drive and with your version of DOS.

ECHO (BATCH COMMAND)
Display a Message
Versions 2.0 and later

Page 321

The Echo command sends a message to the standard output device (usually the display), controls whether DOS displays commands as it carries them out (echo on), or displays the status of echo (on or off). DOS turns echo on when it starts carrying out the commands in a batch file, unless the file is started by another batch file that has turned echo off.

> **echo on off <message>**
>
> *on* tells DOS to display each command as it is carried out.
> *off* tells DOS not to display each command as it is carried out.
> <message> is a message to be sent to standard output.
>
> If you enter an Echo command with no parameters (just type *echo*), DOS displays the status of echo (either *ECHO is on* or *ECHO is off*).
>
> To avoid displaying a line in a batch file, start the line with the @ symbol (versions 3.3 and later). To echo blank lines to the screen and improve the appearance of a batch file, either type *echo* followed immediately by a period (*echo.*) or type *echo*, hold down the Alt key, and press 255 on the numeric keypad.

Examples

To turn echo on:

```
echo on
```

To turn echo off:

```
echo off
```

To display a blank line, the message *Put the backup diskette in drive A*, and another blank line:

```
@echo.
@echo Put the backup diskette in drive A
@echo.
```

To display the echo status:

```
C:\>echo
```

EDIT
Create or Change Text Files
Version 5.0

Page 245

The Edit command starts the MS-DOS Editor, a text editor that allows you to choose from menus to create, change, and save files. Edit is new with version 5.0 and is included with DOS as an alternative to the line-oriented Edlin text editor that has been part of DOS since version 1.

The MS-DOS Editor, called Edit for short in this book, is described in Chapter 11, "Creating and Editing Files of Text." The program's on-screen help can also be used both for learning and as a reference tool. Edit offers two types of help: general information and context-sensitive help that can be requested after a command is chosen.

Note: In order to run Edit, DOS must be able to find the file QBASIC.EXE. Be sure this file is in the command path.

edit <filename> /B /G /H /NOHI

<filename> is the name of an existing file you want to view or edit. Omit <filename> to start Edit without loading a file into memory.

/B starts Edit in monochrome if you have a color monitor.

/G used with a CGA display and adapter causes Edit to update the screen contents as rapidly as possible. If this parameter produces white streaks or dots on the screen, restart the editor without /G.

/H causes Edit to display as many lines per screen as your monitor can manage.

/NOHI tells Edit that your display does not support high-intensity characters (bright white, for example).

The following lists briefly describe each of the menus used with Edit.

File menu: Used for creating, loading, saving, and printing files. It also quits the editor. The File commands are:

▶ New—creates a new file. If another document is on the screen, Edit prompts you to save or close the open file or to cancel the File New command.

▶ Open—opens an existing file. This command causes the editor to display a dialog box. The dialog box asks for the name of the file to open and also includes a list of other drives and directories you can choose from if the file is not on the current drive or in the current directory.

▶ Save—saves the current file under the name already assigned to it. If the file has not been named, the editor asks you to name it.

▶ Save As—both names and saves a file. This command produces a dialog box in which you enter the name you want to give the file and, optionally, choose a different drive, directory, or both in which to save the file.

▶ Print—prints the current file. This command produces a dialog box in which you can choose to print the entire document or a selected portion of it.

▶ Exit—quits the editor. If you choose File Exit before saving the latest changes to a file, the editor prompts you to save or close the file or to cancel the command.

Edit menu: Lets you rearrange a file by cutting, copying, and inserting text in different locations. When you cut text, you delete it from the document; when you copy text, you duplicate it in another part of the document. Edit temporarily stores cut or copied text in a special area of memory called the Clipboard. The Edit commands are:

▶ Cut—deletes selected text to the Clipboard, where it remains until replaced by other text you cut or copy.

▶ Copy—copies selected text to the Clipboard, where it remains until replaced by other text you cut or copy.

▶ Paste—inserts the text most recently cut or copied to the Clipboard in the document at the cursor location.

▶ Clear—deletes selected text without placing it on the Clipboard. Text deleted with this command cannot be retrieved.

Search menu: Searches the current document for a string of characters you specify. Searches begin at the current cursor position and cycle back to the beginning of the document if necessary. The commands on the Search menu are:

▶ Find—searches for a particular string. This command produces a dialog box that asks you to specify the string, choose to match or ignore uppercase and lowercase letters, and either limit the search to complete words (occurrences of the string surrounded by blanks) or include occurrences found as part of other words (for example, *whole* in *wholesome*).

▶ Repeat Last Find—repeats the last search. If no earlier search has been performed, this command searches for the next occurrence of the word the cursor is on (or the word to the left of the cursor if it is between words).

▶ Change—replaces one string with another. This command produces a dialog box that allows you to specify the string to change and the string to change it to, whether to match or ignore uppercase and lowercase, whether to limit the search to whole words, and whether the editor is to confirm before making each change.

Options menu: Controls the screen and lets you set the path to Edit's online help (stored in a file named EDIT.HLP). The Options commands are:

▶ Display—controls three screen features: color, the display of scroll bars at the side and bottom of the screen, and the number of spaces in each tab.

▶ Help Path—sets the path to EDIT.HLP.

Help menu: At the top right corner of the screen, provides access to online help. The Help commands are:

▶ Getting Started—includes help on using Edit, help on getting help, and help on starting the editor with various options.

▶ Keyboard—tells you about the keystrokes used with Edit.

▶ About—displays version and copyright information about Edit.

EDLIN
Create or Modify a Text File
Versions 1.0 and later

Page 263

Edlin is the line-oriented text editor shipped with all versions of DOS since 1.0. It includes a variety of commands for inserting, deleting, changing, copying, and moving lines. Each line can be up to 253 characters long. In addition to the Edlin commands, you can use the DOS editing keys to edit individual lines.

Edlin is called a line-oriented editor because it displays a line number at the beginning of each line; these numbers are for reference only and are not part of the file. Edlin renumbers lines after any command that changes the sequence or number of lines in the file, to maintain an unbroken sequence.

When you enter the Edlin command (type *edlin* followed by a file name) at the system prompt, Edlin loads the file to be edited (or creates it, if it's a new file), displays an asterisk (its prompt), and waits for a command.

Most Edlin commands consist of a single character preceded by one or more parameters (usually line numbers). The command characters can be entered in either uppercase or lowercase, and you can enter more than one command on a line by separating them with semicolons.

Just as DOS keeps track of a current drive and current directory, Edlin keeps track of the *current line,* which is the target for many commands if you don't specify a line number. Many of the Edlin commands operate on a range of lines, which you define by specifying the beginning and ending line numbers.

All Edlin commands that accept a line number or range of line numbers recognize the following symbolic references:

#	means the line after the last line in the file
.	(a period) means the current line
+ or –	specifies line numbers relative to the current line; for example, +3 means three lines past the current line

When you end an editing session and write a revised file back to disk, Edlin renames the original version to give it the extension BAK, thus saving a backup copy of the original. If a file with the same name and the extension BAK exists on the same disk, Edlin deletes the existing file before renaming the original.

To start Edlin, you enter the Edlin command at the DOS system prompt.

edlin <filename> /B

<filename> is the name of the text file to be created or changed. If the file exists, Edlin copies it into memory. If the file doesn't exist, Edlin creates it. Except in version 3.3, Edlin won't edit a file whose extension is BAK. To edit a file whose extension is BAK, first change the extension with the DOS Rename command.

/B causes Edlin to ignore any Control-Z (end-of-file) characters in the file.

Brief descriptions of Edlin commands follow, with examples showing representative uses of each.

Append: Reads additional lines of a file into memory. Use Append when a file is larger than 75 percent of available memory.

<lines>a

<lines> specifies the number of lines to append.

For example, to append 200 lines to the file in memory:

```
*200a
```

Copy: Copies one or more lines from one place in a file to another.

<from>,<to>,<target>,<count>c

<from> is the number of the first line to be copied; <to> is the number of the last. <target> is the number of the line *above* which the lines are to be copied. <count> specifies how many times the lines are to be copied. If you omit <from>, <to>, or both, be sure to type their trailing comma(s) in your command.

The following examples assume that line 20 is the current line. To copy lines 20 through 25 above line 5:

```
*20,25,5c
```

To copy line 20 above line 30:

```
*20,20,30c
```

or, using symbolic references:

```
*,,+10c
```

Delete: Deletes specified lines from a file.

<from>,<to>d

<from> is the number of the first line to be deleted; <to> is the number of the last. If you omit <from>, be sure to type its trailing comma in your command. If you omit both <from> and <to> and simply type *d*, Edlin deletes the current line.

The following examples assume that line 20 is the current line. To delete lines 20 through 25:

```
*20,25d
```

or, using symbolic references:

```
*,+5d
```

To delete the current line:

```
*d
```

Edit: Not strictly a command. To edit a line, type the line number and press Enter. You can edit the current line by typing a period and pressing Enter. You can edit the line that follows the current line by just pressing Enter.

<line> or .

<line> is the number of the line to be edited.

The following examples assume that line 20 is the current line. Pressing the Enter key is represented by <Enter>. To edit line 25:

```
*25<Enter>
```

or, using symbolic references:

```
*+5<Enter>
```

To edit the current line (line 20):

```
*.<Enter>
```

To edit line 21:

```
*<Enter>
```

End Edit: Ends the editing session and writes the current file to disk. (To end the session without saving the file, you use the Quit command, described later.)

```
e
```

The End Edit command has no parameters. To end the editing session and save the current file:

```
*e
```

Insert: Enters new lines into the file being edited. Edlin prompts with the number of the new line and continues to prompt until you press Ctrl-C to stop inserting lines.

<target>i

<target> is the line before which the new line(s) are to be inserted. If you don't specify <target>, the lines are inserted above the current line. To add lines to the end of the file, you can specify <target> as # or as a number larger than the highest line number in the file.

The following examples assume that line 20 is the current line. To insert lines after line 20:

```
*21i
```

To insert lines at the beginning of the file:

```
*1i
```

To insert lines at the end of the file:

```
*#i
```

List: Displays one or more lines of the file.

<from>,<to>l

<from> is the number of the first line to be displayed; <to> is the number of the last. If you don't specify <from>, Edlin starts 11 lines before the current line. If you don't specify <to>, Edlin displays one screenful starting with <from>. If you omit <from>, be sure to type the trailing comma in your command. If you omit both <from> and <to> and simply type *l*, Edlin displays one screenful centered around the current line.

The following examples assume that the current line is 30. To list lines 30 through 40:

```
*30,40l
```

To list one screenful centered around the current line:

```
*l
```

Move: Moves one or more specified lines from one location in a file to another, deleting them from the original location.

<from>,<to>,<target>m

<from> is the number of the first line to be moved; <to> is the number of the last; <target> is the line above which the line or lines are to be moved. If you omit <from>, Edlin starts with the current line. If you omit <to>, Edlin stops with the current line. If you omit <from>, <to>, or both, be sure to type the trailing comma(s) in your command.

The following examples assume that line 20 is the current line. To move lines 20 through 25 above line 5:

```
*20,25,5m
```

To move line 20 above line 30:

```
*20,20,30m
```

or, using symbolic references:

```
*,,30m
```

Page: Displays up to one screenful of a file at a time.

<from>,<to>p

<from> is the number of the first line to be displayed; <to> is the number of the last. If you omit <from>, Edlin starts with the line after the current line. If you omit <to>, Edlin displays one screenful starting with <from>. If you omit <from>, be sure to type the trailing comma. If you omit both <from> and <to> and simply type *p*, Edlin displays one screenful, starting with the line after the current line.

The following examples assume that the current line is 30. To display lines 30 through 40:

```
*30,40p
```

To display one screenful, starting with the line after the current line:

```
*p
```

Quit: Ends an editing session without saving the current file. The Quit command has no parameters. To avoid inadvertent loss of a file, however, Edlin prompts for confirmation before quitting.

q

To quit the editing session without saving the current file:

`*q`

Edlin responds:

Abort edit (Y/N)?

Press Y to quit; press N to remain in Edlin.

Replace: Replaces one character string with another in one or more lines of a file. You can tell Edlin to prompt for confirmation before each replacement by including a question mark (?) in the command.

<from>,<to>?r<string1><Ctrl-Z or F6><string2>

<from> is the number of the first line in which the string is to be replaced; <to> is the number of the last. The ? tells Edlin to prompt before replacement. <string1> is the string to be replaced; <string2> is the replacement string. You must separate the two strings by pressing Ctrl-Z or the F6 key. If you omit <from>, be sure to type the trailing comma in your command.

The following examples assume that line 20 is the current line. To replace all occurrences of *company* with *corporation* in lines 21 through 30:

`*21,30rcompany<Ctrl-Z>corporation`

To replace all occurrences of *March* with *April* from line 21 through the end of the file, requesting a prompt before each replacement:

`*21,#?rMarch<Ctrl-Z>April`

Search: Searches a file for a specified string of characters. Because the file might contain more than one occurrence of the string, you can tell Edlin to prompt for confirmation before stopping the search.

<from>,<to>?s<string>

<from> is the number of the first line to be searched; <to> is the number of the last. The ? tells Edlin to prompt for confirmation before ending the search. <string> is the string to search for. If you omit <from>, be sure to type the trailing comma in your command.

The following examples assume that line 20 is the current line. To find the first occurrence of *value* in lines 21 through 30:

`*21,30svalue`

To find a particular occurrence of *value*, searching the entire file and instructing Edlin to prompt for confirmation:

```
*1,#?svalue
```

Transfer: Merges the contents of another file into the current file.

<target>t<filename>

<target> is the number of the line above which the incoming file will be transferred. If you don't specify <target>, Edlin assumes the current line. <filename> is the name of the file whose contents are to be transferred. In versions 3 and later, you can include a directory path with <filename>.

The following example assumes that line 20 is the current line. To merge the contents of REPORT.DOC above line 20:

```
*20treport.doc
```

or

```
*treport.doc
```

Write: Starting at the beginning of the current file, writes a specified number of lines from memory to disk. Write makes room for more lines to be read into memory with the Append command.

<lines>w

<lines> specifies the number of lines to write. If you omit <lines>, Edlin writes lines until available memory is 25 percent full.

For example, to write 200 lines to disk:

```
*200w
```

EMM386
Enable and Disable Expanded Memory
Version 5.0

The version 5 EMM386 command works with the EMM386.EXE device driver described in the following entry. You can use the EMM386 command to control access to expanded memory on a computer with an 80386 or 80486 microprocessor.

EMM386 on off auto

on enables access to expanded memory controlled by the EMM386.EXE device driver.

off suspends access to expanded memory, making this type of memory temporarily unavailable to programs requesting it.

auto provides access to expanded memory only if a program requests it.

This command includes two additional parameters, *w=on*, and *w=off*, that apply to a computer with a Weitek coprocessor. If you need this additional support, refer to the documentation that came with your version of DOS.

EMM386.EXE
Simulate Expanded Memory and
Provide Access to Upper Memory Blocks

Page 371

EMM386.EXE is the name of a device driver included with version 5 of DOS. This program has two functions: to treat extended memory as if it were expanded memory, and to provide access to the upper memory area located between 640 K and 1 MB. As its name implies, EMM386.EXE requires a computer based on the 80386 (or 80486) microprocessor.

To use EMM386.EXE (or the related EMM386 command), you must tell DOS this device driver exists by including a Device command in your CONFIG.SYS file. EMM386.EXE includes a number of parameters, most of which are useful primarily to programmers and are beyond the scope of this book. The basic form for identifying the device driver is:

device=<path>emm376.exe <size> ram noems

<path> specifies the path to the file EMM386.EXE. Most likely, it is C:\DOS. If you don't specify <path>, DOS looks in the root directory of the system disk.

<size> specifies the amount of extended memory, in kilobytes, that you want to use as if it were expanded memory. You do this for programs that can use expanded memory but not extended memory. The amount you need depends on the memory requirements of your programs. <size> can be any value from 16 through 32768. If you don't include <size>, DOS assumes 256; if you specify a value that can't be divided evenly by 16, DOS rounds the value down to the nearest multiple of 16.

ram allows you to use both expanded memory and blocks of memory (UMBs) in the upper memory area.

noems provides access to the upper memory area, but not to any expanded memory. Use either *ram* or *noems* if you plan to load device drivers or programs into reserved memory with the Devicehigh configuration command or the Loadhigh command.

Example

Because memory management is a complex task for DOS, you include several related commands in CONFIG.SYS along with the Device command you use to identify EMM386.EXE. The following example shows a sample CONFIG.SYS file that includes the commands you need. In this example, the Dos command is used both to load DOS into high memory and to enable DOS to use UMBs. The Device command identifying EMM386.EXE requests access to the upper memory area but not to expanded memory, and the sample Devicehigh command loads the ANSI.SYS device driver into reserved memory.

```
dos=high,umb
device=c:\dos\himem.sys
device=c:\dos\emm386.exe noems
devicehigh=c:\dos\ansi.sys
```

ERASE

Erase a File

See Delete.

EXE2BIN

Convert an Executable (EXE) File to COM Format

Versions 1.0 and later

The Exe2bin command converts a program command file from EXE format to COM format. Exe2bin is an advanced DOS command, usually used by programmers, and a description of its use is beyond the scope of this book; if you need details, refer to the DOS *Technical Reference* or the *Programmer's Reference* manual.

EXIT

Leave COMMAND.COM

Versions 2.0 and later

Page 231

The Exit command leaves the currently active version of COMMAND.COM and returns control of the system to the program from which that version was started. Essentially, the Exit command returns you to a prior task.

COMMAND.COM is the part of DOS that interacts with you by waiting for and responding to commands. When you or a program activates COMMAND.COM, you start a version of it, adding a new layer to the processes DOS keeps track of in the system. For example, if you're using the DOS Shell and leave it by choosing Command Prompt from the Main window, you start a new version of COMMAND.COM. That's why you must type *exit* to return to the Shell. You're exiting one copy of COMMAND.COM and returning to the program from which you started it.

The Exit command has no parameters:

exit

The command has no effect if COMMAND.COM was activated by a Command command with the /P (for *permanent*) parameter.

EXPAND

Expand Compressed DOS Files

Version 5.0

Expand is the name of a utility program that can be used to transfer individual DOS files from the original DOS diskettes to a working DOS disk, such as a fixed disk. This program is included with DOS because command files in version 5 are stored on the DOS diskettes in a special compressed format. Compressed files have extensions ending in an underscore (for example, COMMAND.CO_). They are not usable in compressed form, and they cannot be transferred to a working DOS disk with Copy, Replace, or a similar command. Expand decompresses such a file, at the same time placing the file in a target disk or directory you specify.

> **expand <source> <target>**

<source> is the drive, path, and file name of the compressed file you want to expand. You cannot use wild cards to expand more than one file at a time.

<target> is the destination drive, path and file name of the expanded file. When you expand a file, use the same file name, but replace the underscore with the letter needed to form a recognizable DOS extension; for example, change CO_ to COM, SY_ to SYS, or EX_ to EXE.

Example

Suppose you deleted the SMARTDRV.SYS and RAMDRIVE.SYS files from your \DOS directory because your computer did not have either extended or expanded memory and you wanted to reduce the amount of storage space needed by DOS on the fixed disk. You recently added an extra-memory board and now want to reinstate the two files you deleted. To expand the files and place them in C:\DOS, first place your DOS diskette labeled *Disk 1* in drive A and type *type a:packing.lst ¦ more* to see which DOS diskette contains the files. Then place the DOS diskette with SMARTDRV.SY_ and RAMDRIVE.SY_ in drive A and type:

```
C:\>expand a:smartdrv.sy_ c:\dos\smartdrv.sys
```

and

```
C:\>expand a:ramdrive.sy_ c:\dos\ramdrive.sys
```

FASTOPEN

Speed Up File Access

Versions 3.3 and later

Page 383

The Fastopen command tells DOS to keep in memory the storage locations of subdirectories and files on one or more fixed disks that have been used during the current session. When the Fastopen command is used, DOS checks in memory before searching the disk whenever it is told to find a file or a subdirectory. If the file or subdirectory has already been used, its disk location is in memory, and DOS can go directly to the storage location, instead of searching through each directory in the path. Fastopen cannot be used to keep track of files stored on diskettes or on a network drive.

If you and your applications tend to use the same files or directories over and over, the Fastopen command can make your system noticeably faster. You can enter the Fastopen command only once during a session with DOS, so if you want to increase or decrease the number of files and directories Fastopen tracks, you must restart your system.

fastopen <drive>=<files> /X

<drive> is the drive letter, followed by a colon, of the fixed disk whose files and subdirectories you want DOS to track. The drive letter must refer to a fixed disk.

<files> is the number of file and subdirectory locations DOS is to keep in memory. The number of files must be separated from <drive> by an equal sign. You can specify up to 999 files; each file requires about 50 bytes of memory. If you don't specify <files>, DOS keeps track of the last 48 files and subdirectories (this number varies in different releases of DOS).

/X keeps Fastopen information in expanded memory (versions 4 and 5).

Because your CONFIG.SYS or AUTOEXEC.BAT file might already include a Fastopen command, check their contents before entering the command at the system prompt. If you do use Fastopen and find that it does speed your system, you can put the command in either CONFIG.SYS or AUTOEXEC.BAT in the forms shown in the following examples.

Examples

To keep track of the last 30 files and subdirectories used on the fixed disk in drive C, you can type the following command or put it in AUTOEXEC.BAT:

```
fastopen c:=30
```

Assuming that the file FASTOPEN.EXE is in C:\DOS, the following command in CONFIG.SYS is equivalent to the command in the preceding example:

```
install=c:\dos\fastopen.exe c:=30
```

FC (FILE COMPARISON)
Compare Two Files
Versions 2.0 and later, primarily non-IBM releases

The File Comparison command (fc) compares two files and sends the differences to standard output—normally the display. By redirecting output, you can also send the results of a comparison to a file or to another device, such as a printer.

Note: Another way to compare files is with the Compare command, available in IBM versions of DOS and in Microsoft's versions 3.3 and later. See the entry on Compare.

You can use FC to compare either text files or command files (program files with such extensions as EXE, COM, and SYS). Depending on the parameters you specify, you can compare files either line by line or byte by byte.

In a line-by-line comparison, FC starts by reading as many lines from each file as will fit in the portion of memory it uses (enough to hold 100 lines, unless you specify otherwise). It then compares the lines of the first file with the lines of the second. If it finds any differences, it displays the last line in each file that matched, the lines that don't match, and the first lines in each file that once again match.

When it finds differences, FC assumes that the lines of the two files are no longer synchronized—they don't correspond on a one-to-one basis. Unless you specify otherwise, FC looks for two sequential matching lines before it once again assumes the files are synchronized. If none of the succeeding lines in memory match up, FC displays the message *Resync failed. Files are too different* (***Files are different*** in some versions of DOS).

In a byte-by-byte, or binary, comparison, FC compares the two files from beginning to end. It does not display mismatched lines, but it does tell you which bytes, counting from the beginning of the file, are different, and it tells you what their coded values are in the hexadecimal (base-16) numbering system. If one file is shorter than the other, FC displays the message *FC: FILEx longer than FILEy* at the end of the comparison. Binary comparisons are primarily useful for checking nontext files, such as programs.

The FC command includes the following parameters:

fc /A /B /C /L /LB*n* /N /*nnnn* /T /W <filename1> <filename2>

/A tells FC to abbreviate its report, displaying only the first and last lines of each group of matched/mismatched lines (versions 3.2 and later).

/B specifies that the files are to be compared byte by byte. If you use /B, you cannot use any parameters other than <filename1> and <filename2>.

/C tells FC to ignore differences between uppercase and lowercase.

/L tells FC to compare the files as ASCII text. The command assumes this parameter for all text files (those without program-file extensions, such as COM, SYS, and EXE).

/LB*n*, where *n* is a number you supply, specifies how many lines FC reads into memory. If you omit *n* (specify just /LB), FC assumes 100.

/N tells FC to display line numbers in its report of an ASCII comparison.

/*nnnn*, where *nnnn* is a number you supply, tells FC how many matching lines it must find after a mismatch to assume the files again correspond on a line-by-line basis. If you don't specify /*nnnn*, FC assumes 2 lines (3 in versions through 3.2).

/T tells FC to treat tabs as tabs rather than as strings of spaces.

/W tells FC to convert tabs and consecutive spaces within a line to a single space.

<filename1> and <filename2> are the names of the files to be compared. Each can include a drive letter and a path, and you can include wildcard characters.

Examples

To compare two text files (C:\CLIENTS\MEMO.DOC and A:MEMO.DOC) line by line, using the values FC assumes:

```
C:\>fc c:\clients\memo.doc a:memo.doc
```

To compare the same files, displaying line numbers as part of the output:

```
C:\>fc /n c:\clients\memo.doc a:memo.doc
```

To compare the files, ignoring case and redirecting the output to the printer:

```
C:\>fc /c c:\clients\memo.doc a:memo.doc > prn
```

To perform a byte-by-byte comparison of two nontext files (Q1.DAT and JAN-MAR.DAT):

```
C:\>fc /b q1.dat jan-mar.dat
```

FCBS (CONFIGURATION COMMAND)
Set Maximum Open File Control Blocks (FCBs)
Versions 3.0 and later, IBM releases 3.1 and later

One of the two ways DOS keeps track of file usage is by means of small blocks of information called file control blocks, or FCBs. The FCBS configuration command lets you specify the largest number of files controlled by file control blocks that can be open at the same time when file sharing is in effect. The FCBS command also lets you protect some or all of the open files from being automatically closed. Unless you specify otherwise, DOS assumes four FCB-controlled files, none of them protected from closure.

You're unlikely to need the FCBS configuration command in everyday use of your computer. If you need more information on this command, refer to the documentation that came with your version of DOS.

FDISK
Configure a Fixed Disk
Versions 3.2 and later, IBM releases 2.0 and later

The Fdisk command prepares a fixed disk for use by DOS and, if you choose, by another operating system as well. In preparing the disk, Fdisk creates one or more independent areas—subsections—called *partitions*.

Computers are usually delivered with the fixed disk already prepared and, often, with DOS already installed and ready to start from the fixed disk. You use Fdisk if your fixed disk is not prepared, or if you decide to change or delete one or more partitions.

Warning: If you use Fdisk to modify a fixed disk that already contains information, be sure to back up any of the information you want to save before using Fdisk. Otherwise, you'll lose it all.

The Fdisk command has no parameters:

fdisk

When you type *fdisk*, you start a program that steps you through available choices and procedures via a series of question-and-answer menus. Fdisk uses a few terms you don't encounter in your everyday use of DOS, so the following definitions might help if you're planning to use Fdisk.

Partition: As mentioned earlier, a partition is a portion of the fixed disk. You can have two types of DOS partitions on a fixed disk: the *primary DOS partition* and an *extended DOS partition*.

The primary DOS partition is the one you dedicate to DOS. Beginning with version 4, the primary DOS partition can be any size, up to the full capacity of a fixed disk. In earlier versions, this partition can be no larger than 32 MB.

The extended DOS partition, available in versions 3.3 and later, lets you create a second partition and thus divide the storage space on a large fixed disk into two smaller units, both of them usable by DOS.

Active partition: This is the partition from which you start DOS. If you want DOS to start from your fixed disk, the primary DOS partition must also be the active partition. Fdisk lets you choose the active partition.

Logical drive: In relation to Fdisk, this is a portion of the extended DOS partition that you use as if it were a separate disk drive. A logical drive is not physically separate from your fixed disk, but DOS treats it as if it were. When you create a logical drive with Fdisk, you (or DOS) assign it a drive letter (such as D:) and a size (such as 20 MB). Each logical drive you create behaves—and can be treated—as if it were a real (physical) disk drive.

Cylinder: This is a way of referring to storage space on a fixed disk. You see this term if you're using Fdisk with version 3.3. The program tells you how large your fixed disk is (in cylinders) and, if you're creating an extended DOS partition, asks you how large the partition should be—again, in cylinders. You can estimate roughly how many cylinders equal a given percentage of your fixed disk by deciding on a percentage and then multiplying the total number of cylinders by that amount.

The actual process of using Fdisk is documented thoroughly in the manual that comes with DOS. Read these details carefully before you prepare or try to change a fixed disk, especially one that already contains programs or data.

FILES (CONFIGURATION COMMAND)
Set Maximum Open File Handles
Versions 2.0 and later

Page 380

One of the two ways DOS keeps track of file usage is by assigning a number called a *handle* to each open file. The Files configuration command sets the maximum number of files controlled by file handles that can be open at one time.

files=<number>

<number> specifies how many files can be open at the same time. It can be from 8 through 255; if you don't specify <number>, DOS assumes 8. Each additional open file above 8 increases the memory used by DOS.

When you install DOS, it might create or modify CONFIG.SYS to include a Files command. If a program you're using requires more open files, edit your CONFIG.SYS file or check the program's documentation for an appropriate Files command. If you need more information on this command, refer to the documentation that came with your version of DOS.

FIND
Search Files for a Character String
Versions 2.0 and later

Page 285

The Find filter command searches one or more files for a character string, and sends each line that contains the string to standard output (usually the display).

find /V /C /N /I "<string>" <filename>

/V finds lines that *don't* contain <string>.

/C sends the total number of lines (the *count*), rather than the lines themselves, to standard output. If you specify both /C and /N, the Find command ignores /N.

/N includes the line number with each line of output.

/I, beginning with version 5, tells Find to ignore uppercase and lowercase differences in the search.

"<string>" is the character string to search for. You must enclose the string in quotation marks. To include a quotation mark in <string>, type two quotation marks.

<filename> is the name of the file or files to be searched. You can specify more than one file name, separating them with spaces. If you omit <filename>, the Find

command searches its standard input; you can either redirect standard input or pipe the output of another command to the Find command. You can include a path, but you cannot use wildcards in <filename>.

Examples

To find all lines that contain the string *Sales* (note the capital *S*) in the file REPORT.DOC in the current directory:

    C:\MKT\WP>find "Sales" report.doc

To find all lines that contain the string *April* in the file LETTERS.DOC in the current directory, include the line numbers, and redirect the output to the printer:

    C:\MKT\WP>find /n "April" letters.doc > prn

With version 5 of DOS, to find all lines in REPORT.DOC that contain the word *company* in any combination of uppercase and lowercase letters:

    C:\MKT\WP>find /i "company" report.doc

In any version of DOS, to find all lines that don't contain the string <DIR> in the output of a Directory command:

    C:\>dir ¦ find /v "<DIR>"

Or, in version 5 only:

    C:\>dir ¦ find /i /v "<dir>"

(Note that the version 5 command *dir /a:-d* would be easier to use here.)

FOR (BATCH COMMAND)
Carry Out a Batch Command Several Times
Versions 2.0 and later

Page 345

The For batch command carries out a DOS command once for each member specified by a set of character strings, such as a set of file names.

    for %%p in (<set>) do <command> <parameters>

%%p is a replaceable parameter that is given the value of each member of <set> by DOS before <command> is carried out. It is represented by two percent signs (%%) followed by any character except one of the redirection symbols: <, >, or ¦.

<set> is a series of strings separated by blanks. <command> is carried out once for each member of <set>. If <set> is empty, <command> isn't carried out. <set> can contain character strings, path names, or file names. If one of the strings is a file name that includes wildcard characters, DOS sets %%p, in turn, to each file name that matches the wildcard character, then carries out <command>.

<command> is any DOS command except another For command. Through version 3.2, you can carry out another batch command without returning to the system prompt, by making <command> a Command command with the /C parameter and specifying the batch file as the string that follows the /C parameter (see the second example below). If you're using version 3.3 or later, you can accomplish the same thing by using the Call command.

<parameters> specifies any parameters needed by <command>.

Note: You can type a For command at the system prompt, rather than enter it in a batch file. If you do, use %p instead of %%p. Everything else is the same.

Examples

To copy up to nine files named in the batch command line to the current directory of the disk in drive A:

```
for %%p in (%1 %2 %3 %4 %5 %6 %7 %8 %9) do copy %%p a:
```

To carry out the batch files named BAT1.BAT, BAT2.BAT, and BAT3.BAT in versions 3.3 and later:

```
for %%p in (1 2 3) do call bat%%p
```

In versions prior to 3.3, the For command would be:

```
for %%p in (1 2 3) do command /c bat%%p
```

If you specified the command to be carried out as *bat%%p* (omitting *command /c*), DOS would return to the system prompt after carrying out BAT1.BAT.

FORMAT
Prepare a Disk
Versions 1.0 and later

Page 104

The Format command prepares a disk for use by DOS. Beginning with version 5, DOS normally carries out a safe format that can be undone with the Unformat command. Through version 4, however, formatting a disk destroys the directory information DOS uses to locate files. That means information previously stored on the disk can no longer be retrieved. Because inadvertent formatting can be inconvenient or can mean the loss of valuable programs and data, DOS does not begin to format a disk until you press Enter to verify that the disk you want to format is in the drive you specified.

Note: With DOS 3.1 and earlier, be careful to specify a drive letter and verify that the disk to be formatted is actually in that drive. If you don't specify the drive, these versions of DOS format the disk in the current drive, even if it's a system disk or a fixed disk.

Don't use Format with a drive affected by a Join or Substitute command. Format cannot be used with a network drive. The following description includes some parameters not mentioned in earlier chapters. Not all parameters are available with all versions of DOS.

format <drive> /1 /4 /8 /F:<size> /N:<sectors> /T:<tracks> /S /B /V:<label> /Q /U

<drive> is the letter of the drive, followed by a colon, that contains the disk to be formatted. Early versions of DOS don't require <drive>, but including the drive letter with every Format command is a good habit to form.

/1, a parameter that maintains compatibility with older computers and early versions of DOS, formats only the first side of a 5.25-inch diskette, even if the disk is in a double-sided drive.

/4 formats a 5.25-inch, 360 K diskette in a 1.2 MB drive. If used with the /1 parameter, /4 formats a 180 K diskette. Diskettes formatted with this parameter in a high-capacity drive do not always work reliably in a 180 K or a 360 K drive.

/8, another parameter that maintains compatibility with older systems, formats a 5.25-inch diskette for 8 sectors per track (320 K diskette capacity).

/F:<size> specifies the capacity (in kilobytes) for which the diskette should be formatted. Valid entries for <size> are 160, 180, 320, 360, 720, 1200, 1440, and (in version 5), 2880. The following examples, using 1200 K as a model, show the various ways you can specify <size>: 1200, 1200K, 1200KB, 1.2, 1.2M, or 1.2MB. /F:<size> is in versions 4 and 5 only.

/N:<sectors> and /T:<tracks> specify the number of sectors and tracks to format, if you want to format less than the maximum capacity of the diskette drive. These parameters are available in versions 3.2 and later. If you specify /N:<sectors>, you must also specify /T:<tracks>. Valid combinations of sectors and tracks for standard diskette sizes are as follows:

Size	Sectors	Tracks
360 K	9	40
720 K	9	80
1.2 MB	15	80
1.44 MB	18	80
2.88 MB	36	80

/S creates a system disk by copying DOS system files to the formatted disk.

/B formats a diskette and reserves space for the DOS hidden files. You can later copy these files to the disk with the System (sys) command. If you specify /B, you cannot specify /S.

/V:<label> in versions 4 and 5 assigns <label> as a volume label to the formatted disk. In earlier versions, /V (without the colon and <label>) tells DOS to prompt for a volume label when formatting is complete.

The remaining two parameters are in version 5 only.

/Q (for *quick*) performs a fast reformat of an already formatted disk. In a quick format, DOS clears away the directory records of previously stored files, but it does not check the disk for unusable areas. The reformatted disk retains the same storage capacity for which it was originally formatted.

/U (for *unconditional*) performs an irreversible format that destroys all previously stored information and cannot be undone with the version 5 Unformat command. An unconditional format is the type normally performed by earlier versions of DOS.

Examples

To format the diskette in drive A for its maximum capacity:

```
C:\>format a:
```

To format the diskette in drive A for its maximum capacity and assign it the volume label LETTERS (versions 4 and 5):

```
C:\>format a: /v:letters
```

To format a system diskette in drive A and assign it a volume label when formatting is complete (versions prior to 4.0):

```
C:\>format a: /v /s
```

After formatting the disk, DOS prompts you to type a volume label of 11 characters or less. You can change or delete this label later with the Volume (vol) command.

To format a 360 K diskette in a 1.2 MB drive (versions 3.2 and later):

```
C:\>format a: /4
C:\>format a: /n:9 /t:40
```

Another way to format a 360 K diskette in a 1.2 MB drive in versions 4 and 5:

```
C:\>format a: /f:360
```

To perform a quick format on a previously formatted disk in drive A (version 5 only):

```
C:\>format a: /q
```

To perform an unconditional format on the disk in drive A, making any existing files unrecoverable:

```
C:\>format a: /u
```

GOTO (BATCH COMMAND)
Jump to a Label
Versions 2.0 and later

Page 325

The Goto batch command tells DOS to jump to a specified label in a batch file and carry out the commands that follow. A label is a line that consists of a colon (:) followed by a string up to eight characters long.

> **goto <label>**

<label> is the label in the batch file you want DOS to jump to.

Example

The line numbers in the following batch file are included only for reference. The batch file includes two labels, *:start* in line 2 and *:end* in line 7. These two labels control the backup procedure performed by the Backup command in line 3.

The If command in line 4 includes a *goto end* command that sends DOS to the label *:end* and ends the backup if an error occurs. The *errorlevel* option of the If command detects errors by checking a special *errorlevel* value that Backup sets to report on each backup it performs (0 is success; 1 through 4 represent different reasons why a backup attempt was not completed). Thus, *goto end* is carried out and the batch file ends if the Backup command in line 3 reports an *errorlevel* of 1 or greater. Otherwise, the *goto start* command in line 6 sends DOS back to line 3, to back up another file, until an error occurs or no more files remain to be backed up.

```
1. @echo off
2. :start
3. backup %1 a:
4. if errorlevel 1 goto end
5. shift
6. goto start
7. :end
```

GRAFTABL
Enable Graphics Character Set
Versions 3.0 and later

Pages 136, 405

The Load Graphics Table command (graftabl) enables DOS to display special characters, such as accented letters, symbols, and line-drawing characters (character codes 128–255). When you use the Graftabl command, DOS can display the characters when the Color Graphics Adapter is in graphics mode. The command is unnecessary with an Enhanced Graphics Adapter, and has no effect when the Monochrome Display Adapter is used. You can use Graftabl only once during a session with DOS.

graftabl <codepage> /status ?

<codepage> is the three-digit number that specifies the code page that DOS is to use. You cannot specify <codepage> in versions prior to 3.3. Valid code pages are:

437	United States
850	Multilingual (Latin I)
852	Slavic (Latin II)—DOS 5 only
860	Portuguese
863	Canada (French)
865	Nordic

/status displays the current code page (versions 3.3 and later). You can abbreviate this parameter as /sta.

? (typed as *graftabl ?*) displays the current code page, a description of the parameters you can use, and a list of the numbers and names of available code pages (version 4). In version 5, typing *graftabl /?* (note the slash) causes DOS to display online help for this command.

Examples

To enable DOS to display the graphics characters in graphics mode:

```
C:\>graftabl
```

DOS reads the table of character definitions into memory and tells you it has done so.

To enable DOS to display the Canadian French character set (code page 863) in graphics mode (versions 3.3 and later):

```
C:\>graftabl 863
```

To display the current graphics code page (versions 3.3 and later):

```
C:\>graftabl /sta
```

GRAPHICS
Enable Printing of a Graphics Display
Versions 3.2 and later, IBM releases 2.0 and later

Page 134

The Graphics command loads a program that DOS keeps in memory to print the display produced by the Color Graphics Adapter (CGA), Enhanced Graphics Adapter (EGA), or Video Graphics Array (VGA) used in a graphics mode. After you enter the Graphics command, pressing Shift-PrtSc enables DOS to print either a color graphics screen or the text-based display produced by a monochrome adapter.

Note: Not all printers can reproduce graphics images. The Graphics command itself is not compatible with Hercules monochrome graphics adapters or with Enhanced Graphics Adapters in enhanced display modes.

The Graphics command can include several parameters or none at all; to see which, if any, are available to you, check the documentation that came with your version of DOS.

graphics <printer> <profile> /R /B /LCD /PB:<id> /C /F /P<port>

<printer> is one of the following printers supported by the Graphics command. If you don't specify <printer>, DOS assumes *graphics*.

color1	IBM Personal Computer Color Printer with a black ribbon or the black band of a color ribbon
color4	IBM Personal Computer Color Printer with a red-green-blue-black ribbon
color8	IBM Personal Computer Color Printer with a cyan-magenta-yellow-black ribbon
compact	IBM Personal Computer Compact Printer (versions prior to 4)
graphics	IBM Graphics Printer, Proprinter, Pageprinter, or Quietwriter
graphicswide	IBM Quietwriter or Proprinter with an 11-inch carriage (versions 4 and 5 only)
thermal	IBM PC Convertible Printer (versions 3.3 and later)
hpdefault	Any Hewlett-Packard PCL printer (version 5 only)
deskjet	Hewlett-Packard DeskJet (version 5 only)
laserjet	Hewlett-Packard LaserJet (version 5 only)
laserjetII	Hewlett-Packard LaserJet Series II (version 5 only)
paintjet	Hewlett-Packard PaintJet (version 5 only)
quietjet	Hewlett-Packard Quietjet (version 5 only)
quietjetplus	Hewlett-Packard Quietjet Plus (version 5 only)
ruggedwriter	Hewlett-Packard Rugged Writer (version 5 only)
ruggedwriterwide	Hewlett-Packard Rugged Writer with wide carriage (version 5 only)
thinkjet	Hewlett-Packard ThinkJet (version 5 only)

<profile> specifies the name of the file that provides detailed information about the printer you're using. The file GRAPHICS.PRO, supplied with DOS, describes all the printers listed for <printer> (versions 4 and 5).

/R prints the screen as you see it on the display: light images on a dark background.

/B prints the background in color. It is valid only if <printer> is *color4* or *color8*.

/LCD prints the image from the liquid crystal display (LCD) screen of the IBM PC Convertible (versions 3.3 and later).

/C centers the printed image on the paper. It works with an image resolution of 640 by 200 or with a 320-by-200 image printed with the /F parameter (versions 3.2 and 3.3 of MS-DOS only; not in IBM releases).

/F (for *flip*) prints a 320-by-200 image sideways by rotating it 90 degrees (versions 3.2 and 3.3 of MS-DOS only; not in IBM releases).

/P <port> specifies the printer port. It can be *1* (LPT1), *2* (LPT2), or *3* (LPT3) (versions prior to 4).

/PB:<id> tells DOS what aspect ratio (ratio of display width to display height) to use when printing a graphics image. Valid entries for <id> are STD, which specifies the aspect ratio of a standard display, and LCD, which specifies that the aspect ratio of an LCD display should be used (versions 4 and 5).

On a noncolor printer, the Graphics command prints the screen with up to four shades of gray. On a color printer, screen colors are reproduced with or without the background color, depending on the Graphics parameter you specify. If the display is in a 640-by-200 or a higher-resolution graphics mode, the printed image is rotated 90 degrees (printed sideways).

Examples

To enable printing a graphics display on an IBM Personal Graphics Printer:

```
C:\>graphics
```

To enable printing a graphics display with a colored background on an IBM Personal Computer Color Printer with an RGB ribbon:

```
C:\>graphics color4 /b
```

To enable printing a graphics display on a Hewlett-Packard LaserJet Series II, reversing the image so that a reverse-video image (white on black) is printed:

```
C:\>graphics laserjetII /r
```

HELP
Command Help
Version 5

Page 64

Beginning with version 5, DOS provides online help with command formats. Requesting help for a particular command causes DOS to display a description of the command, the form in which it is typed, and a list of parameters (if any) with descriptions of what they do. Parameter descriptions do not include the values DOS accepts for variables (those shown in angle brackets in this book, as in Format /F:<size>).

Help can be requested either by typing:

```
help <command>
```

or by typing:

```
<command> /?
```

<command>, in either request, is any DOS command other than a configuration command or an Edlin, MS-DOS Editor, or DOS Shell command.

Example

To request online help for the Diskcopy command:

```
C:\>help diskcopy
```

or

```
C:\>diskcopy /?
```

DOS displays:

```
Copies the contents of one floppy disk to another.

DISKCOPY [drive1: [drive2:]] [/1] [/V]

   /1   Copies only the first side of the disk.
   /V   Verifies that the information is copied correctly.

The two floppy disks must be the same type.
You may specify the same drive for drive1 and drive2.
```

HIMEM.SYS
Manage Extended Memory
Version 5.0

Page 371

HIMEM.SYS is a device driver, included with version 5 of DOS, that manages extended memory (memory above 1 MB). As a memory manager, HIMEM.SYS ensures that applications don't attempt to use the same portions of extended memory. Equally important, HIMEM.SYS enables version 5 of DOS to load a large part of itself into the portion of extended memory known as the High Memory Area (HMA). The ability to run DOS ''high'' helps conserve conventional memory (0 K to 640 K) for other programs and for data.

device=<path>himem.sys

<path> is the path to the directory containing HIMEM.SYS. If you don't include <path>, DOS assumes the device driver is in the root directory of the startup drive.

Note: HIMEM.SYS accepts a number of parameters that refine its behavior. You can, for example, specify the amount of memory an application must require if it is to use the HMA. These parameters are beyond the scope of this book; if you need them, refer to the documentation that came with your version of DOS.

Example

The following example shows the two commands needed in CONFIG.SYS to identify HIMEM.SYS to DOS and to enable DOS to run in high memory. The example assumes that HIMEM.SYS is in a \DOS directory.

```
dos=high
device=c:\dos\himem.sys
```

HIMEM.SYS and the Dos command shown here are also needed if you want to use the upper memory area (640 K to 1 MB) for loading device drivers and programs. Additional examples are in the entries on EMM386.EXE and the Devicehigh, Dos, and Loadhigh commands.

IF (BATCH COMMAND)
Deciding Whether to Carry Out a Batch Command
Versions 2.0 and later

Page 323

The If batch command tests a condition and carries out another command if the condition is met.

if not <condition> <command>

not reverses the meaning of <condition>. That is, <command> is carried out only if <condition> is *not* true.

<condition> is the condition to be tested. Using <condition>, a batch file can be used to check the outcome of a command such as Backup or Restore (with the *errorlevel* option); check whether a file exists; or check whether two strings are identical. <condition> takes one of the following forms:

errorlevel <number>	True if *errorlevel* is equal to or greater than <number>. *errorlevel* represents a special value that is set by some DOS commands (and other programs) to indicate whether or not they were completed successfully.
exist <filename>	True if <filename> exists in the specified directory.
<string1>==<string2>	True if <string1> and <string2> are identical; remember, uppercase and lowercase are different. Notice that two equal signs separate the strings. This form of the If command can be used to compare file names, replaceable parameters entered on the command line with the batch command, or character strings.

<command> is the command to be carried out. It can be any DOS command, including another If command.

Examples

To jump to the label :*end* if *errorlevel* is equal to or greater than 1:

```
if errorlevel 1 goto end
```

(For a sample batch file using this command, see the Goto batch command.)

To copy the file named in the first replaceable parameter from the disk in the current drive to the disk in drive A if the file doesn't exist on the disk in drive A:

```
if not exist a:%1 copy %1 a:%1
```

INPUT/OUTPUT REDIRECTION
Redirecting Standard Input and Standard Output

Page 280

Unless instructed otherwise, DOS takes its input from standard input (usually the keyboard) and sends its output to standard output (usually the screen). You can redirect standard input and output, however, to a file or a device by using the symbols <, >, and >>. The < and > symbols redirect the input or output of a command or program.

The < symbol redirects input. For example, to tell the Sort filter command to read its input from the file named LIST.DOC, you would type *sort < list.doc*.

Similarly, you redirect output with the > symbol. For example, to send the output of a Directory command to a file named DIRFILE.DOC in the current directory, you would type *dir > dirfile.doc*. If there were no file named DIRFILE.DOC, DOS would create it. If a file named DIRFILE.DOC already existed, DOS would replace its contents with the output of the Directory command.

You can, however, tell DOS to *add* output to the end of an existing file by using the symbols >>. For example, to add the output of the Directory command to an existing file named DIRFILE.DOC, you would type *dir >> dirfile.doc*. If the file didn't exist, DOS would create it, as in the previous example, which used the > symbol.

You can redirect input and output from and to devices as well as files, and you can redirect both the input and output of a program. For example, to tell the Sort command to read its input from the file LIST.DOC and write its output to the printer (PRN), you would type *sort < list.doc > prn*.

Rather than redirecting output to a file or device, you can send the output of a command or program to the input of another command or program by separating the program or command names with a vertical bar (¦). Because the programs or commands are logically connected, this connection is called a *pipe*.

Pipes are used primarily with the filter commands: Find, More, and Sort. These commands read standard input and write to standard output, so they can be combined through redirection and pipes in a variety of useful ways. For example, *dir ¦ sort* sends the output of the Directory command to the input of the Sort command.

You can combine redirection and piping: For example, you could pipe the output of the Directory command to the Sort command, pipe the output of the Sort command to the Find command and, finally, redirect the output of the Find command to the printer by typing *dir ¦ sort ¦ find ".DOC" > prn*.

INSTALL (CONFIGURATION COMMAND)
Load a Command from CONFIG.SYS
Versions 4 and 5

The Install command loads into memory the command file for any of the following four DOS commands: Fastopen, Keyboard (keyb), National Language Support Function (nlsfunc), and Share. Once loaded, these command files remain in memory until you restart your computer. Install helps DOS manage your computer's use of memory.

> **install=<filename> <cmdparms>**

<filename> is the name of the command file to be installed. You must include the extension (COM or EXE) and can include a drive letter and path.

<cmdparms> represents the parameters, if any, of the command to be installed.

Examples
Assuming that all DOS files are in the C:\DOS directory, the following command in CONFIG.SYS would tell DOS to keep track of the last 50 files opened on the fixed disk (drive C):

```
install=c:\dos\fastopen.exe c:=50
```

Assuming that all DOS files are in the C:\DOS directory, the following commands in CONFIG.SYS would tell DOS to provide national language support and start the system with the French keyboard layout:

```
install=c:\dos\nlsfunc.exe
install=c:\dos\keyb.com fr,,c:\dos\keyboard.sys
```

JOIN
Join a Disk Drive to a Directory
Versions 3.0 and later

Page 386
The Join command connects one disk drive to an empty directory on a second drive. DOS then treats the disk in the joined drive as if it were a directory on the disk in the drive to which it is joined.

503

join <drive> <pathname> /D

<drive> is the drive that is to be joined to a directory on the second drive. The complete directory structure of <drive> is joined, starting at the root. Once you join <drive> to a directory on another drive, you cannot use the letter of <drive> in any DOS command. If you do, DOS responds *Invalid drive specification.*

<pathname> is the drive letter and path name of the drive and directory to which <drive> is to be joined. The directory must be a subdirectory of the root directory. If the directory doesn't exist, the Join command creates it; if the directory does exist, it must be empty. You cannot join <drive> to the root directory of another drive.

/D disconnects any join involving <drive>. The specified directory remains on the disk until it is removed with a Remove Directory command (rd).

If you omit all parameters (type just *join*), DOS displays any joins in effect.

Note: You should avoid using the Assign, Backup, Diskcopy, Format, Restore, and Substitute commands on a drive to which another drive is joined. If you want to use one of these commands, or if you need to use the drive that is joined, delete the join with the /D parameter. Join cannot be used with a network drive.

Examples

To join drive B to C:\DRIVEB:

```
C:\>join b: driveb
```

To delete the join from the preceding example:

```
C:\>join b: /d
```

Assume that you joined drive A to C:\DRIVEA and drive B to C:\DRIVEB. To display the joins in effect:

```
C:\>join
```

DOS displays:

```
A: => C:\DRIVEA
B: => C:\DRIVEB
```

KEYB
Select a Keyboard Layout
Versions 3.3 and later

Pages 137, 402

The Keyboard command (keyb) selects a keyboard layout that matches the layout used in the country you specify. Keyb replaces the Keyb*xx* command used in releases through 3.2. If you have one of those versions of DOS, refer to the entry KEYB*xx*, following this one.

keyb \<code\>,\<codepage\>,\<keybfile\> /ID:\<kbdid\>

\<code\> is one of the following two-letter keyboard codes:

Country	Keyboard Code	Code Page(s)	Keyboard ID
Belgium	be	437,850	
Brazil	br	437,850	
Canada (French)	cf	863,850	
Czechoslovakia (Czech)	cz	852,850	
Czechoslovakia (Slovak)	sl	852,850	
Denmark	dk	865,850	
Finland	su	437,850	
France	fr	437,850	120,189
Germany	gr	437,850	
Hungary	hu	852,850	
Italy	it	437,850	141,142
Latin America	la	437,850	
Netherlands	nl	437,850	
Norway	no	865,850	
Poland	pl	852,850	
Portugal	po	860,850	
Spain	sp	437,850	
Switzerland (French)	sf	437,850	
Switzerland (German)	sg	437,850	
Sweden	sv	437,850	
United Kingdom	uk	437,850	166,168
United States	us	437,850	
Yugoslavia	yu	852,850	

\<codepage\> is a three-digit number that specifies the code page that DOS is to use. Valid code pages for each keyboard are listed in the preceding table. For more information on code pages, refer to Chapter 18, ''DOS Is an International System.''

\<keybfile\> is the name of the system file that contains the keyboard layouts. If you don't specify \<keybfile\>, DOS assumes that the file is named KEYBOARD.SYS and that it is stored in the root directory of the system disk. If, as is likely, this file is in your DOS directory, you must include the path to the file.

/ID:<kbdid> is a three-digit code that specifies a keyboard layout to be used when a country has more than one keyboard ID, as listed in the preceding table. If you don't specify /ID:<kbdid>, and more than one keyboard ID is listed for the country specified, DOS assumes the first keyboard ID listed (versions 4 and 5).

If your computer was manufactured for use in the United States, you can return to the U.S. keyboard layout after entering a Keyb command by pressing Ctrl-Alt-F1. To return to the keyboard you defined with the Keyb command, press Ctrl-Alt-F2.

Examples

To select the French keyboard layout, let DOS assume the value for the code page, and tell DOS that the keyboard definition file is KEYBOARD.SYS in the C:\DOS directory:

```
C:\>keyb fr,,c:\dos\keyboard.sys
```

Notice the two commas following *fr*; if you omit <codepage>, you must still type the comma that would follow, to show DOS that you omitted it.

To display the currently active keyboard code and its code page, as well as the code page currently being used by CON:

```
C:\>keyb
```

If you had selected the U.S. keyboard and code page 850 for the keyboard and console, DOS would respond:

```
Current keyboard code: US   code page: 850
Current CON code page: 850
```

KEYBxx
Select a Keyboard Layout
Version 3.2, IBM releases 3.0 through 3.2

Pages 137, 390

The Keyboard command (keyb*xx*) in versions of DOS prior to 3.3 loads a program that DOS keeps in memory to change the keyboard layout to match the keyboard used in a particular country.

If you specify a keyboard layout other than the one you normally use, you can return to the layout DOS assumes by pressing Ctrl-Alt-F1. You can also switch back to the other keyboard layout by pressing Ctrl-Alt-F2.

The Keyb*xx* command has six forms, one for each keyboard that DOS supports. Each begins with *keyb*; you replace the *xx* with one of the following two-letter codes:

Description	Code	Typed As
Dvorak keyboard (non-IBM versions of DOS)	dv	keybdv
France	fr	keybfr
Germany	gr	keybgr
Italy	it	keybit
Spain	sp	keybsp
United Kingdom	uk	keybuk

Example

To select the French keyboard layout:

```
C>keybfr
```

LABEL
Change or Delete the Volume Label of a Disk
Versions 3.1 and later, IBM releases 3.0 and later

Page 116

The Label command displays, adds, changes, or deletes the volume label of a disk. DOS provides two ways to assign a volume label: the /V parameter of the Format command, which you use when preparing a disk for use, and the Label command, which you can use at any time on any formatted disk. To change or delete an assigned volume label, however, you must use the Label command.

The Label command has two parameters:

label <drive><newlabel>

<drive> is the letter, followed by a colon, of the drive containing the disk whose volume label is to be affected.

<newlabel> is the volume label you want to assign to the disk in <drive>. The label can be up to 11 characters long; it can include spaces as well as any characters that are valid for a file name. If you specify <newlabel>, DOS assigns the label to the disk in <drive>, whether or not the disk already has a volume label. If you omit <newlabel> (type just *label*, or *label* plus a drive letter), DOS displays the volume label (if there is one) of the disk in the current or specified drive, then prompts you to type a new volume label or to press Enter. If you press Enter and the disk already has a volume label, DOS asks if you want to delete the current label.

Note: You cannot use the Label command on a network drive. You should also avoid using it on a drive affected by the Assign, Join, or Substitute command. If you just want to display the volume label of a disk, use the Volume (vol) command.

Examples

To assign the volume label CLIENT LIST to the disk in drive A:

```
C:\>label a:client list
```

To display the volume label of the disk in drive A:

```
C:\>label a:
```

DOS responds:

```
Volume in drive A is CLIENT LIST
Volume Serial Number is 3F68-1AFF
Volume label (11 characters, ENTER for none)?
```

If you type a label, DOS renames the disk. If you press Enter, DOS displays:

```
Delete current volume label (Y/N)?
```

To delete the volume label, press Y; to leave the label unchanged, press N.

LASTDRIVE (CONFIGURATION COMMAND)
Define the Highest Drive Letter

Versions 3.0 and later

Page 381

The Lastdrive configuration command specifies the highest drive letter that DOS recognizes as valid. If you don't use the Lastdrive command, DOS assumes five drive letters, A through E. Using Lastdrive, you can specify letters up to Z—for example, on a system with two diskette drives, one or more fixed disks, and several RAM disks, or on a system with a large fixed disk divided into a number of sections (called logical drives), each referred to by a different drive letter. You can also use Lastdrive if you need one or more unique drive letters (such as X) to refer to disk drives on a network.

```
lastdrive=<letter>
```

<letter> specifies the highest drive letter that DOS recognizes. It can be any letter from A through Z. If <letter> specifies fewer disk drives than the actual number attached to the computer, DOS ignores the Lastdrive command.

Example

To allow eight drive letters, include the following in CONFIG.SYS:

```
lastdrive=h
```

LOADHIGH (LH)
Load Programs into the Upper Memory Area
Version 5.0

Page 378

The Loadhigh command, abbreviated *lh*, tells DOS to load a program into the portion of memory known as the upper memory area, which is used in units called upper memory blocks (UMBs). When you use Loadhigh, you can increase the amount of conventional memory available.

Loadhigh is useful for loading the types of programs known as TSRs (for terminate and stay resident). Such programs stay in memory even when they are not actively working. You probably want to reserve the maximum possible amount of conventional memory for applications, so TSRs are natural candidates for loading into the upper memory area. You can use Loadhigh with the following DOS programs: Doskey, the DOS Shell, Keyb, Graphics, Nlsfunc, Mode, Share, Print, and Append.

The Loadhigh command requires a computer with at least 350 K of extended memory, and it requires a memory-management program that can make UMBs available. If your computer has an 80386 or 80486 microprocessor, you can use the EMM386.EXE device driver described in this appendix.

In addition, because the Loadhigh command makes use of memory that is normally unavailable to DOS, your CONFIG.SYS file must include a Dos command and two Device commands, all of which tell DOS at startup that memory beyond 640 K is accessible. These commands are shown in the example for this entry.

> **loadhigh <filename> <parameters>**

<filename> is the name of the program you want to load into reserved memory. Include a drive letter and path (if necessary) if the program file is not in the current search path.

<parameters> represents any parameters that <filename> requires.

You use a separate Loadhigh command for each program to be loaded into reserved memory. If there isn't enough upper memory to load a program, DOS loads the program into conventional memory instead. If you load the same program or programs into upper memory whenever you start up, you can put the appropriate Loadhigh command(s) in your AUTOEXEC.BAT file.

Example

Assuming that all DOS files are in the C:\DOS directory and you want access to all available upper memory, these commands must be in CONFIG.SYS if you intend to load programs into the upper memory area:

```
dos=umb
device=c:\dos\himem.sys
device=c:\dos\emm386.exe noems
```

The Device commands identify two device drivers, HIMEM.SYS and EMM386.EXE, that DOS needs in order to manage non-conventional memory. The Dos command enables DOS to maintain access to reserved memory after startup.

To load Doskey into reserved memory:

```
C:\>loadhigh doskey
```

To load Doskey into the upper memory area each time you start your system, put this Loadhigh command in AUTOEXEC.BAT.

MD (MAKE DIRECTORY)
Make a New Directory
Versions 2.0 and later

Page 151

The Make Directory command (md or mkdir) creates a new subdirectory.

md <drive><path>

<drive> is the letter, followed by a colon, of the drive containing the disk on which the directory is to be created. If you omit <drive>, DOS creates the directory on the disk in the current drive.

<path> is the path name of the subdirectory to be created. If <path> begins with a backslash (\), DOS makes the new directory a subdirectory of the root directory of the disk in the current or specified drive; if <path> doesn't begin with a backslash, DOS makes the new directory a subdirectory of the current directory. There is no absolute limit to the number of levels of subdirectories you can create, but a good practical limit is about four or five; beyond this, a multilevel directory structure can become more confusing and unwieldy than helpful. The maximum length of a path name from the root directory is 63 characters, including backslashes.

Note: Because the Assign, Join, and Substitute commands mask the real identities of directories, you shouldn't create directories when those commands are in effect.

Examples

To create a subdirectory named WP in the *current* directory of the current drive:

```
C:\ENG>md wp
```

To create a subdirectory named WP in the *root* directory of the current drive:

```
C:\DOS>md \wp
```

To create a subdirectory named WP in the directory \MKT of the disk in drive A:

```
C:\DOS>md a:\mkt\wp
```

MEM (MEMORY)
Display Memory Use
Versions 4.0 and later

Page 122

The Memory command displays the amount of memory installed and available for use, including extended and expanded memory and memory in the upper memory area. It can also display the name, location, size, and type of each program in memory.

mem /program /debug /classify

/program specifies that the name, location, size, and type of each program in memory be displayed. If you have version 5, you can type this parameter as */p*.

/debug specifies that additional detail beyond that provided by the */program* parameter be included in the report. If you have version 5, you can type this parameter as */d*.

/classify reports on use of conventional memory and the upper memory area used by the Loadhigh and Devicehigh commands. Unlike the */program* and */debug* parameters, */classify* gives the size of programs in decimal as well as hexadecimal. It also summarizes memory use and reports the largest available block in the upper memory area.

Examples

To display the types and amount of memory installed and available:

```
C:\>mem

    655360 bytes total conventional memory
    655360 bytes available to MS-DOS
    515856 largest executable program size

   2097152 bytes total contiguous extended memory
         0 bytes available contiguous extended memory
    983040 bytes available XMS memory
           MS-DOS resident in High Memory Area
```

This is the display produced by version 5 of DOS on a system with 2 MB of extended memory, a 1024 K Smartdrive disk cache in extended memory, and DOS loaded into the High Memory Area. Your report will differ to reflect the way your system is set up. For example, if your computer has expanded memory, the report tells you how much *EMS* memory is in the system and how much is currently free. If you have version 4, the lower portion of the report is less detailed.

To see a more detailed report showing the name and size of each program loaded into memory, you could use the version 5 */classify* option as shown on the next page.

```
C:\>mem /c

Conventional Memory :

    Name              Size in Decimal          Size in Hex
 ------------     ----------------------      -------------
    MSDOS            15984    ( 15.6K)           3E70
    SETVER             400    (  0.4K)            190
    HIMEM             1184    (  1.2K)            4A0
    ANSI              4192    (  4.1K)           1060
    SMARTDRV         14576    ( 14.2K)           38F0
    EGA               3280    (  3.2K)            CD0
    COMMAND           3392    (  3.3K)            D40
    MOUSE            10288    ( 10.0K)           2830
    FREE                64    (  0.1K)             40
    FREE               256    (  0.3K)            100
    FREE            601456    (587.4K)           92D70

 Total   FREE :     601776    (587.7K)

 Total bytes available to programs :    601776    (587.7K)
 Largest executable program size :      601456    (587.4K)

    2097152 bytes total contiguous extended memory
          0 bytes available contiguous extended memory
     983040 bytes available XMS memory
            MS-DOS resident in High Memory Area
```

(Some of the lines in the preceding example are shortened to fit on the page.)

To see a very detailed report that not only shows the names and sizes of programs but gives their locations and tells you what types of programs they are, you would type either *mem /p* or *mem /d*.

MIRROR
Save Disk Information for File Recovery
Version 5.0

Pages 77, 204

The Mirror command, new with version 5, is a disk- and file-recovery program. Mirror saves disk-storage information that you can use to unformat an inadvertently formatted diskette or fixed disk, rebuild a damaged fixed disk, or recover deleted files. The command is named Mirror because it creates special files that duplicate the directory and disk-storage information DOS uses internally to keep track of files and their storage locations on disk. Depending on the parameters you specify, the Mirror command can help you record the latest file and directory structure on the disk you specify; track the storage locations of files you delete; or store information about the way a fixed disk is set up for use by DOS.

mirror <drive> /1 /T<drive>-<files> /partn /U

<drive> is the letter, followed by a colon, of the drive whose file and directory in-formation you want to record. You can specify more than one drive letter, separating them with spaces. If you don't specify <drive>, the Mirror command records informa-tion about the disk in the current drive. For each drive you specify, Mirror creates a read-only file named MIRROR.FIL in the root directory. This file, which can be sur-prisingly large for a fixed disk, contains the information needed to rebuild the disk or to recover files and directories in the root directory.

/1 (the numeral 1) tells Mirror to keep only the latest information about the disk in the drive you specify. If you don't use /1 and Mirror finds an earlier version of MIR-ROR.FIL, it renames the old file MIRROR.BAK and creates a new MIRROR.FIL for the latest disk information. MIRROR.BAK then becomes a backup in case the new MIRROR.FIL is unusable.

/T<drive>-<files> tells Mirror to load a program that records the storage loca-tions of files you delete. When you use this feature, known as *delete tracking*, Mirror saves information about all the files you delete while delete tracking is in effect. This information is stored in a system file named PCTRACKR.DEL. If you inadvertently delete a needed file, you can use PCTRACKR.DEL and the Undelete command to try to recover the file.

<drive> is the letter (without a colon) of the drive for which you want to track de-leted files; you must include this parameter. <files> is the number of deleted files you want to track. If you choose to include <files>, you can specify any number from 1 through 999, separating it from <drive> with a hyphen. If you don't specify <files>, Mirror assumes a certain number depending on the size of the disk, as shown in the following table:

Disk Size	Number of Files	Size of PCTRACKR.DEL
360 K	25	5 K
720 K	50	9 K
1.2 MB	75	14 K
1.44 MB	75	14 K
20 MB fixed disk	101	18 K
32 MB fixed disk	202	36 K
Fixed disk larger than 32 MB	303	55 K

Notice that PCTRACKR.DEL can require a fair amount of storage in its own right.

/partn (for *partition*) tells Mirror to save information about the way a fixed disk is set up. DOS uses this information, called a *partition table,* to find and use a fixed disk. Because you need this information only if the partition table is damaged, but DOS can-

not recognize the fixed disk without the partition table, Mirror saves partition information on a diskette rather than on the fixed disk itself. The information is stored in a file named PARTNSAV.FIL.

/U (for *unload*) removes the delete-tracking program from memory so that Mirror no longer records the storage locations of files you delete from disk.

Note: Do not attempt to use the Mirror command with a drive affected by the Join or Substitute command. If you plan to use delete tracking with an assigned drive (Assign command), assign the drive first.

Examples

To record disk-storage information for drives C and D:

```
C:\>mirror c: d:
```

Mirror responds with a message like this (the copyright line is incomplete):

```
Creates an image of the system area.

Drive C being processed.

Drive D being processed.

The MIRROR process was successful.
```

A Directory command shows the file MIRROR.FIL in the root directory of each drive.
To start delete tracking for the current drive:

```
C:\>mirror /tc
```

As in the preceding example, Mirror displays a message describing its response. As soon as a file on this drive is deleted, Mirror will create PCTRACKR.DEL to hold information about it and other deleted files.

To stop delete tracking for the current drive:

```
C:\>mirror /u
```

Mirror responds *Deletion-tracking software removed from memory.*
To record partition information about the fixed disk (drive C):

```
C:\>mirror /partn
```

Mirror responds with the message *Disk Partition Table saver* and a message asking you to insert a formatted diskette in the drive in which you want to save the table. (Unless you specify otherwise, Mirror assumes drive A.) When you press Enter to carry out the command, Mirror saves the partition table on the diskette and, if all goes well, responds:

```
Successful
```

MODE

Control Device Mode

Versions 3.2 and later, IBM releases 1.0 and later

The Mode command is used in several different ways to enable DOS to work with the display and with printer and communications ports. In versions 3.3 and later, the Mode command is also used to set code-page information that enables DOS to display and print accented and foreign-language characters. Mode has eight basic uses:

▶ Set display characteristics, such as monochrome instead of color, or 40 columns instead of 80 columns.

▶ Set number of display lines and columns (versions 4 and 5).

▶ Set keyboard repeat rate (versions 4 and 5).

▶ Set communications parameters for a serial communications port.

▶ Set line width and spacing for a parallel printer attached to a parallel port or tell DOS to use a printer attached to a parallel port other than LPT1.

▶ Connect a serial printer by redirecting output from a parallel port (such as LPT1) to a serial port (such as COM1).

▶ Check the status of system devices.

▶ Prepare and select code pages for national language support (versions 3.3 and later).

Each of these uses is described separately in the following entries.

MODE

Set Display Characteristics

Versions 3.2 and later, IBM releases 2.0 and later

This form of the Mode command selects a display adapter, either Monochrome or Color Graphics. If you select a Color Graphics Adapter, you can also set the width of the display and enable or disable color. If the image on a display isn't centered, you can use Mode to shift the image left or right and display a test pattern.

mode <method>,<shift>,T

<method> selects the Monochrome or Color Graphics Adapter and specifies the width and color characteristics of the display attached to the Color Graphics Adapter. <method> can be specified as one of the values listed on the next page.

Value	Characteristics
mono	Monochrome Display Adapter
40	Color Graphics Adapter, 40-column display
80	Color Graphics Adapter, 80-column display
co40	Color Graphics Adapter, color enabled, 40-column display
co80	Color Graphics Adapter, color enabled, 80-column display
bw40	Color Graphics Adapter, color disabled, 40-column display
bw80	Color Graphics Adapter, color disabled, 80-column display

<shift> can be specified as either *l* or *r* to shift left or right an off-center image on a display attached to the Color Graphics Adapter. The image is shifted two columns if the display width is 80 characters, one column if the display width is 40 characters. <shift> has no effect on an EGA or VGA display, or on a display attached to a Monochrome Display Adapter.

T displays a test pattern after shifting the image so that you can see whether the display is centered. It also displays a prompt asking whether you can see the leftmost (or rightmost) character in the pattern. If you reply *n*, the Mode command shifts the image and displays the prompt again, continuing until you reply *y*. DOS then returns to the system prompt.

Examples

To select the display attached to the Color Graphics Adapter, enable color, and set the display to 80 columns:

```
C>mode co80
```

To select the display attached to the Color Graphics Adapter, disable color, set the display to 80 columns, shift the display two columns to the right, and display a test pattern:

```
C>mode bw80,r,t
```

Note the commas.

To select the display attached to the Monochrome Display Adapter:

```
C>mode mono
```

MODE
Set Display Lines

Versions 4.0 and later

Page 124

This form of the Mode command lets you specify whether 40 or 80 columns and 25, 43, or 50 lines should be displayed on the screen. The command is effective only if the line DEVICE=ANSI.SYS (preceded by a path if necessary) is included in your CONFIG.SYS file, and if the display attached to your system can display the number of lines you specify. You can set either columns or lines, or both, with the command.

mode con cols=<columns> lines=<lines>

CON is the name of the console device; the display is the output portion of CON (the keyboard is the input portion of CON).

cols=<columns> specifies the number of columns in a line. <columns> can be either 40 or 80.

lines=<lines> specifies the number of lines displayed on the screen. <lines> can be 25, 43, or 50.

Note: If you specify 43 or 50 lines and an application program, such as a word processor, resets the display to 25 lines whenever it returns to DOS, you can avoid the need to enter the Mode command each time by starting the application program with a batch file that ends with a Mode command that sets the number of display lines to the number you prefer.

Example

To set the number of display lines to 43 and leave the number of columns unchanged:

```
C:\>mode con lines=43
```

MODE
Set Keyboard Repeat Rate

Versions 4.0 and later

Page 124

This form of the Mode command lets you control how long the keyboard waits before starting to repeat when you hold down a key, and how quickly the character is repeated. You must specify both parameters.

mode con rate=<speed> delay=<pause>

CON is the name of the console device; the keyboard is the input portion of CON (the display is the output portion of CON).

rate=<speed> specifies the speed of the repeat action. <speed> can be from 1 through 32. A value of 1 specifies the slowest rate, about 2 repetitions per second; 32 specifies the fastest rate, about 30 repetitions per second.

delay=<pause> specifies how long the keyboard should wait, after you press a key, before starting to repeat. <pause> represents units of a quarter of a second, and can range from 1 through 4; a value of 1 causes a delay of 0.25 second, and a value of 4 causes a delay of one second.

Example

To set the keyboard repetition rate to 10 and the delay to 0.5 second, type:

```
C:\>mode con rate=10 delay=2
```

MODE
Set Serial Communications Parameters
Versions 3.2 and later, IBM releases 1.1 and later

Page 128

This form of the Mode command sets the communications parameters for a serial port. You use these parameters in situations such as setting up the port for a modem or a serial printer.

In versions 4 and 5, the command and its parameters are entered as shown below. An alternative command format that can be used with all versions of DOS is described later in this entry.

mode <port> baud=<rate> parity=<type> data=<databits>
stop=<stopbits> retry=<action>

<port> is the name of the serial port whose communications parameters are to be set. <port> can be COM1, COM2, COM3, or COM4. You must specify <port>.

baud=<rate> specifies the baud rate (speed of transmission). <rate> can be 110, 150, 300, 600, 1200, 2400, 4800, 9600, or 19200 (if the system is capable of supporting that speed). You must specify <baud>, but only the first two digits are required.

parity=<type> specifies the type of error checking to be performed. <type> can be *n* for none, *o* for odd, *e* for even, *m* for mark, or *s* for space. If you don't specify parity, DOS assumes *e*.

data=<databits> specifies the number of electrical signals used to represent one character (such as *a*). <databits> can be 5, 6, 7, or 8. If you don't specify <databits>, DOS assumes 7.

stop=<stopbits> specifies the number of electrical signals that mark the end of each character. <stopbits> can be 1, 1.5, or 2. If you don't specify <stopbits>, DOS assumes 2 if the baud rate is 110; otherwise, it assumes 1.

retry=<action> specifies how the Mode command should respond when the serial port is busy. Possible values are *e* for error, *b* for busy, *p* for keep trying, *r* for ready, and *n* for no action. If you don't specify <action>, the Mode command assumes *n* (*e* in DOS versions prior to 5). Unless the instructions for a program suggest otherwise, don't specify this parameter. You should also avoid it if you use the Mode command over a network.

With any version of DOS, including versions prior to 4.0, you can also use the following form of the Mode command to set serial communications parameters. If you omit any parameter when you use this form of the command, be sure to include the following comma.

mode <port> <baud>,<parity>,<databits>,<stopbits>,P

<port> is the name of the serial port whose parameters are to be set. As with the preceding form of the command, <port> can be COM1, COM2, or (with versions 3.3 and later) COM3 or COM4. You must specify <port>.

<baud> is the baud rate. It can be any of the values listed for <baud> in the preceding form of the command, but 19200 is available only in versions 3.3 and later.

<parity> is the type of error checking performed. It can be *n*, *o*, or *e* in any version of DOS and can also be *m* or *s* in versions 4 and 5.

<databits> is the number of signals per character. It can be 7 or 8 in any version of DOS and can be 5, 6, 7, or 8 in versions 4 and 5.

<stopbits> is the number of signals marking the end of each character. It can be 1 or 2 in any version of DOS and can be 1, 1.5, or 2 in versions 4 and 5.

P, in versions through 3.3, tells DOS to try continuously to send output to the serial port if the device attached to the port is not ready to receive data (for example, if the device is busy or is not turned on). Specify P when a printer is attached to the serial port. If DOS is waiting for the printer and you want to return to the system prompt, press Ctrl-C or Ctrl-Break to cancel continuous retries. The P parameter is equivalent to the retry=b parameter in versions 4 and 5.

Examples

To set COM1 to 1200 baud, 8 data bits, and no parity, letting DOS assume a value for stop bits and retries, use the following command in versions 4 and 5:

```
C:\>mode com1 baud=1200 data=8 parity=n
```

For the same settings in any version of DOS:

```
C:\>mode com1: 1200,n,8
```

To set COM2 to 2400 baud, no parity, and continuous retries, letting DOS assume values for data bits and stop bits, use the following command in versions 4 and 5:

```
C:\>mode com2 baud=2400 parity=n retry=b
```

Or, in earlier versions of DOS:

```
C:\>mode com2: 2400,n,,,p
```

(Note the commas showing that values for data bits and stop bits are omitted.)

MODE

Set Parallel Printer Width and Spacing
Versions 3.2 and later, IBM releases 1.0 and later

Page 126

This form of the Mode command sets the number of characters per line and the number of lines per inch for a printer attached to a parallel port. In versions 4 and 5, you can use the following form of the command. An alternative command format that can be used with all earlier versions of DOS is described later in this entry.

mode <printer> cols=<width> lines=<spacing> retry=<action>

<printer> is the name of the parallel printer port: LPT1, LPT2, or LPT3. You must specify <printer>.

cols=<width> specifies the maximum number of characters that are to be printed on a line. <width> can be 80 or 132. If you don't specify <width>, DOS assumes 80.

lines=<spacing> specifies the number of lines per vertical inch. <spacing> can be 6 or 8. If you don't specify <spacing>, DOS assumes 6.

retry=<action> specifies how the Mode command should respond when the parallel port is busy. Possible values are *e* for error, *b* for busy, *p* for keep trying, *r* for ready, and *n* for no action. If you don't specify <action>, the Mode command assumes *n* (*e* in DOS versions prior to 5). Unless the instructions for a program suggest otherwise, don't specify this parameter. You should also avoid it if you use the Mode command over a network.

With any version of DOS, including versions prior to 4.0, you can also use the following form of the Mode command to set printer width and spacing:

mode <printer> <width>,<spacing>,P

<printer>, <width>, and <spacing> are the same parameters described earlier in this entry. If you use this form of the command, be sure to include the trailing comma if you omit <width> or <spacing>.

P, in versions prior to 4, tells DOS to continuously try to send output to the printer, even if the printer is busy or not ready. If DOS is waiting for the printer and you want to return to the system prompt, press Ctrl-C or Ctrl-Break to cancel continuous retries. The P parameter is equivalent to the retry=b parameter in versions 4 and 5.

Examples

To set LPT1 to 132 characters per line and 8 lines per inch, letting DOS assume a value for retries, use the following form of the Mode command in versions 4 and 5:

```
C:\>mode lpt1 cols=132 lines=8
```

Or, in any version of DOS:

```
C:\>mode lpt1: 132,8
```

To set LPT2 to 8 lines per inch and specify continuous retries, use the following form of the Mode command in versions 4 and 5:

```
C:\>mode lpt2 lines=8 retry=b
```

Or, in earlier versions of DOS:

```
C:\>mode lpt2: ,8,p
```

MODE
Redirect Parallel Printer Output
Versions 3.2 and later, IBM releases 1.1 and later

Page 131

This form of the Mode command redirects output from a parallel port to a serial port. Before using a serial printer, you must set the communications parameters of the serial port as described previously under the heading ''MODE: Set Serial Communications Parameters,'' and then redirect output from a parallel port to the serial port with the following form of the Mode command:

mode <printer>=<port>

<printer> is the name of the parallel printer whose output is to be redirected. <printer> can be LPT1, LPT2, or LPT3.

<port> is the name of the serial communications port to which the parallel printer port is to be redirected. If you're using 3.2 or an earlier version of DOS, <port> can be COM1 or COM2. If you're using version 3.3 or later, <port> can be COM1, COM2, COM3, or COM4.

To cancel redirection, omit the equal sign and <port> from the Mode command (that is, type just *mode <printer>*).

Examples

To redirect output from LPT1 to COM2:

```
C:\>mode lpt1:=com2:
```

To cancel redirection of LPT1:

```
C:\>mode lpt1:
```

MODE
Check Device Status
Versions 4 and 5

Page 131

Beginning with version 4, this form of the Mode command enables you to request a report on the status of any or all devices on your system.

mode <device> /status

<device> is the name of the device you want to check on, such as CON, LPT1, or COM1. If you omit <device>, DOS reports on all the devices it recognizes.

/status tells DOS you want to check on device status. You can abbreviate this parameter as */sta*, and you can omit it from the command altogether unless you are checking on a parallel printer whose output you've redirected.

Example

To check the status of a parallel printer attached to LPT1 whose output has been redirected to COM2, with no retries if the port is busy:

```
C:\>mode lpt1 /sta

Status for device LPT1:
----------------------
LPT1: rerouted to COM2:
Retry=NONE

Code page operation not supported on this device
```

(The last line means that the device has not been set up for international language support, as described in the following entries.)

MODE
Preparing a Code Page
Versions 3.3 and later

Page 400

This form of the Mode command defines the code page or code pages to be used with a hardware device. To use this form of the Mode command, you must already have installed code-page switching; for details, see Chapter 18, ''DOS Is an International System.''

mode <device> cp prep=((<codepage>) <filename>)

<device> is the name of the device for which the code page or code pages are to be prepared. It can be CON, PRN, LPT1, LPT2, or LPT3.

<codepage> is the code page to be used with <device>. If you specify more than one code page, separate the numbers with blanks. Note that the code-page numbers are enclosed in their own set of parentheses. You can use the following code-page numbers: 437 (United States); 850 (multilingual, or Latin I); 852 (Slavic, or Latin II—version 5 only); 860 (Portuguese); 863 (Canadian French); and 865 (Nordic).

<filename> is the name of the code-page information file DOS needs to prepare the code page for <device>. A code-page information file has the extension CPI. The following files are standard in DOS versions 3.3 and later:

EGA.CPI	Enhanced Graphics Adapter (EGA) or Video Graphics Array (VGA)
4201.CPI	IBM Proprinter and Proprinter XL or compatible
4208.CPI	IBM Proprinter X24E Model 4207 and Proprinter XL24E Model 4208 or compatible (versions 4 and 5)
5202.CPI	IBM Quietwriter III printer or compatible
LCD.CPI	IBM PC Convertible liquid crystal display (LCD)

Example

To prepare code pages 437 and 850 for an EGA or compatible display, assuming that EGA.CPI, the code-page information file, is in the C:\DOS directory:

```
C:\>mode con cp prep=((437 850)c:\dos\ega.cpi)
```

MODE
Selecting a Code Page
Versions 3.3 and later

Page 404

This form of the Mode command selects a code page for a device. To use this form of the Mode command, you must already have installed code-page switching; for details, see Chapter 18, "DOS Is an International System."

mode <device> cp select=<codepage>

<device> is the name of the device for which the code page is to be selected. It can be CON, PRN, LPT1, LPT2, or LPT3.

<codepage> is the three-digit number of the code page to be used with <device>. You can use the following code-page numbers: 437 (United States); 850 (multilingual, or Latin I); 852 (Slavic, or Latin II—version 5 only); 860 (Portuguese); 863 (Canadian French); or 865 (Nordic). <codepage> must be one previously prepared with the *cp prepare* option of the Mode command.

Example

To select code page 850 for the console:

```
C:\>mode con cp select=850
```

MODE
Displaying the Code-Page Status
Versions 3.3 and later

Page 404

This form of the Mode command displays the status of the code pages. To use this form of the Mode command, you must already have installed code-page switching; for details, see Chapter 18, "DOS Is an International System."

mode <device> cp /status

<device> is the name of the device whose code-page status is to be displayed. It can be CON, PRN, LPT1, LPT2, or LPT3.

/status is optional.

Example

To display the status of the console device:

```
C:\>mode con cp
```

MODE
Restoring a Code Page That Was Lost
Versions 3.3 and later

Page 405

This form of the Mode command restores a code page that was selected for a device, then erased from memory. To use this form of the Mode command, you must already have installed code-page switching; for details, see Chapter 18, "DOS Is an International System."

mode <device> cp refresh

<device> is the name of the device whose most recently selected code page is to be restored. It can be CON, PRN, LPT1, LPT2, or LPT3.

Example

To restore the most recently selected code page for the printer that is attached to the LPT2 port:

```
C:\>mode lpt2 cp refresh
```

MORE
Display a File One Screenful at a Time
Versions 2.0 and later

Page 289

The More filter command reads standard input (normally the keyboard) and sends lines to standard output (normally the display); after each screenful of lines it displays the line -- *More* -- and waits for you to press a key.

Because the input and output of the More command can be redirected, input can also come from a file, a device other than the keyboard, or the output of another command. Likewise, you can redirect the output of the More command to a file or a device other than the display.

Thus, by redirecting or piping output to the More command, you can display a file one screenful at a time, pressing a key to see the next screenful. To stop displaying, you press Ctrl-Break. The More command has no parameters:

more

Examples

To display the current directory one screenful at a time:

```
C:\>dir | more
```

To display the file REPORT.DOC one screenful at a time, the More command can be used in either of two ways. The first uses the redirection symbol < to get input from the file REPORT.DOC:

```
C:\MKT\WP>more < report.doc
```

The second pipes output from the Type command to the More command:

```
C:\MKT\WP>type report.doc | more
```

NLSFUNC (NATIONAL LANGUAGE SUPPORT FUNCTION)
Support National Language and Conventions
Versions 3.3 and later

Page 399

The National Language Support Function command (nlsfunc) enables DOS to use code-page switching and loads the file that contains country-specific information, such as date format, time format, and currency symbol. You must enter the Nlsfunc command before you can use the Change Code Page (chcp) command.

nlsfunc <countryfile>

<countryfile> is the name of the country information file (COUNTRY.SYS in most versions of DOS). If you omit <countryfile>, DOS assumes the file is the one specified in the Country configuration command in CONFIG.SYS; if there is no Country configuration command in CONFIG.SYS, DOS assumes that the file is named COUNTRY.SYS and looks for it in the root directory of the current drive.

Examples

The following command, typed at the system prompt (C:\>), starts the national language support program and tells DOS to use the file COUNTRY.SYS in the C:\DOS directory:

```
c:\>nlsfunc c:\dos\country.sys
```

If you have version 4 or 5 of DOS, you can place the following Install command in CONFIG.SYS to load the national language support program and specify the file COUNTRY.SYS (both stored in the C:\DOS directory) at startup:

```
install=c:\dos\nlsfunc.exe c:\dos\country.sys
```

Note: If you have version 3.3 of DOS, you can load national language support at startup by placing the command shown in the first example (nlsfunc c:\dos\country.sys) in AUTOEXEC.BAT.

PATH
Define the Command Path
Versions 2.0 and later

Page 162

The Path command tells DOS where to search for a command file (a file whose extension is COM, EXE, or BAT) that isn't in the current directory. A command path becomes part of the DOS environment, so it is available to every program.

path <drive><path> ;

<drive> is the letter, followed by a colon, of the drive containing the disk on which you want DOS to look for command files (such as c:).

<path> is the path name of the directory that you want DOS to search for command files. You can enter a series of path names, separated by semicolons. If you omit <drive> and <path> but include the semicolon, DOS deletes any paths in effect.

If you enter the Path command with no parameters (type just *path*), DOS displays the current command path. If no path has been specified, DOS displays *No path*.

Include a Path command in AUTOEXEC.BAT if application programs or batch files on your fixed disk are stored in separate subdirectories.

Examples

To tell DOS to search the root directory and the directories named \DOS,\WINDOWS, and \WORD of the current drive for command files:

```
C:\>path c:\;c:\dos;c:\windows;c:\word
```

To display the command path:

```
C:\>path
```

For the command path in the preceding example, DOS responds:

PATH=C:\;C:\DOS;C:\WINDOWS;C:\WORD

To delete the command path:

```
C:\>path ;
```

PAUSE (BATCH COMMAND)
Temporarily Stop a Batch File
Versions 1.0 and later

Page 322

The Pause batch command displays the message *Press any key to continue...* (*Strike a key when ready...* in versions before 4) and waits for you to press a key before carrying out any more commands. You can cancel a batch file while it is paused by pressing Ctrl-C.

The Pause command also lets you include a message to be displayed before *Press any key to continue....*

pause <message>

<message> is the message to be displayed before *Press any key to continue....*

Examples

To temporarily stop a batch file:

pause

To temporarily stop a batch file and echo the message *Put the data disk in drive B and* before the *Press any key to continue...* message:

```
@echo off
echo Put the data disk in drive B and
pause
```

When DOS carries out the commands in the batch file, it displays the following messages and waits for any key to be pressed:

```
Put the data disk in drive B and
Press any key to continue . . .
```

527

PRINT
Print a File

The Print command loads the DOS Print program, which manages a queue of files waiting to be printed. The print program, also known as a *print spooler,* can print the files in the queue while another program is running. It does this by using small portions of the computer's processing time.

The Print command is used in two forms. You use the first when you load the print program and set up its operating characteristics, and you use the second to manage the contents of the print queue. These forms are described separately in the following two entries.

PRINT
Set Operating Characteristics
Versions 2.0 and later

Page 95

The first time you enter the Print command after you start DOS, you can define the operating characteristics of the print program with the command:

print /D:<printer> /Q:<size> /B:<size> /S:<slice> /M:<max> /U:<wait>

/D:<printer> specifies the name of the print device. If you do not specify <printer> in the first Print command you enter after starting the system, DOS prompts you for the device name by displaying *Name of list device [PRN]:*. You can specify LPT1, LPT2, LPT3, COM1, COM2, AUX, or PRN. If you're using version 3.3 or later, you can also specify COM3 or COM4. If you press Enter without specifying a device, DOS assumes PRN. If you use /D to name the print device, it must be the first parameter in the Print command (versions 3.0 and later).

/Q:<size> specifies how many files can be in the print queue. The range is 4 through 32; if you don't specify /Q:<size>, DOS assumes 10.

/B:<size> specifies the number of bytes, up to 16384, in the print buffer (an area of memory used for data by the Print program). If you don't specify /B:<size>, DOS assumes 512 bytes (versions 3.0 and later).

/S:<slice> specifies the length of time (time slice), measured in ticks of the computer's internal timer, that Print is allowed to control the computer. <slice> can be a value from 1 through 255; if you don't specify /S:<slice>, DOS assumes 8 (versions 3.0 and later).

/M:<max> specifies how long, again in ticks of the computer's internal timer, that Print can take to print one character. <max> can be from 1 through 255; if you don't specify /M:<max>, DOS assumes 2 (versions 3.0 and later).

/U:<wait> specifies how many timer ticks Print waits before giving up its time slice if the printer is busy or unavailable. <wait> can be from 1 through 255; if you don't specify /U:<wait>, DOS assumes 1 (versions 3.0 and later).

Because DOS assumes values for all these parameters, you needn't use any of them unless you want to change these assumed values. Depending on such factors as how often you use the Print command, how many files you typically put in the print queue, the average length of the files you print, and the size of your printer's buffer, you may be able to improve overall system performance by experimenting with some of the values that DOS assumes.

Example

To specify COM1 as <printer>, a queue that can hold up to 16 files, and a buffer size of 2048 bytes:

```
C:\>print /d:com1: /q:16 /b:2048
```

Note: Remember that you define these characteristics the first time you enter a Print command. To change the operation of the Print command if your AUTOEXEC.BAT file already contains a Print command, edit your AUTOEXEC.BAT file and restart your computer.

PRINT
Manage the Print Queue
Versions 2.0 and later

Page 91

Files are placed in the print queue in the order in which you specify them in the Print command, and they are printed in the same order. You can add files to and delete files from the print queue in the same command.

DOS continues printing a file until it reaches an end-of-file marker (Ctrl-Z), then stops, even if it has not reached the actual end of the file, and goes on to the next file in the queue. After printing a file, DOS advances the paper to the top of the next page.

print <filename> /P /C /T

<filename> is the name of the file to be added to or deleted from the print queue. You can use wildcard characters to print a set of files with similar file names or extensions, and you can specify more than one file in a single Print command, separating the file names with blanks. In versions 3.0 and later, you can also include a path name.

/P adds to the print queue the preceding and all subsequent files in the command line up to a /C parameter. If you enter a Print command with a file name but no other parameter, DOS assumes /P.

/C deletes from the print queue the preceding and all subsequent files in the command line up to a /P parameter. If one of the deleted files is being printed, DOS prints

File <filename> *canceled by operator*, sounds the printer's bell (if there is one), and advances the paper to the top of the next page.

/T terminates printing. DOS deletes all files from the print queue, cancels any file being printed, prints *All files canceled by operator*, sounds the printer's bell, and advances the paper to the top of the next page.

If you enter the Print command with no parameters, DOS displays the names of the files in the print queue.

Examples

To add all files in the current directory with the extension DOC (or as many as the queue will hold) to the print queue:

```
C:\MKT\WP>print *.doc
```

To remove the file named REPORT.DOC from the print queue and at the same time add the files named SLSRPT.DOC and SLSFCST.DOC to the print queue:

```
C:\MKT\WP>print report.doc /c slsrpt.doc /p slsfcst.doc
```

To cancel printing and remove all files from the print queue:

```
C:\MKT\WP>print /t
```

PROMPT
Set the System Prompt
Versions 2.0 and later, IBM releases 2.1 and later

Page 381

The Prompt command defines the system prompt, which recent versions of DOS normally display as the current drive and directory, followed by a greater-than sign (such as *C:\>*). If you change the system prompt, you can include any character DOS can display, and such items of system information as the time and date, in addition to the current drive and current directory.

prompt <string>

<string> is a string that defines the new prompt. It can contain any character DOS can display, plus any number of the following two-character codes, which tell DOS to include specific information in the prompt (each code must begin with a dollar sign):

Code	Information Displayed
$t	The time
$d	The date (preceded by the day of the week)
$p	Current directory of the current drive
$v	DOS version number
$n	Current drive
$g	A greater-than sign (>)
$l	A less-than sign (<)
$b	A vertical bar (¦)
$q	An equal sign (=)
$h	A backspace (which erases the previous character)
$e	An Escape character
$_ (underscore)	Start a new line
$$	A dollar sign ($)

If any other character follows the $, DOS ignores both characters.

If you enter a Prompt command with no parameters, DOS sets the system prompt to display the current drive followed by a greater-than sign (for example, *C>*).

Examples

Each of the following examples shows a Prompt command followed by the prompt it produces (<space> represents pressing the Spacebar once):

To set the system prompt to display the word *Command* followed by a colon:

```
C:\>prompt Command:<space>
Command: _
```

To change the prompt from the preceding example to show the time—with six backspaces to erase seconds and hundredths of seconds—followed by a blank space, the date, and a colon:

```
Command: prompt $t$h$h$h$h$h$h<space>$d:<space>
16:07 Wed 10-16-1991: _
```

Finally, to reset the system prompt to the usual display (current drive and directory, followed by a greater-than sign):

```
16:07 Wed 10-16-91: prompt $p$g
c:\>_
```

531

QBASIC
Start the QBasic Interpreter
Version 5.0

The Qbasic command, new with version 5 of DOS, starts the program that enables you to use MS-DOS QBasic, the successor to the GW-BASIC and BASICA programming languages shipped with earlier versions of DOS. When you use the Qbasic command, you start the QBasic interpreter, a menu-based program. You use the interpreter to create QBasic programs, and the interpreter translates them into a form the computer can carry out. The QBasic interpreter includes online help; it does not teach you to program, but it does help you learn to use QBasic and the interpreter.

RAMDRIVE.SYS
Create a RAM Drive in Memory
Versions 3.2 and later

Page 375

Note: In IBM releases of DOS, the RAM-disk program is called VDISK.SYS. The following description applies to both RAMDRIVE.SYS and VDISK.SYS. Differences between the two are noted where appropriate.

RAMDRIVE.SYS (and VDISK.SYS) are programs that create a RAM disk by setting aside a certain portion of the computer's memory and treating it as if it were a disk drive. To install a RAM disk, you add a Device command to CONFIG.SYS that identifies the RAM-disk program and specifies the size and characteristics of the RAM disk. You can create more than one RAM disk by including a Device command for each in CONFIG.SYS.

When you create a RAM disk, DOS assigns the first available drive letter to it. DOS normally assumes five available drive letters, A through E. If you need a drive letter higher than E, you should include or modify a Lastdrive command in CONFIG.SYS.

A RAM disk is faster than a physical disk drive because it is electronic—there are no moving parts. Because it is not a physical unit, however, a RAM disk has two characteristics that affect the way you use your system. First, you must be sure to save the contents of a RAM disk on a diskette or a fixed disk. If you don't, any information it contains will be lost when you shut the system down. Second, the memory used for a RAM disk is unavailable for other use. If your system has extended or expanded memory, you can use either for a RAM disk without reducing conventional memory available to applications and data. If your system has 640 K (or less) of conventional RAM, however, you should consider the memory needs of your programs and data and balance those needs against the extra speed provided by a RAM disk.

The CONFIG.SYS Device command format and parameters for RAMDRIVE.SYS are described below. Differences for IBM's VDISK.SYS are noted.

device=ramdrive.sys <size> <sector> <directory> /E /A

RAMDRIVE.SYS (or VDISK.SYS) is the name of the RAM-disk program. Include a drive letter and path name if the program is not in the current directory of the system disk. For example, specify *c:\dos\ramdrive.sys* if the program is in the C:\DOS directory.

<size> specifies the size, in kilobytes, of the RAM disk. If you don't specify <size>, DOS assumes 64 K. If you do specify <size>, acceptable minimum and maximum values for different versions of DOS are:

▶ Version 5: minimum = 16 K, maximum = 4096 K (4 MB)

▶ Earlier Microsoft releases: minimum = 16 K, maximum = all of available memory.

▶ Earlier IBM releases: minimum = 1 K, maximum = all of available memory.

<sector> specifies the size, in bytes, of each RAM-disk sector. Acceptable values for <sector> in different versions of DOS are listed below:

▶ Version 5: 128, 256, or 512. If you don't specify <sector>, DOS assumes 512.

▶ Microsoft version 4: 128, 256, 512, or (in some releases) 1024. If you don't specify <sector>, DOS assumes 512.

▶ Microsoft version 3: 128, 256, 512, or (in some releases) 1024. If you don't specify <sector>, DOS assumes 128.

▶ IBM versions 3 and 4: 128, 256, or 512. If you don't specify <sector>, DOS assumes 128.

<directory> specifies the number of directory entries the root directory can hold. Acceptable values are 2 through 1024 in Microsoft releases of DOS, 2 through 512 in IBM releases. If you don't specify <directory>, DOS assumes 64. Each directory entry requires 32 bytes; if the entries you specify require a fraction of a sector, DOS increases the number to fill the final sector.

/E tells DOS to create the RAM disk in extended memory. If you use extended memory, any required Device command identifying this memory to DOS must precede the RAM-disk command in CONFIG.SYS.

/A tells DOS to create the RAM disk in expanded memory (additional memory conforming to the Lotus-Intel-Microsoft Expanded Memory Specification). If you use expanded memory, any required Device command identifying this memory to DOS must precede the RAM disk command in CONFIG.SYS.

Note: In IBM's release of version 4, this parameter is /X, not /A. If you want to use version 4 to install a RAM disk in expanded memory, check your documentation for details.

Examples

The following examples show equivalent Device commands for RAMDRIVE.SYS and VDISK.SYS. Such commands would be included in CONFIG.SYS. All examples assume RAMDRIVE.SYS or VDISK.SYS is in the C:\DOS directory.

To create a 64 K RAM disk, using all the values that DOS assumes:

```
device=c:\dos\ramdrive.sys
device=c:\dos\vdisk.sys
```

To create a 4 MB RAM disk in expanded memory, specifying 512-byte sectors and 224 directory entries:

```
device=c:\dos\ramdrive.sys 4096 512 224 /a
device=c:\dos\vdisk.sys 4096 512 224 /a
```

(Substitute /x for /a in the second command with IBM's version 4 of DOS.)

To create a 1 MB RAM disk in extended memory, specifying 512-byte sectors and 112 directory entries:

```
device=c:\dos\ramdrive.sys 1024 512 112 /e
device=c:\dos\vdisk.sys 1024 512 112 /e
```

RECOVER
Recover Files from a Damaged Disk
Versions 2.0 and later

The Recover command attempts to reconstruct files from a disk that has damaged sectors or a damaged directory. It names the recovered files FILE*nnnn*.REC, where *nnnn* is a sequence number that starts with 0001. Recovered files may include extraneous material at the end, which you'll need to edit out of the file.

The Recover command excludes data from all damaged sectors; recovered files may or may not be complete and may or may not be usable by an application program. Files can be recovered from subdirectories, but they are placed in the root directory of the disk, not in the subdirectory in which they were originally saved.

Note: Recover cannot be used on a network, nor can it be used with a drive affected by a Join or Substitute command.

    recover <filename>

<filename> is the name of the file to be recovered. If you specify a drive letter rather than a file name, DOS assumes that the directory of the disk in the drive is damaged and recovers the directory as a single file containing the names of the files it originally contained. The original directory is erased, however, so don't use this form of the command unless you're sure the directory is unusable.

Examples

To recover the file named REPORT.DOC in the current directory of the current drive:

```
C:\MKT\WP>recover report.doc
```

To recover as many files as DOS can fit into the root directory of the disk in drive B:

```
C:\>recover b:
```

REM (BATCH COMMAND)
Include a Remark in a Batch File

Versions 1.0 and later

Page 301

The Remark batch command (rem) lets you include remarks in a batch file. Remarks are displayed if echo is on and are not displayed if echo is off.

rem <remark>

<remark> is the remark.

Note: You can also insert rem *at the beginning of a line in your AUTOEXEC.BAT or CONFIG.SYS file. When you do this, you tell DOS to ignore the line during startup. Using the Rem command in this way allows you to disable a command in AUTOEXEC.BAT or CONFIG.SYS, yet keep the command in case you decide to reinstate it later.*

Example

The following batch command includes the remark *This batch file requires the data disk* in a batch file:

```
rem This batch file requires the data disk
```

REMOVE DIRECTORY (RD)
Remove a Directory

Versions 2.0 and later

Page 157

The Remove Directory command (rd or rmdir) removes a subdirectory. You cannot remove the current directory or the root directory, nor can you remove a directory that contains files.

rd <drive><path>

<drive> is the letter, followed by a colon, of the drive containing the disk with the directory to be removed (such as c:).

<path> is the path name of the directory that is to be removed.

Note: Because the Assign, Join, and Substitute commands can mask the actual subdirectory names, you shouldn't remove a directory with the RD command when any of these commands are in effect.

Examples

The following examples assume that the current directory is C:\.

To remove the subdirectory C:\MKT:

`C:\>rd mkt`

To remove the subdirectory C:\MKT\WP:

`C:\>rd \mkt\wp`

To remove the subdirectory \WORD\LETTERS from the disk in drive A:

`C:\>rd a:\word\letters`

RENAME (REN)
Change the Name of a File
Versions 1.0 and later

Page 82

The Rename command (ren) changes the name of a file or a set of files. The renamed file must be in the same directory as the original, and can't be given the name of an existing file in the same directory. You cannot rename a directory.

ren <oldname> <newname>

<oldname> is the name of the file to be renamed. You can include a drive and path, and you can use wildcards (* or ?) to specify a set of files.

<newname> is the new name to be assigned to the file. If you include a drive letter or path name, DOS responds *Invalid parameter* or *Invalid filename or file not found* and doesn't change the name. If <newname> is the same as the name of an existing file, DOS responds *Duplicate file name or file not found* and leaves <oldname> unchanged.

Examples

To change the name of the file REPORT.DOC to FINALRPT.DOC:

`C:\MKT\WP>ren report.doc finalrpt.doc`

To change the name of the file FINALRPT.SAV to FINALRPT.DOC:

`C:\MKT\WP>`ren finalrpt.sav *.doc

To change the names of all files named REPORT in the directory D:\MKT\WP to the name FINALRPT, keeping the same extension:

`C:\>`ren d:\mkt\wp\report.* finalrpt.*

REPLACE
Replace or Add Files on a Disk
Versions 3.2 and later

Page 181

The Replace command lets you copy files selectively, either by replacing files that already exist on the target disk or by adding files to the target. The Replace command can also search subdirectories on the target disk for files to be replaced. The Replace command does not affect files with the hidden or system attribute.

replace <source> <target> /A /S /R /P /W /U

<source> is the name of the file to be copied. You can use wildcard characters to copy a set of files with similar file names or extensions.

<target> specifies where <source> is to be copied. You can include a drive letter and path name, but not a file name.

/A (for *add*) copies only the files in <source> that don't exist in <target>. This lets you add files to <target> without replacing files that already exist. If you don't specify /A, only files specified in <source> that also exist in <target> are copied. If you specify /A, you cannot specify /S or /U.

/S applies the Replace command to all subdirectories contained in <target>. If you specify <target> as the root directory of a disk, the Replace command is applied to every subdirectory on the disk. If you specify /S, you can't specify /A.

/R extends replacement to include read-only files in <target>.

/P prompts for confirmation before replacing or adding each file.

/W waits and prompts you to press a key before the Replace command begins. This gives you a chance to put in the correct diskette before starting to replace or add files on it.

/U replaces only files in the target drive or directory that are older than their counterparts in the source drive or directory.

When it finishes, Replace sets *errorlevel* to one of the following values:

0	Completed normally.
1	There was an error in the command line (versions 3.3 and earlier).
2	No files were found to replace.

3	The source or destination path name was entered incorrectly or does not exist.
5	A read-only file was encountered in <target>, but the /R parameter was not included in the command.
8	Not enough memory.
11	Command-line error (versions 4 and 5).
15	The command includes an invalid drive letter.

You can check this value with the *errorlevel* option of the If batch command and use the outcome of the replace procedure to control the behavior of a batch file.

Examples

To replace all files whose extension is DOC in the directory C:\MKT\WP and all its subdirectories with the files whose extension is DOC on the disk in drive A and prompt for confirmation before each file is copied:

```
C:\>replace a:*.doc c:\mkt\wp /s /p
```

To add all files from the disk in drive A whose extension is DOC and that don't exist in the current directory on the disk in the current drive:

```
C:\MKT\WP>replace a:*.doc /a
```

RESTORE
Restore Backed-Up Files
Versions 2.0 and later

Page 194

The Restore command copies files that were backed up with the Backup command, restoring them from the backup disk to the original disk. Files are restored to the directories from which they were backed up, so the same directory structure must exist on the disk to which the files are restored. If you have a series of backup diskettes, DOS prompts for them, as they are needed, in the same sequence in which they were backed up with the Backup command.

The Restore command includes a number of parameters that help you fine-tune the restoration procedure, but not all parameters are available in all versions of DOS. Check the documentation that came with your version of DOS to determine which parameters you can use.

restore <drive> <filename> /S /P /B:<date> /A:<date> /M /N /E:<time> /L:<time> /D

<drive> specifies the drive that contains the backup disk from which files are to be restored. If you don't specify a drive letter, the files are restored from the disk in the current drive.

<filename> specifies the file or files to be restored. You can include a drive letter and path, and can use wildcard characters to restore a set of files with similar names or extensions. If you don't specify a path, the files are restored to the current directory.

/S restores files from all subdirectories of the specified directory.

/P causes DOS to prompt for confirmation before restoring a read-only file or a file that has changed since it was backed up. In versions 3.3 and later, the Restore command does not affect the system files (IO.SYS and MSDOS.SYS) that DOS needs in order to function. In earlier versions, the /P parameter causes DOS to prompt when it encounters hidden as well as read-only files, so you can use this parameter to avoid replacing the system files with copies from a different version of DOS.

/B:<date> restores only files that were created or changed on or before <date>.

/A:<date> restores only files that were created or changed on or after <date>.

/M restores only files that have been changed since they were backed up.

/N restores only files that don't exist on the target.

/E:<time> restores only files that were created or changed earlier than <time>.

/L:<time> restores only files that were created or changed later than <time>.

/D, in version 5 only, displays the names of all files on the backup disk that match <filename>.

When it is finished, Restore sets one of the following *errorlevel* values:

0	Completed normally.
1	No files were found to restore.
3	The restore process was canceled because the user pressed Ctrl-C or Ctrl-Break.
4	A system error occurred and the restore process was stopped.

You can check this value with the *errorlevel* option of the If batch command and thus use the outcome of the restore procedure to control the behavior of a batch file.

Warning: Trying to restore files that were backed up when an Assign, Substitute, or Join command was in effect can damage the directory structure of the disk.

Examples

To restore the file named REPORT.DOC from the disk in drive A to the directory \MKT\WP (from which it was backed up) on the disk in drive C:

```
C:\>restore a: c:\mkt\wp\report.doc
```

To restore all files in the root directory and all subdirectories on the disk in drive A to the same subdirectories on the disk in drive C:

```
C:\>restore a: c:\ /s
```

With version 5, to see a list of all files on the disk in drive A that were backed up from C:\MKT\WP and would be restored by specifying *.DOC:

```
C:\>restore a: c:\mkt\wp\*.doc /d
```

To restore the files in the preceding example, prompting for confirmation if the file has changed since it was backed up or if the file is read-only:

```
C:\>restore a: c:\mkt\wp\*.doc /p
```

SELECT
Start the Installation Program
Version 4

In version 4, the Select command starts the DOS installation program, which prompts you for information about how to set up your operating system and then installs DOS either on your fixed disk or on diskettes. The DOS version 4 Install diskette contains an AUTOEXEC.BAT file that automatically starts the Select program. To start the program, put the DOS Install diskette in drive A and turn the system on (or, if the system is running, press Ctrl-Alt-Del).

SELECT
Create a Country-specific System Diskette
Version 3.3, IBM releases 3.0 through 3.3

Page 391

The Select command creates a system diskette tailored to the date format and keyboard layout of a particular country.

select <source> <target> <country> <keyboard>

<source> is the letter, followed by a colon, of the drive that contains the DOS system diskette; it must include the system files, COMMAND.COM, the Format command, and the Xcopy command. <source> must be either drive A or drive B; if you don't specify <source>, DOS assumes drive A (versions 3.2 and 3.3).

<target> is the letter, followed by a colon, of the drive that contains the target diskette. If you don't specify <target>, DOS assumes drive B (versions 3.2 and 3.3).

<country> is the three-digit code, corresponding to the long-distance telephone prefix, of the country whose date and time format you want to use.

<keyboard> is the two-letter code for the keyboard layout you want to specify.

Valid country and keyboard codes through version 3.3 are listed in the following table (not all are available in all versions of DOS).

Country	Country Code	Keyboard Code
Australia	061	US
Belgium	032	BE
Canada (English)	001	US
Canada (French)	002	CF
Denmark	045	DK
Finland	358	SU
France	033	FR
Germany	049	GR
International (English)	061	—
Israel	972	—
Italy	039	IT
Latin America	003	LA
Middle East (Arabic)	785	—
Netherlands	031	NL
Norway	047	NO
Portugal	351	PO
Spain	034	SP
Sweden	046	SV
Switzerland (French)	041	SF
Switzerland (German)	041	SG
United Kingdom	044	UK
United States	001	US

When you create a system diskette with the Select command, DOS also creates a CONFIG.SYS file and an AUTOEXEC.BAT file containing Date, Time, and Version commands. In version 3.2, if you specify a country whose keyboard file is not on the source diskette, DOS prompts you to insert the correct diskette. Once a country-specific diskette is created, you can use it to start DOS with the date format and keyboard layout appropriate to that country.

Example

To create a system diskette for France and the French keyboard layout:

```
select 033 fr
```

SET
Change or Display an Environment Variable
Versions 2.0 and later

The Set command changes or displays the value assigned to an environment variable. The environment is an area of memory in which DOS keeps track of such information as the command path and definition of the system prompt. You can also use the Set command to define replaceable parameters for use with batch files. Set commands are usually included in AUTOEXEC.BAT.

    set <variable>=<value>

    <variable> is the name of the variable you want to affect. One common variable is *temp*, which gives the path to a directory where applications can store temporary files. Another variable, useful in version 5 of DOS, is *dircmd*, which can be used to specify how DOS should display the output of the Directory command.

    <value> is the string to be assigned to <variable>.

    Although you don't need the Set command for everyday use, it can be helpful in refining your use of DOS. If you need more information, refer to the documentation that came with your version of DOS.

Examples

To use C:\TEMP for temporary files, create the directory and include the following command in AUTOEXEC.BAT:

```
set temp=c:\temp
```

In version 5, to change the normal Directory command display to a wide format, with directories grouped before file names, you can include the following command in AUTOEXEC.BAT:

```
set dircmd=/w /o:g
```

To override the wide format, you would type a Directory command as *dir /-w*.

SETUP
Install DOS
Version 5.0

The Setup command, in version 5 only, starts a program that installs DOS on your system. To start Setup, place the first DOS disk in drive A and start or restart the system. The installation procedure itself is simple and almost entirely self-contained. If you need information on Setup, refer to the brief description in Appendix A or to the documentation that came with DOS.

SET VERSION (SETVER)
Set DOS Version Number
Version 5.0

The Setver command lets you make version 5 of DOS appear to be a different (earlier) version to an application that requires a different version of DOS. Version requirements for different programs are kept internally by DOS in a format called a version table. You are unlikely to need this command in your everyday use of DOS. If you do use it, first consult your documentation and the application's vendor to verify that you can use Setver without risk to your data.

setver <path> <application> n.nn /delete /quiet

<path> is the drive and path to the DOS file named SETVER.EXE, which loads the version table into memory. The version 5 Setup program ensures that DOS will automatically load SETVER.EXE at startup by placing a Device command in CONFIG.SYS. To display the version table, type *setver* or *setver* <path>.

<application> is the file name and extension of the program for which you want to set the DOS version number.

n.nn is the DOS version number you want to specify (for example, 4.01).

/delete tells DOS to remove a file from the version table. Use this parameter with caution.

/quiet keeps messages from being displayed. You can use this parameter only with */delete*.

Example

To let PROGRAM.EXE use version 5 of DOS as if it were version 3.3:

```
setver program.exe 3.3
```

SETVER.EXE
Load Version Table
Version 5.0

SETVER.EXE is a device driver provided with version 5 that loads the MS-DOS version table into memory. The version table is a list of program names and the versions of DOS under which they were designed to run. SETVER.EXE and the related Setver command are used with programs that expect to work with a particular (earlier) version of DOS, such as version 3.3.

SETVER.EXE is loaded into memory with a Device command, which should be placed in your CONFIG.SYS file by the DOS Setup program.

device=setver.exe

SETVER.EXE is the name of the device driver. If you must add the command to CON-FIG.SYS, precede the file name with a drive and path if the file is not in the current directory—for example, specify *c:\dos\setver.exe* if the file is in your \DOS directory.

SHARE
Allow Files to Be Shared
Versions 3.0 and later

The Share command allows files to be shared by more than one program. If your computer is part of a network, you must enter a Share command before joining the network. Consult with the administrator of your network for information on how to use the Share command.

If your computer isn't part of a network, you probably don't need to use the Share command.

SHELL (CONFIGURATION COMMAND)
Specify the Command Processor
Versions 2.0 and later

The Shell configuration command specifies the command processor—the program that receives your instructions at the keyboard and relays them to the appropriate DOS program—that DOS is to use. Unless you specify otherwise with a Shell command, DOS uses the program named COMMAND.COM. If you need to use a different command processor, the program requiring it should give you instructions on its use.

Note: The Shell command is not the same command that starts the DOS Shell in versions 4 and 5. To start the Shell, you type dosshell *at the system prompt.*

SHIFT (BATCH COMMAND)
Move Batch Parameters One Position Left
Versions 2.0 and later

Page 343
The Shift batch command moves the command-line parameters entered with a batch command one position to the left; the leftmost parameter is lost, and all other parameters move one position left. You can use the Shift command to process more than 10 replaceable parameters in a batch file.

shift

Example

The following batch file, named SHIFT_IT.BAT, uses the Shift command to process as many parameters as you can enter in the command line. The line numbers are shown only for reference:

```
 1.  @echo off
 2.  echo %0
 3.  shift
 4.  :start
 5.  if "%0"=="" goto all_done
 6.  echo %0 %1 %2
 7.  shift
 8.  shift
 9.  shift
10.  goto start
11.  :all_done
12.  echo ALL DONE
```

The Echo command in line 2 displays the name of the batch file, and the Shift command in line 3 shifts all command-line parameters one position to the left; the previous %0 (the name of the batch file) is lost, what was %1 becomes %0, what was %2 becomes %1, and so forth. Line 5 checks the leftmost parameter to see if there is one. If there isn't, the command *goto all_done* ends the batch file. If there is a leftmost parameter, line 6 displays the three leftmost parameters, lines 7 through 9 shift the parameters three positions to the left, and line 10 goes back to repeat the process.

Entering the SHIFT_IT batch command with the following parameters produces the display shown below:

```
C>shift_it 1 2 3 4 5 6 7 8 9 10 11 12 13 14 15
shift_it
1 2 3
4 5 6
7 8 9
10 11 12
13 14 15
ALL DONE
```

SMARTDRV.SYS
Create a Disk Cache in High Memory
Versions 4 (Microsoft releases) and 5

Page 373

The SMARTDRV.SYS device driver creates a disk cache in either extended or expanded memory. A disk cache is an area of memory that DOS uses to store information recently read from disk. Using a disk cache can speed operations significantly because DOS can retrieve information directly from memory much faster than it can find the information on a disk. You create a disk cache by placing a Device configuration command in CONFIG.SYS. Whether you use extended or expanded memory, the Device command that creates a disk cache must follow a Device command that identifies for DOS the program that manages your system's extended or expanded memory.

device=smartdrv.sys <size> <minsize> /A

SMARTDRV.SYS is the name of the device driver. Include a drive and path if SMARTDRV.SYS isn't in the root directory of your startup disk.

<size> is the size of the disk cache, in kilobytes. <size> can be any value from 128 to 8192 (8 MB). If you don't specify <size>, the cache is set to 256 K. In creating the cache, SMARTDRV rounds <size> to the nearest multiple of 16. If there is not enough memory for the size you specify, it creates a smaller cache using the memory available.

<minsize>, in version 5 only, is the smallest you want the cache to be, again in kilobytes. You don't have to specify <minsize> unless you're using Microsoft Windows version 3.0 or later. Windows might reduce the cache to suit its own needs, even if that means reducing <size> to 0.

/A tells SMARDTRV to create the cache in expanded memory. If you don't specify /A, it creates the cache in extended memory.

Example

The following example shows the two commands needed to create a 1024 K disk cache (minimum size 256 K) in extended memory with version 5 of DOS:

```
device=c:\dos\himem.sys
device=c:\dos\smartdrv.sys 1024 256
```

The commands assume the device drivers named are in the C:\DOS directory. HIMEM.SYS is the version 5 extended memory manager; specify your own if you use a different one.

SORT
Arrange Lines of a File
Versions 2.0 and later

Page 283

The Sort filter command reads lines from standard input, arranges (sorts) them in alphabetic or numeric order, and writes the sorted lines to standard output.

In version 2, uppercase and lowercase letters are treated separately, so *Zurich* comes before *aardvark* in a sorted list. In versions 3.0 and later, however, uppercase and lowercase letters are treated identically, so *aardvark* comes before *Zurich*.

The input and output of the Sort command normally come from the keyboard and go to the display. Both, however, can be redirected from or to a file or device, or piped from or to another command. For example, you can redirect input to a file to sort the lines of the file, then redirect the output to another file to store the sorted version on disk. The largest file that the Sort program can handle is 64 K. If you redirect both the input to and the output from the Sort command to a file, use different file names; sorting a file to itself can destroy the contents of the file.

sort /R /+<column>

/R sorts the file in reverse order (Z to A instead of A to Z, or highest number to lowest number).

/+<column> specifies the column on which the sorting is to be based; if you don't specify /+<column>, DOS assumes 1.

Examples

To sort the lines of a file named CLIENTS.LST and display the result:

```
C:\MKT>sort < clients.lst
```

To sort the file CLIENTS.LST in reverse order, placing the result in the file named CLIENTS.SRT:

```
C:\MKT>sort /r < clients.lst > clients.srt
```

STACKS (CONFIGURATION COMMAND)
Reserve Memory for Temporary Program Use

Versions 3.2 and later

The Stacks configuration command tells DOS how much memory to reserve for its own temporary use. Some application programs may require a Stacks command in CONFIG.SYS, and should tell you how to do it; otherwise, you shouldn't need to use this command.

SUBSTITUTE (SUBST)
Treat a Directory as a Disk Drive

Versions 3.1 and later

Page 385

The Substitute command (subst) tells DOS to treat a subdirectory as if it were an additional disk drive in your system. This lets you use subdirectories with an application program that doesn't recognize path names or use a drive letter in place of a long subdirectory name, because you can substitute a drive letter for a path to a subdirectory.

subst <drive> <pathname> /D

<drive> is the letter, followed by a colon, of the drive to be substituted for <pathname> (such as c:). <drive> cannot be the current drive. If you specify <drive>, you must also specify <pathname>.

<pathname> is the path to the subdirectory for which <drive> is to be substituted; <pathname> must begin at the root directory (start with \). If you include a drive letter in <pathname>, it must be different from the letter you specified for <drive>. You must specify at least a backslash to name the root directory.

/D deletes a substitution, returning the drive letter to its original meaning. Do not use this parameter from within the substituted drive or directory.

If you enter the Substitute command with no parameters (type just *subst*), DOS displays all substitutions in effect.

If you substitute a drive letter for one subdirectory, then want to substitute the same drive letter for a different subdirectory, you must first delete the original substitution.

If you want to use several subdirectories, enter a Substitute command for each subdirectory and use a different drive letter for each. If you need drive letters beyond E (the highest letter DOS recognizes unless you specify otherwise), add or edit a Lastdrive configuration command in CONFIG.SYS to tell DOS the highest drive letter.

Note: Because the Substitute command masks the actual type of disk drive from DOS, you shouldn't use the Assign, Backup, Check Disk, Diskcomp, Diskcopy, Fdisk, Format, Join, Label, or Restore command when a substitution is in effect. Because the Substitute command can mask the true directory structure, you should also avoid using the Change Directory, Make Directory, Remove Directory, and Path commands when a substitution is in effect. If you want to use one of these commands, delete the substitution. The Substitute command cannot be used with a network drive.

SWITCHES (CONFIGURATION COMMAND)
Block Enhanced Keyboard Functions
IBM release 4, DOS version 5.0

The Switches configuration command prevents DOS from using the additional keys on the enhanced keyboard. You would most likely need the Switches command only if pressing one of the additional keys on the enhanced keyboard caused problems with one of your application programs.

switches=/K

/K tells DOS not to use the enhanced keyboard functions.

SYSTEM (SYS)
Transfer System Files
Versions 1.0 and later

The System command (sys) copies the DOS system files—IO.SYS and MSDOS.SYS or IBMBIO.COM and IBMDOS.COM, depending on whose version of DOS you're using—from the disk in the current drive to a formatted disk. The system files are hidden and have special storage requirements. You don't see them in the output of the Directory command, but they must be present on any disk from which you want to start DOS. Except in version 5 of DOS, the System command does not copy COMMAND.COM, which must also be on a startup disk. If you don't have version 5, you must copy COMMAND.COM with the Copy command.

You use the System command to transfer the DOS system files to a fixed disk, to a formatted blank diskette, or to a disk (such as an application diskette) on which space has been reserved especially for these files. You can also use the System command to replace existing system files with a newer version (3.3 and earlier versions, however, require the new system files to fit into the space occupied by the older files).

> **sys <source> <drive>**

<source> specifies where the system files are to be copied from. You can specify a drive letter and a directory path name. If you don't specify <source>, DOS copies the system files from the current drive (versions 4 and 5).

<drive> is the letter of the drive, followed by a colon, that contains the disk to which the system files are to be copied (such as c:).

Note: The System command cannot be used on a network drive.

Example

To copy the system files from the disk in drive C to a diskette in drive A:

```
C:\>sys a:
```

TIME
Change or Display the System Time
Versions 1.0 and later

Page 18

The Time command displays the time maintained by DOS, to the hundredth of a second, and prompts you to enter a new time. The time is displayed and entered according to a 12-hour or a 24-hour clock, depending on the custom of the country specified in the Country command in CONFIG.SYS. If you're using version 4 or 5 in a country, such as the United States, that normally uses a 12-hour clock, you can specify the time in

12-hour format, followed by an *a* or a *p* (for example, *10:15a* or *3:15p*), or in 24-hour format (for example, *15:15* for 3:15 P.M.).

The command form shown here uses the traditional United States format (hours:minutes:seconds).

time <hh:mm><:ss><.xx>

<hh:mm> is the new time to be set. <hh> is the hour (1 through 24 or 1 through 12 AM or PM) and <mm> is minutes (0 through 59). <hh> and <mm> are separated by a colon (:).

<:ss> specifies seconds (0 through 59), preceded by a colon (:). If you don't specify <:ss>, DOS assumes 0.

<.xx> specifies hundredths of a second (0 through 99), preceded by a decimal point (.). If you don't specify <.xx>, DOS assumes 0.

If you enter the Time command with no parameter (type just *time*), DOS displays the current time and prompts you to enter the new time. You can either enter the new time, or just press the Enter key to leave the time unchanged. If your system does not keep the time current when the computer is switched off, consider putting Date and Time commands in your AUTOEXEC.BAT file.

Note: The Time command might not permanently change the system clock on computers with built-in or add-on clock/calendars. If you have a system with a built-in clock/calendar (such as the IBM PC/AT or a compatible) and the Time command does not permanently change the time, use the SETUP program on your Diagnostics disk. If you have an add-on clock/calendar, use the software that came with the clock/calendar card.

Examples

To set the time to 6:00 A.M.:

```
C:\>time 6:00
```

Or, in version 4 or 5:

```
C:\>time 6:00a
```

To set the time to 6:00 P.M.:

```
C:\>time 18:00
```

Or, in version 4 or 5:

```
C:\>time 6:00p
```

To display the current time and respond to the prompt for a new time:

```
C:\>time
```

DOS responds:

```
Current time is  6:02:01.60p
Enter new time: _
```

Or, if you're not using version 4 or 5:

```
Current time is 18:02:01.60
Enter new time: _
```

Type the new time or press the Enter key to leave the current time unchanged.

TREE
Display a Directory Structure
Versions 3.2 and later, IBM releases 2.0 and later

Page 163

The Tree command shows the structure of a disk or directory by displaying the directory and subdirectory names and, optionally, the names of the files in each directory. In versions 4 and 5, the Tree command diagrams the structure of a disk or a multilevel directory by using line-drawing and box-drawing characters. Earlier versions produce a list of directory names and, if requested, file names.

tree <drive><path> /F /A

<drive> is the letter of the drive, followed by a colon, that contains the disk whose directory structure is to be displayed.

<path> is the path to a specified directory. If you omit <path>, DOS displays the current directory of the specified drive.

/F displays a list of the files in each directory.

/A specifies that alternative characters (plus signs, hyphens, and vertical bars) be used to draw the tree diagram so that it can be printed by printers that don't support the line-drawing and box-drawing characters (versions 4 and 5).

Note: You can also display a list of the directories and files on a disk with the /V option of the Check Disk command.

Examples

Assume that the root directory of the disk in drive C contains four directories: DOS, MKT, MFG, and ENG; \MKT and \ENG, in turn, contain subdirectories named WP and SPREAD. To display this directory structure, type:

```
C:\>tree
```

In versions 4 and 5, DOS displays the following diagram:

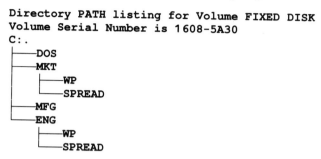

```
Directory PATH listing for Volume FIXED DISK
Volume Serial Number is 1608-5A30
C:.
├────DOS
├────MKT
│       ├───WP
│       └───SPREAD
├────MFG
└────ENG
        ├───WP
        └───SPREAD
```

To print the diagram using the alternative characters, add the /A parameter and redirect the output to the printer:

```
C:\>tree /a > prn
```

DOS prints the following diagram:

```
Directory PATH listing for Volume FIXED DISK
Volume Serial Number is 1608-5A30
C:.
+---DOS
+---MKT
¦    +---WP
¦    \---SPREAD
+---MFG
\---ENG
     +---WP
     \---SPREAD
```

To display the directory structure of the disk in drive B, including all file names and pausing after each screenful:

```
C:\>tree b: /f ¦ more
```

TYPE
Display a File
Versions 1.0 and later

Page 70

The Type command sends a file to standard output. If you don't redirect standard output, the file is displayed.

type <filename>

<filename> is the file to be sent to standard output. The Type command doesn't accept wildcard characters.

Note: Some files include characters other than alphabetic and numeric characters and punctuation marks. Program files are one example; another is a word processor document that includes special formatting codes designed to be read by programs, rather than by people. If you use the Type command to display such a file, you'll probably see unintelligible characters and hear occasional beeps. Don't worry; your computer can handle the display, even though the results might be meaningless to you.

Examples

To display the file named REPORT.DOC in the current directory:

        C:\MKT\WP>type report.doc

To print the file REPORT.DOC from the directory \MKT\WP on the disk in drive A:

        C:\DOS>type a:\mkt\wp\report.doc > prn

VDISK.SYS
Define a RAM Disk

The device driver VDISK.SYS is used with the Device configuration command to create a virtual disk drive in your computer's memory. This file is in IBM's releases of DOS starting with version 3.0. The equivalent MS-DOS file is called RAM-DRIVE.SYS. Refer to that entry if your system includes VDISK.SYS.

UNDELETE
Recover Deleted Files
Version 5.0

Page 79

The Undelete command restores files deleted with the Delete command, replacing them on the drive and in the directory from which they were removed. Available in version 5 only, Undelete can work with the delete-tracking feature of the Mirror command (also new in version 5) or by using the directory-storage information maintained by DOS. Of the two, delete tracking is more accurate, but both methods can be effective.

Although Undelete can save you considerable time and aggravation when you've inadvertently deleted one or more needed files, files *cannot always* be completely recovered. When you delete a file, DOS assumes that its storage space is available for saving other files. Undelete can succeed only if DOS has not yet reassigned the file's disk space to another file. Once DOS uses the space formerly occupied by a deleted file, the original information is lost and cannot be recovered by any means. For this reason, it is important to undelete files as soon as possible—preferably before any other files have been saved on the same disk.

undelete <filename> /dt /dos /all /list

<filename> is the name of the file or files you want to restore. You can specify a drive and path, and you can use wildcards (* or ?) to specify a set of files. If you don't include <filename>, Undelete assumes you want to recover files in the current directory of the current drive.

/dt tells Undelete to recover deleted files recorded by the delete-tracking feature of the Mirror command. To use this parameter, you must already have started delete tracking. Undelete can then try to recover any files subsequently deleted. The /dt parameter causes Undelete to display the name of each deleted file it finds and prompt you to confirm the recovery. If the only parameter you specify is <filename>, Undelete assumes /dt if a delete-tracking file exists. For details on delete tracking, refer to the description of the Mirror command.

/dos tells Undelete to use the information recorded by DOS to recover deleted files. When you use this parameter, Undelete prompts for confirmation before recovering each file it can restore. Because DOS clears the first character in the name of a deleted file, you are also asked what the first character should be before the file is undeleted. If the only parameter you specify is <filename>, Undelete assumes /dos if a delete-tracking file does not exist.

/all tells Undelete to recover all deleted files without stopping at each and prompting for confirmation. If a delete-tracking file exists, /all causes all recoverable files to be restored under their original file names. If a delete-tracking file does not exist, /all causes all recoverable files to be restored with # or another unique character as the first character in the file name. You can then use the DOS Rename command to replace the # symbol with an appropriate character.

/list tells Undelete to display a list of the files it can recover. Unrecoverable files are marked with a double asterisk (**).

Note: If you need to restore a deleted subdirectory, you can try the Unformat command.

Examples

To undelete all recoverable files in the current directory of the current drive, using the delete-tracking file and prompting for confirmation each time:

```
C:\MKT>undelete /dt
```

To undelete all recoverable files with the extension DOC in the directory C:\MEMOS, using the DOS record of deleted files and prompting for confirmation each time:

```
C:\>undelete \memos\*.doc /dos
```

To undelete all recoverable files with the extension DOC in the directory C:\MEMOS, not prompting for confirmation:

```
C:\>undelete \memos\*.doc /all
```

To list all deleted files in the directory C:\MEMOS and to note which can be recovered:

```
c:\>undelete \memos /list
```

UNFORMAT
Undo a Disk Format
Version 5.0

Pages 109, 205

The Unformat command, new with version 5, helps you undo the effects of formatting either a diskette or a fixed disk. With Unformat, you can restore a disk, its files, and its directories to their status before the disk was formatted. Like the complementary Mirror command, Unformat provides a safeguard against accidental loss of programs and data.

Unformat restores a disk by reconstructing the file-storage information on it in either of two ways: by referring to a disk-storage information file created by the Mirror command, or by referring directly to storage information recorded on the disk by DOS. Of these two methods, using the Mirror file is preferable because it gives Unformat a more reliable reference to work from.

Unformat cannot always restore a disk completely, however, especially if you have not used the Mirror command recently to create an information file that accurately reflects the current state of the disk. Losing the contents of any disk can be severe, so you should use Mirror regularly to track file storage...just in case. Because no prior files, including the Unformat command file, can be read from a fixed disk you've formatted by mistake, you should also keep on hand a DOS startup diskette containing UNFORMAT.COM and a current copy of the system's CONFIG.SYS file for use in gaining access to the disk after formatting.

Note: Unformat cannot restore a disk formatted with the /U parameter of the Format command.

unformat <drive> /J /L /test /partn /P /U

<drive> is the letter, followed by a colon, of the drive containing the disk to unformat (such as c:). <drive> cannot refer to a network drive.

/J checks the disk in <drive> for disk-information files recorded by the Mirror command, but it does not unformat the disk at the same time. If you use /J, Unformat tries to verify that the contents of the Mirror files agree with the information it finds on the disk. Because of the way Unformat searches the disk, it can find a Mirror file even after the disk has been formatted. It cannot work, however, if you have used the Fdisk command to partition a fixed disk.

/test checks the disk in <drive>, but does not use files recorded by the Mirror command. Like the /J parameter, */test* examines the state of the disk but does not actually unformat it.

/L causes Unformat to react in one of two ways, depending on whether you also use the */partn* parameter:

▶ If you specify /L without the */partn* parameter, Unformat assumes there is no Mirror file and searches the disk directly, listing all the files and directories it finds in the root directory. This parameter causes Unformat to first search the disk and then ask if you're sure you want to restore it. Because Unformat cannot fully recover fragmented files (files stored in separate areas on the disk), it displays the name of each fragmented file and asks whether you want to truncate or delete it. You must choose one or the other, and in either case, you can expect to lose at least some information. If you don't use /L, Unformat normally displays only the names of files and subdirectories that are fragmented and are not fully recoverable.

▶ If you specify /L with the */partn* parameter, Unformat displays the disk's partition table (information about the way the disk is set up for use by DOS).

/partn without the /L parameter tells Unformat to restore the disk's partition table. To do this, Unformat must have access to a file named PARTNSAV.FIL, which you create with the Mirror command and keep on a diskette, separate from the fixed disk.

/P tells Unformat to send its messages to the printer attached to LPT1.

/U tells Unformat to rebuild the disk without using the Mirror file.

Examples

To use the Mirror information file and check on the inadvertently formatted fixed disk in drive C without actually unformatting the disk:

```
A:\>unformat c: /j
```

To check on the inadvertently formatted fixed disk in drive C without the use of a Mirror file and without actually unformatting the disk:

```
A:\>unformat c: /test
```

To unformat the fixed disk in drive C, using the Mirror file (and a startup system diskette in drive A:

```
A:\>unformat c:
```

To unformat the fixed disk in drive C, without using a Mirror file (but with the help of a startup system diskette in drive A:

```
A:\>unformat c: /l
```

To display the partition table of the fixed disk in drive C without unformatting the disk:

```
A:\>unformat c: /partn /l
```

To rebuild a damaged partition table on the fixed disk in drive C:

```
A:\>unformat c: /partn
```

To unformat an inadvertently formatted diskette in drive A, using the Mirror file:

```
C:\>unformat a:
```

VER (VERSION)
Display the DOS Version Number
Versions 2.0 and later

Page 381
The Version command (ver) displays the DOS version number, which consists of the major version number, a period, and the minor version number (such as 4.01).

The Version command has no parameters.

ver

Example

To display the DOS version number:

```
C:\>ver
```

For version 5, DOS responds with a message like this:

```
MS-DOS Version 5.0
```

VERIFY
Verify Data Written to Disk
Versions 2.0 and later

The Verify command turns the verify feature of DOS on or off. The verify feature confirms that data is correctly written to disk. Storing data on a disk takes a bit longer when Verify is on. Setting Verify on is equivalent to using the /V parameter of the Copy command. DOS assumes Verify is off unless you specify otherwise.

verify on off

on turns Verify on.
off turns Verify off.

If you enter a Verify command with no parameters (type just *verify*), DOS displays the current status of Verify (*VERIFY is on* or *VERIFY is off*).

557

Examples

To turn Verify on:

```
C:\>verify on
```

To display the status of Verify:

```
C:\>verify
```

DOS responds:

VERIFY is on

or

VERIFY is off

VOL (VOLUME)
Display the Volume Label of a Disk
Versions 2.0 and later

Page 117

The Volume command (vol) displays the volume label and, in versions 4 and 5, the serial number of a disk.

vol <drive>

<drive> is the letter, followed by a colon, of the drive containing the disk whose volume label is to be displayed. If you omit <drive>, DOS displays the volume label of the disk in the current drive.

Example

To display the volume label of the disk in the current drive:

```
C:\>vol
```

If the disk's volume label is FIXED DISK, DOS responds as follows:

```
Volume in drive C is FIXED DISK
Volume Serial Number is 1608-5A30
```

If the disk has no volume label, DOS responds:

```
Volume in drive A has no label
Volume Serial Number is 3433-1BC6
```

XCOPY
Copy Files and Directories Selectively
Versions 3.2 and later

Page 184

The Xcopy command lets you copy only files whose archive attribute is on, or files that have changed since a particular date. You can also use the Xcopy command to copy files not only from the source directory but also from all the subdirectories it contains; if the corresponding subdirectories don't exist on the target disk or directory, the Xcopy command creates them. Xcopy is thus particularly useful in duplicating a directory structure from one disk to another.

xcopy <source> <target> /A /M /E /P /S /V /W /D:<date>

<source> is the name of the file to be copied. You can use wildcard characters to copy a set of files with similar file names or extensions. You must include <source>, specifying at least a drive letter.

<target> specifies where <source> is to be copied. You can include any combination of drive letter, path name, and file name.

/A copies only those files whose archive attribute is on, but leaves the archive attribute unchanged.

/M copies only those files whose archive attribute is on, then turns off the archive attribute of the source files. Turning the archive attribute off is useful for backup procedures because it tells DOS (or any other program, such as a backup utility) that the file hasn't been changed since it was last backed up, and therefore doesn't need to be archived again.

/E creates subdirectories on <target> even if they are empty on <source>. If you use /E, you must also use /S.

/P prompts for confirmation before copying each file specified in <source>.

/S applies the Xcopy command to all subdirectories contained in <source> unless the subdirectories are empty. If you specify <source> as a drive letter or as the root directory of a disk, the Xcopy command is applied to every subdirectory on the disk.

/V verifies that the copy of the file on <target> was stored correctly. This option can slow the operation of the Xcopy command somewhat, but it's good insurance if you're copying critical data and must be certain that it was copied correctly.

/W waits and prompts you to press a key before the Xcopy command begins. This gives you a chance to put in the correct diskette before starting to copy files.

/D:<date> copies only files whose date of creation or last change (as displayed by the Directory command) is the same as or later than <date>.

Examples

To copy all the files whose archive attribute is on from the directory C:\MKT\WP to the disk in drive A and turn off the archive attribute of the source files:

```
C:\>xcopy \mkt\wp a: /m
```

To copy all the files whose archive attribute is on from the directory C:\MKT\WP and all subdirectories that contain files to the disk in drive A and turn off the archive attribute of the source files:

```
C:\>xcopy \mkt\wp a: /s /m
```

To copy all the files that have changed since October 16, 1991, from the directory D:\MKT\WP and all subdirectories that contain files to the disk in the current drive, prompting for confirmation before each copy:

```
C:\>xcopy d:\mkt\wp /d:10-16-91 /s /p
```

To copy all the files and directories on the disk in drive A to the disk in drive B, including all empty subdirectories:

```
C:\>xcopy a:\ b:\ /s /e
```

XMAEM.SYS
Emulate IBM PS/2 80286 Expanded Memory Adapter
Version 4

XMA2EMS.SYS
Manage Lotus-Intel-Microsoft Expanded Memory
Version 4

XMAEM.SYS and XMA2EMS.SYS are device drivers that enable version 4 of DOS to use memory beyond the normal maximum of 640 K. Because these programs are for use by specific computer models and memory expansion boards, follow the instructions in the manual that came with your computer or memory expansion board when using these commands.

INDEX

Special Characters

\# (EDLIN last line symbol)
266, 478

\$ (DOSKEY macro commands)
314, 472

\$ (PROMPT operator) 382

% (batch replaceable parameter)
302, 493

% (DOSSHELL parameter) 238

%% (batch replaceable
parameter) 345, 492

* (DOSSHELL directory
operator) 229

* (EDLIN prompt) 264

* (wildcard character) 43, 62–63

+ (COPY file-combining
operator) 74

+ (DOSSHELL directory
operator) 212, 229

– (DOSSHELL directory
operator) 212, 229

. (current directory symbol)
153, 464

. (EDLIN current line symbol)
478

.. (parent directory symbol)
153, 464

... (DOSSHELL symbol) 217

: (batch file label operator) 325

< (redirection operator) 50, 288,
291, 502

> (redirection operator) 52, 280,
288, 502

>> (redirection operator) 289,
502

? (wildcard character) 43, 63–64

@ (batch display-suppression
operator) 321

\ (canceled command symbol)
29

\ (path name separator) 149

\ (root directory symbol) 145,
147, 149

^ (control key symbol) 31

¦ (piping operator) 51, 289, 291,
502–3

4201.CPI file 400, 523

4208.CPI file 400, 523

5202.CPI file 400, 523

A

accented characters 138, 390

access, file/directory. *See*
attributes, file/directory

access, speeding up disk. *See*
disk buffers; disk caches;
FASTOPEN command

allocation units 45, 103, 447

Alternate key (Alt) 30
DOSSHELL use of *213*
DOS use of 30

Alt-Esc keys 232

Alt-F1 keys 251

Alt-Minus keys 251

Alt-Plus keys 251

Alt-Tab keys 232

ANSI.SYS device driver
command reference 434
Devicehigh command and
reserved memory use by
379
installing 380, 461
MODE command and 126

APPEND command 168–69,
378–79, 434–35

application-based file systems
357–58

application programs 4

archive attributes 176–79

archiving files with batch files
320–32, 343–44, 347

arrow keys. *See* direction keys

ASCII (American Standard
Code for Information
Interchange) 90, 221

ASSIGN command 384–85, 436

asterisk wildcard character (∗)
43, 62–63

attrib. *See* ATTRIBUTE
command (attrib)

ATTRIB.EXE file 83

ATTRIBUTE command (attrib)
84–87, 176–81, 437–38

attributes, file/directory
archive status 176–79
changing 84–87, 437–38
displaying status of 176–81
hidden status 86–87, 176,
179–81
read-only status 84–85

AUTOEXEC.400 file 368,
415–16

AUTOEXEC.BAT file
batch file commands 441
CONFIG.SYS and 368
creating 306–9
described 305–6
DOS installation 415–16
paths 162–63
root directory requirement 202

AUX device name 121

Auxiliary devices. *See* serial
ports

B

backing up files/directories
188–94, 364–65,
438–40

Backspace key 15, 18

BACKUP.001 file 190

BACKUP command 188–94,
364–65, 438–40

BACKUPID.@@@ file 190
BACKUP.LOG file 189, 197, 439
BAS extension *60*
Basic language 230, 532
batch files. *See also* files
  archiving files with 320–32,
    343–44, 347
  calling other 348–49,
    444–45, 449
  canceling 303–5
  chaining 336–39
  changing command sequences
    in 325–27, 496
  command reference 440–41
  conditional execution
    323–25, 501–2
  copying files between
    directories with 342–43
  creating, with COPY 300–301
  creating, with DOSKEY
    312–13
  deleting files with 311,
    340–41
  described 298
  displaying blank lines
    330–32, 339
  displaying directories of
    subdirectories with 341
  displaying long directories
    with 339–40
  displaying messages with
    ECHO 321, 330–32, 339,
    474–75
  displaying messages with
    PAUSE 322–23, 527
  displaying messages with
    REMARK 301–2, 535
  displaying multiple files with
    349–50
  displaying sorted directories
    with 352–54
  DOS command search order
    and 298–99
  labels 325
  macros vs. 311–12
  menu systems 360–64
  printing files with 310
  searching through files with
    334–39, 350–52

batch files, *continued*
  shifting command-line
    parameters 343–44,
    544–45
  starting DOS with (*see*
    AUTOEXEC.BAT file)
  using replaceable parameters
    to repeat commands
    302–3, 345–47,
    492–93
  wildcard characters and
    327–28
BAT extension *60*, 298
baud rate 129, 130
bibliographic index 366–67
booting DOS. *See* starting DOS
BREAK command 441–42. *See
    also* Ctrl-Break keys
BREAK configuration
    command 442. *See also*
    Ctrl-Break keys
Break key 30
buffers, disk 380, 442–44
BUFFERS configuration
    command 380, 442–44
built-in commands 40
bytes 24–25

C

caches, disk 373–74, 545–46
CALL batch command
    348–49, 444–45
capital inventory 367–68
cd. *See* CHANGE DIRECTORY
    command (cd)
CGA (Color Graphics Adapter)
    125, 136, 405, 496–97,
    515–16
chaining batch files 336–39
chains 447
CHANGE CODE PAGE
    command (chcp) 403–4,
    445
CHANGE DIRECTORY
    command (cd) 25–26,
    146–47, 152, 446
characters. *See also* keyboards;
    keys
  accented 138, 390

characters, *continued*
  ASCII 90, 221
  enabling display of graphics
    136, 405, 496–97
  foreign language (*see* code
    pages)
  hexadecimal 90, 221
  system prompt definition 382
  wildcard 43–44, 62–64,
    327–28
character strings 52
chcp. *See* CHANGE CODE
    PAGE command (chcp)
CHECK DISK command
    (chkdsk) 113–15, 166–68,
    446–48
CHKDSK.COM file 166
CHKDSK.EXE file 166
CLEAR SCREEN command
    (cls) 21, 123, 448–49
Clipboard, EDIT program
    257–58
clock, system. *See* date; time
cls. *See* CLEAR SCREEN
    command (cls)
clusters 447
code pages. *See also* foreign
    languages
  changing 403–4, 445
  date/time/currency/decimal
    formats 401–2, 456–58
  described 136, 393–97
  displaying status of 404–5,
    524
  enabling code-page switching
    399, 525–26
  keyboard layouts 402–3,
    504–6
  preparing 400–401, 522–23
  restoring 405, 524
  selecting 404, 523–24
  setting up code-page switching
    397–403
  specifying display drivers
    397–98, 400, 406–7
  specifying printer drivers
    398–99, 400, 406–7
  using code-page switching
    403–5

code pages, *continued*
  valid combinations of country codes, keyboard codes, and *396*
Color Graphics Adapter. *See* CGA
COM1–COM4. *See* serial ports
combining text files 74–75, 455–56
COM extension *60*
COM files, converting EXE files to 485
COMMAND.COM file 202, 417
COMMAND command 449
command files. *See* batch files; commands, DOS; DOSKEY program; program files
command history. *See* DOSKEY program
command level 14
command macros. *See* DOSKEY program
command processors
  COMMAND.COM file 202, 417
  exiting current version of 485
  loading new copy of 449
  specifying 544
command prompt. *See* prompt, system
Command Prompt Program Item, DOSSHELL program 230
commands, DOS
  canceling 29, 30, 31–32
  configuration (*see* CONFIG.SYS configuration file)
  described 7
  editing, 292
  entering 14–16
  external vs. internal 40–41
  file management 58
  help on 64–65, 499–500
  history/macros (*see* DOSKEY program)

commands, DOS, *continued*
  parameters (*see* parameters, command-line)
  redirecting input/output of (*see* input/output redirection)
  search order 298–99
  search paths (*see* paths)
  sorting output of 546–47
  user-defined (*see* batch files; DOSKEY program)
  wildcard characters 43–44, 62–64
command search path 162–63, 526–27
communications parameters 128–30, 518–20
communications ports. *See* serial ports
COMPARE command (comp) 87–90, 450–51. *See also* FILE COMPARISON command (fc)
compatibility. *See also* versions, DOS
  backup files 189, 190, 440
  defined 6, 7
  diskettes 103–4
  RESTORE command 194
COMP.COM file 83
compressed files, expanding 486
computer files, tracking 365–66
condensed print 126–28
CON device name 46, 59, 121
CONFIG.400 file 368, 415–16
CONFIG.SYS configuration file
  AUTOEXEC.BAT and 368
  code-page switching (*see* code pages)
  command reference 451–52
  device drivers 369–80, 461–62, 463
  disk buffers 380, 442–44
  disk caches 373–74, 545–46
  DOS installation 415–16
  highest drive letter 381, 508
  memory management (*see* memory)
  open files 380–81, 491

CONFIG.SYS configuration file, *continued*
  RAM drives 375–77, 532–34, 553
  root directory requirement 202
  unformatting requirement 206
consoles. *See also* keyboards; screens
  changing 458–59
  control program (*see* ANSI.SYS device driver)
  creating batch files from 300–301
  creating text files from 46–47, 60–62
  displaying status of 131–33, 522
CONTROL.001 file 190
Control key (Ctrl) 30–33
conventional memory 123, 369–70
COPY command
  combining files 74–75
  command reference 452–56
  copying files 70–73
  copying files between directories 148–49, 342–43
  copying files to devices 73–74, 454–55
  copying from devices to files/ devices 133–34, 455
  creating batch files 300–301
  creating text files 46–47, 60–62
  printing files with 47–48, 267–68
copying diskettes 110–11, 468–69
copying files. *See* COPY command; File List, DOSSHELL program; REPLACE command; XCOPY command
country codes. *See also* foreign languages
  code-pages *396*
  date/time/currency/decimal formats 389, 401

country codes, *continued*
  keyboard layouts *137–38*
  system diskettes *388*
COUNTRY configuration
  command 389, 401–2,
  456–58
COUNTRY.SYS file 399, 401,
  526
CPI extension 395
creating files. *See also* EDIT
  program; EDLIN program
  batch 300–301
  text 46–47, 60–62
Ctrl-* keys 229
Ctrl-Alt-Del keys *31,* 36
Ctrl-Alt-F1 keys 140, 391, 506
Ctrl-Alt-F2 keys 140, 391, 506
Ctrl-Break keys
  canceling batch files 303–5
  EDLIN use of 265
  function 30, 31–32
  handling 441–42
Ctrl-C keys. *See* Ctrl-Break keys
Ctrl-Esc keys 231
Ctrl-F1 keys 251
Ctrl-Ins keys 257
Ctrl key 30–33
Ctrl-Num Lock keys 29, 31
Ctrl-P keys 32
Ctrl-PrtSc keys 30, *31,* 32–33
Ctrl-T keys 295, 315
Ctrl-Z keys 46, 60, 133, 270
CTTY command 458–59
currency formats 389, 401–2,
  456–58, 540–41
current directory (.)
  changing 25–26, 146–47, 152,
    446
  defined 149
  symbol 153, 464
  as system prompt 146, 152–53
current drive 14, 19–20
cursor 16, 246
cursor-movement keys. *See*
  direction keys
cut and paste 257

D

data bits 129, 130
data files. *See* files
data search path 168–69,
  434–35
date
  changing 17–18, 459–60
  formats 389, 401–2,
    456–58, 540–41
  starting DOS 13
DATE command 17–18,
  459–60
dead keys 138, 390
decimal formats 389, 401–2,
  456–58, 540–41
DELETE command (del, erase)
  49, 76–81, 460
Delete key (Del) 30
delete tracking
  installing 77–78, 512–14
  undeleting files with 79–81,
    553–55
deleting files
  with batch files 311, 340–41
  with DELETE 49, 76–81, 460
  with DOSSHELL 221–23
department-based file systems
  358–59
DEVICE configuration
  command 369–80,
  397–99, 461–62
device drivers 369–80,
  461–62, 463
DEVICEHIGH configuration
  command 378, 379–80, 463
devices. *See also* consoles;
  display adapters; parallel
  ports; printers; serial ports
  code-page switching (*see* code
    pages)
  copying files to 73–74,
    454–55
  copying from, to files/devices
    133–34, 455
  described 46, 120, 369
  displaying status of 131–33,
    522

devices, *continued*
  drivers 369–80, 461–62, 463
  names 46, 47, 59, 121–*22*
  redirection and 51, 53, 280,
    502
dialog boxes 219, 239
dir. *See* DIRECTORY command
  (dir)
direction keys
  activating 29–30
  DOSKEY use of 33–34
  DOSSHELL use of 217
  EDIT use of 246–48
  Up Arrow 16, 18
directories. *See also* tree-
  structured file systems
  access, controlling (*see*
    attributes, file/directory)
  backing up 189–91, 438–40
  backing up, with batch files
    364–65
  changing 25–26, 146–47, 152,
    446
  copying files between 148–49
  copying files between, in
    DOSSHELL 219–20
  copying files between, with
    batch files 342–43
  creating 143–45, 151–52, 510
  current (*see* current directory)
  described 24–25, 149
  displaying (*see* DIRECTORY
    command)
  displaying, in DOSSHELL
    224–28
  displaying, of subdirectories
    341
  displaying long, with batch
    files 339–40
  displaying sorted, in
    DOSSHELL 223–24
  displaying sorted, with batch
    files 352–54
  DOS subdirectory 25,
    201–2, 417–18
  entries *27,* 149
  joining disk drives to 386,
    503–4

directories, *continued*
  naming, as disk drives 385,
    547–48
  parent 153
  path names (*see* paths)
  removing 157–59, 535–36
  removing, in DOSSHELL
    222–23
  restoring, from backup
    194–200, 538–40
  root 142, 145, 147, 149
  scrolling, in DOSSHELL
    217–18
  selecting, in DOSSHELL 217
  subdirectories 25–26, 142, 149
  symbols 149, 153–57, 464
DIRECTORY command (dir)
  command reference 464–66
  file-only displays 69
  multiple-directory displays
    154–62
  parameters 66–67, 87, 159, 363
  pausing displays 26–27, 68
  printing displays 51–52
  sorting displays 69
  sorting displays with batch
    files 352–54
  specific files/sets of files and
    42–44, 160–62
  wide displays 66–68
directory entries 27, 149
disk access speedup. *See* disk
    buffers; disk caches;
    FASTOPEN command
disk buffers 380, 442–44
disk caches 373–74, 545–46
DISK COMPARE command
    (diskcomp) 112–13,
    467–68
DISKCOPY command 110–11,
    468–69
disk drives
  capacities 25, 102
  current 14, 19–20
  defining characteristics of 474
  defining highest letter for 381,
    508
  joining, to directories 386,
    503–4

disk drives, *continued*
  naming directories as 385,
    547–48
  routing operations to different
    384–85, 436
diskettes. *See also* disks
  backup tips 99–100
  capacities 102, *104*
  comparing 112–13, 467–68
  composition of 100–101
  copying 110–11, 468–69
  displaying contents of backup
    196–97
  formatting (*see* FORMAT
    command; SELECT
    command)
  formatting, during backup 188
  handling 98–99
  information storage method
    100–*102*
  system (*see* system disks)
disk files. *See* files
disk operating system. *See* DOS
disks. *See also* diskettes; fixed
    disks
  capacities 25, 102
  displaying status of 113–15,
    166–68, 446–48
  formatting (*see* FORMAT
    command; SELECT
    command)
  installing/upgrading DOS (*see*
    versions, DOS)
  RAM/virtual (*see* RAM
    drives)
  recovering files from damaged
    534–35
  saving recovery information
    107–8, 203–5, 512–14
  system (*see* system disks)
  types 5
  unformatting 109–10,
    205–7, 555–57
  verifying data written to
    557–58
  volume labels (*see* labels, disk
    volume)
  volume serial numbers 103

Disk Utilities Program Group,
    DOSSHELL program
    240–42
display adapters. *See also*
    screens
  changing display
    characteristics 515–16
  changing display columns/
    lines 124–26, 339–40, 517
  code pages 397–98, 400,
    405–6
DISPLAY.SYS device driver
    379, 397–98, 461
DOS
  commands (*see* commands,
    DOS)
  compatibility (*see*
    compatibility)
  configuration (*see*
    CONFIG.SYS
    configuration file)
  described 4–8
  disk management (*see* disks)
  editors (*see* EDIT program;
    EDLIN program)
  files (*see* files)
  foreign language support (*see*
    foreign languages)
  installing/upgrading (*see*
    versions, DOS)
  loading, into extended memory
    372–73, 469–71,
    500–501
  memory management (*see*
    memory)
  prompt (*see* prompt, system)
  root directory files, 202
  shell (*see* DOSSHELL
    program)
  starting (*see* starting DOS)
  subdirectory for 25, 201–2,
    417–18
  undeleting files with, vs.
    MIRROR 81, 553–54
  unformatting disks with, vs.
    MIRROR 555–57
  versions (*see* versions, DOS)
DOS configuration command
    372–73, 469–71

DOSKEY program
  command parameters 312
  command reference 471–73
  creating batch files 312–13
  creating macros 314–15
  editing commands 293–94
  macros vs. batch files 311–12,
    361
  repeating commands 18, 33–36
  replaceable parameters
    314–16
  reserved memory use with
    378–79, 509–10
  saving macros 315–16
  starting 16
  using multiple commands
    295–96
DOSSHELL.INI file 220–21
DOSSHELL program
  command reference 473
  File List 216–29
  File menu 216–23, 233–43
  Help menu 214–16
  keyboard/mouse use in 213
  Options menu 221–25,
    231–32
  Program List 230–43
  starting 210–13
  starting DOS with/without
    11–13
  text mode vs. graphics mode 211
  Tree menu 229
  View menu 210, 223, 225–26
  view options 225–28
  window, parts of 211–12
DOS subdirectory 25, 201–2,
  417–18
dot-matrix printers. *See* printers
DRIVE PARAMETERS
  configuration command
    (drivparm) 474
DRIVER.SYS device driver
  379, 461
drives. *See* disk drives; RAM
  drives; tape drives
drivparm. *See* DRIVE
  PARAMETERS
  configuration command
    (drivparm)

E

ECHO batch command 321,
  330–32, 339, 474–75
EDIT.COM file 248
Edit menu, EDIT program 256,
  257–58, 476
editors. *See* EDIT program;
  EDLIN program
EDIT program
  changing screen options
    261–62
  command reference 475–77
  copying/moving text 257–58
  copying text from another file
    260–61
  deleting text 256
  editing files 257–58
  entering text 252
  exiting 256–57
  inserting text 252–53
  inserting vs. overstriking 260
  keyboard/mouse use in
    246–48
  margins 253–54
  printing files 254
  replacing text 259
  saving files 254–56
  searching files 258
  selecting text 247–48
  starting 248
  Survival Guide help 248–52
EDLIN.COM file 92
EDLIN program
  canceling edits 269
  command reference 477–83
  copying lines 275–76
  copying lines from another file
    276–77
  creating files 264–65
  deleting lines 268
  editing files 268
  editing keys 272–75
  editing lines 270–75
  ending/saving edits 267
  entering lines 265
  inserting lines 264–65,
    266–67
  listing lines 266
  moving lines 274–75

EDLIN program, *continued*
  paging lines 267
  printing files 267–68
  replacing strings 270–72
  searching lines 269–70
  starting 264
EGA (Enhanced Graphics
  Adapter)
  changing display columns/
    lines 124–*26*, 339–40, 517
  code pages 397–98, 400,
    406–7, 523
EGA.CPI file 400, 523
EGA.SYS 379, 461
EMM386 command 483–84
EMM386.EXE device driver
  371–72, 461, 484–85
end-of-file character 46, 60, 133
Enhanced Graphics Adapter.
  See EGA
Enter key 15
environmental variables 542
erase. *See* DELETE command
  (del, erase)
errorlevel values
  BACKUP command 439
  batch file testing of 501–2
  REPLACE command 537–38
  RESTORE command 539
Escape key (Esc) 29, 251
EXE2BIN command 485
EXE extension *60*
EXE files, converting, to COM
  files 485
EXIT command 230–31, 232,
  485
EXPAND command 486
expanded memory
  described 123, 370
  disk caches 373–74, 545–46
  emulating IBM PS/2 560
  enabling/disabling 483–84
  FASTOPEN use of 383–84
  LIM EMS 370, 560
  RAM drives 375–77,
    532–34
  simulating, with extended
    memory 371–72, 484–85

extended memory
  described 123, 370
  disk caches 373–74, 545–46
  DOS in 372–73, 469–71,
    500–501
  managing 371, 500–501
  RAM drives 375–77,
    531–33
  simulating expanded memory
    with 371–72, 484–85
extensions. *See* names/
  extensions, file
external commands 41

F

F1 function key 215, 249
F2 function key 292
F3 function key 258, 292
F4 function key 292
F6 function key 60, 133, 251,
  270
F10 function key 212
FASTOPEN command
  383–84, 486–87, 503
fc. *See* FILE COMPARISON
  command (fc)
FCBS configuration command
  489
FDISK command 489–91
FILE000X.CHK files 116
FILE COMPARISON
  command (fc) 487–89. *See
  also* COMPARE command
  (comp)
file control blocks 489
file handles 380–81, 491
File List, DOSSHELL program
  copying files 219–20
  deleting files 221–23
  displaying directories 226–27
  displaying directory structures
    229
  displaying files 220–21
  displaying files in sorted order
    223–24
  file information options
    224–25
  finding files 227–28
  scrolling directories 217–18

File List, DOSSHELL program,
    continued
  selecting directories 217
  selecting files 218–19
file-management applications.
    See record-management
    applications
File menu, DOSSHELL
    program
  File List 216–29
  Program List 233–43
File menu, EDIT program
  254–57, 475–76
files. *See also* batch files;
    program files; text files
  access, controlling (*see*
    attributes, file/directory)
  access, speeding up (*see* disk
    buffers; disk caches;
    FASTOPEN command)
  archiving, with batch files
    320–32, 343–44, 347
  backing up 188–94, 438–40
  backing up, with batch files
    364–65
  comparing 87–90, 450–51,
    487–89
  copying 48–49, 70–73,
    175–76, 453–56
  copying, in DOSSHELL
    219–20
  copying directory structure
    and 174–75, 184–87,
    559–60
  copying/replacing 181–84, 418,
    537–38
  creating/editing (*see* EDIT
    program; EDLIN program)
  delete tracking 77–78
  deleting 49, 76–81, 460
  deleting, in DOSSHELL
    221–23
  deleting, with batch files 311,
    340–41
  described 6
  finding, in DOSSHELL
    227–28
  fragmented 113–14

files, *continued*
  names/extensions (*see* names/
    extensions, file)
  recovering, from damaged
    disks 534–35
  renaming 82–83, 536–37
  restoring, from backup
    194–200, 538–40
  saving recovery information
    for 512–14
  search paths for (*see* paths)
  selecting, in DOSSHELL
    218–19
  sharing 544
  specifying number of open
    380–81, 491
  structures/systems (*see*
    directories; tree-structured
    file systems)
  system 416–17, 549
  types 40–41
  undeleting 77–78, 79–81,
    553–55
FILES configuration command
  380–81, 491
filters. *See* FIND filter
  command; MORE filter
  command; SORT filter
  command
FIND filter command 52–53,
  283, 285–88, 334–39,
  491–92
fixed disks. *See also* disks
  access, speeding up (*see* disk
    buffers; disk caches;
    FASTOPEN command)
  backing up files/directories
    187–94, 438–40
  backing up files/directories
    with batch files 364–65
  described 172
  directory structures (*see*
    directories; tree-structured
    file systems)
  installing applications
    173–76, 201–2
  installing/upgrading DOS (*see*
    versions, DOS)
  maintenance 207

fixed disks, *continued*
  partitions (*see* partitions, fixed
    disk)
  restoring files/directories
    194–200, 538–40
FOR batch command 345–47,
  492–93
foreign languages
  character sets (*see* code pages)
  country-specific system
    diskettes 391–92, 540–41
  date/time/currency/decimal
    formats 389, 401–2,
    456–58, 540–41
  keyboard layouts 136–40,
    390–91, 402–3, 504–7,
    540–41
  overview 388–89
FORMAT.COM file 103, 188
FORMAT command
  BACKUP command and 188
  command reference 493–95
  diskette capacities 103–4
  diskettes 44–46
  parameters 104–6
  reformatting/quick formatting
    105, 108–9
formatting disks. *See* FORMAT
  command; SELECT
  command
fragmented files 113–14
function keys. *See also individual*
  function key names
  DOS command-editing 292
  DOSKEY use of 33–36
  DOSSHELL use of 213, 217
  EDIT Survival Guide use of
    251
  EDLIN use of 272–75

G

GOTO batch command
  325–27, 496
graftabl. *See* LOAD
  GRAPHICS TABLE
  command (graftable)
GRAFTABL.COM file 122

graphics
  enabling display of 136,
    496–97
  enabling printing of 134–35,
    497–99
GRAPHICS.COM file 122
GRAPHICS command 134–35,
  378–79, 497–99
GRAPHICS.PRO file 498

H

hard disks. *See* fixed disks
hardware 4
hardware code page 394
HELP command 64–65,
  499–500
HELP.EXE file 65
help features
  DOS commands 64–65,
    499–500
  DOSSHELL program 214–16
  DOSSHELL program items
    237
  EDIT program 248–52, 477
Help menu, DOSSHELL
  program 214–16
Help menu, EDIT program
  248–52, 477
help text, DOSSHELL program
  item 237
Hercules Display Adapter *125*
Hewlett-Packard LaserJet Plus
  printer 20, 32, 135, 498
hexadecimal number system 90,
  221
hidden attributes 86–87, 176,
  179–81
High Memory Area (HMA) 123,
  372. *See also* extended
  memory
HIMEM.SYS device driver 371,
  462, 500–501
history, command. *See*
  DOSKEY program
HLP extension *60*

I

IBM-compatible 7
IBM keyboards *15, 28, 33–34*

IBM Proprinters 135, 398–401,
  406–7, 498, 523
IBM PS/2 computers 406–7, 560
IF batch command 323–25,
  501–2
incompatibility. *See*
  compatibility
index, DOSSHELL help
  214–16
index, bibliographic 366–67
initializing disks. *See* FORMAT
  command, SELECT
  command
input, standard 281
input/output redirection
  appending redirected output to
    files 289, 502
  command reference 502–3
  described 280–81
  devices and 51–52, 53, 280,
    288
  filter commands and 50–53,
    281–91
  parallel printer output 131, 521
  piping and 51, 289–91, 335–36
  redirecting both input and
    output 288–89
INSTALL configuration
  command 399, 503
installing/upgrading DOS. *See*
  versions, DOS
internal commands 40
international formats. *See*
  foreign languages
inventory 367–68
IO.SYS file 549

J

JOIN command 386, 503–4

K

keyb. *See* KEYBOARD
  command (keyb)
KEYBOARD command (keyb)
  136–40, 402–3, 503, 504–6
KEYBOARD command
  (keyb*xx*) 136–40, 390–91,
  506–7

keyboards. *See also* consoles; keys
  blocking functions of enhanced 548
  control program (*see* ANSI.SYS device driver)
  DOSSHELL use of 213
  EDIT use of 246–48
  layouts 136–40, 390–91, 402–3, 504–7, 540–41
  PC/AT and PC/XT *15, 28, 33–34*
  repeat rate 124, 517–18
KEYBOARD.SYS file 139, 505
keyb*xx. See* KEYBOARD command (keyb*xx*)
keys. *See also* keyboards
  dead 138, 390
  direction (*see* direction keys)
  DOS command-editing 292
  DOSKEY use of 33–36, *293*
  DOSSHELL shortcut 238
  DOSSHELL use of 212, 213, 215, 217, 229
  EDLIN editing 272–75
  function (*see* function keys)
  screen-printing 20, 30, 32–33
  special 14–16, 28–33

L

LABEL command 116, 507–8
labels, batch file 325
labels, disk volume
  changing/deleting 116, 507–8
  defined 102–3
  displaying 117, 558
  formatting and 45
languages, foreign. *See* foreign languages
laser printers 20, 32, 126
LASTDRIVE configuration command 381, 508
LCD (Liquid Crystal Display) 134–35, 398, 400, 523
LCD.CPI file 400, 523
lh. *See* LOADHIGH command (lh)

LIM EMS (Lotus-Intel-Microsoft) Expanded Memory Specification 370, 560. *See also* expanded memory
line editor. *See* EDLIN program
Liquid Crystal Display. *See* LCD
LOAD GRAPHICS TABLE command (graftabl) 136, 405, 496–97
LOADHIGH command (lh) 377–79, 509–10
loading DOS. *See* starting DOS
look-ahead buffers. *See* disk buffers
LPT1–LPT3 device names. *See* parallel ports

M

macros. *See* DOSKEY program
MAKE DIRECTORY command (md, mkdir) 143–45, 151–52, 510
margins, EDIT program 253–54
MCGA (Multicolor Graphics Array) *125*
md. *See* MAKE DIRECTORY command (md, mkdir)
MDA (Monochrome Display Adapter) *125*
mem. *See* MEMORY command (mem)
MEM.EXE file 122
memory
  balancing, during DOS installation 414
  conventional 123, 369–70
  disk buffers 380, 442–44
  disk caches 373–74, 545–46
  displaying use of 122–23, 373, 378, 511–12
  expanded (*see* expanded memory)
  extended (*see* extended memory)
  RAM drives 375–77, 532–34, 553

memory, *continued*
  reserved (*see* reserved memory)
  reserving, for temporary program use 547
  types of 369–73
MEMORY command (mem) 122–23, 373, 378, 511–12
menu systems 361–64. *See also* Program List, DOSSHELL program
messages
  displaying, with ECHO 321, 330–32, 339, 474–75
  displaying, with PAUSE 322–23, 527
  displaying, with REMARK 301–2, 535
  MIRROR command
  command reference 512–14
  delete tracking 77–78
  saving disk partition information 203–5
  saving disk recovery information 107–8, 203–5
  undeleting files and 79–81
MIRROR.FIL file 108, 109, 205, 513
mkdir. *See* MAKE DIRECTORY command (md, mkdir)
MODE.COM file 122
MODE command
  batch file use of 310
  changing display characteristics 126, 515–16
  changing display columns/lines 124–26, 339–40, 517
  changing keyboard repeat rate 124, 517–18
  command reference 515–24
  connecting serial printer 131, 521
  displaying/changing code-page status 404–5, 522–24
  displaying device status 131–33, 522

MODE command, *continued*
  parallel printer width/spacing
    126–28, 310, 520–21
  preparing code page 400–401,
    522–23
  reserved memory use with
    378–79
  restoring code page 405, 524
  selecting code page 404,
    523–24
  setting serial communications
    parameters 128–30, 518–20
Monochrome Display Adapter.
  See MDA
MORE filter command 50–51,
  289–90, 525
mouse
  DOSSHELL use of 213
  EDIT use of 246–48
moving files. *See* COPY
  command; File List,
  DOSSHELL program;
  REPLACE command;
  XCOPY command)
MS-DOS. *See* DOS
MS-DOS Editor. *See* EDIT
  program
Multicolor Graphics Array. *See*
  MCGA

N

names/extensions, file
  changing 82–83, 536–37
  path names 145, 149
  special extensions 59–60, 202
  valid 24, 41, 58–60
national language support. *See*
  code pages
NATIONAL LANGUAGE
  SUPPORT FUNCTION
  command (nlsfunc) 399,
  503, 525–26
nlsfunc. *See* NATIONAL
  LANGUAGE SUPPORT
  FUNCTION command
  (nlsfunc)
Numeric Lock key (Num Lock)
  29–30

O

online help. *See* help features
operating system. *See* DOS
Options menu, DOSSHELL
  program 221–25, 231–32
Options menu, EDIT program
  261–62, 477
output. *See* input/output
  redirection; printing;
  screens
output, standard 280

P

page frame 370
paging with Edlin 267, 481
parallel ports. *See also* printers
  displaying status of 132–33,
    522
  printer parameters 126–28,
    310, 520–21
  redirecting output to serial
    ports from 131, 521
parameters
  command 26, 42
  command, DOSSHELL
    program item 237–38
  communications 128–30,
    518–20
  replaceable (*see* replaceable
    parameters)
  shifting commands 343–44,
    543–44
parent directory (..) 153, 464
parity 129
parking fixed disks 207
partitions, fixed disk
  configuring 489–91
  rebuilding 205–7, 555–57
  saving recovery information
    203–5, 512–14
passwords, DOSSHELL
  program 235, 237
paste, cut and 257
PATH command 162–63,
  306–9, 526–27
paths
  command search 162–63,
    306–9, 526–27
  data search 168–69, 434–35

paths, *continued*
  described 145, 149
  DOSSHELL program items
    238
PAUSE batch command
  322–23, 527
Pause key 30, 31
pause messages, DOSSHELL
  program item 238
PCTRACKR.DEL file 77,
  512–14
PC/AT and PC/XT keyboards *15,
  28, 33–34*
permanent commands 40
phone-list 281–96, 334–39
Photo Graphic Adapter *125*
piping 51, 289–91, 335–36,
  502–3
ports. *See* parallel ports; serial
  ports
prepared code page 394
PRINT.COM file 82
PRINT command 48, 91–95,
  528–30
printers. *See also* parallel ports;
  printing
  changing width/spacing for
    parallel 126–28, 310,
    520–21
  code pages 398–99, 400,
    406–7
  copying files to 47–48,
    267–68
  graphics support *135*
  laser 20, 32
  redirecting command output to
    51–52, 280
  redirecting parallel printer
    output to serial 131, 521
PRINTER.SYS device driver
  379, 397–98, 462
printing. *See also* printers
  command output 51–52, 280
  files, with COPY command
    47–48, 267–68, 454
  files, with EDIT program 254
  files in queues 91–95, 528–30
  screens 20, 30, 32–33

printing, *continued*
  screens, graphics 134–35,
    497–99
print queue. *See* PRINT
  command
Print Screen key (PrtSc, Print
  Scrn) 20, 30, 32–33
PRN device name 47, 121
program files. *See also* files;
    Program List, DOSSHELL
    program
  converting EXE programs to
    COM 485
  described 4, 40
  displaying memory use by
    122–23, 373, 379, 511–12
  expanding compressed 486
  search paths (*see* paths)
  terminate-and-stay-resident
    378–79, 509
program groups 230
program items 233
Program List, DOSSHELL
    program
  adding program groups
    236–37
  adding program items 233–34
  changing program items
    234–35
  deleting program groups
    242–43
  deleting program items 235
  designing dialog boxes 239
  Disk Utilities Program Group
    240–42
  selecting program group 233
  specifying command
    parameters 237–38
  specifying paths 238
  specifying pause messages 238
  specifying shortcut keys 238
  starting programs 230–31
  switching programs 231–32
  testing program items 239–40
prompt, system
  changing 36–37, 381–83,
    529–31
  current directory as 146,
    152–53

Program List, DOSSHELL
    program, *continued*
  current drive as 14
  defined 14
  invisible 382
PROMPT command 36–37, 146,
    152–53, 381–83, 530–31
properties, DOSSHELL
    program item 234–35
Proprinters 138, 398–401,
    406–7, 498, 522
PS/2 computers 406–7, 560

Q

QBasic 230, 532
question mark wildcard
    character 43, 63–64
queue, print. *See* PRINT
  commmand
quick formatting disks 105,
    108–9, 495

R

RAM (random access memory)
    369–70
RAM drives
  advantages 207, 375
  creating 375–77, 462, 532–34
  drawbacks 376
  RAMDRIVE.SYS 375–77,
    532–34
  VDISK.SYS 376, 553
RAMDRIVE.SYS device driver
    375–77, 379, 462, 531–34
rd. *See* REMOVE DIRECTORY
  command (rd, rmdir)
read-only attributes 84–85,
    437–38, 465
rebooting DOS *31,* 36
record-management
  bibliographic files 366–67
  capital inventory files 367–68
  telephone files 281–96,
    334–39
  text files 365–66
RECOVER command 534–35
redirection. *See* input/output
  redirection

reformatting disks 105, 108–9
regular memory 123
REMARK batch command
    (rem) 301–2, 535
REMOVE DIRECTORY
    command (rd, rmdir)
    157–59, 535–36
RENAME command (ren)
    82–83, 536–37
replaceable parameters
  batch files 302–3, 345–47,
    492–93
  DOSKEY macros 314, 472
REPLACE command 181–84,
    418, 537–38
rerouting. *See* input/output
  redirection
reserved memory
  described 370
  device drivers/command files
    in 372–73, 377–80, 463,
    509–10
  enabling 371–72, 484–85
  managing 377–80
  TSR programs in 378–79,
    509–10
restarting DOS *31,* 36
RESTORE command 194–200,
    538–40
restoring files/directories
    194–200, 538–40
rmdir. *See* REMOVE
    DIRECTORY command
    (rd, rmdir)
root directory
  defined 142, 149
  required DOS files 202
  symbol 145, 147, 149

S

screens. *See also* consoles;
    display adapters
  clearing 21, 123, 448–49
  control program (*see*
    ANSI.SYS device driver)
  displaying graphics characters
    136, 497–99
  pausing displays 29–30, 31,
    50–51, 525

screens, *continued*
   printing 20, 30, 32–33
   printing graphics images
      134–36, 497–99
scroll bar 218
scroll box 218
Scroll Lock key 30
searching text files. *See* FIND
   filter command
Search menu, EDIT program
   258–59, 476–77
search paths. *See* paths
sectors 101–2
SELECT command 391–92,
   540–41
SELECT installation command
   413–16, 540
serial numbers, volume 45, 103
serial ports
   communications parameters
      128–30, 518–20
   described 120
   displaying status of 131–33,
      522
   redirecting output from
      parallel ports to 131,
      521
serial printers 131
SET command 542
SETUP.EXE file 412
SETUP installation command
   412–13, 542
SET VERSION command
   (setver) 543–44
SHARE command 503, 544
SHELL configuration command
   544
shell program. *See* DOSSHELL
   program
Shift-Alt-Esc keys 232
SHIFT batch command
   343–44, 544–45
Shift-Del keys 258
Shift-Enter keys 232
Shift-F9 keys 212
Shift-Ins keys 257
Shift keys 29, 248
Shift-PrtSc keys 20, 30, 32–33
Shift-Tab keys 213

shortcut keys
   DOSSHELL 238
   EDIT 257–58
SMARTDRV.SYS device driver
   373–74, 462, 545–46
software 4
SORT filter command 50,
   283–85, 352–54, 546–47
sorting
   command output 546–47
   directory displays 69, 464–66
   directory displays in
      DOSSHELL 223–24
   directory displays with batch
      files 352–54
   file lines 50, 283–85, 546–47
special keys. *See* keys
spooling. *See* PRINT command
STACKS configuration
   command 547
standard input 281
standard output 280
starting DOS
   with AUTOEXEC.BAT
      305–9
   with date/time 13
   from diskette 10
   with/without DOSSHELL
      11–13
   in high memory 372–73,
      469–71, 500–501
   with other shell programs 14
   restarting *31*, 36
stop bits 129, 130
strings 52
subdirectories. *See also*
   directories; tree-structured
   file systems
   defined 25–26, 142, 149
   directories of 341
   DOS subdirectory 25,
      201–2, 417–18
   grouping in directory listing
      464–66, 542
SUBSTITUTE command
   (subst) 385, 547–48
Survival Guide, EDIT program
   248–52

SWITCHES configuration
   command 548
sys. *See* SYSTEM command
   (sys)
SYS extension *60*
system attributes 87, 176
system clock. *See* date; time
SYSTEM command (sys)
   416–17, 549
system date. *See* date
system disks
   copying system files 416–17,
      549
   country-specific diskettes
      391–92, 540–41
   defined 10
   formatting 493–95
system files 416–17, 549
system memory. *See* memory
system messages. *See* messages
system programs 4
system prompt. *See* prompt,
   system
system setup. *See* starting DOS
system shutdown 21
system time. *See* time

T

Tab key 213
tape drives 474
Task Swapper, DOSSHELL
   program 231–32
telephone file 281–96,
   334–39
temporary commands 41
terminate-and-stay-resident
   programs 378–79, 509–10
text files. *See also* files
   appending redirected ouput to
      289, 502–3
   combining 74–75, 455–56
   copying, to devices 73–74,
      454–55
   copying to, from devices 133,
      455
   creating, with COPY 46–47,
      60–62
   creating/editing (*see* EDIT
      program; EDLIN program)

text files, *continued*
  described 40
  displaying 47, 70, 552–53
  displaying, in DOSSHELL
    220–21
  displaying, with pauses 50–51,
    525
  displaying multiple, with batch
    files 349–50
  printing 47–48
  printing, with batch files 310
  printing, in queues 91–95,
    528–30
  searching through 52–53,
    334–39, 350–52,
    491–92
  sorting lines 50, 53, 283,
    546–47
time
  changing 18–19, 549–50
  formats 389, 401–2,
    456–58, 540–41
  starting DOS 13
TIME command 18–19,
    549–50
tracks 101–*2*
TREE.COM file 164
TREE command 163–68,
    551–52
Tree menu, DOSSHELL
    program 229
tree-structured file systems. *See
    also* directories
  application-based 357–58
  backing up 364–65, 438–40
  batch files and macros for
    360–64
  copying structure of, and files
    174–75, 184–87, 559–60
  department-based 358–59
  described 142

tree-structured file systems,
    continued
  displaying structure of
    163–68, 446–48,
    551–52
  displaying structure of, in
    DOSSHELL 229
  fixed disk tips 201–3
  sample 149–50, 154–57
  setting up 356–64
  user-based 359
TSR programs 378–79,
    509–10
TYPE command 47, 70, 551

U

UNDELETE command 79–81,
    553–55
UNFORMAT command
    109–10, 205–7, 555–57
Up Arrow key 16, 18
upgrading DOS. *See* versions,
    DOS
upper memory blocks (UMBs).
    See reserved memory
user-based file systems 359
user-defined commands. *See*
    batch files; DOSKEY
    program

V

variables, environmental 542
VDISK.SYS device driver 376,
    462, 557
ver. *See* VERSION command
    (ver)
VERIFY command 557–58
VERSION command (ver) 16,
    381, 557
versions, DOS. *See also*
    compatibility
  compressed files 486

versions, DOS, *continued*
  described 6
  displaying version numbers 16,
    381, 557
  emulating earlier 543–44
  foreign language support 388
  installation programs 540, 542
  installing/upgrading version 3
    416–20
  installing/upgrading version 4
    413–16
  installing/upgrading version 5
    412–13
  time formats 19
VGA (Video Graphics Array)
  changing display columns/
    lines 124–*26*, 339–40, 517
  code pages 397–98, 400, 406,
    522–23
View menu, DOSSHELL
    program 225–28
virtual disks. *See* RAM drives
VOLUME command (vol) 117,
    558
volume labels. *See* labels, disk
    volume
volume serial numbers 45, 103

W, X

wildcard characters 43–44,
    62–64, 327–28
windows
  parts of DOSSHELL 211–12
  sizing EDIT help 251–52
  switching EDIT 251
word processing. *See* EDIT
    program
XCOPY command 174–75,
    184–87, 559–60
XMA2EMS.SYS device driver
    462, 560
XMAEM.SYS device driver
    462, 560

VAN WOLVERTON

A professional writer since 1963, Van Wolverton has had bylines as a newspaper reporter, editorial writer, political columnist, and technical writer. He wrote his first computer program—one that tabulated political polls—for the *Idaho State Journal* in Pocatello, Idaho, in 1965. His interests in computers and writing have been intertwined ever since. As a computer professional, Wolverton has worked at IBM and Intel and has written software documentation for national software companies, including Microsoft Corporation. He is the author of SUPERCHARGING MS-DOS and HARD DISK MANAGEMENT, a Microsoft Quick Reference, and he was a contributor to THE MS-DOS ENCYCLOPEDIA. Wolverton and his wife, Jeanne, live in a twenty-first–century log cabin near Alberton, Montana.

The manuscript for this book was prepared and submitted to Microsoft Press in electronic form. Text files were processed and formatted using Microsoft Word.

Principal word processors: Debbie Kem and Judith Bloch
Principal proofreader: Shawn Peck
Principal typographer: Lisa Iversen
Principal illustrator: Rebecca Geisler-Johnson
Cover designer: Thomas A. Draper
Cover color separator: Rainier Color

Text composition by Microsoft Press in Times Roman with display type in Kabel Bold, using the Magna composition system and the Linotronic 300 laser imagesetter.

Printed on recycled paper stock.